THE LEGO® BOOK

LONDON, NEW YORK,
MELBOURNE, MUNICH, DELHI

For DK
Senior Editor Alastair Dougall
Senior Designer Lisa Sodeau
Designers Owen Bennett, Jon Hall, Mark Richards, and Clive Savage
Design Manager Ron Stobbart
Publishing Manager Catherine Saunders
Art Director Lisa Lanzarini
Publisher Simon Beecroft
Publishing Director Alex Allan
Pre-Production Producer Andy Hilliard
Producer Louise Daly
Senior Producer Melanie Mikellides

For the LEGO Group
Head of the LEGO Idea House Jette Orduna
Assistant Licensing Manager Randi Kirsten Sørensen

For Tall Tree
Editors Rob Colson and Jon Richards
Designers Malcolm Parchment, Ben Ruocco, and Ed Simkins

First published in the United States in 2009. This revised edition published in 2012 by DK Publishing,
375 Hudson Street, New York, New York 10014
10 9 8 7 6 5 4 3 2 1
001-185969-09/12

Discover more at
www.dk.com

THE LEGO® BOOK

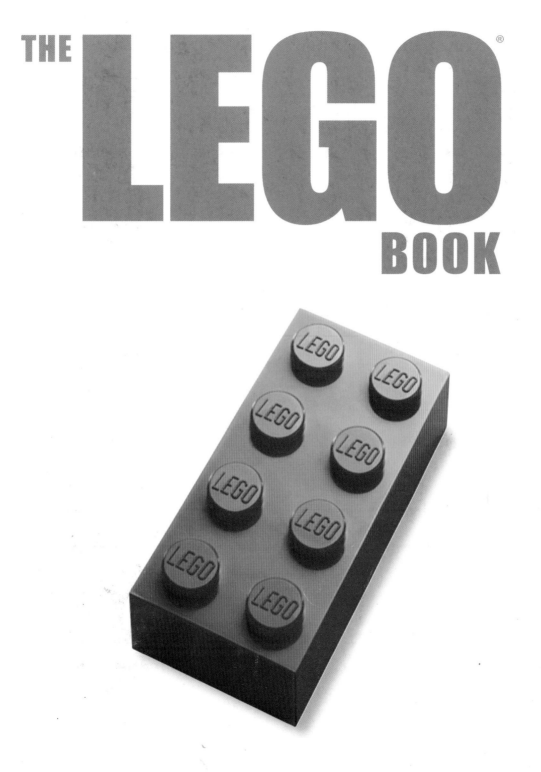

Written by
Daniel Lipkowitz

Contents

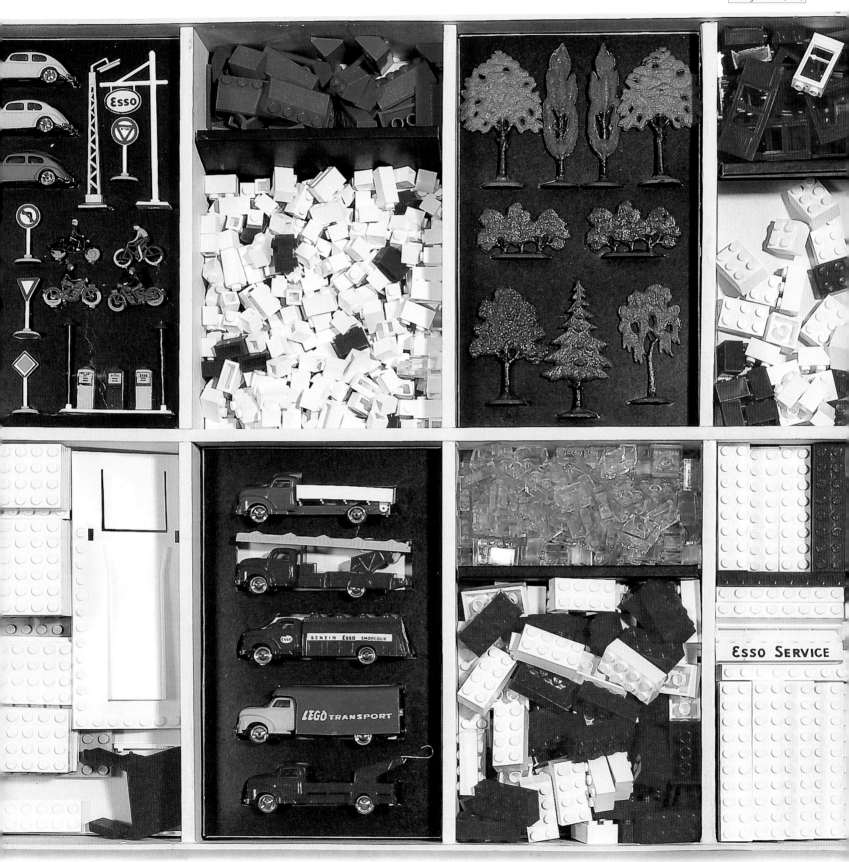

ESSO

BENZIN ESSO SMØREOLIE

LEGO TRANSPORT

ESSO SERVICE

An inspirational leaflet from 1959 shows children some of the countless things they can build with their LEGO bricks.

Foreword

Dear Reader,

On January 28, 1958, the LEGO Group patented the LEGO® brick with its now well-known tubes inside and studs on top. That day marked the beginning of an adventure that we are still on.

Although the LEGO brick is now more than 50 years old, it is as young as ever. We are often asked why the LEGO brick continues to inspire and excite children and adults all over the world. I can think of at least three reasons.

First of all, it's a new toy every day. The possibilities for play really are endless. With just six 2x4 LEGO bricks of the same color, you can build more than 915 million different creations. So LEGO play never stops. A police station today can become a space rocket tomorrow.

Secondly, it's more than a toy; the LEGO brick has educational applications. Of course, children don't deliberately look for a toy that will develop their skills and capabilities. They want a fun toy. But playing with a toy that gives you a real feeling of achievement and pride is fun. LEGO play gives you that feeling. And meanwhile you develop your motor, social, and creative skills—and your curiosity. You develop systematic creativity. That is what we call playful learning.

Thirdly, LEGO bricks foster collaboration and social skills. If you gather together children of different nationalities, who don't understand each other's language, and give them LEGO bricks to play with, they will instinctively begin to build and play with each other. The LEGO brick is a global language!

This book is packed with information about the company that invented the LEGO brick and all the fantastic creations that have so far come from it. There are many, many more creations to come.

What will *you* make next?

Happy reading.

Jørgen Vig Knudstorp
Chief Executive Officer of the LEGO Group

"Only the Best..."

"ONLY THE BEST IS GOOD ENOUGH."
That was the motto of LEGO Group founder Ole Kirk Kristiansen, and he believed in it so strongly that his son Godtfred Kirk Christiansen carved it on a sign and hung it on his father's carpentry workshop's wall. Ole Kirk believed that children deserved to have toys made with the highest quality materials and workmanship, and he was determined that the toys manufactured in his workshop would last and remain just as fun through years of play. Today, the words of the company's founder remain its driving force, and LEGO® products continue to be passed down from one generation to the next, sparking the creativity and imaginations of millions of children and adults all over the world ●

Carved in Danish as a reminder to his employees to never skimp on quality, Ole Kirk's motto has been a guiding principle for the LEGO Group for more than 75 years.

Workers pose for a photograph, taken in the late 1940s. Above their heads, Ole Kirk's motto is proudly displayed upon the workshop wall.

Ole Kirk Kristiansen recreates the patterns for the wooden LEGO duck in 1943 after a fire the previous year destroyed the LEGO workshop and all of the company's designs.

A Family Business

THROUGH THREE generations of family ownership and family management, the LEGO Group has grown from a small local company into one of the world's leading providers of creative, developmental play products. Each generation has contributed to the LEGO® brand's expansion and continued success ●

Workers pose with a range of the first wooden toys in 1932. "It was not until the day that I said to myself, you must choose between your carpentry and the toys that things started to make sense," Ole Kirk recalled.

AN IMAGE OF HOPE

The year 1932 was a difficult one for company founder Ole Kirk Kristiansen, combining Europe's economic depression, looming bankruptcy, and deep personal loss at the death of his wife. While bringing up four young sons on his own, Ole Kirk created a new business: making wooden toys. The years that followed were little easier, often forcing him to borrow money from his family to keep his workshop afloat and maintain his standards for creating the finest possible wooden toys.

This wooden plane is a reconstruction of the one on top of the ladder in the photograph on the left. Today, it symbolizes the company's ability to rise above adversity.

CHILDREN DESERVE THE BEST

The company's toys needed to work and work well, even in the hands of the most enthusiastically active child. From the very start, Ole Kirk was dedicated to quality. He worked under the self-coined motto "Only the best is good enough," and his sons and employees were often reminded that "This is the way we do things" at the LEGO workshop. By choosing a name contracted from "LEg GOdt," or "Play Well" in Danish, Ole Kirk emphasized that the LEGO name needed to represent a standard of quality that would set the company apart from its competitors.

Ole Kirk and his son Godtfred examine a wooden LEGO farm in the late 1940s.

Godtfred Kirk Christiansen (GKC) continued his father's philosophy when, under his leadership, the company changed to concentrate on the new LEGO System of Play in 1955. The need to constantly improve product quality led him to develop the LEGO brick's unique "clutch" principle, and better materials and production technology maintained its precise shape. Godtfred Kirk was a firm believer in the LEGO code of "good play," and in 1963, he introduced the "10 important characteristics" for future LEGO product development.

GKC's Watchwords for the LEGO System

- Unlimited play possibilities
- For girls, for boys
- Enthusiasm for all ages
- Play all year round
- Healthy and quiet play
- Endless hours of play
- Imagination, creativity, development
- Each new product multiplies the play value of the rest
- Always topical
- Safety and quality

Ole Kirk Kristiansen, Godtfred Kirk Christiansen, and Kjeld Kirk Kristiansen at Ole Kirk's 60th birthday party in 1951. Three generations building on each other's achievements!

From early on, Kjeld Kirk Kristiansen realized the potential of LEGO bricks and built his own models, some of which became official sets. Here, Kjeld and his father discuss one of Kjeld's models in 1978.

" Children mean everything to us. Children and their development. And this must pervade everything we do."

Kjeld Kirk Kristiansen, 1996

FOCUS ON CHILDREN

Third-generation company owner Kjeld Kirk Kristiansen created a "system within the system" with his own model for product development, establishing a division to provide each age group of customers with the right toys at the right time in their lives. Kjeld Kirk Kristiansen believed strongly in the LEGO brand and became a driving force to change the consumer's perception of it from just a great construction toy to a world-recognized icon of quality, creativity, and learning. In 1996 he explained: "My grandfather's main drive was the perfection of quality craftsmanship. My father's main focus was on our unique product idea with all its inherent possibilities. I see myself as a more globally oriented leader, seeking to fully exploit our brand potential for further developing and broadening our product range and business concept, based upon our product idea and brand values."

Wooden Toys

THE STORY of one of the world's most successful toy companies began in 1916 when Danish master carpenter Ole Kirk Kristiansen bought a workshop in the little town of Billund and set up a business building houses and furniture. In 1932, with the worldwide Great Depression threatening to close his carpentry shop for good, Ole Kirk turned his skills to creating a range of toys for children. These beautifully made and painted playthings included yo-yos, wooden blocks, pull-along animals, and vehicles of all kinds ●

Yo-yos (1932)

Launched in 1932 as one of the workshop's first wooden toys, the yo-yo enjoyed a brief period of great popularity. When the craze and sales declined, the remaining stock was recycled into wheels for other toys, like the pull-along pony and trap below.

Pony and Trap (1937)

WOODEN BLOCKS

Decorated with colorful painted letters and numbers, LEGO wooden blocks could be stacked and arranged into words to help young children learn the alphabet and spelling. Forerunners of the plastic brick (which appeared in 1949), these blocks date from 1946.

PULL-ALONG TOYS

During the 1930s and 1940s, the company had great success with its wide range of pull-along wooden toy animals for young children. Produced in several different color schemes, this rolling duck, painted to resemble a male mallard, was one of the most popular early LEGO toys.

Duck (1935)

Beak opens and shuts as wheels turn

"Clumsy Hans" (1936)

"CLUMSY HANS"

From the popular "Klods-Hans" fairy tale by Danish writer and poet Hans Christian Andersen, Clumsy Hans bobs up and down on his billy goat as you pull this toy along.

Pull-along cats, released between the mid-1930s and the late 1950s.

This realistic rooster toy was made from 1947 to 1958.

Monkey (1946)

Lever connected to wheels

The moving handle on the car works with the joints built into this wooden monkey's arms and legs to make him rock forward and backward when the wheels turn.

Wagon tray

Train (1935)

Ole Kirk's son Godtfred Kirk Christiansen started designing toys for the company in 1937 at the age of 17. At technical school, he learned to draw concept illustrations for new LEGO products, such as these wooden cars.

WOODEN VEHICLES

The LEGO workshop produced a large number of wooden cars and trucks throughout the 1930s and 1940s, each manufactured and painted to Ole Kirk's standards of high quality. When Denmark was occupied in 1940, the use of metal and rubber in toys was banned, and the company's trademark wooden toys suddenly became even more popular.

Steering wheel linked to front wheels

Covered Truck (1940)

Tractor (1949)

Plank-side Truck (1940)

Plastic Toys

One of the company's first plastic toys was a baby's rattle shaped like a fish. Blending different plastic colors inside the molding machine gave it an eye-catching marbled appearance.

IN 1947, Ole Kirk purchased a plastic injection-molding machine imported from Britain. One of the first in Denmark, the machine cost DKK 30,000, one-15th of the company's entire earnings for the year. Plastic toys were expensive to manufacture, but the risk paid off: by 1951, half of the company's toys were made from plastic ●

LEGO Mursten (1953)

The slits in the bricks enabled builders to insert windows and doors.

BIRTH OF A BRICK

The first LEGO® bricks were produced in 1949 under the name "Automatic Binding Bricks." At first, they were just a handful out of about 200 plastic and wooden toys the company manufactured. Made from cellulose acetate, they resembled today's bricks but had slits on their sides and were completely hollow underneath, without tubes to lock them together. In 1953, they were renamed LEGO Mursten ("LEGO Bricks").

The boy in the white shirt is Ole Kirk's grandson, Kjeld Kirk Kristiansen; the girl is his sister.

CARS AND TRUCKS

A new series of realistic plastic cars based on real auto models started in 1958 with the launch of the company-wide LEGO System of Play. Designed to complement the new Town Plan sets, many of the vehicles included bases and display containers with studs for attaching LEGO bricks.

262 Opel Rekord with Garage (1961)

This plastic car came in a transparent display case with an opening door and LEGO System studs on top.

260 VW Beetle (1958)

Produced in various colors and sizes between 1957 and 1967, the VW Beetle could also be purchased with a showcase box that included a LEGO brick VW logo plate.

CARS AND TRUCKS

With the new plastics technology came the ability to design and produce toys with much greater detail and accuracy than ever before. Colorful cars and trucks were a popular product among children, who could collect and play with all the latest models and styles.

Colorful artwork decorates the box of this 1950s Chevrolet truck collection.

Many toys combined plastic with other materials. This Esso fuel truck had a plastic cab and a painted wooden trailer.

SAMLESÆT TIL *Ferguson* MODEL TRAKTOR

FREMSTILLET AF LEGO · DANMARK

The real Ferguson Model TE20 tractor (nicknamed the "Little Grey Fergie"), illustrated here on the toy's new 1953 packaging, was manufactured from 1946 to 1956.

Just like the real thing, the LEGO Ferguson Tractor was designed to pull a variety of farming attachments.

Originally sold fully assembled, the tractor was released again in 1953 with the option of putting it together yourself.

FERGUSON TRACTOR (1952)

One of the company's biggest early successes in plastic toys was the Ferguson Tractor. Its highly-detailed plastic-injection mold cost as much to make as the price of a real tractor, but with 75,000 pieces sold in its first year alone, the gamble quickly paid off. The increasing popularity of industrialized farming in Europe meant that the Ferguson Tractor arrived during a time when more and more farmers were switching from horses to tractors, making it a must-have toy for the 1950s child. The profits that the toy tractor earned made it possible for the company to invest in its still new and unproven plastic bricks.

Realistic color scheme

Ferguson logo

Front wheels connected to steering wheel

Detailed wheels and rubber tires

Work Hard, Play Well

THE LEGO GROUP has been making its famous bricks for over half a century, but its story doesn't begin there. Presented here is a timeline of the company's earliest days, from the birth of its founder, to its humble beginnings in a carpentry workshop in the Danish village of Billund, the move to producing wooden and then plastic toys, the birth of the first LEGO® bricks, and the dawn of the revolutionary LEGO System of Play ●

Ole Kirk aged 20 years old.

1891
● Ole Kirk, founder of the LEGO Group, is born at Omvrå near Filskov, not far from the village of Billund in Denmark.

Ole Kirk's 1936 motto for the company.

1935
● The business manufactures the first LEGO wooden duck, and markets "Kirk's Sandgame," its first construction toy.

1936
● Ole Kirk coins the company motto, "Only the best is good enough." His son Godtfred Kirk Christiansen carves Ole Kirk's motto and hangs it on the workshop wall.

1937
● Godtfred Kirk Christiansen begins designing models for the company at the age of 17.

1939
● The LEGO factory hires its 10th employee.

1942
● A fire destroys the factory and Ole Kirk's life's work. A new toy factory is built, and he remakes all of the lost designs himself.

1950
● On his 30th birthday, Godtfred Kirk Christiansen is appointed Junior Managing Director of the company.

1952
● The LEGO Ferguson tractor is released.
● A building base with 10 x 20 studs is sold for use with the interlocking bricks.

1952
● A new LEGO manufacturing plant is built at the cost of DKK 350,000.

1953
● "Automatic Binding Bricks" are renamed "LEGO Bricks" ("LEGO Mursten" in Danish). The LEGO name is molded onto every brick.

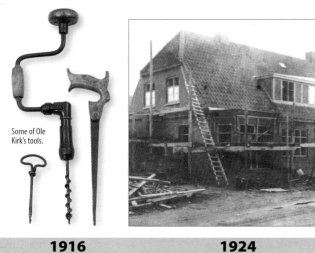

Some of Ole Kirk's tools.

LEGO

1916
● Ole Kirk buys the Billund Joinery Manufacturing and Carpentry Workshop and sets up business as a self-employed carpenter and joiner.

1924
● Ole Kirk's three sons play with matches and the workshop burns down! He builds a larger one, renting out the remaining space.

1932
● Ole Kirk starts to manufacture and sell wooden toys.

1934
● Ole Kirk holds a competition among his employees to name the company, with a bottle of wine as the prize. He wins it himself with the name "LEGO," short for "LEg GOdt," or "Play Well" in Danish. Coincidentally, the word can also mean "I put together" in Latin.

Illustrations of animals and people added more possibilities.

The first bricks have no logo

AUTOMATIC BINDING BRICKS

1943
● The company gains its 43rd employee.

1946
● New LEGO products include wooden blocks with painted letters and numbers.

1947
● Ole Kirk imports a plastic injection- molding machine from the UK.
● The company produces its first plastic toys, including a ball for infants and Monopoli, an educational road safety game.

1948
● The firm now employs 50 people.
● New products include a pinball game.

1949
● "Automatic Binding Bricks," the company's first plastic interlocking bricks, are produced. The company now makes about 200 plastic and wooden toys, including a new plastic fish and sailor.

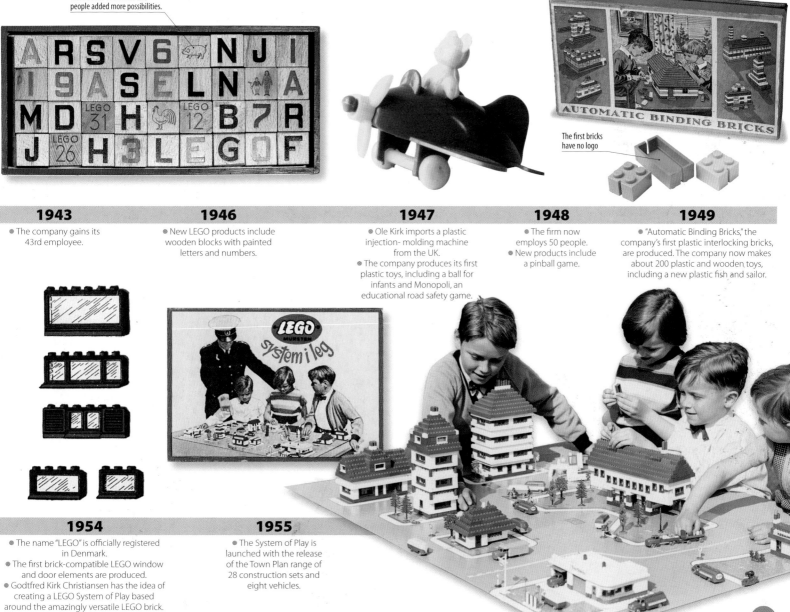

1954
● The name "LEGO" is officially registered in Denmark.
● The first brick-compatible LEGO window and door elements are produced.
● Godtfred Kirk Christiansen has the idea of creating a LEGO System of Play based around the amazingly versatile LEGO brick.

1955
● The System of Play is launched with the release of the Town Plan range of 28 construction sets and eight vehicles.

The LEGO® System of Play

The first LEGO System set was "Town Plan No. 1."
Appearing on its packaging was young Kjeld Kirk
Kristiansen, son of GKC and the grandson of company
founder Ole Kirk Kristiansen.

1954 WAS A YEAR in which Godtfred Kirk Christiansen (GKC)
did a lot of thinking about the future of the LEGO Group.
Returning from a toy fair in Britain, he got talking to a colleague,
who pointed out that there was no *system* in the toy industry.
That was all the inspiration GKC needed. He decided to create
a structured system of products. Reviewing all the toys made by
the company, he saw that the LEGO® brick was the best choice
for this project. The LEGO System of Play launched the following
year with the Town Plan range of construction sets ●

Of the System of Play, GKC
wrote: "Our idea is to create a
toy that prepares the child
for life, appeals to the
imagination, and develops
the creative urge and joy of
creation that are the driving
force in every human being."

Town Plan No.1 (1955)

Additional Town Plan
boards were sold
separately

A GROWING SYSTEM

The idea behind the LEGO System was that every element should connect to every other
element; the more bricks, the more building possibilities. With Town Plan, children could make
their towns bigger and better with each new set, and thanks to the included extra building ideas
(pictured below left), they could make more than just what was pictured on the box.

Pre-assembled, realistic
1950s cars and trucks

HOTEL

TOWN PLAN

The original Town Plan No. 1 set included everything children
needed to assemble their own realistic town centers, from a
colorful street board to citizens, cars and trucks, and lots of red,
white, and blue LEGO bricks. The first street boards were soft
plastic; they were changed to wooden fiberboard in 1956.

A NEW TOWN PLAN

In 2008, the company celebrated the 50th anniversary of the patenting of the modern LEGO brick with a new version of the classic Town Plan set. The special-edition set let kids and collectors create a town center from the 1950s, with a movie theater, gas station, and town hall.

In honor of the LEGO brick's golden anniversary, the set included three metallic gold bricks built into the town's central fountain.

Kjeld Kirk Kristiansen, now the owner of the company, reprised his childhood starring role by appearing on the new Town Plan set's packaging.

Built from 1,981 pieces, 10184 Town Plan (2008) included a newly-married minifigure bride and groom, elements in rare shapes and colors, and a letter from Kjeld Kirk Kristiansen. Its movie theater had a ticket booth, seats, a popcorn machine, and LEGO themed posters.

The gas station included a garage, a carwash, and pumps for filling up the set's pair of 1950s-style brick-built automobiles.

Detailed traffic signs

Painted crossing guards directed traffic

Esso gas station

TREES AND TRAFFIC SAFETY

Town Plan models came with pre-molded and painted trees, people, vehicles, and road signs. Produced in collaboration with the Danish Road Safety Council, the sets helped teach traffic safety to children in an era when automobile ownership was steeply on the rise.

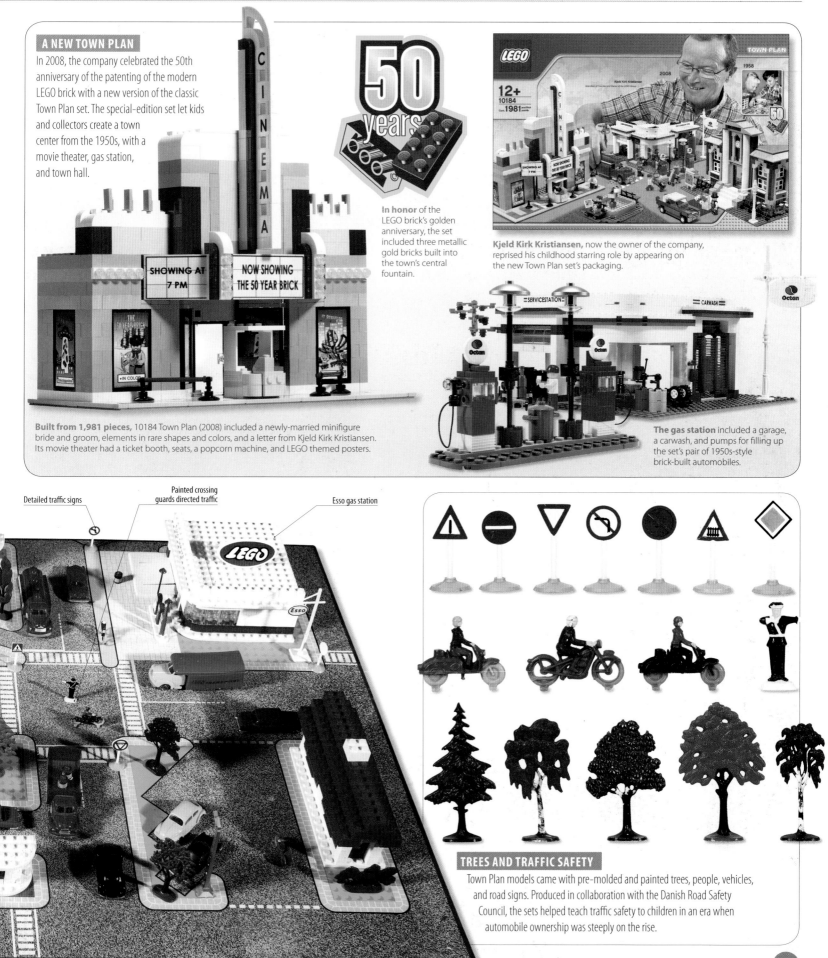

A Worldwide System

THANKS TO THE NEW LEGO® System of Play, the company was no longer just another toy manufacturer. It now had a unique brand identity all its own, and a mission to bring its message of creative fun to the rest of the world. It wasn't easy to convince the first few international markets to gamble on importing plastic bricks, but by the end of the 1960s, the LEGO name was known in every household, with sets for preschoolers and even its very own theme park ●

1956
● The first foreign sales company, LEGO Spielwaren GmbH, is founded in Hohenwestedt in Germany.

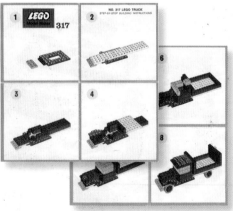

Fire destroys the wooden toy stock.

Production concentrates on plastic products.

1958
● Ole Kirk passes away and Godtfred Kirk Christiansen becomes head of the company.
● The company now has 140 employees.
● The first sloping roof-tile bricks are produced.

1959
● The LEGO Futura department is established to conceive, plan, and oversee the design of new LEGO sets.
● LEGO divisions are founded in France, the UK, Belgium, and Sweden.
● New products include BILOfix wood and plastic construction toys.

1960
● A fire destroys the workshop where the company's wooden toys are made. A decision is made to stop making wooden toys and focus entirely on the LEGO System.
● LEGO divisions are established in Finland and the Netherlands. Approximately 400 employees now work at the company headquarters in Billund.

The 1966 version has a 4.5 volt motor.

Just one of 1967's millions of LEGO sets.

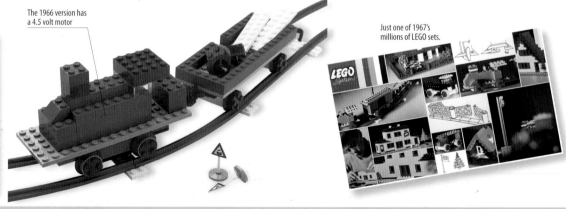

1964
● LEGO model sets with building instructions are produced.
● LEGO products are sold in the Middle East.
● LEGO bricks are exhibited at the Danish pavilion of the New York World Fair.
● The Ole Kirk Foundation is established to help support the arts and other cultural activities.

1965
● LEGO product sales start in Spain.
● The company now has more than 600 employees.

1966
● The first battery-powered LEGO Train sets are launched.
● LEGO products are now sold in 42 countries.
● The first official LEGO Club begins in Canada.

1967
● More than 18 million LEGO sets are sold during the year.
● The LEGO® DUPLO® building system is patented in August.
● There are now 218 different LEGO element shapes.
● A LEGO Club is founded in Sweden.

The LEGO brick patent application.

The new interlocking brick

1957
- The LEGO Group celebrates its Silver Jubilee.
- New products include bricks with light-bulbs and VW Beetles in eight colors.

1957
- The LEGO brick is updated with a new stud-and-tube interlocking system that increases building possibilities and improves model stability.

1958
- The LEGO brick's interlocking principle is patented at 1:58 pm on January 28th.

The LEGO airplane at Billund Airstrip.

The launch of LEGO bricks in the US.

1961
- The design for a LEGO wheel is discovered in a product developer's drawer. Wheels are released the next year, letting children build rolling vehicles of all kinds.

1961
- Godtfred Kirk Christiansen buys a small airplane, and a landing field is built outside Billund.
- LEGO sales begin in the US and Canada through a license agreement with the Samsonite Corp. luggage company.
- The first LEGO preschool lines are launched: Terapi I, II, and III.
- LEGO Italy is established.

1962
- LEGO products are first sold in Singapore, Hong Kong, Australia, Morocco, and Japan.
- LEGO Australia is established.

1963
- ABS (acrylonitrile butadiene styrene) replaces cellulose acetate as the material used to make LEGO bricks. It is more color-fast and allows better molding.
- Billund airport officially opens.
- LEGO Austria is established.

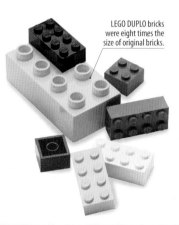

LEGO DUPLO bricks were eight times the size of original bricks.

1968
- The first LEGOLAND® park opens in Billund on June 7th. 625,000 people visit in the first year.
- LEGO DUPLO bricks are test-marketed in Sweden.

1969
- The LEGO DUPLO range for children under five years old is launched internationally.
- A 12-volt motor is added to the LEGO Train series.

Bricks for Everyone

THE 1970s saw LEGO® products branch out in new ways. Creating construction toys that girls, boys, and experienced builders of all ages would enjoy became a key goal, and all of the company's products and brands were brought together under an iconic new logo. LEGO people appeared for the first time, leading up to the minifigures that LEGO fans know today, and the classic LEGO Play Themes were born ●

MINI-WHEEL CAR AND TRUCK SET

348 | STEP-BY-STEP BUILDING INSTRUCTIONS | **LEGO** Model Maker

1970
● The company now has almost 1,000 employees in Billund.
● Small car sets are sold at pocket-money prices.

200 C

US Presidents Washington, Jefferson, Roosevelt, and Lincoln

1974
● The first LEGO people are released, with round heads, movable arms, and bodies built from bricks.
● The best-selling #200 LEGO Family set included a father, mother, son, daughter, and grandmother.

1974
● A brick replica of Mount Rushmore is constructed in LEGOLAND® Billund by Danish artist Bjørn Richter.
● The park receives its 5 millionth visitor.
● LEGO Spain is established.

1978
● The first three LEGO Play Themes are introduced.
● The LEGO Castle theme features medieval knights and castles.

1978
● The first modern-style minifigures with printed faces and movable arms and legs appear.
● The LEGO Town theme lets children build modern buildings and vehicles.
● LEGO baseplates with road markings are produced.

1978
● The LEGO Space theme lets builders' imaginations run wild with outer space adventures.
● A LEGO Club is founded in the UK with a magazine titled *Bricks 'n' Pieces*.
● LEGO Japan is established.

The tugboat was one of the first floating LEGO ships.

Hollow, watertight sections

1971
- LEGO sets for girls are launched, including dolls' houses and furniture.

1972
- 1.8 billion LEGO bricks and other elements have been produced.

1973
- A new LEGO logo unifies all of the company's products

1973
- The first LEGO ship designed to float is released.
- LEGO Systems Inc. USA and LEGO Portugal are established.

The Expert Series featured more realistic details for experienced builders.

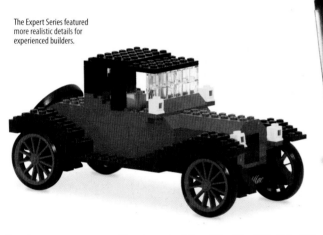

DUPLO figures came with different colors and faces.

1975
- The Expert Series of vintage car models is released.
- The LEGO Group now has 2,500 employees.
- LEGO USA moves from Brookfield, Connecticut, to its present location of Enfield, Connecticut.
- A new, smaller LEGO figure is launched with a blank face and non-moving arms and legs.

1977
- The LEGO Technic series of mechanical models is launched.

1977
- LEGO® DUPLO® sets with door, window, and figure elements are launched.

LEGO SCALA featured necklaces and bracelets that girls could build and customize.

The animal-headed characters of LEGO FABULAND sets had easy-to-construct buildings and vehicles.

1979
- Kjeld Kirk Kristiansen, Godtfred Kirk Christiansen's son and Ole Kirk's grandson, is appointed President and Chief Executive Officer of the company.

1979
- New products include the FABULAND™ series for young builders and LEGO® SCALA™ jewelry.

Building the Future

IN THE 1980s, the company invested heavily in technology, education, and the global community. It sponsored international events like building competitions and awards, developed durable new products for infants and toddlers, created special sets for school programs, and incorporated light and sound into many of its models. New products included buckets full of LEGO® pieces for creative building without instructions, the LEGO Maniac ruled the television screen, and the LEGO Pirates set sail ●

1980
- The LEGO Educational Products Department is established in Billund.
- The LEGO® DUPLO® rabbit logo is used for the first time.
- 70% of Western European families with children under 14 now have LEGO bricks in their home.

Posable arms and legs

1983
- The LEGO DUPLO Baby series is launched, along with new big DUPLO figures with movable arms and legs.
- The company now has 3,700 employees worldwide.

1984
- The first international LEGO building competition is held in Billund. Children from 11 countries take part.
- LEGO Brazil and LEGO Korea are established.
- LEGO Castle gains its first factions: the Black Falcons and Crusaders.

1985
- The LEGO Prize is founded as an international annual award for exceptional efforts on behalf of children anywhere in the world.
- The company has about 5,000 employees worldwide.

1986
- LEGO Technic Computer Control launches in schools.
- The LEGO Technic figure is created.
- The LEGO Group is granted the title "Purveyor to Her Majesty the Queen" on April 16, the birthday of Queen Margrethe of Denmark.

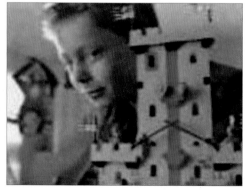

1987
- New products include the motorized LEGO Space Monorail Transport System
- *Brick Kicks*, the official LEGO Club magazine, is mailed to the homes of LEGO Club members across the US.

1988
- The first official LEGO World Cup building championships are held in Billund in August. 38 children from 14 countries take part.
- The "Art of LEGO" exhibition tours the United Kingdom.
- LEGO Canada is established.

1988
- The "LEGO Maniac" bursts on the scene in a series of TV commercials with a memorable tune, becoming a LEGO mascot for years to come.

1981

- The first LEGO World Show takes place in Denmark.

1982

- The LEGO Group celebrates its 50th anniversary.
- The LEGO DUPLO Mosaic and LEGO Technic I educational lines launch.
- LEGO South Africa is established.

Bricks in buckets.

Here they are: The big new LEGO® and DUPLO buckets.
A special offer for more elements. And much space to store a lot more.

1986

- Electronic Light & Sound kits are added to LEGO Town and LEGO Space.

1987

- The LEGO Club starts in Germany, Austria, Switzerland, France, and Norway.
- Buckets are sold containing basic LEGO and LEGO DUPLO elements.
- Launch of the Space sub-themes Blacktron and Futuron.

1989

- The LEGO Pirates theme launches with 11 models.
- Ole Kirk Kristiansen is inducted into the Toy Industry Hall of Fame, USA.

The LEGO Pirates sets quickly became best-sellers.

1989

- The first LEGO Space Police series arrives in stores.

LEGO® Catalogs

SINCE THE DEBUT of the LEGO® System of Play, the company's mission has been to let parents and children know about all of the different ways to play with LEGO bricks. For decades, colorful, informative, and fun-filled LEGO brand catalogs have displayed all of the very latest exciting LEGO sets and themes. Here is just a small selection of catalogs, all of which have inspired, or continue to inspire, LEGO fans around the world to new heights of creativity ●

1959

1974

1963

1981

1984

1969

1981

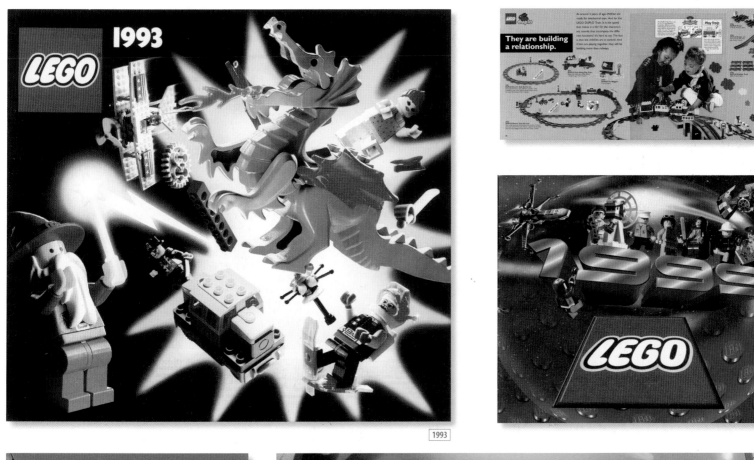

1993

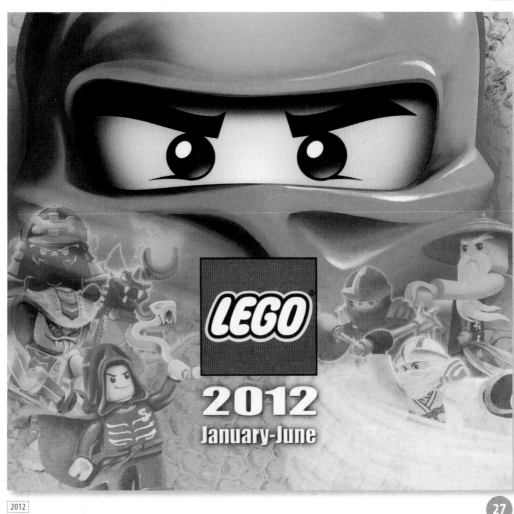

2004

Full Speed Ahead!

THE 1990s were a time of big risks for a company that had become one of the world's largest toy manufacturers. The decade saw the opening of stores that sold only LEGO® products, a branded clothing shop, the first LEGO video games, the launch of the official LEGO website, the release of a high-tech building system for constructing programmable robots, and a leap into licensed themes with the record-smashing debut of LEGO® *Star Wars*® ●

1990

- The LEGO Group is now one of the world's ten largest toy manufacturers, and the only one of the ten in Europe.
- LEGOLAND® Billund gets over 1 million visitors in a single year.
- LEGO Malaysia is established.
- The Model Team series and the LEGO® DUPLO® Zoo are launched.

DUPLO PRIMO figures

1993

- A LEGO building event takes place in Red Square in Moscow, Russia.
- LEGO Space travels to the Ice Planet 2002.

1994

- The United Nations Commission on Human Rights (UNCHR) uses LEGO minifigures as part of an awareness campaign.
- The LEGO® BELVILLE™ line of building sets for girls is released.
- LEGO Mexico is established.
- LEGO products are advertised on Chinese television for the first time.
- The company has 8,880 employees worldwide.
- *Brick Kicks* becomes *LEGO Mania* magazine.

1995

- Godtfred Kirk Christiansen passes away.
- Weekly LEGO programs air on TV in Latvia and Lithuania.
- LEGO events and exhibitions take place in Latvia, Peru, Hungary, Switzerland, Denmark, Greenland, the US, Canada, Italy, and Ecuador.
- LEGO Aquazone and DUPLO® PRIMO™ are launched.

1997

- More than 300,000 children take part in a LEGO building event at Kremlin Palace in Moscow, Russia.
- The LEGO Kids Wear shop opens in Oxford Street, London, UK.

1998

- The company adopts the slogan "Just Imagine…"
- Japanese Emperor Akihito and Empress Michiko visit LEGOLAND Billund.
- The LEGO® MINDSTORMS® and Znap lines launch.

1998

- The LEGO logo is updated.
- The LEGO Space Insectoids appear.
- The LEGO Adventurers explore Egypt.

IMAGINATION CENTER

1991

- The company now has 7,550 employees and 1,000 injection-molding machines at the five LEGO factories.
- New products include the LEGO Town Harbor sets, Technic flex-system elements, and transformer-controlled 9-volt trains.

1991

- The LEGO System Brick Vac helps pick bricks up off the floor.
- The LEGO Town Nautica series starts.

1992

- The first LEGO Imagination Center opens at the Mall of America in Bloomington, Minneapolis, USA.
- The world's largest LEGO Castle is built on Swedish television out of more than 400,000 bricks.
- The second LEGO World Cup Final in Billund features 32 children competing from 11 countries.
- Paradisa and Res-Q sets are released for LEGO Town.

Fort LEGOREDO, the wildest Wild West set of them all!

1996

- LEGOLAND® Windsor opens in the UK.
- The official LEGO website, www.LEGO.com, goes online.
- LEGOLAND Billund receives its 25-millionth visitor.

1996

- LEGO Western and LEGO Time Cruisers are launched.

1997

- The *LEGO Island* computer game is released.
- A new LEGO Imagination Center opens in Disney Village, Florida, USA.
- The first LEGO® MINDSTORMS® Learning Center opens at the Museum of Science and Industry in Chicago, Illinois, USA.

The first year's sets included models from the classic trilogy and the brand-new prequel movie.

1999

- LEGOLAND® California opens in Carlsbad, CA, USA.
- Fortune Magazine names the LEGO brick one of the "Products of the Century."
- The LEGO World Shop opens at www.LEGO.com.
- New LEGO themes include Rock Raiders, LEGO® DUPLO® Winnie the Pooh and Friends™, and one of the biggest ever: LEGO® *Star Wars*®.

New Worlds to Discover

LICENSES ABOUNDED during the first few years of the new millennium, as everything from super heroes to talking sponges moved from the big and small screens to the construction toy aisle. The first LEGO® figures based on real people were produced, changing the familiar yellow face of the minifigure forever. The company even created its own new worlds with original science fiction and fantasy themes complete with stories that were told through books, comics, and movies ●

2000

- The British Association of Toy Retailers names the LEGO brick "Toy of the Century."
- LEGO Studios launches, letting budding film-makers build and animate their own LEGO movies.
- The LEGO Sports theme launches with LEGO Soccer/Football.
- Disney's Baby Mickey™ sets are released.

2002

- LEGOLAND® Deutschland opens in Günzburg.
- "Play On" replaces "Just Imagine…" as the company slogan.
- LEGO® Spider-Man™ swings into action to accompany the new movie.

2002

- *LEGO Mania* magazine becomes *LEGO Magazine*.
- LEGO Spybotics sets invade homes.
- LEGO® DUPLO® becomes LEGO Explore and introduces LEGO® Bob the Builder™ sets.
- LEGO Brand Retail stores open in Germany, England, and Russia.

2002

- Galidor: Defenders of the Outer Dimension, based on the TV series, features action figures with swappable body parts.
- LEGO Island Xtreme Stunts sets based on the video game arrive.
- LEGO Racers teams compete in the Racing Drome, with an accompanying video game.

2003

- The LEGO minifigure celebrates its 25th birthday.
- LEGO Sports NBA Basketball and Hockey sets join the game.

2004

- LEGO EXPLORE is replaced by three building systems for the very young: LEGO DUPLO, BABY, and QUATRO.
- The US LEGO Club creates the premium LEGO BrickMaster program.

2004

- LEGO Factory lets builders create models online and buy the pieces to make them.
- The LEGO Group partners with Ferrari to create a line of licensed LEGO Racers sets.
- Several traditional LEGO brick colors are retired and new colors are introduced.
- LEGO Dora the Explorer sets explore the globe.

2005

- The LEGO System of Play celebrates its 50th anniversary.
- The LEGOLAND parks are sold to the Merlin Entertainments Group. The LEGO Group owners maintain a shareholding in Merlin Entertainments Group.
- The first LEGO® *Star Wars®* videogame is released to rave reviews.
- The third BIONICLE movie, *Web of Shadows*, is released on DVD.
- LEGO World City is renamed LEGO City.
- LEGO Dino Attack and LEGO Dino 2010 roar to life.

2005

- LEGO DUPLO introduces Thomas and Friends™ building sets.
- The LEGO Vikings set sail.
- The LEGO Group sets up its LEGO Ambassador program to create closer ties between the company and adult LEGO fans.

2000
- The LEGO KNIGHTS' KINGDOM series launches.
- LEGO Writing office and school supplies are introduced.
- LEGO Mosaic lets you create your face in LEGO bricks.
- Action Wheelers brings racing action into younger hands.
- LEGO Arctic unleashes the first LEGO polar bear.
- The LEGO Adventurers travel to Dino Island.

2001
- The BIONICLE® line launches worldwide with a huge publicity campaign.
- The magic of LEGO® Harry Potter™ begins.
- Jack Stone rescues his city from natural disasters in a new "4 Plus" figure scale for younger builders.
- The LEGO Dinosaurs line is hatched.

2001
- LEGO® SERIOUS PLAY™ is founded to help businesses learn creative thinking through the use of LEGO bricks and building.
- Life on Mars takes LEGO Space to the Red Planet.

2001
- The LEGO Alpha Team battles to save the world from the evil Ogel.
- LEGO Racers starts its engine with a line of crashing mini-cars with alien drivers.

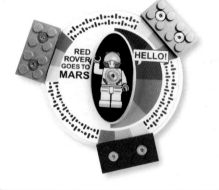

Kids could build a jungle for Dora and Diego to explore.

2003
- LEGO Discovery NASA sets based on modern space exploration are released. LEGO Minifigure astrobots Biff Starling and Sandy Moondust—or pictures of them, at least—become the first Earthlings to reach the planet Mars aboard the NASA rovers *Spirit* and *Opportunity*.
- LEGO Town becomes LEGO World City.

2003
- The CLIKITS™ line of buildable jewelry is released.
- The BIONICLE film *Mask of Light* is released to DVD.
- LEGO Designer and LEGO Gravity Games lines are launched.
- A record-breaking 1.63 million people visit LEGOLAND Billund.

2003
- LEGO® Dora the Explorer™ sets are released under LEGO Explore.
- Little Robots™ toys are released in Europe based on the TV series.
- www.LEGO.com receives about 4 million visitors per month.

2004
- The second LEGO KNIGHTS' KINGDOM series features an original story, complete with story and activity books, online comics and a collectible card game.
- *BIONICLE 2: Legends of Metru Nui* is released on DVD.

2005
- LEGO *Star Wars*: Revenge of the Brick airs on television.
- LEGO Racers shrinks race cars down into pocket-sized Tiny Turbos.

2006
- The new LEGO® EXO-FORCE™ theme begins, inspired by Japanese giant-robot comics and animation.
- LEGO® MINDSTORMS® NXT is launched.
- LEGO® Batman™ leaps onto the scene.

2006
- LEGO sets based on the Nickelodeon cartoons SpongeBob SquarePants™ and *Avatar: The Last Airbender*™ are released.
- Remote-controlled LEGO Trains replace the classic electric system.

2006
- LEGO *Star Wars* II: The Original Trilogy video game is released.

And Beyond!

THE COMPANY CELEBRATED its 75th anniversary in 2007, and things only got bigger from there. LEGO® construction returned to outer space, and classic Castle, Pirates, and underwater themes made triumphant comebacks as well. Licensed lines were a huge success with blockbuster video games and sets based on some of the biggest properties around, from comic books to hobbits. These years also saw a boom for ninja, the debut and demise of LEGO Universe, and the 30th anniversary of the one and only LEGO minifigure ●

2007

- The LEGO Group celebrates its 75th anniversary.
- LEGO Mars Mission brings back LEGO Space sets for the first time since 2001's Life on Mars.
- More classic themes return in the form of new LEGO Castle and LEGO Aqua Raiders product lines.

2008

- LEGOLAND Discovery Center Chicago opens in Schaumberg, IL.
- LEGO Stores begin offering a monthly mini-model build event.
- The LEGO Architecture theme introduces special-edition microscale models of famous buildings.

2009

- LEGO Power Miners is launched.
- LEGO Pirates and LEGO Space Police return with all-new sets.
- LEGO Games is launched.

2009

- The LEGO *Star Wars* theme celebrates its 10th anniversary with special packaging and minifigures.
- The LEGO Indiana Jones 2: The Adventure Continues video game adds new levels from the fourth movie and the original trilogy.
- LEGO Rock Band puts a minifigure spin on the Rock Band series of music video games.

2009

- The LEGO Agents upgrade to Agents 2.0.
- LEGO City branches out into the countryside with LEGO Farm sets.
- LEGO fans use the LEGO Design byME program to build virtual 3D models and then order them online with a custom box and building instructions.

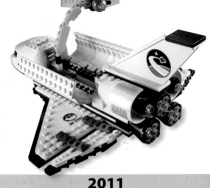

2011

- LEGO *Pirates of the Caribbean*™ sets include ships, locations, and characters from the blockbuster movies.
- The LEGO Games sub-theme of Heroica introduces buildable games that can be combined into one giant adventure.

2011

- Hero Recon Team lets builders create their own Hero Factory characters online and order the parts through the mail.
- Hero Factory and Ninjago specials air on television.
- After a decade, LEGO® DUPLO® Winnie the Pooh™ sets return.

2011

- LEGOLAND® Florida becomes North America's second LEGOLAND theme park.
- A LEGOLAND Discovery Center opens in Texas.
- LEGOLAND California adds a new *Star Wars* section to its MINILAND display.
- LEGO *Star Wars* III: The Clone Wars introduces video game missions based on the computer-animated television series.

2011

- LEGO *Pirates of the Caribbean*: The Video Game includes gameplay from all four movies.
- LEGO City gains a new spaceport with sets developed in conjunction with NASA.
- LEGO sets are launched into space aboard the Space Shuttle *Endeavour*.
- The LEGO Master Builder Academy program teaches how to build like the LEGO professionals.

Indy's whip, hat, and bag were all-new pieces for 2008.

2007

- The LEGO® Star Wars®: The Complete Saga video game lets gamers play through a brick-ified version of all six films.
- The Modular Buildings series of models for advanced builders launches with the Café Corner set.
- Mr. Magorium's Big Book, a set containing nine different models, is released to coincide with the movie Mr. Magorium's Wonder Emporium.
- LEGO Creator sets introduce LEGO Power Functions, electronic modules that add motors, lights, and remote-controlled movement to models.

2008

- Kjeld Kirk Kristiansen is inducted into the Toy Industry Hall of Fame, USA.
- LEGO Magazine becomes LEGO Club Magazine.
- The first issue of LEGO Club Jr. magazine is sent to younger club members in the US.

2008

- The LEGO® Indiana Jones™, LEGO® Speed Racer™, and LEGO Agents themes are launched.
- LEGO Indiana Jones and LEGO® Batman™ videogames are released.

2008

- The 50th anniversary of the patent of the stud-and-tube LEGO brick is celebrated with a worldwide building contest.
- The 30th birthday of the LEGO minifigure is commemorated with the "Go Miniman Go!" internet campaign and fan-video showcase.

2010

- The LEGO Group and Disney resume their partnership with the release of sets based on the Toy Story films, Cars (in LEGO® DUPLO® form) and Prince of Persia.
- Underwater action returns with LEGO Atlantis sets.
- The LEGO Castle theme continues with new LEGO Kingdoms sets.
- The LEGO Minifigures line launches with its first series of 16 characters.

2010

- LEGO World Racers takes builders on a frenetic, action-packed race through different environments.
- The long-running BIONICLE line comes to an end with the release of six BIONICLE Stars commemorative sets, each including a piece of extra golden armor to upgrade the Tahu figure.
- The Hero Factory theme continues the BIONICLE building style with an all-new universe and story.
- Harry Potter sets are produced for the first time since 2007.

2010

- LEGO® Ben 10™ buildable action figures are made in conjunction with Cartoon Network.
- Video game players magically build their way through the first four movies in LEGO® Harry Potter™: Years 1–4.
- The LEGO Universe massively multiplayer online game lets players create minifigure avatars and adventure together in a world of quests and construction.
- A direct-to-video movie, The Adventures of Clutch Powers, is the first full-length film to star minifigures.

2011

- Extraterrestrials invade Earth in the LEGO Alien Conquest theme.
- LEGO Ninjago puts a whole new spin on martial-arts action.
- The legacy of the LEGO Adventurers lives on with the heroes of the Pharaoh's Quest theme.

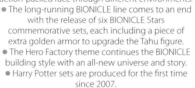

2011

- The LEGO CUUSOO partnership lets fans vote for models to be considered for release as LEGO sets.
- LEGO Harry Potter: Years 5–7 completes the video game retelling of the movie series.
- Life of George is released as an iPhone/iPod Touch application that interacts with a LEGO set.
- The year ends with the opening of LEGO ReBrick, a social media platform for LEGO fans aged 13 and over.

2012

- World-famous heroes and villains take the LEGO world by storm with the debut of the LEGO DC Universe Super Heroes and LEGO Marvel Universe Super Heroes themes.
- The new LEGO® The Lord of the Rings™ theme brings the epic movie world of Middle-earth to life with bricks, battling, and lots of short-legged minifigures.
- The LEGO Friends theme introduces a new line of building sets aimed at girls.

2012

- The LEGO City Police move out to the forest.
- Dinosaurs threaten the modern world once again with LEGO Dino.
- The LEGO Monster Fighters battle classic monster villains to prevent the sun from being forever extinguished.
- LEGO Ninjago gets an entire season of half-hour television episodes.

2012

- LEGO Universe, LEGO Design byME, and Hero Recon Team close down.
- LEGO CUUSOO voting leads to the production of a LEGO® Minecraft™ licensed model.
- LEGO DUPLO Disney Princess sets are released.
- New LEGOLAND Discovery Centers open in Kansas City and Atlanta.

The LEGO® Brick Patent

WHEN THE LEGO GROUP launched the LEGO® System of Play in 1955, it realized that the new LEGO brick had to be as perfect a building toy as possible. Bricks needed to lock together firmly to make stable models, but also come apart easily. CEO Godtfred Kirk Christiansen was determined to perfect the brick's quality and clutch power and fulfill the company's belief that it should be possible to build virtually *anything* with LEGO elements. At 1:58 pm on January 28, 1958, he finally submitted an application in Copenhagen, Denmark, for a patent for the improved LEGO brick and its building system ●

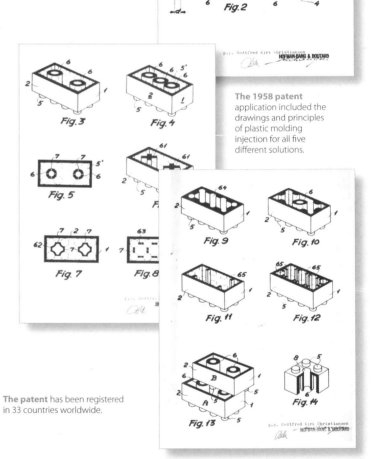

The **1958 patent** application included the drawings and principles of plastic molding injection for all five different solutions.

The **patent** has been registered in 33 countries worldwide.

KONGERIGET DANMARK

DIREKTORATET FOR PATENT- OG VAREMÆRKEVÆSENET

attesterer herved, at Godtfred Kirk Christiansen af Billund den 28. januar 1958 kl. 13.58 hertil har indleveret en ansøgning om patent i Danmark på et legetøjsbyggeelement.
(Ans. pr. 1958 nr. 289).

Vedhæftede fotokopi med tilhørende tegninger er overensstemmende med den med ansøgningen fulgte beskrivelse med tilhørende 3 tegninger.

Patentafdelingen, København, den 21. januar 1959.

F. Neergaard-Petersen.
direktøren.

Betalt med 24.00 kr.

Form. 119. 3000. Maj 58

THE STUD-AND-TUBE SOLUTION

The company developed several possible ways to improve the brick's clutch power. The first added three tubes to the underside of the current LEGO brick, creating a perfect three-point connection with the studs on top of the next brick below. Alternative solutions included bricks with two tubes or even crosses inside, with a total of five potential connection methods.

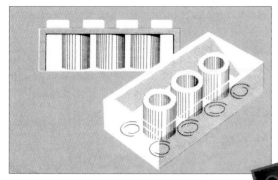

Godtfred Kirk Christiansen's favorite solution, the three-tube clutching system devised in 1957, became the final model for the new and improved LEGO brick.

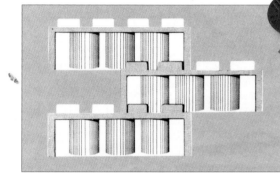

All 2 x 4 LEGO bricks manufactured since 1958 have been produced to the exact same measurements as the three-tube version described in the original patent.

BRICK VARIATIONS

Godtfred Kirk Christiansen's stud-and-tube solution continues to form the cornerstone of LEGO building. Today, LEGO elements are produced in thousands of different shapes, colors, and sizes, but each and every one of them is precisely designed to connect with the original brick, two studs wide and four studs long, that was patented on that famous day in 1958.

UNLIMITED POSSIBILITIES

The patented clutching ability of the LEGO brick gives builders of all ages an almost infinite variety of ways to express their imagination and creativity through construction. Each brick in the system can be connected to every other brick in multiple configurations, and as more bricks are added, the possibilities grow exponentially.

Two eight-stud LEGO bricks can be combined in 24 ways.

Three eight-stud LEGO bricks can be combined in 1,060 ways.

Six eight-stud LEGO bricks can be combined in 915,103,765 ways.

With eight bricks, the possibilities are virtually endless.

THE LEGO® BRICK

● LEGO® elements are part of a universal system and are all compatible with each other; bricks from 1958 fit bricks made 50 years later ● At 1:58 pm on January 28th, 1958, the company received a patent to manufacture LEGO bricks ● Since 1963, LEGO elements have been manufactured from ABS (acrylonitrile butadiene styrene), which is scratch and bite-resistant ● Bricks are made using small-capacity, precision-made molds ● Inspectors check the bricks for shape and color; only an average of 18 out of every million fails the test ● 36 billion LEGO bricks are produced each year. That's 68,000 every minute ● Six red eight-stud bricks can be combined in 915,103,765 different ways ● There are 4,200 different LEGO brick shapes ● The LEGO brick's 50th anniversary was celebrated in 2008 ● 40 billion LEGO bricks stacked together would reach the Moon ● There are 80 LEGO bricks for every person in the world

Top view showing studs.

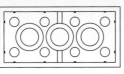

Bottom view showing tubes.

LEGO® Elements to Remember...

1949	**1953**	**1954**	**1955**
The first plastic bricks are launched. Forerunners of the true LEGO® brick, they are named Automatic Binding Bricks.	The first LEGO baseplate for building.	LEGO beams and windows.	Trees and small plastic vehicles for LEGO System of Play.

1968	**1969**	**1970**	**1974**	**1977**
Magnetic coupling brick.	LEGO® DUPLO® brick.	Cogwheel.	LEGO Family building figures.	LEGO DUPLO people.

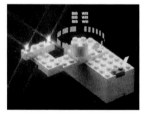

1986	**1989**	**1990**	**1990**	**1990**	**1993**
LEGO Light & Sound elements.	LEGO Pirates parrot and monkey.	Coupling.	LEGO DUPLO zoo animals.	LEGO Technic motor.	LEGO Castle series dragon.

2003	**2003**	**2004**	**2005**	**2006**	**2006**
LEGO Technic motor.	CLIKITS™ elements.	LEGO QUATRO brick.	LEGO DUPLO figures become more realistic.	LEGO® EXO-FORCE™ elements.	LEGO® MINDSTORMS® NXT programmable brick.

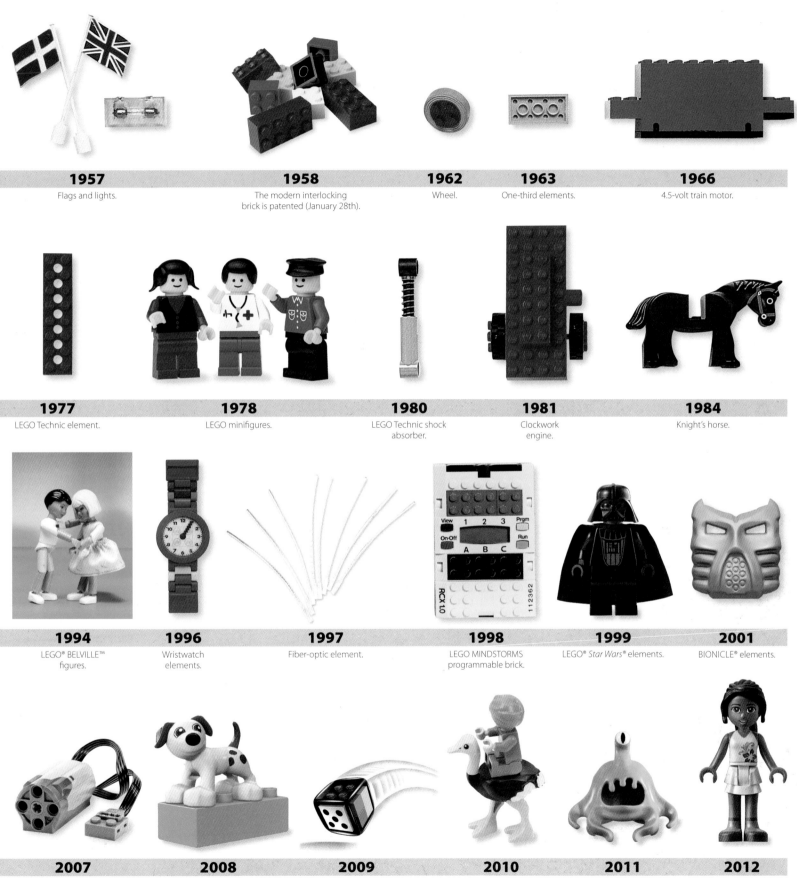

1957
Flags and lights.

1958
The modern interlocking brick is patented (January 28th).

1962
Wheel.

1963
One-third elements.

1966
4.5-volt train motor.

1977
LEGO Technic element.

1978
LEGO minifigures.

1980
LEGO Technic shock absorber.

1981
Clockwork engine.

1984
Knight's horse.

1994
LEGO® BELVILLE™ figures.

1996
Wristwatch elements.

1997
Fiber-optic element.

1998
LEGO MINDSTORMS programmable brick.

1999
LEGO® Star Wars® elements.

2001
BIONICLE® elements.

2007
Power Functions motor.

2008
LEGO DUPLO animals.

2009
LEGO Games.

2010
Rideable ostrich.

2011
Brain-sucking Alien Clinger.

2012
LEGO Friends mini-dolls.

THE LEGO® MINIFIGURE

● The first LEGO® minifigures were made in 1978 for the new Town, Castle, and Space themes ● Minifigures are also known as "minifigs" ● Minifigure feet and legs have holes to let them connect to LEGO bricks when standing or sitting. Their heads have a stud on top to attach hair, hats, helmets, or other LEGO pieces ● Minifigures are made up of nine pieces, but are usually packaged in 3: head, body with arms, and legs ● Until 1989, all minifigures had the same smiling expression. That year, the new Pirates series added different faces as well as hook-hands and peg legs ● The first non-yellow standard minifigures were released in 2003 when the LEGO Group launched licensed characters from sports, television, and movies with more realistic skin tones ● Minifigures with two-sided faces that could change expression by turning their heads around were introduced with the LEGO® Harry Potter™ Professor Quirrell minifigure ● In 2005, electronics were added to minifigures, letting *Star Wars*® lightsabers and police flashlights light up when the figure's head was pressed down ● Some characters have their own unique bodies, such as the skeletons from LEGO Castle, droids from LEGO® *Star Wars*®, BIONICLE® heroes and villains, and aliens from Life on Mars and Mars Mission ● In 2008, the LEGO Group celebrated the 30th birthday of the minifigure with the worldwide "Go Miniman Go!" multimedia event. Fans joined in by uploading their own minifigure movies ● About 4 billion minifigures have been produced—more than 10 times the population of the USA!

An early ancestor of the LEGO minifigure, with a simple three-piece body, a faceless yellow head and no separate arms or legs, first appeared in sets in 1975.

Making LEGO® Bricks

THE LEGO® Kornmarken factory at the company headquarters in Billund, Denmark, opened on June 24th, 1987 after 18 months of construction. Today, the giant factory is constantly in motion, operating 24 hours a day and seven days a week. Its workers and state-of-the-art machinery produce about 2.4 million plastic bricks every hour. Approximately 16 billion LEGO elements were made there in the year 2007 alone ●

The Kornmarken factory building is big enough for a 20 km half-marathon race to be run inside it. It's so big inside that employees often use special scooters and other vehicles to get from place to place quickly.

BRICK BY BRICK BY BRICK...

1 A LEGO brick begins life as a pile of tiny plastic granules, each about the size of a grain of rice. The granules are shipped to Denmark from Italy, the Netherlands, and Germany. There are currently about 55 basic granule colors, which can be mixed to make additional colors.

2 The granules are sucked up from large plastic containers into one of the factory's 14 silos.

A silo can hold up to 33 tons (30 tonnes) of granules, but usually contains about 29 tons (26 tonnes). 50 tons (45 tonnes) of granules can be processed every 24 hours.

3 The granules travel along pipes to one of the 12 molding halls, which contain a total of 775 molding machines.

4 The granules are fed down pipes directly into the molding machines. A single person, backed

up by maintenance technicians, looks after 72 molding machines. The machines are computer-controlled and made in Germany and Austria. A warning light on top of the machine turns on to indicate any problems in the molding process.

5 Inside the molding machines, the granules are heated to a temperature of 455°F (235°C), which melts them together into a toothpaste-

like mass of gooey plastic. The molds then apply 28 to 165 tons (25 to 150 tonnes) of pressure (depending on the element being produced) to shape each individual brick to an accuracy of 0.0002 in (0.005 mm), which is necessary to make sure that every LEGO brick fits together with the rest. In 10–15 seconds, the bricks harden and cool. Leftover plastic is recycled.

Bricks that chance to fall onto the factory floor are also recycled. The new bricks are automatically ejected from the molds.

6 The bricks travel along a short conveyor belt, dropping into boxes at the end.

7 When a box is full of newly made bricks, the molding machine transmits a signal to a nearby robot along wires embedded

in the floor of the factory.

8 The robot travels to the machine, collects the box, puts a lid on it, stamps the box with the all-important barcode that enables this particular batch to be identified in future operations, and places it on a conveyor belt. This leads to the distribution warehouse.

9 The box travels along the conveyor belt to the distribution warehouse. The high-level warehouse has space for 424,000 boxes of LEGO® bricks. A logical motion machine, powered by compressed air, finds the boxes according to their barcodes and selects which ones are needed for an order. When certain boxes of bricks are needed to make up a LEGO set, the logical motion machine selects and grabs the correct ones.

10 The machine places the boxes on a conveyor belt that leads to a truck. The boxes are then driven to the packing, assembling, and decoration department.

11, 12 Assembly machines then attach arms and hands to minifigure bodies, tires to wheels, and so on.

13 Painting machines add faces to heads and complex patterns to decorated elements.

14 The finished LEGO pieces are then

13

From 1978 to 1989, all LEGO minifigures had the same expression: a smile and two dots for eyes. Today, there are so many different faces that the factory has to keep track of all the ones being made on a particular day!

Some heads even get an extra face painted on the back so you can turn it around and change our mood!

Printing inks used to make up colors for different features on bodies and faces.

14 **15**

16

17 **18** **19**

transported in trays to the packaging department. Vibrating machines sort the piles of elements into their individual shapes, which are collected in bins. Each bin contains one type of element. Boxes called cassettes move along a conveyor belt beneath the bins. As each cassette arrives beneath a bin, the correct number and type of element drops into it.

15 The elements are then bagged or stored in clear plastic display trays. Each bag is weighed twice to make sure that it contains the right number and type of elements.

16 Machines send the bags of elements, along with the set's instruction booklet, down chutes to fall into boxes on a packing line.

17 LEGO workers check that the bags of elements lie flat so that box lids close tightly.

18, 19 The boxed LEGO sets are picked up by robotic arms and packed into cardboard boxes for transportation to stores.

Designing a LEGO® Set

HOW DO THE LEGO® set designers come up with all of those wonderful models and minifigures? The first step is finding inspiration. The design team gathers material from many different sources—even from their own experiences. The LEGO City team worked at a fire station for a day to learn more about fire-fighting and fire trucks, and the LEGO Power Miners team took a trip to an underground mine ●

BRAINSTORMING

Once they have their inspiration, the LEGO design team members get together for a Design Boost session, where they come up with ideas for story, models, characters, and any new elements that might be needed. The Design Lead and Marketing Lead refine the models and agree on their price points, making sure that each model is unique, but works as part of the overall series.

New LEGO characters start out as a blank minifigure template.

A graphic designer makes a quick sketch and adds color with markers or a computer.

Once the design is approved, the decoration is finalized on the computer so a test print can be made.

CREATING NEW ELEMENTS

If the set needs a new LEGO element, the model designer works with a part designer or engineer to produce it. Rounded pieces like animals and minifigure hair are hand-sculpted and scanned into a computer for the engineer to finalize, while simple shapes like bricks and wheels are built directly on the computer using 3D software.

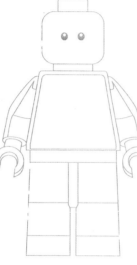

The 2007 LEGO Castle skeleton horse was first created as a 3D computer model. All new elements are measured and checked to make sure they are child-safe and fit into the LEGO System.

MODEL DEVELOPMENT

A team of four to eight Model Builder designers is assigned to start developing the final models. They make multiple versions of each one to test different functions and colors. All through the process, the models are tested with kids to find out what they like best or want to see added —it's their opinions that matter the most when designing a new LEGO set!

Realistic exhaust stack, light, and horn details

EARLY CONCEPTS

After the initial brainstorming, some ideas for new sets and minifigures are turned into hand-drawn illustrations or clay character models, while others are built out of LEGO bricks as conceptual "sketch models." If an element isn't available in the right color, the designers paint it themselves.

8258 Crane Truck (2009)

Gears and transmissions control crane functions

Creating a LEGO Technic model is one of the toughest challenges there is for a set designer. All of the parts have to line up with perfect precision to make the mechanical functions work properly when the model is put together.

V8 engine pistons move when vehicle rolls

Built-in safety clutch protects gears from damage

FINAL STEPS

The model is nearly done! Now it has to be approved by a Model Committee of expert builders, engineers, part designers, and building-instruction developers. If they find any problems, the designer has to start over again. Once approved, the model is taken apart piece by piece by the instructions team, who use a 3D computer program to create the building steps.

The LEGO® Logo

SINCE ITS CREATION in 1934, the LEGO® logo has undergone many changes. By 1953, what was affectionately nicknamed the "sausage logo"—rounded, black-outlined white letters, and a red background—already resembled today's distinctive brand. By the early 1970s, the logo looked almost as it does today; a slight modification in 1998 brought it up to date ●

1934

1946

1950

1953

1955

1955

1958

1958

1936

1946

1953

1953

1956

1958

1958

1964

1972

1998

Inspirational building leaflet included in
LEGO model boxes between 1963 and 1964.

LEGO® Play Themes

EVEN THOUGH all of the sets in the LEGO® System of Play were designed to be compatible within one big creative LEGO universe, there were some types of models that kids wanted more and more of. More trains! More castles! More cities! More spaceships! Answering the call in 1978 were the first three LEGO Play Themes, each full of sets based on a popular subject and populated by the brand-new, fully-posable LEGO minifigures. LEGO Castle had medieval knights, kings, and fortresses. LEGO Town had buildings, roads, cars, and trucks. LEGO Space had rockets, rovers, and lunar bases. No matter what your favorite theme was, now you could collect and construct it to build your own LEGO world ●

LEGO® City

IT TAKES A TOWN to make a city. A LEGO® Town, that is! In contrast to fantastical themes like LEGO Castle and LEGO Space, LEGO Town has offered a familiar slice of real life ever since it first came on the scene in 1978. Spinning out of sets like 1972's Police Heliport and the original 1955 Town Plan, the Town theme let builders create their own modern cities full of airports, police stations, construction sites, shops, restaurants, and more. Known today as LEGO City, this once-little town is bigger and busier than ever before ●

LEGO® Town & City

With a moving piston and bucket, the Fire Station truck's folding, telescoping ladder worked just like the real thing.

Fire truck from 7945 Fire Station (2007)

SOME THINGS never go out of style in the big city. While LEGO® Town and LEGO City sub-themes may have come and gone over the years, no brick-built metropolis is complete without these classic civic fixtures: a police department, a fire station, an airport, a hospital, and a busy construction crew to ensure the city keeps on growing ●

FIRE

For more than 50 years, the fearless firefighters of LEGO City have been extinguishing blazes and saving LEGO cats from LEGO trees with the help of extending ladders, wind-up hoses, and an ever-growing assortment of fire trucks, fire stations, and rescue gear!

Not everyone rides in the truck. When there's an emergency in LEGO City, the Fire Chief speeds to the scene in his personal car.

POLICE

When danger calls, the LEGO City Police are always on the scene. These dedicated officers never stop patrolling the streets of LEGO City, protecting its citizens night and day. From their modern police station, they can monitor radio bands, dispatch vehicles to emergencies, scan the crime computer, and keep watch on the prison in case of break-outs.

7744 Police Headquarters (2008)

Radio mast

7892 LEGO City Hospital (2006)

The most common procedure at this hospital? Emergency minifigure reassembly!

The operating room had everything a LEGO doctor could need. Just don't ask about the chainsaw in the corner.

HOSPITAL

Though it's had fewer releases than the other major sub-themes, the LEGO City Hospital is a vital part of city life. Complete with all the latest innovations in minifigure medical care, it even had a helicopter pad and off-road vehicle for the biggest emergencies in and out of town.

POLICE

7893 Passenger Plane (2006)

Angled wing tips

Tool kit

Did you know that the airport has its own fire department? 7891 Airport Firetruck (2006) and others are always on hand in case of emergencies.

AIRPORT

Whether you're taking a vacation or just arriving in town for the first time, the LEGO City Airport is the place to go when you need to fly. With dozens of different helicopters, passenger planes, and jumbo jets to choose from, not to mention baggage carts, runway strips, air traffic control towers, and a friendly crew of pilots, mechanics, and flight attendants, you'll never have a delayed departure!

In 2008, the police department finally got something it had needed for a long time: the first-ever LEGO City handcuffs.

Searchlight

The 2008 Police Headquarters featured 953 elements, including five police officers, one crook, and a police dog.

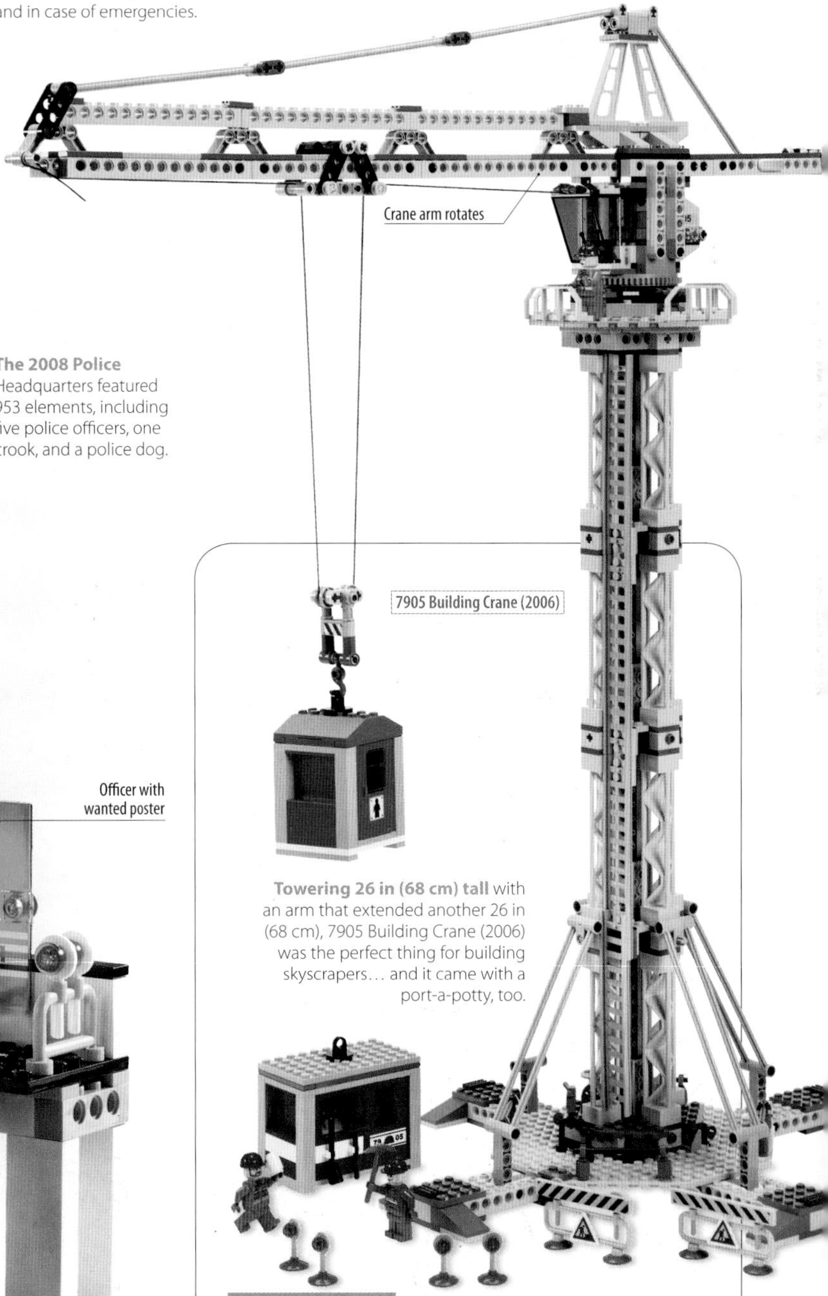

Crane arm rotates

7905 Building Crane (2006)

Towering 26 in (68 cm) tall with an arm that extended another 26 in (68 cm), 7905 Building Crane (2006) was the perfect thing for building skyscrapers… and it came with a port-a-potty, too.

Officer with wanted poster

CONSTRUCTION

They may not have a station of their own, but these hard-working, hard-hatted city heroes make up for it by building all the rest. With cranes, bulldozers, cement mixers, dump trucks, haulers, loaders, and more to use in their projects, it's a wonder the LEGO City Construction crew ever gets any sleep at all!

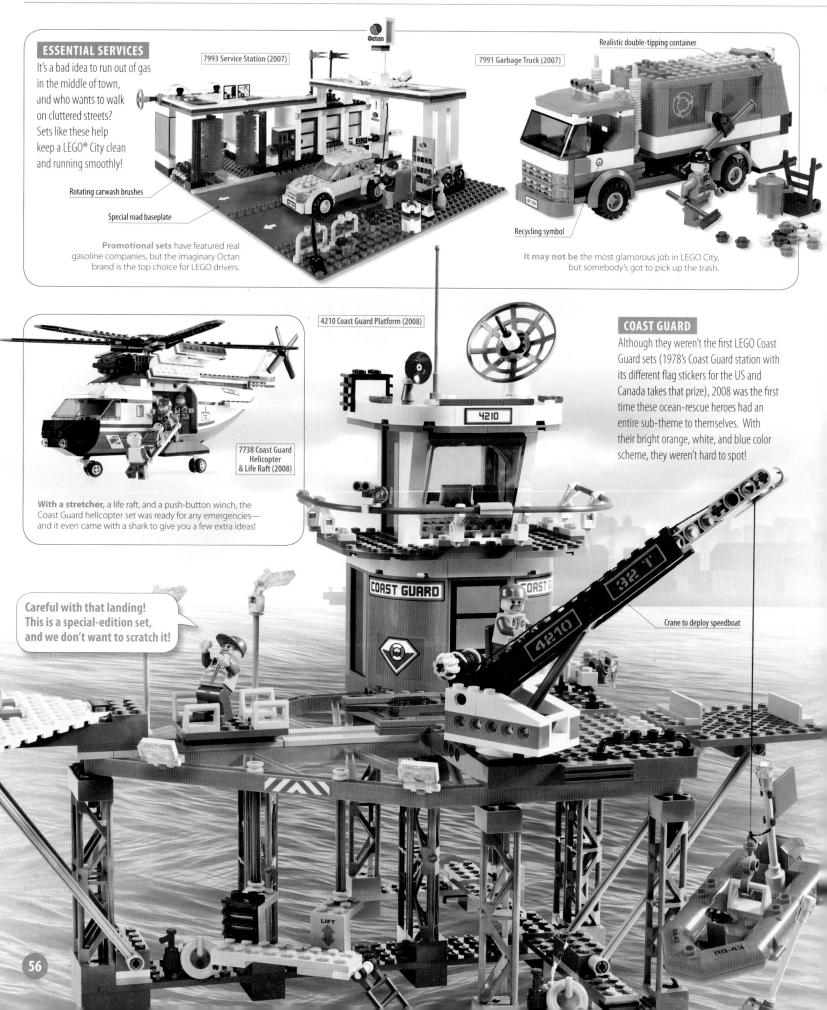

ESSENTIAL SERVICES

It's a bad idea to run out of gas in the middle of town, and who wants to walk on cluttered streets? Sets like these help keep a LEGO® City clean and running smoothly!

7993 Service Station (2007)

Rotating carwash brushes

Special road baseplate

Promotional sets have featured real gasoline companies, but the imaginary Octan brand is the top choice for LEGO drivers.

Realistic double-tipping container

7991 Garbage Truck (2007)

Recycling symbol

It may not be the most glamorous job in LEGO City, but somebody's got to pick up the trash.

4210 Coast Guard Platform (2008)

7738 Coast Guard Helicopter & Life Raft (2008)

With a stretcher, a life raft, and a push-button winch, the Coast Guard helicopter set was ready for any emergencies—and it even came with a shark to give you a few extra ideas!

COAST GUARD

Although they weren't the first LEGO Coast Guard sets (1978's Coast Guard station with its different flag stickers for the US and Canada takes that prize), 2008 was the first time these ocean-rescue heroes had an entire sub-theme to themselves. With their bright orange, white, and blue color scheme, they weren't hard to spot!

Careful with that landing! This is a special-edition set, and we don't want to scratch it!

4210

COAST GUARD

Crane to deploy speedboat

LIFT

7637 Farm (2009)

DAS GOLDENE SCHAUKELPFERD
Familie&Co
2009
Sieger in der Kategorie
"Für Künstler und Baumeister"

Pier crane raises,
lowers, and spins 360°

7994 LEGO City Harbor (2007)

City Lines dock office

FEEDING THE CITY

Out in the country near LEGO City, the farmer and his family get up at sunrise to plow the fields, empty the silo, and fill the barn with fresh bales of hay. This set included a dog, a cat, a rat, and the first spotted LEGO cows!

Ship is 23 in (58 cm) long

With a special one-piece hull, this cargo ship really floated on water.

Anchor with working winch

OUT ON THE DOCK

Things are always bustling down at the city harbor pier. Who has time to nap when there are fish to catch, containers to deliver, and big cargo ships to load and unload?

EVERYDAY PLACES

And that's not all! With houses, shops, restaurants, garages, race tracks, deep-sea divers, road rescue crews, extreme sports teams, Outback explorers, and even a space port or two, there have probably been enough LEGO Town and LEGO City sets released since 1978 to fill a real city!

6376 Breezeway Cafe (1990)

The busy City Corner set included a skater and bike shop, a 2-story pizzeria, and a businessman to chase after the bus when he was running late for work.

6372 Town House (1982)

7641 City Corner (2009)

Auto mechanic	Skateboarder	Builder	Photographer	Waiter
Swimmer	Security guard	Firefighter	Robber	Pedestrian	Doctor

CITIZENS OF THE CITY

Meet the inhabitants of LEGO Town and LEGO City! They include cooks, crooks, divers, drivers, mailmen, mechanics, news reporters, office workers, delivery boys, and lots of other familiar city faces. And they always do their jobs with a smile!

7731 Mail Van (2008)

City Outskirts

THERE'S MORE TO LEGO® City than just what's in the city. From a bustling modern space center where rockets and space shuttles blast into orbit, to a forest full of cops, robbers, and the occasional hungry bear, these sets are just a small sampling of the activity and fun that you can discover outside the city limits •

The shuttle's cargo was a brick-built Hubble Space Telescope!

3367 Space Shuttle (2011)

CITY IN SPACE

Built on a LEGO road baseplate, the biggest set in 2011's LEGO City space sub-theme starred a 14 in (35 cm) tall rocket. Builders could fuel it up, use tools to make last minute changes, roll it into position at the launch platform, load a pilot or cargo on board, count down, and then blast off for adventure.

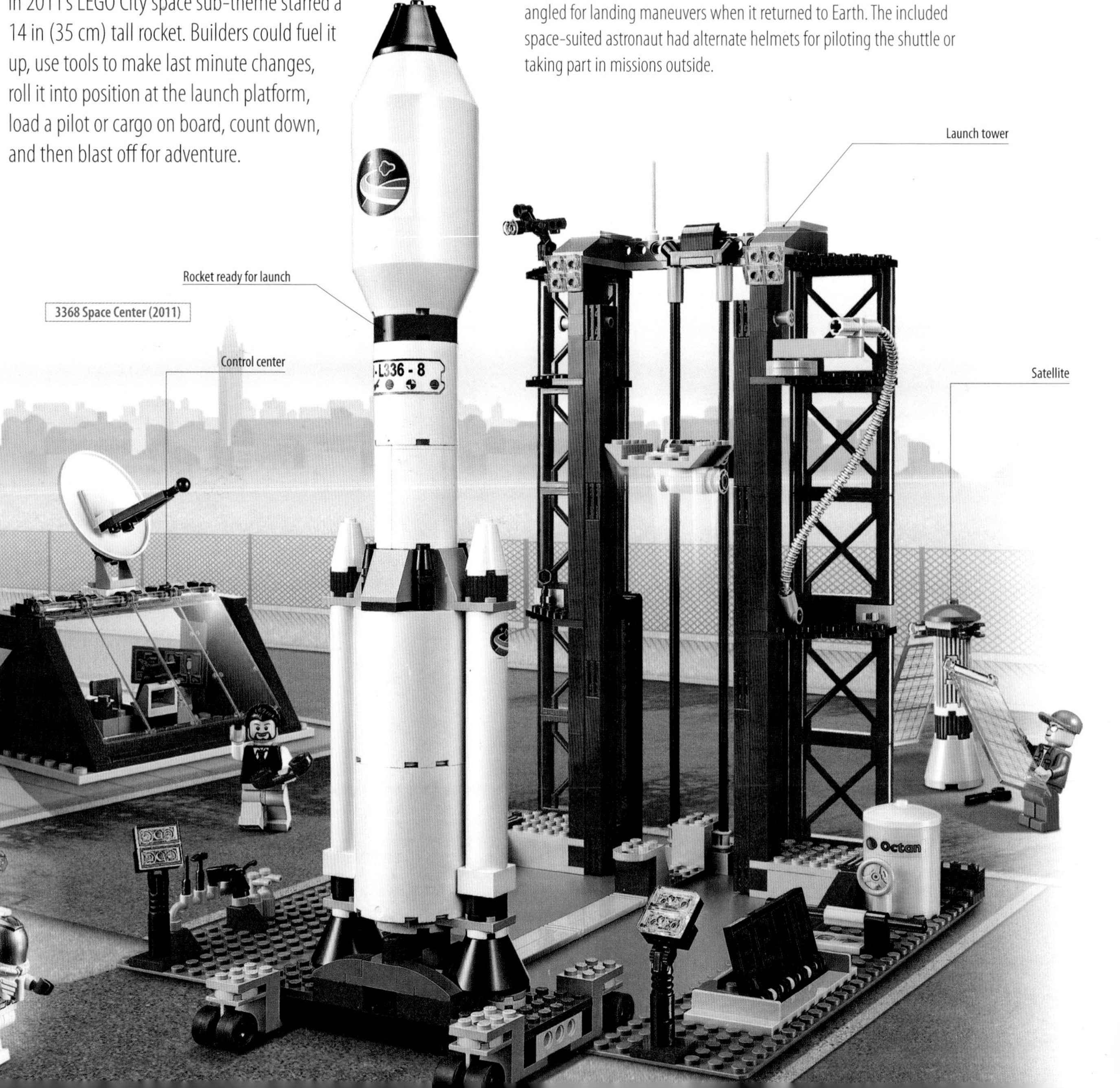

SPACE SHUTTLE

The LEGO City space shuttle had opening cargo bay doors and a hinged robotic arm for deploying or retrieving satellites. Its rear wing flaps could be angled for landing maneuvers when it returned to Earth. The included space-suited astronaut had alternate helmets for piloting the shuttle or taking part in missions outside.

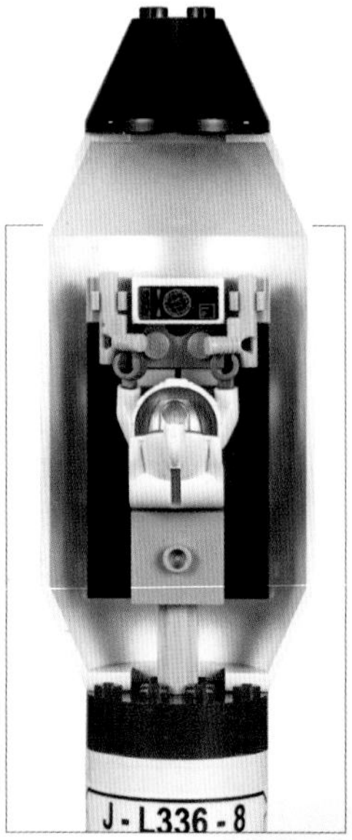

Accessed by a launch platform elevator, the cockpit had interchangeable parts to hold an astronaut or a folded-up satellite.

J - L 336 - 8

Rocket ready for launch

3368 Space Center (2011)

Control center

Launch tower

Satellite

Back-up crew

Astronaut with helmet

58

COUNTRY TRIP

Released as a special-edition set in the City Farm line, this four-wheel drive auto pulled a trailer with a LEGO horse inside. The horse's rider wore a smart riding jacket and helmet, while the 4WD driver was more relaxed in plaid. The model also included a fence for jumping.

Horse could wear a saddle

7635 4WD with Horse Trailer (2009)

WIND POWER

LEGO City went green with this model, which let you drive the disassembled wind turbine to its destination on the extending transport truck with escort traffic car, then connect the blades, motor, and tower together to start generating clean wind power for the city.

7747 Wind Turbine Transport (2009)

FLYING IN STYLE

Whether driving or flying, this is the way to travel! Another special-edition model in the US, this set featured a private helicopter and a stretch limousine to carry its V.I.P.s (very important passengers). To get them there, they had both a chopper pilot and their very own chauffeur.

3222 Helicopter and Limousine (2010)

LEGO building got a little recursive with this 2010 model of a LEGO delivery truck. Its trailer was full of tiny LEGO City boxes… including one for the truck itself!

INTO THE WOODS

The LEGO City theme took a detour off the beaten path in 2012, which saw a change of scene from the city streets to the trees of the nearby LEGO City Forest. Builders were introduced to a brave team of forest police, who used their off-road vehicles and knowledge of nature to track down fugitive crooks.

The woodsy-looking forest police station had a tall communications tower for keeping in touch with civilization.

Secret mailbox escape hatch

Hollow rock for hiding stolen loot

3221 LEGO® Truck (2010)

LEGO set boxes made from bricks with stickers

Police helicopter

Police truck

4440 Forest Police Station (2012)

The forest police sets introduced a brand-new LEGO bear. Its hind legs and neck were jointed to let it walk on four or two legs—much to the dismay of these crooks.

4438 Robbers' Hideout (2012)

Working crane

MINE, ALL MINE

LEGO City struck gold with its 2012 mining sets. At the big mine, you could use the drilling machine to break up rocks, drive them out to the crane, load them onto the conveyor belt, and haul them away.

Drilling machine

4204 The Mine (2012)

What do you get when you build flame elements onto trees? A forest fire! Fortunately, the Fire Plane could dump a tank-full of clear blue "water" bricks to put out the blaze.

4209 Fire Plane (2012)

Sets to Remember

374 Fire Station (1978)

6335 Indy Transport (1996)

6414 Dolphin Point (1995)

600 Police Car (1978)

1656 Evacuation Team (1991)

376 Town House With Garden (1978)

1572 Super Tow Truck (1986)

6356 Med-Star Rescue Plane (1988)

6365 Summer Cottage (1981)

6380 Emergency Treatment Center (1987)

6336 Launch Response Unit (1995)

6441

ages/edades
9+
10159
LEGO City
Airport
cont. 863 pcs/pzs

6441 Deep Reef Refuge (1997)

10159 City Airport (2004)

6473

8-12

6473 RES-Q Cruiser (1998)

5-12
7239

7239 Fire Truck (2004)

6435

5-10

6435 Coast Guard HQ (1999)

5-12
7634

7634 Tractor (2009)

5-12
7734

7734 Cargo Plane (2008)

7+
7034

World City

7034 Surveillance Truck (2003)

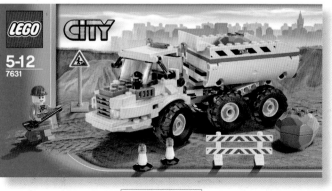

5-12
7631

7631 Dump Truck (2009)

5-12
7279

7279 Police Minifigure Collection (2011)

LEGO® Train

ALL ABOARD!

Train conductor (2003)

This conductor's jacket bears the LEGO Train logo.

IT'S BEEN SPEEDING down the tracks since 1966. It's driven on blue rails, gray rails, metal rails, and plastic rails. It's been powered by hand, clockwork, batteries, electricity, and remote control. From old-time steam locomotives to modern bullet trains, here comes that classic among classics: the famous LEGO® Train ●

080 Basic Building Set with Train (1967)

RIGHT ON TRACK

This 700-piece Universal Building Set model included one of the first LEGO trains. It had to be pushed along by hand, but could be motorized with a 4.5-volt battery box borrowed from another train set.

7740 12V Passenger Train (1980)

INTER-CITY EXPRESS

This German inter-city engine with an electric 12-volt motor and two passenger cars was introduced in 1980, the year when the LEGO Train theme was redesigned with gray tracks and a more realistic model style.

Most LEGO train cars were connected to the engine and each other by articulated magnetic couplers; the earliest trains used a hook-and-eye system.

RUNNING ON BLUE RAILS

Between 1966 and 1979, LEGO train sets ran on blue rails. The first models were basic push-along trains, but 4.5-volt battery motors quickly followed, and in 1969, the latest LEGO trains were powered by 12-volt electrified tracks. Trains of this period were small and low on detail.

182 4.5v Train Set with Signal (1975)

116 Starter Train Set with Motor (1967)

Thanks to the LEGO System of Play, boats, aircraft, buildings, and trains from different years combine together.

Blue LEGO train tracks were simple rails with white cross-tie bricks to hold them off the ground.

113 Motorized Train Set (1966)

10020 Santa Fe Super Chief (2002)

SANTA FE SUPER CHIEF

Originally sold as a numbered limited edition of 10,000, this locomotive was based on the real *Super Chief* luxury passenger train. It could be upgraded with additional cars or a motor.

LEGO Train logo

4513 Grand Central Station (2003)

RAIL NETWORK

Along with train engines and cars of all shapes and sizes, LEGO Train sets have included a number of stations, level crossings, cargo cranes, a train wash, and an engine shed.

Track-side pizzeria

6399 Airport Shuttle (1990)

9-VOLT MONORAIL

This LEGO Town monorail was powered by the 9-volt electric current that would become a new standard for LEGO Train rails starting in 1991.

NIGHT TRAIN

Inspired by classic steam engines, the Emerald Night was a LEGO Train fan's dream come true. It measured 27 in (68 cm) long, featured piston-action wheels and an opening coal tender and dining car, and could be motorized by adding Power Functions parts.

The Emerald Night took a year and a half to develop with input from top train fans. It included two new sizes of big train wheels and elements in new and rare colors.

10194 Emerald Night (2009)

REMOTE CONTROL

In 2006, LEGO Trains returned to plastic rails and battery-powered motors, but now they had infrared remote controls that could turn on an engine's lights, change its speed, and even toot its horn. 2009 saw the further introduction of Power Functions technology, rechargeable motor batteries, and new flexible tracks.

My Own Train was hosted by Engineer Max and Conductor Charlie, who also came with the 10133 BNSF GP-38 Locomotive set in 2005.

7897 Passenger Train (2006)

This motorized train would start and stop automatically when you blew the whistle (lying on rear car).

118 Electronic Train (Forward-Stop) (1968)

MY OWN TRAIN

From 2001 to 2003, the LEGO My Own Train website let builders create and order their own custom trains from two sizes and five colors of classic steam locomotives, as well as several types of rolling stock cars.

10205 My Own Train (2002)

Conductor Charlie

Engineer Max

LEGO® Castle

1978 WAS A HISTORIC YEAR
for the LEGO Group—it embarked on a fantasy-filled journey back to the days of kings, queens, knights, and legends. Starting with a simple yellow fortress, the world of LEGO® Castle soon grew to include entire kingdoms, as well as armies of sword-wielding warriors that were at times chivalrous, villainous, swashbuckling, or downright spooky. Prepare for a blast from the past with these sets straight from the days of knightly yore ●

For King and Castle!

375 Castle (1978)

Classic Castles

FROM THE ORIGINAL yellow castle with its brick-built horses to today's catapult-covered fantasy fortresses, the LEGO® Castle theme has been letting builders create their own medieval kingdoms for more than 30 years. Take an historical tour of some of the most famous castles of the past and present, and then turn the page to discover even more of the world of LEGO Castle ●

THE FIRST CASTLE

Here's where it all began! The famous "Yellow Castle" was the very first castle made for the LEGO System of Play. With its tall towers, crank-raised drawbridge and four factions of knights to attack or defend it, it already had many of the classic features of later LEGO castles.

6086 Black Knight's Castle (1992)

One of the most realistic LEGO castles, the home of the Black Knights included rare yellow Tudor-patterned wall pieces and four knights with lances and flags, mounted on horses and ready to joust.

You might think that this piece only works as a dragon's wing, but see p. 190 and you might just spot it somewhere else!

7094 King's Castle Siege (2007)

KING'S CASTLE SIEGE

Besieged by an evil wizard's skeleton warriors and a fire-breathing dragon, the King of the Western Kingdom fought back with knights, catapults, and a golden sword. The 2007–2009 LEGO Castle series was praised by fans for its return to classic building styles and castle design, including a working drawbridge and portcullis.

The 2007 Skeleton Warriors were redesigned from the original loose-limbed LEGO Castle skeletons to have scarier skulls and more posable limbs

8877 Vladek's Dark Fortress (2005)

Bad guys need homes, too. When the evil Vladek conquered the kingdom of Ankoria, he built his own fortress, complete with launching fireballs and an enchanted mask for the heroes to knock off its central tower.

Watch out if you walk from the treasure room to the prison tower. This bridge is booby-trapped to flip upside-down and send attackers flying!

Catapult flings LEGO bricks at the enemy

Break-away wall for battle damage or secret escapes

6097 Night Lord's Castle (1997)

The lair of the dreaded Fright Knights and their leader, Basil the Bat Lord, was also home to Willa the Witch and a black dragon. Spooky surprises included a secret rotating wall, a locking dungeon door, and a skull that appeared inside a crystal ball.

8781 Castle of Morcia (2004)

From the second LEGO® KNIGHTS' KINGDOM™ series, King Mathias's magical castle had reversible details to let you transform it from good and blue to evil and red when the villainous Vladek took control.

6082 Fire Breathing Fortress (1993)

Starring Majisto the wizard and his glow-in-the-dark wand, the Dragon Masters series jumped into the world of fantasy and magic. This set featured a rock-dropping dragon head, a cage for captured dragons, and a sneaky spy from the Wolfpack Renegades.

6098 King Leo's Castle (2000)

From the first LEGO KNIGHTS' KINGDOM series, this fairy tale-style castle had modular towers on a raised baseplate. It belonged to the Lion Knights, who defended it with the sword-swinging Princess Storm against Cedric the Bull's warriors.

Knights & Legends

THERE'S MUCH MORE to LEGO® Castle than just castles! The theme has included hundreds of buildings, vehicles, and scenes, as well as more than a dozen groups of minifigure characters, from the chivalrous Royal Knights and the swashbuckling Forestmen to the savage Wolfpack Renegades and the creepy Fright Knights ●

7093 Skeleton Tower (2007)

WILY WIZARDRY

The first LEGO Castle theme to be titled "LEGO Castle" on the packaging launched in 2007. It featured a kingdom under attack by The Evil Wizard, who was served by a horde of skeleton warriors and dragons.

6067 Guarded Inn (1986)

A CASTLE CLASSIC

Hailed by many fans as the best LEGO Castle set of all time, 1986's Guarded Inn is a rare civilian setting with a cozy tavern and section of wall that can be connected to other castle models. It includes a knight on horse, two guards, and a maiden to tend the inn and pour refreshments. It proved so popular that it was re-released in 2001 as the first in a series of LEGO Legends.

| LEGOLAND Castle (1978–1983) | Black Falcons (1984–1992) | Crusaders (1984–1992) | Forestmen (1987–1990) | Black Knights (1988–1994) | Wolfpack Renegades (1992–1993) | Basil the Bat Lord Fright Knights (1997–1998) | Cedric the Bull KNIGHTS' KINGDOM I (2000) | Jayko KNIGHTS' KINGDOM II (2004–2006) |

A-VIKING WE SHALL GO

The LEGO Vikings set sail in 2005 with a collection of sets full of bold, bearded warriors, vehicles built for battle, and a mighty walled fortress. With their horned helmets, fireball launchers, and monsters from the mists of Norse mythology like the Fenris Wolf and Nidhogg dragon, these Vikings may not have been quite historically accurate, but they did have some of the longest LEGO set names of all time!

7018 Viking Ship Challenges the Midgard Serpent (2005)

Flexible sea serpent

Longboat measures 19 in (48 cm) long with a 12-in (30-cm) sail

3053 Emperor's Stronghold (1999)

NINJA KNIGHTS

Despite their unusual non-European setting, the Ninja sets were an official part of the LEGO Castle theme. With their ornate temples, sword-wielding samurai, and bands of stealthy (and occasionally flying) ninja mercenaries, they added a distinctly Eastern flair and plenty of brand-new pieces to the Castle collection.

6066 Camouflaged Outpost (1987)

8701 King Jayko (2006)

MERRY MEN

With their feathered caps, green clothes, bows and arrows, and treetop hideouts, the Forestmen bore quite a resemblance to a famous merry band of outlaws from English folklore!

Once a reckless young knight, Jayko the Swift became King of Morcia.

LEGO® KNIGHTS' KINGDOM™

The second of two LEGO Castle themes named KNIGHTS' KINGDOM, the 2004–2006 series revolved around the magical kingdom of Morcia. The tale was told through storybooks and online comics, and the sets included both minifigure-scale models, and larger action figures with thumb-driven battle moves.

8702 Lord Vladek (2006)

The scorpion-themed Vladek had mystical powers and a legion of Shadow Knights at his command.

8780 Citadel of Orlan (2004)

Each knight had his own animal icon, armor color, and special skill.

PERILOUS PITFALLS

When the dark knight Vladek took over the kingdom and kidnapped the king, Jayko the Swift, Santis the Strong, Danju the Wise, and Rascus the Joker had to brave the traps of this ancient ruin—including whirling axes, swinging vines, a collapsed bridge, and a giant serpent—to find the one magical artifact that could defeat their foe.

7009 The Final Joust (2007)

The king's finest knight and the wizard's black skeleton rider battled for the fate of the kingdom in this set that included a new skeleton horse element.

NEW FRIENDS AND FOES

Originally made up entirely of humans and the occasional dragon, the population of LEGO Castle swelled with the introduction of the evil Skeleton Warriors, the stout and stalwart Dwarves, the greedy Trolls, and the huge but dim-witted Giant Trolls.

7036 Dwarves' Mine (2007)

LEGO® Kingdoms

WHEN THE THEME CALLED LEGO® Castle ended, the question on every castle-builder's mind was: what next? The answer arrived in 2010 with LEGO Kingdoms. Gone were the trolls and dwarves of the fantasy era. In their place came a tale of two rival medieval kingdoms, the good Lion Knights and the wicked Dragon Knights—not to mention the villagers stuck in the middle ●

7947 Prison Tower Rescue (2010)

PRINCESS IN PERIL

Smart and brave but a bit clumsy, the Princess of the Lion Kingdom had a habit of getting captured by the Dragon Knights and locked up in their prison tower. Fortunately, there were always loyal Lion Knights ready to ride to the rescue. LEGO Kingdoms introduced new armor that transformed knightly horses into horned battle-steeds.

The princess also had a habit of escaping on her own if the knights didn't arrive fast enough.

What would a modern LEGO Castle be without catapults? The King's Castle was defended by three of them.

KING'S CASTLE

The castle of the Lion Knights had a modular design that let builders arrange its walls and towers in different configurations. Its drawbridge could be raised and lowered, and a turning crank controlled the gatehouse's portcullis to keep enemies outside—such as the three Dragon Knights who came in the set.

King's royal tower

Drawbridge mechanism

Lion Knight with crossbow

Blazing torch

Dragon Knight

Lion Knight with glaive

7946 King's Castle (2010)

Rotating windmill blades

Spinning the rooster weathervane raised or lowered the barn's basket, and the crank-powered windmill had moving gears and a tipper box inside.

Farmer

Milkmaid

Goats

Dragon Knight raiders

Chickens

Pig

Horse-drawn cart

7189 Mill Village Raid (2011)

VILLAGERS

The Dragon Knights didn't limit their plundering to castles. They also raided this village mill and farm in search of hidden treasure. The brave farmers fought back with pitchforks, apples, booby traps, and a barnyard full of animal friends, including brand-new LEGO goats and chickens. The barn could open up on a secret flowerbox hinge.

THE BIG EVENT

With 1,575 pieces, this was the largest model to date in the LEGO Kingdoms theme. The Kingdoms Joust set included a six-roomed castle, nine minifigures, two weapon tents, a royal viewing box, a jousting fence, and two horses. Even better, you could combine two sets to make an even bigger scene!

Among the contents: a nobleman, a princess, a squire, a frog, and a knight who resembled the classic Black Falcons.

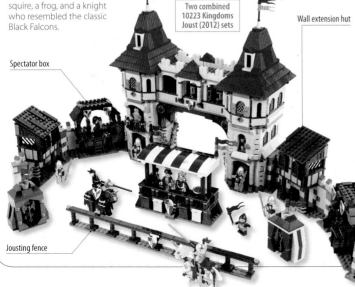

Spectator box

Two combined 10223 Kingdoms Joust (2012) sets

Wall extension hut

Jousting fence

YE OLDE SMITHY

Those Dragon Knights just didn't give up! This set depicted a Dragon Kingdom knight's attack on a blacksmith's shop. Spinning the water-wheel made the hammer pound on the anvil to forge new weapons.

6918 Blacksmith Attack (2011)

Given all of the fighting gear in the shop, the evil knight might have made an error in judgment.

A KINGLY CARRIAGE

The King's Carriage Ambush set introduced new torso and leg decoration for the wise and noble Lion King. He'd need his chromed sword when a pair of Dragon Knights launched a forest sneak attack with their lever-activated hammer in an attempt to capture a king's ransom in treasure.

The royal treasure chest was filled with gold, jewels, and precious trinkets.

7188 King's Carriage Ambush (2011)

A Medieval Village

PRODUCED IN 2008 as a special-edition exclusive for the online LEGO® Shop and LEGO Brand Stores, the Medieval Market Village was the biggest town-themed LEGO Castle set ever made. The designers consulted with Castle fans and filled the model with colorful characters, brand-new animals, and rare and classic elements ●

Cock-a-doodle doo! We're the first buildable LEGO chickens!

10193 Medieval Market Village (2008)

Both buildings open up to show the furnished rooms inside!

Mm-mm. I'm glad they rediscovered this classic LEGO turkey piece!

Male and female villagers

Peasant boy

Medieval peasant

King's soldier

Tavern maid

Village blacksmith

VILLAGE PEOPLE

The 1,601-piece set featured a tavern, a blacksmith's shop, a feast of plastic food, the return of the original LEGO Castle hood element, and eight minifigures including a pair of soldiers to guard the king's treasure... or fill themselves up with turkey!

We've also got the first LEGO cow, a brick-built tree, stables, tables, a duck, and more!

Spinning the water-wheel makes my hammer strike the anvil!

Sets to Remember

375 Castle (1978)

383 Knight's Tournament (1979)

6074 Black Falcon's Fortress (1986)

6077 Forestmen's River Fortress (1989)

6034 Black Monarch's Ghost (1990)

6030 Catapult (1984)

6059 Knight's Stronghold (1990)

6049 Viking Voyager (1987)

1584 Knight's Challenge (1988)

6062 Battering Ram (1987)

6048 Majisto's Magical Workshop (1993)

6090 Royal Knight's Castle (1995)

6037 Witch's Windship (1997)

Blacksmith Shop
Schmiedewerkstatt

3739

AGES/EDADES
10+

Building Toy
Jouet de Construction
Juguete para Construir

Cont. 622 pcs/pzs

Original design by Daniel Siskind

3739 Blacksmith Shop (2002)

8702 Lord Vladek (2006)

8823 Mistlands Tower (2006)

6093 Flying Ninja Fortress (1998)

8780 Citadel of Orlan (2004)

7041 Troll Battle Wheel (2008)

8876 Scorpion Prison Cave (2005)

6096 Bull's Attack (2000)

7187 Escape from the Dragon's Prison (2011)

7094 King's Castle Siege (2007)

7949 Prison Carriage Rescue (2010)

LEGO® Space Themes

THE LEGO GROUP had launched beyond the bounds of planet Earth as early as the simple "Space Rocket" model of the 1950s, but 1978 was the year when LEGO® Space themes finally blasted off. From the space scooters and lunar buggies of the early classic sets to the sci-fi stylings of Futuron, Insectoids, and LEGO Space Police, LEGO Space has been exploring the stars for more than 30 years with over 200 spaceships, robots, moon bases, and other models in its interstellar armada ●

You're under arrest for grand theft spaceship and leaving the scene of a black hole!

Classic LEGO® Space Sets

THE EARLIEST LEGO® Space sets in 1978 let kids build a future that seemed just around the corner. The theme became more sci-fi in 1984 with Blacktron and Futuron, the first of many Space sub-series with their own unique vehicle designs, colors, astronauts, and model functions. With new series released almost every year through 2001, these sets are the classic era of LEGO Space and beyond ●

The sleek black spaceships of Blacktron made it one of the most popular LEGO Space sub-themes. It later provided bad guys for the 1989 Space Police, and was revisited with a second series in 1991.

6954 Renegade (1987)

6990 Monorail Transport System (1987)

FAST FORWARD

Futuron carried on in the spirit and color scheme of the original Space sets. Its battery-powered, 9-volt monorail transported blue and yellow astronauts around their home base on a distant moon or planet.

1789 Star Hawk II (1995)

TO THE STARS

The Unitron theme saw only four sets released in 1994 and 1995, but even this short-lived series had a distinct style. With their translucent blue windows and yellow-green weapons, the high-tech Star Hawk II spaceship, crater cruiser, monorail transport base and Zenon space station were unified by cockpit pods that could be detached and exchanged between vehicles.

Communications dish

Rear laboratory section

OUT OF THIS WORLD

The earliest LEGO Space sets were a mix of simple science-fiction spaceships, lunar bases, rockets and rovers that weren't too far removed from the real space technology of the 1970s and 1980s, like the Uranium Search Vehicle with its 16 wheels.

6928 Uranium Search Vehicle (1984)

All-terrain wheels

HEY, MISTER SPACEMAN!

With space suits, helmets, and air tanks in white, red, yellow, blue, and black, the colorful astronauts of the original LEGO Space series explored the universe in peace and harmony, with no names or stories beyond what builders imagined themselves.

MINIFIGURE ASTRONAUTS

From M:Tron to Exploriens, U.F.O., and RoboForce, each LEGO Space series had its own astronauts. One rare pair was Biff Starling and Sandy Moondust, "astrobots" produced as a tie-in with NASA's 2003 Mars Exploration Rover mission.

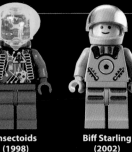

Space Police II (1992)

Insectoids (1998)

Biff Starling (2002)

6986 Mission Commander (1989)

SPACE POLICE

Piloting blue and black vehicles with clear red windows and interchangeable prison cells, the Space Police arrived in 1989 to battle the villains of Blacktron. They returned with a second series in 1992, and again in 2009 after LEGO Space was relaunched.

Rocket booster

Classic Space logo

497 Galaxy Explorer (1979)

LL 928

EXPLORING A GALAXY

The classic of classic LEGO spaceships and a favorite for Space fans, the Galaxy Explorer was built in the traditional blue and grey color scheme with yellow windows and details. It included a decorated base plate with a communications tower and launch pad.

7314 Recon-Mech RP (2001)

RED PLANET ADVENTURE

Life on Mars brought things closer to home with the story of a crashed shuttle team and a planet of mech-driving Martians for them to battle or befriend. Apart from a licensed Discovery Channel theme in 2003, it was the last LEGO Space series for six years.

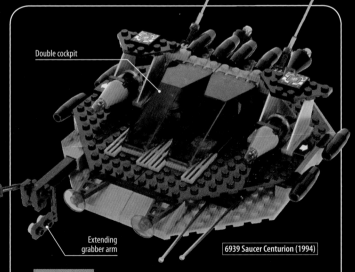

Double cockpit

Extending grabber arm

6939 Saucer Centurion (1994)

SPY GUYS

In 1994, Spyrius joined the bad guys of Blacktron as the latest villains to menace the LEGO Space universe. Until 1996, these data-stealing agents used giant and minifigure-sized robots to do their dirty work all over the galaxy. The Saucer Centurion, the Spyrius flagship, could split down the middle to deploy an android-driven space buggy.

DEEP FREEZE

In 1993, LEGO builders went on an interstellar journey to the distant future of 2002. Ice Planet 2002 took place on the frozen world of Krysto, where clear neon orange parts reigned supreme, jetpacks gave way to skis, and lasers were replaced by ice-cutting chainsaws.

Magnetic rocket crane

6898 Ice-Sat V (1993)

LEGO® Mars Mission

THE LAST TIME LEGO® space explorers traveled to Mars in 2001's LEGO Life on Mars theme, they encountered a friendly Martian civilization. In 2007, they returned to a Red Planet filled with precious energy crystals and menaced by a mysterious alien armada. The result was the first new LEGO Space theme in six years: Mars Mission ●

Crystal-powered extraterrestrial weaponry

Distinctive black and green alien color scheme

SPACE STATION

The astronauts' base on Mars included a research lab, containment pods for alien prisoners, and a hand pump to move captured aliens through the base's transport tubes or launch missiles at alien attack ships. The tubes could also be attached to the base's shuttle to load aliens on board and blast them into orbit.

7690 MB-01 Eagle Command Base (2007)

ALIENS ON MARS

Who were the hostile aliens? They emerged from fissures in the planet's surface, but they weren't Martians. They glowed in the dark and used crystals to power their sinister technology. In the theme's second year, they were joined by bigger, tougher commanders with more posable bodies.

Alien commander

CRYSTAL CLASH

Everyone on Mars wanted the planet's energy crystals. The humans' vehicles had drills, saws, and claws for mining them, while the aliens' ships were equipped with sci-fi weapons to steal them.

Mining Robot from 7646 ETX Alien Infiltrator (2008)

7647 MX-41 Switch Fighter (2008)

Dropship pilot

Miner

Crystal

Wings and nosecone fold up to convert to six-wheeled Mars rover

NEW TECHNOLOGY

In 2008, the battle for Mars got even tougher when the newest human and alien vehicles gained the ability to transform between different modes. Each one was built with parts that could move or detach to change land vehicles into air fighters or split one model apart into several.

ALIEN TECH

The aliens' ultimate attack vehicle included five glowing alien warriors and could split apart into a command saucer, two scout ships, and a strike fighter. To combat it, the set came with a defense station with two astronauts and pump-blasted foam missiles.

7691 ETX Alien Mothership Assault (2007)

Shuttle attaches as cockpit and drill becomes top-mounted cannon

7649 MT-201 Ultra-Drill Walker (2008)

MULTI-PURPOSE WALKER

Another special-edition set, the MT-201 could be converted from a mining base with a powerful spinning drill into a 4-legged mech walker with a detachable observation shuttle and a launching missile. It also came with a small enemy vehicle to fight.

Gear-driven rotating drill

THREE VEHICLES IN ONE

With independent suspension for its six wheels, a giant drill for mining crystals, a firing launcher and the ability to separate into three vehicles to fight an alien attack ship, the special-edition MT-101 was one of the most popular Mars Mission sets.

7699 MT-101 Armored Drilling Unit (2007)

Cockpit becomes armed flying vehicle

Instructions included for motorizing with LEGO Power Functions parts

7645 MT-61 Crystal Reaper (2008)

CRYSTAL REAPER

The MT-61 was designed to collect crystals from Martian rocks, but with its giant spinning saw blades, blasters, and gripping hands, it was no slouch in the alien-fighting department. It included three astronauts, two aliens, an alien commander, an alien strike-ship, and a deploying rover.

Treads rotate and saw-blades and crystal scoops spin when model rolls

LEGO® Space Police

IN 2009, the Space Police made their long-awaited return. Piloting sleek black-and-white patrol spaceships and packing an arsenal of freeze-ray blasters and prison pods, these brave defenders of the interplanetary peace had the tough job of chasing down an assortment of crooks from all sectors of the galaxy and bringing them to justice ●

Space Biker Gang markings

LIGHT-SPEED HEIST

Toting a safe full of stolen gold bars, the Skull Twins thought they could make a quick getaway aboard their Skull Interceptor. But even though the alien brothers broke every speed limit in the universe, they couldn't evade the long arm of the intergalactic law.

SPACE CHASE

The nano-second the First Galactic Bank's alarm sounded, the Space Police were on the move in the VX-Falcon Pursuit Cruiser. Siren blazing and lights flashing, the pilot hit his turbo-rockets and blasted off at near-lightspeed after the fleeing space criminals. All it took was a few well-placed freeze-rays and both the pilfered gold and the Skull Twins were safely back in Space Police custody.

5973 Hyperspeed Pursuit (2009)

Modular prison pod

Freeze-ray blasters

COSMIC CROOKS

Slizer, heavy-metal hyper-crook with a penchant for satellite theft and galactic graffiti.

The Skull Twins, identical clone brothers with a double dose of disregard for the law.

Snake, arachnoid astro-punk who once stole a prototype Space Police laser.

Squidman, gold-crazed mollusk menace wanted for gold robbery, forging, and smuggling.

Kranxx, Space Biker leader wanted galaxy-wide for grand theft spacecraft and robot rustling.

Frenzy, four-armed space lizard known for illegally impersonating a Venusian.

LEGO® Alien Conquest

Detachable escape craft

7051 Tripod Invader (2011)

Clinger and Alien Trooper

Panicked human citizen

THE HISTORY of LEGO® Space is full of astronauts blasting off from Earth to explore the outer reaches of the galaxy and encountering all kinds of alien life forms along the way. But in 2011, for the first time ever, they came to visit us—and they weren't friendly. As saucers and tripods swept across the world, only the A.D.U. stood between our planet… and alien conquest ●

Alien Pilots have hyper-tuned reflexes

Transparent neon-green elements

Brainpower-fueled technology

WALK AND RULE

The three-legged Tripod Invader had posable legs, a swiveling disintegrator cannon, a prison pod for captured humans, and a bumper sticker reading, "WE'VE BEEN TO EARTH." Removing the civilian's hair and attaching an Alien Clinger (a.k.a. Pluuvian Brain-Beast) over his head would drain his brainpower and control him.

8-14
7065
batteries included

7065 Alien Mothership (2011)

MOTHERSHIP

Hypaxxus-8 oversaw the invasion from his giant saucer along with his pet Clinger, Captain Ploovie. Spinning the mothership's outer ring (built from curved track elements) produced an eerie electronic sound. It also had a jointed capture claw to grab a reporter for an exclusive interview.

The News Reporter may have gotten a little too close to her story this time.

The alien commander was a megalomaniac with gold epaulettes, a torso covered with medals, and a translucent brain. His empress was released as the Alien Villainess in the eighth series of the LEGO Minifigures line.

Hypaxxus-8

7052 UFO Abduction (2011)

UFO could land on top of a minifigure to "capture" it

THE INVADERS

Under the leadership of the tentacled Commander Hypaxxus-8, the invasion fleet included dim-witted Alien Troopers, hyperactive Alien Pilots, and the cybernetic Alien Android. They came to kidnap humans and steal our brainpower to use as spaceship fuel.

THE A.D.U.

Earth's protectors were the Alien Defense Unit (A.D.U.), an elite fighting force that used the latest tech to strike back against the invaders. Their base was the Earth Defense HQ, a massive armored truck with firing rockets in front and a mobile laboratory in back. The articulated sections could snap together for a compact transport mode.

The shuttle's decals included an homage to a late fan builder who went by the nickname "nnenn".

Interceptor Shuttle on launch rack

The HQ's lab trailer was loaded with equipment and scanners for studying captured aliens and freeing Clinger victims. Panels on its sides could be folded out to reveal flip-up satellite dishes for detecting alien attacks.

Rescue vehicle with stretcher

Mini UFO

7066 Earth Defense HQ (2011)

Alien containment pod

OUR HEROES

The A.D.U. forces included the grizzled Sergeant, the cocky Pilot, the loyal Soldier, the brainy Computer Specialist, the eccentric Scientist (in white), and the enthusiastic but hapless Rookie. Most wore uniforms in a brand-new shade of blue and carried a double-barreled blaster.

Alien Troopers had big mouths and tiny brains

7049 Alien Striker (2011)

The Computer Specialist's small scout car battled an even smaller alien mini hover-bike.

Alien prisoners could be stowed in the Jet-Copter's detachable pod.

SKY PROTECTOR

The Jet-Copter was the only vehicle fast enough to catch flying saucers, though it might have met its match in a UFO that could split into a pair of flyers. Although the website listed this as the A.D.U. Pilot's favorite vehicle, it actually came with the Rookie.

7067 Jet-Copter Encounter (2011)

Wingtip cannons

7050 Alien Defender (2011)

Sets to Remember

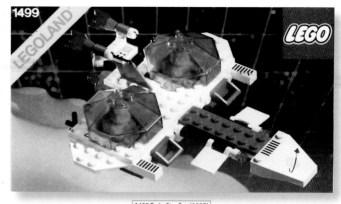

493 Space Command Center (1978)

305 2 Crater Plates (1979)

6954 Renegade (1987)

1499 Twin Starfire (1987)

454 Landing Plates (1979)

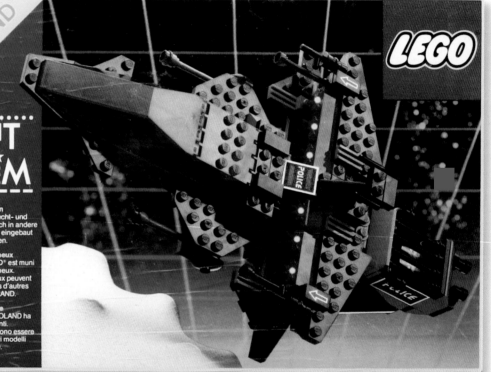

LIGHT ★★ SYSTEM

Licht System
Mit elektrischen Leucht- und Blinkelementen, die auch in andere LEGOLAND® Modelle eingebaut werden können.

Système Lumineux
Ce modèle LEGOLAND® est muni de flashes lumineux. Les éléments lumineux peuvent être incorporés dans d'autres modèles LEGOLAND.

Sistema luce
Questo modello LEGOLAND ha luci intermittenti. Gli elementi luce possono essere inseriti anche in altri modelli LEGOLAND.

483 Alpha-1 Rocket Base (1979)

6781 SP-Striker (1989)

6989 Mega Core Magnetizer (1990)

6930 Space Supply Station (1983)

6877 Vector Detector (1990)

6887 Allied Avenger (1991)

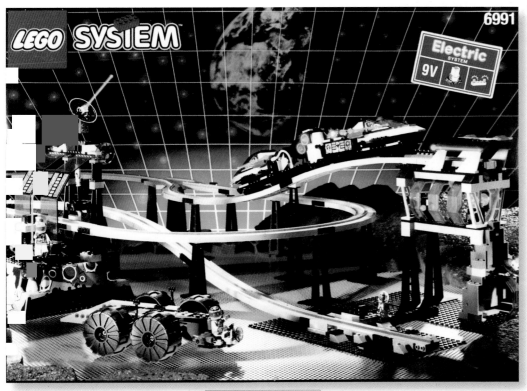

6991 Monorail Transport Base (1994)

7315 Solar Explorer (2001)

7699 MT-101 Armored Drilling Unit (2007)

6939 Sonar Security (1993)

6982 Explorien Starship (1996)

1793 Space Station Zenon (1995)

7697 MT-51 Claw-Tank Ambush (2007)   7647 MX-41 Switch Fighter (2008)

5972 Space Truck Getaway (2009)

6975 Alien Avenger (1997)

6907 Sonic Stinger (1998)

8399 K-9 Bot (2009)

7052 UFO Abduction (2011)

LEGO® Pirates

YO HO HO! The first eleven LEGO® Pirates sets set sail in 1989, and they quickly became the most popular LEGO theme of the time. Filled with daring buccaneers with hook-hands and peg-legs, square-sailed sailing ships, tropical islands full of hidden treasure, and imperial soldiers in hot high-seas pursuit, LEGO Pirates is still an enduring favorite for kids and grown-up fans alike. Best of all, it was up to you to decide which of the scurvy swashbucklers were the good guys and which were the bad guys ●

On The High Seas

SHIPS AHOY! A pirate captain has to have a ship, and the LEGO® Pirates theme was filled from the start with gallant galleons, cutlass-laden clippers, and ramshackle rafts. Through more than 20 years of ocean-going excitement and fun, these stalwart sea vessels have helped their crews do what they do best: loot, fight, and have a swashbucklingly good time on the high seas.

A PIRATE'S PRIZE

The fan-favorite Black Seas Barracuda is considered by many to be the best classic LEGO pirate ship. With Captain Redbeard at the helm, it sailed the Seven Seas with four cannons, five secret compartments, and seven piratical crew members, plus a parrot and monkey.

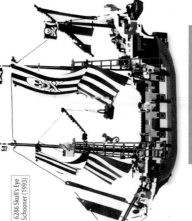

6286 Skull's Eye Schooner (1993)

A SKULL'S EYE BROADSIDE

Even bigger than the Black Seas Barracuda, this three-masted pirate ship boasted a quartet of deck cannons that could rotate from one side to the other, making it a dangerous foe to sail alongside.

Fabric sails

7070 Catapult Raft (2004)

Eight years after the last LEGO Pirates set, the 2004 LEGO 4+ Pirates series reintroduced the theme for younger deckhands with bigger figures and models for quicker, easier construction.

6285 Black Seas Barracuda (1989)

IMPERIAL SOLDIERS

When the LEGO Pirates first set sail in 1989, they were opposed by the blue-uniformed Imperial Soldiers. The soldiers were led by Governor Broadside, whose Caribbean Clipper was named the Sea Hawk in its UK release.

6274 Caribbean Clipper (1989)

After an absence of 12 long years (apart from three 2001 re-releases), minifigure-scale LEGO Pirates sets finally returned in 2009 with an all-new series of models and a new pirate captain.

6240 Kraken Attackin' (2009)

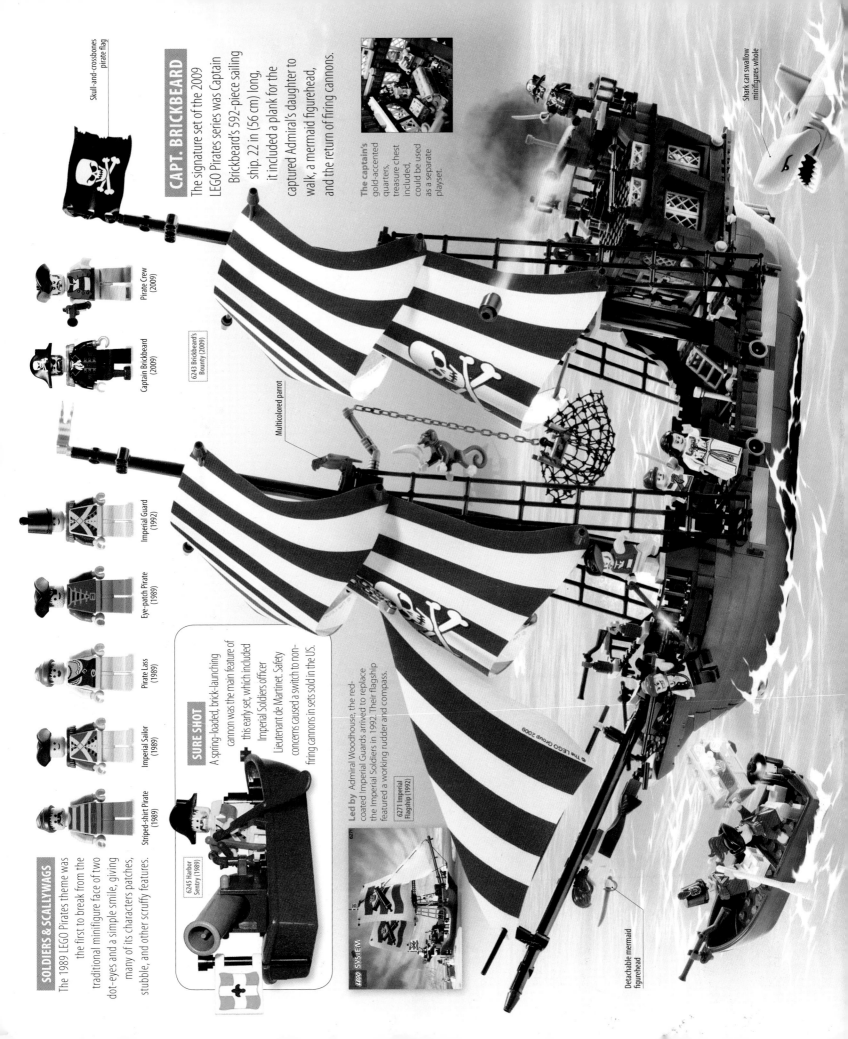

SOLDIERS & SCALLYWAGS

The 1989 LEGO Pirates theme was the first to break from the traditional minifigure face of two dot-eyes and a simple smile, giving many of its characters patches, stubble, and other scruffy features.

Skull-and-crossbones pirate flag

Pirate Crew (2009)

Captain Brickbeard (2009)

6243 Brickbeard's Bounty (2009)

Imperial Guard (1992)

Eye-patch Pirate (1989)

Pirate Lass (1989)

Imperial Sailor (1989)

Striped-shirt Pirate (1989)

CAPT. BRICKBEARD

The signature set of the 2009 LEGO Pirates series was Captain Brickbeard's 592-piece sailing ship. 22 in (56 cm) long, it included a plank for the captured Admiral's daughter to walk, a mermaid figurehead, and the return of firing cannons.

The captain's gold-accented quarters, treasure chest included, could be used as a separate playset.

Multicolored parrot

Shark can swallow minifigures whole

© The LEGO Group 2009

Detachable mermaid figurehead

SURE SHOT

A spring-loaded, brick-launching cannon was the main feature of this early set, which included Imperial Soldiers officer Lieutenant de Martinet. Safety concerns caused a switch to non-firing cannons in sets sold in the US.

6245 Harbor Sentry (1989)

Led by Admiral Woodhouse, the red-coated Imperial Guards arrived to replace the Imperial Soldiers in 1992. Their flagship featured a working rudder and compass.

6271 Imperial Flagship (1992)

LEGO SYSTEM

Treasure Islands

What good is plundered pirate treasure without somewhere to bury it? The world of the LEGO® Pirates is full of exotic desert islands, pirate hideouts, and soldier outposts, forts, and prisons. The theme has even had a band of tropical islanders, who weren't too thrilled about their new piratical neighbors digging up their beautiful beaches ●

CAPTAIN REDBEARD

Captain Redbeard was the original leader of the LEGO Pirates. Known as Captain Roger in some countries, he was the first minifigure to sport a hook-hand and peg-leg, and was often accompanied by his parrot, Pupsy.

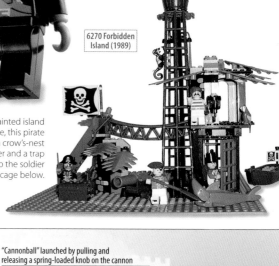

6270 Forbidden Island (1989)

Built on a painted island baseplate, this pirate hideaway had a crow's-nest lookout tower and a trap door to drop the soldier into the cage below.

Governor Broadside

6276 Eldorado Fortress (1989)

MEET THE GOVERNOR

One of only two sets to include the rare Governor Broadside figure, this sturdy portside fortress swarmed with loyal Imperial Soldiers, each of them ready to arrest and imprison any pirates daring or foolish enough to try to steal the Governor's treasure.

"Cannonball" launched by pulling and releasing a spring-loaded knob on the cannon

SHIPWRECKED

Long ago, the pirate king's ship ran aground on an uncharted island, and Captain Brickbeard built his hideout inside the wreck. Invading soldiers had to get past a collapsing bridge, a slashing sword trap, and a skull launcher.

6253 Shipwreck Hideout (2009)

NEW ENEMIES

Although they wore red coats like the 1992 Imperial Guards, the 2009 theme's soldiers were not given a formal name. They did, however, get their own base: a fortress prison built above the sea, complete with a new Admiral figure to lead the troops, a Captain Brickbeard wanted poster, and a jail cell with a monkey guard that the pirate prisoner could bribe with a banana.

Crane with working winch to load and unload treasure

6242 Soldiers' Fort (2009)

Following the Imperial Soldiers and Imperial Guards came the Imperial Armada, a new faction of soldiers inspired by Spanish conquistadors.

6244 Armada Sentry (1996)

6278 Enchanted Island (1994)

In 1994, the pirates met the Islanders. Led by King Kahuka, the Pacific Islands-inspired tribe didn't take kindly to trespassing buccaneers.

CAPTAIN IRONHOOK

The second LEGO Pirates captain was Captain Ironhook, introduced in 1992 and shown in command of the 6268 Renegade Runner in 1993. Not as stylishly dressed as Captains Redbeard or Brickbeard, the tattered Ironhook battled the Royal Guards and Islanders, and occasionally gained or lost a peg-leg. He was last seen aboard 1996's 6289 Red Beard Runner.

This set included a new island baseplate, a fish roasting over a fire, a catapult, and a treasure map.

6241 Loot Island (2009)

TREASURE HUNTERS

A skull marked the spot on this almost-deserted island where a castaway guarded a hidden treasure. When both a pirate and soldier arrived, it was a three-way race to find the golden chest.

Dark green crocodile with moving jaw and tail

Imperial Flagship

AFTER YEARS of the LEGO® Pirates ruling the seas, the Imperial navy finally struck back in 2010 with the biggest LEGO sailing ship of them all. Stretching 30 in (75 cm) from bowsprit to stern and standing 24 in (60 cm) tall at the top of its main-mast, the enormous Imperial Flagship was built from 1,664 LEGO pieces ●

The ship's flag resembled that of the classic Imperial Guards. This exclusive set was the last one released in the LEGO Pirates theme... at least for now.

Fabric sails

10210 Imperial Flagship (2010)

Aft mast

Pennant flag

PIRATE PURSUIT

Watch out, Captain Brickbeard! The flagship was crewed by its captain, four soldiers, a lieutenant, the ship's cook, and the captain's daughter. No wonder the famous pirate ended up shackled in the brig —but could he get loose, steal the captain's gold, and make his escape?

Frying pan

The captain's daughter had a reversible face (and sometimes an alternate dress piece). The cook had short legs and a large knife.

Rifle

Peg leg

The ship included four firing, wheeled cannons, eight cannon hatches (four on each side), and plenty of ammunition.

DECK TOUR

Realistic and detailed in its design, the Imperial Flagship was covered with doors and hatches, railings, and intricately assembled decorations. It had a working anchor winch, a captain's quarters, a galley, and a brig (with a resident rat to keep the pirate prisoners company).

Clips on the base of the ship's wheel held a golden telescope and a sextant for plotting a safe course across the waves.

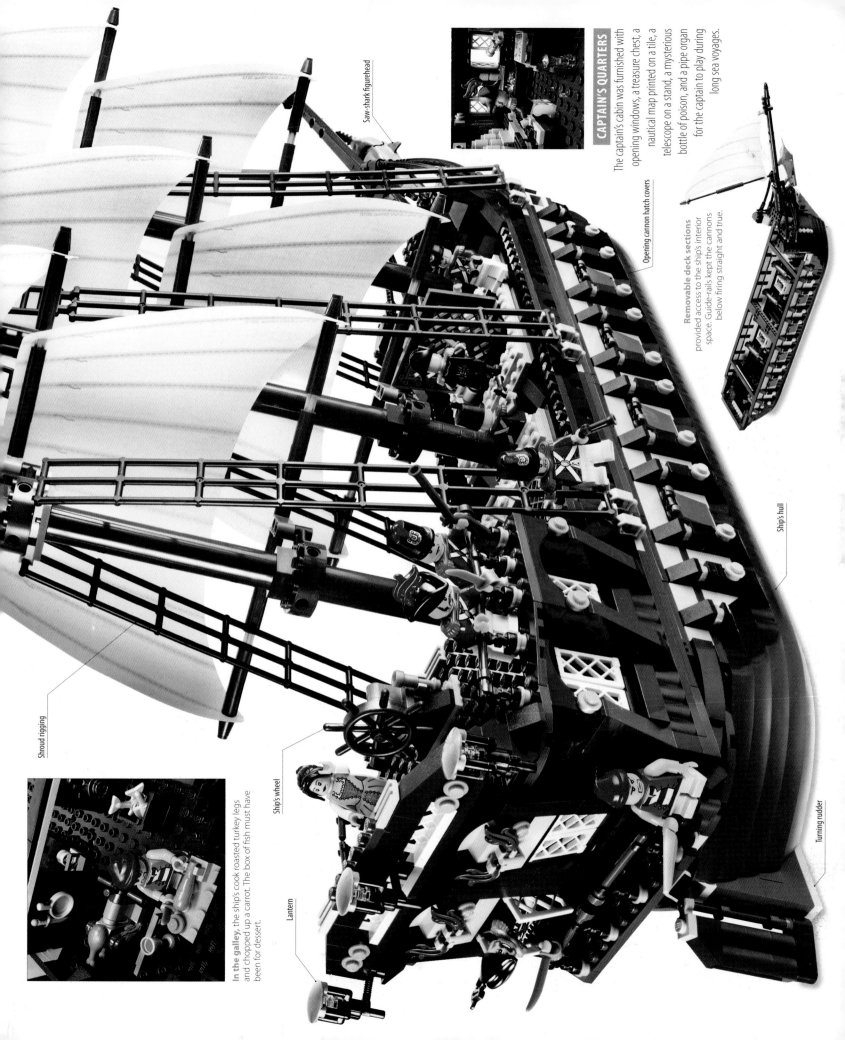

Saw-shark figurehead

CAPTAIN'S QUARTERS
The captain's cabin was furnished with opening windows, a treasure chest, a nautical map printed on a tile, a telescope on a stand, a mysterious bottle of poison, and a pipe organ for the captain to play during long sea voyages.

Opening cannon hatch covers

Removable deck sections provided access to the ship's interior space. Guide-rails kept the cannons below firing straight and true.

Ship's hull

Shroud rigging

Ship's wheel

In the galley, the ship's cook roasted turkey legs and chopped up a carrot. The box of fish must have been for dessert.

Lantern

Turning rudder

Sets to Remember

6235 Buried Treasure (1989)

1696 Pirate Lookout (1992)

6268 Renegade Runner (1993)

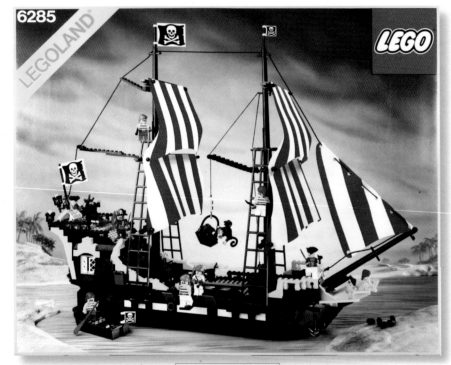
6285 Black Seas Barracuda (1989)

6256 Islander Catamaran (1994)

6262 King Kahuka's Throne (1994)

6236 King Kahuka (1994)

6273 Rock Island Refuge (1991)

6252 Sea Mates (1993)

6237 Pirates' Plunder (1993)

6267 Lagoon Lock-up (1991)

6279 Skull Island (1995)

6280 Armada Flagship (1996)

6290 Pirate Battle Ship / Red Beard Runner (2001)

8397 Pirate Survival (2009)

1747 Pirates Treasure Suprise (1996)

6296 Shipwreck Island (1996)

6253 Shipwreck Hideout (2009)

6248 Volcano Island (1996)

6204 Buccaneers (1997)

6232 Skeleton Crew (1996)

8396 Soldier's Arsenal (2009)

6249 Pirates Ambush (1997)

7072 Captain Kragg's Pirate Boat (2004)

7071 Treasure Island (2004)

7074 Skull Island (2004)

6241 Loot Island (2009)

LEGO® Adventures

JOURNEY TO A WORLD of buildable adventures, where the good guys are good, the bad guys are bad, and there's always another battle for the fate of the city, the ocean, or the planet waiting just around the corner. These classic and modern LEGO® themes have taken kids of all ages from the Earth's inner core to a near future filled with rampaging dinosaurs, and even on a wild trip through time itself. Fasten your supercar seat belt and power up your giant robot, because the LEGO adventures are just getting started ●

Another adventurer?

Around the Globe

YOU CAN'T HAVE ADVENTURE without adventurers! From 1998 until 2003, the LEGO® Adventurers traveled the globe in search of discoveries and danger—and they found plenty of both. Though the names of his friends and enemies often changed, you always knew that wherever Johnny Thunder and company went, exciting adventure was sure to follow ●

This hot-air balloon carried the Adventurers over the Himalayas in the 2003 LEGO Orient Expedition series.

Crate of adventure tools

7415 Aero Nomad (2003)

LEGO ADVENTURERS

In 1998, a new hero arrived in the LEGO universe. Johnny Thunder, dashing explorer from Australia, was joined by the wise Dr. Kilroy and intrepid reporter Miss Pippin Reed. Together, they were the LEGO Adventurers, and for five years and four series of LEGO sets, their travels took them on exciting 1920s-era adventures all over the world.

ADVENTURES IN EGYPT

The first series to feature the Adventurers took place in Egypt during the golden age of archaeology. Joined by their pilot friend Harry Cane, Johnny and his friends explored tombs, temples, and pyramids, encountering mummies, skeletons, scorpions, and nefarious criminals along the way.

5988 Pharaoh's Forbidden Ruins (1998)

AMAZON

In 1999, the Adventurers returned for a journey deep into the Amazon jungle. There, they braved colorful tribal warriors and perilous pitfalls while racing to find treasures before the villainous Señor Palomar and Rudo Villano could get their hands on them. At least Pippin had a good story to take back to World Magazine!

1271 Jungle Surprise (1999)

5934 Track Master/Dino Explorer (2000)

DINO ISLAND

2000 saw Johnny and his friends visit a lost island inhabited by dinosaurs, where they built a research compound and kept Lord Sinister and his allies from stealing the creatures.

LEGO ORIENT EXPEDITION

The final LEGO Adventurers theme saw Johnny and his friends journey across India, China, and Tibet as they faced a tyrannical Maharaja, a ruthless emperor, a wild Yeti, and their old enemy Lord Sam Sinister in search of explorer Marco Polo's long-lost treasure.

Fireworks

To find the Golden Dragon statue, the Adventurers had to make it past the traps and guards in Emperor Chang Wu's Dragon Fortress.

7414 Elephant Caravan (2003)

The Adventurers' new friend Babloo and his elephant Giri.

ALSO KNOWN AS...

The Adventurers often had different names in different countries. Johnny Thunder was also known as Sam Grant and Joe Freemann, Dr. Kilroy as Dr. Charles Lightning and Professor Articus, and Pippin Reed as Pippin Read, Gail Storm, and Linda Lovely. Even in the same country, things could change: the original Sam Sinister later became Slyboots, while the second Lord Sinister also went by Baron von Barron, Sam Sanister, Evil Eye, and Mr. Hates!

7419 Dragon Fortress (2003)   Lord Sinister   Printed 3-D baseplate

One place you don't expect to find evil mummies is up in the sky—but that's exactly where Jake Raines ran across them in his search for the Soul Diamond.

7307 Flying Mummy Attack (2011)

7306 Golden Staff Guardians (2011)

ANCIENT TREASURES

Each of the treasures gave Amset-Ra a different power, like the Golden Staff that increased the might of his mummy servants. If he could gather all six, the pharaoh would become unstoppable. That's why it was up to the luckless Mac to get it first!

PHARAOH'S QUEST

The Adventurers' spirit lived on in the 2011 theme Pharaoh's Quest, which pitted a new team of period adventure heroes against a resurrected Egyptian king with an army of mummy warriors and living stone monsters. The heroes' task was to find six ancient treasures and prevent Pharaoh Amset-Ra from conquering the world.

Like Johnny Thunder, Gail Storm and Professor Lightning before them, Jake Raines, Mac McCloud, Professor Hale and Helena Skvalling all had weather-related names.

7327 Scorpion Pyramid (2011)

MUMMIES

Amset-Ra's legions included Mummy Warriors, winged and falcon-helmeted Flying Mummies, a Mummy Snake Charmer, and the elite, jackal-headed Anubis Guards who protected his pyramid. Each type was stronger than the last.

Scarab shield

Mummy Warrior from 7306 Golden Staff Guardians (2011)

CREATURES OF STONE

7326 Rise of the Sphinx (2011)

Even more dangerous than the pharaoh's warriors were the ancient guardians that protected his treasures: giant beasts that looked like stone statues until they sprang to life to attack the enemies of Amset-Ra. They included a mighty sphinx that crouched above the Temple of Anubis, hiding place of the Golden Sword.

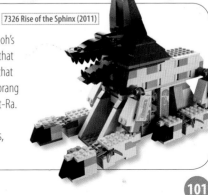

6497 Twisted Time Train (1997)

Worlds of Adventure

FROM THE ROOTIN', tootin' cowboys of the Wild West to the dangerous world of 2010, from the time-cruising travels of the eccentric Dr. Cyber to battles with dinosaurs in the modern-day jungle… when you're building a LEGO® adventure, your imagination can take you anywhere you want to go, or even anywhen—past, present, or future ●

TIME TRAVEL

In 1996, Dr. Cyber, his sidekick Tim, and their monkey friend were the LEGO Time Cruisers, bold adventurers who traveled across the centuries in wacky hat-powered contraptions with parts that moved and spun when their wheels turned. 1997 introduced their rivals, Tony Twister and Professor Millennium, also known as the artifact-stealing Time Twisters.

WILD WESTERN

From 1996 to 1997, the LEGO Western theme took builders back to the American frontier of the 1800s and the age of round-ups, showdowns, and cattle rustling. With models full of cowboy minifigures, locations, and accessories but no official story to set the scene, kids were free to make up their own tall tales and adventures set in the exciting days of the Wild West.

6755 Sheriff's Lock-Up (1996)

The infamous outlaw Flatfoot Thompson

The brave sheriff and his faithful steed

Card shark Dewey Cheatum

Z-1 Kinetic Launcher

LEGO DINO 2010

In the year 2010, science finally brought extinct dinosaurs back to life. When they broke loose and escaped into the jungle, it was up to a team of fearless dino hunters to track down and recapture the gigantic creatures before they could cause any harm to the outside world.

Light-up eyes and mouth

7297 Dino Track Transport (2005)

7476 Iron Predator vs. T-Rex (2005)

LEGO DINO ATTACK

In the near future, mutated monsters from the prehistoric past suddenly appeared and started laying waste to cities all across the globe. Enter the LEGO Dino Attack team: a rag-tag band of scientists, adventurers, and soldiers whose mission was to fight back against the rogue reptiles and end their threat once and for all.

In an unusual split launch, these 2005 themes offered two different spins on the same basic models. Some countries received the conflict-heavy Dino Attack, with vehicles covered in sci-fi weaponry and firing projectiles, while others had the more peaceful Dino 2010 with its nets, cages, and capture gear.

Rotating treads

Big enough to carry the tyrant-lizard king himself, this transport chopper included a rolling scout vehicle and a harness designed to lift the largest dino in the line.

5886 T-Rex Hunter (2012)

LEGO DINO

Two years after 2010 (but seven years after LEGO Dino 2010), dinosaurs once again materialized in the jungle and threatened the nearby city. Another group of daring dino hunters was sent to subdue, capture, and study them, armed with powerful tranquilizer weapons and a fleet of heavily armored all-terrain vehicles.

Commanded by Josh Thunder, descendant of Johnny Thunder, the LEGO Dino team's base was built to contain even the toughest T-Rex. The Dino Defense HQ included opening gates, a crane with capture net, a communications center and lab, two vehicles, and three ferocious dinosaurs.

5887 Dino Defense HQ (2012)

JUNGLE CHASE

Sometimes it takes more than tranq rifles to catch a dinosaur. This off-roader's crew had to lure a ravenous Raptor in close with the most low-tech trap of all: a roasted turkey leg. Then they just needed to snare it with the lasso and somehow get it back to base.

5884 Raptor Chase (2012)

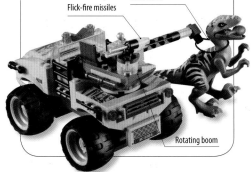

Flick-fire missiles

Lasso snare

Rotating boom

5885 Triceratops Trapper (2012)

THREE-HORNED TROUBLE

The spikes on the bumper of this heavy-duty truck were no match for the horns of an angry Triceratops. That's why it carried a set of flick-fire tranquilizer missiles in front and a reinforced cage in back. Dino team member "Tracer" Tops was just the minifigure for the job.

Where did the dinosaurs come from, and why were they here? The answer was revealed in the pages of *LEGO® Club Magazine*: it was all part of a plot by Commander Hypaxxus-8 of the Alien Conquest theme!

5883 Tower Takedown (2012)

Pteranodon bait stick

Tranq refilling station

Jet boat

Under the Sea

LEGO SYSTEM
6160
7-12

6160 Sea Scorpion (1998)

LEGO AQUAZONE

Running from 1995 to 1998, LEGO Aquazone was the overall name for several underwater sci-fi themes, including the crystal-hunting Aquanauts, their enemies the Aquasharks, the Aquaraiders, the Hydronauts, and the fearsome fish-like Stingrays.

LEGO SYSTEM
6180
8-12

6180 Hydro Search Sub (1998)

THE VAST OCEANS of the LEGO® world are filled with mysteries to explore, unknown dangers to face, and amazing new discoveries to make. Forget about outer space—for these brave divers, the deep blue sea is the real final frontier ●

LEGO AQUA RAIDERS

In 2007, the popular LEGO underwater theme returned when the Aqua Raiders dove into danger deep within the mysterious Bermuda Triangle. Piloting hi-tech submarines and other undersea vehicles, this team of valiant explorers searched every cave and fissure on the ocean floor in their quest for long-lost sunken treasure.

With snapping claws, spiny legs, and an armored shell, this giant lobster was one tough crustacean…

… but the Aqua Raiders underwater exploration rover took it on with the help of working treads, a robot arm, and a saw-blade drill.

7772 Lobster Strike (2007)

7773 Tiger Shark Attack (2007)

Collapsing mast

Magnetic Clamp

7776 The Shipwreck (2007)

Spinning turbines

SUB 76

With a powerful thrashing tail and chomping jaws, this tiger shark was more than a match for the included battle submarine.

CREATURES OF THE DEEP

Unlike many past underwater teams, the new generation of Aqua Raiders didn't fight other minifigures. Instead, they faced off against an entire marine menagerie of hostile sea life, from a deep-sea anglerfish with glowing fangs to a base-invading giant squid with a skeleton trapped in its see-through stomach.

7774 Crab Crusher (2007)

8077 Atlantis Exploration HQ (2010)

Sea-scooter docking platform

Spinnning drill

In the second year of the Atlantis theme, the crew were joined by excavation specialist Dr. Brains from the LEGO Power Miners. Yellow parts replaced neon green on the team's new vehicles.

7984 Deep Sea Raider (2011)

Primary viewing dome

THE CREW

The Atlantis crew were mission commander Captain Ace Speedman, first mate Lance Spears, tech pro Axel Storm, apprentice Bobby Buoy, marine biologist Dr. Jeff "Fish" Fisher, and Atlantis expert Professor Samantha (Sam) Rhodes.

Treasure keys could be used to activate special functions in Atlantis models. This one revealed the legendary Golden King, ruler of the lost city.

7985 City of Atlantis (2011)

8061 Gateway of the Squid (2010)

8079 Shadow Snapper (2010)

The Shadow Snapper was an oversized turtle with a spiked shell and massive claws. It was available in a limited-edition set along with a small combat sub, diver, and treasure key.

LEGO ATLANTIS

In 2010, the LEGO Atlantis theme sent a team of bold salvage divers on a mission to locate the famous sunken city of Atlantis. In futuristic undersea vehicles, they combed the ocean for long-lost treasure keys, battling fish-men and monstrous sea beasts that were determined to keep them from finding their goal.

RUINS OF ATLANTIS

The Gateway of the Squid was the team's first major archaeological find. A treasure key unlocked its gates, though you'd think they could just swim over them. Either way, they'd have to escape the giant squid's rotating jaws and the Squid Warrior's octopus prison cage.

8060 Typhoon Turbo Sub (2010)

The spectacular Portal of Atlantis featured an opening shark-jaw entrance, detachable shark statue guardians, a Portal Emperor minifigure, and a gateway that opened with five treasure keys.

8078 Portal of Atlantis (2010)

WARRIORS AND GUARDIANS

The crew faced fierce underwater humanoids such as the Manta Warrior, Shark Warrior, and Squid Warrior; 2011's evil Dark Guardians; and giant sea creatures covered with glowing Atlantean runes, including a huge black shark known as the Guardian of the Deep. The beginning of the LEGO Atlantis story was told in a half-hour television special, and other parts in magazine comics and online games.

A slider flipped the Typhoon Turbo Sub's propellers around to reveal a grabber claw and a firing torpedo. It would need them to defeat the Shark Warrior that guarded the yellow Atlantis treasure key!

Rough and Tough

WHETHER THEY'RE MINING for energy crystals in deep space, battling monsters at the Earth's core, or racing across the planet's most hostile terrain, these hard-working heroes laugh at danger and don't mind getting down and dirty. It's all part of a day's work when you're on one of the roughest, toughest teams of LEGO® minifigures around ●

THE CRYSTALS

Underwater, underground, or in outer space, LEGO explorers always seem to run into energy crystals. These ones packed some serious power —if a rock monster ate one, it would vibrate so much it created earth-shaking rumblings!

LEGO POWER MINERS

In 2009, mysterious rumblings from deep beneath the ground threatened to shake apart the surface world. To fix the problem, a courageous team of miners tunneled down to a subterranean kingdom full of glowing crystals and mischievous rock monsters. It was up to the Power Miners to dig up the crystals, stop the monsters, and save the planet!

Double-geared rotating planetary drill

Adjustable drilling platform

Team leader Doc

Heavy-duty spiked wheels

8-12

LEGO ROCK RAIDERS

A decade before the Power Miners took on their mission, the space-traveling LEGO Rock Raiders were flung across the galaxy to a distant planet, where they dug for energy crystals and battled alien rock creatures. Their adventures were chronicled in books and video games.

4970 Chrome Crusher (1999)

THE MONSTERS

The underground world of the Power Miners was filled with monsters of all sizes, shapes, and colors. Each had its own troublemaking personality, from the pint-sized rock monsters and their hot-headed lava cousins, to the boulder-tossing bullies Geolix and Tremorox, all the way up to the titanic Crystal King and Eruptorr, ruler of the molten core.

Geolix

Meltrox

The Crystal King

Eruptorr

Cavern-illuminating floodlights

TITANIUM COMMAND RIG

The LEGO Power Miners' mobile base was this gigantic digging machine. Its forward-mounted drill had sections that rotated in different directions as the massive vehicle rolled forward. A few quick turns and snaps converted it into a vertical drilling platform built to bore into the cave floor below in search of crystals.

Veteran miner Duke

World-famous scientist Brains

Rock monster containment cage

8190 Claw Catcher (2010)

INTO THE CORE

In 2010, the Power Miners dug even deeper, discovering a volcanic world full of raging lava monsters. Building a base called Lavatraz, they outfitted their vehicles with water blasters and donned silver anti-heat armor to put out the monsters' fire and calm things down.

The Thunder Driller was the team's most vital vehicle. Not only was it how they reached the underground caverns, but it was also their only way to get back home when the job was done.

Glaciator rock monster

8964 Titanium Command Rig (2009)

Double-geared drill

Emergency toolbox (with banana)

8960 Thunder Driller (2009)

LEGO WORLD RACERS

The World Racers theme of 2010 pitted the fearless X-treme Daredevils team against the lowdown, cheating Backyard Blasters in high-speed racing competitions in different vehicles and environments all over the globe. With set names like Snake Canyon, Wreckage Road, and Jagged Jaws Reef, you knew these guys meant business!

8864 Desert of Destruction (2010)

Missiles, harpoons, chainsaws, mines, dynamite, fish-launchers, and ball-blasting cannons were all within the rules for the World Racers' armed and armored rides.

REX-Treme, DEX-Treme, and MAX-Treme faced off against Bart, Billy Bob, and Bubba Blaster for the World Race championship.

4791 Alpha Team Sub-Surface Scooter (2002)

4791

MISSION DEEP SEA

In 2002, LEGO Alpha Team: Mission Deep Sea brought our heroes beneath the waves, where the newly hook-handed Ogel was creating an army of mutated sea life to do his bidding.

Extreme Action

WHEN EVIL MASTERMINDS hatched sinister schemes… when giant robots rampaged through the streets… when mad scientists threatened to take over the world… these LEGO® themes were there! Filled with battle-function models and larger-than-life heroes, they took adventure to a new level of excitement ●

In 2004, the LEGO Alpha Team took a trip south to icy Antarctica, where Ogel was plotting to freeze time itself. A secret Alpha Mode let the team's latest vehicles reveal new forms and hidden weapons.

Orb-collecting crane

Evil skeleton drone

4746 Mobile Command Center (2004)

4742 Chill Speeder (2004)

ALPHA MODE

With Agent Flex at the controls, the speedy Chill Speeder could convert from a snowmobile into an all-terrain walker to help the team search for Ogel's ice orbs.

Dash Justice, the heroic leader of LEGO Alpha Team.

LEGO ALPHA TEAM

On the land, in the air, even at the bottom of the sea, Dash Justice and the agents of LEGO Alpha Team were always ready to foil the planet-conquering schemes of the evil Ogel (say it backwards!) and his mind-control orbs.

8634 Mission 5: Turbocar Chase (2008)

TURBO POWER

Move over, bad guys—Agent Chase was at the wheel of his turbocar with a stolen laptop full of Dr. Inferno's latest evil plans! The spider-legged Spy Clops was only one of the villains Chase and his fellow agents fought. They also crossed paths with the likes of Break Jaw, Gold Tooth, and Slime Face.

Rare silver-coated elements

TGD-2000

Pop-up laser blasters

Articulated robo-limbs

HOT SPOT

In true evil-genius fashion, Dr. Inferno made his super villain base inside an active volcano. The set included Agents Chase, Trace, and Fuse, as well as the spiky-haired doctor and hench-persons Fire Arm and Claw-Dette. Lots of translucent orange elements simulated blazing-hot lava.

8637 Mission 8: Volcano Base (2008)

Giant laser cannon

Satellite dish

Remote-controlled arm

The other Agents had to rescue the captured Fuse before Claw-Dette dropped him into the lava pit.

8635 Mission 6: Mobile Command Center (2008)

Stealth plane

The Agents' headquarters was packed with spy gear, a light-up mission projector, and a prison for Dr. Inferno.

Armor plating

Spy car 1

Spy car 2

Jet-boat stores under trailer

8970 Robo Attack (2009)

In the theme's second year, its name changed to Agents 2.0 and the action moved to the city. The Agents got new body armor… and Dr. Inferno got a giant robot to crush his enemies.

LEGO AGENTS

Wherever the maniacal Dr. Inferno struck, the LEGO Agents were on the case. The specially trained super-spies battled the bad doctor and his cybernetic henchmen with an arsenal of cutting-edge vehicles and gadgets. Their missions took them all over the world, from jetpack battles on snowy mountaintops to high-speed escapes from secret lairs.

8971 Aerial Defense Unit (2009)

The Agents 2.0 got a big new toy, too: a helicopter with a geared dual rotor and a mission to destroy Magma Commander's satellite broadcaster and magma-drones.

LEGO® Monster Fighters

SPOOKY CREATURES have been a part of the LEGO® universe since the first ghost minifigure appeared in 1990, but this is definitely their biggest starring role. Monsters of all kinds abound in 2012's LEGO Monster Fighters theme, including vampires, swamp creatures, mummies, werewolves, and zombies. Standing against them was a band of heroes who battled to save the world from eternal night ●

Spear

9461 The Swamp
Creature (2012)

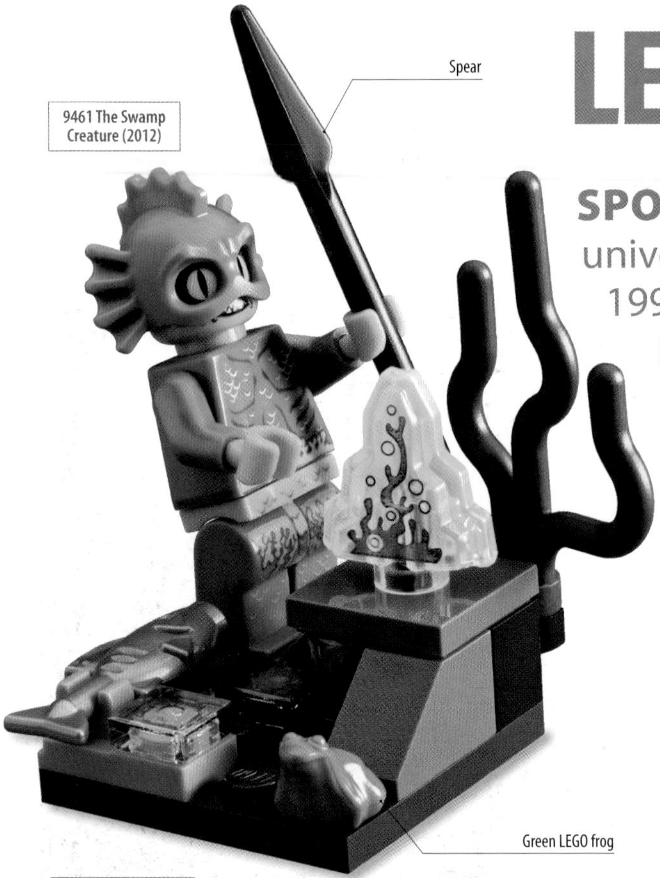

Green LEGO frog

FISHY FIEND

LEGO Monster Fighters sets included decorated, transparent moonstones for the heroes to try to capture. The amphibious Swamp Creature guarded its stone from biker Frank Rock and his swamp boat. Its mask could be removed to reveal a fully painted face underneath, and its small section of underwater terrain included a clipped-on fish for a forever-midnight snack.

VAMPYRE'S CASTLE

When Lord Vampyre collected the six moonstones and placed them in his castle's tower window, he would gain the power to eclipse the sun forever. It was up to Dr. Rodney Rathbone, Major Quinton Steele, Jack McHammer, Ann Lee, and Frank Rock to shine some light on his dark designs.

Man-bat henchman

9468 Vampyre Castle (2012)

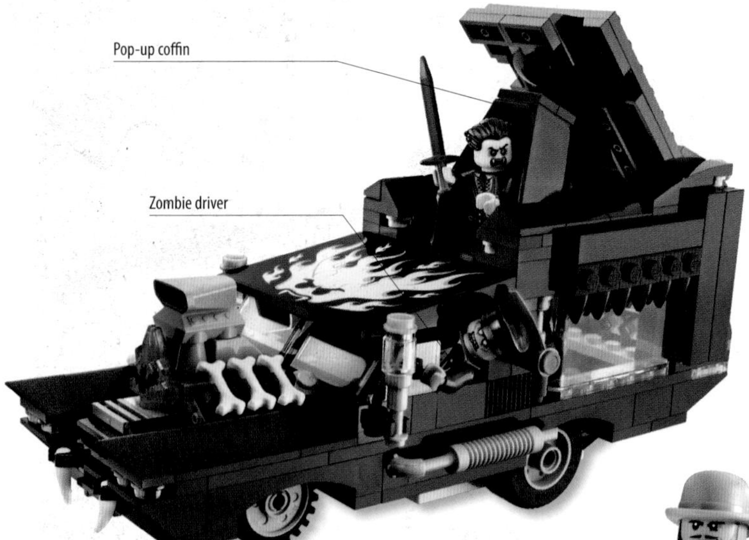

An unfortunate guest

Pop-up coffin

Zombie driver

Mechanical leg

9464 The Vampyre Hearse (2012)

Red moonstone

Single driving glove

Dueling rapier

REVVED-UP RIDE

Lord Vampyre's personal hot-rod hearse had a pair of fangs in front and a six-bone-cylinder engine on its hood that was powered by the red moonstone. Turning a lever made the main villain pop up through the top of the car in his coffin to launch a surprise attack on his foes.

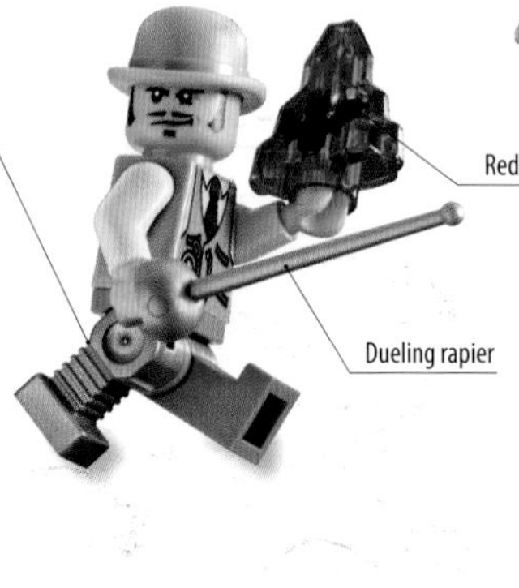

Dr. Rodney Rathbone, the bowler-hatted British leader of the heroes, had a mechanical right leg to replace the one lost in a past monster battle.

The Zombie Driver, Lord Vampyre's most loyal and obedient servant, was rotten to the core... literally.

A special mechanism built into the castle tower made the moonstones swing open simultaneously to activate their evil power when the moon-dish in the middle was pushed forward.

Spire bat

Vampyre's Bride

Dr. Rodney Rathbone

Moonstone eclipse device

Lord Vampyre

GHOST BUSTERS

Pulling three cars full of glow-in-the-dark ghosts, the ghoulish Ghost Train locomotive could only be stopped by the heroes' flick-missile-firing airplane. The barrel on the plane's back was designed for containing captured ghosts. The Monster Fighters also faced a werewolf, a crazy scientist and his monster, a chariot-driving mummy, and a graveyard full of zombies.

Ghost-sucking vacuum

Frank Rock

Ann Lee carried a spare crossbow bolt in her hair in case of emergencies.

Rolling the ghost train made the wings on its cars flap up and down.

Ectoplasmic exhaust

Jack McHammer

Lord Vampyre's coffin

The heroes customized their vehicles with special gear to help them battle the monsters and counter their fearsome supernatural powers. Mixing vintage and hi-tech elements gave the models a steampunk flair.

Double-barreled bumper blasters

This auto's back-mounted cannon could aim and fire a net to snare Lord Vampyre's winged minions.

9467 The Ghost Train (2012)

111

LEGO® EXO-FORCE™ Universe

INSPIRED BY Japanese manga and animation, the LEGO® EXO-FORCE™ theme introduced a new world of giant robot action in 2006. With courage, skill, and pointy hair, the human pilots used battle machines to fight an evil robot army for control of their mountain home ●

Many EXO-FORCE sets featured instructions for alternate and combination models. The giant Mountain Warrior was assembled out of the pieces of the Stealth Hunter and Grand Titan battle machines.

THE EXO-FORCE comics were illustrated in the popular style of Japanese manga. Pictured here are Takeshi (left) and Hikaru (right).

Something's wrong. We need to get back to the Golden City!

POWERING UP

The LEGO EXO-FORCE story was told through books, TV mini-episodes, and a series of comics on the LEGO.com website. The 40 comic chapters formed a three-year saga that brought the battle for Sentai Mountain to life for readers all over the world.

MOUNTAIN OF MYSTERY

The LEGO EXO-FORCE story took place on Sentai Mountain, a towering peak split in two by unknown forces during the first robot rebellion. With humans trapped on one side and robots on the other, their battle machines clashed on the narrow bridges that spanned the divide. What lay at the base of the mountain was unrevealed.

Double-strength armor plating

Battlefield repair tool

Two light-up bricks for twice the firepower

Pilot Takeshi

7701 Grand Titan (2006)

7700 Stealth Hunter (2006)

Although the theme's models also included vehicles and buildings, most sets were battle machines, piloted robotic combat armor that could walk, run, fight hand-to-hand, and sometimes fly. Both sides in the conflict tried to create stronger battle machines to win the war between the humans and the robots.

THE GOOD GUYS

Presenting the heroes of the LEGO EXO-FORCE team: cool-headed marksman Hikaru, reckless warrior Takeshi, eccentric inventor Ryo, and fun-loving flyer Ha-Ya-To. They were joined by Hitomi, the proud, sword-wielding granddaughter of Sensei Keiken, the team's wise commander and mentor.

Hitomi

Sensei Keiken

Most of the 2006 EXO-FORCE sets had a built-in light-up brick. Pulling a lever on the battle machine pressed the button on the brick, sending light through a flexible clear tube to make weapons glow red.

Mountain Warrior

Ha-Ya-To　　Hikaru　　Ryo　　Takeshi　　EXO-FORCE pilot

8113 Assault
Tiger (2008)

2008 battle machine sets included weapons that could transform into mini-robots to help the pilots.

INTO THE JUNGLE

The 2008 LEGO EXO-FORCE story ended on a cliffhanger: with Sensei Keiken captured by the robots and taken deep into the mountain's jungle, could the heroes and their newest battle machines rescue their leader in time?

With just a quick turn of the head, my expression changes from calm to battle-rage!

THE GOLDEN CITY

In 2007, with their Sentai Fortress HQ in ruins, the EXO-FORCE team retreated to the legendary Golden City, home of an ancient civilization. There they discovered more powerful battle machines to fight the robots, and codes to unlock the city's secrets.

Triple turbojet engines

Heavy laser cannon

Ha-Ya-To upgraded his ride in a major way with the Aero Booster, a battle machine with a huge detachable rocket pack.

Firing missile launcher

8106 Aero
Booster (2007)

The first year's story ended with a climactic battle as Meca One unleashed his ultimate weapon, the Striking Venom battle tank. Only the courage of the entire EXO-FORCE team—and a lucky shot from Takeshi's Grand Titan—saved the day.

Rotating laser
machine cannons

Rapid-fire energy
disc launcher

Light-up brick

11 in (28 cm) tall

18 in (46 cm) wide

Piledriver legs

Iron Drone
defender

Meca One pilot

Shovel claw

7707 Striking Venom (2006)

THE BAD GUYS

There were three main types of robots: mass-produced, copper-colored Iron Drones, smarter silver Devastator commanders (available with several different secondary colors), and Meca One, the golden leader of the robot forces.

Meca One   Devastator   Iron Drone

GOLDEN IDOL

Built as a simple mining machine, Meca One gained awareness and reprogrammed his fellow robots to revolt. Not content with driving humanity off his half of the mountain, the mechanical tyrant sent wave after wave of battle machines across the bridges to destroy LEGO EXO-FORCE once and for all.

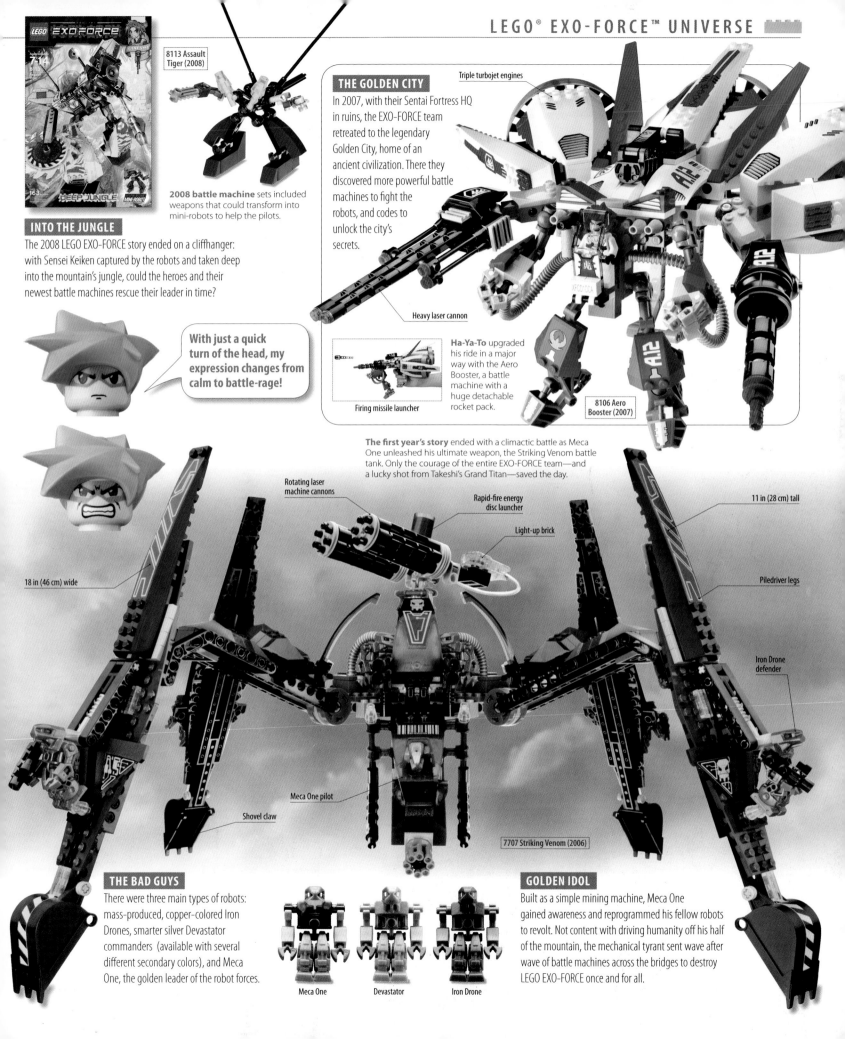

LEGO® Ninjago

LONG AGO, the mystical world of Ninjago was created by the first Spinjitzu master using four golden weapons: the Scythe of Quakes, the Nunchucks of Lightning, the Shurikens of Ice, and the Sword of Fire. Launched in 2011, the LEGO® Ninjago: Masters of Spinjitzu theme took classic LEGO ninja figures and gave them a whole new spin ●

Removable ninja mask

Golden katana

2111 Kai (2011)

SPINNERS

Kai and his fellow ninja warriors could be found in standard LEGO construction sets, but they were also sold individually with top-like spinners. The rules: two players spin their minifigures toward each other while shouting "Ninja GO!" The ninja that stayed on its spinner was the winner of the showdown.

Spinjitzu spinner

Bone hand with jointed fingers

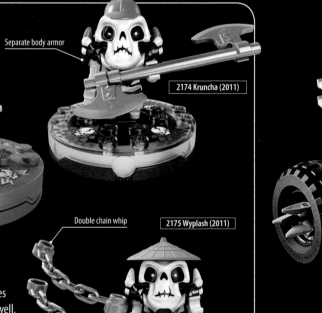

Individualized skull features

Separate body armor

2174 Kruncha (2011)

Driver's seat

Double chain whip

2175 Wyplash (2011)

2173 Nuckal (2011)

GENERALS

The ninja team's skeleton enemies were available with spinners as well, including the bigger and tougher generals who served their arch-enemy, Lord Garmadon. Spinner sets included a variety of weapons, cards, and bricks that could be used to modify play for more challenging duels.

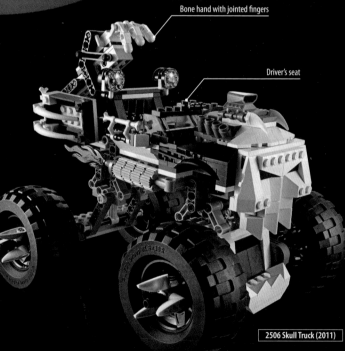

2506 Skull Truck (2011)

SKELETON VEHICLES

Although the world of Ninjago was based on a fantasy version of feudal Japan, the Skulkin villains emerged from the underworld with their own fleet of skeleton-themed vehicles. The massive Skull Truck featured chomping jaws, a bone hand that could be launched to capture ninja, two rib-cages, and a working suspension system.

Ninja side of arena

Skeleton side of arena

Skull archway entrance

Weapon rack

BATTLE ARENA

Some Ninjago sets were about spinning, some were about building, and some were both. The Ninjago Battle Arena could be built into a ring for spinner duels, complete with an armory of 14 different weapons and a pair of ball-shooters that you could use to try to knock your opponent's minifigure off its spinner.

2520 Ninjago Battle Arena (2011)

Ball shooter

THE DRAGONS

Four powerful elemental dragons guarded the legendary weapons. Toward the end of the two-part Ninjago TV special in 2011, they befriended the ninja heroes, upgrading them to DX (Dragon Xtreme) versions with new uniforms, and helped take them to confront Lord Garmadon.

Spreading wings

Posable limbs

NINJA VS. SKELETON

Pull lever to activate ninja-slammer

Subordinate to the generals were the skeleton troops, who had normal-sized minifigure heads but shared the same body pieces. Chopov's Skull Motorbike could swing its skull down to smash an unwary ninja flat.

Flame-spewing exhaust

Jay with Nunchucks of Lightning

2259 Skull Motorbike (2011)

LORD GARMADON

Lord Garmadon was the evil brother of the ninja team's teacher, Sensei Wu. His underworld fortress included four-armed skeleton king Samukai, Kai's sister Nya, and other figures. The skull above the gate could detach as a giant spider.

2505 Garmadon's Dark Fortress (2011)

Lightning ball shooter

2521 Lightning Dragon Battle (2011)

LEGO® Ninjago: Year 2

THE DEFEAT OF THE SKELETONS was only the start of the adventure. In 2012, the theme returned with the emergence of five ancient tribes of snake-like Serpentine, set free by Lord Garmadon's young son Lloyd Garmadon. The ninja had to master new powers to save their world from the giant serpent called the Great Devourer ●

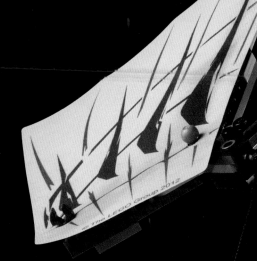

AIR SHIP

A theme of most of the 2012 ninja sets was transformation: vehicles that could convert into different modes for attack or disguise. The *Destiny's Bounty* became the team's new headquarters after their original home was destroyed by the Serpentine. Its sail unfolded into wings at the flick of a switch. Its rear spikes rotated to become flight thrusters.

In the second season of the TV series, the ship was much larger and contained an entire training facility and computer center.

Four-armed Lord Garmadon

Moving figurehead jaw

9446 Destiny's Bounty (2012)

THE GREEN NINJA

Who would become the prophesied Green Ninja? It turned out to be Lloyd himself, who discovered his heroic destiny in time for the final battle with the Great Devourer when it was summoned by the Serpentine leader Pythor.

9443 Rattlecopter (2012)

RISE OF THE SNAKES

The five Serpentine tribes were the Hypnobrai, Fangpyre, Anacondrai, Venomari, and Constrictai. Each tribe had its own staff and symbol.

Snake bombs   Fang-Suei   Lloyd Garmadon   Kai ZX

Spitta   Rattla   Fangdam

Retractable anchor

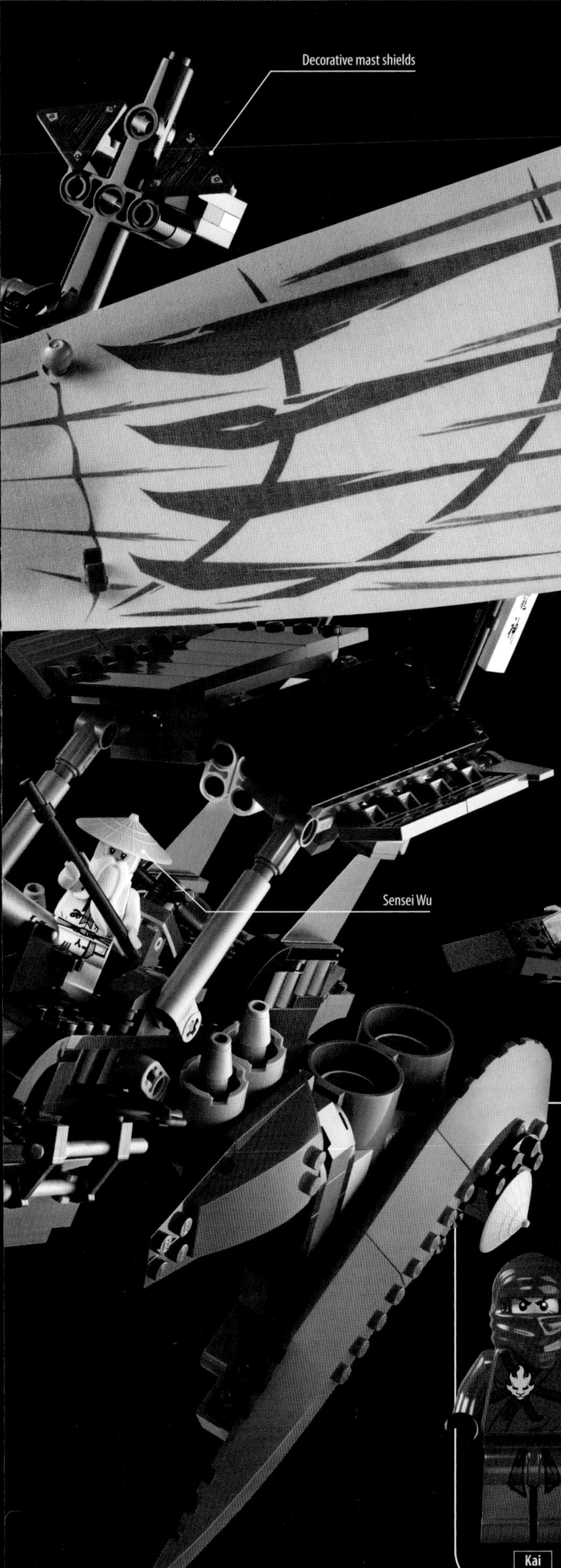

Decorative mast shields

SAMURAI X

The masked Samurai X was secretly Nya, who proved that a samurai and her giant sword-wielding mech could be every bit as good at saving the day as a ninja… or even four of them.

Samurai helmet crest

Sail converts from sea to air modes

Robotic armor plating

Opening cockpit

9448 Samurai Mech (2012)

Sensei Wu

VEHICLES

The world of Ninjago got a little more hi-tech in the second year. Jay's Storm Fighter jet could swing its wings back to reveal a set of golden sword blades.

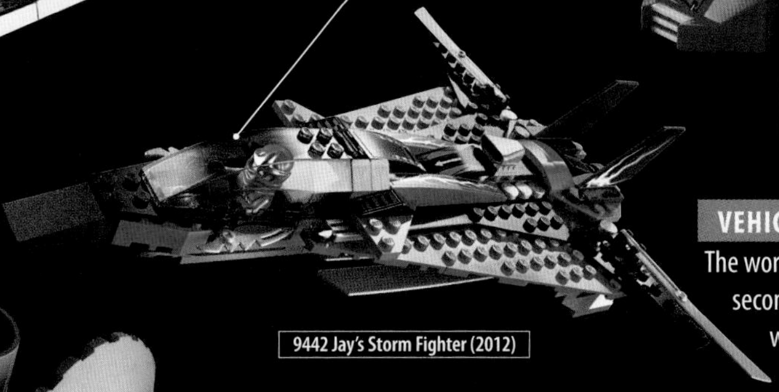

9442 Jay's Storm Fighter (2012)

NINJA EVOLUTION

As the ninja heroes gained new Spinjitzu skills and abilities, their looks changed as well. Their NRG forms represented their ultimate elemental powers—fire for Kai, lightning for Jay, earth for Cole, and ice for Zane.

| Kai | Kai DX | Kendo Kai | Kai ZX | NRG Kai |

Sets to Remember

6195 Neptune Discovery Lab (1995)

6190 Shark's Crystal Cave (1996)

6769 Fort Legoredo (1996)

6494 Magic Mountain Time Lab (1996)

5978 The Sphinx Secret Surprise (1998)

5956 Expedition Balloon (1999)

4980 Tunnel Transport (1999)

6776 Ogel Control Center (2001)

4797 Ogel Mutant Killer Whale (2002)

7419 Dragon Fortress (2003)

7475 Fire Hammer vs. Mutant Lizards (2005)

7298 Dino Air Tracker (2005)

7713 Bridge Walker and White Lightning (2006)

8107 Fight for the Golden Tower (2007)

8118 Hybrid Rescue Tank (2008)

7775 Aquabase Invasion (2007)

8961 Crystal Sweeper (2009)

8634 Mission 5: Turbocar Chase (2008)

8898 Wreckage Road (2010)

7985 City of Atlantis (2011)

8970 Robo Attack (2009)

8191 Lavatraz (2010)

7327 Scorpion Pyramid (2011)

9464 The Vampyre Hearse (2012)

2507 Fire Temple (2011)

9450 Epic Dragon Battle (2012)

5887 Dino Defense HQ (2012)

119

LEGO® Racers

LEGO® RACING started with a Formula 1 car model in 1975 and a racetrack-themed Town series in the 1980s, but it wasn't until LEGO Racers revved up in 2001 that brick-built cars and trucks were designed with real speed and competition in mind. With vehicles that have ranged from pint-sized Tiny Turbos to stunt-driving Power Racers, LEGO Racers just keeps on going ●

Built to burn rubber!

4584 Hot Scorcher (2002)

DROME RACERS

In 2002, everything had a story—even LEGO Racers! Set in the year 2015, its racecar-driver heroes and villains vied for fame and fortune in the dangerous Drome, run by the mysterious Dromulus and his pet robot monkey Monkulus. A video game and comics told the tale of these multi-scaled race cars with pull-back motors.

R/C RACING

With an infrared remote control, this 133-piece RC racer set included instructions for building it as a 4x4 off-road vehicle, a dune buggy for pit racing, or a fast track car. It could swap wheels with other LEGO Racers sets for different surfaces and speeds.

4589 RC-Nitro Flash (2002)

Three infrared channels let up to three people race their cars at the same time without interference.

RADICAL RACERS

The first LEGO Racers sets were very different from the rest. Shredd, Surfer, Spiky, Duster, and their rivals were toothy monsters whose simple, eight-piece cars were built to send their drivers flying on impact.

Each set came with a storage container that doubled as a high-speed slammer launcher.

4570 Shredd (2001)

TINY TURBOS

The Tiny Turbos sub-theme of LEGO Racers launched in 2005. Similar in scale to other small race car toys, these pocket-sized cars and trucks came in tire-shaped transport cases and had smooth, free-spinning tires for maximum speed when pushed or rolled down a ramp. Releases have included classic muscle cars, police cruisers, and city street racers with glow-in-the-dark elements.

6111 Street Chase (2006)

The different fold-out tracks could be combined and rebuilt into even bigger and better raceways!

BUILDABLE RACETRACKS

The 2009 Tiny Turbos series included vehicle two-packs with storage containers that unfolded to make T-shaped stretches of racetrack. LEGO pieces and racing signs were included to build environment-themed tracks, including an ice rally, a bumpy desert road, and a stock car raceway.

EXTREME ICE RALLY

STAGE 5

8124 Ice Rally (2009)

8146 Nitro Muscle (2007)

Turning the nitro booster in back steered the front tires.

The body frame flipped open for access to the detailed interior.

MUSCLE MANIA

With oversized rear wheels, an exposed engine and metallic racing decals, the Nitro Muscle may be the most vividly colored LEGO Racers set of all. This nitro-burning "funny car" drag racer stretched more than 15 in (38 cm) long and was largely constructed from LEGO® Technic beams and curved body plates.

Blast-off hood and engine

Fly-apart body

Roof lights

9094 Star Striker (2012)

2012 revisted some old concepts with monster truck models that ejected their minifigure drivers when they crashed.

POWER RACERS

LEGO Power Racers models used a combination of standard bricks and LEGO Technic pieces to construct racing vehicles with built-in functions. Some had pull-back motors or power-slammer launchers, some had flip-out glider wings or came with ramps and flaming hoops, and some—like this big green pick-up truck— were made for crashing.

Stunt-action bumper

8141 Off-Road Power (2007)

Big rubber off-road tires

Interior designed to be as accurate as possible to that of the real supercar.

LAMBORGHINI

2009 brought a **brand**-new license into the LEGO Racers fold. The 1:17 scale Lamborghini Gallardo LP560-4 could be built as either a coupe or a spyder model, and featured working doors, a detailed engine with opening cover, a retractable top, and special Lamborghini wheel rims.

STUNT ACTION

Part of an assortment built to perform different stunts, the Action Wheelie had an oversized rear spoiler that made it speed forward while popping a wheelie when you pulled it back and let go. Other stunt racers could jump, spin, and drive on their side wheels.

8169 Lamborghini Gallardo LP560-4 (2009)

8667 Action Wheelie (2006)

POWER SLAMMERS

With extra-wide tires and glow in the dark headlights and wheel discs for night racing, this motorcycle looked pretty fast on its own . . . but when you put the bike in front of its launcher and slammed the lever down with your fist, it really went flying!

8645 Muscle Slammer Bike (2005)

Decorative BIONICLE® elements include Bohrok-eye headlights, a fire-sword exhaust, and silver Toa feet on the sides.

LEGO® Ferrari

IN 2004, Italian sports car manufacturer Ferrari S.p.A. joined the LEGO® Racers team, and brought Ferrari's famous Formula One race cars, premium sports cars, and an international reputation for speed and quality. The bright red Ferrari sets quickly became a popular LEGO license for both young auto fans and grown-up enthusiasts, with a growing collection of racing toys and detailed replicas in multiple scales, and even a pair of LEGO® DUPLO® sets for the youngest builders ●

8375 Ferrari F1 Pit Set (2004)

The classic yellow minifigure face means that this Scuderia Ferrari racing team member isn't based on a real person.

8142 Ferrari 248 1:24 (2007)

Special racing tires

Details and functions included working jacks and a mid-mounted engine with support frame.

8143 Ferrari 1:17 F430 Challenge (2007)

COLORS OF VICTORY

The LEGO model of the aerodynamic Ferrari F430 included optional parts to make either the standard sports car version in yellow or the lighter, faster racing-edition F430 Challenge with a red body, sponsor logos, and different rims on the wheels.

FERRARI FORMULA ONE

In 2004 and 2007, the series included 1:24 scale versions of Ferrari's famous Formula One race cars with pull-back motors. The 2007 version had an updated construction and sponsorship decals to match the latest real vehicle. Despite appearances, there are no minifigures included with the set, as it's too large to be in-scale; instead, the driver's head and helmet are directly attached to the cockpit.

RACING CREW

Everybody may know the drivers, but the hard-working Scuderia Ferrari pit crew received their due at last in several garage and pit sets that included them and all their tools and equipment. After all, somebody has to keep those race cars tuned-up and ready to break records!

This set also came with two Ferrari F1 racers and a full garage with fuel pit, driver stations, and a service bike.

8144 Ferrari 248 F1 Team (2007)

8155 Ferrari F1 Pit 1:55 (2008)

SMALLER SPEEDSTERS

In 2008, Ferrari sets went pocket-sized with a garage, fuel pit, trucks, and F1 racers in the same small scale as the LEGO Racers Tiny Turbos.

4693 Ferrari F1 Race car (2004)

LEGO DUPLO FERRARI

Little kids like to race, too! This officially licensed Ferarri car for ages 3–6 came pre-assembled as a single piece, but young builders could build on top of the rear spoiler or put together the winner's stand and stack the shining trophy on top when they won the preschool championship. 4694 Ferrari F1 Racing Team, released the same year, included a car, truck, mechanic, and race pit.

PIT STOP

This set from the first year of LEGO Ferrari featured a racing pit with a custom road plate, six helmeted mechanics, spare tires for quick mid-race replacements, tools for on-the-go repairs, and instructions for rebuilding it into a Ferarri F1 starting grid.

8375 Ferrari F1 Pit Set (2004)

2556 Ferrari Formula 1 Racing Car (1997)

FIRST OFF THE GRID

Meet the very first LEGO Ferrari set! This Model Team racer (above) for experienced builders was only available at Shell gas stations as a special promotional purchase.

Driver and passenger seats

Technic body frame

GRAND TOURER

This model of Ferrari's 2-seat Gran Turismo flagship coupe used flexible LEGO Technic rod elements to replicate the real auto's curves. Built from 1,340 pieces, it was 18 in (46 cm) long and had a working front-wheel steering system and a V12 engine with moving pistons.

8145 Ferrari 599 GTB Fiorano 1:10 (2007)

Doors, hood, and trunk all opened for access to interior details.

8156 Ferrari FXX 1:17 (2008)

RARE RACER

Only 30 of the real Ferrari FXX racing cars were ever produced. Fortunately, it was a lot easier to get hold of the LEGO version, which had an opening rear engine cover and front trunk, and doors that swung up just like the ones on the real thing.

Some builders bought this set just to get the rare chrome-coated winner's trophy!

8389 M. Schumacher & R. Barrichello (2004)

A DARING DUO

The 2009 LEGO Ferrari series starred the newest drivers on the Scuderia Ferrari racing team. Finnish driver Kimi Räikkönen won first place in the 2007 Drivers' World Championship, and Brazilian-born Felipe Massa took second place in 2008, making them the latest tough team to beat.

DESIGNATED DRIVERS

The 2004 Scuderia Ferrari racing team became LEGO minifigures in this all-star winner's podium set. It featured multiple-record-smashing driver Michael Schumacher and 2000 German Grand Prix winner Rubens Barrichello, both with flesh-toned faces, authentically decorated helmets and jackets, and approved real-world likenesses.

8168 Ferrari Victory (2009)

LEGO® Sports

LEGO Basketball minifigures had springs built into their legs and specially designed arms to let them hold, throw, and dunk balls.

> Let's see your Castle figures do THIS!

3427 NBA Slam Dunk (2003)

ATHLETIC COMPETITION and brick construction go together better than you'd think. Between 2000 and 2006, the LEGO® Group produced several model series based on real sports. These licensed themes were filled with unique minifigures and action features to let builders show off their skills ●

LEGO SOCCER

Released as LEGO Soccer in some countries and LEGO Football in others, this was the first, largest, and longest-lived of the LEGO Sports themes. With over 25 sets made between 2000 and 2006, its models included international team buses, training stations, and fields with minifigure bases that could be rotated to aim and tapped with a finger to "kick" a ball.

3569 Grand Soccer Stadium (2006)

Stadium measures 22 in (55 cm) long and 14 in (35 cm) wide

LEGO BASKETBALL

Launched in 2003, the NBA-licensed LEGO Basketball theme's models enabled builders to reproduce their favorite flashy basketball moves. Sets included street hoops with lever-activated slam-dunking features and courts with full teams.

3432 NBA Challenge (2003)

3544 Game Set (2003)

LEGO HOCKEY

Licensed by the NHL and NHLPA, the first LEGO Hockey sets in 2003 used chunky BIONICLE® style elements to build tough robotic players that swung their sticks when you slammed down on their heads. Different sets could execute slap shots, flip shots, passes, and other hockey moves.

The Basketball theme featured the first minifigures based on real personalities.

FAMOUS FIGURES

Although the generic team members in LEGO Basketball sets kept their familiar yellow faces, the company tried something new for minifigures based on real NBA players: realistic skin tones. This soon became standard for licensed figures across all LEGO themes.

Shaquille O'Neal (2003)   Paul Pierce (2003)

LEGO hockey puck

SECOND PERIOD

In its second year, LEGO Hockey shifted to a smaller scale. Similar to other LEGO Sports themes, the 2004 hockey sets let builders play against their friends by controlling rival minifigure players on a stadium-like base. No actual teams or players were licensed, and ice hockey figures wore only the NHL logo on their padded jerseys.

3578 NHL Championship Challenge (2004)

Long rods moved the hockey figures' bases and activated flippers to pass or shoot the puck.

Sliding base with flipper

URBAN SHOWDOWN

3579 NHL Street Hockey (2004)

Only two LEGO Hockey sets were made in the new style: 3578 NHL Championship Challenge, with an ice rink and two four-figure teams, and 3579 NHL Street Hockey for those who favored a one-on-one face-off on the mean city streets.

The street hockey set was also licensed from the NHL.

GRAVITY GAMES

In a tie-in with the summer edition of the extreme-sports Gravity Games, LEGO Sports released this skateboarding park with customizable vertical ramps and railings. The set included a special "stunt stick" that could be attached to a minifigure skater to create mid-air tricks and stunts.

Curved ramp pieces

3537 Skateboard Vert Park (2003)

Sets could be combined to make bigger parks.

Modular design

3538 Snowboard Boarder Cross Race (2003)

Snowboard launcher

Airborne snowboarder

COLD COMPETITION

Made for the winter Gravity Games, this competitive snowboarding set featured a snowy mountain slope with launchers at the top for two minifigures on boards. Set them loose and they slid down the hill toward the finish line at the bottom, flying and bouncing into the air thanks to the course's built-in obstacles and stunt ramps.

The snowboards were weighted to keep the minifigures upright and moving down the slope.

Each minifigure comes randomly packed inside a sealed bag (a different color for each series), so you never know which one you'll get!

Collectible Minifigures

FOR MORE THAN 30 YEARS, LEGO® themes have been filled with colorful minifigures. Kids and grown-up fans both love them—so why not give them even more to love? Starting in 2010, the LEGO Minifigures collection has swelled the population of the brick-built world, 16 collectible characters at a time ●

Cowboy

Twin six-irons

Nurse

Zombie

Deep Sea Diver

Flippers for swimming

Skater

Rolling skateboard

Super Wrestler

Forestman

Robot

Magician

Ninja

Demolition Dummy

Tribal Hunter

New pompom elements

Circus Clown

SERIES 1

Released in May 2010, the first series of LEGO Minifigures provided new citizens for classic themes such as City, Castle, Space, and Western, along with totally original creations like the Super Wrestler, Circus Clown, and Zombie. Common categories across multiple series include sports, monsters, sci-fi, and historical warriors.

Cheerleader

Caveman

Each minifigure includes a base and signature accessories. Some are classic LEGO elements, while others are totally new and exclusive.

8683 LEGO Minifigures Series 1 (2010)

Series 2 featured the sombrero-wearing Maraca Man, a Mime with two extra heads for added expressions, a Spartan Warrior, a Pop Star, and the totally retro Disco Dude.

8684 LEGO Minifigures Series 2

Breakout stars of Series 3 included the Hula Dancer, an Elf warrior, a cybernetic Space Villain with a Blacktron II logo, a Baseball Player, and the Gorilla Suit Guy.

8803 LEGO Minifigures Series 3

SERIES 4

To give some extra character to the characters, the collectible minifigures have their own individual bios on the LEGO website. Series 4's update revealed the Hazmat Guy's job concerns, the Artist's compulsion to paint (and paint on) everything he sees, the Kimono Girl's love of haiku verse, and the Monster's desire to help people build.

8804 LEGO Minifigures Series 4

Lawn Gnome's fishing pole

Gold Viking horns

Silver Soccer Player trophy

Street Skater board with new printing

Punk Rocker's new electric guitar

Spaceman

Electro-Zapp blast

8805 LEGO Minifigures Series 5

SERIES 5

Series 5 added lots of brand-new LEGO pieces, including the Small Clown's cream pie and bowler hat, the Lizard Man's removable mask and tail, the Gladiator's helmet and sword, the Detective's deerstalker cap, the Gangster's opening violin case, and the Zookeeper's chimpanzee.

SERIES 6

Things got even more wild in Series 6, which introduced a Leprechaun with a pot o' gold, a Clockwork Robot with a wind-up key, the universe-saving Intergalactic Girl, the pajama-clad Sleepyhead, a smoke-tailed Genie, and the torch-bearing Lady Liberty.

8827 LEGO Minifigures Series 6

Genie can hold or attach to his magic lamp

Removable tiara holds veil in place

SERIES 7

Still going strong as of 2012, Series 7's lineup featured (among others) a brave Aztec Warrior, a kilted Bagpiper, a Computer Programmer with a laptop, a Bride with a bouquet and veil, an armored member of the Galaxy Patrol, and the enigmatic Bunny Suit Guy.

8831 LEGO Minifigures Series 7

BIONICLE®

IT WAS A TRICKY PUZZLE: How could the LEGO Group break into the world of action figures without losing what made its products so distinctly LEGO® sets? The company tested the water with the Technic-themed, robotic Slizers (a.k.a. ThrowBots) in 1999, and the rolling RoboRiders the following year. The success of these "constraction" sets led to the development of an all-new, entirely original LEGO theme called BIONICLE®. Launched in 2001 to great acclaim, the "Biological Chronicle" blended technology with mythology to create a universe filled with buildable heroes, creatures, and villains, with a story that was told through comic books, novels, movies, and online games and animations. It quickly became one of the most unique and popular LEGO themes of all time ●

The Legend Begins

MONTHS BEFORE the first toys were released in 2001, the BIONICLE® story emerged through an intriguing series of teaser ads and a popular online adventure game. The setting was a mysterious tropical island called Mata Nui, where bio-mechanical villagers were under attack from fierce creatures controlled by an evil being called the Makuta. When all seemed lost, six heroes arrived who were prophesied to save the universe from darkness. The BIONICLE legend had begun ●

Each Toa Nuva's tools had a double function. The magma swords of Tahu Nuva, Toa of Fire, could also attach to his feet to make a lava surfboard.

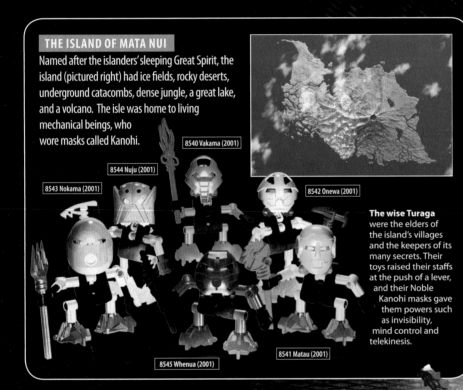

THE ISLAND OF MATA NUI
Named after the islanders' sleeping Great Spirit, the island (pictured right) had ice fields, rocky deserts, underground catacombs, dense jungle, a great lake, and a volcano. The isle was home to living mechanical beings, who wore masks called Kanohi.

8540 Vakama (2001)

8544 Nuju (2001)

8543 Nokama (2001)

8542 Onewa (2001)

The wise Turaga were the elders of the island's villages and the keepers of its many secrets. Their toys raised their staffs at the push of a lever, and their Noble Kanohi masks gave them powers such as invisibility, mind control and telekinesis.

8545 Whenua (2001)

8541 Matau (2001)

THE TOA
The six Toa came to the island in canisters—matching their toys' packaging—that washed up on shore from the endless sea. Imbued with elemental powers and wearing Great Kanohi masks, they were figures of legend to the islanders, who believed that the heroes were destined to awaken the Great Spirit Mata Nui and save the universe from Makuta's evil.

8568 Pohatu Nuva (2002)

8567 Lewa Nuva (2002)

8566 Onua Nuva (2002)

THE VILLAGERS
The villagers of Mata Nui lived in six villages, one for each of the island's elemental themes. Originally known as Tohunga, they were renamed the Matoran in honor of Mata Nui following the defeat of the invading Bohrok.

8595 Takua and Pewku (2003)

Once called the Chronicler, Takua would later be transformed by the Mask of Light into the Seventh Toa, Takanuva.

The Toa battled Makuta, the Rahi, and other threats to the island. In the theme's second year, they became the Toa Nuva (pictured below) and gained new armor, tools, and enhanced mask powers.

Collectible Kanohi came with sets and in assorted mask packs

8538 Muaka & Kane-Ra (2001)

THE RAHI

From the mosquito-like Nui Rama to the mighty Kane-Ra bull, the beasts of the BIONICLE universe were collectively called Rahi. In the theme's first year, five sets of Rahi were sold in two-packs, each with instructions for combining the pieces into a new, larger creature. The models were designed with Technic action features that let them battle Toa and each other by knocking off their opponents' masks.

Ice blades convert to skis

8571 Kopaka Nuva (2002)

8570 Gali Nuva (2002)

MAKUTA

The dark being known as the Makuta had been trying to dominate the inhabitants of Mata Nui for centuries before the arrival of the Toa. He used infected masks to control wild Rahi, set the Bohrok swarm loose on the island, and unleashed the reptilian Rahkshi to prevent the discovery of the Toa of Light.

8593 Makuta (2003)

THE SWARM

The six breeds of insect-like Bohrok were the first Toa-sized BIONICLE villain sets. They could curl up and hibernate inside their plastic containers, or attack with lunging heads and rubbery parasite "brains" called krana. These controlled heroes by taking the place of their masks.

8562 Gahlok (2002)

Aqua axes become swimming fins

131

New Islands, New Adventures

AT THE CONCLUSION of 2003's *BIONICLE™: Mask of Light* movie, the heroes of Mata Nui discovered a second island deep beneath their own. For the first time, the BIONICLE story departed from its original home, first in an ancient tale from the high-tech city of Metru Nui , and then with an epic quest that led from the imperiled island of Voya Nui to sunken Mahri Nui, and finally to Karda Nui at the heart of the BIONICLE world ●

8605 Toa Matau
(2004)

THE VISORAK INVASION

The flashback continued as the Toa Metru were transformed into savage, mutated Toa Hordika and battled the spider-like Visorak. The Metru Nui chronicles were animated in the movies *BIONICLE® 2: Legends of Metru Nui* (2004) and *BIONICLE® 3: Web of Shadows* (2005).

The six Rahaga (2005), companions to the Toa Hordika

Lifeblade measures 5 in (13 cm) long

TOA METRU

The rediscovery of Metru Nui led the Turaga to tell a tale from 1,000 years before, when they were the Toa Metru, guardians of the ancient island city. Like the Toa Nuva, their sets' tools could be reconfigured into travel forms, and their action figures were the first BIONICLE heroes to feature articulated elbows, knees, and heads.

Axonn's axe could cut through stone, fire energy blasts, and return to his hand when thrown

8733 Axonn (2006)

IGNITION

In 2006, the BIONICLE story returned to its present when six Matoran villagers traveled to Voya Nui and became the Toa Inika. They fought the mercenary Piraka for the Mask of Life that could save the Great Spirit Mata Nui. These BIONICLE figures lacked Technic-style gear mechanisms, focusing instead on new parts and posability.

The robotic guard Maxilos was secretly the evil Makuta in disguise

8924 Maxilos and Spinax (2007)

INTO THE DEEPS

In 2007, the Toa Inika followed the Mask of Life into the sea, transforming into the aquatic Toa Mahri and defending a lost underwater city from squid-launching Barraki warlords. Their sets featured air hoses, diving masks, and rapid-fire Cordak blasters. At the end of the year, Toa Matoro sacrificed himself to save Mata Nui, but the story wasn't over yet...

A friend to the Toa Inika, Axonn even had articulated fingers.

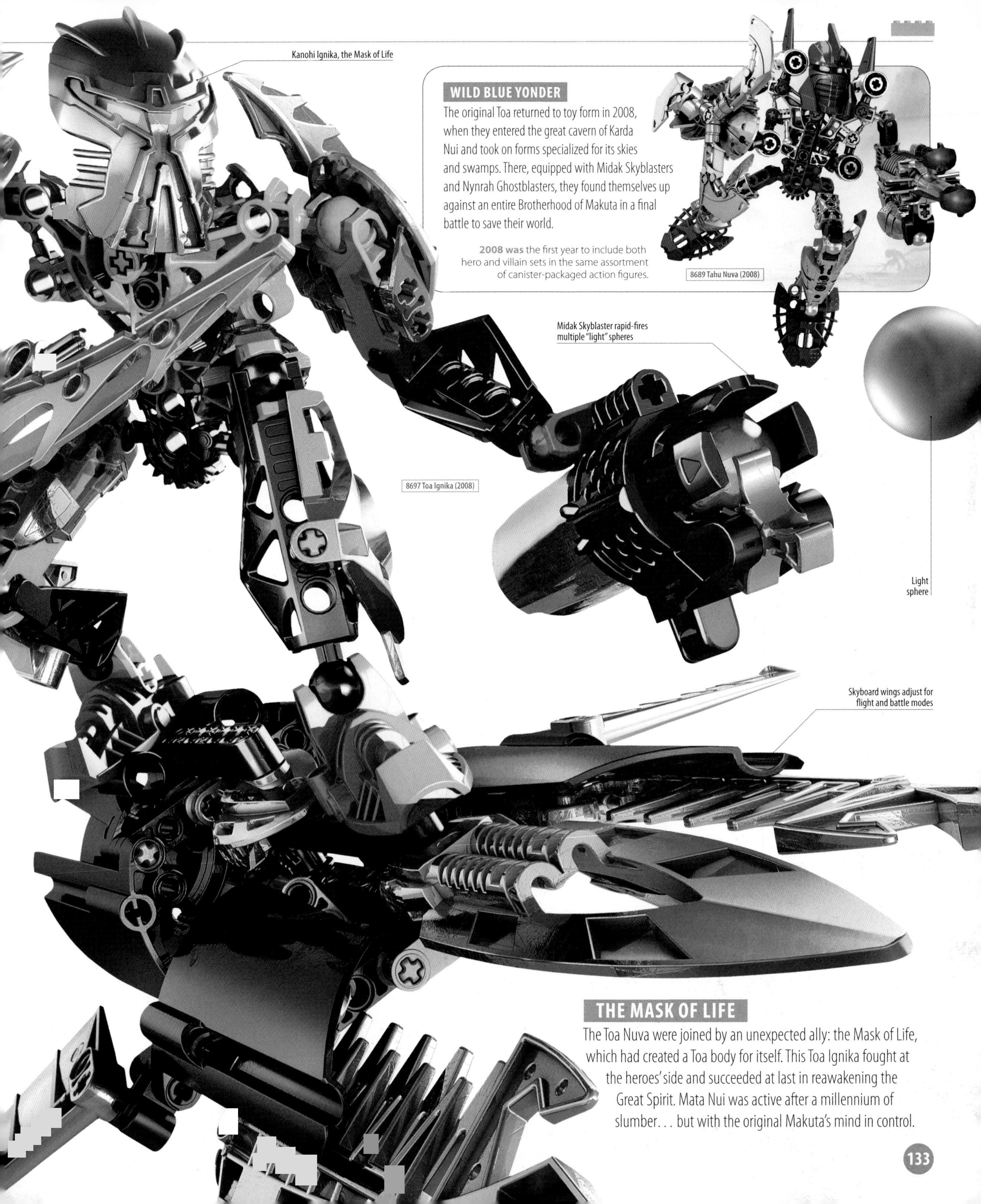

Kanohi Ignika, the Mask of Life

WILD BLUE YONDER

WILD BLUE YONDER

The original Toa returned to toy form in 2008, when they entered the great cavern of Karda Nui and took on forms specialized for its skies and swamps. There, equipped with Midak Skyblasters and Nynrah Ghostblasters, they found themselves up against an entire Brotherhood of Makuta in a final battle to save their world.

2008 was the first year to include both hero and villain sets in the same assortment of canister-packaged action figures.

8689 Tahu Nuva (2008)

Midak Skyblaster rapid-fires multiple "light" spheres

8697 Toa Ignika (2008)

Light sphere

Skyboard wings adjust for flight and battle modes

THE MASK OF LIFE

The Toa Nuva were joined by an unexpected ally: the Mask of Life, which had created a Toa body for itself. This Toa Ignika fought at the heroes' side and succeeded at last in reawakening the Great Spirit. Mata Nui was active after a millennium of slumber... but with the original Makuta's mind in control.

Endings and Beginnings

AFTER EIGHT YEARS of mystery, the biggest secret of the BIONICLE® universe was at last revealed: the Great Spirit Mata Nui was a space-faring robot 40 million feet (12,200 km) tall, and the story's islands and cities were all parts of his colossal body. Now, in 2009, Mata Nui would have an adventure of his own ●

8978 Skrall (2009)

A NEW WORLD

The ancient, shattered world of Bara Magna was populated by Agori villagers, mighty Glatorian warriors, nomadic Bone Hunters, and ferocious beasts. Perhaps most dangerous of all were the warlike Skrall, a tribe of fearless rock warriors who lived for conflict and the conquest of their savage planet.

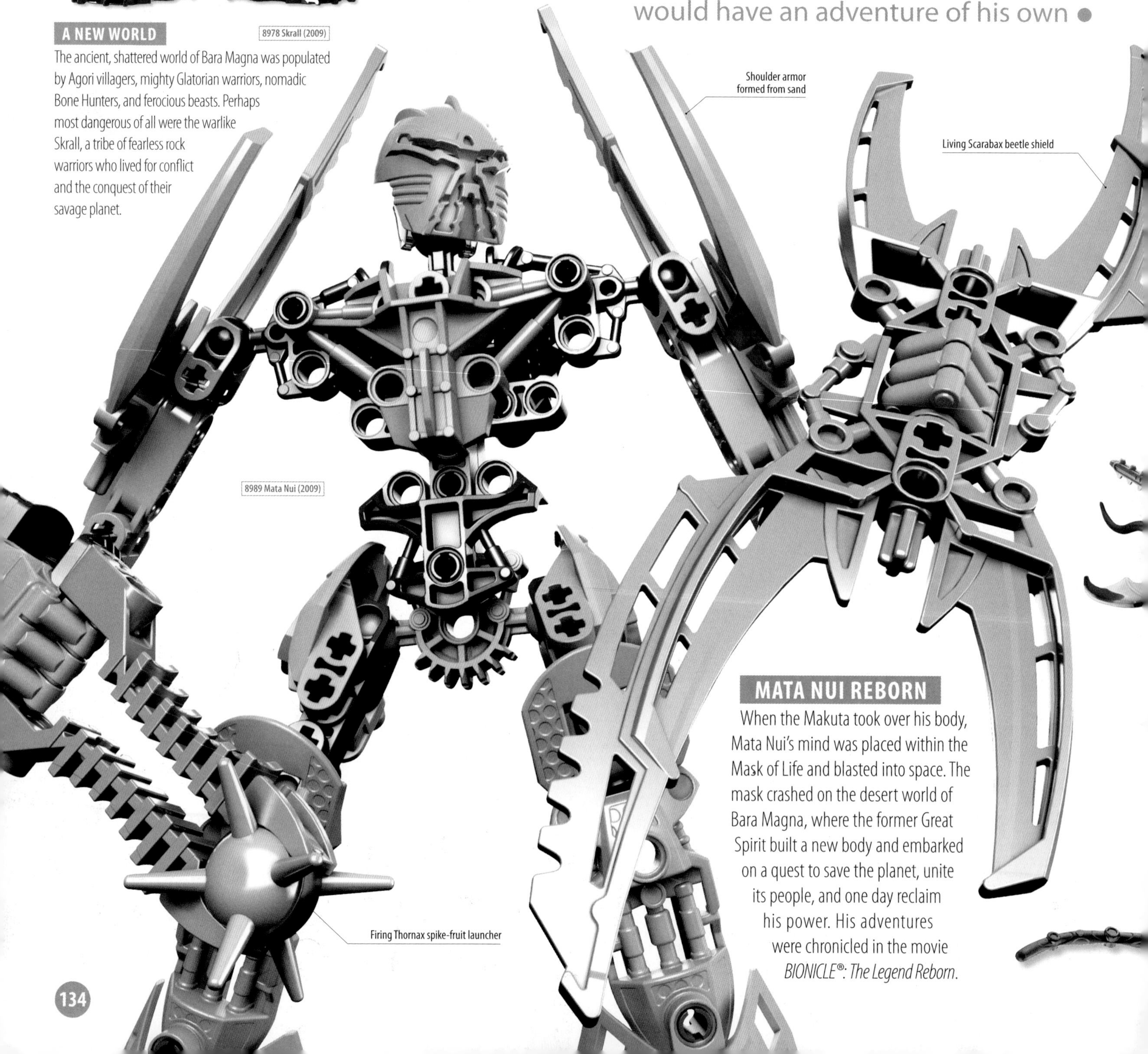

Shoulder armor formed from sand

Living Scarabax beetle shield

8989 Mata Nui (2009)

MATA NUI REBORN

When the Makuta took over his body, Mata Nui's mind was placed within the Mask of Life and blasted into space. The mask crashed on the desert world of Bara Magna, where the former Great Spirit built a new body and embarked on a quest to save the planet, unite its people, and one day reclaim his power. His adventures were chronicled in the movie *BIONICLE®: The Legend Reborn*.

Firing Thornax spike-fruit launcher

Thornax launcher

Flame claws

BATTLE WHEELS

Glatorian and other large 2009 sets had built-in wheels for playing an action figure game against friends. Thornax strikes on figures, vehicles, and canisters made life counters tick down until only one was left standing as the winner.

8979 Malum
(2009)

THE GLATORIAN

To avoid all-out war between villages, territorial conflicts on Bara Magna were settled in combat arenas. Each tribe employed warriors called Glatorian to fight duels on their behalf. The hot-tempered Malum was a gladiator for the Fire Tribe until he broke the rules of the arena and was exiled into the wastelands.

The BIONICLE universe was filled with imaginative alien vehicles packed with action features, from the Bohrok-punching Boxor and the Exo-Toa battle armor of the theme's earliest years, to the rocket-powered flyers of Karda Nui and the post-apocalyptic, scrap-metal desert rollers of Bara Magna.

8993 Kaxium V3
(2009)

SMALL HEROES, BIG BATTLES

It was difficult to create full-sized scenes featuring the large action figures, but minifigure-scaled BIONICLE sets enabled builders to create giant vehicles, huge monsters, fortresses, and battle scenes from the sagas of Metru Nui, Voya Nui, and Mahri Nui.

8927 Toa Terrain Crawler (2007)

Mutant sea squid

Rapid-fire Cordak blaster

Mini Toa Mahri with posable arms, waist, and head

LEGO® Hero Factory

IN EARLY 2010, the BIONICLE® universe came to an end with the release of the BIONICLE Stars, new versions of six characters from the nine-year history of the theme. In its place rose LEGO® Hero Factory, a new story about an immense factory in futuristic Makuhero City, where robot heroes were manufactured to protect the galaxy ●

7164 Preston Stormer (2010)

Preston Stormer, a.k.a. "The Pro," was a seasoned veteran and the leader of the Alpha 1 Team. The six main 2010 heroes had real first names and carried large weapons on their hands and arms.

FIRST GENERATION

The first Hero Factory heroes were smaller than traditional BIONICLE Toa and made use of the same construction style as the BIONICLE Stars, with snap-on armor and jointed heads, shoulders, wrists, hips, and ankles. In the center of the chest was the Hero Core that provided each robot's personality and power source.

FALLEN HERO

Von Nebula was once the hero Von Ness until his cowardice made him desert during a vital mission. Gaining a hatred for Hero Factory, he recruited a team of interplanetary villains and set in motion a grand scheme for revenge.

7145 Von Nebula (2010)

At 156 pieces, Von Nebula was the largest individual character released in the theme's first year. His Black Hole Orb Staff had spinning blades and in the story could generate black holes.

NEED A LIFT?

The Drop Ship was a light-speed transport vehicle that the factory used to carry heroes to their assigned missions on remote planets. It had trigger-activated wings and could pick up or drop the "Hero Pod" canisters that the heroes came inside. It included a pilot figure.

LEGO Technic structure

7160 Drop Ship (2010)

The Drop Ship was much bigger in the four-part *Hero Factory: Rise of the Rookies* animated miniseries, with a cockpit that had room for four.

H4 Force Ball shooter

NEW KID ON THE BRICK

A newly built, latest-model hero with a supercharged Hero Core, William Furno was placed in charge of a group of rookies under the training of the Alpha 1 Team. Competitive and impulsive, he was eager to prove himself to Stormer and the other veterans.

Furno was released twice in 2010: as a standard canister figure and with a different body design in the Furno Bike set, where he rode a fiery, ball-shooting motorcycle.

7158 Furno Bike (2010)

THE UPGRADE

In 2011, the heroes underwent an upgrade, gaining enhanced armor and abilities. Furno's fellow rookies Surge and Breez were joined by two new team members: tech-head Nex and weapons specialist Evo. The reinforcements really came in handy against renegade mining bots under the command of the powerful Fire Lord.

The characters' 2.0 upgrade was reflected in the hero figures' new, larger designs. These added elbow and knee articulation and armor that snapped onto ball joints instead of LEGO® Technic connections.

2068 Nex 2.0 (2011) 2067 Evo 2.0 (2011) 2141 Surge 2.0 (2011) 2142 Breez 2.0 (2011)

ORDEAL OF FIRE

The 2011 Hero Factory story kicked off with a mission to Tanker Station 22, which was under siege by a group of energy-siphoning fuel thieves. The mission was communicated in multiple ways: through a television episode, a comic book adapted by BIONICLE writer Greg Farshtey, and an online game on the Hero Factory website.

Drilldozer was one of the Fire Lord's three hench-bots. He carried a large turbine drill and a firing Lava Sphere shooter. His body was protected by molten spikes.

Nitroblast was the smartest of the three hench-bots and utterly loyal to the Fire Lord. His blowtorch was powered by the plasma container on his shoulder.

The insectile Jetbug had bladed mandibles and rocket-powered wings on his back. Like the others, he was a mid-sized model in between the smaller heroes and the giant Fire Lord.

2192 Drilldozer (2011) 2194 Nitroblast (2011) 2193 Jetbug (2011)

SAVAGE PLANET

In the second half of 2011, the heroes' new mission took them to the jungle world of Quatros, where the evil Witch Doctor was using Quaza spikes to control the local robotic wildlife.

The Witch Doctor had been Dr. Aldous Witch, a Hero Factory instructor who became obsessed with the Quaza Stone used to make Hero Cores.

2283 Witch Doctor (2011)

BEASTLY BOTS

Several of the heroes (including first-year veterans Stormer, Stringer, and Bulk) were upgraded again for their jungle assignment, gaining animal features and a new 3.0 designation. They also gained a new member: the lion-armored Rocka.

Starting in 2011, the Hero Factory sets included armor pieces with printed decoration specific to each character.

2143 Rocka 3.0 (2011)

KING-SIZED HERO

To deal with the titanic Witch Doctor, Rocka temporarily upgraded to this giant-sized body. At more than 11 in (29 cm) tall, Rocka XL was armed with a ball shooter and his double-blade claw combo tool.

At 174 pieces, Rocka XL had nearly six times the part count of the Rocka 3.0 figure.

2282 Rocka XL (2011)

Hero Factory: Breakout

HERO FACTORY doesn't just make heroes. It's also a prison for the most powerful and dangerous criminals from all across the galaxy—and at the beginning of 2012, the prisoners broke loose. It was up to the heroes to recapture them and stop the new villain Black Phantom from shutting the factory down for good ●

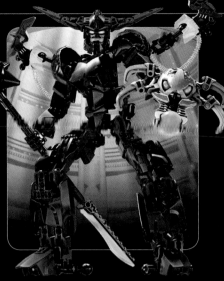

6203 Black Phantom (2012)

Black Phantom was armed with twin saber strikers, a double-ended staff, and a detachable arachnix drone.

BAGGED BOTS

2012 marked the first time since the beginning of the BIONICLE® universe that no "buildable figure" sets were sold in plastic canisters. Instead, many of the new Hero Factory heroes and villains came in two different sizes of heavy-duty resealable bags, or traditional boxes like Black Phantom.

Coming in at 39 pieces including his electricity shooter, plasma gun, and extra shoulder armor, Surge's latest upgrade was one of the smaller bagged sets.

6217 Surge (2012)

TOXIC FOE

Each of the heroes was paired up against a specific villain. Evo was sent to take on Toxic Reapa, whose toxic waste-spewing arms contaminated anything he touched. Online instructions showed how to combine both sets into a single super model.

6201 Toxic Reapa (2012)

Toxic Reapa hails from the planet Z'chaya. His sinister scheme was to infect the larvae on his home world and create an army of evil insects... unless Evo caught him first.

SOLO STYLE

With so many escaped villains on the loose, the factory's Mission Managers took the rare step of breaking up its teams and sending heroes out individually to round up the fugitives one by one. Each hero was given a shiny new set of hi-tech Hero Cuffs to use in catching the bad guys.

LAST LINE OF DEFENSE

With the other heroes scattered across the galaxy and Hero Factory locked down, Rocka—the only hero who hadn't yet been sent out on a mission—discovered that Black Phantom had stayed inside to destroy the hero-building Assembly Tower. Only he could save the factory... if he managed to survive the saboteur's booby traps.

6202 Rocka (2012)

Rocka was one of the larger-sized bagged sets. Built from 55 pieces, he was taller and more armored than his smaller teammates, like Evo and Surge. Of course, the 124-piece Black Phantom towered over him, too!

HEART OF A HERO

The most physically strong member of the Alpha 1 Team, though not the brightest, Dunkan Bulk helps to keep the task-oriented Stormer from getting too obsessed with rules and regulations. He's gone on many missions with his fellow veteran, the sonic-powered Jimi Stringer. This was his fourth design, counting a 2010 two-pack with exclusive villain Vapor.

During the year-long Breakout story, Bulk was armed with a laser-targeted missile launcher, a plasma shooter, and high-impact shoulder armor.

6223 Bulk (2012)

GAME POINTS

Each 2012 set included a Hero Core with a code printed on the back. Entering the code into the online *Hero Factory: Breakout* game earned points that could be used to upgrade the player's hero character. Bigger sets (like the deluxe-sized Breez) came with more points.

Natalie Breez is a nature-loving aerial ace. She can turn the blades of her hex shield sideways to act as a steering wing for her rocket boots.

6227 Breez (2012)

Razor spike

Plasma ball shooter

6222 Core Hunter (2012)

Core Hunter's predatory pursuits were aided by his plasma shooter, six-eyed multi-vision mask, and armor covered with razor spikes, but most dangerous of all was the Hero Core remover tool on his left arm.

Hero Core remover

Stealthy armor plating

THE FACTORY

Rising like a silver shark's fin high above the buildings of Makuhero City—home to a million mechanical citizens—Hero Factory's Assembly Tower was the brainchild of Akiyama Makuro, the oldest known robot in the universe. In the real world, kids could tune in to the Hero Factory FM podcast and even call in with trouble reports for the heroes.

SPEEDY SLICER

Freed from prison, Speeda Demon didn't look back—he just burned rubber to the ice planet Kollix IV on his nitro rocket motorbike. It was up to Stormer XL to put the brakes on his getaway.

6231 Speeda Demon (2012)

The lightning-fast Speeda Demon was double trouble for the heroes thanks to the wing-blades gripped in the extra hands on his shoulders.

CORE COLLECTOR

Another former Hero Factory operative, the cruel Core Hunter waited a long time to strike back at his one-time allies. The breakout gave him just the opportunity he needed to return to his favorite hobby: stalking heroes and stealing their Hero Cores for his collection.

Sets to Remember

8548 Nui-Jaga (2001)

8534 Tahu (2001)

8557 Exo-Toa (2002)

8525 Masks (2001)

8568 Pohatu Nuva (2002)

8596 Takanuva (2003)

8811 Toa Lhikan and Kikanalo (2004)

8759 Battle of Metru Nui (2005)

8918 Carapar (2007)

8755 Keetongu (2005)

8764 Vezon & Fenrakk (2006)

8723 Piruk (2006)

BIONICLE
AXALARA T9

Ages/edades
10-16
8943
Cont. 693 pcs/pzs

www.BIONICLE.com

8943 Axalara T9 (2008)

BIONICLE
PHANTOKA
VAMPRAH

Ages/edades
7-16
8692
Cont. 49 pcs/pzs

WARNING: CHOKING HAZARD. Toy contains small parts and a small ball. Not for children under 3 years.

8692 Vamprah (2008)

BIONICLE
TOA MATA NUI

www.BIONICLE.com

Ages/edades
8-16
8998
366

LIMITED EDITION

8998 Toa Mata Nui (2009)

BIONICLE
TUMA

Ages/edades
8-16
8991
188

8991 Tuma (2009)

HERO FACTORY

Ages/edades
6-16
7164
17 pcs/pzs

STORMER

7164 Preston Stormer (2010)

BIONICLE
TAHU
STARS

Ages/edades
6-16
7116
19 pcs/pzs

COLLECT THE GOLDEN BIONICLE

www.BIONICLE.com

7116 Tahu (2010)

HERO FACTORY

Ages/edades
7-16
7148
50

MELTDOWN

WARNING: CHOKING HAZARD. Toy contains small parts and a small ball. Not for children under 3 years.

7148 Meltdown (2010)

HERO FACTORY

Ages/edades
6-16
2183
30 pcs/pzs

STRINGER 3.0

2183 Stringer 3.0 (2011)

HERO FACTORY

Ages/edades
9-16
6203
124 pcs/pzs

BLACK PHANTOM
+500 GAME POINTS

6203 Black Phantom (2012)

HERO FACTORY

Ages/edades
9-16
2282
174 PCS/PZS

ROCKA XL

2282 Rock XL (2012)

HERO FACTORY

VOLTIX
+300 GAME POINTS

7-14
6283

6283 Voltix (2012)

LEGO® Creator

WHAT WILL YOU MAKE with a box full of bricks without any themes, characters, or stories? Just about anything! They've been called LEGO® Creator, Designer Sets, X-Pods, and Inventor. They may come with instructions and model ideas, but creative sets like these all represent the same thing: classic LEGO construction without rules or limitations ●

CREEPY CRAWLIES

If you liked scaring your little brother or sister, this was the LEGO Creator set for you. It could be assembled into a giant spider, a big bug, or a slithering cobra, each with multiple points of movement and pointy fangs.

4994 Fierce Creatures (2008)

Articulated spider legs

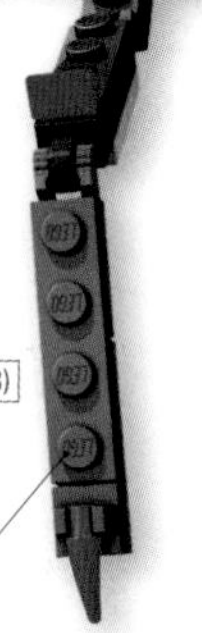

Flapping wings

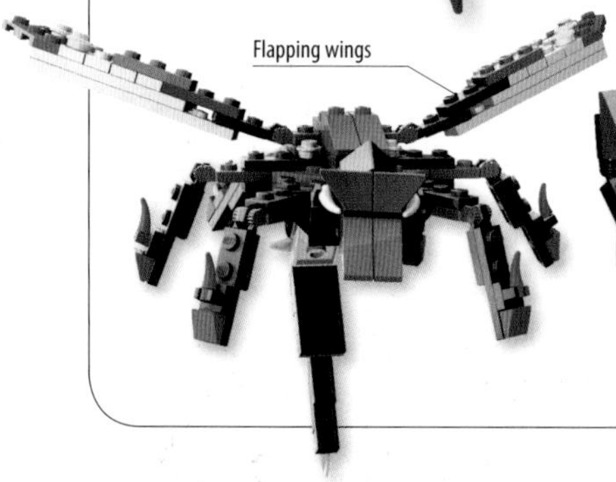

POWER PACKED

Thanks to built-in gears and Power Functions motors, some LEGO Creator sets have the power to move, light up, and make noise on command. The Ferris Wheel model could spin around and around at the push of a switch.

4957 Ferris Wheel (2007)

Retracted roof cover

CREATIVE CRUISING

LEGO construction never had more speed and style than with this convertible sports car with ninja sword windshield wipers, adjustable seats and mirrors, and 2 in (5 cm) rubber tires. It also had opening doors, a V8 engine under the hood, and bonus building instructions to convert it into a truck cab or a working mini-loader.

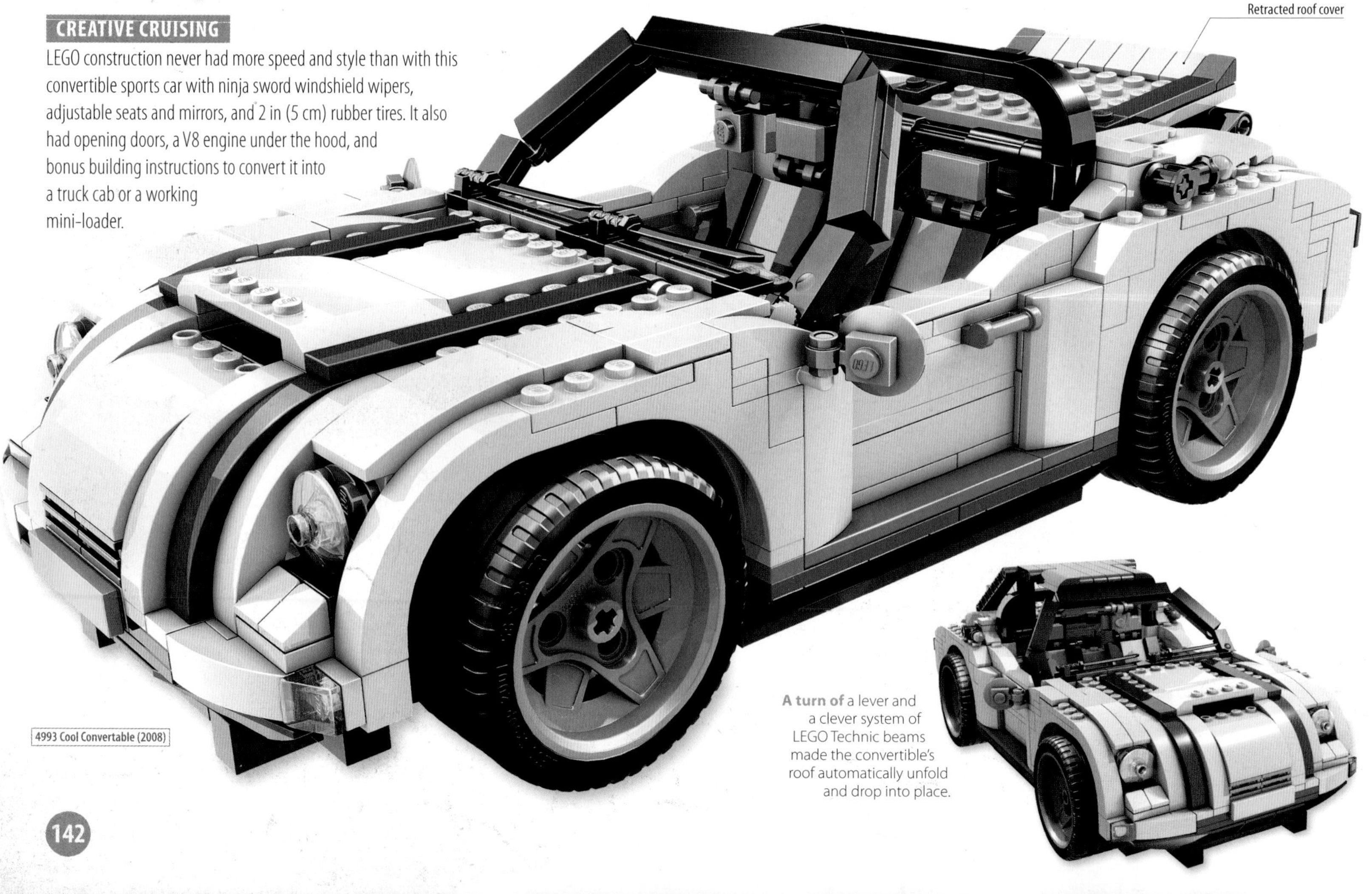

4993 Cool Convertable (2008)

A turn of a lever and a clever system of LEGO Technic beams made the convertible's roof automatically unfold and drop into place.

Wingspan measures 11 in (27 cm)

6745 Propeller Power (2009)

Helicopter with triple-bladed spinning propeller.

Vertical/short take-off and landing (V/STOL) jump jet.

TAKE TO THE AIR

This 247-element LEGO Creator model kit could be built as any of three different air vehicles: a classic propeller plane with a radial engine and retractable landing gear, a three-bladed modern helicopter, and a Harrier-style military jet… plus anything else the builder could come up with!

A popular color, yellow dominated the color schemes of seven LEGO Creator sets produced between 2006 and 2008.

Working landing gear

3 ½-story apartment building alternate model

GO WILD!

If it ran, crawled, slithered, or flew, you could construct it with this Designer Set. The Wild Collection included an Idea Book with instructions for 63 different animals that you could build using its 487 colorful pieces.

Parrot

Bumblebee

Snail

Songbird

Sea turtle

With a bit of imagination, even just a small handful of pieces can make a pocket-sized LEGO model.

4101 Wild Collection (2003)

REBUILDABLE BUILDINGS

This Creator beach house was enormously popular among LEGO City fans. Not only did the set feature details like a patio table, BBQ grill, flower bed, mailbox, satellite TV dish, and interior with stairs, fireplace, and an opening skylight, it had alternate instructions to turn it into an apartment building or a café.

4996 Beach House (2008)

DINO MIGHT

This mechanical dinosaur model included Power Functions motors in two different sizes, plus an infrared remote control and receiver to make it walk, move its arms, and roar with the help of a built-in sound brick. The spines on its back glowed in the dark, too!

4958 Monster Dino (2007)

6751 Fiery Legend (2009)

FIRE FLYER

A light-up brick made the flames in this posable dragon's mouth glow. It came with instructions for rebuilding it into a sinuous Asian dragon or a mean-looking ogre with a spiked hammer. A 2006 set, 4894 Mythical Creatures, was similar to this one, but with additional model instructions and a green color scheme.

SUPER-SONIC

The main model for this 3-in-1 Creator set was a modern supersonic jet. Its wing flaps and tail-fins were adjustable for aerial maneuvers, but its coolest function was the lever on top. Pulling it made the two rear engine thrusters light up as if the jet were rocketing through the sky.

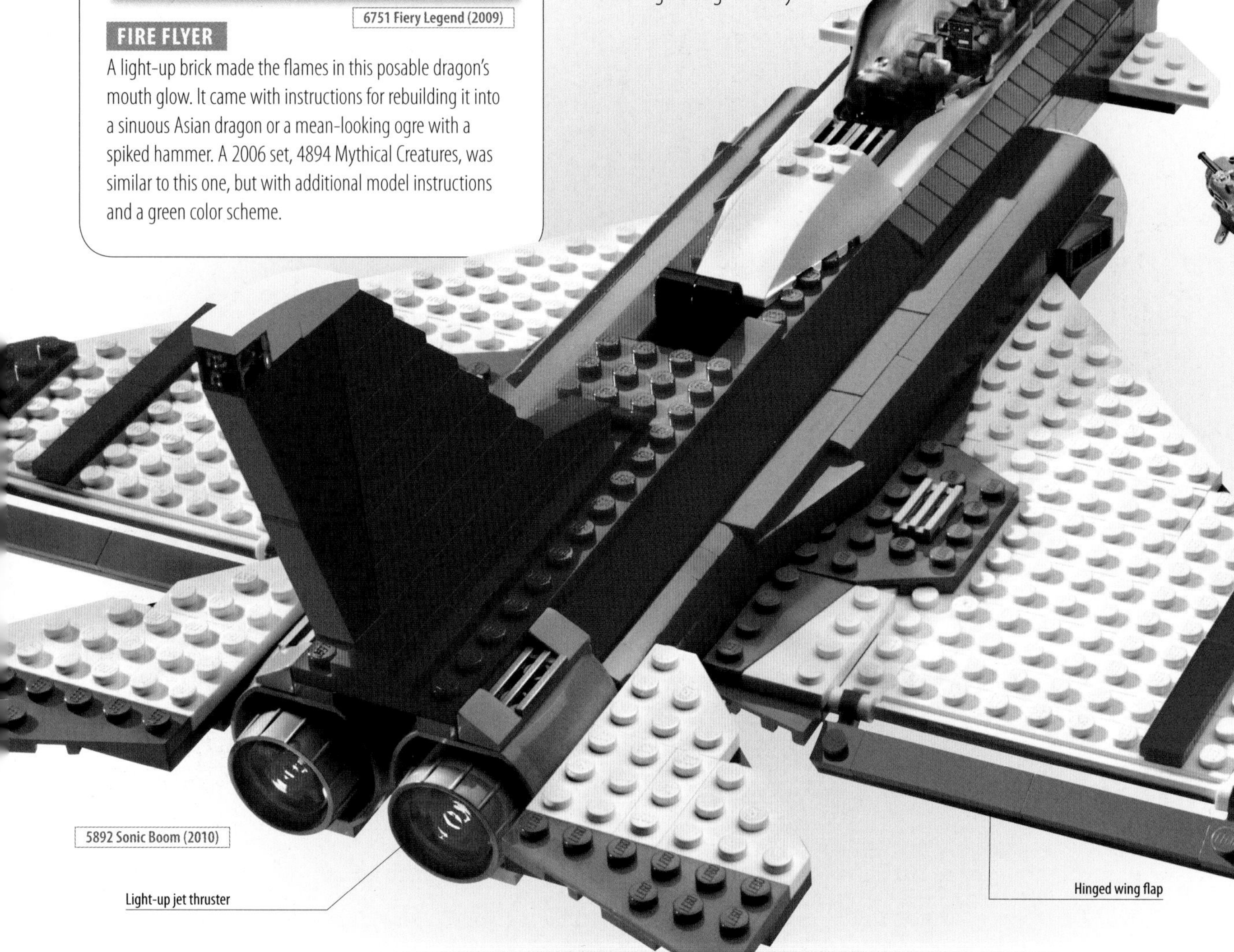

Opening canopy

The kit's second set of building steps let you convert the jet into a twin-propeller plane. It also had light-up engines.

The third set of steps was for a speedboat model with spinning rear propellers and lights to brighten dark seas.

5892 Sonic Boom (2010)

Light-up jet thruster

Hinged wing flap

TOOTHY SMILES

Carnivores were the order of the day for this 416-piece set from 2010. Its star model was an 18 in (45 cm) long crocodile with a thrashing tail and jaws that opened and closed when you moved a lever hidden among its scales. When you were done, you could rebuild it into either of two other predatory beasts.

The LEGO designers researched different animals to decide which ones to include in the set.

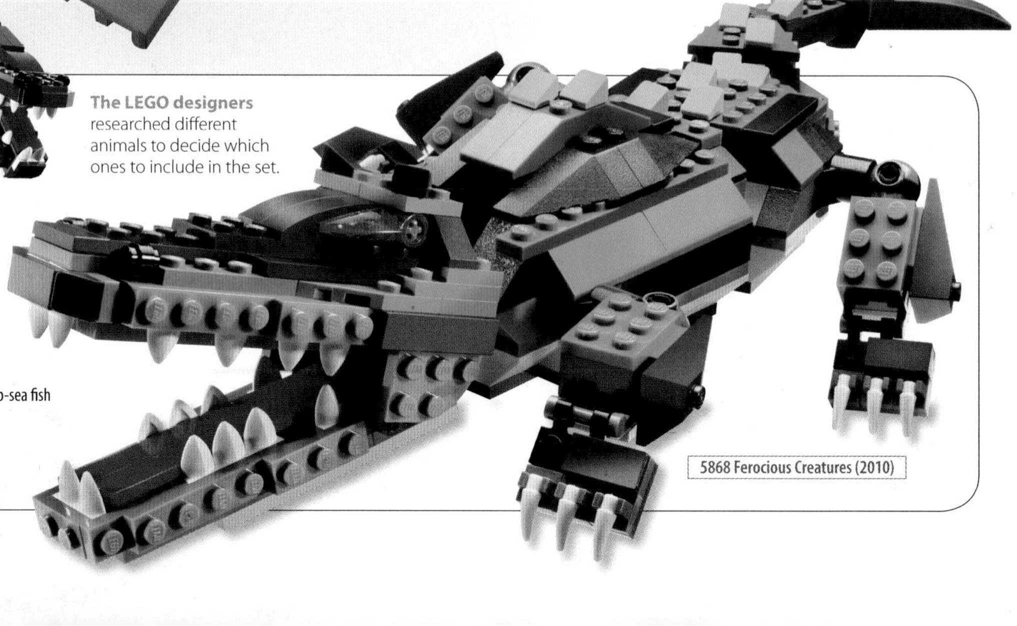

Dinosaur

Deep-sea fish

5868 Ferocious Creatures (2010)

FEATURES & FUNCTIONS

This LEGO Creator set was designed with Technic-style functions like working steering and suspension, a self-winding winch, and opening doors and tailgate panels. The main truck model's construction used an interesting method in which several bricks temporarily stabilized the chassis during the building process, and then came off to become part of the trailer.

Roof lights

Quad bike

Articulated trailer

5893 Offroad Power (2010)

Two of the set's models included extra vehicles for more play options. This transport truck carried a removable digger on its back.

Winch automatically retracts

Thanks to its big tires, the dune buggy alternate model was suited for driving over sandy beaches and other rough terrain.

TO THE RESCUE

A Power Functions light brick made the Rescue Robot's translucent yellow eye light up when it arrived to save the day. It co-starred with the LEGO City firefighters in a crossover *LEGO Club Magazine* comic in which it grew to a giant size and ran amok trying to help people.

An alternate model was a Robocat with a glowing nose.

The first Creator set to come with a minifigure, the Log Cabin was a forest getaway with a kayak and campfire.

5766 Log Cabin (2011)

You could also build a riverside hut with a brook and bridge, or a country retreat with a duck pond.

5764 Rescue Robot (2011)

A LIGHT IN THE DARK

This set let you build a striped lighthouse with a dock and the lighthouse-keeper's home on a small island. A crank on the side of the tower turned the mirror inside to rotate the light and warn passing ships away from the rocky shore. It even included buildable sea gulls!

5770 Lighthouse Island (2011)

The other models were a boathouse and a seafood restaurant with a light-up grill.

THE LEGO® WHEEL

● 2012 was the 50th anniversary of the release of the original LEGO® wheel ● The earliest known design drawings for the LEGO wheel date from 1958 ● The original LEGO wheel was a thin gray rubber tire around a red plastic hub with four studs and a connecting axle on the back. It could be built into models using a specially designed 2x4 brick with holes for the axle ● The first LEGO set with wheels was no. 400. Released in 1962, it was an accessory kit that included 4 wheels, 2 axle bricks, a tow-bar, and a base plate to let builders add rolling movement to their brick creations ● Until then, car models had to sit on square LEGO bricks ● The original wheel kit sold 820,400 sets in 1967 ● The first wheeled LEGO auto model was no. 315, a 40-piece black car released in 1963 ● The smallest LEGO wheel with a hub and tire was made in 1969. It was 0.57 in (1.44 cm) across ● The biggest LEGO wheel was made in 2000. It was 4.22 in (10.72 cm) across ● Today, the LEGO Group produces more than 300 million rubber tires per year, making it one of the biggest tire manufacturers in the world!

The larger wheel on the left was launched in 1963 with set no. 316 "Farm Tractor" and a new accessory kit, featuring large and small wheels, plus turntables.

On the Move

VEHICLES of all kinds have been part of the LEGO Group's success story since the very start. Having always wanted to be an auto mechanic, Godtfred Kirk Christiansen enjoyed designing toy cars for his father's workshop in the 1930s, and the tremendous sales of the Ferguson Tractor in the early 1950s led to the rise of the LEGO® brick and its unlimited possibilities for new transportation models. Rolling, floating, and flying, these are just a small sample of the amazing variety of LEGO vehicles out there ●

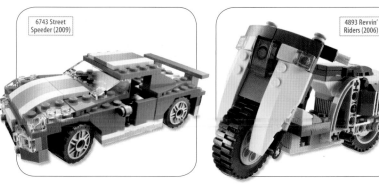

6743 Street Speeder (2009)

4893 Revvin' Riders (2006)

7893 Passenger Plane (2006)

8420 Street Bike (2005)

Rear wheel with drive chain and working suspension

7990 Cement Mixer (2007)

4939 Cool Cars (2007)

8635 Mission 6: Mobile Command Center (2008)

4995 Cargo Copter (2008)

7344 Dump Truck (2005)

7899 Police Boat (2006)

POLICE 7899

7944 Fire Hovercraft (2007)

7734 Cargo Plane (2008)

8292 Cherry Picker (2008)

7739 Coast Guard Patrol Boat & Tower (2008)

Opening gull-wing doors

Off-road tires with steering system and motorized suspension

8297 Off-Roader (2008)

Extending ladder for emergency rescue

7239 Fire Truck (2004)

4955 Big Rig (2007)

4896 Roaring Roadsters (2006)

7890 Ambulance (2006)

8434 Aircraft (2004)

Cargo Plane from 4997 Transport Ferry (2008)

Mini Loader from 4993 Cool Convertible (2008)

Hovercraft from 4953 Fast Flyers (2007)

Especially for Girls

OF COURSE, there's no rule that says that LEGO® construction is just for boys, and there are plenty of girls who play with exactly the same sets as the other half of the population. But some do prefer construction with a pinker tone, and so we present a sampling of LEGO sets specifically designed for girls ●

5808 The Enchanted Palace (1999)

Glittery, translucent tower

LEGO® BELVILLE™

Starting in 1994, LEGO BELVILLE introduced a new scale of bigger, multi-jointed figures. With sets that combine traditional LEGO bricks with decorative pink and purple pieces, shiny glitter and lots of horses to ride, the theme included both models of everyday life and scenes from fairy tales and fantasy. A 2005 series featured sets based on classic Hans Christian Andersen stories such as "The Little Mermaid," "The Snow Queen," "The Princess and the Pea," and "Thumbelina."

5585 LEGO® Pink Brick Box (2008)

THINKING PINK

A favorite among grandmothers at holiday time, this sturdy storage box came with fences, windows, doors, flowers, and lots of pink bricks mixed in with its 216 pieces for hours of building with a colorful twist.

6411 Sand Dollar Café (1992)

PARADISA

A sub-theme of LEGO Town that ran from 1992 to 1997, the seaside adventures of Paradisa took place at a tranquil tropical resort. In pastel-colored sets, Paradisa minifigures enjoyed sailing, windsurfing, beach-side barbecues, and playing with friendly dolphins. The color scheme and settings made Paradisa a very popular theme among girls.

6414 Dolphin Point (1995)

7538 Totally CLIKITS Fashion Bag and Accessories (2005)

This set included jewelry, school supplies, and a fashion bag to carry them.

CLIKITS™

A line of buildable, customizable jewelry and accessories, the CLIKITS™ theme featured sets with such fashionable items as photo frames, bracelets, and purses, each with connection points to let girls decorate and redesign them with a collection of hearts, stars, seashells, and other shapes.

Our website let girls decorate virtual rooms and build digital bracelets to send to their friends!

Each of the CLIKITS girls had her own color-coordinated pieces and unique decorations.

4307 Finger Rings (1980)

LEGO® SCALA™

CLIKITS wasn't the only line of buildable LEGO jewelry. In 1979, the first LEGO® SCALA™ series let girls use decorated tiles to create their own unique rings, necklaces, bracelets, and even a hand mirror. The theme was retired the following year, but it wouldn't be the last time the SCALA name appeared...

4336 Mirror (1980)

3149 Happy Home (2000)

HOUSE AND GARDEN

Unused since 1980, LEGO SCALA was brought back in 1997 as the name of a new dollhouse-style theme. Its characters, including Caroline, Christian, Marie, and Baby Thomas, were larger and more traditional fashion dolls than the stylized inhabitants of LEGO BELVILLE. Sets included fabric clothing packs and constructable scenes of gardens, homes, and neighborhood shops.

Foam foliage

4828 Princess Royal Stables (2007)

FAIRY-TALE FUN

With a princess, a prince, and three ponies with brushable hair, this LEGO® DUPLO® set was full of fun to spark the imagination of preschool girls.

3061 City Park Café (2012)

LEGO® Friends

LAUNCHED IN 2012, the LEGO® Friends theme was designed to provide a fun play experience for girls who couldn't find a perfect match for their building interests in the rest of the LEGO assortment. Its new "mini-doll figures" are slightly taller than minifigures, but they can hold the same objects, connect to the same bricks, and even swap hairstyles ●

OUT AT THE CAFÉ

The theme centers on the daily lives of five friends who live in the fictional Heartlake City. Its sets feature classic LEGO building, with lots of new elements, accessories, and colors. The City Park Café is a favorite hangout for all of the girls, and the only set to include Marie (in pink).

The café served everything from burgers to freshly-baked cupcakes and pie.

INVENTION LAB

3933 Olivia's Invention Workshop (2012)

Each of the friends has her own personality and interests. Olivia loves science, nature, and inventions, so her workshop is full of tools, collection jars, and even a microscope, not to mention her custom-built robot.

LEGO Friends mini-dolls have jointed heads, shoulders, and single-piece legs to let them sit or stand.

Emma (with black hair) wants to be a clothing and jewelry designer. She's also into interior decorating, horseback riding, and martial arts.

3187 Butterfly Beauty Shop (2012)

BEAUTY SHOP

This salon at the center of Heartlake City comes stocked with a variety of bows and clips that can be attached to mini-doll hair, as well as lipsticks, sunglasses, and a hairdryer. It even has a fashion head display with a spare hair piece for the ultimate makeover.

OLIVIA'S HOUSE

Along with her lab and tree house, Olivia comes in the biggest set in the theme's first year: the house where she lived with her parents and pet cat. Complete with a kitchen, bathroom, living room, bedroom, and rooftop patio, the house also included her mom Anna and dad Peter—the first male mini-doll figure.

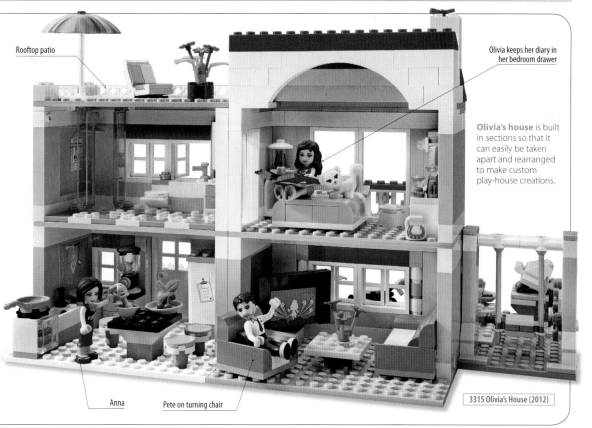

Rooftop patio

Olivia keeps her diary in her bedroom drawer

Olivia's house is built in sections so that it can easily be taken apart and rearranged to make custom play-house creations.

The front yard had a mailbox, vegetable garden, lawnmower, swing set, and an outdoor grill for barbecues with friends and family.

Anna

Pete on turning chair

3315 Olivia's House (2012)

3932 Andrea's Stage (2012)

Boom box

Singer and song-writer Andrea is already on her way to being a star. Her music stage lets her put on a whole performance with the help of a microphone stand, a piano, a boom box, and an entrance with multicolored "lights".

Piano with bench and glass

Movable stage light

ROAD TRIP

Stephanie's car was built just like any other LEGO vehicle, but in colors that delivered on many girls' preferences. It came with her puppy Coco, a carwash stand with a lamp-post, faucet and bucket, and even a tiny MP3 player printed on a LEGO tile.

3183 Stephanie's Cool Convertible (2012)

3942 Heartlake Dog Show (2012)

PET PARADE

The Heartlake Dog Show featured a podium with a runway, a canine obstacle course with a see-saw and hurdle, a grooming station, prize ribbons, and a trophy for the winning pooch. It also had a plate of bones and a camera for snapping photos of well-trained pets.

Mia loves animals, whether training them or fixing them up when they're not feeling well.

Younger Builders

EVERY GREAT BUILDER has to start somewhere. Seeing the need for building play designed for young children, the LEGO Group has produced a number of toys over its history that are geared toward tots and toddlers. Since 1969, the most famous of these has been the wide range of LEGO® DUPLO® products: sets for kids aged 18 months and up that are full of big, rounded bricks suitable for small hands and big imaginations ●

It's a LEGO® DUPLO® World!

THE MOST WELL KNOWN and enduring of the LEGO® construction systems for younger builders, LEGO® DUPLO® sets have bigger pieces that are easy for small fingers to handle, assemble, and take apart. Designed for children between 1½ and 6 years old, these sets have been inspiring preschool creativity and helping children to develop early motor skills for more than 40 years ●

2940 Fire Truck (1992)

Standard 2x4 LEGO System brick

THE LEGO DUPLO BRICK

The LEGO DUPLO brick is twice as tall, twice as long, and twice as wide as a LEGO brick. The earliest DUPLO elements produced in 1969 had shorter studs and slightly different connectors underneath, but just like the modern version, they were fully compatible with standard LEGO pieces.

TOOLS FOR TOTS

For preschoolers who wanted to use tools just like their parents, the DUPLO TOOLO sets of the 1990s had vehicles with yellow connection joints that could be locked or unlocked with play tools that made satisfying clicking sounds when turned. In 2009, the building system returned with brand-new sets featuring the same beloved, child-safe screwdrivers and wrenches.

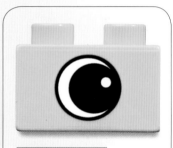

JUST IMAGINE...

DUPLO pieces with special shapes, colors, and painted decorations mean that toddlers can build just about anything they can imagine, from buildings to animals to vehicles that float, roll, and fly.

LOGO (1978)

LOGO

The DUPLO rabbit was first used on packaging in 1979. In 1997, it was redesigned with a friendlier appearance to match the new PRIMO elephant logo for infant toys. It disappeared in 2002, when DUPLO was merged into the new LEGO Explore theme for young children, but returned when the DUPLO name appeared once again in 2004.

LOGO (1997)

The second rabbit logo was designed to be cute, colorful, and make eye contact with the viewer.

FIRST FIGURES

The DUPLO name did not always appear on young-builder packaging during the 1970s. Some boxes were labeled PreSchool, and others had no secondary title at all. This is when the first preschool human and animal figures were introduced, with decorated faces and simple, single-piece bodies.

537

537 Mary's House (1977)

Rooftop TV antenna

2770 Furnished Playhouse (1986)

By the mid-1980s, new DUPLO figures came in two sizes and could sit down and hold objects; however, the original-style figures continued to appear in sets into the next decade.

11 12 1 10 2 9 3 8 4 7 6 5

One-piece wall with sliding door

LEGO DUPLO PLAYHOUSE

In 1986, a DUPLO playhouse building set was released, featuring an assortment of family characters and furniture that could be used to assemble the interior of a rebuildable home. Separate accessory sets included parts for a bathroom, kitchen, living room, and extra wall and roof pieces. The concept would be visited again for several years during the 1990s.

A DAY AT THE ZOO

Everybody knows that kids love animals. That's why the DUPLO Zoo theme has returned over and over again with sets full of vehicles, environments, and lots of baby and grown-up animals.

A selection of animals and characters from various 1990s Zoo sets.

This stretched-out pooch doesn't just carry bricks. Thanks to its collar, it can connect to them too!

5503 DUPLO® Dog (2005)

BRICK COLLECTIONS

As a toddler grows, so does his or her DUPLO brick collection. Parents can get extra pieces in a variety of handy storage containers, from sturdy plastic buckets to this friendly dachshund storage tube that came with 32 bricks inside its see-through cylinder body.

All aboard for the big top!

LEGO DUPLO TRAINS

Another recurring favorite is DUPLO trains, which have their own track system and have been around since 2700 Preschool Freight Train in 1983. Built from 12 pieces, this circus train from the LEGO Ville daily life series had wheels with pistons that really moved when you pushed it forward, the latest style of DUPLO figure, and a baby elephant to ride in the back.

3770 My First Train (2005)

Building plate

Carrying handle

Safe rubber
brick scooper

5359 Block-O-Dile (2004)

PICKING UP THE PIECES

"I eat blocks!" boasted this handy storage case and pick-up tool, which solved every parent's greatest sore-feet dilemma by gobbling up stray DUPLO pieces left lying on the floor. It also included a collection of extra bricks and had a studded plate on top that kids could use as a building surface.

5593 Circus (2008)

PREHISTORIC PLAY

Dinosaurs and cave-people playing together? It could only happen in the DUPLO Dino Valley. This happy stone-age family had scaly friends to ride, a cozy cave with stackable cave-art bricks, fabric clothes, a canoe, a giant fish and a roasting steak with DUPLO studs for building.

LEGO duplo
3-6
5598

5598 Dino Valley (2008)

BIG TOP, BIG BRICKS

When the circus train comes to LEGO Ville, here's where it arrives! The big top DUPLO circus was filled with friendly figures and features, including an acrobat with a horse and high-wire, a teeter-tottering elephant, a launching cannon, a monkey with a swing, a wheel-spinning, cake-throwing clown, and a ringmaster with a trained lion act.

BUCCANEERS AT BATHTIME

At a time when there hadn't been a single new LEGO Pirates set in years, preschoolers got to have all the fun with the DUPLO Pirates. This giant pirate ship not only floated, but also had wheels to roll across the floor. With a monkey in the rigging, a working winch for swinging from the sails, a firing cannon, a treasure chest and prison hold, and a plank for sending landlubbers to the deepest depths of the tub, plenty of big kids must have pined after this one.

7880 DUPLO Big
Pirate Ship (2006)

WHAT'S A ZOOTER?

Goozle, Wazo, and Tez weren't only some of the weirdest-looking things in the LEGO DUPLO series—they were the Zooters, constructible creatures with a fabulous mix of claws, tentacles, and suction-cup feet. Kids aged three and up could disassemble and combine them to create a host of unique imaginary friends.

Goozle and Tez
may have been your everyday aliens, but Wazo had a special feature: his head could record and play back speech and sounds!

3265 Wazo (2001)

3264 Tez (2001)   3263 Goozle (2001)

SORT AND BUILD

This sturdy storage box included blue, yellow, and red sorting plates that doubled as a lid. Young builders could use the plates to identify the color-coded bricks that they'd need to make an elephant, giraffe, or parrot model, and even see a picture of the right way to put them together.

5506 LEGO DUPLO Large Brick Box (2010)

Boxes of basic DUPLO bricks can add new possibilities to a collection or just kick off some imaginative creative play. Many include inspirational building booklets.

LEGO VILLE

The busy LEGO Ville Supermarket was full of ways for kids to interact with their creations. They could pick out fruits, vegetables, and other foods, roll them over to the check-out counter, and help the clerk ring them up on a register that really made sounds.

LEGO City's younger cousin, LEGO Ville has been letting kids build fun everyday scenes since 2004.

5683 Market Place (2011)

5604 Supermarket (2008)

BAKING FUN

The 55 colorful DUPLO pieces in this set (including special meringue, muffin, and candle bricks) let young bakers prepare a buildable feast of delicious-looking desserts of all shapes and sizes. The box's lid even doubled as a serving tray.

6785 Creative Cakes (2012)

How's this for a fiery steed?

4776 Dragon Tower (2004)

Dragon with movable wings and jaws

LEGO DUPLO CASTLE

The DUPLO Castle series let kids build their own fortresses full of ferocious dragons, tough-looking knights, and hidden trap doors and treasures. The most impressive was 4785 Black Castle (2005), which, with 386 extra-large pieces, was one of the biggest DUPLO sets of all time. It included pictures that showed how to rebuild it into a 5½ ft (170 cm) tower.

Fire piece fits in dragon's mouth

A KNIGHTLY FIGURE

Unlike LEGO minifigures, DUPLO figures can't be taken apart. The modern figure has separated legs (which still move as a single piece), hands with visible fingers, rotating shoulders and head, and a little round bump for a nose. It often has a permanently-attached hat or hair and comes in three sizes: adult, child, and a new baby figure introduced in 2009.

This flail is perfect for gently bopping rival knights on the noggin.

The armor and helmet really come in handy when you fall off your dragon.

shield to block
ne… at least of
sort.

ASSEMBLING ANIMALS

This series of animal-building sets featured unusual parts like accordion hinges for flexible necks and bodies, heads with opening mouths, and pull-string tails, designed to give young children a more physically interactive experience with their creations. Lots of extra bricks (some with painted-on eyes) were included to let kids make even more wild creatures than the ones on the box.

Originally released under the LEGO Explore "Explore Imagination" brand for children aged 1½ and up, these sets were re-packaged for 2–5-year-olds when DUPLO returned the next year.

3515 African Adventures (2003)

Sets to Remember

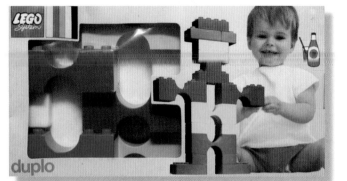

514 Pre-School Building Set (1972)

010 Building Set (1973)

524 LEGOVILLE Set (1977)

534 Passenger Boat (1978)

2623 Delivery Truck (1980)

2705 Play Train (1983)

2355 Basic Set "Vehicles" (1984)

2629 Tractor and Farm Tools (1985)

2770 Furnished Playhouse (1986)

2458 Barnyard (1990)

1583 Clown Bucket (1992)

2679 DUPLO Aiport (1993)

2338 Kitty Cat's Building Set (1995)

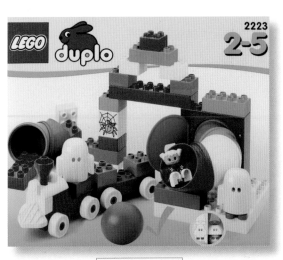

2223 Spooky House (1998)

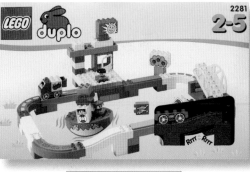

2281 Deluxe Harbor Highway (1999)

4960 Giant Zoo (2006)

2400 Cute Vehicles (2000)

1403 Racing Leopard (2001)

4973 Harvester (2007)

4683 Pony and Cart (2004)

2952 Marie (2001)

4864 Castle (2008)

2971 Action Police Bike (2001)

4691 Police Station (2004)

5604 Supermarket (2008)

5655 Caravan (2010)

6158 Animal Clinic (2012)

2024 Rattle (1983)

Bricks for Baby

THERE HAVE BEEN many LEGO® products designed for younger children, from infants and toddlers to preschoolers almost ready to start building with LEGO® DUPLO® bricks. Some of these baby-safe building and learning toys were experiments that came and went quickly, while others were popular enough to be revisited again and again with different names and colors. Here are just a few of the LEGO items that the smallest builders have played and developed creativity with over the years ●

SHAKE, RATTLE, AND CHEW

This duck rattle may look simple, but it was the result of years of research on how babies play and learn. Because infants instinctively react to a moving eye, the duck's eyes bounced when the rattle was shaken, and the ball in the middle could spin and make sounds. The two grips were added on the advice of a panel of mothers. Studs on top and openings on the bottom allowed the rattle to be attached to a child's DUPLO or LEGO bricks later on.

BABY BRICKS

Colorful LEGO PRIMO and LEGO Baby pieces were made to be safe, sturdy, and simple enough for the smallest builders to stack up and take apart.

Pieces from 5461 Shape Sorter House (2005)

5443 Hanging Rattle (2003)

LEGO PRIMO & LEGO BABY

In 1995, the company unveiled LEGO PRIMO, a line of building toys with big, teething-proof pieces for babies between the ages of six and 24 months. In 1997, it became its own brand as LEGO PRIMO, with a yellow elephant logo and sets that included a shape sorter, a music-making boat, a buildable mouse, and lots of colorful, durable, stackable pieces. PRIMO was renamed LEGO Baby in 2000, merged into LEGO Explore in 2002, became Baby again with a new teddy bear logo in 2004, and was officially discontinued in 2006.

2503 Musical Apple (2000)

Pushing down on the worm in the apple made it pop up and play music.

BOUNCING BUG

A favorite of children aged six to 18 months all over the world, the Bendy Caterpillar would flatten out when pushed down, then spring up again when released for a guaranteed baby laugh. It could also roll around on the floor and came with bug friends that could be stacked up on the bumps on its back.

The caterpillar was also made in dark green and red for LEGO PRIMO in 1997 and yellow and dark green for LEGO Baby in 2001 and LEGO Explore in 2002.

FOR THE YOUNGEST

This smiling-faced LEGO Explore rattle with fabric, string, and soft plastic parts could hang from the railing of a crib or playpen. It was made for newborns under the "Explore Being Me" label.

5465 Bendy Caterpillar (2005)

5470 My First QUATRO Figure Set (2006)

Less than a dozen sets were released between 2004 and 2006, making this not just the first, but the only QUATRO figure ever made.

LEGO® QUATRO™ THEME

As DUPLO bricks were to System bricks, so LEGO® QUATRO™ was to LEGO DUPLO. Made for children aged one to three, its teething-friendly pieces were more rounded and twice as long, wide, and tall as the DUPLO versions. Emblazoned with a blue version of the original PRIMO elephant logo, QUATRO sets were mostly brick collections that focused more on building giant free-form towers than assembling models.

MUSICAL CUTHBERT AND FRIEND

A LEGO PRIMO set for babies aged 0 to 2, Cuthbert the Camel was a music box that children could twist around to wind up and release to make him play a happy, soothing tune. His feet could attach to PRIMO pieces, and his hump was a stud that other compatible elements, including his round-bodied PRIMO figure friend, could stack on top of.

2007 Musical Cuthbert and Friend (1998)

SHAPES & COLORS

Released in the first year of the PRIMO brand after it was split off from the DUPLO one, this set helped babies aged eight to 24 months learn shapes and colors by discovering which pieces fit into which cubes. The cubes could be stacked on top of each other as well as on the green baseplate that served as the packaging lid.

2099 Shape Sorter (1997)

Train cars with bumps for stacking

2974 Play Train (2001)

BABY TRAINS

Made from seven pieces for babies six months and up, this train toy was, like the caterpillar, produced in several different colors for different LEGO Baby brands between 2000 and 2005. It made sounds when you pushed down on the locomotive's smokestack.

LEGO® FABULAND™

FROM THE MOMENT its first sets arrived in 1979, LEGO® FABULAND™ was something different and special. Its simple-to-build models and friendly, funny animal-headed figures filled the gap between LEGO® DUPLO® play and LEGO System, and appealed to boys and girls. FABULAND was also the first LEGO theme to feature storybooks, children's clothing, and even an animated TV series ●

This sturdy paddle steamer was captained by Wilfred Walrus. Mike Monkey swept the deck, and another monkey crew member worked on the engine.

3673 Steamboat (1985)

A WORLD OF MAKE-BELIEVE

LEGO FABULAND was the perfect theme for children who loved to pretend. Its colorful, charming buildings and vehicles were built from large pieces for fast construction, and its houses had rooms that were large enough to play with figures inside.

Lionel Lion (sometimes called Leonard Lion) was the mayor of FABULAND. His Town Hall set also came with his friends Buster Bulldog the fire-fighter and the trouble-making but good-hearted Freddy Fox.

350 Town Hall with Leonard Lion and Friends (1979)

Boat from 3660 Fisherman's Cottage (1985)

FUZZY FRIENDS

Halfway between minifigures and DUPLO figures in scale, the creature cast of FABULAND all had their own names, accessories, and sometimes even hats and uniforms related to particular jobs. Edward Elephant arrived with a rowboat and fisherman's cottage in 1985, while Charlie Cat just tagged along with his friend for a fun fishing trip far from town.

Welcome aboard, Miss Hippopotamus!

3662 Bus (1987)

Bernhard Bear drops in on Billy Bear at the service station, which included a gas pump and car-fixing tools.

3670 Service Station (1984)

STORY BUILDING

Children from the age of 3 and up could use their FABULAND sets to create houses, boats, fairground rides, police and fire stations, and much more. Larger sets included easy-to-follow building guides with stories for parents to read aloud while their children built.

PICTURE BOOKS

"*Lionel Lion, mayor of Fabuland, had invited all his friends to a fancy dress party. All the invitations had been delivered and everyone was very excited—there was going to be a competition for the best fancy dress costume. 'I'll go as a car,' said Max. He found an old cardboard box and painted some wheels on the sides"*. . . and the adventure continued in one of the many FABULAND storybooks!

I like to help all my friends, even the ones who haven't asked yet!

With moving heads, arms, and legs, the citizens of FABULAND included the daydreaming Edward Elephant, friendly Bonnie Bunny, adventure-loving Max Mouse, flower-shop keeper Hannah Hippopotamus, clumsy Clive Crocodile, Lucy Lamb the nurse, and many more.

Bonnie Bunny

Max Mouse

Mike Monkey

A LAND OF DREAMS

After a decade of fun and imagination, the FABULAND theme finally came to an end in 1989. The last sets released were a school room, a carousel, and a park with a slide and swing. But the children who grew up with high-flying Joe Crow and all his friends remember them fondly, and the happy world of LEGO FABULAND still has many fans and collectors today.

Plane from 3671 Airport (1984)

How do you get to FABULAND? "It's not far away—just a little to the left as you go north, or a little to the right as you go south. Edward Elephant lives there, and so do all his friends."

Advanced Building

SO YOU'VE outgrown LEGO®
DUPLO®. You've built everything
that LEGO Creator has to offer.
What's next for the best of the
best LEGO builders? The
following pages reveal
some of the biggest, most
complicated and detailed
LEGO sets ever designed,
from the realistic vehicles
of LEGO Model Team to the
working gears and pistons
of LEGO Technic and the
programmable robots of
MINDSTORMS. Can you
tackle the toughest LEGO
models of all time? The
challenge may be great, but
the results will be worth it ●

LEGO® Technic

DEVELOPED FROM special gear sets and the Expert Builder series of the 1970s, LEGO® Technic adds mechanical motion to LEGO models. By building in gears, axles, and motors, builders can bring their LEGO creations to life with extending crane booms, wheel-linked steering systems, adjustable suspensions, and other realistic functions ●

8300 Action Figures (2000)

LEGO® TECHNIC FIGURES

From 1986 to 2001, many LEGO Technic sets included figures with highly-posable limbs to serve as drivers for large-scale vehicles. Although they had the traditional yellow hands and faces of LEGO minifigures, they towered over their smaller cousins. In true LEGO construction style, they could also be attached to bricks and Technic pieces.

Mechanical actuators raise, lower, and extend articulated arm

857 Motorcycle (1979)

Switch-activated bucket scoop extends and retracts for digging

FORM AND FUNCTION

This bike with sidecar had the brick-built appearance of a classic Model Team set, but the functionality of a Technic model. It featured big rubber wheels, front-wheel steering, a working piston, and an engine with a drive-chain assembled from 26 tiny link elements.

Gear extends crane arm when wheel at base is spun

Early LEGO Technic models had traditional studded pieces, making them resemble LEGO System vehicles more closely than today's streamlined Technic sets.

855 Mobile Crane (1978)

WHEELS & GEARS

Thanks to a clever combination of spinning gears and revolving axles, a trio of wheels built into this Technic crane model could be turned by hand to raise and lower the crane's arm, extend its boom, and drop or retract its lifting cable.

5571 Giant Truck (1996)

LEGO MODEL TEAM

Technic wasn't the only LEGO theme for experienced builders. In 1986, the company launched LEGO Model Team, a series of vehicles built to be as realistic as possible. Made from 1,743 pieces, the super-detailed, large-scale Model Team Giant Truck was until recently the all-time biggest LEGO set.

LEGO TECHNIC TITAN

This 1,884-piece construction vehicle bore little resemblance to its 1978 ancestor. Its functions included six-wheel steering, retractable side outriggers, and an arm lifted by a working pneumatic cylinder and powered by a motor that could extend the crane's length to 18 in (46 cm).

8421 Mobile Crane (2005)

MODERN CONSTRUCTION

Thanks to their heavy-duty appearance and a multitude of moving parts and mechanisms, construction vehicles are some of the most popular Technic sets. Along with a variety of cranes, excavators, and dump trucks, recent years' models have included a motorized bulldozer, a telehandler, and backhoe, front-end, and wheel loaders.

The 8293 Power Functions Motor Set could be added for motorized functions.

9394 Jet Plane (2012)

SMOOTH FLYING

Most modern Technic sets are made from a combination of smooth, non-studded support beams and angled, decorative plates with gearing and other functions built into the middle. This largely brick-less construction system gives Technic models a more realistic shape than other LEGO kits.

Rotating treads built from individual link segments

KING OF THE ROAD

Stretching 26 in (66 cm) long and built out of 1,877 pieces, this monster of a Technic tow truck had working rack-and-pinion steering, a V6 engine with moving pistons and a spinning radiator fan, metallic-finished bricks and custom decals, and a telescopic towing crane with a ratchet-regulated winch.

8285 Tow Truck (2006)

The truck could elevate its crane, extend its boom, and lower its metal hook with controls hidden in the cab's side panels. It had a deployable towing platform with pneumatic lift, and rear stabilizers for heavy loads.

8294 Excavator (2008)

8110 Mercedes-Benz Unimog U 400 (2011)

UNIMOG

The Unimog's 2,048 pieces made it the largest Technic set so far. It had a working suspension system and a switch that let you provide pneumatic Power Functions control to either the grapple crane in back or the recovery winch in front.

Cab platform rotates 360°

Super Models

THEY'RE HUGE! They're realistic! They're made from lots and lots of bricks! These are the ultimate LEGO® models, chosen from among the most amazing (and expensive!) official sets ever made. Behold—the LEGO Super Models ●

3723 LEGO Minifigure (2000)

At a 1:300 scale, the LEGO Eiffel Tower set stood an impressive 42½ in (108 cm) tall. Designed using blueprints of the real tower in Paris and assembled from 3,428 pieces, it was accurate from the lifts at the base to the French flag on top.

10181 Eiffel Tower (2007)

33 in (84 cm) tall from her base to the top of her burning torch, the LEGO model of New York's famous "Lady Liberty" was built from 2,882 bricks, almost entirely colored sand green.

One of the first official LEGO sculptures, this friendly fellow took 1,850 pieces to build and stood 20 in (51 cm) tall, 12 times the size of a regular minifigure. More than just a statue, he had rotating shoulders and hands and a removable cap.

10187 VW Beetle™ (2008)

Based on the iconic "Charlotte" model of 1960, this VW Beetle was picked by LEGO fans as the classic car that they'd most like to have as a set. At 16 in (41 cm) long and 1,626 pieces, it had a movable stick shift, opening doors, hood, trunk, and glove compartment, folding seats, rear engine, spare tire, and windshield wipers.

3450 Statue of Liberty (2000)

10177 Boeing 787 Dreamliner™ (2006)

3451 Sopwith Camel (2001)

This licensed LEGO version of Boeing Commercial Airplanes' next-generation jet airliner was made from 1,197 pieces and included a display stand and information card. Designed using specifications from Boeing, the model was 26 in (66 cm) long, with a 27 in (69 cm) wingspan.

The Sopwith Camel was that rarest of things: a LEGO "war" model. Built from 577 pieces and complete with strings for tension wires, it was a replica of the British World War I fighter plane. It was followed the next year by an arch-rival: the Red Baron's Fokker Dr.I triplane.

This incredibly detailed model of the world-famous "Jewel of India," with an equally incredible piece count of 5,922, was built from the most elements of any LEGO set created so far. Its intricate architecture and decorations required advanced building techniques to construct and incorporated many rare and unusual pieces that were found in few other sets. The model was 20 in (51 cm) wide and 16 in (41 cm) tall.

10189 Taj Mahal (2008)

Modeled after London's real Tower Bridge, the 4,287-piece LEGO version had a working drawbridge, could come apart in sections for storage, and included scaled models of a tiny taxi and a double-decker bus.

10214 Tower Bridge (2010)

10196 Grand Carousel (2009)

10220 Volkswagen T1 Camper Van (2011)

"Make LEGO Models, Not War!" A replica of the 1962 vehicle, the 1,332-piece VW camper van was detailed inside and out with a pop-up roof, plaid textile curtains, and a four-cylinder boxer engine in back.

Built from 3,263 elements, the spectacular Grand Carousel had Power Functions components to make it spin and play music while the horses and swing boats moved up and down. It came with a ride operator and eight passenger minifigures.

Modular Buildings

LEGO® MODULAR BUILDINGS models give experienced fans the chance to assemble highly detailed and realistic buildings, created by expert designers using advanced building techniques. Built with detachable levels for easy customization and access to interiors, the models can be connected together side-by-side to create a street scene, complete with busy minifigure inhabitants ●

10197 Fire Brigade (2009)

FIRE BRIGADE

This model was styled after the vintage fire stations of the 1930s. It had a garage with an opening door for the old-time fire truck, a water tower and bell on the roof, a ping-pong table for the times between emergencies, and even a loyal fire dog.

10211 Grand Emporium (2010)

The Grand Emporium was a three-story department store with a clothing department, housewares section, and top-floor toy shop. Its details included revolving doors, an escalator, and a window washer working outside.

Boy on push-scooter

Four-level townhouse

Rooftop terrace

IN THE BEGINNING

The Modular Buildings series started in 2007 with Café Corner, a 2,056-piece hotel and café. It was followed by Market Street, a LEGO Factory exclusive (see pp.224–25) created by talented fan Eric Brok. The next addition was Green Grocer, which featured apartments built above a neighborhood grocery store.

10190 Market Street (2007)

10185 Green Grocer (2008)

The pet shop came with plenty of LEGO animals: a dog, a cat, two parrots, and a goldfish in a tank, plus a yellow toy frog.

Parrot

Cat

Dog

PET SHOP

This two-building model featured a well-stocked pet store full of animals and supplies, with an upper apartment, kitchenette, and loft above it. Next door was a townhouse with a spiral staircase, a rooftop garden, an attic full of storage boxes, and a room that a painter was just starting to paint with his roller.

Mailbox

10218 Pet Shop (2011)

10182 Café Corner (2007)

Although most Modular Buildings have connectors on their left and right sides, Café Corner and the Grand Emporium are street corners that change the direction of the city block by 90 degrees.

Brick-built hotel sign

TOWN HALL

Bell tower with clock

Unlike most LEGO buildings, Modular Buildings are designed in true scale to minifigures. The Town Hall was the biggest one yet, with 2,766 pieces and an amazing height of 20 in (50 cm). It included the Mayor and his secretary, a bride and groom, a janitor, a reporter, visiting school kids, and a working elevator.

10224 Town Hall (2012)

10230 Mini Modulars (2012)

Made from 1,356 tiny pieces

LEGO bicycle

Available only to members of the LEGO Store VIP program, the Mini Modulars set included the original five Modular Buildings at a much smaller scale.

Spilled rubbish

173

LEGO® MINDSTORMS®

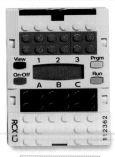

9719 Robotics Invention
System 1.0 (1998)

IN 1984, THE LEGO GROUP formed a unique partnership with the Media Laboratory at the US-based Massachusetts Institute of Technology (MIT). One of the first results was the LEGO® Technic Computer Control for educational products in 1986, but it was in 1998 that the cooperation of research lab and building toy led to a truly revolutionary product: the LEGO® MINDSTORMS® RCX computer brick, which could be used to construct and program moving, working robots ●

THE FIRST GENERATION

The first RCX (Robotic Command System) programmable brick contained an 8-bit microcontroller CPU and 32K of RAM. Users could "build" a program on their home computer and download it to the RCX using an infrared interface. The program told the motors and sensors plugged into the computer brick how to move and bring a robot to life.

UPGRADES

9747 Robotics Invention System 1.5 (1999) and 3804 Robotics Invention System 2.0 (2001) updated the previous versions of LEGO robot technology.

Decorative LEGO
element eyes

RCX 1.0 brick

Gear rotates torso

CUSTOM CREATIONS

By combining Robotics Invention System sensors, motors and the RCX brick with the beams and gears from their LEGO Technic collections, builders could create robots with a virtually endless variety of looks and functions.

9731 Vision
Command
(2000) camera

Rubber tire for mouth

LEGO Technic
gears

This bartender robot was built for the Nuremberg Toy Fair in 2001. It is programmed to recognize green and red cards and serve a BIONICLE® or Jack Stone themed drink depending on which card is presented.

Robotics Invention System robot

3801 Ultimate Accessory Set (2000)

EXPANDING HORIZONS

How do you make a LEGO robot even better? With expansion sets that add even more sensors, motors, elements, and programming possibilities, like this one with a rotational sensor, a glowing lamp and the first LEGO MINDSTORMS remote control.

3800 Ultimate Builder's Set (2001)

NEW COMPONENTS

Requiring the user to already have the basic Robotics Invention System set, the Ultimate Builder's Set included extra parts for even more advanced LEGO MINDSTORMS models and digital building steps for seven new robot

This add-on kit provided an extra gear motor and transparent pneumatic parts, as well as a CD-ROM full of building instructions from the LEGO Master Builders.

LEGO Space Insectoids legs

Rover deployment ramp

This space-age accessory set included pieces and programs to build a Mars Lander and other interplanetary explorers, as well as a Challenge CD with missions for the programmer to complete.

9736 Exploration Mars (2000)

SPORT-BOTS

The RoboSports expansion let you build sports-playing robots, such as this rolling, dunking basketball star. It came with a Challenge CD, a mat to serve as a sports field, an extra motor, and useful elements, including balls and pucks.

Ball-dunking claw

Basketball hoop

9730 RoboSports (1998)

The Robotics Discovery Set had instructions with different difficulty levels, starting with The Bug Book, a guide to making robot insects.

9735 Robotics Discovery Set (1999)

9748 Droid Developer Kit (1999)

MicroScout controller

STARTER SCOUT

The Scout microcomputer brick was included with 9735 Robotics Discovery Set, a 1999 LEGO MINDSTORMS starter kit. The blue Scout had a built-in light sensor and ports for two motors and two additional sensors to be attached.

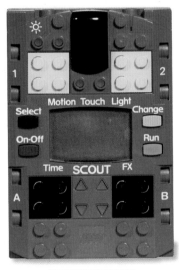

Scout Microcomputer brick

Mars rover with unreleased prototype Vision Command camera

DESIGNING DROIDS

LEGO MINDSTORMS products entered a galaxy far, far away with expansion sets based on the *Star Wars*® movies. The Droid Developer Kit let you make your own rolling R2-D2™ and other droids, while 9754 Dark Side Developer Kit (2000) had parts and instructions for building a walking Imperial AT-AT, a marching Destroyer Droid, and more. Both came with a new MicroScout controller with a built-in motor and light sensor.

"NXT" Generation

EIGHT YEARS after the Robotics Invention System was launched, 8527 LEGO® MINDSTORMS® NXT arrived with the goal of making robot creation simple enough for someone to build and program one in half an hour. The RCX was replaced by the NXT Intelligent Brick, and new motors and sensors were designed to give the latest robots even more capabilities, as well as a sleek, futuristic look ●

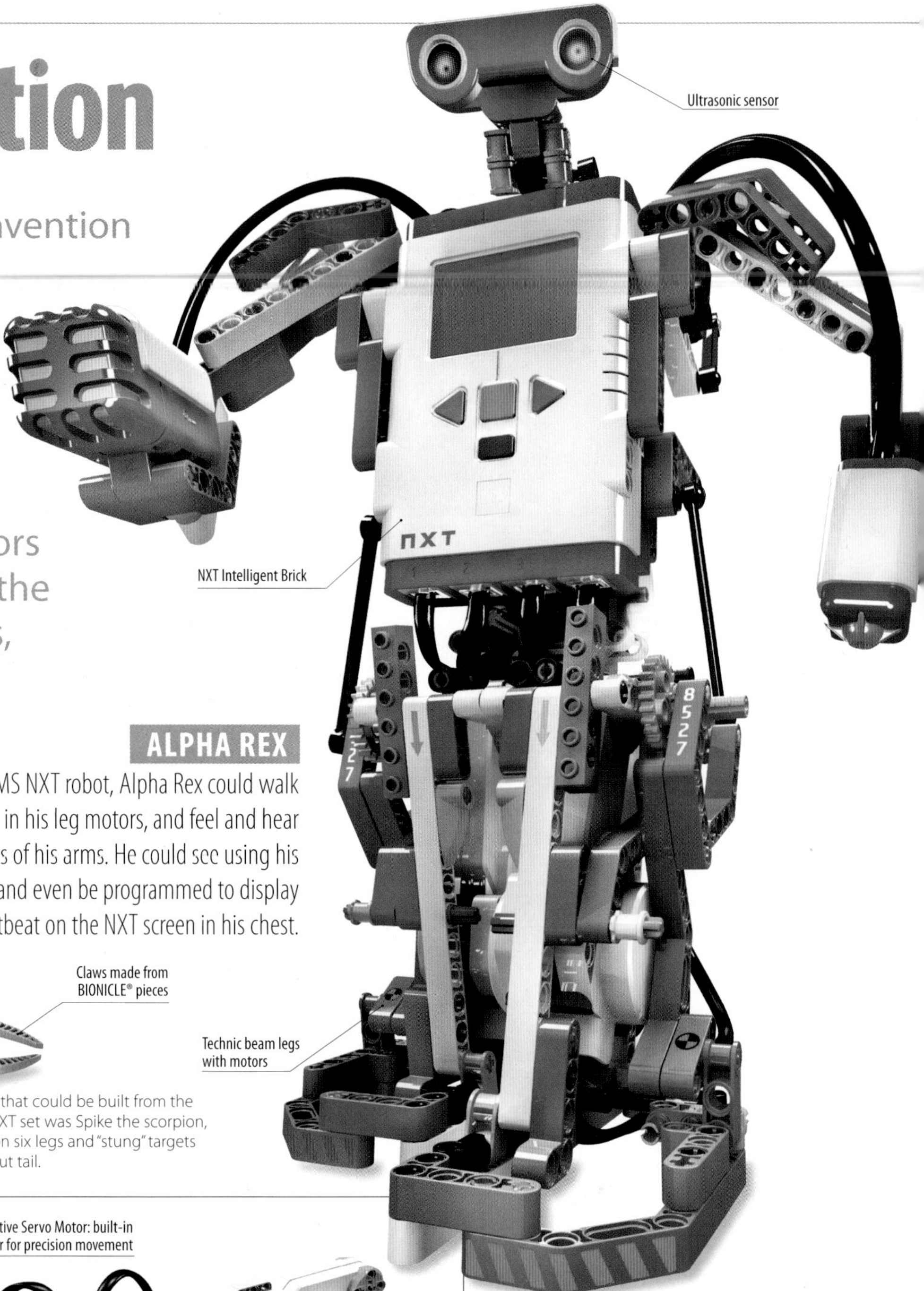

Ultrasonic sensor

NXT Intelligent Brick

ALPHA REX

The signature LEGO MINDSTORMS NXT robot, Alpha Rex could walk with built-in rotation sensors in his leg motors, and feel and hear with the sensors on the ends of his arms. He could see using his ultrasonic-sensor eyes, and even be programmed to display a virtual heartbeat on the NXT screen in his chest.

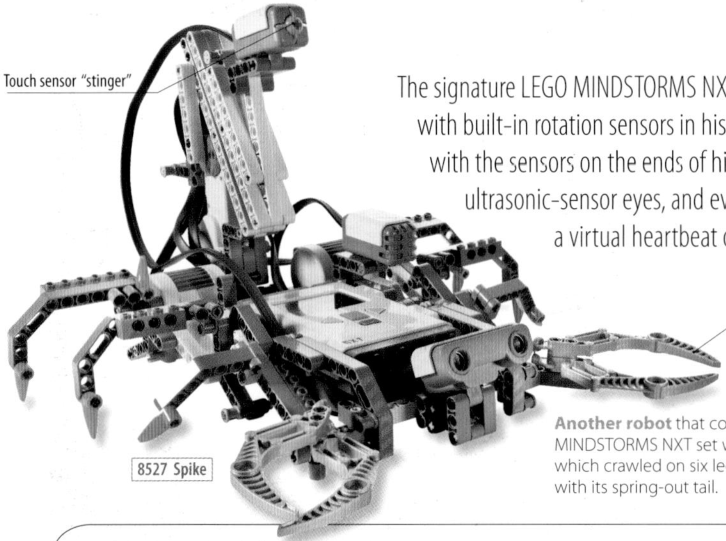

Touch sensor "stinger"

Claws made from BIONICLE® pieces

Technic beam legs with motors

Another robot that could be built from the MINDSTORMS NXT set was Spike the scorpion, which crawled on six legs and "stung" targets with its spring-out tail.

8527 Spike

8527 MINDSTORMS NXT (2006)

The original NXT set included instructions for building the robots Alpha Rex, Spike, TriBot, and the T-56 mechanical arm.

NXT INTELLIGENT BRICK

The NXT is the new generation of programmable bricks, with an ARM 32-bit microprocessor, 256 KB memory, USB 2.0 and Bluetooth support, and a whole array of new and enhanced sensors and motors.

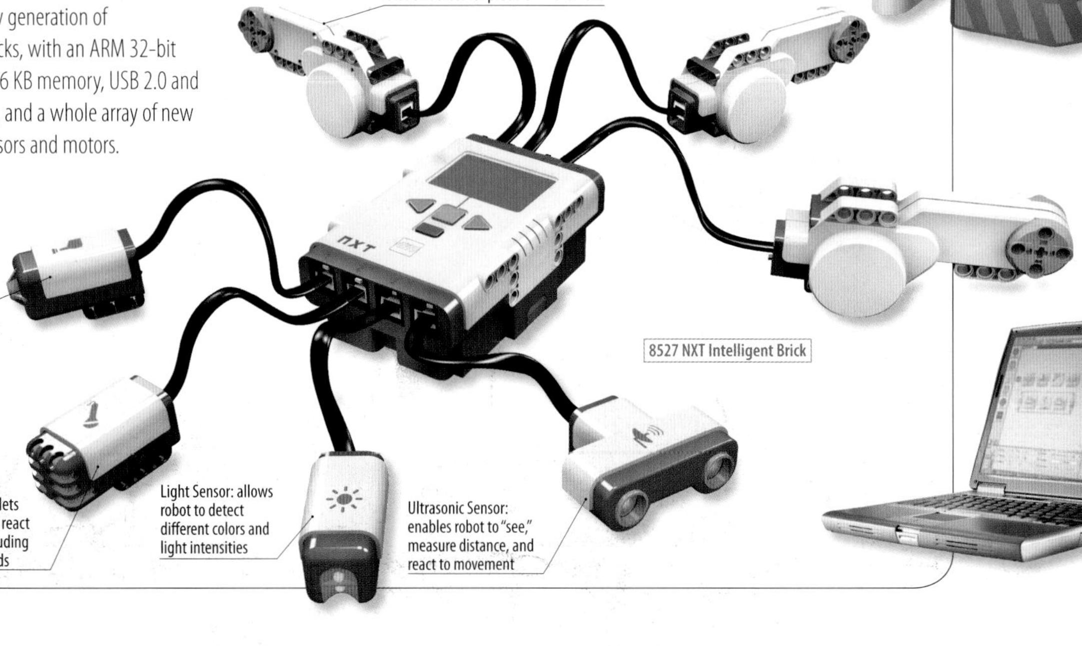

Interactive Servo Motor: built-in rotation sensor for precision movement

Touch Sensor: detects touch and release to let robot "feel" its environment

8527 NXT Intelligent Brick

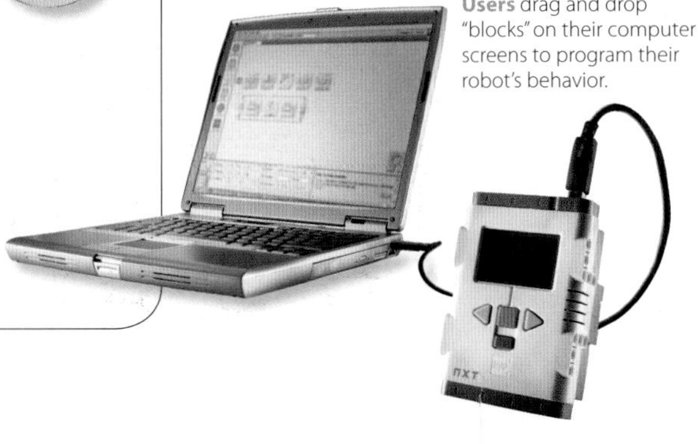

Users drag and drop "blocks" on their computer screens to program their robot's behavior.

Sound Sensor: lets robot hear and react to sounds, including voice commands

Light Sensor: allows robot to detect different colors and light intensities

Ultrasonic Sensor: enables robot to "see," measure distance, and react to movement

When **TriBot** rolled up to a ball, a lever pressed the touch sensor and instructed the claws to close.

TRIBOT

The fast and flexible TriBot was a three-wheeled vehicle that could be programmed to follow a line on the ground and capture objects when commanded out loud.

FIRST LEGO® LEAGUE

Created with the non-profit organization FIRST (For Inspiration and Recognition of Science and Technology), the *FIRST* LEGO® League is an annual program that culminates in a robotic technology tournament for elementary and middle school students from around the world.

Teams are judged based on teamwork, robot design, research presentations, and the performance of their robots on the playing field.

Teams of 5 to 10 players design robots using LEGO MINDSTORMS kits and compete to solve scientific and technical challenges based on real-world issues ranging from alternative energy to space exploration—learning life skills along the way.

ADD-ONS

Additional components, some made by licensed second-party developers, are available at the LEGO online shop, including sensors that measure rotation, detect infrared light, and even tell a robot which way is up or how fast it is accelerating.

MS1034 Compass sensor

The compass sensor measures the Earth's magnetic field to determine which direction a robot is facing.

MS1048 RF ID Sensor

The RF ID sensor uses a key transponder to unlock and activate NXT programs.

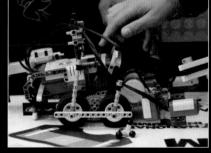

More than 137,000 children in 50 countries have taken part in the FLL program in recent years.

WHAT'S NXT?

Meet the next version of LEGO MINDSTORMS NXT. The 2009 edition of the state-of-the-art LEGO robotics kit came with more customizable programming options, instructions for making even more robots, and all-new technology, including its own color sensor!

8547 MINDSTORMS NXT 2.0 (2009)

The all-new, all-different Alpha Rex was bigger, sturdier, and had even more built-in and programmed options.

FIRST also runs a *FIRST* Robotics Competition and a *FIRST* Tech Challenge for high schoolers, and the Junior *FIRST* LEGO League for kids aged 6–9.

FIRST *Championship photography by Adriana Groisman. Other photography courtesy of students, volunteers, and sponsors.*

Licensed Themes

WHO WOULDN'T want to build the characters, vehicles, and worlds from their favorite TV shows and movies? It was only a matter of time before LEGO® sets started to branch out into some of the biggest licenses around. As early as the 1970s, the company was making branded gas station models and airlines were selling LEGO kits of their jets. However, in 1999, with the release of LEGO® *Star Wars*®, licensed LEGO themes really took off. Since then, we've seen LEGO® Batman™, LEGO® Mickey Mouse™, LEGO® SpongeBob SquarePants™, LEGO® Spider-Man™, and many more ●

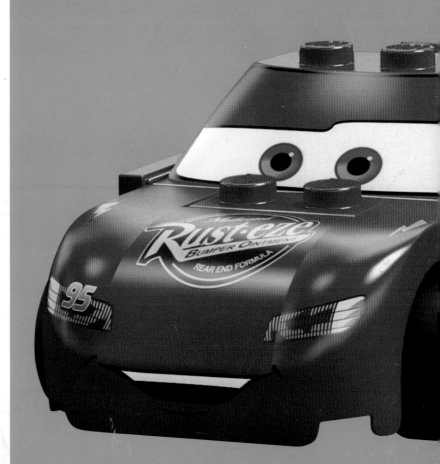

LEGO® *Star Wars*®

THE LEGO GROUP'S first licensed property in more than 40 years, LEGO® *Star Wars*® launched in 1999. With constructible classic vehicles and the whole cast of famous heroes, villains, aliens, and droids rendered in minifigure style for the first time ever, the theme was an immediate success with builders of all ages—and it's still proving very popular ●

7961 Darth Maul's Sith Infiltrator™ (2011) was the third minifigure-scale version of the ship. It introduced a soft-plastic cap to give Darth Maul his fierce Zabrak horns.

STAR WARS: EPISODE I *THE PHANTOM MENACE*

RACE FOR FREEDOM

One of the first sets released from the *Star Wars* prequel trilogy, Mos Espa Podrace let builders pit young Anakin Skywalker and his custom Podracer against rivals Sebulba and Gasgano in a race for his freedom in the perilous Boonta Eve Classic Podrace. With lots of unusual elements and colors, it remains a popular set among LEGO fans. Just like in the movie, Sebulba's orange Podracer was equipped with sneaky gadgets to sabotage his opponents' vehicles.

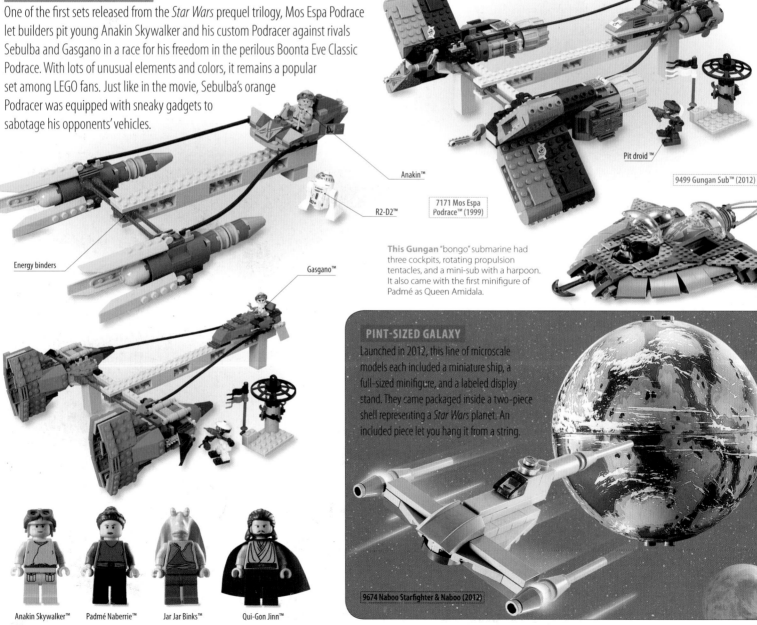

Sebulba™

Anakin™

R2-D2™

Energy binders

Gasgano™

Pit droid™

9499 Gungan Sub™ (2012)

7171 Mos Espa Podrace™ (1999)

This Gungan "bongo" submarine had three cockpits, rotating propulsion tentacles, and a mini-sub with a harpoon. It also came with the first minifigure of Padmé as Queen Amidala.

PINT-SIZED GALAXY
Launched in 2012, this line of microscale models each included a miniature ship, a full-sized minifigure, and a labeled display stand. They came packaged inside a two-piece shell representing a *Star Wars* planet. An included piece let you hang it from a string.

9674 Naboo Starfighter & Naboo (2012)

Anakin Skywalker™

Padmé Naberrie™

Jar Jar Binks™

Qui-Gon Jinn™

STAR WARS: EPISODE II *ATTACK OF THE CLONES*

7153 Jango Fett's *Slave I*™ (2002)

Stabilizer fin

Hidden missile launcher

Rotating laser cannon

Cargo ramp

Boba Fett™

Jango Fett™

This set was the only place to get the Jango Fett and young Boba Fett minifigures.

7163 Republic Gunship™ (2002)

Super battle droids and destroyer droid

SLAVE I

Episode II introduced bounty hunter Jango Fett and his all-new, earlier version of the familiar *Slave I* starship. The prequel-era LEGO *Slave I* had a new canopy window piece, dropping bombs, secret compartments, a magnetic cargo container, and gravity-activated rotating cockpit and wings, creatively tipped with a BIONICLE® foot piece to replicate the mechanical detail of the movie ship.

REPUBLIC GUNSHIP

Straight from the final battle on the planet Geonosis, the LEGO Republic Gunship had a 15 in (38 cm) wingspan, movable side laser turrets, a detachable top section, a magnetic tool-box, opening troop bay doors, and hidden compartments. Popular for its many features and a high count of droid and clone trooper minifigures, it also included a mysterious unnamed Jedi Knight to help battle the Separatists. A new, even bigger version of the Republic Gunship was made in 2008 for *The Clone Wars* line.

STAR WARS: EPISODE III *REVENGE OF THE SITH*

SPACE BATTLE

The Jedi Knight who would soon become Darth Vader blasted off one last time as a good guy aboard Anakin Skywalker's new Eta-2 interceptor, closely pursued by a Separatist vulture droid that could convert from flight to walking mode. With both hero and villain vehicles included, this set let builders reenact the blazing battle in the skies above Coruscant from the opening scenes of Episode III.

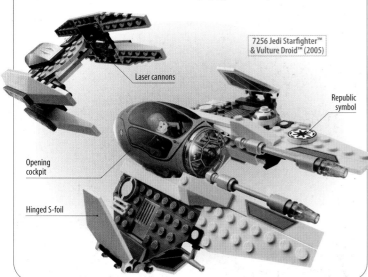

7256 Jedi Starfighter™ & Vulture Droid™ (2005)

Laser cannons

Opening cockpit

Hinged S-foil

Republic symbol

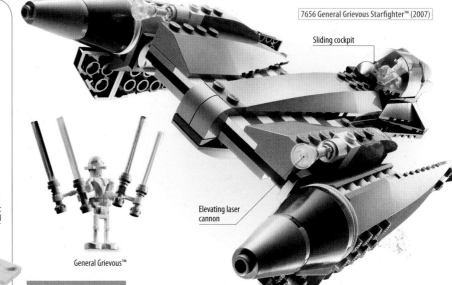

7656 General Grievous Starfighter™ (2007)

Sliding cockpit

Elevating laser cannon

General Grievous™

GRIEVOUS THREAT

General Grievous, the cyborg commander of the Separatist droid army, piloted this modified Belbullab-22 starfighter during the Clone Wars, but it was Obi-Wan Kenobi who flew away with it after their final battle on Utapau. The model had a slide-open cockpit, flip-up laser cannons, and a tail fin that folded down for landing. A new version was released for *The Clone Wars* in 2010.

Storage clips on the bottom of the model held the four-armed general's four stolen Jedi lightsabers.

STAR WARS: EPISODE IV *A NEW HOPE*

**10179 Ultimate Collector Series
Millennium Falcon™ (2008)**

Main sensor

Exhaust vent

Laser cannon

Cargo bay

Docking
ring

Maintenance
access bay

Forward
floodlight

Cockpit

THE *MILLENNIUM FALCON*

This is it: the biggest LEGO® set ever made! Measuring a whopping 33 in (84 cm) long, 22 in (56 cm) wide, and 8 in (20.3 cm) tall, the Ultimate Collector Series *Millennium Falcon* was built out of 5,195 pieces using the detailed steps in its 311-page, spiral-bound instructions manual. With incredible movie-accurate details and moving parts, it quickly became the centerpiece of many a *Star Wars* fan's collection… provided they could find a surface large enough to display it!

Features included rotating top and bottom laser turrets, a moving sensor dish, an extending boarding ramp, five minifigures, and a display card with technical information about the ship.

9492 TIE Fighter™ (2012) included detailed wing panels, flick-firing missiles, an exclusive droid, and a new helmet for its Death Star Trooper.

Chewbacca™   Han Solo™

Luke Skywalker™   Princess Leia™   Obi-Wan Kenobi™

TATOOINE

You'll never build a more wretched hive of scum and villainy. 2004's Mos Eisley Cantina set provided lots of LEGO firsts: the first-ever Dewback riding lizard, the first-ever sandtrooper, and the first-ever Greedo minifigure. The desert planet grew with 2012's Droid Escape set, which updated a model from 11 years earlier with new versions of the escape pod, fugitive droids R2-D2 and C-3PO, and a pair of Sandtroopers with a swoop bike.

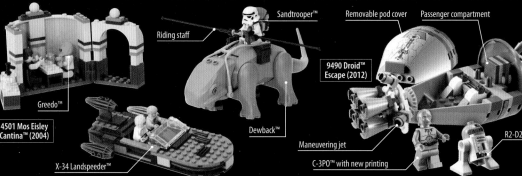
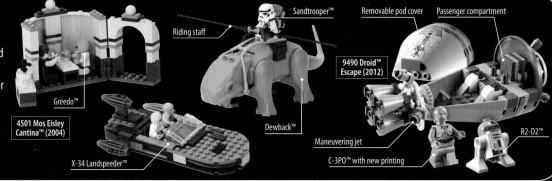

Greedo™

**4501 Mos Eisley
Cantina**™ (2004)

X-34 Landspeeder™

Riding staff

Sandtrooper™

Dewback™

Removable pod cover   Passenger compartment

9490 Droid™
Escape (2012)

Maneuvering jet

C-3PO™ with new printing

R2-D2™

Tractor beam targeting array

Command bridge

STAR DESTROYER

Blasting out of the opening scene of the original *Star Wars* movie, the Ultimate Collector Series Imperial Star Destroyer model stretched nearly 38½ in (98 cm) long and was made from more than 3,100 pieces. Built more for display than play, it took even advanced builders many hours to assemble the gigantic starship, parts of which were held together with magnets. This model pioneered the use of tiny LEGO elements known as "greebles" to create intricate detail.

Rebel Blockade Runner

Quad laser

Turbolaser turret

10030 Ultimate Collector Series Imperial Star Destroyer™ (2006)

The MINI collection brought a whole new scale to LEGO *Star Wars*. The first series, including 4484 MINI X-wing vs. TIE Advanced (2003), came with pieces to make two pocket-sized models, plus part of a bonus TIE Bomber that could be fully assembled when you collected all 4 sets.

STAR WARS: EPISODE V *THE EMPIRE STRIKES BACK*

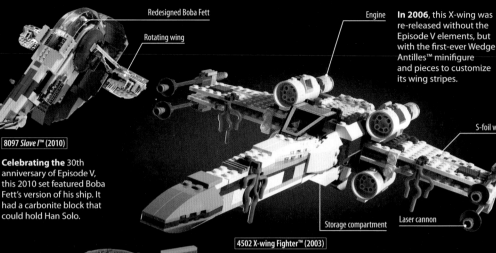

Redesigned Boba Fett

Rotating wing

Engine

In 2006, this X-wing was re-released without the Episode V elements, but with the first-ever Wedge Antilles™ minifigure and pieces to customize its wing stripes.

S-foil wing

Storage compartment

Laser cannon

4502 X-wing Fighter™ (2003)

10178 Motorized AT-AT Walker™ (2007)

Opening cockpit

8097 *Slave I*™ (2010)

Celebrating the 30th anniversary of Episode V, this 2010 set featured Boba Fett's version of his ship. It had a carbonite block that could hold Han Solo.

Luke Skywalker™

Yoda™

Yoda's hut opened up to reveal his bed, stew pot, and a secret compartment for his lightsaber.

X-WING FIGHTER

A LEGO X-wing fighter set was released with the first wave of *Star Wars* sets in 1999, but the new 2003 version was a major improvement. It was bigger, had better colors, and was more accurate to the movies, plus it came with detachable swamp muck and Yoda's Dagobah hut. The wings were even geared to open and close when you turned a piece on the back of the model!

IMPERIAL WALKER

The winner of a 2006 fan vote to decide the next exclusive LEGO *Star Wars* set, the second minifigure-scale AT-AT (All Terrain Armored Transport) included a LEGO Power Functions motor and battery box. The flip of a switch enabled it to walk forward or back and move its head. Clever builders added an infrared receiver to make their walkers remote-controlled.

STAR WARS: EPISODE VI *RETURN OF THE JEDI*

10143 Death Star II™ (2005)

RETURN TO TATOOINE

The LEGO version of Jabba's sail barge was packed with fun play features. You could move the blaster cannon and sails, use the mini-catapult to launch Boba Fett into the air, extend the skiff's gangplank to feed pesky Rebels to the hungry Sarlacc, and open the sides to reveal Jabba the Hutt himself, complete with throne room, prison, and even a well-stocked kitchen.

Jabba's 2012 palace included (among others) majordomo Bib Fortuna, dancing girl Oola, monkey-lizard Salacious Crumb, and an all-new Jabba on his throne above the Rancor pit.

9516 Jabba's Palace™ (2012)

Forward sail

Jabba the Hutt™

The Sail Barge came with eight characters, including Lando Calrissian™ in skiff guard disguise, Princess Leia as Jabba's prisoner, Jedi Luke Skywalker, Han Solo, a Gamorrean guard, and R2-D2™ with a drink tray.

Lando™ in disguise

Desert Skiff

THE SECOND DEATH STAR

An Ultimate Collector Series model designed for assembly by advanced builders 16 and up, the *Death Star II* was made from 3,449 pieces and measured 19 in (48 cm) across and 25 in (63.5 cm) high on its display stand. It included translucent pieces to create a firing superlaser beam and a tiny Star Destroyer built to scale with the giant battle station.

Drive thrust system

6210 Jabba's Sail Barge™ (2006)

Sarlacc™

STAR WARS: THE CLONE WARS®

In 2008, *Star Wars*® hit both big and small screens with *The Clone Wars*, an action-packed new computer animated series that took place between the events of Episode II and Episode III. Naturally, the LEGO Group followed suit with buildable versions of the new vehicles and characters!

R2-D2™

Laser cannon

7669 Anakin's Jedi Starfighter™ (2008)

Flick-launching missile

JEDI STARFIGHTER

Released at the beginning of 2008 (or the end of 2007 in some stores) as a special preview for the new series, Anakin's latest Jedi starfighter featured a few differences from the Episode II version, such as a central astromech socket for R2-D2, an ejection button to pop the little droid out of the ship, and missiles beneath the wings that could be launched with the flick of a finger. One of only a few LEGO® sets to be sold in multiple boxes within the same country, Anakin's Jedi starfighter was re-released in mid-2008 in new *The Clone Wars*-style packaging.

Heavy blaster

Flick-launching laser cannon

Escape pod

The *Halo* belonged to a team of bounty hunters who sometimes helped the good guys, though they were usually villains in LEGO stories.

7930 Bounty Hunter Assault Gunship (2011)

THE TWILIGHT

This model featured folding wings, flip-out landing gear, a removable emergency escape pod, and a rear cargo hatch with a working winch and tow-cable inside. It included Anakin, R2-D2, and two brand-new characters: Anakin's Jedi apprentice Ahsoka, and Rotta, Jabba the Hutt's stinky offspring.

Main engine

Cockpit

7680 The *Twilight*™ (2008)

The *Twilight's* opening cockpit comfortably seated three… as long as one was a baby alien slug, anyway!

Rotta™

Ahsoka™

Anakin™

REPUBLIC TANK

This store-exclusive model of the TX-130S Hover Tank was armed with rotating laser cannon turrets, an elevating gunner seat, and flip-out flick-missile launchers. It also had hidden wheels that made it look like the tank was floating when it rolled along the ground.

Medium laser

Turret hatch

Clone trooper gunner

Heavy laser cannon

7679 Republic Fighter Tank™ (2008)

Opening cockpit

Clone trooper

Some LEGO *Star Wars* fans build their own Clone Wars armies by collecting extras of sets like this one, which included a walker vehicle with three clone troopers, a clone gunner, and officer gear.

8014 Clone Walker Battle Pack (2009)

These two clone troopers became the misadventure-prone 1137 and 1139 in a series of comic web-animations.

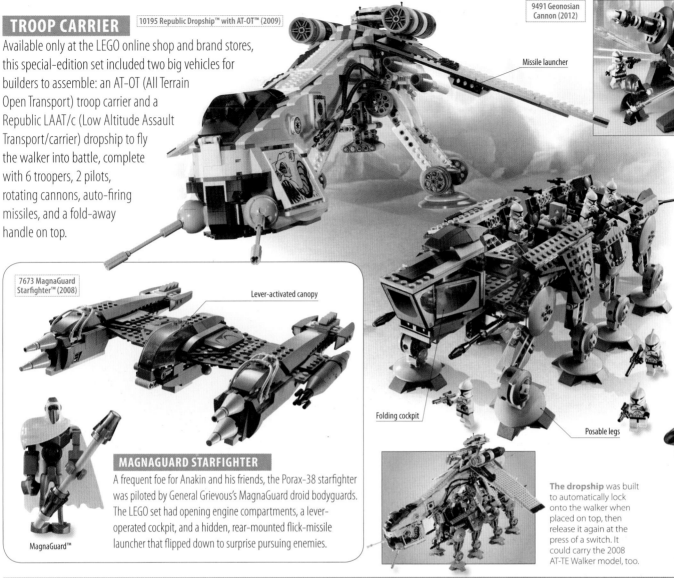

TROOP CARRIER

10195 Republic Dropship™ with AT-OT™ (2009)

Available only at the LEGO online shop and brand stores, this special-edition set included two big vehicles for builders to assemble: an AT-OT (All Terrain Open Transport) troop carrier and a Republic LAAT/c (Low Altitude Assault Transport/carrier) dropship to fly the walker into battle, complete with 6 troopers, 2 pilots, rotating cannons, auto-firing missiles, and a fold-away handle on top.

9491 Geonosian Cannon (2012)

Missile launcher

Featuring an LR1K sonic cannon from the Separatist world of Geonosis, this set included Jedi General Barriss Offee, Clone Commander Gree, a bug-like Geonosian Warrior, and a mindless Geonosian Zombie.

7673 MagnaGuard Starfighter™ (2008)

Lever-activated canopy

MAGNAGUARD STARFIGHTER

A frequent foe for Anakin and his friends, the Porax-38 starfighter was piloted by General Grievous's MagnaGuard droid bodyguards. The LEGO set had opening engine compartments, a lever-operated cockpit, and a hidden, rear-mounted flick-missile launcher that flipped down to surprise pursuing enemies.

MagnaGuard™

Bounty hunter Cad Bane was a new villain introduced in the TV series. He made his first appearance as a minifigure in 8098 Clone Turbo Tank (2010).

Folding cockpit

Posable legs

The dropship was built to automatically lock onto the walker when placed on top, then release it again at the press of a switch. It could carry the 2008 AT-TE Walker model, too.

Cad Bane™

CHARACTER MODELS

JEDI MASTER

This Ultimate Collector Series model let you build the diminutive Jedi Master himself out of more than 1,000 LEGO pieces. Standing 14 in (36 cm) tall from the tips of his toes to the top of his head when completed, the LEGO Yoda had a rotating head and wore his blissl flute around his neck. Mastery of the Force not included!

7194 Yoda™ (2002)

DARING DROID

Plucky astromech R2-D2 joined the ranks of the Ultimate Collector Series with this 2012 model. Built from a whopping 2,127 pieces, the 12 in (31 cm) high droid featured opening body panels with hidden tools, a swiveling dome, and a retractable third leg, plus a data plaque and his own minifigure.

Photoreceptor eye

Holographic projector

Spacecraft linkage control arms

Fold-out circular saw (hidden behind panel)

Adjustable legs

10225 R2-D2™ (2012)

SITH APPRENTICE

Looming more than 17 in (43 cm) tall, this life-sized bust of the deadly Darth Maul took 1,860 LEGO pieces to complete, almost all of them black or red. Detailed down to the tiny silver stud in one ear, the sinister Sith Lord came packaged in a black and white box as a LEGO Store exclusive. This is the set that paved the way for all Ultimate Collector Series Star Wars models to come!

10018 Darth Maul™ (2001)

STAR WARS®: THE EXPANDED UNIVERSE

THE OLD REPUBLIC

There's much more to *Star Wars* than just what you see on the screen. Beyond the movies and television series, there's a whole expanded universe full of video games, comic books, novels, and other tales. Blasting out of the *Star Wars: The Old Republic* online role-playing game, the *Fury*-class Interceptor transported the Sith Lord Darth Malgus and his Sith troopers in their war against the original Republic more than 3,000 years before the events of the *Star Wars* films.

Opening cockpit

9497 Republic *Striker*-class Starfighter™ (2012)

Wings sweep forward for cruising

9500 Sith™ *Fury*-class Interceptor™ (2012)

Like Darth Vader long after him, Darth Malgus was a mighty dark side warrior kept alive by a cybernetic respirator.

HEROES OF THE PAST

A distant ancestor of the X-wing, the *Striker*-class starfighter flew for the Old Republic during the Great Galactic War. The LEGO® model had wings that repositioned for flight or attack, flick-fire missiles, and a spot for lightsaber storage.

The set included Jedi Master Satele Shan, an armored Republic Trooper, and old-time astromech droid T7-O1.

The player's character was Galen Marek, code-named Starkiller. Also included were pilot (and love interest) Juno Eclipse and a battle-damaged Darth Vader.

Vader's broken helmet was a black Aquazone mask flipped on its side!

Rotating wings

VADER'S SECRET

The *Star Wars: The Force Unleashed* video game series let you play as Darth Vader's secret apprentice, and ultimately choose between the light and dark sides of the Force. The *Rogue Shadow* was the stealthy ship that carried the apprentice on his missions across the galaxy. Its wings and engines rotated together for flight and landing modes.

Blaster cannon

7672 *Rogue Shadow*™ (2008)

IMPERIAL ARMADA

The *Star Wars* movies are full of TIE (twin ion engine) variations: Darth Vader's TIE Advanced, the twin-hulled TIE Bomber, the speedy TIE Interceptor, and the standard TIE starfighter that makes up most of the Empire's squadrons. The Expanded Universe also had the powerful three-winged TIE Defender that first appeared in the *Star Wars: TIE Fighter* video game.

The TIE Defender included a TIE Pilot with a new helmet to sit in the fighter's spinning cockpit, plus a Stormtrooper to stand guard outside.

7664 TIE Crawler™ (2007)

8087 TIE Defender™ (2010)

TIE CRAWLER

Another unusual variant was the TIE Crawler, which traded in its wings for giant treads to become a land-roving century tank. It included flip-out blasters, a pair of black-armored Shadow Stormtroopers, and the ability to stand up on its treads to get a higher view of the battlefield.

Maintenance hatch

DROPSHIP

With a squad of three Stormtroopers and a Shadow Stormtrooper, the Imperial Dropship used its detachable troop platform to get the Empire's forces into combat quickly. Rather than a comic or game, it came straight from the minds of the LEGO designers.

Solar wing array

Laser cannon

TIE/D from 10131 TIE™ Collection (2004)

The TIE/D was a unique type of TIE fighter— it didn't have a pilot! Instead, it was controlled by an internal (and removable) droid brain.

7667 Imperial Dropship™ (2008)

SCOUT SPEEDER

The Rebel Scout Speeder was a battle pack set including four Rebel Troopers and a removable heavy blaster cannon. Like the Dropship, it was an original LEGO design.

7668 Rebel Scout Speeder™ (2008)

MERRY SITH-MAS!

A holiday tradition that started in 2011, LEGO *Star Wars* advent calendars let builders count down to Christmas with 24 buildable micro-vehicles, accessories and minifigures— including 2012's exclusive Santa-garbed Darth Maul and snow-droid R2-D2!

9509 LEGO® *Star Wars*® Advent Calendar (2012)

LEGO® *Indiana Jones*™

IN 2008, adventure got a new name: LEGO® *Indiana Jones!* With the release of a long-awaited fourth Indy movie, the whip-wielding, globe-trotting, all-action archeologist hero finally arrived in minifigure form ●

Indiana Jones (2008)

Pilot Jock and his pet snake weren't originally planned for this set, but the LEGO designers and Lucasfilm agreed that he was an important addition to

Skull carving

Flexible plastic pipes let the giant boulder roll down after Indy, just like in the movie!

Rolling boulder

Seaplane

René Belloq

Skeleton

7623 Temple Escape (2008)

Golden idol

Booby traps included collapsing walls, shooting spears, slashing swords, tumbling rocks, a pit to swing over, and a spider web.

Satipo

Obelisk tower

Russian vehicle

7627 Temple of the Crystal Skull (2008)

THRILLING ESCAPE

Straight from the opening scene of the first Indiana Jones film, *Raiders of the Lost Ark*™, the Temple Escape set stretched 21 in (53 cm) long and let builders construct and play with all of the deadly traps and daring escapes from the famous adventurer's debut. Actors Harrison Ford (Indiana Jones) and Alfred Molina (Indy's guide Satipo) both got their second minifigure characters with this set. Upside-down baby dinosaur elements were used to decorate the temple entrance.

A piece that you won't find in any other LEGO set: the golden Chachapoyan fertility idol of Peru!

Indiana Jones™

Mutt Williams

Irina Spalko

Russian soldier

Ugha Warrior™

TEMPLE OF AKATOR

From *Indiana Jones and the Kingdom of the Crystal Skull*™, the peril-filled Temple of Akator included a whirling circle of crystal skeletons to enable you to reenact the exciting ending of the movie.

Fuel truck

German pilot

German mechanic

Indiana Jones

Marion Ravenwood™

7683 Fight on the Flying Wing (2009)

FLYING WING

As German soldiers prepare to leave Egypt with the Ark of the Covenant, Indiana Jones and Marion try to keep their experimental plane from taking off. The LEGO version had a 23 in (58 cm) wingspan, spinning propellers, an opening cockpit, and a hidden cargo hold.

JONES & SON

This small set from *Indiana Jones and the Last Crusade*™ was the only one from the third movie in the theme's first year. It included a German checkpoint, two motorcycles, and the first-ever minifigure of Indy's dad, Professor Henry Jones, Sr.

7620 Motorcycle Chase (2008)

Prof. Jones's Grail diary

Falling rocks

Booby-trapped altar

Snakes! Why did it have to be snakes?

FINDING THE ARK

"Why did it have to be snakes?" Trapped underground in the Well of Souls, Indy and Marion have to find a way to escape and recover the Ark. Fortunately, there's a handy statue that they can tip over to break the wall and get away!

Look closely and you may notice a few *Star Wars* characters hidden among the wall carvings (they were there in the movie, too).

7621 The Lost Tomb (2008)

The Ark of the Covenant

MINE CART CHASE

The first year of LEGO *Indiana Jones* had no models from the second movie, *Indiana Jones and the Temple of Doom*™. Fortunately, 2009 more than made up for it with this set, which used all-new LEGO track elements to re-create the film's thrilling roller-coaster mine cart chase.

Indiana Jones™

Willie Scott

Short Round

Mola Ram

7199 The Temple of Doom (2009)

Mine cart

Rock bin trap

Pull the lever to drop "rocks" on the Thuggee guards below!

Sloped track

Lava plume

Sankara Stones

LEGO® Batman™

Batman (2008)

IN 2006, the Dark Knight™ arrived in the world of LEGO® construction. LEGO® Batman™ brought all of his famous vehicles and gadgets with him for the battle against crime. His toughest foes also came along for the ride through 13 sets, a video game, and even a computer-animated TV mini-movie ●

THE BATMOBILE™

Almost as big as life, this super-sleek, super-detailed version of Batman's most classic vehicle took 1,045 elements to build and stretched over 17½ in (45 cm) long and 6 in (15 cm) wide. Its black-on-black-on-black design made it challenging to keep track of pieces while putting it together.

Turning the steering wheel raised the front bat-shield, revealing hidden intakes for an extra burst of speed!

Angled bat-wing fins

Opening cockpit

Bat-shield battering ram

Built with jet technology, the Batmobile's fiery turbines spun as it rolled forward!

Headlights

Gold Bat-symbol hubcaps

Low-riding chassis

7784 The Batmobile™: Ultimate Collectors' Edition (2006)

ARKHAM ASYLUM™

This special-edition set included three of Batman's most fearsome foes, plus high-security prison cells to contain them until the next big breakout. Fortunately, the Dark Knight had help in the form of Nightwing, the grown-up original Robin.

7785 Arkham Asylum™: (2006)

The fright-faced Scarecrow's head was made of a special translucent plastic that really glowed in the dark!

Guard   The Riddler™   Batman™   Nightwing™   Poison Ivy™   Scarecrow™

7886 The Batcycle™: Harley Quinn's Hammer Truck (2006)

THE BATCYCLE™

With a giant-sized crush on The Joker, prank-playing Harley Quinn™ is more a pest than a super villain… but when she went on a crime spree in her big-wheeled hammer-slammer truck, it was still up to Batman and his speedy cycle to bring the mischievous jester to justice.

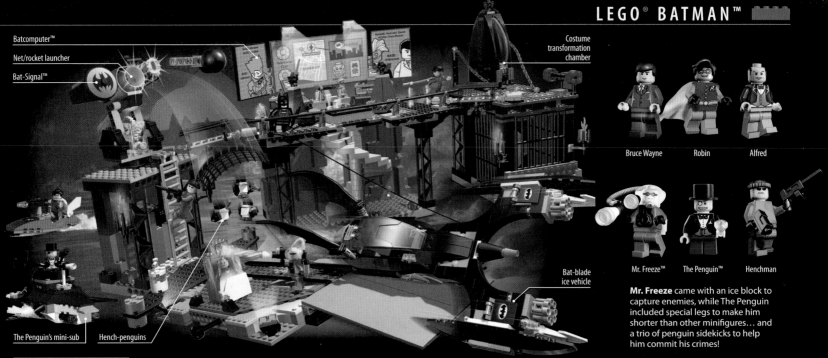

Batcomputer™
Net/rocket launcher
Bat-Signal™

Costume
transformation
chamber

Bat-blade
ice vehicle

The Penguin's mini-sub   Hench-penguins

7783 The Batcave™: The Penguin™ and Mr. Freeze's Invasion (2006)

Bruce Wayne   Robin   Alfred

Mr. Freeze™   The Penguin™   Henchman

Mr. Freeze came with an ice block to capture enemies, while The Penguin included special legs to make him shorter than other minifigures… and a trio of penguin sidekicks to help him commit his crimes!

THE BATCAVE™

Built from 1,075 pieces, Batman's secret underground lair contained everything a caped crime-fighter needed to battle evil, from a detective lab filled with captured clues to training weights, a costume quick-change chamber, and a rotating vehicle repair bay. This was also the only set to include minifigures of Bruce Wayne (Batman's billionaire secret identity) and his faithful butler Alfred.

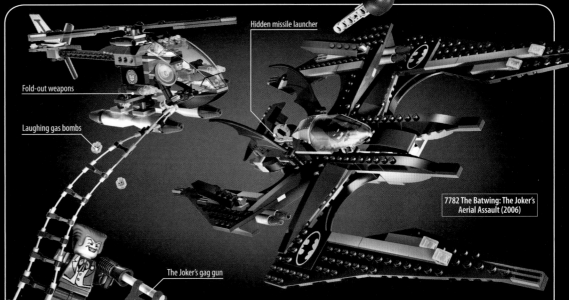

Hidden missile launcher

Fold-out weapons

Laughing gas bombs

7782 The Batwing: The Joker's Aerial Assault (2006)

The Joker's gag gun

Batman's archenemy The Joker was definitely cuter as a minifigure than the crazed clown had ever been before!

7888 The Tumbler™: The Joker's Ice Cream Surprise (2008)

THE BATWING™

Styled in the shape of Batman's classic symbol, the Batwing could split its wings apart to reveal slide-out rockets and launch a pop-up missile hidden behind the cockpit. A direct hit on The Joker Copter's spotlight dropped the ladder and The Joker into the waters of Gotham City™ Harbor below.

THE TUMBLER™

The only movie-based model in the line, the armored Tumbler looked like it drove right off the screen of *Batman Begins* and *The Dark Knight*. Included was The Joker's Ice Cream Van, which launched a surprise missile out of the back doors when you pushed the cone on the roof.

Batman has worn a few different costumes over the years. The LEGO minifigures followed suit with multiple comic and movie-styled versions.

Batman's special crime-fighting equipment included Batarangs and Bat-cuffs for catching the bad guys.

LEGO® DC Universe™ Super Heroes

LEGO® BATMAN™ returned in 2012, but he was not alone. The LEGO DC Universe Super Heroes theme gave the LEGO designers license to create sets featuring superpowered heroes and villains from all across the DC Universe, starting with some of the biggest names around. Most of the boxes included pack-in comics that provided a story for the models inside ●

4528 Green Lantern (2012)

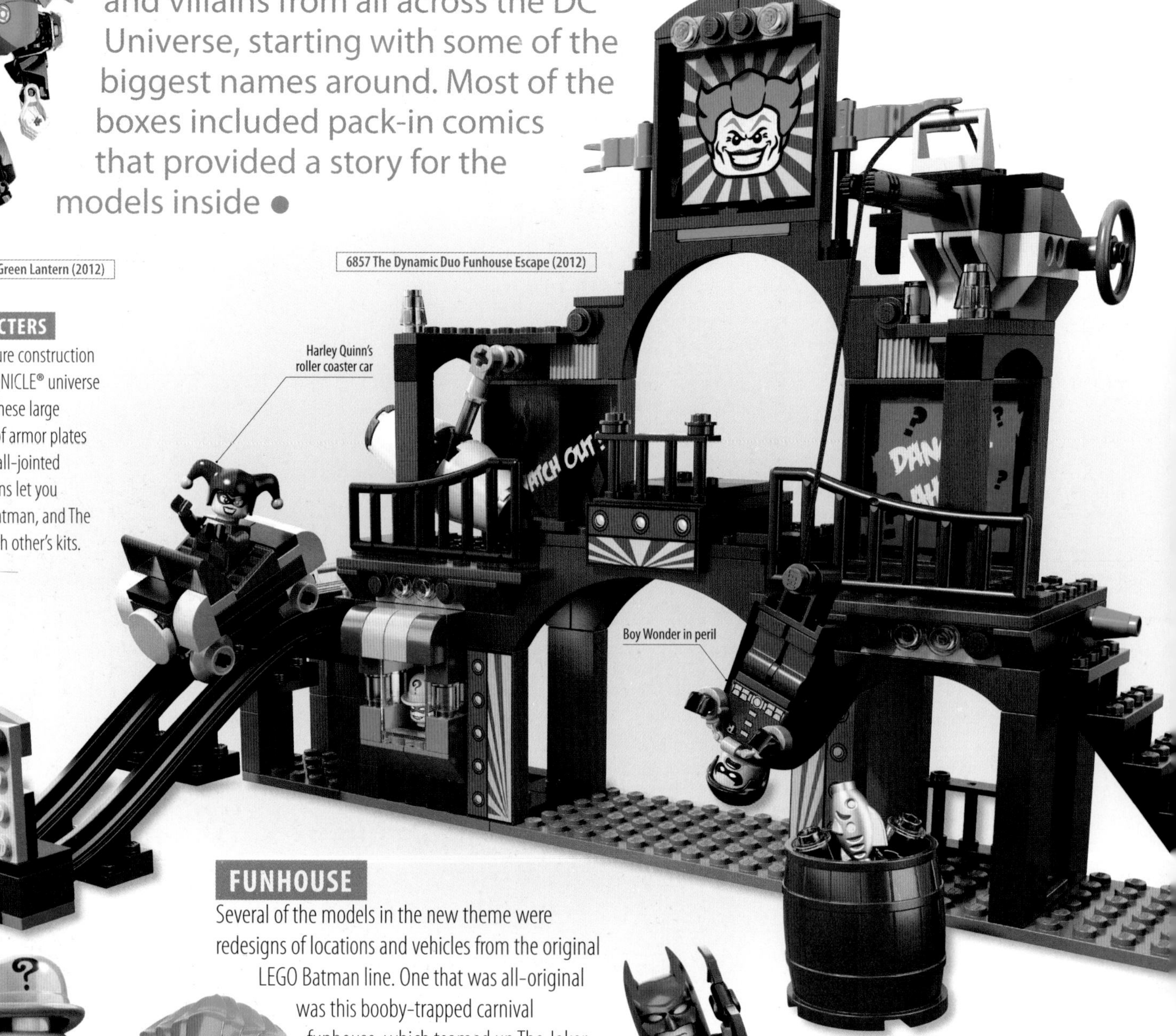

6857 The Dynamic Duo Funhouse Escape (2012)

BUILDABLE CHARACTERS

Drawing on the action figure construction style pioneered for the BIONICLE® universe and LEGO® Hero Factory, these large characters were built out of armor plates snapped onto a posable ball-jointed skeleton. Online instructions let you upgrade Green Lantern, Batman, and The Joker with pieces from each other's kits.

Harley Quinn's roller coaster car

Boy Wonder in peril

FUNHOUSE

Several of the models in the new theme were redesigns of locations and vehicles from the original LEGO Batman line. One that was all-original was this booby-trapped carnival funhouse, which teamed up The Joker, The Riddler, and Harley Quinn in an attempt to defeat the Dynamic Duo once and for all.

The Riddler's new (but classic) costume included a bowler hat and a crowbar for his question-mark cane.

The Joker had a new look, too—along with a double-sided face with a toothy grin on the other side.

Rubber tires

Batman had to reach Robin on his Batcycle before his sidekick was dunked in a barrel full of Joker toxin.

Printed coin

Bundle of dynamite

Opening canopy

6864 The Batmobile and the Two-Face Chase (2012)

TWO-FACE CHASE

Batman's updated Batmobile had a pair of flick-firing missiles behind its cockpit. It pursued Two-Face, who had traded in his cartoon-inspired black and white suit from 2006 for something a bit brighter and drove an armored tow truck to match. Like many of the villains from both themes, Two-Face had henchmen who dressed in his personal color scheme.

The set also included a section of a Gotham City bank with a blast-out window and a safe for Two-Face's truck to tow away.

Lex Luthor at the controls

Golden Lasso of Truth

6860 The Batcave (2012)

BATCAVE REVISITED

The new Batcave had a few changes. It had more colors, a containment tank for Poison Ivy, a drill tank for Bane, and an awesome drop-down elevator that transformed Bruce Wayne into Batman. It also included Robin with a grappling gun and a new Batcycle for the Dark Knight.

Translucent green Kryptonite elements

Red fabric cape

SUPERPOWERS

The first DC super heroes to join Batman's battle against brick-related crime were Superman and Wonder Woman (plus a convention-exclusive Green Lantern). They battled evil genius Lex Luthor and his Kryptonite-powered mech, which had posable fingers for grabbing minifigures. All three characters (and lots more) were featured in the LEGO *Batman 2: DC Super Heroes* video game.

6862 Superman vs. Power Armor Lex (2012)

193

LEGO® Marvel Super Heroes

2012 WAS CERTAINLY a super-powered year, featuring not just one giant comic-book license for the LEGO Group, but two. The LEGO® Marvel Universe Super Heroes theme opened up the action-packed worlds of Marvel comics and movies to LEGO building, starting with sets based on *The Avengers* film, the *Ultimate Spider-Man* TV series, and the comic book adventures of the uncanny X-Men ●

Thor

6869 Quinjet Aerial Battle (2012)

Black Widow

Loki's scepter

Iron Man

Mini-jet drone

Detachable repulsor ray elements

Alien chariot

4529 Iron Man™ (2012) and 4597 Captain America™ (2012)

BUILDABLE CHARACTERS

The Marvel Super Heroes buildable characters line kicked off with three mighty sets: the invincible Iron Man, the star-studded Captain America, and the incredible Hulk. Instructions for super-model combinations could be downloaded from the LEGO website.

The Hulk figure could move at the shoulders and wrists.

AVENGERS ASSEMBLE!

Most of the first-year Marvel sets were inspired by the blockbuster *The Avengers* movie. The heroes' iconic vehicle was the Quinjet, a supersonic transport with adjustable wing-tips, firing flick-missiles, and a prison pod for arch-enemy Loki or his alien foot soldier. It was the only 2012 set to include superspy team member Black Widow.

6868 Hulk's Helicarrier Breakout (2012)

HULK SMASH

This interior section of S.H.I.E.L.D.'s flying helicarrier base featured an exploding containment cell for the captured Loki to escape from, launching fuel canisters, and a small jet piloted by Avengers archer Hawkeye. The star of the show, though, is the giant-sized Hulk figure!

6873 Spider-Man's Doc Ock Ambush (2012)

Spider-Man

Iron Fist

Vent for Spidey to sneak in

Doc Ock with articulated cyber-tentacles

Missile-firing octo-car

SPIDER-MAN™ RETURNS

This super villain laboratory was based on the *Ultimate Spider-Man* animated series, in which Spider-Man trained to be a better super hero. It came with new versions of Spider-Man and Doctor Octopus, and the first-ever minifigure of Spidey's fellow rookie, Iron Fist.

CAPTAIN AMERICA™

Un-frozen World War II hero Captain America raced into action on his patriotic motorcycle. The small set also included two aliens and their invasion equipment. Although there had been many LEGO shields before, Cap's decorated shield was a brand-new piece.

6865 Captain America's Avenging Cycle (2012)

X-MEN

Marvel's most famous band of mutants was represented by lone member Wolverine in this set, which pitted the quick-healing, metal-clawed hero against the master of magnetism Magneto and Deadpool, a mentally-unhinged mercenary flying his own helicopter into battle.

6866 Wolverine's Chopper Showdown (2012)

As part of the new LEGO Group policy for licensed characters, the *Spider-Man 2* minifigures had realistic skin colors instead of the classic universal yellow.

Mary Jane

Peter Parker

Spider-Man™

Aunt May

Doc Ock™

SPIDER-MAN™

The first LEGO® Spider-Man™ movie theme in 2002 was part of LEGO® Studios, with models that were designed both to build scenes from the film and to act out movie-making action stunts. One announced set, 1375 Wrestling Scene, was mysteriously never released.

1374 Green Goblin™ (2002)

Spider-Copter from 4858 Doc Ock's Crime Spree (2004)

Several *Spider-Man 2* sets were made as part of the LEGO 4 plus series for younger builders, with larger-scale "mid-figures" and construction based on bigger and fewer elements.

Not all of the *Spider-Man 2* sets came directly from scenes in the movie. This one, in which Spider-Man foils a heist by cycle-riding robbers, could happen on any day in the life of the friendly neighborhood web-slinger.

Spidey's web-line— a re-colored LEGO vine!

DIAMONDS

YARICK ST.

Cycle-jumping ramp

SPIDER-MAN™ 2

Although the LEGO Studios theme had come to an end by the time the sequel was in theaters, models based on *Spider-Man 2* were produced as their own stand-alone sets.

4853 Spider-Man's Street Chase (2004)

195

LEGO® Harry Potter™

Harry Potter™ (2004)

THE LEGO® HARRY POTTER™ theme began in 2001 with the theatrical release of *Harry Potter and the Sorcerer's Stone* and featured sets based on the entire *Harry Potter* film series. Starring the movies' characters, the models conjured an enchanted world of moving staircases, hidden rooms, and magical creatures ●

HOGWARTS™ EXPRESS

The second LEGO® model of the magic locomotive that carried Harry and his friends to school at Hogwarts was produced for the third movie, *Harry Potter and the Prisoner of Azkaban*. It was almost identical to 2001's 4708 Hogwarts Express, but had slightly fewer pieces, a smaller Hogsmeade™ train station, and minifigures with the new flesh-toned hands and faces required for licensed LEGO characters.

A motorized version with a larger station and tracks was available the same year.

4758 Hogwarts Express (2004)

Dementor™

Professor Lupin

The winged Thestral made use of a skeleton horse designed earlier by the company but never before used in sets.

Thestral

5378 Hogwarts™ Castle (2007)

HOGWARTS™ CASTLE

The buildable star of the LEGO Harry Potter theme was unquestionably Hogwarts Castle, with over a dozen different castle and classroom sets produced over the course of the series. The 2007 version was the only LEGO model released for the fifth film, *Harry Potter and the Order of the Phoenix*.

Greenhouse

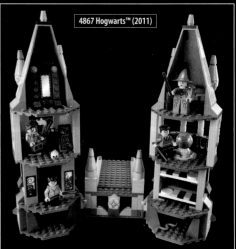

4867 Hogwarts™ (2011)

The latest brick incarnation of the famous school of wizardry included two castle towers and an exploding bridge in between.

The Mandrakes in the castle's greenhouse included their own unique minifigure heads.

Harry Potter™

Ron Weasley™

Hermione Granger™

Draco Malfoy™

Professor Dumbledore™

Professor Snape™

Professor Umbridge™

Death Eater

Hagrid™

Mandrake plant

TRIWIZARD TOURNAMENT™

When Harry took part in the Triwizard Tournament in 2005's *Harry Potter and the Goblet of Fire*, he was given the dangerous task of stealing a golden egg from a fire-breathing dragon. The LEGO version of the scene gave Harry a magnet to scoop up the egg in a flash, a catapult to "magically" launch his flying broom to him, and a spectator stand that collapsed when the enraged Hungarian Horntail pulled on its chain.

4767 Harry and the Hungarian Horntail (2005)

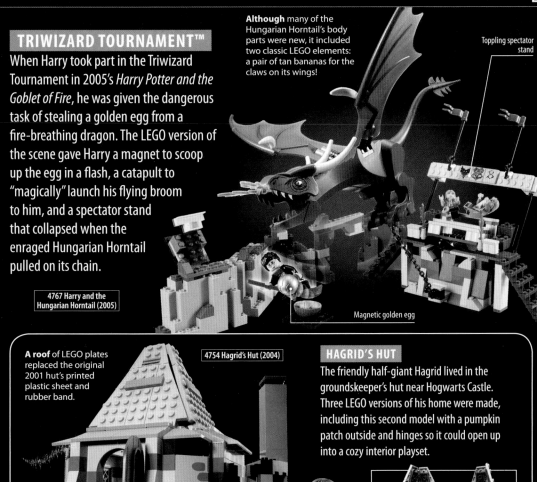

Although many of the Hungarian Horntail's body parts were new, it included two classic LEGO elements: a pair of tan bananas for the claws on its wings!

Toppling spectator stand

Magnetic golden egg

4755 Knight Bus (2004)

KNIGHT BUS™

Thinking he was being stalked by the mysterious Grim, Harry caught an emergency ride to Hogwarts aboard the Knight Bus. The set's rare purple pieces were prized among collectors. A new version of the bus was released in 2011.

A roof of LEGO plates replaced the original 2001 hut's printed plastic sheet and rubber band.

4754 Hagrid's Hut (2004)

HAGRID'S HUT

The friendly half-giant Hagrid lived in the groundskeeper's hut near Hogwarts Castle. Three LEGO versions of his home were made, including this second model with a pumpkin patch outside and hinges so it could open up into a cozy interior playset.

10217 Diagon Alley (2011)

DIAGON ALLEY™

The biggest set in the theme, the special-edition Diagon Alley featured highly detailed versions of Ollivanders Wand Shop, Borgin and Burkes, and Gringotts Wizarding Bank. It was built from 2,025 pieces and came with 11 minifigures.

YOU-KNOW-WHO

When Lord Voldemort™ made his long-awaited return to the land of the living in *Harry Potter and the Goblet of Fire*, the 548-piece LEGO Graveyard Duel model captured the fateful scene of the evil wizard's resurrection and confrontation with Harry. The set had opening graves, secret compartments, snakes, skeletons, tombstones, a spooky bat-filled tree, a crypt with an underground tomb, caretaker's tools, and even a garbage can.

Opening grave

Tom Riddle's tomb

Pop-up skeleton

Lucius Malfoy with reversible Death Eater face

4766 Graveyard Duel (2005)

The resurrected, snake-eyed Lord Voldemort had a glow-in-the-dark head.

SpongeBob (2006)

Nickelodeon™ Sets

IN THE US AND ABROAD, Nickelodeon™ is one of the most popular children's television networks. With its imaginative shows and world-famous original characters, "Nick" proved the perfect partner for the LEGO Group. Their team-up has led to a series of themes for fun-loving builders ●

The LEGO® SpongeBob™ minifigure's pants were even squarer than usual!

Antenna eyelashes

Spinning eyes

SPONGEBOB SQUAREPANTS™

When the evil Plankton took over SpongeBob's brain, wacky adventures were in store for Bikini Bottom's silliest citizen. The only LEGO® SpongeBob set not in minifigure scale, this buildable version stood over 11.5 in (29 cm) tall. He could spin his eyes, launch jellyfish bubbles from his mouth, and change expression from happy to sad.

Gears, controls, and a picture on the wall… it looks like Plankton's planning on staying!

Changeable mouth

Square pants

3826 Build-a-Bob (2006)

Posable arms

3834 Good Neighbors at Bikini Bottom (2009)

HOWDY, NEIGHBORS!

Like his television namesake, LEGO SpongeBob lives in a big orange pineapple under the sea. The second of two LEGO models of SpongeBob's house, this one includes a reef blower for SpongeBob, a boat with a marshmallow launcher for Patrick, and yet another headache for poor old Squidward—but at least his head is a brand-new piece this time!

LEGO SpongeBob characters come in all shapes and sizes. Gary is built out of tiny LEGO pieces, including an upside-down pair of green cherries for his eyes.

Gary the snail   SpongeBob   Patrick   Squidward

KRUSTY BUT NEVER RUSTY

SpongeBob works here at the Krusty Krab, where his boss Mr. Krabs fiercely guards the secret formula for Krabby Patties from his rival Plankton. The LEGO version had a safe for the formula, a trash bin out back, and a patty-flipping grill to toss burgers at SpongeBob's long-suffering neighbor and fellow employee, Squidward.

Krabby Patty

Plankton

THE KRUSTY KRAB

ENTER

Mr. Krabs

3825 The Krusty Krab (2006)

THE MANY FACES OF SPONGEBOB

The animated SpongeBob is one expressive fellow, so the minifigures followed suit with a whole range of zany faces. Can you spot the robot imposter?

AVATAR: THE LAST AIRBENDER™

Nickelodeon's animated martial arts adventure had many incredible locations and fantastic vehicles, but only one of each became a LEGO set. The Air Temple included an armory, catapult, disc-firing Fire Nation tank, a three-wheeled spinning lock on the gate, and a launcher to send young hero Aang flying into the air on his glider.

3828
Air Temple
(2006)

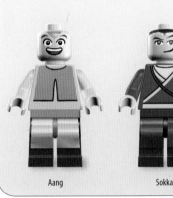

Abandoned temple of the long-vanished Airbenders.

Removable glider wings

The TV show's element-controlling powers were represented with classic LEGO pieces like Aang's transparent radar-dish air shield and the Firebender's plume of flame.

Aang with air glider staff

IRONCLAD SHIP

The scarred and exiled Prince Zuko pursued Aang and his friends aboard this mighty ironclad warship. Over 18 in (46 cm) long and 12 in (30 cm) high, the LEGO model had a fireball catapult, a furnace, and a removable prison beneath the deck, and a prow spike that swung down for boarding other ships.

Prince Zuko

Katara

Firebender

3829 Fire Nation Ship (2006)

Aang

Sokka

Momo

7333 Dora and Diego's Animal Adventure (2004)

Working "flying fox" zip-line

Jaguar cub

The LEGO Dora the Explorer sets included lots of colorful outdoor elements to build park, jungle, and island scenes.

DUPLO tree-top with building studs

DORA THE EXPLORER™

Dora is ready to explore the world with help from her cousin, Diego! The LEGO Group's first Nickelodeon™ license provided tons of new adventures for children. The LEGO® Explore series (a brief re-branding of LEGO® DUPLO®) let preschool children put together Dora and Diego's world and create adventures for them and their animal friends.

Rocking raft

Swiper the sneaky fox

Push-button sound box

The LEGO Group & Disney

LEGO Mickey Mouse (2000)

IN 1999, the LEGO Group joined with the Walt Disney Company to produce construction toys for younger builders based on some of Disney's classic characters. But those sets featuring Mickey Mouse™ and Winnie the Pooh™ were not the first team-up between the two companies, nor would they be the last: in 2010, the partnership resumed with new sets based on some of Disney's biggest action and adventure properties ●

THE FIRST EVER TOYS

The LEGO Group's very first licensed Disney products were a set of inflatable bathing rings released in 1956, featuring characters like Mickey Mouse and Lady from Lady and the Tramp. That same year, a painted wooden pull-toy of Mickey's faithful pooch Pluto was manufactured by the company's wooden toy department, along with a rifle, musket, and cabin based on Disney's new Davy Crockett film.

Pull-string attached to collar

427 Pluto pull-toy (1956)

Classic LEGO® logo

Pluto's legs moved when the wheels rolled.

The fully painted Mickey and Minnie figures could sit, stand, and move their heads and arms.

4165 Minnie's Birthday Party (2000)

MICKEY & FRIENDS

Five LEGO® sets were produced in 2000 for Disney's Mickey Mouse theme, making use of large pieces so that young builders could put them together quickly and easily. Each included a Mickey figure and one or more classic cartoon-styled vehicles. In this set, decorative stickers transformed bricks into letters, animal friends, and even a slice of birthday

Extra pieces

Mickey's jalopy

4178 Mickey's Fishing Adventure (2000)

FISHY TALE

This bucket set included Mickey, Minnie, a shark, and about 100 elements for plenty of water-themed adventures. One of the suggested models was a paddleboat that might have been inspired by the 1928 Disney cartoon *Steamboat Willie*, Mickey Mouse's very first with sound.

2594 Disney's Baby Mickey & Minnie (2000)

Three sets were produced under the LEGO® Baby brand for infants aged six to 24 months. They featured one-piece baby versions of Mickey and Minnie and big, simple, stackable bricks.

WINNIE THE POOH™

With 15 sets released between 1999 and 2001, the LEGO® DUPLO® Winnie the Pooh™ series was the longest-lasting line produced under the original Disney license. The sets for toddlers aged two and up (plus one for 18-month-olds) included posable Winnie the Pooh figures and stationary versions of his friends Piglet, Eeyore, and Tigger. In 2011, three new DUPLO sets were released, featuring a redesigned Pooh along with his house, a picnic, and a fishing expedition for the newly-articulated Tigger and Piglet.

Treetop elements

As everyone knows, Winnie the Pooh lives under the name of Mr. Sanders—literally! This 2011 set had an opening door, a slide, plenty of honey, and even a clear yellow DUPLO brick with a bee printed on it.

Bee brick

Piglet can sit and move his arms

DUPLO brick table

Front door

5947 Winnie the Pooh's House (2011)

Eeyore with DUPLO stud for building or riding

Pot of honey

2979 Winnie the Pooh Build and Play (2001)

This unique set included a Pooh figure and a circular pop-up playset with dividers that recreated four different parts of the Hundred Acre Wood.

TOY STORY™ & CARS™

Little kids could get in on the big-screen adventure with these DUPLO sets based on the worlds of the *Toy Story* and *Cars* movies. They included many of the same characters and locations as the models for bigger builders, but with all the fun and chunky charm of LEGO DUPLO bricks and building.

Sheriff's office

5657 Jessie's Round-Up (2010)

5817 Agent Mater (2011)

Heroic horse Bullseye had a big stud on his back to let DUPLO figures ride him around.

Agent Mater came apart for extra building fun. His child-safe firing cannon could knock over the included target bricks.

6151 Sleeping Beauty's Room (2012)

DISNEY PRINCESS

2012 saw the release of LEGO DUPLO sets based on the Disney Princesses. Snow White and Cinderella joined Sleeping Beauty, whose fairy-tale room came with a bed so she could get plenty of rest.

Disney Action

FROM THE DESERTS of ancient Persia to the stormy seas of the Caribbean, these LEGO® themes captured some of the most exciting moments of movie action ever shown on screen. They also provided fans with new parts, and new minifigures of many of their favorite movie stars and monsters ●

YO HO, YO HO!

Disney, action, and pirates—could there be a more classic combination for a new LEGO theme? First teased with a Jack Sparrow minifigure hidden in a *Prince of Persia* display at San Diego Comic-Con 2010, the LEGO *Pirates of the Caribbean™* line of ships and playsets sailed into port the next year in time for the fourth film in the blockbuster series. Also released were a video game and a series of animations detailing Captain Jack's tall tales.

FAMOUS FIEND

The *Queen Anne's Revenge™* was the infamous real-world pirate Blackbeard's ship. Of course, the real Blackbeard probably couldn't turn pirates into zombies, or control his ship's rigging with a magic sword.

Blackheard's pirate flag

Main mast

Fearsome crimson sails

Firing cannon

Several different costume variations for Captain Jack were made. This one had cannibal king paint on both faces of his reversible head.

4182 The Cannibal Escape (2011)

A PIRATE'S LIFE

Full of action features like runaway mill wheels, launching nets, rotating cave walls, and collapsing lighthouse towers, the LEGO *Pirates of the Caribbean* theme packed as much of the thrills and fun of the celebrated movies as possible into its models. Printed and painted elements abounded, from Captain Jack Sparrow's elaborate hat and hair pieces to his ever-present compass.

A colorful collection of characters included pirates, zombie pirates, and mutated sea-life pirates.

Hadras from 4183 The Mill (2011)

Removable captain's cabin

4195 Queen Anne's Revenge™ (2011)

Skeleton ship details

The ship featured three brick-firing cannons, a working anchor, and seven minifigures including Blackbeard™ and his daughter Angelica (who has a bone to pick with Jack), plus a tiny Jack Sparrow voodoo doll!

PAINT IT BLACK

The latest set created for the theme was the long-awaited *Black Pearl*, Captain Jack's beloved (and frequently misplaced) pirate ship. Released in November 2011, it was built from 804 pieces.

4184 *The Black Pearl* (2011)

The set included Jack Sparrow, Will Turner, Joshamee Gibbs, and exclusive figures of Davy Jones, Bootstrap Bill, and the shark-headed Maccus, plus the black figurehead on its prow.

THE ROGUE RETURNS

Accompanying sets based on the original movie trilogy were models for the new *Pirates of the Caribbean: On Stranger Tides*. One depicted Captain Jack's attempt to escape from King George's soldiers in a frantic chase through the streets of London.

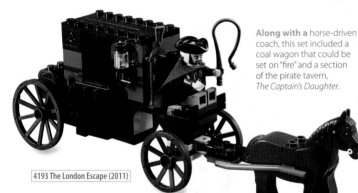

Along with a horse-driven coach, this set included a coal wagon that could be set on "fire" and a section of the pirate tavern, *The Captain's Daughter*.

4193 *The London Escape* (2011)

FINAL BATTLE

The Fountain of Youth model let you recreate the climactic duel between Blackbeard and Jack's sometimes-foe, sometimes-ally Captain Barbossa, who had gained a new peg-leg since his last minifigure appearance.

4192 Fountain of Youth (2011)

An interesting piece was the reverse-flowing waterfall that hid the fountain's sanctuary, printed on a curtain-like plastic sheet.

PRINCE OF PERSIA™

The first action theme produced under the partnership was for the 2010 film *Prince of Persia: The Sands of Time*. Based on the best-selling series of video games, the movie chronicled the quest of Prince Dastan to clear his name and save his empire from a plot to use the fabled Sands of Time to rewrite

Collapsing balcony

Dastan is tricked into attacking the sacred city of Alamut. During the battle, he gains possession of a mysterious dagger.

Princess Tamina

The Dagger of Time

7571 The Fight for the Dagger (2010)

WILD RACE

Sets were based on scenes from throughout the movie. In this one, Dastan takes part in a chaotic, high-speed ostrich race. The model also included the wily Sheik Amar, a spectator stand, and a weapons rack.

7572 Quest Against Time (2010)

7570 The Ostrich Race (2010)

NO TIME TO LOSE

In the catacombs beneath Alamut, Dastan has to run a gauntlet of traps to reach the Sandglass of Time before his treacherous uncle Nizam.

ALAMUT CITY

The largest set in the theme depicted the walled city and palace of Alamut, where several of the movie's major battle scenes took place. The gate was defended by catapults and barrels of boiling oil. Studs on the sides of the walls helped builders recreate Dastan's unique parkour-based fighting style by letting him run and jump on vertical surfaces.

7573 Battle of Alamut (2010)

Buzz Lightyear minifigure fits inside cockpit

7593 Buzz's Star Command Spaceship (2010)

Disney Adventure

THE WALT DISNEY COMPANY is traditionally known for its all-ages animated movies and family adventures, and its modern partnership with computer animation studio Pixar has produced more than a dozen beloved feature films. At the top of the list are the *Toy Story*™ and *Cars*™ movies, some of the most popular and successful animated pictures of all time ●

OFF-SCREEN ADVENTURES

Not all of the *Toy Story* sets depicted events directly from the movies. Buzz's spaceship was based on the outer-space adventures of the "real" Buzz Lightyear, Space Ranger, while Woody's western town represented the world of the fictional old-time *Woody's Roundup* TV series, complete with co-stars Jessie, Bullseye, and Stinky Pete the Prospector.

Gold mine

TOY STORY™

In the world of the *Toy Story* movies, your playthings are secretly alive, and have their own adventures whenever you're out of the room. Woody, Buzz, and many of their friends (and foes) starred in LEGO® sets based on the first two films at the beginning of 2010.

PIZZA PLANET

The Pizza Planet restaurant chain's delivery truck cameos in almost every Pixar movie. The exclusive pizza-launching LEGO version recreated the scene from *Toy Story 2* when the toy heroes try to drive the human-scaled vehicle, with comic results.

7598 Pizza Planet Truck Rescue (2010)

7594 Woody's Roundup! (2010)

Stinky Pete

Jessie and Woody had extra-long arms and legs

7591 Construct-a-Zurg (2010)

BUILDABLE FIGURES

For kids who wanted something bigger to play with, there were constructable action figures of Buzz Lightyear and his arch-nemesis, the Evil Emperor Zurg. Both included a green alien sidekick.

7595 Army Men on Patrol (2010)

ARMY OF FUN

The minifigure Army Men were much more posable than the classic toys they were based on. Containing a medic, a minesweeper, two riflemen, and a Jeep, this set was small and inexpensive enough that you could buy extras and build your own toy army.

7592 Construct-a-Buzz (2010)

Buzz had moving wings, a retractable visor, and a flick-fire missile to simulate his laser.

At 9 in (23 cm) tall, the special-edition Zurg had a rotating waist and a sphere-shooting cannon.

BAD BEAR

Toy Story 3 sets were released in the summer of 2010. To avoid spoiling secret villain Lotso's true role, his minifigure's official description made him sound like a new friend for Buzz and Woody.

7789 Lotso's Dump Truck (2010)

TRAIN CHASE

Recreating the thrilling opening sequence of *Toy Story 3*, this 584-piece set let you build a toy steam locomotive with three magnetically-linked cars. It included an exclusive version of piggy bank pal Hamm play-acting as the evil Dr. Porkchop. His hat and cork were both removable.

One-piece head and hat

7597 Western Train Chase (2010)

Evil Dr. Porkchop

Rex the friendly dinosaur

Buzz Lightyear to the rescue!

Bulleye's legs are posable

Slammer-powered car launcher

Combination gas station/carwash

CARS™

First launched as a line of LEGO® DUPLO® sets in 2010, the *Cars* movies made their System-scale debut in 2011. Models were based on characters and locations from both films, including Radiator Springs's V8 Café, which came with a whopping six characters from the original movie: Lightning McQueen, Mater, Sarge, Fillmore, Sally, and café owner Flo.

SPY GAMES

In *Cars™ 2*, tow truck Mater is mistakenly recruited as a spy to help take down a globe-spanning plot. The LEGO theme echoed the movie's international flavor with models set in Japan and England, where the Big Bentley clock tower had a flying-car launcher.

8487 Flo's V8 Café (2011)

COOL CARS

To reflect the hi-tech gear and gadgets used by the characters in the sequel, sets included a variety of equipment built into their car models, from Agent Mater's jet thrusters to superspy Finn McMissile's propeller-powered submarine mode. Other sets let you assemble McMissile in standard, hydrofoil, flight, weaponized, and police car disguise configurations.

8426 Escape at Sea (2011)

8639 Big Bentley Bust Out (2011)

BIG WHEELS

Several detailed, larger-scale character sets were released, too. The 242-piece Ultimate Build Lightning McQueen gave the starring race car gold wheel hubs and his World Grand Prix decorations. Mater and rival F-1 racer Francesco were also made in Ultimate Build scale. Lightning and Francesco included pit crew forklift helpers, while Mater had removable spy gear.

8484 Ultimate Build Lightning McQueen (2011)

LEGO® *The Lord of the Rings*™

FANS ALL OVER the world had demanded it for years, and in 2012 they finally got their wish with the first LEGO® sets based on the epic *The Lord of the Rings* movie trilogy. From Gandalf's arrival in the Shire to the battle of *Helm's Deep*, you could collect the entire Fellowship of the Ring and take them on adventures through *Middle-earth*. And that was only the beginning, because LEGO® *The Hobbit: An Unexpected Journey* sets were just behind ●

Rohan™ soldier

Éomer™

9472 Attack on Weathertop™ (2012)

WORLD OF MIDDLE-EARTH

The LEGO® *The Lord of the Rings*™ theme featured many new elements, including weapons, armor, and horses that could rear up on their hind legs... not to mention the golden One Ring itself, which could fit around the top of a minifigure's hand. Its brick-built locations were full of bold heroes, savage enemies, and interactive details that really captured the action and atmosphere of the movies.

THE RING AND THE WRAITHS

Entrusted with the legendary One Ring, *Frodo* is menaced by fearsome, faceless *Ringwraiths* among the ruins of *Weathertop*. Only the blazing torch and sword of the ranger *Aragorn* can save him. This set's model of an ancient stone fortress included fellow hobbit Merry and opened on hinges so you could explore its interior.

9471 Uruk-hai™ Army (2012)

Armored hook-launching ballista

MINES OF MORIA

The Moria Orcs wielded cruel and jagged weapons and shields.

On their quest to destroy the Ring and end the Dark Lord Sauron's power, the Fellowship are attacked by a horde of Orcs and a giant Cave Troll. The LEGO set recreated the battle in *Balin's Tomb*, complete with a skeleton for Pippin to knock down a well and cause all the trouble.

Cave Troll with club

Book of Mazarbul

9473 The Mines of Moria™ (2012)

The Hornburg tower

9474 The Battle of Helm's Deep™ (2012)

Siege ladder hooks onto wall

Uruk-hai bomb in culvert

Fearless Dwarf Gimli

Haldir the Wood Elf

Besieged by an army of ferocious *Uruk-hai* warriors, the defenders of *Helm's Deep* fight back in *The Two Towers*. An additional set let you add to the model's walls and armies.

Berserker Uruk-hai™

Gollum was an entirely new minifigure with a unique crouching body and jointed arms. A levered catapult let you fling him into action.

Crank under abdomen extends or retracts web-line

Halberd weapon

Uruk-hai™ helm

9471 Uruk-hai™ Army (2012)

9470 Shelob™ Attacks (2012)

FRIEND OR FOE?

Desperate to get his hands on the Ring, the treacherous *Gollum* leads *Frodo* and his companion *Samwise Gamgee* into a deadly trap in *The Return of the King*. The giant spider *Shelob* had eight posable legs and a web-line that could wrap around poor *Frodo*, whose minifigure included an alternate face to show him paralyzed by her sting.

ARMY OF EVIL

Created in the Orc Forge (which was released as an exclusive LEGO set), *Uruk-hai* are tougher than normal Orcs and have no fear of daylight. Several varieties of Uruk-hai minifigures were made, including warriors, a berserker, and their general, *Lurtz*.

207

LEGOLAND®

LEGO® FANS have always constructed their own LEGO worlds, but until the first LEGOLAND® theme park opened in Billund, Denmark, in 1968, they never had one big enough to walk around in! Today, LEGOLAND Parks, Discovery Centers, water parks, and hotels can be found all around the world. Filled with the miniature cities and monuments of MINILAND, thrilling LEGO themed rides, enormous brick-built sculptures, and spectacular, specially built models, they're both a fan and a family's dream come true ●

A 2012 map of LEGOLAND® Billund guides visitors to all of the theme park's areas and attractions, including MINILAND, Pirate Land, Adventure Land, the Imagination Zone, LEGOREDO® Town, the new Polar Land, and much more.

Park Design

AS THE LEGO® BRICK'S fame grew in the 1960s, so did the number of visitors to the company's Billund headquarters. When Godtfred Kirk Christiansen realized that more than 20,000 people a year were coming to admire the elaborate LEGO sculptures that decorated the factories, he decided to create an outdoor display. Envisioned as a small garden, it became the first ever LEGOLAND® Park ●

THE FIRST PARK

The original LEGOLAND Park opened on June 7, 1968 and quickly became Denmark's most popular tourist attraction outside its capital city, Copenhagen. It originally took up nearly 125,000 sq ft (38,100 sq m), but doubled in size over the next 30 years.

PARKS AROUND THE WORLD

With the success of LEGOLAND® Billund came the idea to create more parks in other countries. LEGOLAND Parks opened in Windsor, UK, in 1996, followed by California, USA, in 1999, Günzburg, Germany, in 2002, Florida, USA, in 2011, and Malaysia in 2012.

Based on a LEGOLAND® Windsor model, these concept sketches depict a moving, water-shooting dinosaur sculpture designed for the main entrance at LEGOLAND® California.

Brick-built dinosaur sculpture

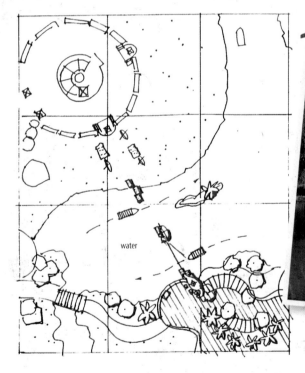

water

The final display closely resembles the concept artwork, except that the dinosaur construction worker has changed from green to red.

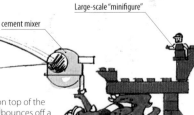

Animation

Family boat ride

Large-scale "minifigure"

cement mixer

A construction worker on top of the dinosaur blasts water that bounces off a cement mixer to splash passing boats.

RIDES AND ATTRACTIONS

The LEGOLAND Parks are filled with constantly changing themed areas, interactive rides, and seasonal events, from LEGOLAND Windsor's transport-themed Traffic section with its Driving School and Fire Academy rides, and the wild rides and coasters of LEGOLAND® California's Dino Island and Castle Hill, to LEGOLAND® Deutschland's Imagination area featuring the Build & Test Center, Kids' Power Tower, and Pedal-A-Car ride.

Each car of the Pedal-A-Car attraction at LEGOLAND Deutschland holds four passengers.

LEGOLAND® Malaysia is the sixth LEGOLAND Park and the first to be built in Asia. Divided into seven themed areas, its 76 acres of adventure are packed full of more than 40 rides, shows, and attractions.

Under construction (left), the elevated ride track circles around LEGOLAND Deutschland's Imagination section, giving riders a spectacular view of the Park.

As they pass over MINILAND, Pedal-A-Car passengers can look down over a scale model of Bavaria's Neuschwanstein Castle built from more than 300,000 LEGO bricks.

LEGOLAND® Florida, the world's largest LEGOLAND Park, incorporates the gardens from the former Cypress Gardens amusement park. A water park was added in 2012.

MAKING MODEL MAGIC

Around every corner of a LEGOLAND Park is an amazing LEGO sculpture. The Parks are home to thousands of models of buildings, people, and animals, built from millions of LEGO bricks. Each LEGOLAND Park has its own team of model designers and builders who take care of the Park's existing sculptures and create all-new ones.

LEGOLAND Deutschland model builders built a scale replica of Munich Airport entirely out of LEGO bricks!

A LEGOLAND model builder assembles a 1:20-scale model of an Airbus A380 passenger airliner in the German Park's workshop.

Finishing touches are added on-site to LEGOLAND Deutschland's MINILAND Munich Airport display. Every morning, the model builders tour the Park to check, repair, and clean all of its models.

MINILAND Areas

The heart of every LEGOLAND® Park is its unique MINILAND display. Constructed out of millions of bricks by the LEGOLAND Master Model Builders and populated by brick-built citizens, these constantly evolving and expanding 1:20-scale dioramas let visitors explore famous landmarks from their home countries and around the world, all in one amazing place ●

BILLUND

At the original MINILAND in LEGOLAND® Billund, 20 million bricks have been used to create scenes of European life, with sections representing Denmark, Sweden, Germany, Norway, Finland, and more. Passengers on the Miniboat ride sail past Thailand's Wat Phra Keo Temple, and Park guests can take in the entire amazing display from the top of a rotating panoramic tower.

WINDSOR

Almost 40 million bricks went into building LEGOLAND® Windsor's MINILAND, which features city scenes from London and across Europe and the US, complete with traffic noises and moving cars, buses, and trains. A newer addition is a space exploration section with a 1:20 scale version of America's Cape Canaveral and the John F. Kennedy Space Center.

Famous London landmarks at MINILAND UK include Canary Wharf, 30 St. Mary's Axe, the Lloyd's Building, City Hall, and the Millennium Bridge.

Copenhagen Nyhavn Harbor's red roofs are perfectly reproduced in LEGO® bricks.

The largest part of MINILAND Billund is the Port of Copenhagen, with moving miniature ships that travel 8,500 nautical miles a year.

MALAYSIA

The centerpiece of the new LEGOLAND® Malaysia is its spectacular MINILAND display, which features scaled replicas of famous Asian towns and landscapes, assembled from over 25 million LEGO bricks with great care and detail.

Motion technology lets the people, animals, cars, ships, trains, and airplanes of LEGOLAND Malaysia's MINILAND move at the touch of a button, together with location-appropriate background sounds.

GÜNZBURG

MINILAND at LEGOLAND® Deutschland includes miniature models of Berlin (like the Reichstag), the financial district of Frankfurt, a church and dairy from a Swabian village, Neuschwanstein Castle, and Munich's famous airport and Allianz Arena. The Park's Venice display contains St. Mark's Cathedral and the Doge's Palace, while canals, drawbridges, and turning windmills adorn the Netherlands area. Attendees can interact with the 25-million-brick world by pressing buttons and moving joysticks to bring its intricate scenes to life.

An evening stroll in the Swiss city of Lucerne reveals glowing electric lights inside the miniature buildings and street lamps.

Miniature divers are captured in mid-leap (and mid-cannonball) at a Berlin swimming pool in MINILAND Deutschland. The swimmers and sunbathers may be plastic, but the water is real.

FLORIDA

LEGOLAND® Florida's display, known as MINILAND USA, includes models of Daytona International Speedway; a pirate battle at Pirate Shores; and sections of Florida, California, Las Vegas, Washington DC, and New York City, with such sights as Times Square, the Empire State Building, and the Bronx Zoo.

The Capitol Building and the Statue of Liberty together? Only at MINILAND USA!

500 photos from every angle were taken to get the details of San Francisco's famous Steiner Street houses exactly right.

Realistically decorated gabled roof

Victorian clapboard architecture

CARLSBAD

At LEGOLAND® California, mini-ice skaters enjoy a New York winter in Central Park, and New Orleans comes alive at Halloween with a cemetery filled with spooky skeletons. MINILAND Las Vegas has hotels, a wedding chapel, and a working monorail, and giant miniature crowds gather on the steps of the Capitol Building in Washington DC every four years for the inauguration of the next President of the 23 million bricks of MINILAND.

Watch out for the moving cable cars! A LEGOLAND Master Model Builder works on a street scene in the MINILAND San Francisco display.

LEGO® *Star Wars*® MINILAND

It took the LEGOLAND® Model Builders 143 hours and 19, 200 pieces to design and build the MINILAND *Millennium Falcon*™.

TATOOINE™

In the *Star Wars* Episode IV display set on the desert planet of Tatooine, visitors can tour the Mos Eisley spaceport and watch the animated band play inside the Cantina where Luke Skywalker and Obi-Wan Kenobi first met Han Solo — currently being cornered by the bounty hunter Greedo — and his loyal co-pilot Chewbacca.

The *Star Wars* MINILAND models were initially developed by eight model designers and two animation electricians at LEGOLAND® Deutschland.

MINILAND areas usually represent locations from the real world, but that all changed in 2011 when the California, Billund, and Deutschland LEGOLAND® Parks opened the world's first Star Wars® MINILAND displays! Built out of more than 1.5 million LEGO® bricks, each attraction features seven different scenes from the Star Wars® movies and The Clone Wars TV series ●

The Theed Royal Palace is built out of more than 15,000 LEGO bricks

Cliff-side tower

Statues of famous Naboo philosophers

Green tile roof

Theed Hangar

In a climactic scene from *Star Wars* Episode I, the battle droid forces of the Trade Federation march into battle against the *Gungan* army on Naboo, with the capital city of Theed in the background.

Anakin Skywalker, Obi-Wan Kenobi, Qui-Gon Jinn, and Darth Maul can all be found inside the Theed Hangar.

Fambaa with deflector shield generator

Gungan battle wagon

Gungan "bongo" sub

I was expecting someone... a little taller

NEW ARRIVALS

The original California *Star Wars* MINILAND display was updated in 2012 when new models were added to each of the seven scenes, including a Jawa sandcrawler on Tatooine, a Rebel ion cannon in the Episode V Hoth diorama, and an immense Opee Sea Killer from Naboo's aquatic core.

The Opee's prey-catching tongue has snared a fleeing Gungan sub, which was built with multicolored lights in front.

AROUND THE GALAXY

A fourth LEGO® Star Wars® MINILAND was added in 2012 at LEGOLAND Windsor Resort in the UK. As the first indoor MINILAND at a LEGOLAND Park, it features 2,000 LEGO models built at a 1:20 scale and takes visitors on a chronological tour of the Star Wars® saga with immersive special effects like sound, climate changes, and video.

Darth Vader came face to helmeted face with himself at the new MINILAND *Star Wars* Gallery, which features 3 foot (0.9 m) tall LEGO brick minifigures of famous characters from the saga.

Repulsorlift AATs reinforce the droid army

Battle droids deploy from a Trade Federation MTT

The displays come to life with button-activated movement, lights, and sound effects straight from the movies.

OPENING DAY

Actress Carrie Fisher (Princess Leia) made a special appearance at the grand opening of LEGOLAND California's *Star Wars* MINILAND on March 31, 2011. Costumed characters and voice actors from *The Clone Wars* also attended.

A young fan used a lightsaber to break the ribbon and officially open the attraction.

Allianz Arena

No pressure... I'm only being watched by 30,000 fans!

PROUDLY DISPLAYED in MINILAND at LEGOLAND® Deutschland in Günzburg, Germany, is the Allianz Arena, one of the biggest LEGO® buildings in the world. Constructed from more than a million LEGO bricks, the 1:50-scale model of Munich's famous soccer stadium is 16.5 ft (5 m) long, 15 ft (4.5 m) wide, and 3.3 ft (1 m) high, and weighs in at 1.5 tons ●

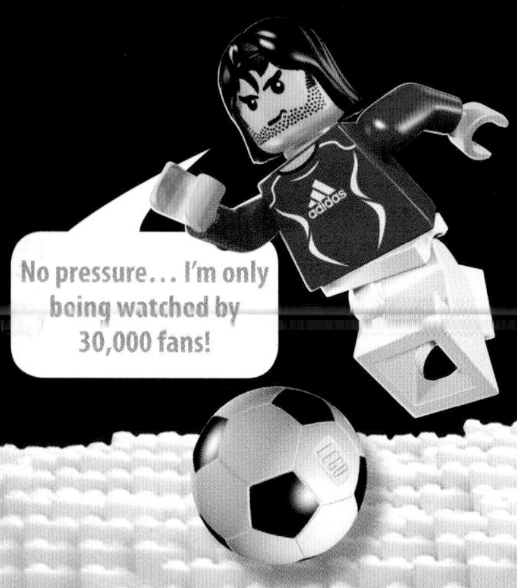

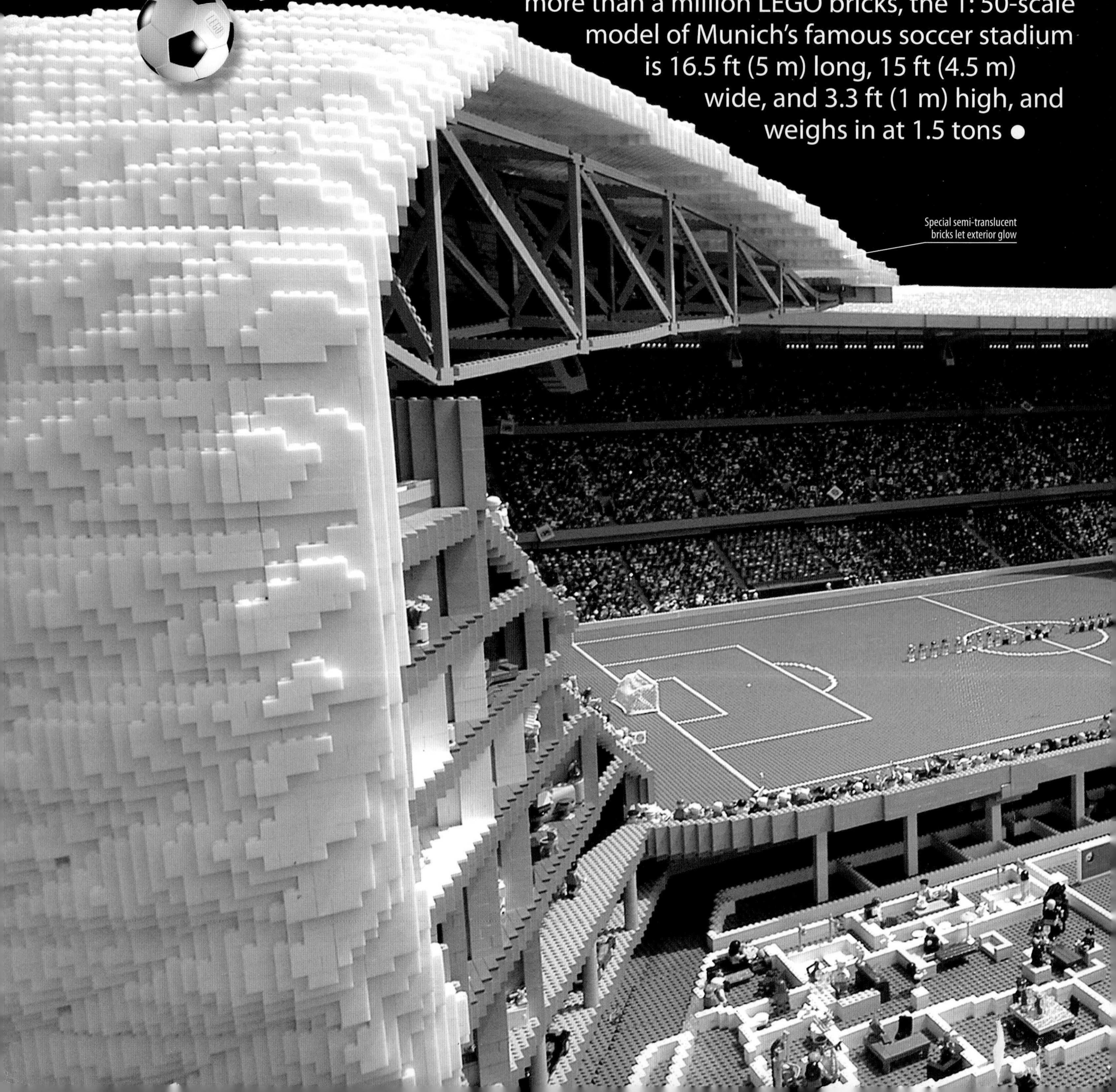

Special semi-translucent bricks let exterior glow

Even at its smaller than MINILAND-standard minifigure scale, the arena model is enormous next to a pair of LEGOLAND Deutschland's smaller visitors. Button controls on the nearby columns activate special moving features inside the model.

When the sun sets and night falls, 5,000 LEDs (Light-Emitting Diodes) illuminate the MINILAND Allianz Arena in red or blue to represent the colors of the Bayern Munich and 1860 Munich soccer teams—just like the real thing!

30,000 minifigure spectators

Luxury VIP suites

Stadium cafeteria

Soccer fans enter above the four-level parking garage

MAKING A STADIUM

Each minifigure in the bleachers and on the playing field was posed and placed by hand before the model's first appearance on May 12th, 2005. Park visitors received an exclusive LEGO brick to commemorate the occasion.

A LEGO Master Model Builder adds finishing touches to the pitch in the LEGOLAND workshop.

Discovery Centers

VISITING A LEGOLAND® Discovery Center is like jumping into the world's biggest box of LEGO® bricks. With locations open in Germany, the USA, the UK, and Japan, plus even more on the way, these big indoor attractions feature plenty of LEGO themed fun, including MINILAND displays, 4D cinemas, interactive rides, party rooms, school workshops, and much more.

A giraffe built out of LEGO bricks welcomes visitors to the USA's first Discovery Center just outside of Chicago. They'll find more wildlife like snakes, parrots, and monkeys at the Jungle Adventure Trail inside, along with other curious characters and a quiz to unlock the jungle's hidden secrets.

PICTURE THIS...

The first LEGOLAND Discovery Center opened in Berlin, Germany, in 2007. But before a Discovery Center can be built, it first has to be designed. Concept images help to create the latest additions to the LEGOLAND family.

Concepts show the development of the Factory Tour and LEGO Friends areas at the Chicago Discovery Center. A visit will reveal the difference between ideas and reality!

DRAGON RIDE

At the Berlin Discovery Center, kids can climb aboard a giant green dragon for a twisting, turning ride through a medieval castle full of moving LEGO characters and models. Try to spot the red dragon hidden somewhere along the way.

I didn't keep my hands inside the dragon ride, so the King and Queen sent me to the tickle torture room!

MODEL WORKSHOP

A real live LEGOLAND Master Model Builder hosts the Discovery Center's Model Builders Workshop, where young LEGO fans can get a hands-on tutorial from the experts and learn how to create their very own brick masterpieces.

Today's new generation of LEGO builders might just become tomorrow's new generation of LEGO Master Builders!

MINILAND AREAS

Every good LEGOLAND experience needs its iconic MINILAND! At the Chicago/Schaumburg Discovery Center, the main attraction is a miniature scale model of Chicago built from nearly 1.5 million LEGO bricks. Filled with lights and sound, the city is made up of models ranging from a parking meter constructed from only three tiny pieces to the gigantic Willis Tower, built from 190,000 bricks and weighing in at over 200 lbs (90.7 kg).

4D MOVIES

Hold on tight, because four-dimensional LEGO films pop right off the screen at the LEGOLAND Discovery Center four-dimensional Cinema, with state-of-the-art 3D special effects and an interactive theater environment guaranteed to keep audiences on the edge of their seats.

Chicago's Navy Pier shoreline on Lake Michigan, complete with its famous Ferris wheel and carousel, is captured in bricks of all shapes and colors.

SOFT PLAY ZONE

Need to let off some steam? Kids can get physical in the Soft Play Zone, full of stackable, oversized LEGO bricks, a multi-colored jungle gym, and a big climbing wall. It's excitement, entertainment, and exercise all rolled into one.

You've never played with LEGO bricks like these ones before!

Safety helmet

Every stage of manufacturing is on display on the LEGO Factory Tour.

Quality control worker

FACTORY TOUR

At the Factory Tour, visitors get a close-up look at the process by which LEGO bricks are made, from the raw materials all the way to the colorful finished product. You can even get an exclusive LEGO Factory brick to take home as a special souvenir!

EGO Factory brick

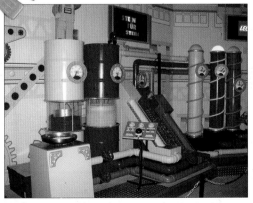

The factory comes alive with moving machines, animated workers, and authentic sound effects.

A LEGO® World

FROM INTERNATIONAL fan clubs to action-packed video games, from minifigure movies to artists' studios, the LEGO® brick has definitely made the leap from simple plastic construction toy to global phenomenon. Every day, people around the world are finding new ways to move beyond the instruction booklets and make their passion for LEGO building a part of their lives. Read on to discover how some of them show off and share their love of imagination, creativity, and that famous little brick ●

Soft, bouncy
outer layer

Four red LEGO
studs per side

The LEGO Dice
(technically a die)
can be customized
for use in different
games.

LEGO® Dice from 3841
Minotaurus (2009)

Swap tiles to change
the game

LEGO® Games

ALTHOUGH LICENSED LEGO® games have existed for years, it wasn't until 2009 that game-playing was able to fully capture the fun and imagination of LEGO building. That's when the company launched LEGO Games, a line of tabletop games that players can assemble out of LEGO bricks, play together with their friends and family, and then—if they want to—change the pieces around to make up completely new games of their own ●

MICROFIGURES

With the new gaming system came a new type of LEGO character: the microfigure! Standing a miniscule two bricks tall, microfigures are single-piece game tokens with printed details to give them personality. They can connect to LEGO bricks on the top and bottom.

Microfigures from 3841 Minotaurus (2009)

LEGO® WORLDS

Some LEGO Games take place inside the familiar worlds of the LEGO play themes. In the City Alarm game, players become LEGO City Police officers or robbers in a chase through a micro-sized LEGO City that includes a lighthouse, a coffee shop, and even a pizzeria.

3865 City Alarm (2012)

GUESS THE MODEL

In Creationary, you roll the LEGO Dice to select a category of vehicles, buildings, nature, or things, and then build your assigned object from a randomly picked card using a collection of 338 LEGO pieces… all while your fellow players try to guess what you are making. A 2011 booster pack added more cards, categories, and pieces.

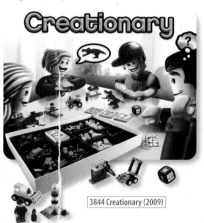

3844 Creationary (2009)

The funny thing with Creationary is that if you are really good, people will guess your model before you get to finish building it!

3843 Ramses Pyramid (2009)

Created by famous board game designer Reiner Knizia, Ramses Pyramid won a Toy Innovation 2009 award. A sequel, Ramses Return, came out in 2011.

PYRAMID OF PERIL

The heroes of LEGO Pharaoh's Quest and the Adventurers aren't the only ones who have to deal with troublesome mummy kings. In 2009's Ramses Pyramid, groups of two to four players compete to unlock crystal-coded layers and climb to the top of the pyramid to defeat Ramses and take his golden crown.

3845 Shave A Sheep (2010)

WILD AND WOOLY

Released as Wild Wool in the USA, Shave A Sheep is an addictively simple game in which players roll the LEGO Dice to grow wool on their sheep, shave the wool that has already grown, swap sheep with another player, or send the wolf to scare off all of an opponent's wool.

Goblin General

Waterfall

When the Gobl[...]
control of Draida Bay[...]
the Barbarian and Wizar[...]
Crystal of Deflection ar[...]
the tide. HEROICA™ ga[...]
can be built together
to create an entire
game world.

Goblin Warrior

Hero Pack – don't run
out of life points!

Barbarian

3857 Draida Bay (2011)

LEGO plate sail

3848 Pirate Plank (2010)

WALK THE PLANK

Forced to walk the plank by the big-hatted captain, your job is to make your fellow buccaneers hop into the shark-filled water first and end up the last pirate standing. The LEGO designers had a lot of fun creating the game's miniature-scale pirate ship. It even has a tiny cannon!

Micro-sized pirates for
a micro-sized ship

Players are encouraged to change the rules each time they play. For example, you can let pirates hop across planks, or take the extra skull-and-crossbones tile off the sail to use on the LEGO Dice.

HEROICA™

Introduced in 2011, HEROICA is designed to make board games that can be played like video games and role-playing games. Each game pits player heroes like the Knight, Ranger, Druid, and Rogue against evil warriors and monsters in a quest to capture relics and free the world of HEROICA from darkness.

3860 Castle Fortaan (2011)

TEAM UP TO WIN

Not all LEGO Games call for head-to-head competition. In the LEGO Ninjago game, groups of two to four players can play individually as they look for hidden golden weapons, swing on ropes, and battle guards with the help of a buildable spinner—and if they find all four before the Skeleton General can steal any away, everybody wins the game at the same time!

Time to roll the bones!

3856 Ninjago (2012)

LEGO® HARRY POTTER™

The Harry Potter Hogwarts game lets you take on the role of a student wizard and race around moving staircases and secret passages, searching the classrooms to collect your homework. The first student to get back to their common room wins.

3862 Harry Potter™
Hogwarts™ (2010)

Although you play as a nameless student from one of Hogwarts' four houses, the game also comes with microfigures of Harry Potter, Hermione, Ron, Draco, and Dumbledore.

Digital Designer

THE ULTIMATE

DREAM of the LEGO® fan: to get to see your creation transformed into a real LEGO set. On the LEGO Factory and LEGO Design byME websites, builders could use a program called LEGO Digital Designer to build models on their computers, upload them to inspire other fans, and order the pieces online to build their creations in person. A few lucky fans even had their models produced and sold as official LEGO Factory sets ●

THE CONTEST

In 2005, the LEGO Group offered a challenge to the fan community: to construct micro-scale models using LEGO Digital Designer, with weekly rounds of voting to decide the winners. The highest-scoring models became the very first LEGO Factory sets.

5524 Airport (2005)

The **10 winning fan-created models** were combined into three LEGO Factory sets. They were sold online and in LEGO Brand Stores.

5526 Skyline (2005)

Detail from 5525 Amusement Park (2005)

FACTORY ORIGINALS

Every model released under the LEGO Factory brand was created by talented LEGO fans, working together with professional model designers to make sure that their creations had the stability and ease of building of all official LEGO sets.

10200 Custom Car Garage (2008)

The set included both printed instructions and a CD to help builders get started with LEGO Digital Designer.

Browse each step or animate the entire process

Fan expertise helped the Custom Car Garage make use of special building techniques seen in few other LEGO models.

Removable V8 racing engine

Current piece selection

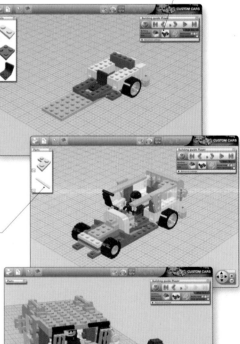

Custom decals

The complete set included three custom hot rod cars with drivers, a mechanic with tools, a racing garage with a removable roof and working repair lift, and six modular engines that could be swapped from car to car.

Classic hot rod styling

Rotating view to see every angle

MAKING TRAINS

With few LEGO Train sets released to stores these days, LEGO Factory became a haven for train builders around the world. The website featured train-building tips, fan files, and a timeline of LEGO train models from 1964 to the present, while LEGO Digital Designer included parts to help hobbyists build their perfect engines and rolling stock cars.

The many uses of robot minifigure parts

Symmetrical fore-aft design

Designed with the help of many fans, the Hobby Train included more than 1,000 pieces.

Compatible with classic 9V electric train system

10183 Hobby Train Set (2007)

The Hobby Train set came with instructions for one train model and a link to online building steps for 29 more.

SPACE MODELS

Fans of LEGO Space blasted off again with these LEGO Factory sets inspired by the classic era of the theme. Featuring the heroic Star Justice team and the evil Space Skulls, the multi-model collections were designed by a pair of adult builders.

10192 Space Skulls (2008)

The Space Skulls were skull-faced space villains with a singular technological theme.

Star Justice included spaceships, a rolling transport, a base, and a crew of astronauts and robots.

"Studs Not On Top" construction style

Spaceship from 10191 Star Justice (2008)

LEGO® DESIGN BYME

In 2009, LEGO Factory became LEGO Design byME. As before, builders could use Digital Designer to design models online, create names, packaging, and auto-generated building steps, and then purchase their creations. In 2011, Design byME added Hero Recon Team, which let you do the same with Hero Factory parts. In 2012, both ordering services closed down, although LEGO Digital Designer remained available for online use.

DESIGNING YOUR OWN MODEL

At LEGOfactory.com, users can download the free LEGO Digital Designer program and use its pre-programmed modules and a large palette of LEGO elements and colors to drag, drop, and rotate pieces as they build new models on their computer screens. When they are done, they can upload the digital model to an online gallery, design a custom box for their creation, and mail-order the pieces to be delivered to their homes.

With a huge variety of current LEGO pieces, the possibilities for what you could make in LDD are quite literally endless.

Don't see the car you want? Go online and build it yourself!

LEGO Factory packaging featured a computer-rendered image of the model with options for different backgrounds, special effects, and even comic speech balloons.

Hosted by team leader Merrick Fortis, Hero Recon Team recruited the best and the brightest fan-designed heroes. Its parts included a black and silver chest plate that could not be found in retail sets.

LEGO Island (1997)

The one that started it all, 1997's LEGO Island introduced the world to pizza delivery boy Pepper Roni, the deconstructing Brickster, and an island full of fun missions.

LEGO® Video Games

FROM LEGO® ISLAND to famous licenses like *Star Wars®* and *Batman™*, LEGO video games have been letting fans race, adventure, and play in the worlds of LEGO bricks for over 15 years. Here are some of the growing number of video game titles that have been produced so far ●

LEGO Batman 2: DC Super Heroes (2012)

BIG NAME GAMES

The LEGO Group's biggest successes in the video games field have definitely been its games based on licensed properties. With four LEGO *Star Wars* titles and other familiar names including Batman, Indiana Jones™, Harry Potter™, and Pirates of the Caribbean™, they present well-known stories and characters with a uniquely silly LEGO twist.

The whole minifigure Justice League teamed up to battle Lex Luthor and the Joker in LEGO Batman 2: DC Super Heroes.

STARTING SMALL

The earliest LEGO video games had simple concepts. LEGO Chess gave you the option of playing chess with a Western or a Pirates theme, LEGO Creator let you build with standard pieces or special "Action Bricks" and then bring your models to animated life, and in LEGO Loco you could build a town and railway system.

LEGO Chess (1998)

LEGO Creator (1998)

LEGO Loco (1998)

LEGO Friends (1999)

Although it had little to do with bricks or building, in LEGO Friends (no relation to the play theme) you arranged music and dance routines for a band of teenaged friends.

ROCK RAIDERS

Different games inspired by the LEGO Rock Raiders theme were produced for the PC and PlayStation platforms. Both gave you control of the expedition's mining team and provided you with the objective of collecting energy crystals, surviving in a hostile alien environment, and finally making your way home.

LEGO Rock Raiders (1999)

LEGO My Style Kindergarten (2000)

LEGO My Style Kindergarten used learning buddies to introduce concepts of music, math, language, and art to younger children who were just discovering those subjects in school.

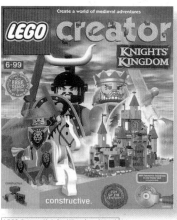

LEGO Creator Knights' Kingdom (2000)

The second LEGO Creator game let kids create a medieval kingdom—or bring it tumbling down with a Destructa Brick.

LEGO Stunt Rally (2000)

In this racing game, you could collect power-ups to help you win, or unlock elements to build your own tracks.

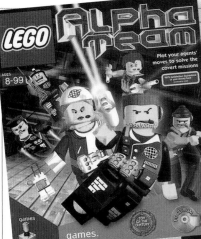

SECRET AGENT ACTION

LEGO Alpha Team had you take on the role of Dash Justice as you solved puzzles, rescued your teammates, and thwarted the world-domination plans of the evil Ogel with the help of special items like chutes, trampolines, lasers, and anti-gravity generators.

LEGO Alpha Team (2001)

No minifigures were injured in the playing of this video game, though a few Ogel-controlled drones may have been lightly singed.

Galidor: Defenders of the Outer Dimension (2002)

GALIDOR

Based on the TV series, the Galidor game let you play as hero Nick Bluetooth and travel between the worlds of the Outer Dimension, using your limb-morphing "glinching" power to help your friends and battle the evil tyrant Gorm. The game could also interact with the Kek Powerizer toy.

BIONICLE® GAMES

BIONICLE® has been the company's most prolific video game franchise to date. Its epic storyline and biomechanical heroes came to life in five different titles released between 2001 and 2006. It also had two popular online games that let players explore the island and mysteries of Mata Nui on their web browsers.

The first BIONICLE game, Tales of the Tohunga (later renamed Quest for the Toa) was produced exclusively for the Game Boy Advance in 2001. You played as a Mata Nui villager on a mission to summon the mighty Toa and save your island.

BIONICLE: Tales of the Tohunga (2001)

BIONICLE Heroes (2006)

A third-person action game, BIONICLE Heroes let you play as different Toa and use their element-controlling powers to battle the Piraka and other classic BIONICLE foes.

SEQUELS

A number of LEGO video games proved popular enough to earn follow-ups. In addition to the four LEGO Creator and five BIONICLE games, there have been three LEGO Island Games and two LEGO Battles games, including a Ninjago-themed sequel.

LEGO Racers 2 (2001)

LEGO Racers 2 had courses from the Adventurers, Arctic, and Life on Mars themes.

LEGO Island 2: The Brickster's Revenge (2001)

Pepper and the Brickster returned in LEGO Island 2 and again in Island Xtreme Stunts.

LEGO UNIVERSE

Launched in late 2010, LEGO Universe was a multiplayer online game that let LEGO fans from around the globe create their own minifigure characters and team up to quest their way through different worlds of brick-based adventures. However, lower than expected sales led to the game's demise in early 2012.

LEGO Universe (2010)

Making a LEGO® Video Game

WHAT GOES IN THE MIX? It all starts when the game developers work together with the LEGO Group to find the characters and worlds that would work best for a new game. They boil the chosen LEGO® theme down to its most important elements, and then the development and publishing teams meet to discuss the best way to blend them together ●

Every frame of character movement is created by professional animators. Sometimes they do it twice!

Each character, vehicle, or object made of LEGO elements in the game is built on a computer using a digital library of every LEGO piece ever made.

Illustrated storyboards set up the visual story and the timing of action and jokes for the game's programmers to animate later on.

Suddenly, an alarm bell sounds and Catwoman is caught in a spotlight. She looks startled.

Catwoman runs to the end of the ledge and leaps off...

Catwoman makes her escape by leaping and somersaulting across the rooftops.

EARLY CONCEPTS

Once the game's key features are decided, it's time to create a concept framework. A small team of programmers and designers works on new abilities and functions for the game, while the art and animation teams work up ideas for the characters, the environments they'll inhabit, and the game's storyline.

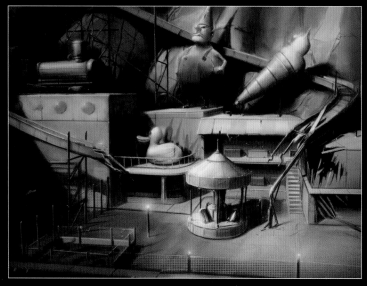

Early in the design process, concept paintings are created to help establish the mood and locations for the final game.

FROM PAPER TO PIXELS

Some of the initial illustrated designs make it into the game, while others are changed or removed if they don't seem quite right. The result is a "First Playable" prototype that lets the designers test their ideas in a simpler version of the game.

KID TESTING

Now it's time for the biggest test of all: will kids like it? Kid testing is important because new players may notice problems with gameplay that the designers have missed. Thanks to their feedback, the team can create a better game for everybody.

Nearly finished character and vehicle models are tested in a simplified game world before the final details are added.

A 3 D "wire frame" game environment.

The wire-frame filled in, with shading added.

The final rendered version has light, color, and detailed textures.

Rough wire-frame rendering

Two-Face™ and the rest of Batman's cast of characters are scripted and animated to be true to their comic selves… plus a bit of uniquely brick-ified LEGO humor.

Two faces, two personalities

FILLING IN THE DETAILS

With the overall design in place, even more animators, artists, and programmers join the team. They help create the rest of the game's environments, characters, story events, levels, and puzzles.

This **LEGO® Batman™: The Videogame** cake was created for the game's big 2008 launch party in New York City. Complete with edible sugar dough minifigures, it weighed a whopping 300 lbs!

THE PUBLICITY MACHINE

Now the game is in full production, and it's up to the marketing and promotional teams to decide how to introduce it to the world, whether through magazines, online, or other media. Screenshots, trailers, interviews, and playable demos are released in the months leading up to the game's debut to whet the public's appetite.

Every part of the game, even early packaging concepts, has to be approved by the LEGO Group and other partners.

More than 30 LEGO video games have been released since the original *LEGO Island* in 1997.

Bricks on Film

The main LEGO Studios set included a real camera, actors, a rampaging dinosaur, special effects props, a city street stage, and a minifigure film-making crew. More sets could be added to create new stunts and action scenes.

BRICKS... CAMERA... ACTION! From official LEGO® movies to themed sets that enable builders to create animations of their own, and on to an entire industry of amazing fan-made films, LEGO building and the world of movie-making have forged a beautiful friendship destined to last for years to come ●

LEGO® STUDIOS

In 2000, the LEGO Group teamed up with the world-famous director Steven Spielberg to create a new kind of LEGO theme. LEGO Studios wouldn't just be about construction and play, but making video stories using the principle of stop-motion animation. In this process, a camera takes a single picture of a model or scene, which is then moved slightly and photographed again. By repeating this over and over and then playing back the shots in sequence, the many still pictures blend together to make an animated LEGO movie.

Building for dramatic escapes

Only two sets were made for the LEGO Studios *Jurassic Park III* line, which starred adventurer Johnny Thunder in scenes based on the making of the movie. Many of the animal pieces came from the 2001 LEGO Dinosaurs theme.

1370 Raptor Rumble Studio (2001)

Movie director (with a suspicious similarity to Mr. Spielberg)

Stage light

The working LEGO Studios camera came with software and a wire to connect it to a computer for digital stop motion filming. And, of course, you could build on it, too!

Break-apart road plate and flames for disaster scenes

Attack of the Monster Tree!

All of the monster-movie minifigures (even the monsters!) had reversible faces, allowing filmmakers to change a character's mood depending on the dramatic situation.

1349 LEGO® & Steven Spielberg MovieMaker Set (2000)

T. rex stunt foot for close-up shots

Wolfman transforms with removable mask and switchable torso parts

MONSTER MOVIES

In 2002, the newest theme for LEGO Studios was monsters, monsters, monsters! With models like 1381 Vampire Crypt, 1382 Scary Laboratory, and 1383 Curse of the Pharaoh, these spooky sets let budding directors create their very own tall tales of thrills and chills.

1380 Werewolf Ambush (2002)

LEGO MOVIES

On the internet, on television, and on home video, made with old-fashioned stop-motion and cutting-edge computer animation, these movies and mini-movies are all official LEGO films created by and for the LEGO Group!

LEGO® Indiana Jones: *Raiders of the Lost Brick™* (2008)

LEGO® Batman™: *Bricks, Bats & Bad Guys* (2006)

Go Miniman Go! (2008)

LEGO® *Star Wars*®: *The Han Solo Affair* (2002)

LEGO® Spider-Man™: *The Peril of Doc Ock* (2004)

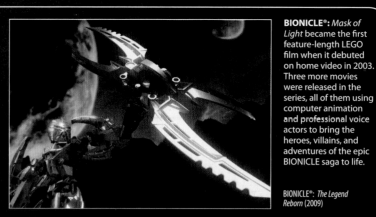

BIONICLE®: *Mask of Light* became the first feature-length LEGO film when it debuted on home video in 2003. Three more movies were released in the series, all of them using computer animation and professional voice actors to bring the heroes, villains, and adventures of the epic BIONICLE saga to life.

BIONICLE®: *The Legend Reborn* (2009)

To celebrate the theatrical release of *Star Wars:* Episode III *Revenge of the Sith*, this five-minute, computer-animated mini-movie was broadcast on television in May, 2005. Featuring a comedic look at the events of the movie, it ended with the credits rolling over a clone trooper orchestra with Darth Vader as conductor.

LEGO® *Star Wars*®: *Revenge of the Brick* (2005)

FAN FILMS

Even before LEGO Studios, fans were making their own animations starring LEGO minifigures. Often called Brickfilms, here are just a few examples of the thousands of great LEGO fan films out there!

Jane's Brai atively animated by Chris Salt by Adam Buxton.

Curt Werline's "Alabama Jones and the Lost Topping of Doom."

Steffen Troeger's "E.A.R.T.H. 2.0," an animated warning about the threat of pollution.

*The Fastest and Funniest LEGO **Star Wars** Story Ever Told* was a two-minute stop-motion short that sped through the original movie trilogy at a breakneck pace. Placed online on May the Fourth, 2010, it got over 7 million views and was followed a year later by a prequel edition.

The Adventures of Clutch Powers was the first full-length movie to feature minifigures. Released directly to video in 2010, it starred action hero and explorer Clutch Powers, a character created for the film.

LEGO Ninjago followed a two-episode miniseries in 2011 with an entire season of computer-animated TV adventures in 2012. The story followed the ninja team from trainees to full-fledged heroes.

THE PADAWAN MENACE

Written by Emmy Award-winning writer Michael Price and produced by the Australian visual effects company Animal Logic, LEGO® *Star Wars*®: *The Padawan Menace* (2011) was a 22-minute feature broadcast around the world in 2011. The DVD and Blu-ray video release included extras like the short film *Bombad Bounty* and a compilation of animations based on *The Clone Wars*.

Created in close collaboration with Lucasfilm, *The Padawan Menace* featured the voice of original actor Anthony Daniels as C-3PO and cameos by Darth Vader and George Lucas himself. The first edition video included an exclusive Young Han Solo minifigure.

Special Edition Sets

THE MODELS on these pages are all special editions, some created for milestone anniversaries, others to thrill the most experienced builders, and some just to look good. If you have any of them in your collection, consider yourself one lucky LEGO® fan ●

3443 LEGO Mosaic (2000)

Sold directly from the LEGO website between 2000 and 2005, LEGO Mosaic let builders use the online Brick-o-Lizer to transform their own photographs into step-by-step instructions for assembling mosaics out of thousands of black, white, and gray LEGO pieces.

4999 Vestas Wind Turbine (2008)

Rotating turbine

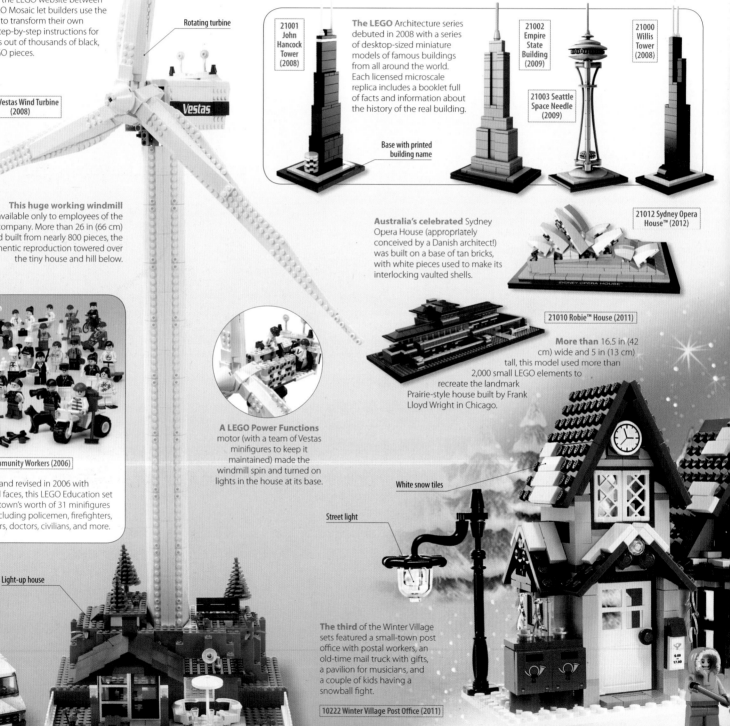

This huge working windmill was available only to employees of the Vestas company. More than 26 in (66 cm) high and built from nearly 800 pieces, the authentic reproduction towered over the tiny house and hill below.

The LEGO Architecture series debuted in 2008 with a series of desktop-sized miniature models of famous buildings from all around the world. Each licensed microscale replica includes a booklet full of facts and information about the history of the real building.

21001 John Hancock Tower (2008)

21002 Empire State Building (2009)

21003 Seattle Space Needle (2009)

21000 Willis Tower (2008)

Base with printed building name

Australia's celebrated Sydney Opera House (appropriately conceived by a Danish architect!) was built on a base of tan bricks, with white pieces used to make its interlocking vaulted shells.

21012 Sydney Opera House™ (2012)

21010 Robie™ House (2011)

More than 16.5 in (42 cm) wide and 5 in (13 cm) tall, this model used more than 2,000 small LEGO elements to recreate the landmark Prairie-style house built by Frank Lloyd Wright in Chicago.

9247 Community Workers (2006)

Released in 2005 and revised in 2006 with different pieces and faces, this LEGO Education set contained a whole town's worth of 31 minifigures with accessories, including policemen, firefighters, construction workers, doctors, civilians, and more.

A LEGO Power Functions motor (with a team of Vestas minifigures to keep it maintained) made the windmill spin and turned on lights in the house at its base.

White snow tiles

Street light

The third of the Winter Village sets featured a small-town post office with postal workers, an old-time mail truck with gifts, a pavilion for musicians, and a couple of kids having a snowball fight.

10222 Winter Village Post Office (2011)

Light-up house

Maintenance van

852293 Giant Chess Set (2007)

Brick-built figure bases

Knights' castle tower

Troll fortress

Dwarven mine

Extra weapons and shields

Decorative dragon head

Packaged in a gigantic book-shaped box, the biggest (and most expensive) LEGO chess set ever made measured 17 in (43 cm) long on each side, was built from 2,481 pieces, and included 33 figures. The board doubled as a playset, with dungeons, armories, and rolling siege-tower rooks to play with in between games.

Skeleton dungeon

King

Queen

Knight

Wizard (Bishop)

30029 Pudsey Bear (2011)

Bandage

Pudsey Bear, the mascot of the BBC Children in Need program, was created as a 95-piece LEGO set in 2011, polka-dot bandage and all. All profits from his sale were donated to charity.

5522 LEGO Golden Anniversary Set (2008)

This 2008 creative building set celebrated the 50th anniversary of the LEGO brick with a special-edition golden brick and classic retro-style packaging.

Gold-topped collections like this 1,000-piece tub marked the golden anniversary of the LEGO System of Play in 2005.

4496 50th Anniversary Tub (2005)

LIMITED EDITION

To commemorate the 25th anniversary of the LEGO logo, the company released limited-edition sets in clear, glittery buckets with an exclusive silver brick inside.

Christmas wreath

The first in a series of seasonal exclusive models, the Winter Toy Shop let builders create a snow-covered, old-fashioned toy store with miniature toys in the windows, and a Christmas tree and singing carolers outside.

10199 Winter Toy Shop (2009)

Snowy roof plates

Bakery shop sign

The Winter Village theme continued with a cozy bakery full of treats for a frosty day. It also had a tree-seller's stand and cart, and a frozen pond for ice skaters.

10216 Winter Village Bakery (2010)

Fashion & Style

SOME PEOPLE wear their love of LEGO® bricks and building on their sleeves… and on their wrists, keys, and kitchen tables, too! With so many choices of apparel and accessories, there's something out there to suit every LEGO lifestyle ●

Minifigure head salt and pepper shakers

EXTENDED LINE

Have you ever seen a LEGO lollipop maker? How about salt and pepper shakers shaped like minifigure heads? With key chains, coat racks, children's costumes, and more, these unique Extended Line items were produced for sale at the LEGOLAND® Parks, the LEGO Brand Stores, and the online LEGO Shop (shop.LEGO.com).

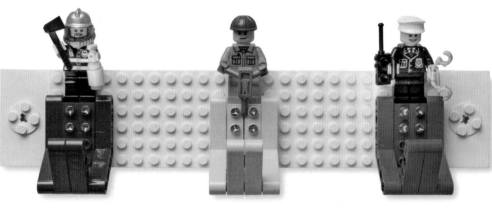

Coat rack with building studs and LEGO City minifigures

Ninjago minifigure keychain

LEGO brick backpack with zippered stud pockets

LEGO Castle children's knight costume

Drinking mug with 3D brick detail

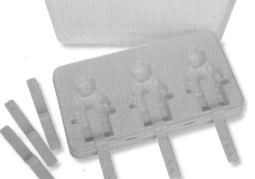

Minifigure-shaped ice pop mold

LEGO Friends jewelry box

LICENSED ITEMS

These products were all created by outside companies under licenses from the LEGO Group. They include watches with wristbands that you can make longer or shorter, link by link, colorful pens with LEGO themed beads to build and rearrange, and even light-up minifigure lanterns and brick-styled home electronics for the biggest LEGO fans.

Classic LEGO watch
with multi-piece band

LEGO wallet

LEGO® DUPLO® board book

LEGO Friends
bracelets

LEGO® DUPLO® t-shirt

LEGO City
Police cap

LEGO 2x4 brick coin bank

Insulated minifigure lunch bag

LEGO City kids' watch

Brick-styled MP3 player

Light-up minifigure lantern

DK BOOKS

The LEGO Group and Dorling Kindersley Publishing have teamed up to create a number of large, high-quality books—in fact, you're holding one in your hands right now! Full of detailed photos and information about LEGO models and minifigures, these best-selling titles and many more have been published in multiple languages and countries around the globe.

LEGO® Star Wars®: The Visual Dictionary (2009)

The LEGO® Ideas Book (2011)

"50 Years of the LEGO® Brick" book

The LEGO® Club

THE FIRST official LEGO® Club was created by the company's Canadian division in 1966. It was followed the next year by LEGO Sweden. Today, the LEGO Club provides building inspiration and behind-the-scenes information to 4 million club members around the world ●

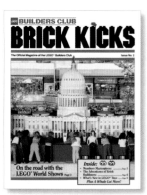

Membership card mailed to US LEGO Club members in 2007.

INSIDE FEATURES

Games, articles, contests, kids' creations, building steps and more fill the pages of the LEGO Club magazine, with national editions shipping four to six times a year to more than a dozen countries.

The US LEGO Club kicked off in July 1987 with the eight-page, quarterly *Brick Kicks* newsletter.

LEGO UK mailed the first issue of *Bricks 'n Pieces* to collectors in December 1974.

MEET MAX!

Max first appeared as the host of European editions of *LEGO Magazine* in 2007 before becoming the modern mascot of the world-wide LEGO Club. As a minifigure, he has the inside scoop on all the latest company news and upcoming themes. In 2010, Max was slightly redesigned and released as a real figure for the first time!

Max appears in stop-motion adventures as part of the LEGO Club Show. The online series features music videos, interviews, and on-the-scene reports from all around the world of LEGO building.

BRICK BUILDMORE

"The Adventures of Brick Buildmore" premiered in the very first issue of *Brick Kicks*. Together with his friend Bridget and faithful dog Comet, Brick solved problems the good old-fashioned way: by building!

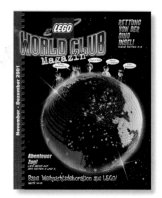

The UK LEGO Technic Club's magazine shipped four times a year between 1994 and 2000.

LEGO World Club Magazine was first available by subscription in Germany in 1997.

Illustrated, photographed, and even computer-generated comics are a permanent staple of LEGO Club magazines, offering stories and play ideas to help readers get started on their own adventures.

The bilingual *Innovations* replaced the Canadian club's *LEGO Design News* in 1990.

THE LEGO® MANIAC

Based on a series of live-action television commercials, Jack the LEGO Maniac originally introduced the Summer 1989 issue of *Brick Kicks*. He eventually lost his name and became the host of the newly relaunched *LEGO Mania Magazine*, starring in comics in which his imagination took him on adventures inside of his LEGO sets.

In the US, *LEGO Mania Magazine* took over from *Brick Kicks* at the end of 1994…

… switched to plain *LEGO Magazine* in May of 2002 with a big feature on LEGO® *Star Wars*®…

… became the unified face of the LEGO Club around the world…

…and was finally retitled *LEGO Club Magazine* in 2008.

LEGO® BRICKMASTER

The US-based BrickMaster program was launched in November 2004 as a premium version of the free LEGO Club. Subscribers paid an annual fee to receive a larger magazine, exclusive LEGO sets, and other rewards for the company's biggest fans. The last issue of *LEGO BrickMaster* shipped in November 2010.

20003 Dinosaur (2008)

Exclusive T-shirts are given out to club members who attend in-person LEGO Club Meetings at LEGO Brand Stores across the US.

Other versions of *LEGO Club Magazine* include an in-school edition and *Club Jr.* for children under 7.

The official Club website at www.LEGOclub.com is regularly updated with news stories, downloadable building instructions, an online gallery for club members' Cool Creations, an interactive version of the magazine, LEGO Club TV videos, and more.

LEGO.com

WITH THE GOAL of giving fans the ultimate LEGO® experience, the official company website at LEGO.com is one of the most-visited internet sites of any toy manufacturer in the world. With 21 local sites, the award-winning website welcomes visitors that hail from more than 200 countries, from Togo to Tajikistan. At the last count, LEGO.com had more than 14 million unique visitors per month! And yes, the site has a store, too ●

The introductory homepage is the site's one-stop starting place. Along with information, games, and activities for LEGO fans, it features links to customer service, a company history and timeline, official press releases, and sections for parents and educators.

COMIC BUILDER

Have you ever wanted to create a comic? The LEGO.com Comic Builder lets you tell your own story. You can choose a panel layout, drop in backgrounds, and design your own action with a cast of LEGO minifigures and vehicles. It even lets you add dialogue, pose characters, and add special effects just like a real comic book—and then print it out to show your friends your comic creation!

The comic-building fun starts when you click on this big blue button!

SHOPPING FOR BRICKS

LEGO.com/shop, the official LEGO shop, sells the latest sets by mail order to customers from more than 23 countries around the world. Featured items include LEGO Exclusives and Hard-to-Find sets, LEGO Lifestyle and Licensed products like books, stationery, and clothing, and a well-stocked Pick A Brick selection for custom model creation!

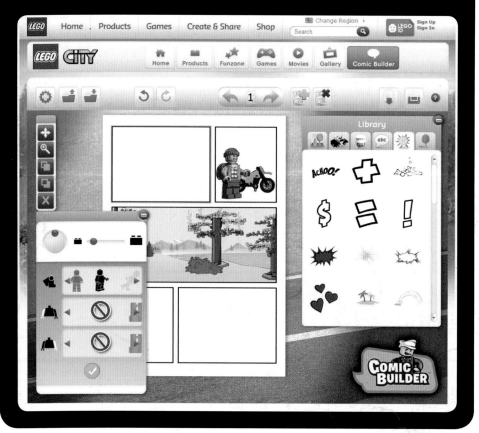

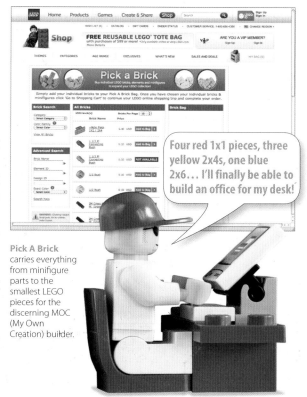

Four red 1x1 pieces, three yellow 2x4s, one blue 2x6… I'll finally be able to build an office for my desk!

Pick A Brick carries everything from minifigure parts to the smallest LEGO pieces for the discerning MOC (My Own Creation) builder.

GAMES TO PLAY

Whatever your preference, from action and adventure to puzzle-solving, stories, or strategy, the LEGO website likely has a free online game to suit your tastes. The single and multi-player selections are constantly expanded as new themes are released, so there's almost always something new.

In the Ninjago Viper Smash game, players hone their Spinjitzu skills by using game cards and special ninja attacks to battle snake-like Serpentine warriors.

THEME PAGES

Each current LEGO theme has its own section on LEGO.com with characters and stories, online games, and downloadable extras like wallpaper, TV commercials, and videos.

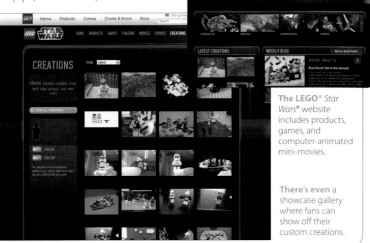

The LEGO® *Star Wars*® website includes products, games, and computer-animated mini-movies.

There's even a showcase gallery where fans can show off their custom creations.

LEGO.com has preschool games to help even the youngest computer-using builders develop their coordination and pattern-matching skills.

ANIMATIONS & ADVENTURES

From exciting new adventures in a galaxy far, far away to the latest get-rich schemes of the LEGO City crooks, LEGO.com is always packed with stop-motion and computer-animated stories starring models and minifigures from the company's many famous themes.

Computer animation brings the LEGO City Police and other memorable characters from the world of LEGO building to life!

INTERACTION

Ever wanted to talk to other LEGO builders? From the LEGO Club website to moderated message boards, LEGO.com has lots of ways for fans to connect and communicate in an online environment built to be friendly and safe for children of all ages.

KIDS GET ALL THE FUN. I DEMAND MESSAGE BOARDS FOR MINIFIGURES!

LEGO.com/club lets builders upload their Cool Creations and share their masterpieces with the entire world.

The LEGO Message Boards cover topics from favorite LEGO themes to high scores in the site's online games.

LEGO Message Boards

The LEGO Message Boards are a safe and fun online community, because every post is reviewed by a real person before it goes live.

You can read as many comments as you'd like, but before you post, you will have to agree to the house rules and to the terms of use. Ask your parent or guardian to help you. To check if the Message Board is available in your language please change your region.

Since each post is read by a real person, it takes some time for your message to appear, so be patient, and have fun!

Some Good Message Board Advice

Play it safe

Stay on topic

Don't give out your real name or phone number!

Be yourself, have fun and visit often

Play nice

LEGO® Education

PLAYFUL LEARNING. It's what LEGO® Education is all about. Established in 1980, and designed in collaboration with education experts, the LEGO Education program offers a wide variety of constructive experiences for teachers, students and children 18 months and older. With guides and activity packs, free early-learning activities available for download at LEGOeducation.com, and a catalogue of products, the program engages creative minds and teaches children the importance of learning by making ●

LEGO Education ABC 123 sets help to develop early mathematical skills and literacy. Mosaic-building kits provide a fun, creative way for young children to start recognizing shapes, colors, letters, and numbers, and the patterns that they can form together.

ROLE PLAY

Filled with pieces that represent familiar people, objects, and locations, LEGO Education Play Theme sets encourage children to act out different scenes from real life. By playing on their own or with friends and family, they learn to understand the needs and feelings of others while improving their own social and emotional skills.

9215 Dolls Family Set (2007)

Sets include illustrated story starter cards to inspire role play ideas.

NOW I GET IT!

Cooperative play helps children explore different situations and learn to respect each others' points of view.

CREATIVE CONSTRUCTION

With enough LEGO pieces at hand, a child can create anything. That's why LEGO Education Creative Construction sets include large collections of colorful bricks and special elements to help stimulate younger children's imaginations, self-expression, and creativity through rules-free building. Products range from boxes of basic bricks, building plates, windows, and wheels to entire DUPLO® town collections and huge, award-winning LEGO SOFT bricks, designed to develop motor skills and spatial awareness in children ages 2 and up.

LEGO SOFT bricks are oversized, durable, and washable pieces that let children create life-sized figures, walls, towers, and anything else that they can think up and build.

9020 LEGO® SOFT Starter Set (1998)

Kids can make creatures and buildings with tubes of all lengths and shapes using the 9076 Tubes Experiment Set (2007), then roll balls through them to find out what happens.

MACHINES & MECHANISMS

These kits and CD-ROM activity packs give students the parts, instructions, and inspiration they need to build both simple and powered machine models with mechanical functions like spinning gears, wheels, and axles. By learning how things work through construction and play, they gain a better understanding of the machines around them every day.

Students use the machines they build to measure time, distance, speed, weight, and more in lesson plans that help them explore energy and how forces affect motion.

This core machine-construction set includes almost 400 LEGO Technic elements and instructions for assembling 14 models with functions that range from studying gearing mechanisms to calibrating and capturing wind. An optional pneumatics set adds even more to build and learn.

Valve

Pump

Air tank

9686 Simple & Powered Machines Set (2009) with Pneumatics Add-On Set

LEGO® SERIOUS PLAY™

It's not just children who can learn from playing with LEGO bricks. LEGO SERIOUS PLAY is a workshop program in which a certified facilitator helps guide business teams to communicate and work together better by using LEGO construction as a metaphor for their shared strategies and goals. The program has been so successful that a classroom version is being developed as well.

A visual representation of workers at cross-purposes before a Serious Play course.

Everyone on the team contributes and participates in building landscape models, telling stories and playing out possible business scenarios through the medium of LEGO bricks.

ROBOTICS

LEGO® Education WeDo™ kits let elementary school students aged 7 to 11 get a head start on robotics by building models, hooking up computer-controlled sensors and motors, and using a simple programming tool to create behavior and overcome curriculum-based challenges with their robot inventions.

WeDo themes include Amazing Mechanisms, Wild Animals, Play Soccer, and Adventure Stories, covering topics within science, technology, mathematics, and language.

9580 LEGO® Education WeDo™ Construction Set (2009)

USB cable

Power Functions M-Motor

Soccer activity goalkeeper

Brick-built LEGO Technic lever arm

The WeDo Construction Set comes with more than 150 elements, including a motor, motion and tilt sensors, and a LEGO USB hub for connecting the model to a computer.

LEGO® MINDSTORMS®

Students over 8 can learn more complex robotics skills with LEGO® MINDSTORMS® Education sets. Activity packs teach them how to program and control robots built with the NXT Intelligent Brick, test and modify life-like behavior, and analyze their robots' sensor data afterwards.

Developed by Tufts University's Center for Engineering Educational Outreach, the LEGOengineering.com website provides teachers with an online community and resources to help create new classroom activities.

LEGO MINDSTORMS Education activity packs are developed by Carnegie Mellon University's Robotics Academy and include video tutorials, worksheets, and teacher introduction materials.

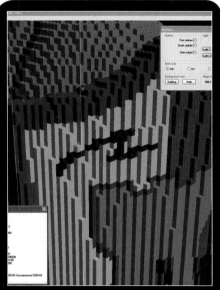

Ridged grip for leverage

Created in 1988, the LEGO brick separator is a LEGO Master Builder's best friend. This simple, one-piece plastic tool can pop any brick off a model, no matter how tightly wedged-in it may be. A new orange version was released in 2012 that's compatible with LEGO Technic axles, too.

Studs above and tubes below

LEGO® Master Builders

HAVE YOU EVER SEEN a spectacular LEGO® sculpture and wondered who built it? Chances are, it was a team of LEGO Master Builders. Rigorously tested and selected for their creative construction skills, the LEGO Master Builders work at the LEGO model shops, where they assemble an incredible variety of models for in-store use, parks, special projects, and events all around the world ●

The Connecticut, USA, model shop team assembles a 12 ft (3.7 m) long scale model of the newest LEGO factory in Monterrey, Mexico.

LEGO Master Builders can zoom in to make changes to individual bricks. Before digital building, they would have had to take apart the entire model first.

DIGITAL BRICKS

The LEGO Master Builders once used half-scale prototypes to design their giant brick sculptures, but these days they use special computer programs to digitally create models before they start assembling the real thing.

THE MODEL SHOP

Here's where the LEGO magic happens! With model shops in Denmark, the USA, the Czech Republic, and at the LEGOLAND® Parks, the hard-working LEGO Master Builders are always in the middle of creating something new and amazing. Their workspaces are filled with LEGO models, giant building tables, and racks of bricks in every shape, size, and color imaginable.

LEGO Master Builders love to use specialized pieces in unusual ways. Here, one works on a space monster made out of parts that started as a giant LEGO snake.

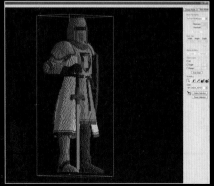

Zoomed out, the model is revealed as a LEGO knight. Purple highlights areas still being worked on.

A LEGO Master Builder works near the prototype heads for a band of singing robots.

LIGHT, SOUND, & MOVEMENT

This 47,000-piece model of the Hollywood Bowl amphitheater, built over the course of 600 hours for LEGOLAND® California's MINILAND, glows with rainbow-colored electric lights that change to the beat of "The LEGO Symphony." Models with moving and light-up features are a specialty of the LEGO Master Builders.

All built and ready for lift-off!

MASTER DESIGNS

Built at the Kladno model shop in the Czech Republic, this huge statue of an ancient Egyptian pharaoh was designed as a hand-drawn sketch and then constructed brick-by-virtual-brick in full scale on a computer before the first two plastic elements were ever snapped together.

A nose on a minifigure? Built from about 2,400 bricks and standing 2 ½ feet (80 cm) tall, these smiling characters are known as LEGO Friends.

Giant LEGO Friend version of a LEGO Mars Mission astronaut

Mechanized moving jaw

This animatronic *Tyrannosaurus rex* head was built with an articulated, pneumatic metal framework inside that could automatically open and close its toothy jaws.

BUILT TO LAST

Models that will be placed on display outdoors must be sturdy and long-lasting. Some larger models are built hollow with a custom metal frame inside to support the weight of their thousands of bricks. Permanent models are usually glued together to make sure no birds or passers-by make off with stray pieces.

New Horizons

YOU DON'T BECOME a company as enduring and globally-celebrated as the LEGO Group without trying a few experiments, using a lot of imagination, and thinking a little bit outside the box of bricks. What lies ahead for the future of creative construction, and which young stars will rise to become the next generation of building pioneers? Programs like these were developed to answer just those questions—and provide a whole lot of learning and fun along the way ●

Low-gain antenna

21101 Hayabusa (2012)

Junichiro Kawaguchi, real-life Project Manager for the Hayabusa, was included when it was released as a LEGO CUUSOO set.

LEGO® CUUSOO

"Where wishes come true" is the motto of LEGO® CUUSOO, a crowd sourcing experiment devoted to turning fans' dream LEGO projects into reality. The LEGO CUUSOO ("Imagination") website lets builders upload their model ideas and gather support from the online community. When an idea reaches 10,000 votes, the LEGO Group formally considers it for release as an official LEGO set.

The second of two Japan-exclusive CUUSOO sets, the *Hayabusa* ("Falcon") was an unmanned spacecraft launched in 2003. It was designed to travel to an asteroid, collect samples from its surface, and return them to Earth for study.

Sampler

Titanium alloy pressure hull

SONAR housing

しんかい 6500

The builders of winning concepts get more than accolades—they also receive a 1% royalty on the sales of their set.

SHINKAI 6500

The first LEGO CUUSOO model was based on the Shinkai 6500, a real submarine with the greatest depth range of any manned research vehicle in the world. As the first concept to receive the originally required 1,000 votes, it was released as a 412-piece set in a limited edition of 10,000 sold exclusively in Japan.

21100 Shinkai 6500 (2011)

LIFE OF GEORGE

The first interactive Life of George set is designed to work with iOS and Android apps of the same name. Players follow George on his travels around the world as he challenges them to build specific models as fast as they can, then capture their creations with their digital device's camera.

The set includes 144 LEGO bricks and a special play mat to photograph models against.

21200 Life of George (2011)

Builders are graded on time and accuracy, and can compete in two-player mode. You can also create your own album to challenge your friends.

High-gain antenna

Solar cell paddle

LEGO® MINECRAFT

Based on the immensely popular online game, LEGO Minecraft Micro World was the first idea submission to earn 10,000 votes on the new global LEGO CUUSOO website—and it took less than three days to do it. The model was made up of four cube-like vignette sections that could be taken apart and rearranged to build different landscapes.

21102 LEGO® Minecraft Micro World (2012)

The Minecraft model included buildable "Micro Mobs" of Steve (the player's avatar in the game) and a deadly Creeper.

LEGO® MASTER BUILDER ACADEMY

Founded in 2011, "LEGO MBA" is a multi-level program designed to teach LEGO fans to be better builders by learning the techniques of the official LEGO Master Builders and model designers. Members train with a series of themed kits, each containing a handbook and a collection of bricks. An online site (LEGOmba.com) lets them upload creations and test their knowledge of new skills.

LEGO MASTER BUILDER ACADEMY

20200 LEGO® Master Builder Academy Kit 1: Space Designer (2011)

By the time members reach Level 3, they're experienced enough to make their own new story-telling adventure models.

20206 LEGO® Master Builder Academy Kit 7: The Lost Village (2012)

Each kit includes buildable accessories for that level's exclusive LEGO MBA minifigure.

LEVEL 1

LEVEL 2

LEVEL 3

LEGO® Brick Art

SOME ARTISTS paint on canvas. Others carve stone or weld metal. But a special few create art using the unique medium of LEGO® bricks and imagery. The work of these talented "Brick Artists" and others like them is a remarkable visual testament to the creative nature of LEGO building and the unlimited ways that it allows people to express themselves ●

"Reflection" (right) "is about seeing oneself in brick," Sawaya says. "As an artist, I tend to see the world in little rectangles, a lot like LEGO bricks."

"Red"
August 2005

"Reflection"
August 2006

EGO LEONARD

In August 2007, a giant minifigure washed ashore on a beach in the Netherlands. Standing 8 ft (2.5 m) tall and carrying the enigmatic message "NO REAL THAN YOU ARE" on his shirt, the mysterious, ever-smiling Ego Leonard claimed to hail from a virtual world without rules or limitations, and to want to see "all the beautiful things that are there to admire and experience in your world."

Newspapers and internet blogs around the world marveled at "the Giant LEGO Man" and wondered where he had come from.

In November 2008, the Dutch artist had an art show in, appropriately enough, the Brick Lane Gallery in London, England.

NATHAN SAWAYA

Brick artist Nathan Sawaya is a full-time freelance builder based in New York. His imaginative life-sized LEGO sculptures and giant mosaic portraits have been featured on television and in a North American touring museum exhibit titled "The Art of the Brick®."

"Blue"
January 2006

"Yellow"
February 2006

METAMORPHOSIS

Sinking into or emerging from a pile of bricks, opening up to reveal the inner nature, and even putting oneself together piece by piece, Nathan Sawaya's "Red," "Yellow," and "Blue" all represent transitions.

"I create art out of LEGO bricks to show people things they have never seen before, nor will they ever see anywhere else," the artist says.

"The Ant and the Shoe" (left) tells a fairy tale of tough friendship, while "Two Short Orders" spells financial trouble for a cook and an investor.

"The Ant and the Shoe" February 2009

"Two Short Orders" October 2008

SEAN KENNEY

Sean Kenney is a full-time artist, officially-licensed LEGO Certified Professional, and self-described "professional kid" who has made LEGO creations for television shows, museums, galleries, celebrities, stores, and companies all over the world. He builds his artwork at a New York City studio containing more than a million LEGO bricks.

"The Walker" 1989

ANDREW LIPSON & DANIEL SHIU

Andrew Lipson is a LEGO builder and Technic fan who creates clever working mechanisms and mathematical brick sculptures. Together with fellow builder Daniel Shiu, he designs and constructs 3D recreations of the Dutch graphic artist M.C. Escher's mind-bendingly impossible, physics-defying illustrations, including Escher's "Relativity" in LEGO bricks

© A. Lipson 2003

MOSAIC ART

Creating artistic mosaics and murals from LEGO bricks is a time-honored hobby for many. Up close, the two-dimensional designs are clearly patterns of solid squares and rectangles, but as you move further away, the shapes and colors become increasingly real. LEGO mosaic artists use everything from scientific graph paper to cross-stitch needlework computer programs to turn photos and paintings into building blueprints.

A LEGO mosaic of the "Mona Lisa," Leonardo da Vinci's famous 16th century masterpiece, was created in 1993 to show how basic brick colors could be combined to create subtle shades.

JØRN RØNNAU

Danish artist Jørn Rønnau grew up playing with the very first LEGO bricks. He describes "The Walker," which is made from 120,000 elements, as "an intuitive self-portrait... partly a robot, built from all kinds of special grey pieces, wheels, antennas, fire hoses, ladders, shovels, etc. He can hardly move his feet... but he is surely trying!"

"Li" (2008)

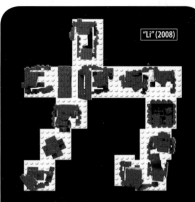

NICHOLAS FOO

Singapore-based artist Nicholas Foo is Asia's first LEGO Certified Professional. His Miniland-scale creation "Li," dedicated to the survivors of China's 2008 Sichuan earthquake, is made up of five small scenes that link together to form the Chinese character for strength and perseverance through adversity.

"Li—Renewal": planting a new beginning.

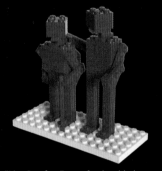

"Li—Comfort": care for the elderly.

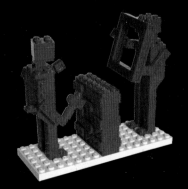

"Li—Rebuild": the reconstruction of homes.

Curved roof design inspired by the builder's own covered cart model

BANK

Fan Builders

ALL OVER THE WORLD, grown-ups are rediscovering their childhood love of LEGO® building—except for the ones who never lost it to begin with! With incredible talent and imagination, these AFOLs, or Adult Fans of LEGO, are pioneering new building techniques and detailing, attending fan groups and conventions, and showing off their passion for the LEGO brick every day ●

SOLAR FLARE

Lino Martins, an AFOL from the US, built this bright and sunny classic 1960s station wagon in MINILAND scale for his LEGO car-builder group. It was displayed along with a friend's night-themed car and their Rockabilly band drivers at the Brickcon08 fan convention.

THE BANK

Polish LEGO fan Paweł Michalak was inspired by the official Café Corner set (see p. 172) to create his own model in the Modular Buildings style. "The Bank" was built for the LUGPol (LEGO User Group—Poland) "Klocki Zdrój" diorama.

Nannan Zhang's tiny, high-tech Yamamura Bike was built to race through the streets of a futuristic city.

COLOGNE CATHEDRAL

Here's one dedicated AFOL! It took Jürgen Bramigk two long years to build this 10 ft (3 m) high model of Cologne Cathedral from his native Germany. Assembling it took about 900,000 LEGO bricks in different shades of gray.

Maciej Karwowski based his HD Bobber on the custom stripped-down motorcycles of the 1950s.

DAY AT THE STABLES

Marcin Danielek's model of a two-story country house with an attached horse stable includes details like a pile of chopped firewood, a dog chasing a cat up a tree, and a clever use of LEGO pieces to let a skirt-wearing minifigure sit down.

"CATCH UP!"

A 1955 San Francisco diner purchased by an eccentric billionaire and turned into a motorcycle and moped shop, this whimsical model was built by Jamie Spencer using custom decals and pieces from his LEGO City, LEGO Castle, and LEGO® Star Wars® collections.

Decals on model were custom-made by the builder

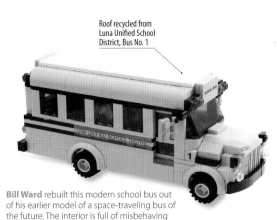

Roof recycled from Luna Unified School District, Bus No. 1

Bill Ward rebuilt this modern school bus out of his earlier model of a space-traveling bus of the future. The interior is full of misbehaving students and one very annoyed driver.

NOPPINGEN

German fan Rainer Kaufmann grew up with the LEGO sets of the 1970s and rediscovered building almost 20 years later. His expansive Noppingen town display started as a one-man project, but has grown to include models made by his fellow builders.

Terrace overhang built from "log wall" pieces

Rainer's Townhouse 3 model includes a sidewalk and section of street in front, and terraces overlooking a small yard at the back.

Lemming lives in the town of Noppingen. He loves walking, riding his bicycle, eating pizza, and showing tourists around his hometown.

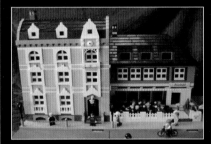

Marvelous old houses like these are common in Noppingen. Lemming's was completely renovated and looks like new.

His favorite place is the balcony of his second-floor apartment. From there, he can look around and see the entire town.

PICTURE STORIES

Many AFOLs like to build models that tell stories. Some are single-scene vignettes; others, like Rainer's "Lemming Presents his House" story, are created as a series of changing pictures.

Fan-tasy & Sci-fi

OFFICIAL LEGO® SETS have to contain a fixed number of bricks, but there's no limit to the number of LEGO elements fan builders can use in their custom creations. Fan models can be as huge and as detailed as the builder desires. That really comes in handy when making other-worldly creations like spaceships and monsters ●

THE TOWER OF BROTHERS

Once upon a time in a long-forgotten land, two brothers fought against each other in a crumbling tower. Maciej Karwowski's LEGO Castle fan contest-winning model is filled with spiral staircases, a hanging chandelier, and an intricate use of small bricks to create an age-worn look.

Maciej used lots of small LEGO pieces to make his tower look like the site of an ancient battle.

Uneven stones from LEGO tiles

GOLDFISH BALLOON

Wafting, drifting, swimming in the vast sky... Goldfish Balloon! Japanese builder Sachiko Akinaga has been building for more than 25 years and is known for her beautifully colorful and imaginative LEGO brick creations. Her portfolio of artistic models includes a car with a food-themed town hiding inside, an Earth Park with a motorized escalator and color-changing fountain, and a fortune-telling elephant.

Creeping vines

Ruined road

Membranes made from LEGO glider wings

DRAGON FOREST

Bryce McGlone excels at using LEGO elements to create organic-looking shapes like robots and monsters. His Dragon Forest diorama, displayed at the BrickWorld 2007 LEGO fan convention, incorporates standard bricks with Technic parts to make a fierce mythical beast and rider.

LL-X2 VANGUARD

Chris Giddens, the fan designer of the LEGO Factory Star Justice set (p. 224), has his own style of retro-future sci-fi building that he calls "Pre Classic Space." Built in 2003, his LL-X2 Vanguard cruiser is a galactic peacekeeper starship with internal details that include a built-in fighter bay and a crew of bold space explorers.

Six heavy XLT deep space thrusters

In **Marcin Danielek's** vertical "Double Trouble" vignette, a team of dwarven miners encounters unexpected surprises both above and beneath the ground.

Marcin Danielek's "The Final Voyage" was the Medieval Journey winner in an online fan contest. Clever building techniques created the look of a half-submerged sea monster and floating debris and minifigures.

STINGER LIGHT FIGHTER

This sleek starcraft was Australian fan Aaron Andrews's first LEGO spaceship model in more than 20 years. He built it with an opening cockpit, a female astronaut pilot, and fold-down landing gear.

Hungry cave worm

DOUBLE TROUBLE

Building in solid or similar colors with elements of many different shapes and sizes can add realistic detail and complexity to a custom LEGO model.

Jointed arms with powerful claws

INTERPLANETARY PROBE

Dan Rubin was inspired by the shapes of real-world insects when he built this biomechanical emissary of a mysterious alien race. Its sensitive gray internal mechanisms are protected by armor plating made from tan LEGO pieces.

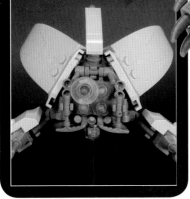

EXO-SUIT

Some MOC ("My Own Creation") makers like to specialize in a particular type of model, and UK builder Peter Reid's specialty is definitely his robots and "Neo-Classic Space" spacecraft. Unusual pieces and construction methods make his outer space exo-suit model really stand out in a crowd.

All-terrain legs

Index

Updated Edition

THE GHETTO UNDERCLASS

Social Science Perspectives

Edited by William Julius Wilson

An ANNALS publication, sponsored by the
American Academy of Political and Social Science

SAGE PUBLICATIONS
International Educational and Professional Publisher
Newbury Park   London   New Delhi

This is an updated and reprinted edition of the ANNALS (January 1989).

For information address:

SAGE Publications, Inc.
2455 Teller Road
Newbury Park, California 91320

SAGE Publications Ltd.
6 Bonhill Street
London EC2A 4PU
United Kingdom

SAGE Publications India Pvt. Ltd.
M-32 Market
Greater Kailash I
New Delhi 110 048 India

Printed in the United States of America

Library of Congress Cataloging-in-Publication Data

Main entry under title:

The ghetto underclass : social science perspectives / edited by
 William Julius Wilson—Updated ed.
      p. cm.
   "An ANNALS publication, sponsored by the American Academy of
 Political and Social Science."
   Includes bibliographical references and index.
   ISBN 0-8039-5272-4 (pbk.)
   1. Urban poor—United States. 2. Inner cities—United States.
 3. Urban policy—United States. 4. Afro-Americans—Economic
 conditions. 5. Afro-Americans—Social conditions. 6. United
 States—Race relations. I. Wilson, William J., 1935- .
 HV4045.G54 1993
 362.5'0973—dc20   93-25061

      95 96 97 10 9 8 7 6 5 4 3 2

Sage Production Editor: Astrid Virding

Contents

1

The Underclass:
Issues, Perspectives, and Public Policy

By WILLIAM JULIUS WILSON

ABSTRACT: This chapter critically reviews the chapters in this book and integrates some of their major issues. Attention is given to the substantive arguments advanced by each author and how they relate to the points raised by the other authors. In conclusion, the policy recommendations put forth in several of the articles are assessed. The chapter then turns to a critical discussion of the major studies on the underclass and the inner-city ghetto since the publication of the original version of these papers in the *Annals*.

A MacArthur prize fellow, William Julius Wilson is the Lucy Flower University Professor of Sociology and Public Policy at the University of Chicago. He is the author of Power, Racism, and Privilege; The Declining Significance of Race; *and* The Truly Disadvantaged; *the editor of* Sociology and the Public Agenda; *and the coeditor of* Through Different Eyes.

NOTE: Parts of this chapter appeared in somewhat different form in William Julius Wilson, "Public Policy and the Truly Disadvantaged," in *The Urban Underclass*, eds. Christopher Jencks and Paul E. Peterson (Washington, DC: The Brookings Institution, 1991), pp. 460-482. Used by permission.

1

DURING the decade of the 1970s, significant changes occurred in ghetto neighborhoods of large central cities; however, they were not carefully monitored or researched by social scientists during the 1970s and early 1980s. In the aftermath of the controversy over Daniel Patrick Moynihan's report on the black family, scholars, particularly liberal scholars, tended to shy away from researching any behavior that could be construed as stigmatizing or unflattering to inner-city minority residents. The vitriolic attacks and acrimonious debate that characterized this controversy proved to be too intimidating to liberal scholars. Accordingly, for a period of several years, and well after this controversy had subsided, the problems of social dislocation in the inner-city ghetto did not attract serious research attention. This left the study of ghetto social dislocations to conservative analysts who, without the benefit of actual field research in the inner city, put their own peculiar stamp on the problem, so much so that the dominant image of the underclass became one of people with serious character flaws entrenched by a welfare subculture and who have only themselves to blame for their social position in society.

Since the mid-1980s, however, as the nation's awareness of the problems in the ghetto has been heightened by a proliferation of conservative studies and sensational media reports, the problems of inner-city ghettos have once again drawn the attention of serious academic researchers, including liberal social scientists. Accordingly, an alternative or competing view to that of the dominant image of the underclass is slowly emerging, a view more firmly anchored in serious empirical research and/or thoughtful theoretical arguments. The work of some of the social scientists responsible for this different perspective is included in this book.

ANALYSIS OF INNER-CITY SOCIAL DISLOCATIONS

The chapter by Wacquant and Wilson sets the tone for most of the research contributions in this book. In contrast to discussions of inner-city social dislocations that strongly emphasize the individual attributes of ghetto residents and a so-called culture of ghetto poverty, Wacquant and Wilson draw attention to the structural cleavage separating ghetto residents from other members of society and to the severe constraints and limited opportunities that shape their daily lives. In highlighting a new socio-spatial patterning of class and racial subjugation in the ghetto, Wacquant and Wilson argue that the dramatic rise in inner-city joblessness and economic exclusion is a product of continuous industrial restructuring.

Lawrence Mead challenges this view in an argument based on the selective use of secondary sources. Mead maintains that since opportunities for work are widely available, the problem of inner-city joblessness cannot be blamed on limited employment opportunities; rather, it is inconsistent work, not a lack of jobs, that largely accounts for the high poverty and jobless rates in the inner city. Mead speculates that there is a disinclination among the ghetto underclass both to accept and to retain available low-wage jobs because they do not consider menial work fair or obligatory.

This thesis is seriously undermined by the evidence Kasarda has amassed on urban industrial transition. Carefully analyzing data from the Census Public Use Microdata

Sample Files, Kasarda demonstrates that although employment increased in every occupational classification in the suburban rings of all selected Northern metropolises, blue-collar, clerical, and sales jobs declined sharply between 1970 and 1980 in the central cities even though there was substantial growth in the number of managerial, professional, and higher-level technical and administrative support positions. These occupational shifts have contributed to major changes in the educational composition of central-city jobholders: precipitous net declines in slots filled by persons with poor education and rapid increases in slots filled by those with at least some college training.

These changes are particularly problematic for the black urban labor force, which remains overrepresented among those with less than a high school education—for whom city employment has rapidly expanded. Kasarda points out that from 1950 to 1970 there were substantial increases in the number of blacks hired in the urban industrial sector who had not graduated from high school, but after 1970 "the bottom fell out in urban industrial demand for poorly educated" labor. As Wacquant and Wilson put it, "A high school degree is a *condition sine qua non* for blacks for entering the world of work."

Challenging the orthodox thesis put forth by economists that it is entirely race rather than space that determines the differential black employment rates, Kasarda's data show that not only have blacks with less than a high school education in the suburban ring experienced considerably lower unemployment than their counterparts in the central city but that these city-suburban differences have actually widened since 1969. Finally, Kasarda's data reveal that compared with lesser-educated whites, less-educated blacks must endure considerably longer commuting time in reaching suburban jobs and are highly dependent on private vehicles to reach such jobs. Likewise, Wacquant and Wilson point out that "not owning a car severely curtails [the] chances [of ghetto blacks when they compete] for available jobs that are not located nearby or that are not readily accessible by public transportation."

The arguments put forth by Sullivan reinforce those of Wacquant and Wilson and of Kasarda on the impact of macroeconomic changes on inner-city neighborhoods and on poor blacks. Sullivan, like Wacquant and Wilson, is concerned that a heavy stress on individual causation neglects the mounting evidence of the relationship between increasing joblessness and the dismal employment prospects in the inner city. He notes that too great an emphasis on structural causation leads one to ignore the significance of culture and therefore leaves us unaware of the unique collective responses or adaptations to economic disadvantage, prejudice, and the problems of raising a family and socializing children under such conditions. Accordingly, Sullivan's article relates data on cultural processes to the structural constraints of the political economy and to the different individual choices and strategies within these neighborhoods. Sullivan attempts to analyze the collective adaptations of different ethnic groups to similar yet distinctive problems in obtaining an income and raising and supporting children. Whereas he is able to show a strong relationship between poor female-headed households and an overall lack of decent jobs in the two minority neighborhoods under study, he does not clearly establish the linkage between culture and macro-structural concerns. Nonetheless, his analysis does strongly suggest that some of the effects of macro-structural

constraints may be mediated by traditional ethnic values.

Sullivan's subtle cultural analysis should not be confused with the culture-of-poverty perspective on inner-city social dislocations. The term *culture of poverty* was introduced by the late Oscar Lewis to describe the configuration of cultural traits that tend to emerge, he argued, in class-stratified and highly individuated capitalist societies that have few, if any, of the characteristics of a welfare state: a sizable unskilled labor force that is poorly paid; high rates of unemployment and underemployment; few organizations, if any, to protect the interests of the poor; and advantaged classes who emphasize the value of upward mobility and the accumulation of wealth and who associate poverty with personal inadequacy or inferiority. Lewis argued that these conditions constitute powerful and enduring constraints on the experiences of the poor. As the poor learn to live within these constraints they develop a design for living—a culture of poverty—that is crystallized and is passed on from generation to generation. According to Lewis's formulation, then, the ultimate cause of the culture of poverty is the constraints imposed on the poor in highly individualistic class-stratified capitalist societies, and the principal reason for its stability and persistence is the transmission of this culture from one generation to the next. As Lewis put it, "By the time slum children are age six or seven, they have usually absorbed the basic values and attitudes of their subculture and are not psychologically geared to take full advantage of changing conditions or increased opportunities which may occur in their lifetime."[1]

It is the cultural-transmission thesis of the culture of poverty that has received the most critical attention. As Ulf Hannerz noted, it is debatable, but certainly possible, that the father's deserting of mothers and children, a high tolerance for psychological pathology, and an unwillingness to defer gratification are products of cultural transmission. It is much more difficult, however, to entertain the idea that unemployment, underemployment, low income, a persistent shortage of cash, and crowded living conditions directly stem from cultural learning.[2]

Hannerz argued that Lewis's work on cultural transmission had generated a great deal of confusion because he failed to draw a clear distinction between causes and symptoms, between what counts as objective poverty created by structural constraints and what counts as culture as people learn to cope with objective poverty. By failing to make this distinction clear, argued Hannerz, the notion of a culture of poverty tends to be used in a diluted sense as "a whole way of life." Emphasis is then placed not on the structural constraints or the ultimate origins of culture but on the "modes of behavior learned within the community."[3]

But, as Hannerz noted, it is possible to recognize the importance of macro-structural constraints—that is, to avoid the extreme notion of the culture of poverty—and still see "the merits of a more subtle kind of cultural analysis of life in poverty." The point that Hannerz raised 20 years ago is still an open and crucial question today,

1. Oscar Lewis, "Culture of Poverty," in *On Understanding Poverty: Perspectives from the Social Sciences*, ed. Daniel Patrick Moynihan (New York: Basic Books, 1968), p. 188.

2. Ulf Hannerz, *Soulside: Inquiries into Ghetto Culture and Community* (New York: Columbia University Press, 1969).

3. Ibid., pp. 179-80. For an example of the extended—and thus unrigorous—use of the culture-of-poverty concept as "a whole way of life," see Edward Banfield, *The Unheavenly City*, 2nd ed. (Boston: Little, Brown, 1970).

namely, whether there is a difference between "a person who is alone in being exposed to certain macro-structural constraints" and a person "who is influenced both by these constraints and by the behavior of others who are affected by them."[4] Ghetto-specific practices such as overt emphasis on sexuality, idleness, and public drinking "do not go free of denunciation" in inner-city ghetto neighborhoods. But because they occur much more frequently there than in middle-class society, in major part because of social organizational forces, the transmission of these modes of behavior by precept, as in role modeling, is more easily facilitated.[5] The term I have used to refer to this process is *social isolation*, which implies that contact between groups of different class and/or racial backgrounds is either lacking or has become increasingly intermittent and that the nature of this contact enhances the effects of living in a highly concentrated poverty area.[6]

Unlike the concept of culture of poverty, social isolation does not postulate that ghetto-specific practices become internalized, take on a life of their own, and therefore continue to influence behavior even if opportunities for mobility improve. Rather, it suggests that reducing structural inequality would not only decrease the frequency of these practices but also make their transmission by precept less efficient.

In this book, Elijah Anderson's article on sex codes among black inner-city youths graphically depicts the problems of social isolation in the inner city and provides persuasive arguments on the relationship between ghetto-specific practices and structural inequality. Anderson points out that young black men in the inner city, facing limited job prospects, cannot readily assume the roles of breadwinner and reliable husband. They therefore "cling to the support" provided by their peer groups, and they back away from enduring relationships with girlfriends. The lack of employment opportunities not only impoverishes the entire community but strips the young men "of the traditional American way of proving their manhood, namely, supporting a family." Given the paucity of conventional avenues of success in the isolated inner city, the young ghetto male affirms his manhood through peer-group interaction. His esteem is enhanced, that is, he becomes a man, if he can demonstrate that he has had casual sex with many women and has gotten one or more of them to "have his baby."

As Anderson emphasizes, casual sex is really not so casual. In the inner-city peer-group status system, it carries a special meaning. Inner-city adolescents "engage in a mating game," states Anderson. The girl dreams of having a home and a family with a husband who can provide financial support. The boy, without a job or employment prospects, knows he cannot fulfill that role. He nonetheless convinces the girl to have sex with him, often leading to out-of-wedlock pregnancy, and therefore achieves "manhood in the eyes of his peer group." In the subculture of the ghetto, argues Anderson,

people generally get married "to have something." This mind-set presupposes a job, the work ethic, and, perhaps most of all, a persistent sense of hope for, if not . . . a belief in, an economic future. . . . [F]or so many of those who . . . become unwed mothers and

---

4. Hannerz, *Soulside*, p. 182.

5. Ibid., p. 184.

6. William Julius Wilson, *The Truly Disadvantaged: The Inner City, the Underclass, and Public Policy.* (Chicago: University of Chicago Press, 1987).

fathers, there is little hope for a good job and even less for a future of conventional family life.

The impact of employment in the inner city is a central theme in the article by Testa and his coauthors. Drawing on survey data collected by the University of Chicago's Urban Poverty and Family Structure Project, Testa and his colleagues find that employed fathers are 2½ times more likely than nonemployed fathers to marry the mother of their first child. This finding supports the hypothesis that male joblessness is a central factor in the trends involving never-married parenthood in the ghetto. Indeed, these findings reveal that the effect of male employment on marriage is strong not only among inner-city black men but among inner-city white, Puerto Rican, and Mexican men as well. Moreover, their unique data set demonstrates that high school graduates are more likely to marry than high-school dropouts, suggesting, therefore, that the marriage decisions of inner-city couples are shaped both by current economic realities and by long-term economic prospects.

Although McLanahan and Garfinkel also support the view that the rise in male joblessness in the inner city is a major contributor to the growth of female headship of families, they likewise note the contribution of welfare to the growth of mother-only families. More specifically, when analyzing the social and economic situations of black, single mothers who are weakly attached to the labor force and are concentrated in Northern ghettos, they argue that "too heavy a reliance on welfare can facilitate the growth of an underclass." McLanahan and Garfinkel maintain that Aid to Families with Dependent Children (AFDC) and other means-tested public assistance programs reduce the likelihood of marriage

and promote female headship in the inner city and therefore weaken the labor force attachment of poor single mothers. Recognizing that the existing research reveals that welfare has a very small effect on the aggregate growth of female-headed families, they nonetheless maintain that its impact on the poorer half of the population is greater. They estimate that between 20 and 30 percent of the growth of mother-only families among the lower half of the income distribution can be accounted for by "the threefold increase in AFDC and welfare-related benefits between 1955 and 1975."

But it is difficult really to separate the effects of welfare on family formation and labor-force attachment from the effects of the overwhelming joblessness that has plagued the inner city since 1965 and especially since 1970. As David Ellwood has pointed out elsewhere, "Welfare benefits rose sharply until about 1973, but they have fallen since then."[7] Adjusted for inflation, the welfare package—AFDC plus food stamps—was 22 percent less in 1984 than it was in 1972.[8] During the decade of the 1970s, the decade in which the real dollar value of welfare declined steadily after 1972, we nonetheless witnessed the sharpest rise in inner-city joblessness and related social dislocations such as the concentration of poverty, poor female-headed families, and welfare receipt.[9]

7. David T. Ellwood, *Poor Support: Poverty in the American Family* (New York: Basic Books, 1988), p . 209.

8. Sheldon Danziger and Peter Gottschalk, "The Poverty of Losing Ground," *Challenge*, May-June 1985.

9. Wilson, *Truly Disadvantaged*; Loïc J. D. Wacquant and William Julius Wilson, "Poverty, Joblessness, and the Social Transformation of the Inner City," in *Welfare Policy for the 1990s*, eds. P. Cottingham and D. Ellwood (Cambridge, MA: Harvard University Press, 1989), pp. 70-102.

Although McLanahan and Garfinkel state that joblessness is the single most important factor in the rise of mother-only families, they fail to address the complex relationship between joblessness, family formation, and welfare.[10] Joblessness aggravates both single-parent family formation and welfare receipt. If welfare receipt is related to the formation of single-parent families and labor-force attachment—although careful empirical research has yet to establish this relationship firmly—it is best seen as a mediating variable or as part of a matrix of constraints and opportunities, a matrix that does not necessarily produce a single outcome but rather a set of behavioral outcomes.[11]

As shown in Wacquant and Wilson's article, blacks who live in the ghetto are confronted with a different matrix of constraints and opportunities from that confronted by blacks who live in low-poverty areas. These include differences in the class structure, availability of employment, economic and financial capital, poverty concentration, and social capital. For all these reasons, greater significance is attached to the availability of welfare in the ghetto than in the low-poverty areas. As reported by Wacquant and Wilson, welfare mothers who live in the ghetto are far less likely to expect to be welfare-free within less than a year and far more likely to anticipate needing assistance for more than 5 years than welfare mothers who reside in low-poverty areas. Wacquant and Wilson argue, therefore, that "those unable to secure jobs in low-poverty areas have access to social and economic supports to help them avoid the public-aid rolls that their ghetto counterparts lack." Indeed, the mere fact of living in a ghetto or an extreme-poverty area could increase one's uneasiness about entering the job market. "We all remember the anxiety of getting our first job," Thomas Corbett, of the Institute for Research on Poverty, has stated elsewhere. "For a woman who has been out of the job market for years, or maybe has never had a job, that anxiety can be greatly compounded. And many of these people live in isolated inner-city neighborhoods, where there aren't many role models to offer skills at coping with the job market,"[12] As one welfare mother seeking a job in Chicago put it, "I get so nervous and scared going out looking for a job. Meeting all them strange folks, you know. And I never know how to talk to 'em."[13] Such feelings are likely to be far more prevalent in socially isolated ghetto neighborhoods than in other areas of the city.

It is important, therefore, in any discussion of welfare's contribution to the growth of an urban underclass, to consider public assistance programs as part of the overall matrix of constraints and opportunities. The most important variable in this matrix, as so many of the chapters in this book demonstrate, is employment opportunities.

Decreasing employment opportunities are centrally related to the dramatic impoverishment of Puerto Ricans in large urban centers. In this book, Marta Tienda points out that since 1970 Puerto Ricans have witnessed a precipitous decline of jobs that they traditionally filled and an overall economic

---

10. *Joblessness* here does not refer simply to unemployment but to non-labor-force participation as well.

11. Claude S. Fisher, *Networks and Places: Social Relations in the Urban Setting* (New York: Free Press, 1977).

12. Quoted in Dirk Johnson, "Anti-Poverty Program Seeks to Build Self-Esteem" *New York Times*, 21 Feb. 1988, p. 13.

13. Ibid.

decline and industrial restructuring in areas where they are concentrated. As a result, the labor market position of Puerto Ricans represents the bottom of the ethnic hiring queue. Whereas Mexicans have been preferred laborers in agricultural jobs, at least in recent years, Puerto Ricans, except for women in the garment and textile industries, have never been preferred workers for specific jobs. But Tienda argues that the massive industrial restructuring of the Northeast has wiped out many unskilled and unionized blue-collar jobs, so much so that not only have the employment opportunities of Puerto Rican youths and men of prime working age been severely limited, but the job prospects of Puerto Rican women in the textile and garment industries have diminished as well.

If social scientists tend to emphasize the impact of changes in the organization of the American economy on lives of urban minorities, the general public has identified the growing presence of immigrants, particularly immigrants from the poorer Latin American countries, as a prime factor in the labor market displacement of American-born groups, particularly black Americans.

But, as shown in Robert Reischauer's succinct article, there is "little evidence that immigrants have had any significant negative impacts on the employment situation of black Americans." Reischauer is aware that the data on which this conclusion is based are old and are not sufficiently detailed to isolate localized or regional effects or to capture the effects of recent immigration in cities such as Los Angeles, Miami, New York, Houston, San Francisco, and Chicago. Moreover, he raises the possibility that the effects of immigration could have been much greater on working conditions and internal migration, labor-force participation, and fringe benefits, which

have received less attention from researchers, than on the dimensions that have been the focus of current studies—unemployment, wages, and earnings. Nonetheless, "the existing evidence suggests that immigration has not been a major factor contributing to the emergence of the urban underclass."

The increasing problems of social dislocation among the underclass have been accompanied by a rise in the homeless population. As Rossi and Wright reveal in their chapter, the recent increase of the literally homeless population is associated with a number of macro processes—including changes in the demand for low-skilled workers, which have led to a drastic reduction in the market for casual labor and have made it more difficult for the homeless to pay rent and buy food; changes in the level and coverage of income-maintenance support programs, which have decreased access of the homeless to the cheapest available rentals, have discouraged their families from subsidizing them, and have reduced their probability of receiving adequate institutional care; and sharp declines in the quality and quantity of low-cost housing in urban areas across the country.

It is interesting to note that all of these macro processes have also adversely affected the poor nonhomeless population in urban areas. Accordingly, comprehensive programs to address the problems associated with urban poverty in general will benefit not only the nonhomeless residents of the inner-city ghetto but the urban homeless population as well.

POLICY OPTIONS: A CRITICAL ASSESSMENT

Several of the chapters discussed in the previous section draw out the policy impli-

cations of their analyses. Kasarda outlines a series of practical steps to reduce the spatial isolation from jobs that match the skills of inner-city residents, including a computerized job-opportunity network, job-search assistance, temporary relocation assistance, housing vouchers for low-income citizens, stricter enforcement of fair-hiring and fair-housing laws, and a review of public assistance programs to determine whether they help anchor the poor to distressed areas.

Sullivan's chapter outlines some policy initiatives in which inner-city males are seen "as important parts of the solution and not merely as the sources of the problem." Among these are those programs that include males in services designed to prevent unwanted pregnancy, more imaginative child-support enforcement in order to encourage young fathers to accept paternity, and "an overall program of intensive and comprehensive services for inner-city children and adolescents."

McLanahan and Garfinkel believe that more universal programs—including full employment, health care, child care, child support assurance systems, and children's allowances—are needed to replace the current welfare system, provide aid to single mothers, and thereby "retard the growth of an underclass." Rossi and Wright put forth several recommendations to address the problems of the literally homeless, including creating more generous programs of income maintenance, offering broader coverage for disability programs, increasing the supply of low-cost housing, providing more low-skilled employment opportunities for the extremely poor, developing measures to reduce "the prevalence of disabling conditions among young adult males," and supporting charitable organizations that serve the homeless.

Except for Kasarda's notion of the need for computerized employment networks, none of these suggestions represents entirely new recommendations. The question is, how effective are recommended programs such as these likely to be in addressing the problems spelled out by the respective authors? And if introduced, how much support are they likely to receive from the American public? For possible answers to these questions I turn to a critical discussion of the chapters by Hochschild, Mead, and Nathan.

Jennifer Hochschild believes that the "problem of severe poverty and its attendant behaviors and emotions can be solved only when Americans choose actually, not merely rhetorically, to open the opportunity structure to all, regardless of their race, class, or gender." The fervor of the 1960s to enhance opportunities for the disadvantaged did not last long enough to fulfill its promises to all the poor. Although all minorities and women benefited in legal and normative terms, only the more advantaged tended to benefit socially, economically, and politically. By the 1980s, little of the 1960s' political commitment to erase inequality remained.

What Hochschild would like to see is a new political commitment to promote social and economic mobility among the estranged poor. In this regard, she has little faith in programs such as income maintenance, workfare, or social services because they do not change the "structural conditions that create the gap between the promise and practice of equal opportunity." She is also not enthusiastic about programs that are designed to provide jobs for men and not for women. What she ought to make clear, however, is that one must be careful not to confuse a now popular explanation

of the rise of poor female-headed black families—namely, that the increase of poor black female-headed households is associated with male joblessness—with a policy prescription that more jobs should be made available for men. Indeed, some authors in this book who used this explanation and at the same time called for the creation of jobs for both men and women as a major policy recommendation have been unfairly charged with gender bias because of careless interpretations of their work.[14] Nonetheless, Hochschild is certainly correct when she emphasizes that any program that is designed to increase the employment of men without simultaneously increasing the employment for women "reifies a patriarchal social structure in which women are dependent upon . . . men."

What is needed, she argues, are programs that enable the estranged poor to enter the mainstream of society, programs that "involve a wide array of activities aimed at changing skills, views, and life circumstances." Such programs would include steps to provide employment for inner-city youth, reform public schools and facilitate the transition from school to work, reduce racial and gender discrimination, remove barriers between jobs in the primary and secondary labor markets, reduce teenage pregnancies and births, increase the political control of previously disenfranchised people, and provide more political control over industrial relocation and plant closings. Such programs would be costly, she points out, because they would be intensive, long lasting, and comprehensive. They would also be politically vulnerable if they are not "submerged economically and politically in the horizontally redistributive

component." In other words, wherever possible, programs that would help the estranged poor should "build on Americans' support for social policies that give everyone a chance for at least some success."

Of the programs recommended by contributors to this book and discussed in the previous section, Sullivan's proposal of intensive and comprehensive services for inner-city adolescents and children, McLanahan and Garfinkel's package of universal programs, and Kasarda's recommendation for stricter enforcement of fair-hiring and fair-housing laws come closest to meeting the criteria for successful programs outlined in Hochschild's chapter.

In direct contrast to Hochschild's comprehensive recommendation for bringing the underclass or the estranged poor into the mainstream of American society is Lawrence Mead's program of mandatory workfare. Although, as I have indicated previously, serious questions can be raised about Mead's assumptions concerning the reasons for the entrenched poverty in the inner city, especially when his arguments are contrasted with those of Kasarda's, Mead's focus on mandatory workfare as a solution to inner-city social dislocations is also problematic. Mead's program is based on the assumption that a mysterious welfare ethos exists that encourages public assistance recipients to avoid their obligations as citizens to be educated, to work, to support their families, and to obey the law. In other words, and in keeping with the dominant American belief system on poverty, *it is the moral fabric of individuals, not the social and economic structure of society, that is taken to be the root of the problem.*[15]

---

14. A typical example of this type of scholarship is Adolph Reed, "The Liberal Technocrat," *Nation*, 6 Feb. 1988, pp. 167-70.

15. Wacquant and Wilson, "Poverty, Joblessness, and the Social Transformation of the Inner City" (Italics in original).

There is no existing rigorous research to support this view. As shown in the chapters in this book by Wacquant and Wilson and by Kasarda, in particular, the spatial patterning and basic timing of rising social dislocations, including welfare receipt, in recent years contradict it.

Aside from the questionable reasoning that underlies Mead's recommendation for mandatory workfare, a work-welfare program that is not part of a broader framework to stimulate economic growth and a tight labor market remains at the mercy of the economy. As Robert Reischauer has pointed out elsewhere:

In recessionary periods, when jobs are scarce throughout the nation, a credible emphasis on work will be difficult to maintain. Unskilled welfare recipients will realize that they stand little chance of competing successfully against experienced unemployed workers for the few positions available. In regions of the country where the economy is chronically weak, this dilemma will be a persistent problem. Evidence from one such area, West Virginia, suggests that work-welfare programs can do little to increase the employment or earnings of welfare recipients if the local economy is not growing. A public sector job of last resort may be the only alternative in such cases.[16]

I am not suggesting that the so-called new-style workfare programs, described in Richard Nathan's chapter, that include an array of training and employment activities and services are without merit. But they represent, in Nathan's words, "incremental" programs and therefore fall far short of the comprehensive reform package recom-

mended by Jennifer Hochschild. Nonetheless, for Nathan, the emphasis on new-style welfare reflects a liberal-conservative consensus that is quite compatible with the American process. Nathan argues that this consensus is in part based on the recognition that—given the structure of American federalism and the central role of state governments in establishing and administering the major institutions providing social services—"it will take a long time to achieve change, that even then only some people will be affected, and that the politics involved are very difficult." Nathan believes, therefore, that it is necessary now to concentrate on the institutional dimension of the policy changes in order to address the problems of the ghetto underclass, especially the implementation of new programs and strategies to promote and facilitate institutional change. He also believes that both evaluation research and consultive arrangements could be useful in furthering this process.

But the history of social change in the United States has not always reflected a slow incremental process. Despite the structure of American federalism, despite the American political process, and despite the important role of the individual states, the major reforms of the New Deal, the comprehensive legislation of the civil rights movement, and the broadbased policies of the Great Society programs were all achieved within a short period of time. As Jennifer Hochschild so aptly put it:

American citizens may be willing to do more . . . than is normally assumed in order really to open the system to all. So far, the American policymaking system has made a lot of wrong choices, but there is no reason why we cannot change our course, and lots of reasons why we should.

16. Robert D. Reischauer, "Welfare Reform: Will Consensus Be Enough?" *Brookings Review*, 5:8 (Summer 1987). See also Wacquant and Wilson, "Poverty, Joblessness, and the Social Transformation of the Inner City."

THE ECONOMY, WEAK LABOR-
FORCE ATTACHMENT,
AND THE INNER-CITY NEIGHBORHOOD:
A RESEARCH UPDATE

Since the publication of the *Annals* issue on the ghetto underclass (Vol. 501, January 1989), a number of studies have appeared that provide a direct test of many of the major theoretical arguments outlined in *The Truly Disadvantaged* and that complement many of the studies included in this book. I should like to organize my discussion of these studies around three topics, namely, (1) the economy and weak labor-force attachment in the inner city; (2) weak labor-force attachment and the inner-city neighborhood environment; and (3) social theory and the concept of *underclass*. But first let me present a brief summary of the major arguments advanced in *The Truly Disadvantaged*.

A synopsis of the truly disadvantaged

I argue in *The Truly Disadvantaged* that historical discrimination and a migration to large metropolises that kept the urban minority population relatively young created a problem of weak labor-force attachment among urban blacks and, especially since 1970, made them particularly vulnerable to the industrial and geographic changes in the economy.[17] The shift from goods-producing to service-producing industries, the increasing polarization of the labor market into low-wage and high-wage sectors, innovations in technology, the relocation of manufacturing industries out of central cities, and periodic recessions have forced up the rate of black joblessness (unemployment and nonparticipation in the labor market), despite the passage of anti-

17. William Julius Wilson, *The Truly Disadvantaged*.

discrimination legislation and the creation of affirmative action programs. The rise in joblessness has in turn helped trigger an increase in the concentrations of poor people, a growing number of poor single-parent families, and an increase in welfare dependency.

These problems have been especially evident in the ghetto neighborhoods of large cities, not only because the most impoverished minority populations live there but also because the neighborhoods have become less diversified in a way that has severely worsened the impact of the continuing economic changes.

Especially since 1970, inner-city neighborhoods have experienced an outmigration of working- and middle-class families previously confined to them by the restrictive covenants of higher-status city neighborhoods and suburbs. Combined with the increase in the number of poor caused by rising joblessness, this outmigration has sharply concentrated the poverty in inner-city neighborhoods. The number with poverty rates that exceed 40 percent—a threshold definition of "extreme poverty" neighborhoods—has risen precipitously. And the dwindling presence of middle- and working-class households has also removed an important social buffer that once deflected the full impact of the kind of prolonged high levels of joblessness in these neighborhoods that has stemmed from uneven economic growth and periodic recessions.

In earlier decades, not only were most of the adults in ghetto neighborhoods employed but black working and middle classes brought stability. They invested economic and social resources in the neighborhoods, patronized their churches, stores, banks, and community organizations, sent their children to the local schools, reinforced

societal norms and values, and made it meaningful for lower-class blacks in these segregated enclaves to envision the possibility of some upward mobility.

However, today the ghetto features a population whose primary predicament is joblessness reinforced by growing social isolation. Outmigration has decreased the contact between groups of different class and racial backgrounds and thereby concentrated the adverse effects of living in impoverished neighborhoods. These concentration effects, reflected, for example, in the residents' self-limiting social dispositions, are created by inadequate access to jobs and job networks, the lack of involvement in quality schools, the unavailability of suitable marriage partners, and lack of exposure to informal "mainstream" social networks and conventional role models.

Accordingly, *The Truly Disadvantaged* argued that the factors associated with the recent increases in social dislocation in the ghetto are complex. They cannot be reduced to the easy explanations of a "culture of poverty" that have been advanced by those on the right, or of racism, posited by those on the left. Although the ghetto is a product of historical discrimination and although present-day discrimination has undoubtedly contributed to the deepening social and economic woes of its residents, to understand the sharp increase in these problems requires the specification of a complex web of other factors, including shifts in the American economy.

The economy and weak labor-force attachment in the inner city

In my attempt in *The Truly Disadvantaged* to examine empirically the problem of the growing concentration of poverty, I used census tracts as proxies for nonpoverty and inner-city areas. The latter was divided

into poverty, high-poverty, and extreme poverty neighborhoods. Most of my analysis of concentrated poverty focused on areas of extreme poverty, that is, those in which at least 40 percent of the people are poor. More recent studies have followed this lead by defining ghettos as those areas with poverty rates of at least 40 percent. The ghetto poor are therefore identified as those among the poor in the inner city who reside in these extreme poverty neighborhoods.[18]

18. See Wacquant and Wilson, "Poverty, Joblessness, and the Social Transformation of the Inner City"; and Paul A. Jargowsky and Mary Jo Bane, "Ghetto Poverty in the United States, 1970-1980," in *The Urban Underclass*, eds. Christopher Jencks and Paul E. Peterson (Washington, DC: The Brookings Institution, 1991), pp. 342-356. In discussing the correspondence between ghetto neighborhoods and extreme poverty census tracts in Chicago, Wacquant and Wilson state: "Extreme-poverty neighborhoods comprise tracts with at least 40 percent of their residents in poverty in 1980. These tracts make up the historic heart of Chicago's black ghetto: over 82 percent of the respondents in this category inhabit the west and south sides of the city, in areas most of which have been all black for half a century and more, and an additional 13 percent live in immediately adjacent tracts. Thus when we counterpose extreme-poverty areas with low-poverty areas, we are in effect comparing ghetto neighborhoods with other black areas, most of which are moderately poor, that are not part of Chicago's traditional black belt" (p. 16). Jargowsky and Bane use the same rationale on a national level: "Based on visits to several cities, we found that the 40 percent criterion came very close to identifying areas that looked like ghettos in terms of their housing conditions. Moreover, the areas selected by the 40 percent criterion corresponded rather closely with the judgments of city officials and local census bureau officials about which neighborhoods were ghettos" (pp. 8-9).

Of course, not all the residents who reside in ghettos are poor. In the 10 largest American cities, as of 1970, the number of Hispanic residents (poor and nonpoor) residing in ghetto areas tripled between 1970 and 1980; the number of blacks doubled.

Paul Jargowsky and Mary Jo Bane's research reveals that the proportion of the poor who reside in ghetto neighborhoods varies dramatically by race. Whereas only 2 percent of the non-Hispanic white poor lived in ghettos in 1980, some 21 percent of black poor and 16 percent of Hispanic poor resided there. And almost a third of all metropolitan blacks lived in a ghetto in 1980. Sixty-five percent of the 2.4 million ghetto poor in the United States are black, 22 percent Hispanic, and 13 percent non-Hispanic and other races. Thus, to speak of the ghetto poor in the United States is to refer primarily to blacks and Hispanics. This has both descriptive and theoretical significance.

What is not revealed in *The Truly Disadvantaged* and what is clearly spelled out by Jargowsky and Bane is that the increase of ghetto poverty occurred mainly in only two regions of the country: the Midwest and the Northeast. Moreover, only 10 cities accounted for three fourths of the total rise of ghetto poverty during the 1970s. One third of the increase was accounted for solely by New York City, and one half by New York and Chicago together. By adding Philadelphia, Newark, and Detroit, two thirds of the total increase is accounted for. The others in the top 10 were Columbus, Ohio; Atlanta; Baltimore; Buffalo; and Paterson, New Jersey. Of the 195 standard metropolitan areas in 1970 that recorded some ghetto poverty, 88 experienced decreases in the number of ghetto poor by 1980. Those with the largest decreases were Texas cities with significant declines in Hispanic ghetto poverty and Southern cities with sharp drops in black ghetto poverty.

The focus of *The Truly Disadvantaged*, however, was on the increase in ghetto poverty. The question is why did this increase occur and why was most of it confined to the large industrial metropolises of the Northeast and Midwest? Because these two regions experienced massive industrial restructuring and loss of blue-collar jobs. Cities of the frostbelt suffered overall employment decline because "growth in their predominantly information-processing industries could not numerically compensate for substantial losses in their more traditional industrial sectors, especially manufacturing."[19] Cities in the sunbelt experienced job growth in all major sectors of the economy (manufacturing, retail and wholesale, white-collar services, and blue-collar services) between 1970 and 1986.

In *The Truly Disadvantaged*, I maintained that one result of these changes for many urban blacks has been a growing mismatch between the location of employment and residence in the inner city. Although studies based on data collected before 1970 did not show consistent or convincing effects on black employment as the result of this spatial mismatch, the employment of inner-city blacks relative to suburban ones has clearly deteriorated since then.[20] Recent research conducted mainly by urban and labor economists strongly shows that the decentralization of employment is continuing and that employment in manufacturing, most of which is already suburbanized,

19. John D. Kasarda, "Structural Factors Affecting the Location and Timing of Urban Underclass Growth," *Urban Geography* 11:241 (1990).

20. Harry J. Holzer, "The Spatial Mismatch Hypothesis: What Has The Evidence Shown?" Paper presented at a conference on *The Truly Disadvantaged*, Northwestern University, October 1990. For a study based on earlier data, see David T. Ellwood, "The Spatial Mismatch Hypothesis: Are There Teenage Jobs Missing in the Ghetto?" in *The Black Youth Employment Crisis*, eds. Richard B. Freeman and Harry J. Holzer (Chicago: University of Chicago Press, 1986), pp. 147-148.

has decreased in central cities, particularly in the Northeast and Midwest. Blacks living in central cities have less access to employment, as measured by the ratio of jobs to people and the average travel time to and from work, than do central-city whites. Unlike most other groups of workers, less-educated central-city blacks receive lower wages than less-educated suburban blacks. And the decline in earnings of central-city blacks is positively associated with the extent of metropolitan job decentralization.[21]

But are the differences in employment between city and suburban blacks mainly the result of changes in the location of jobs? It is possible that in recent years the migration of blacks to the suburbs has become much more selective than in earlier years, so much so that the changes attributed to the job location are really caused by this selective migration.[22] The pattern of black migration to the suburbs in the 1970s was similar to that of whites during the 1950s and 1960s in the sense that it was concentrated among the more educated and younger city residents.[23] However, in the 1970s this was even more true for blacks, creating a situation in which the education and income gaps between city and suburban blacks seemed to expand and that between city and suburban whites

seemed to contract.[24] Accordingly, if one were to control for personal and family characteristics, how much of the employment gap between city and suburbs would remain?

This question was addressed in a study by James E. Rosenbaum and Susan J. Popkin of the Gautreaux program in Chicago.[25] The design of the program permitted them to contrast systematically the employment experiences of a group of low-income blacks who had been assigned private apartments in the suburbs with the experiences of a control group with similar demographic characteristics and employment histories who had been assigned private apartments in the city. The authors' findings support the spatial mismatch hypothesis. After controlling for personal characteristics (including family background, family circumstances, human capital, motivation, length of time since the respondent first moved to the Gautreaux program—all before the move—and education after moving), they found that those who moved to apartments in the suburbs were significantly more likely than those moving to apartments in the city to have a job after the move. When asked what makes it easier to obtain employment in the suburbs, nearly all the respondents mentioned the availability of jobs.

The occupational advancement of the more disadvantaged urban minority members has also been severely curtailed by industrial restructuring. In this book, John Kasarda draws on data to show that "the bottom fell out in urban industrial demand

21. Holzer, "The Spatial Mismatch Hypothesis."

22. Christopher Jencks and Susan E. Mayer, "The Social Consequences of Growing Up in a Poor Neighborhood: A Review." Unpublished paper, Center for Urban Affairs and Policy Research, Northwestern University, 1989.

23. William Frey, "Mover Destination Selectivity and the Changing Suburbanization of Whites and Blacks," *Demography*, 22:223-243 (May 1985); and Eunice S. Grier and George Grier, "Minorities in Suburbia: A Mid-1980s Update." Report to the Urban Institute Project on Housing Mobility, March 1988.

24. Holzer, "The Spatial Mismatch Hypothesis."

25. James E. Rosenbaum and Susan J. Popkin, "Employment and Earnings of Low-Income Blacks Who Move to Middle-Class Suburbs," in *The Urban Underclass*, eds. Christopher Jencks and Paul E. Peterson (Washington, DC: The Brookings Institution, 1991), pp. 342-356.

for poorly educated blacks," particularly in the goods-producing industries in Northeast and Midwest cities. And data collected from the Chicago Urban Poverty and Family Life Survey show that efforts by out-of-school inner-city black men to obtain blue-collar jobs in the industries in which their fathers had been employed have been hampered by industrial restructuring. "The most common occupation reported by the cohort of respondents at ages 19 to 28 changed from operative and assembler jobs among the oldest cohorts to service jobs (waiters and janitors) among the youngest cohort."[26]

Finally, a recent study shows that although black employment in New York City declined by 84,000 in durable and nondurable goods manufacturing—industries whose workers have lower levels of education—from 1970 to 1987, black employment increased by 104,000 in public administration and professional services—industries whose workers are more highly educated.[27] Thus, if industrial restructuring has reduced opportunities for the least educated blacks, it may have improved opportunities for those more highly educated.

As I pointed out in *The Truly Disadvantaged*, manufacturing industries have been a major source of black employment in the 20th century. Unfortunately, these industries are particularly sensitive to a slack economy, and blacks lost a considerable number of jobs during the recession-plagued decade of the 1970s.[28] A unique test of my argument that many of the employment problems among disadvantaged inner-city youths are the direct result of job losses in local labor markets was provided by Richard Freeman. Examining the employment situation of disadvantaged black youths from 1983 to 1987 in metropolitan areas that had achieved the tightest labor markets by 1987, Freeman found that despite the social problems that beset these youths and "despite the 1980s twist in the American labor market against those with fewer skills, tight labor markets substantially improved their economic position." Although jobless rates remain high among disadvantaged minority youths, dramatic progress occurred during the economic recovery of the late 1980s in the metropolitan areas with the tightest labor markets.[29]

If a tight labor market reduces joblessness among the disadvantaged, it also effectively reduces poverty, as the research by Paul Osterman clearly shows. When Boston experienced full employment in the 1980s, not only was there a significant drop in poverty, but a high percentage of the poor had jobs. However, the strong economy did not significantly affect the prevalence of single-parent families. Was the period that Osterman observed (1980 to 1988) of sufficient length to allow for changes in family formation as a response to changes in the economy to emerge?

26. Mark Testa and Marilyn Krogh, *The Effect of Employment on Marriage Among Black Males in Inner-City Chicago.* Unpublished manuscript, University of Chicago, 1989.

27. Thomas Bailey, "Black Employment Opportunities," in *Setting Municipal Priorities, 1990*, eds. Charles Brecher and Raymond D. Horton (New York: New York University Press, 1989).

28. For a good discussion of this problem, see Frank Levy, *Dollars and Dreams: The Changing American Income Distribution* (New York: Russell Sage Foundation, 1987).

29. Richard B. Freeman, "Employment and Earnings of Disadvantaged Young Men in a Labor Shortage Economy," in *The Urban Underclass*, eds. Christopher Jencks and Paul E. Peterson (Washington, DC: The Brookings Institution), p. 119.

Changes in employment and poverty are likely to appear much sooner following changes in the economy than are changes in family formation because the latter not only represent a more indirect relationship to the economy but a more complex and subtle process of human experience as well.[30]

The relationship between employment and marriage received more detailed attention in a paper by Robert Mare and Christopher Winship. They found only modest support for the hypothesis, emphasized in *The Truly Disadvantaged*, that associates the sharp rise in poor single-parent families with the declining employment status of young black men. "Changes in the employment of young black men," they concluded, "explain approximately 20 percent of the decline in their marriage rates since 1960." Their results are based on national surveys.[31] But unlike *The Truly Disadvantaged*, their paper makes no effort to examine regional differences that may reflect the impact of changes in the industrial economies in the Northeast and Midwest.

The data that would be most relevant for understanding the relationship between employment and marriage decline among the underclass are those collected from inner cities. Since the publication of *The Truly Disadvantaged*, this relationship has been examined more closely with data from the inner-city neighborhoods of Chicago as a part of the Urban Poverty and Family Life Study. The chapter in this book by Mark Testa and his colleagues based on these data shows that black men in inner-city Chicago who have stable work are more

than twice as likely to marry as black men who are jobless.[32]

However, in a more recent study based on these same data, Testa also shows that the decline in marriage among inner-city blacks is not simply a function of the proportion of jobless men. Because the disparity in marriage rates between employed and jobless black men was smaller for older cohorts, it is reasonable to consider the effects of weaker social strictures against out-of-wedlock births. "In earlier years," he comments, "the social stigma of illegitimacy counterbalanced economic considerations in the decision to marry. As the norms of legitimacy weakened, marriage rates dropped precipitously among chronically jobless men as couples no longer felt obliged to legitimate the birth of a child for social reasons."[33]

In *The Truly Disadvantaged*, I related the increasing jobless rate among black men to geographic, industrial, and other shifts in the economy. This hypothesis has drawn criticisms because some observers believed that the focus on impersonal economic forces overlooked willful acts of employment discrimination against racial minorities.[34] Although empirical research on such discrimination is scarce, data from the Chicago Urban Poverty and Family Life Study's survey of employers suggest that inner-city blacks, particularly black men, do indeed face negative attitudes from employers. The Chicago study revealed that many employers consider inner-city workers, especially young black

30. Paul Osterman, "Gains from Growth? The Impact of a Full Employment Economy," pp. 122-134.

31. Robert D. Mare and Christopher Winship, "Socioeconomic Change and the Decline of Marriage for Blacks and Whites," pp. 175-202.

32. Mark Testa et al., see Chapter 6, this volume.

33. Mark Testa, "Joblessness and Absent Fatherhood in the Inner City." Paper presented at the annual meeting of the American Sociological Association, Washington, DC, 1990, p. 22.

34. Bailey op. cit.; and Jennifer Hochschild, "The Politics of the Estranged Poor," *Ethics*, 101: 560-578 (April 1991).

men, to be uneducated, uncooperative, and unstable. Accordingly, employers may practice what economists call statistical discrimination, making judgments about an applicant's productivity, which are often too difficult or too expensive to measure, on the basis of his or her race, ethnic, or class background.[35] Although only a few employers explicitly expressed racist attitudes or a categorical loathing of blacks, many did in fact practice statistical discrimination by screening out black job applicants because of their social class, public school education, and inner-city residence. These factors also served as proxies for judgments about productivity.

However, the practice of statistical discrimination will vary according to the tightness of the labor market. It therefore ought not be analyzed without reference to the overall state of the local or national economy. In a tight labor market, job vacancies are more prevalent, unemployment is of shorter duration, and wages are higher. The pool of potential workers expands because an increase in job opportunities not only lowers unemployment but also draws into the labor force those workers who respond to fading job prospects in slack markets by dropping out of the labor force altogether. Accordingly, the status of disadvantaged minorities improves in a tight labor market because unemployment is reduced, better

jobs are available, and wages are higher. In contrast, employers are—indeed, can afford to be—more selective in recruiting and in granting promotions in a slack labor market. They overemphasize job prerequisites and the importance of experience. In such an economic climate, the level of employer discrimination rises and disadvantaged minorities suffer disproportionately.[36]

Although basic economic transformations and changes in labor markets are important for understanding the life experiences of the urban minority poor, *The Truly Disadvantaged* also argued that the outmigration of higher-income residents from certain parts of the inner city resulted in a higher concentration of residents in ghetto neighborhoods. However, recent studies by Douglas Massey of the University of Chicago have questioned the extent of this outmigration of higher-income blacks from inner-city communities. He states, in a paper written with Mitchell Eggers, "Although the levels of black interclass segregation increased during the 1970s, we could find no evidence that these trends account for the rising concentration of black poverty." He argues that because of persisting segregation, higher-income blacks have been "less able to separate themselves from the poor than the privileged of other groups."[37] Accordingly, an increase in the poverty rate of a highly segregated group will be automatically accompanied by an increase in the concentration of poverty. However, Massey's measures of segregation are census tract averages of Standard Metropolitan Statistical Areas (SMSAs). The use of

---

35. See Joleen Kirschenman and Kathryn M. Neckerman, " 'We'd Love to Hire Them, but . . . ': The Meaning of Race for Employers," in *The Urban Underclass*, eds. Christopher Jencks and Paul E. Peterson (Washington, DC: The Brookings Institution, 1991), pp. 203-234; and Kathryn Neckerman and Joleen Kirschenman, "Statistical Discrimination and Inner-City Workers: An Investigation of Employers' Hiring Decisions." Paper presented at the annual meeting of the American Sociological Association, Washington, DC, 1990.

36. James Tobin, "On Improving the Economic Status of the Negro," *Daedalus* 94:878-898 (1965).

37. Doughlas S. Massey and Mitchell L. Eggers, "The Ecology of Inequality: Minorities and the Concentration of Poverty, 1970-1980," *American Journal of Sociology* 95:1186 (March 1990).

metropolitan averages obscures changes that have occurred in the outmigration of non-poor blacks from the more impoverished inner-city neighborhoods—the focus of analysis in *The Truly Disadvantaged*.

In contrast to the metropolitan averages used in Massey's research, three recent studies designed to test my hypothesis used measures to specifically identify concentrated poverty in particular neighborhoods. And contrary to Massey, they reached conclusions that firmly support the notion that there has been a significant outmigration of higher-income blacks from ghetto poverty areas, thereby contributing to the rise of concentrated poverty in these areas.

Dividing neighborhoods into traditional, emerging, and new poverty areas in Cleveland, Claudia Coulton and her colleagues at Case Western Reserve University found that although more persons became poor in all of these areas during the decade of the 1970s, the most important factor in the growth of concentrated poverty in these areas was the outmigration of the nonpoor.[38]

Paul Jargowsky and Mary Jo Bane of the Kennedy School at Harvard focused their research on Philadelphia, Cleveland, Milwaukee, and Memphis. Using census tracts as proxies for neighborhoods, they designate ghetto neighborhoods (that is, neighborhoods with rates of poverty of at least 40 percent) and nonghetto neighborhoods, and report a significant geographic spreading of ghetto neighborhoods from 1970 to 1980. Areas that had become ghettos by 1980 had been mixed-income tracts in 1970, although they were contiguous to areas identified as ghettos. Their results reveal that a major factor in the growth of ghetto poverty has been the exodus of the nonpoor from mixed income areas: "[T]he poor were leaving as well, but the nonpoor left faster, leaving behind a group of people in 1980 that was poorer than in 1970."[39]

As the population spread out from areas of mixed income, Jargowsky and Bane go on to state, the next ring, mostly areas that were white and nonpoor, became the home of a "larger proportion of the black and poor population. The white nonpoor left these areas, which also lost population overall." Thus, the black middle-class outmigration from the mixed income areas that then became ghettos did not result in a significant decrease in their contacts with poorer blacks because they relocated in areas that at the same time were being abandoned by nonpoor whites, areas that therefore experienced increasing segregation and poverty during the 1970s. Unfortunately, the geographic spread of ghetto poverty cannot be captured in studies such as Massey's that rely on averages at the metropolitan level (i.e., SMSAs).

The most important study on segregation and the geographic spread of concentrated poverty was conducted by the economist Kathryn Nelson of the Department of Housing and Urban Development. Using new data from HUD's American Housing Survey, Nelson identified zones of population within large metropolitan areas and traced the residential mobility among them during the 1980s. The zones of population can be interpreted as proxies for

38. Claudia J. Coulton, Julian Chow, and Shanta Pandey, *An Analysis of Poverty and Related Conditions in Cleveland Area Neighborhoods* (Cleveland, Ohio: Center for Urban Poverty and Social Change, Case Western Reserve University, 1990).

39. Jargowsky and Bane, "Ghetto Poverty in the United States, 1970-1980."

neighborhoods. Because she was able to identify both the current and previous residence for most of the intermetropolitan movers in these areas by zone, Nelson examined "intrametropolitan movers at a finer level of geographic detail than the city-suburb level typically available in Census publications or microdata."[40]

She found that during the 1980s all households, including blacks and other minorities, had high rates of outmigration from the poorest areas. Moreover, she discovered that the movement out of poor ghettos increased "markedly with income, among blacks and other minorities as well as for all households; and that high rates of black outmovement from the poorest areas were higher and more selective by income in the more segregated metropolitan areas." However, she also found that the white exodus from the poorest zones in the more segregated metropolitan areas was even higher than that of blacks and more positively associated with income. This led her to speculate that higher-income blacks in the more segregated metropolitan areas may have fewer nonghetto neighborhoods accessible to them, so that when they leave ghetto areas they have less space to disperse because of patterns of residential segregation and, as Massey's research suggests, are more likely to have poor people as neighbors.

Weak labor-force attachment and the inner-city neighborhood environment

The exodus of higher-income blacks was not only a factor in the growth of ghetto poverty, it also deprived these neighborhoods of structural resources, such as social buffers to minimize the effects of growing joblessness, and cultural resources, such as conventional role models for neighborhood children, therefore further contributing to the economic marginality of the underclass.

In *The Truly Disadvantaged*, I argued that the central problem of the underclass is joblessness reinforced by an increasing social isolation in impoverished neighborhoods, as reflected, for example, in the residents' declining access to job information network systems. Martha Van Haitsma, in an important conceptual paper, has more sharply delineated the relationship between the social environment and experiences in the labor market by distinguishing those persons with weak attachment to the labor force whose social context "tends to maintain or further weaken this attachment."[41] I would like to include this more explicit notion in my framework by equating the social context with the neighborhood.

The term *weak labor-force attachment* as used here does not imply a willingness or desire to work. Rather, I view weak labor-force attachment as a structural concept set in a theoretical framework that explains the vulnerability of certain groups to joblessness. In other words, the concept signifies the marginal position of some people in the labor force because of limited job opportunities or limited access to the informal job network systems. From a theoretical standpoint there are two major sources of weak labor-force attachment: macrostructural processes in the larger society, particularly the economy, and the individual's social environment. The former has been discussed; let me now briefly focus on the latter.

40. Kathryn P. Nelson, "Racial Segregation, Mobility, and Poverty Concentrations." Paper presented at the Annual Meeting of the Population Association of America, Washington, DC, March 22, 1991.

41. Martha Van Haitsma, "A Contextual Definition of the Underclass," *Focus* 12:28 (Spring-Summer 1989).

To understand the unique position of the underclass, it is important to understand the association between attachment to the labor force and the neighborhood context. As Martha Van Haitsma points out, "environments with low opportunity for stable and legitimate employment and high opportunity for alternative income-generating activities, particularly those which are incompatible with regular employment," perpetuate weak labor-force attachment.[42] Poor people who reside in neighborhoods that foster or support strong labor-force attachment are in a much different social context than those with similar education and occupational skills living in neighborhoods that promote or reinforce weak labor-force attachment.

Thus, neighborhoods that have few legitimate employment opportunities, inadequate job information networks, and poor schools not only give rise to weak labor-force attachment but also raise the likelihood that people will turn to illegal or deviant activities for income, thereby further weakening their attachment to the legitimate labor market. A jobless family in such a neighborhood is influenced by the behavior, beliefs, orientations, and social perceptions of other disadvantaged families disproportionately concentrated in the neighborhood. To capture this process I used the term *concentration effects*, that is, the effects of living in an overwhelmingly impoverished environment.

Several recent studies have addressed the hypothesis on concentration effects. Elijah Anderson's research in a ghetto neighborhood of Philadelphia provides ethnographic support by showing how a young woman's proximity to and degree of integration with certain neighborhood peer groups can significantly increase her chances of becoming pregnant.[43] Jonathan Crane, relying on evidence from a unique data set (the Neighborhood Characteristics File from the 1970 Public Use Microdata Sample) provides quantitative support for the hypothesis by showing that neighborhood influence on teenage childbearing and dropping out among both blacks and whites was substantial in inner cities. Consistent with the arguments developed in *The Truly Disadvantaged*, Crane found that "neighborhood effects are much larger at the bottom of the neighborhood distribution than elsewhere."[44] And Susan Mayer supports the hypothesis with data from the High School and Beyond Survey. She finds that teenagers attending schools of low socioeconomic status are more likely to give birth out of wedlock than those with the same socioeconomic background who attend schools of higher socioeconomic status.[45]

In a study of the political behavior of poor people, Jeffrey Berry, Kent E. Portney, and Ken Thomson present evidence that does not support the concentration-effects hypothesis. It is important to note, however, that the cities they selected for analysis included virtually no neighborhoods with a poverty level of 40 percent or more. Moreover, the neighbor-

42. Ibid., p. 7.

43. Elijah Anderson, "Neighborhood Effects on Teenage Pregnancy," in *The Urban Underclass*, eds. Christopher Jencks and Paul E. Peterson (Washington, DC: The Brookings Institution, 1991), pp. 375-398.

44. Jonathan Crane, "Effects of Neighborhoods on Dropping out of School and Teenage Childbearing," in *The Urban Underclass*, eds. Christopher Jencks and Paul E. Peterson (Washington, DC: The Brookings Institution, 1991), pp. 299-320.

45. Susan E. Mayer, "How Much Does a High School's Racial and Socioeconomic Mix Affect Graduation and Teenage Fertility Rates," in *The Urban Underclass*, eds. Christopher Jencks and Paul E. Peterson (Washington, DC: The Brookings Institution, 1991), pp. 321-341.

hoods they identified as poor neighborhoods represented those "that cross the 20 percent threshold." Accordingly, the absence of extreme poverty or ghetto neighborhoods qualifies their conclusion that the concentration of poor blacks does not lead to distinctive patterns of political behavior.[46]

However, a study of concentrated poverty and black politics in Detroit, which divided neighborhoods into those with poverty rates of 0-10 percent, 11-20 percent, 21-30 percent, and at least 31 percent, found that the residents in the most impoverished neighborhoods (i.e., those with poverty rates of at least 31 percent) held significantly "different political attitudes and exhibited different political behavior beyond the impact of individual poverty."[47]

It would also be interesting and important to replicate a recent study by Greg Duncan and Saul Hoffman in areas of extreme poverty. On the basis of national data from the Michigan Panel Study of Income Dynamics, they found that raising AFDC benefit levels increased slightly the chances that a teenager would have a child out of wedlock and would receive AFDC. Nonwelfare opportunities decreased the chances and the effect was much stronger. The teenagers most likely to bear a child, they find, are those with the least to lose.[48] This view

is supported in Anderson's study: "Those who cannot go on to college, who lack an outlook, who fail to find a husband with whom they can pursue the dream and become upwardly mobile, appear to adapt to the situation of closed mobility they see before them."[49] And as Crane's research demonstrates, this is far more likely to happen in an impoverished inner-city neighborhood than in one that is less poor. That is one of many reasons why the neighborhood environment is crucial to my definition of the concept *underclass*.[50]

Social theory and the concept of the underclass

In my formulation, the concept of underclass derives its meaning from a theoretical framework that links structural, social-psychological, and cultural arguments. Simplistic either-or notions of culture and social structure impede the development of a broader theoretical context in which to examine questions recently raised by the ongoing debate on the underclass.

In early studies of the inner city, some observers argued that ghetto-specific behaviors were unique adaptations to the restricted opportunities of the disadvantaged in American society, not a different system of values.[51] Although they discussed the influence of culture—that is, the extent to which people follow their inclinations as

46. Jeffrey M. Berry, Kent E. Portney, and Ken Thomson, "The Political Behavior of Poor People," in *The Urban Underclass*, eds. Christopher Jencks and Paul E. Peterson (Washington, DC: The Brookings Institution, 1991), pp. 357-374.

47. Cathy J. Cohen and Michael C. Dawson, *Neighborhood Poverty and African American Politics*. Unpublished manuscript, 1992, p. 23.

48. Greg J. Duncan and Saul D. Hoffman, "Teenage Underclass Behavior and Subsequent Poverty: Have the Rules Changed," in *The Urban Underclass*, eds. Christopher Jencks and Paul E. Peterson (Washington, DC: The Brookings Institution, 1991), pp. 155-174.

49. Anderson, "Neighborhood Effects on Teenage Pregnancy," op. cit., p. 394.

50. Crane, "Effects of Neighborhoods on Dropping Out of School," op. cit.

51. Kenneth B. Clark, *Dark Ghetto: Dilemmas of Social Power* (New York: Harper & Row, 1965); Lee Rainwater, *Behind Ghetto Walls: Black Families in a Federal Slum* (Chicago: Aldine Press, 1969); and Ulf Hannerz, *Soulside: Inquiries into Ghetto Culture and Community* (New York: Columbia University Press, 1970).

they have been developed by learning from other members of the community—they did not argue that the influence takes on a life of its own or is autonomous in the ghetto. In other words, these authors demonstrated the possibility of seeing the importance of macrostructural constraints (that is, of avoiding the extreme assumption of a culture of poverty) while still recognizing the value of a more subtle cultural analysis of life in poverty. The question Ulf Hannerz raised 20 years ago remains an important research hypothesis today. Is there a fundamental difference between "a person who is alone in being exposed to certain macrostructural constraints" and a person "who is influenced both by these constraints and by the behavior of others who are affected by them"?[52]

What distinguishes members of the underclass from those of other economically disadvantaged groups is that their marginal economic position or weak attachment to the labor force is uniquely reinforced by the neighborhood or social milieu. For this reason, Christopher Jencks's recent discussion of the concept of the underclass is not relevant. Although he has elegantly and impressively laid out the various ways that one can view the underclass, his typology has no underlying theoretical significance. He argues that "what we now call the underclass bears a striking resemblance to what sociologists use to call the lower class." This is not true with the formulation developed in *The Truly Disadvantaged* and further elaborated here. Indeed, I know of no previous studies that attempted to define *lower class* in terms of the dual problem of marginal economic position and social isolation in highly concentrated poverty areas, an important distinction that cannot be captured by using the standard designation

"lower class." In America, the problems this definition of the underclass connotes are more likely to be found in the inner-city ghettos.

Jencks argues that my definition of the underclass also turns out to mean a largely nonwhite population because I emphasize location. However, in my usage, the concept can be theoretically applied not only to all racial and ethnic groups but also to different societies. In the United States, the concept will more often refer to minorities because the white poor seldom live in extreme poverty or ghetto areas. However, there is nothing in the definition that restricts its application to nonwhites. Moreover, in other societies the combination of weak labor-force attachment and social isolation may exist in certain urban environments without the same level of concentrated poverty inherent in American ghettos. For example, there is evidence that the long-term jobless in the inner cities in the Netherlands have experienced sharply decreasing contact with conventional groups and institutions in the larger society despite levels of class and ethnic segregation far below those of American inner cities. This development has prompted several Dutch social scientists to discuss the formation of an underclass in the Netherlands in precisely the theoretical terms that I outlined in *The Truly Disadvantaged*.[53]

52. Hannerz, *Soulside*, p. 184.

53. See, for example, Kees Schuyt, "The New Emerging Underclass in Europe: The Experience of Long-Term Unemployment in Dutch Inner Cities." Paper presented at the Leiden Workshop on Modern Poverty, Unemployment and the Emergence of a Dutch Underclass, University of Leiden, Netherlands, August 1990; Robert C. Kloosterman, "The Making of the Dutch Underclass? A Labour Market View." Paper presented at the Workshop on Social Policy and the Underclass, University of Amsterdam, the Netherlands, August 1990; and Godfried Engbersen, Kees Schuyt, and Jaap Timmer, *Cultures of Unemployment: Long Term Unemployment in Dutch Inner Cities* (Boulder, Colorado: Westview Press, 1993).

Unless the concept of underclass is defined as a part of a theoretical framework, as I have done, its meaning will become hopelessly polluted and, as Herbert Gans has warned, will be used increasingly to discredit the urban minority poor.[54] Indeed, one of my concerns is that because of the atheoretical way that the concept is often defined by scholars and nonscholars alike, its use has become exceedingly controversial, so much so that the debate has often obscured the important theoretical and empirical issues discussed in this book and outlined here.

The crucial question is whether a theoretically defined concept of underclass, which is by its very nature complex, will be overshadowed in the long run by nonsystematic, arbitrary, and atheoretical usages that often end up as code words or ideological slogans, particularly in journalistic descriptions of inner-city behavior. If this proves true, research scholars ought to give serious consideration to dropping the term and carefully selecting another that also allows one to describe and highlight the important theoretical linkage between a disadvantaged group's position in the labor market and its social environment.

54. Herbert Gans, "Deconstructing the Underclass: The Term's Danger as a Planning Concept," *Journal of the American Planning Association,* 56:271-349 (Summer 1990).

2

The Cost of Racial and Class Exclusion in the Inner City

By LOÏC J. D. WACQUANT and WILLIAM JULIUS WILSON

ABSTRACT: Discussions of inner-city social dislocations are often severed from the struggles and structural changes in the larger society, economy, and polity that in fact determine them, resulting in undue emphasis on the individual attributes of ghetto residents and on the alleged grip of the so-called culture of poverty. This article provides a different perspective by drawing attention to the specific features of the proximate social structure in which ghetto residents evolve and try to survive. This is done by contrasting the class composition, welfare trajectories, economic and financial assets, and social capital of blacks who live in Chicago's ghetto neighborhoods with those who reside in this city's low-poverty areas. Our central argument is that the interrelated set of phenomena captured by the term "underclass" is primarily social-structural and that the inner city is experiencing a crisis because the dramatic growth in joblessness and economic exclusion associated with the ongoing spatial and industrial restructuring of American capitalism has triggered a process of hyperghettoization.

Loïc J. D. Wacquant is pursuing doctorates in sociology at the University of Chicago and the Ecole des hautes études en sciences sociales, Paris. He is presently a research assistant on the Urban Poverty and Family Structure Project, investigating the relationships between class, race, and joblessness in the United States.

A MacArthur prize fellow, William Julius Wilson is the Lucy Flower Distinguished Service Professor of Sociology and Social Policy at the University of Chicago. He is the author of Power, Racism, and Privilege; The Declining Significance of Race; The Truly Disadvantaged; *and coeditor of* Through Different Eyes.

NOTE: This article is based on data gathered and analyzed as part of the University of Chicago's Urban Poverty and Family Structure Project, whose principal investigator is W. J. Wilson. We gratefully acknowledge the financial support of the Ford Foundation, the Carnegie Corporation, the U.S. Department of Health and Human Services, the Institute for Research on Poverty, the Joyce Foundation, the Lloyd A. Fry Foundation, the Rockefeller Foundation, the Spencer Foundation, the William T. Grant Foundation, and the Woods Charitable Fund.

A FTER a long eclipse, the ghetto has made a stunning comeback into the collective consciousness of America. Not since the riots of the hot summers of 1966-68 have the black poor received so much attention in academic, activist, and policymaking quarters alike.[1] Persistent and rising poverty, especially among children, mounting social disruptions, the continuing degradation of public housing and public schools, concern over the eroding tax base of cities plagued by large ghettos and by the dilemmas of gentrification, the disillusions of liberals over welfare have all combined to put the black inner-city poor back in the spotlight. Owing in large part to the pervasive and ascendant influence of conservative ideology in the United States, however, recent discussions of the plight of ghetto blacks have typically been cast in individualistic and moralistic terms. The poor are presented as a mere aggregation of personal cases, each with its own logic and self-contained causes. Severed from the struggles and structural changes in the society, economy, and polity that in fact determine them, inner-city dislocations are then portrayed as a self-imposed, self-sustaining phenomenon.

1. For instance, Sheldon H. Danziger and Daniel H. Weinberg, eds., *Fighting Poverty: What Works and What Doesn't* (Cambridge, MA: Harvard University Press, 1986); William Kornblum, "Lumping the Poor: What *Is* the Underclass?" *Dissent,* Summer 1984, pp. 275-302; William Julius Wilson, *The Truly Disadvantaged: The Inner City, the Underclass and Public Policy* (Chicago: University of Chicago Press, 1987); Rose M. Brewer, "Black Women in Poverty: Some Comments on Female-Headed Families," *Signs: Journal of Women in Culture and Society,* 13(2):331-39 (Winter 1988); Fred R. Harris and Roger W. Wilkins, eds., *Quiet Riots: Race and Poverty in the United States* (New York: Pantheon, 1988). Martha A. Gephart and Robert W. Pearson survey recent research in their "Contemporary Research on the Urban Underclass," *Items,* 42(1-2):1-10 (June 1988).

This vision of poverty has found perhaps its most vivid expression in the lurid descriptions of ghetto residents that have flourished in the pages of popular magazines and on televised programs devoted to the emerging underclass.[2] Descriptions and explanations of the current predicament of inner-city blacks put the emphasis on individual attributes and the alleged grip of the so-called culture of poverty.

This article, in sharp contrast, draws attention to the specific features of the proximate social structure in which ghetto residents evolve and strive, against formidable odds, to survive and, whenever they can, escape its poverty and degradation. We provide this different perspective by profiling blacks who live in Chicago's inner city, contrasting the situation of those who dwell in low-poverty areas with residents of the city's ghetto neighborhoods. Beyond its sociographic focus, the central argument running through this article is that the interrelated set of phenomena captured by the term "underclass" is primarily social-structural and that the ghetto is experiencing a "crisis" not because a "welfare ethos" has mysteriously taken over its residents but because joblessness and economic exclusion, having reached dramatic proportions, have triggered a process of hyperghettoization.

Indeed, the urban black poor of today differ both from their counterparts of earlier years and from the white poor in that they are becoming increasingly concentrated in dilapidated territorial enclaves that epitomize acute social and economic marginalization. In Chicago, for instance, the proportion of all black poor residing in extreme-poverty areas—

2. William Julius Wilson, "The American Underclass: Inner-City Ghettos and the Norms of Citizenship" (Godkin Lecture, John F. Kennedy School of Government, Harvard University, Apr. 1988), offers a critical dissection of these accounts.

that is, census tracts with a population at least 40 percent of which comprises poor persons—shot up from 24 percent to 47 percent between 1970 and 1980. By this date, fully 38 percent of all poor blacks in the 10 largest American cities lived in extreme-poverty tracts, contrasted with 22 percent a decade before, and with only 6 percent of poor non-Hispanic whites.[3]

This growing social and spatial concentration of poverty creates a formidable and unprecedented set of obstacles for ghetto blacks. As we shall see, the social structure of today's inner city has been radically altered by the mass exodus of jobs and working families and by the rapid deterioration of housing, schools, businesses, recreational facilities, and other community organizations, further exacerbated by government policies of industrial and urban laissez-faire[4] that have channeled a disproportionate share of federal, state, and municipal resources to the more affluent. The economic and social buffer provided by a stable black working class and a visible, if small, black middle class that cushioned the impact of downswings in the economy and tied ghetto residents to the world of work has all but disappeared. Moreover, the social networks of parents, friends, and associates, as well as the nexus of local institutions, have seen their resources for economic stability progressively depleted. In sum, today's ghetto residents face a closed opportunity structure.

3. A detailed analysis of changes in population, poverty, and poverty concentration in these 10 cities is presented in Loïc J.D. Wacquant and William Julius Wilson, "Poverty, Joblessness and the Social Transformation of the Inner City," in *Reforming Welfare Policy,* ed. D. Ellwood and P. Cottingham (Cambridge, MA: Harvard University Press, forthcoming).

4. See Gregory D. Squires et al., *Chicago: Race, Class, and the Response to Urban Decline* (Philadelphia: Temple University Press, 1987).

The purpose of this article is to begin to highlight this specifically sociological dimension of the changing reality of ghetto poverty by focusing on Chicago's inner city. Using data from a multistage, random sample of black residents of Chicago's poor communities,[5] we show that ghetto dwellers do face specific obstacles owing to the characteristics of the social structure they compose. We begin, by way of background, by sketching the accelerating degradation of Chicago's inner city, relating the cumulation of social dislocations visited upon its South and West sides to changes in the city's economy over the last thirty years.

5. The following is a summary description of the sample design and characteristics of the data for this article. The data come from a survey of 2490 inner-city residents of Chicago fielded by the National Opinion Research Center in 1986-87 for the Urban Poverty and Family Structure Project of the University of Chicago. The sample for blacks was drawn randomly from residents of the city's 377 tracts with poverty rates of at least 20.0 percent, the citywide average as of the last census. It was stratified by parental status and included 1184 respondents—415 men and 769 women—for a completion rate of 83.0 percent for black parents and 78.0 percent for black nonparents. Of the 1166 black respondents who still lived in the city at the time they were interviewed, 405, or 34.7 percent, resided in low-poverty tracts—that is, tracts with poverty rates between 20.0 and 29.9 percent—to which were added 41 individuals, or 3.5 percent, who had moved into tracts with poverty rates below 20.0 percent; 364, or 31.2 percent, lived in high-poverty tracts—tracts with poverty rates of 30.0 to 39.9 percent—and are excluded from the analyses reported in this article; and 356, or 30.5 percent, inhabited extreme-poverty areas, including 9.6 percent in tracts with poverty rates above 50.0 percent. The latter include 63 persons, or 17.7 percent of all extreme-poverty-area residents, dwelling in tracts with poverty rates in excess of 70.0 percent—public housing projects in most cases. All the results presented in this article are based on unweighted data, although weighted data exhibit essentially the same patterns.

DEINDUSTRIALIZATION AND HYPERGHETTOIZATION

Social conditions in the ghettos of Northern metropolises have never been enviable, but today they are scaling new heights in deprivation, oppression, and hardship. The situation of Chicago's black inner city is emblematic of the social changes that have sown despair and exclusion in these communities. As Table 1 indicates, an unprecedented tangle of social woes is now gripping the black communities of the city's South Side and West Side. In the past decade alone, these racial enclaves have experienced rapid increases in the number and percentage of poor families, extensive out-migration of working- and middle-class households, stagnation—if not real regression—of income, and record levels of unemployment. As of the last census, over two-thirds of all families living in these areas were headed by women; about half of the population had to rely on public aid, for most adults were out of a job and only a tiny fraction of them had completed college.[6]

The single largest force behind this increasing social and economic marginalization of large numbers of inner-city blacks has been a set of mutually reinforcing spatial and industrial changes in the country's urban political economy[7] that have converged to undermine the material foundations of the traditional ghetto. Among these structural shifts are the decentralization of industrial plants, which commenced at the time of World War I but accelerated sharply after 1950, and the flight of manufacturing jobs abroad, to the Sunbelt states, or to the suburbs and exurbs at a time when blacks were continuing to migrate en masse to Rustbelt central cities; the general deconcentration of metropolitan economies and the turn toward service industries and occupations, promoted by the growing separation of banks and industry; and the emergence of post-Taylorist, so-called flexible forms of organizations and generalized corporate attacks on unions—expressed by, among other things, wage cutbacks and the spread of two-tier wage systems and labor contracting—which has intensified job competition and triggered an explosion of low-pay, part-time work. This means that even mild forms of racial discrimination—mild by historical standards—have a bigger impact on those at the bottom of the American class order. In the labor-surplus environment of the 1970s, the weakness of unions and the retrenchment of civil rights enforcement aggravated the structuring of unskilled labor markets along racial lines,[8] marking large num-

---

6. A more detailed analysis of social changes on Chicago's South Side is in William Julius Wilson et al., "The Ghetto Underclass and the Changing Structure of Urban Poverty," in *Quiet Riots*, ed. Harris and Wilkins.

7. Space does not allow us to do more than allude to the transformations of the American economy as they bear on the ghetto. For provocative analyses of the systemic disorganization of advanced capitalist economies and polities and the impact, actual and potential, of postindustrial and flexible-specialization trends on cities and their labor markets, see Scott Lash and John Urry, *The End of Organized Capitalism* (Madison: University of Wisconsin Press, 1988); Claus Offe, *Disorganized Capitalism: Contemporary Transformations of Work and Politics*, ed. John Keane (Cambridge: MIT Press, 1985); Fred Block, *Revising State Theory: Essays on Politics and Postindustrialism* (Philadelphia: Temple University Press, 1987); Donald A. Hicks, *Advanced Industrial Development* (Boston: Oelgeschlager, Gun and Hain, 1985); Barry Bluestone and Bennett Harrison, *The Great U-Turn* (New York: Basic Books, 1988); Michael J. Piore and Charles F. Sabel, *The Second Industrial Divide: Possibilities for Prosperity* (New York: Basic Books, 1984).

8. See, for instance, Norman Fainstein, "The Underclass/Mismatch Hypothesis as an Explana-

TABLE 1
SELECTED CHARACTERISTICS OF CHICAGO'S GHETTO NEIGHBORHOOD, 1970-80

Area	Families below Poverty Line (percentage)		Unemployed (percentage)		Female-Headed Families (percentage)		Median Family Income*		Residents with Four-Year College Degree (percentage)	
	1970	1980	1970	1980	1970	1980	1970	1980	1970	1980
West Side										
Near West Side	35	47	8	16	37	66	6.0	7.5	5	13†
East Garfield Park	32	40	8	21	34	61	6.4	9.7	1	2
North Lawndale	30	40	9	20	33	61	7.0	9.9	2	3
West Garfield Park	25	37	8	21	29	58	7.5	10.9	1	2
South Side										
Oakland	44	61	13	30	48	79	4.9	5.5	2	3
Grand Boulevard	37	51	10	24	40	76	5.6	6.9	2	3
Washington Park	28	43	8	21	35	70	6.5	8.1	2	3
Near South Side	37	43	7	20	41	76	5.2	7.3	5	9†

SOURCE: Chicago Fact Book Consortium, *Local Community Fact Book: Chicago Metropolitan Area* (Chicago: Chicago Review Press, 1984).

*In thousands of dollars annually.

†Increases due to the partial gentrification of these areas.

bers of inner-city blacks with the stamp of economic redundancy.

In 1954, Chicago was still near the height of its industrial power. Over 10,000 manufacturing establishments operated within the city limits, employing a total of 616,000, including nearly half a million production workers. By 1982, the number of plants had been cut by half, providing a mere 277,000 jobs for fewer than 162,000 blue-collar employees—a loss of 63 percent, in sharp contrast with the overall growth of manufacturing employment in the country, which added almost 1 million production jobs in the quarter century starting in 1958. This crumbling of the city's industrial base was accompanied by substantial cuts in trade employment, with over 120,000 jobs lost in retail and wholesale from 1963 to 1982. The mild growth of services—which created an additional 57,000 jobs during the same period, excluding health, financial, and social services—came nowhere near to compensating for this collapse of Chicago's low-skilled employment pool. Because, traditionally, blacks have relied heavily on manufacturing and blue-collar employment for economic sustenance,[9] the upshot of these structural economic changes for the inhabitants of the inner

city has been a steep and accelerating rise in labor market exclusion. In the 1950s, ghetto blacks had roughly the same rate of employment as the average Chicagoan, with some 6 adults in 10 working (see Table 2). While this ratio has not changed citywide over the ensuing three decades, nowadays most residents of the Black Belt cannot find gainful employment and must resort to welfare, to participation in the second economy, or to illegal activities in order to survive. In 1980, two persons in three did not hold jobs in the ghetto neighborhoods of East Garfield Park and Washington Park, and three adults in four were not employed in Grand Boulevard and Oakland.[10]

As the metropolitan economy moved away from smokestack industries and expanded outside of Chicago, emptying the Black Belt of most of its manufacturing jobs and employed residents, the gap between the ghetto and the rest of the city, not to mention its suburbs, widened dramatically. By 1980, median family income on the South and West sides had dropped to around one-third and one-half of the city average, respectively, compared with two-thirds and near parity thirty years earlier. Meanwhile, some of the city's white bourgeois neighborhoods and upper-class suburbs had reached over twice the citywide figure. Thus in 1980, half of the families of Oakland had to make do with less than $5500 a year, while half of the families of Highland Park incurred incomes in excess of $43,000.

tion for Black Economic Deprivation," *Politics and Society,* 15(4):403-52 (1986-87); Wendy Wintermute, "Recession and 'Recovery': Impact on Black and White Workers in Chicago" (Chicago: Chicago Urban League, 1983); Bruce Williams, *Black Workers in an Industrial Suburb: The Struggle against Discrimination* (New Brunswick, NJ: Rutgers University Press, 1987).

9. In 1950, fully 60 percent of employed black men and 43 percent of black women in Chicago had blue-collar occupations, skilled and unskilled combined, compared to 48 percent and 28 percent of white men and women, respectively. See "Black Metropolis 1961, Appendix," in St. Clair Drake and Horace R. Cayton, *Black Metropolis: A Study of Negro Life in a Northern City,* 2 vols., rev. and enlarged ed. (originally 1945; New York: Harper & Row, 1962).

10. Rates of joblessness have risen at a much faster pace in the ghetto than for blacks as a whole. For comparative data on the long-term decline of black labor force participation, esp. among males, see Reynolds Farley and Walter R. Allen, *The Color Line and the Quality of Life in America* (New York: Russell Sage Foundation, 1987); Katherine L. Bradbury and Lynn E. Brown, "Black Men in the Labor Market," *New England Economic Review,* Mar.-Apr. 1986, pp. 32-42.

TABLE 2
THE HISTORIC RISE OF LABOR MARKET EXCLUSION
IN CHICAGO'S GHETTO NEIGHBORHOODS, 1950-80

	Adults Not Employed (percentage)		
	1950	1970	1980
City of Chicago	43.4	41.5	44.8
West Side			
Near West Side	49.8	51.2	64.8
East Garfield Park	38.7	51.9	67.2
North Lawndale	43.7	56.0	62.2
South Side			
Oakland	49.1	64.3	76.0
Grand Boulevard	47.5	58.2	74.4
Washington Park	45.3	52.0	67.1

SOURCE: Computed from Chicago Fact Book Consortium, *Local Community Fact Book: Chicago Metropolitan Area*; Philip M. Hauser and Evelyn M. Kitagawa, *Local Community Fact Book for Chicago, 1950* (Chicago: University of Chicago, Chicago Community Inventory, 1953).
NOTE: Labor market exclusion is measured by the percentage of adults not employed, aged 16 years and older for 1970 and 1980, 14 years and older for 1950.

A recent ethnographic account of changes in North Kenwood, one of the poorest black sections on the city's South Side, vividly encapsulates the accelerated physical and social decay of the ghetto and is worth quoting at some length:

In the 1960's, 47th Street was still the social hub of the South Side black community. Sue's eyes light up when she describes how the street used to be filled with stores, theaters and nightclubs in which one could listen to jazz bands well into the evening. Sue remembers the street as "soulful." Today the street might be better characterized as soulless. Some stores, currency exchanges, bars and liquor stores continue to exist on 47th. Yet, as one walks down the street, one is struck more by the death of the street than by its life. Quite literally, the destruction of human life occurs frequently on 47th. In terms of physical structures, many stores are boarded up and abandoned. A few buildings have bars across the front and are closed to the public, but they are not empty. They are used, not so secretly, by people involved in illegal activities. Other stretches of the street are simply barren, empty lots. Whatever buildings once stood on the lots are long gone. Nothing gets built on 47th. . . . Over the years one apartment building after another has been condemned by the city and torn down. Today many blocks have the bombed-out look of Berlin after World War II. There are huge, barren areas of Kenwood, covered by weeds, bricks, and broken bottles.[11]

Duncan reports how this disappearance of businesses and loss of housing have stimulated the influx of drugs and criminal activities to undermine the strong sense of solidarity that once permeated the community. With no activities or organizations left to bring them together or to represent them as a collectivity, with half the population gone in 15 years, the remaining residents, some of whom now refer to North Kenwood as the "Wild West," seem to be engaged in a perpetual

11. Arne Duncan, "The Values, Aspirations, and Opportunities of the Urban Underclass" (B.A. honors thesis, Harvard University, 1987), pp. 18 ff.

bellum omnium contra omnes for sheer survival. One informant expresses this succinctly: "'It's gotten worse. They tore down all the buildings, deterioratin' the neighborhood. All your friends have to leave. They are just spreading out your mellahs [close friends]. It's not no neighborhood anymore.'"[12] With the ever-present threat of gentrification—much of the area is prime lake-front property that would bring in huge profits if it could be turned over to upper-class condominiums and apartment complexes to cater to the needs of the higher-income clientele of Hyde Park, which lies just to the south—the future of the community appears gloomy. One resident explains: "'They want to put all the blacks in the projects. They want to build buildings for the rich, and not us poor people. They are trying to move us all out. In four or five years we will all be gone.'"[13]

Fundamental changes in the organization of America's advanced economy have thus unleashed irresistible centrifugal pressures that have broken down the previous structure of the ghetto and set off a process of hyperghettoization.[14] By this, we mean that the ghetto has lost much of its organizational strength—the "pulpit and the press," for instance, have virtually collapsed as collective agencies—as it has become increasingly marginal economically; its activities are no longer structured around an internal and relatively autonomous social space that duplicates the institutional structure of

the larger society and provides basic minimal resources for social mobility, if only within a truncated black class structure. And the social ills that have long been associated with segregated poverty—violent crime, drugs, housing deterioration, family disruption, commercial blight, and educational failure—have reached qualitatively different proportions and have become articulated into a new configuration that endows each with a more deadly impact than before.

If the "organized," or institutional, ghetto of forty years ago described so graphically by Drake and Cayton[15] imposed an enormous cost on blacks collectively,[16] the "disorganized" ghetto, or hyperghetto, of today carries an even larger price. For, now, not only are ghetto residents, as before, dependent on the will and decisions of outside forces that rule the field of power—the mostly white dominant class, corporations, realtors, politicians, and welfare agencies—they have no control over and are forced to rely on services and institutions that are massively inferior to those of the wider society. Today's ghetto inhabitants

12. In ibid., p. 21.
13. In ibid., p. 28.
14. See Gary Orfield, "Ghettoization and Its Alternatives," in *The New Urban Reality*, ed. P. Peterson (Washington, DC: Brookings Institution, 1985), for an account of processes of ghettoization; and Wacquant and Wilson, "Poverty, Joblessness and Social Transformation," for a preliminary discussion of some of the factors that underlie hyperghettoization.

15. Drake and Cayton, *Black Metropolis.*
16. Let us emphasize here that this contrast between the traditional ghetto and the hyperghetto of today implies no nostalgic celebration of the ghetto of yesteryear. If the latter was organizationally and socially integrated, it was not by choice but under the yoke of total black subjugation and with the threat of racial violence looming never too far in the background. See Arnold Hirsch, *Making the Second Ghetto: Race and Housing in Chicago, 1940-1960* (New York: Cambridge University Press, 1983), for an account of riots and violent white opposition to housing desegregation in Chicago in the two decades following World War II. The organized ghetto emerged out of necessity, as a limited, if creative, response to implacable white hostility; separatism was never a voluntary development, but a protection against unyielding pressures from without, as shown in Allan H. Spear, *Black Chicago: The Making of a Negro Ghetto, 1890-1920* (Chicago: University of Chicago Press, 1968).

comprise almost exclusively the most marginal and oppressed sections of the black community. Having lost the economic underpinnings and much of the fine texture of organizations and patterned activities that allowed previous generations of urban blacks to sustain family, community, and collectivity even in the face of continued economic hardship and unflinching racial subordination, the inner-city now presents a picture of radical class and racial exclusion. It is to a sociographic assessment of the latter that we now turn.

THE COST OF
LIVING IN THE GHETTO

Let us contrast the social structure of ghetto neighborhoods with that of low-poverty black areas of the city of Chicago. For purposes of this comparison, we have classified as low-poverty neighborhoods all those tracts with rates of poverty—as measured by the number of persons below the official poverty line—between 20 and 30 percent as of the 1980 census. Given that the overall poverty rate among black families in the city is about one-third, these low-poverty areas can be considered as roughly representative of the average non-ghetto, non-middle-class, black neighborhood of Chicago. In point of fact, nearly all—97 percent—of the respondents in this category reside outside traditional ghetto areas. Extreme-poverty neighborhoods comprise tracts with at least 40 percent of their residents in poverty in 1980. These tracts make up the historic heart of Chicago's black ghetto: over 82 percent of the respondents in this category inhabit the West and South sides of the city, in areas most of which have been all black for half a century and more, and an additional 13 percent live in immediately

adjacent tracts. Thus when we counterpose extreme-poverty areas with low-poverty areas, we are in effect comparing ghetto neighborhoods with other black areas, most of which are moderately poor, that are not part of Chicago's traditional Black Belt. Even though this comparison involves a truncated spectrum of types of neighborhoods,[17] the contrasts it reveals between low-poverty and ghetto tracts are quite pronounced.

It should be noted that this distinction between low-poverty and ghetto neighborhoods is not merely analytical but captures differences that are clearly perceived by social agents themselves. First, the folk category of ghetto does, in Chicago, refer to the South Side and West Side, not just to any black area of the city; mundane usages of the term entail a social-historical and spatial referent rather than simply a racial dimension. Furthermore, blacks who live in extreme-poverty areas have a noticeably more negative opinion of their neighborhood. Only 16 percent rate it as a "good" to "very good" place to live in, compared to 41 percent among inhabitants of low-poverty tracts; almost 1 in 4 find their neighborhood "bad or very bad" compared to fewer than 1 in 10 among the latter. In short, the contrast between ghetto and non-ghetto poor areas is one that is socially meaningful to their residents.

The black class structure in
and out of the ghetto

The first major difference between low- and extreme-poverty areas has to do

17. Poverty levels were arbitrarily limited by the sampling design: areas with less than 20 percent poor persons in 1980 were excluded at the outset, and tracts with extreme levels of poverty, being generally relatively underpopulated, ended up being underrepresented by the random sampling procedure chosen.

with their class structure (see Figure 1). A sizable majority of blacks in low-poverty tracts are gainfully employed: two-thirds hold a job, including 11 percent with middle-class occupations and 55 percent with working-class jobs, while one-third do not work.[18] These proportions are exactly opposite in the ghetto, where fully 61 percent of adult residents do not work, one-third have working-class jobs and a mere 6 percent enjoy middle-class status. For those who reside in the urban core, then, being without a job is by far the most likely occurrence, while being employed is the exception. Controlling for gender does not affect this contrast, though it does reveal the greater economic vulnerability of women, who are twice as likely as men to be jobless. Men in both

18. Class categories have been roughly defined on the basis of the respondent's current occupation as follows: the middle class comprises managers, administrators, executives, professional specialists, and technical staff; the working class includes both blue-collar workers and noncredentialed white-collar workers; in the jobless category fall all those who did not hold a job at the time of the interview. Our dividing line between middle and working class, cutting across white-collar occupations, is consistent with recent research and theory on class—for example, Erik Olin Wright, *Classes* (New York: Verso, 1985); Nicolas Abercrombie and John Urry, *Capital, Labour and the Middle Classes* (London: George Allen & Unwin, 1983)—and on contemporary perceptions of class in the black community—see Reeve Vanneman and Lynn Cannon Weber, *The American Perception of Class* (Philadelphia: Temple University Press, 1987), chap. 10. The category of the jobless is admittedly heterogeneous, as it should be given that the identity of those without an occupational position is ambiguous and ill-defined in reality itself. It includes people actively looking for work (half the men and 1 woman in 10), keeping house (13 percent of the men and 61 percent of the women), and a minority of respondents who also attend school part- or full-time (16 percent of the males, 14 percent of the females). A few respondents without jobs declared themselves physically unable to work (6 percent of the men, 3 percent of the women).

types of neighborhoods have a more favorable class mix resulting from their better rates of employment: 78 percent in low-poverty areas and 66 percent in the ghetto. If women are much less frequently employed—42 percent in low-poverty areas and 69 percent in the ghetto do not work—they have comparable, that is, severely limited, overall access to middle-class status: in both types of neighborhood, only about 10 percent hold credentialed salaried positions or better.

These data are hardly surprising. They stand as a brutal reminder that joblessness and poverty are two sides of the same coin. The poorer the neighborhood, the more prevalent joblessness and the lower the class recruitment of its residents. But these results also reveal that the degree of economic exclusion observed in ghetto neighborhoods during the period of sluggish economic growth of the late 1970s is still very much with us nearly a decade later, in the midst of the most rapid expansion in recent American economic history.

As we would expect, there is a close association between class and educational credentials. Virtually every member of the middle class has at least graduated from high school; nearly two-thirds of working-class blacks have also completed secondary education; but less than half— 44 percent—of the jobless have a high school diploma or more. Looked at from another angle, 15 percent of our educated respondents—that is, high school graduates or better—have made it into the salaried middle class, half have become white-collar or blue-collar wage earners, and 36 percent are without a job. By comparison, those without a high school education are distributed as follows: 1.6 percent in the middle class, 37.9 percent in the working class, and a substantial

FIGURE 1

THE BLACK CLASS STRUCTURE IN CHICAGO"S LOW- AND EXTREME-POVERTY AREAS

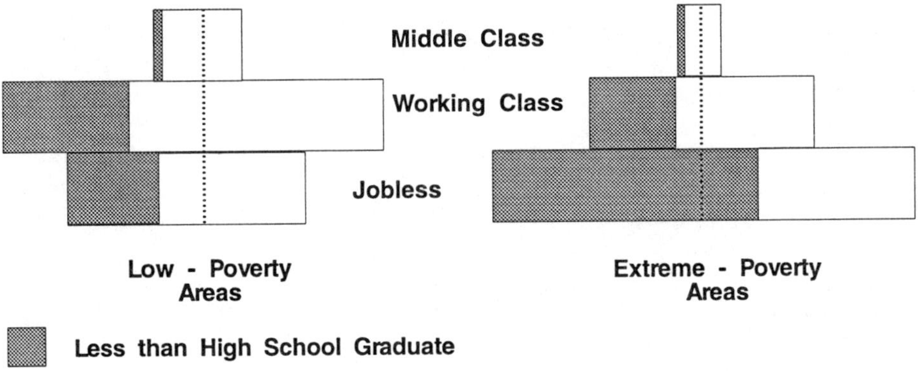

Middle Class

Working Class

Jobless

Low - Poverty
Areas

Extreme - Poverty
Areas

Less than High School Graduate

SOURCE: Urban Poverty and Family Structure Survey.

majority of 60.5 percent in the jobless category. In other words, a high school degree is a *conditio sine qua non* for blacks for entering the world of work, let alone that of the middle class. Not finishing secondary education is synonymous with economic redundancy.

Ghetto residents are, on the whole, less educated than the inhabitants of other black neighborhoods. This results in part from their lower class composition but also from the much more modest academic background of the jobless: fewer than 4 in 10 jobless persons on the city's South Side and West Side have graduated from high school, compared to nearly 6 in 10 in low-poverty areas. It should be pointed out that education is one of the few areas in which women do not fare worse than men: females are as likely to hold a high school diploma as males in the ghetto—50 percent—and more likely to do so in low-poverty areas—69 percent versus 62 percent.

Moreover, ghetto residents have lower class origins, if one judges from the economic assets of their family of orienta-

tion.[19] Fewer than 4 ghetto dwellers in 10 come from a family that owned its home and 6 in 10 have parents who owned nothing, that is, no home, business, or land. In low-poverty areas, 55 percent of the inhabitants are from a home-owning family while only 40 percent had no assets at all a generation ago. Women, both in and out of the ghetto, are least likely to come from a family with a home or any other asset—46 percent and 37 percent, respectively. This difference in class origins is also captured by differential rates of welfare receipt during childhood: the proportion of respondents whose parents were on public aid at some time when they were growing up is 30 percent in low-poverty tracts and 41 percent in the ghetto. Women in extreme-poverty areas are by far the most likely to come from a family with a welfare record.

19. And from the education of their fathers: only 36 percent of ghetto residents have a father with at least a high school education, compared to 43 percent among those who live outside the ghetto. The different class backgrounds and trajectories of ghetto and non-ghetto blacks will be examined in a subsequent paper.

TABLE 3
INCIDENCE OF WELFARE RECEIPT AND FOOD ASSISTANCE AMONG BLACK
RESIDENTS OF CHICAGO'S LOW- AND EXTREME-POVERTY AREAS (Percentage)

	All Respondents		Males		Females	
	Low poverty	Extreme poverty	Low poverty	Extreme poverty	Low poverty	Extreme poverty
On aid when child	30.5	41.4	26.3	36.4	33.5	43.8
Currently on aid	25.2	57.6	13.4	31.8	32.4	68.9
Never had own grant	45.9	22.0	68.6	44.5	31.3	11.9
Expects to remain on aid*						
Less than 1 year	52.9	29.5	75.0	56.6	46.1	25.0
More than 5 years	9.4	21.1	5.0	13.0	10.8	22.0
Receives food stamps	33.5	60.2	22.2	39.1	40.4	70.0
Receives at least one of five forms of food assistance†	51.1	71.1	37.8	45.0	59.6	85.2

SOURCE: Urban Poverty and Family Structure Survey, University of Chicago, Chicago, IL.
*Asked of current public-aid recipients only.
†Including pantry or soup kitchen, government food surplus program, food stamps, Special Supplemental Food Program for Women, Infants and Children, free or reduced-cost school lunches.

Class, gender, and welfare trajectories in low- and extreme-poverty areas

If they are more likely to have been raised in a household that drew public assistance in the past, ghetto dwellers are also much more likely to have been or to be currently on welfare themselves. Differences in class, gender, and neighborhood cumulate at each juncture of the welfare trajectory to produce much higher levels of welfare attachments among the ghetto population (Table 3).

In low-poverty areas, only one resident in four are currently on aid while almost half have never personally received assistance. In the ghetto, by contrast, over half the residents are current welfare recipients, and only one in five have never been on aid. These differences are consistent with what we know from censuses and other studies: in 1980, about half of the black population of most community areas on the South Side and West Side was officially receiving public assistance, while working- and middle-class black neighborhoods of the far South Side, such as South Shore, Chatham, or Roseland, had rates of welfare receipt ranging between one-fifth and one-fourth.[20]

None of the middle-class respondents who live in low-poverty tracts were on welfare at the time they were interviewed, and only one in five had ever been on aid in their lives. Among working-class residents, a mere 7 percent were on welfare and just over one-half had never had any welfare experience. This same relationship between class and welfare receipt is found among residents of extreme-poverty tracts, but with significantly higher rates of welfare receipt at all class levels: there, 12 percent of working-class residents are presently on aid and 39 percent received

20. See Wacquant and Wilson, "Poverty, Joblessness and Social Transformation," fig. 2.

welfare before; even a few middle-class blacks—9 percent—are drawing public assistance and only one-third of them have never received any aid, instead of three-quarters in low-poverty tracts. But it is among the jobless that the difference between low- and extreme-poverty areas is the largest: fully 86 percent of those in ghetto tracts are currently on welfare and only 7 percent have never had recourse to public aid, compared with 62 percent and 20 percent, respectively, among those who live outside the ghetto.

Neighborhood differences in patterns of welfare receipt are robust across genders, with women exhibiting noticeably higher rates than men in both types of areas and at all class levels. The handful of black middle-class women who reside in the ghetto are much more likely to admit to having received aid in the past than their male counterparts: one-third versus one-tenth. Among working-class respondents, levels of current welfare receipt are similar for both sexes—5.0 percent and 8.5 percent, respectively—while levels of past receipt again display the greater economic vulnerability of women: one in two received aid before as against one male in five. This gender differential is somewhat attenuated in extreme-poverty areas by the general prevalence of welfare receipt, with two-thirds of all jobless males and 9 in 10 jobless women presently receiving public assistance.

The high incidence and persistence of joblessness and welfare in ghetto neighborhoods, reflecting the paucity of viable options for stable employment, take a heavy toll on those who are on aid by significantly depressing their expectations of finding a route to economic self-sufficiency. While a slim majority of welfare recipients living in low-poverty tracts expect to be self-supportive within a year and only a small minority anticipate receiving aid for longer than five years, in ghetto neighborhoods, by contrast, fewer than 1 in 3 public-aid recipients expect to be welfare-free within a year and fully 1 in 5 anticipate needing assistance for more than five years. This difference of expectations increases among the jobless of both genders. For instance, unemployed women in the ghetto are twice as likely as unemployed women in low-poverty areas to think that they will remain on aid for more than five years and half as likely to anticipate getting off the rolls within a year.

Thus if the likelihood of being on welfare increases sharply as one crosses the line between the employed and the jobless, it remains that, at each level of the class structure, welfare receipt is notably more frequent in extreme-poverty neighborhoods, especially among the unemployed, and among women. This pattern is confirmed by the data on the incidence of food assistance presented in Table 3 and strongly suggests that those unable to secure jobs in low-poverty areas have access to social and economic supports to help them avoid the public-aid rolls that their ghetto counterparts lack. Chief among those are their financial and economic assets.

Differences in economic and financial capital

A quick survey of the economic and financial assets of the residents of Chicago's poor black neighborhoods (Table 4) reveals the appalling degree of economic hardship, insecurity, and deprivation that they must confront day in and day out.[21] The picture in low-poverty

21. Again, we must reiterate that our comparison excludes *ex definitio* the black upper- and the middle-class neighborhoods that have mushroomed

areas is grim; that in the ghetto is one of near-total destitution.

In 1986, the median family income for blacks nationally was pegged at $18,000, compared to $31,000 for white families. Black households in Chicago's low-poverty areas have roughly equivalent incomes, with 52 percent declaring over $20,000 annually. Those living in Chicago's ghetto, by contrast, command but a fraction of this figure: half of all ghetto respondents live in households that dispose of less than $7500 annually, twice the rate among residents of low-poverty neighborhoods. Women assign their households to much lower income brackets in both areas, with fewer than 1 in 3 in low-poverty areas and 1 in 10 in extreme-poverty areas enjoying more than $25,000 annually. Even those who work report smaller incomes in the ghetto: the proportion of working-class and middle-class households falling under the $7500 mark on the South and West sides—12.5 percent and 6.5 percent, respectively—is double that of other black neighborhoods, while fully one-half of jobless respondents in extreme-poverty tracts do not reach the $5000 line. It is not surprising that ghetto dwellers also less frequently report an improvement of the financial situation of their household, with women again in the least enviable position. This reflects sharp class differences: 42 percent of our middle-class respondents and 36 percent of working-class blacks register a financial amelioration as against 13 percent of the jobless.

Due to meager and irregular income, those financial and banking services that most members of the larger society take

for granted are, to put it mildly, not of obvious access to the black poor. Barely one-third of the residents of low-poverty areas maintain a personal checking account; only one in nine manage to do so in the ghetto, where nearly three of every four persons report no financial asset whatsoever from a possible list of six and only 8 percent have at least three of those six assets. (See Table 4.) Here, again, class and neighborhood lines are sharply drawn: in low-poverty areas, 10 percent of the jobless and 48 percent of working-class blacks have a personal checking account compared to 3 percent and 37 percent, respectively, in the ghetto; the proportion for members of the middle class is similar—63 percent—in both areas.

The American dream of owning one's home remains well out of reach for a large majority of our black respondents, especially those in the ghetto, where barely 1 person in 10 belong to a home-owning household, compared to over 4 in 10 in low-poverty areas, a difference that is just as pronounced within each gender. The considerably more modest dream of owning an automobile is likewise one that has yet to materialize for ghetto residents, of which only one-third live in households with a car that runs. Again, this is due to a cumulation of sharp class and neighborhood differences: 79 percent of middle-class respondents and 62 percent of working-class blacks have an automobile in their household, contrasted with merely 28 percent of the jobless. But, in ghetto tracts, only 18 percent of the jobless have domestic access to a car—34 percent for men and 13 percent for women.

The social consequences of such a paucity of income and assets as suffered by ghetto blacks cannot be overemphasized. For just as the lack of financial

---

in Chicago since the opening of race relations in the 1960s. The development of this "new black middle class" is surveyed in Bart Landry, *The New Black Middle Class* (Berkeley: University of California Press, 1987).

TABLE 1

ECONOMIC AND FINANCIAL ASSETS OF BLACK RESIDENTS OF CHICAGO'S LOW- AND EXTREME-POVERTY AREAS (Percentage)

	All Respondents		Males		Females	
	Low poverty	Extreme poverty	Low poverty	Extreme poverty	Low poverty	Extreme poverty
Household income						
Less than $7,500	27.2	51.1	16.1	33.6	34.5	59.0
More than $25,000	34.1	14.3	41.4	22.7	29.8	10.5
Finances have improved	32.3	21.1	35.7	23.4	30.4	20.1
Financial assets						
Has checking account	34.8	12.2	33.3	17.6	36.4	9.9
Has savings account	35.4	17.8	40.4	26.6	33.1	14.1
Has none of six assets*	48.2	73.6	40.7	63.1	52.6	78.3
Has at least three of six assets*	23.3	8.3	26.8	13.5	21.3	5.8
Respondent owns nothing[†]	78.7	96.6	75.6	93.7	80.5	98.0
Material assets of household						
Owns home	44.7	11.5	49.7	19.8	41.5	7.8
Has a car	64.8	33.9	75.9	51.4	57.7	25.7

SOURCE: Urban Poverty and Family Structure Survey.
*Including personal checking account, savings account, individual retirement account, pension plan, money in stocks and bonds, and prepaid burial.
†Home, business, or land.

resources or possession of a home represents a critical handicap when one can only find low-paying and casual employment or when one loses one's job, in that it literally forces one to go on the welfare rolls, not owning a car severely curtails one's chances of competing for available jobs that are not located nearby or that are not readily accessible by public transportation.

Social capital and poverty concentration

Among the resources that individuals can draw upon to implement strategies of social mobility are those potentially provided by their lovers, kin, and friends and by the contacts they develop within the formal associations to which they belong—in sum, the resources they have access to by virtue of being socially integrated into solidary groups, networks, or organizations, what Bourdieu calls "social capital."[22] Our data indicate that not only do residents of extreme-poverty

22. Pierre Bourdieu, "The Forms of Capital," in *Handbook of Theory and Research for the Sociology of Education,* ed. J. G. Richardson (New York: Greenwood Press, 1986). The crucial role played by relatives, friends, and lovers in strategies of survival in poor black communities is documented extensively in Carol B. Stack, *All Our Kin: Strategies for Survival in a Black Community* (New York: Harper & Row, 1974). On the management of relationships and the influence of friends in the ghetto, see also Elliot Liebow, *Tally's Corner: A Study of Negro Streetcorner Men* (Boston: Little, Brown, 1967); Ulf Hannerz, *Soulside: Inquiries into Ghetto Culture and Community* (New York: Columbia University Press, 1969); Elijah Anderson, *A*

TABLE 5
SOCIAL CAPITAL OF BLACK RESIDENTS OF CHICAGO'S
LOW- AND EXTREME-POVERTY AREAS (Percentage)

	All Respondents		Males		Females	
	Low poverty	Extreme poverty	Low poverty	Extreme poverty	Low poverty	Extreme poverty
Current partner						
Respondent has no current partner	32.4	42.0	23.3	39.1	38.0	43.1
Respondent married*	35.2	18.6	40.9	27.0	31.2	14.9
Partner completed high school	80.9	72.1	83.8	83.0	88.4	71.5
Partner works steadily	69.0	54.3	50.0	34.8	83.8	62.2
Partner is on public aid	20.4	34.2	38.6	45.5	16.2	28.6
Best friend						
Respondent has no best friend	12.2	19.0	14.3	21.1	10.7	18.1
Best friend completed high school	87.4	76.4	83.7	76.3	87.2	76.3
Best friend works steadily	72.3	60.4	77.2	72.8	65.6	54.8
Best friend is on public aid	14.0	28.6	3.0	13.6	20.5	35.3

SOURCE: Urban Poverty and Family Structure Survey.
*And not separated from his or her spouse.

areas have fewer social ties but also that they tend to have ties of lesser social worth, as measured by the social position of their partners, parents, siblings, and best friends, for instance. In short, they possess lower volumes of social capital.

Living in the ghetto means being more socially isolated: nearly half of the residents of extreme-poverty tracts have no current partner—defined here as a person they are married to, live with, or are dating steadily—and one in five admit to having no one who would qualify as a best friend, compared to 32 percent and 12 percent, respectively, in low-poverty areas. It also means that intact marriages are less frequent (Table 5). Jobless men are much less likely than working males to have current partners in both types of neighborhoods: 62 percent in low-poverty neighborhoods and 44 percent in extreme-poverty areas. Black women have a slightly better chance of having a partner if they live in a low-poverty area, and this partner is also more likely to have completed high school and to work steadily; for ghetto residence further affects the labor-market standing of the latter. The partners of women living in extreme-poverty areas are less stably employed than those of female respondents from low-poverty neighborhoods: 62 percent in extreme-poverty areas work regularly

Place on the Corner (Chicago: University of Chicago Press, 1978); Terry Williams and William Kornblum, *Growing up Poor* (Lexington, MA: Lexington Books, 1985).

as compared to 84 percent in low-poverty areas.

Friends often play a crucial role in life in that they provide emotional and material support, help construct one's identity, and often open up opportunities that one would not have without them—particularly in the area of jobs. We have seen that ghetto residents are more likely than other black Chicagoans to have no close friend. If they have a best friend, furthermore, he or she is less likely to work, less educated, and twice as likely to be on aid. Because friendships tend to develop primarily within genders and women have much higher rates of economic exclusion, female respondents are much more likely than men to have a best friend who does not work and who receives welfare assistance. Both of these characteristics, in turn, tend to be more prevalent among ghetto females.

Such differences in social capital are also evidenced by different rates and patterns of organizational participation. While being part of a formal organization, such as a block club or a community organization, a political party, a school-related association, or a sports, fraternal, or other social group, is a rare occurrence as a rule—with the notable exception of middle-class blacks, two-thirds of whom belong to at least one such group—it is more common for ghetto residents—64 percent, versus 50 percent in low-poverty tracts—especially females—64 percent, versus 46 percent in low-poverty areas—to belong to no organization. As for church membership, the small minority who profess to be, in Weber's felicitous expression, "religiously unmusical" is twice as large in the ghetto as outside: 12 percent versus 5 percent. For those with a religion, ghetto residence tends to depress church attendance slightly—29 percent of ghetto inhabitants attend service at least once a week compared to 37 percent of respondents from low-poverty tracts—even though women tend to attend more regularly than men in both types of areas. Finally, black women who inhabit the ghetto are also slightly less likely to know most of their neighbors than their counterparts from low-poverty areas. All in all, then, poverty concentration has the effect of devaluing the social capital of those who live in its midst.

CONCLUSION:
THE SOCIAL STRUCTURING OF
GHETTO POVERTY

The extraordinary levels of economic hardship plaguing Chicago's inner city in the 1970s have not abated, and the ghetto seems to have gone unaffected by the economic boom of the past five years. If anything, conditions have continued to worsen. This points to the asymmetric causality between the economy and ghetto poverty[23] and to the urgent need to study the social and political structures that mediate their relationship. The significant differences we have uncovered between low-poverty and extreme-poverty areas in Chicago are essentially a reflection of their different class mix and of the prevalence of economic exclusion in the ghetto.

Our conclusion, then, is that social analysts must pay more attention to the extreme levels of economic deprivation and social marginalization as uncovered in this article before they further entertain and spread so-called theories[24] about the

23. By this we mean that when the economy slumps, conditions in the ghetto become a lot worse but do not automatically return to the *status quo ante* when macroeconomic conditions improve, so that cyclical economic fluctuations lead to stepwise increases in social dislocations.

24. We say "so-called" here because, more often than not, the views expressed by scholars in this

potency of a ghetto culture of poverty that has yet to receive rigorous empirical elaboration. Those who have been pushing moral-cultural or individualistic-behavioral explanations of the social dislocations that have swept through the inner city in recent years have created a fictitious normative divide between urban blacks that, no matter its reality—which has yet to be ascertained[25]—cannot but pale when compared to the objective structural cleavage that separates ghetto residents from the larger society and to the collective material constraints that bear on them.[26]

It is the cumulative structural entrapment and forcible socioeconomic marginalization resulting from the historically evolving interplay of class, racial, and gender domination, together with sea changes in the organization of American capitalism and failed urban and social policies, not a "welfare ethos," that explain the plight of today's ghetto blacks. Thus, if the concept of underclass is used, it must be a structural concept: it must denote a new sociospatial patterning of class and racial domination, recognizable by the unprecedented concentration of the most socially excluded and economically marginal members of the dominated racial and economic group. It should not be used as a label to designate a new breed of individuals molded freely by a mythical and all-powerful culture of poverty.

regard are little more than a surface formalization of the dominant American ideology—or common-sense notion—of poverty that assigns its origins to the moral or psychological deficiencies of individual poor persons. See Robert Castel, "La 'guerre à la pauvreté' et le statut de l'indigence dans une société d'abondance," *Actes de la recherche en sciences sociales,* 19 Jan. 1978, pp. 47-60, for a pungent critical and historical analysis of conceptions of poverty in the American mind and in American welfare policy.

25. Initial examination of our Chicago data would appear to indicate that ghetto blacks on public aid hold basically the same views as regards welfare, work, and family as do other blacks, even those who belong to the middle class.

26. Let us emphasize in closing that we are not suggesting that differences between ghetto and nonghetto poor can be explained by their residence.

Because the processes that allocate individuals and families to neighborhoods are highly socially selective ones, to separate neighborhood effects—the specific impact of ghetto residence—from the social forces that operate jointly with, or independently of, them cannot be done by simple controls such as we have used here for descriptive purposes. On the arduous methodological and theoretical problems posed by such socially selective effects, see Stanley Lieberson, *Making It Count: The Improvement of Social Theory and Social Research* (Berkeley: University of California Press, 1985), pp. 14-43 and passim.

3

Urban Industrial Transition and the Underclass

JOHN D. KASARDA

ABSTRACT: Major U.S. cities have transformed industrially from centers of goods processing to centers of information processing. Concurrently, the demand for poorly educated labor has declined markedly and the demand for labor with higher education has increased substantially. Urban blacks have been caught in this web of change. Despite improvements in their overall educational attainment, a great majority still have very little schooling and therefore have been unable to gain significant access to new urban growth industries. Underclass blacks, with exceptionally high rates of school dropout, are especially handicapped. Whereas jobs requiring only limited education have been rapidly increasing in the suburbs, poorly educated blacks remain residentially constrained in inner-city housing. Within underclass neighborhoods, few households have private vehicles, which are shown to be increasingly necessary for employment in dispersing metropolitan economies. The implications of interactions among race, space, and urban industrial change are explored. Reasons for the success of recent Asian immigrants in transforming cities are considered, and policies are suggested to rekindle social mobility in the black underclass.

John D. Kasarda is Kenan Professor and Chairman of the Department of Sociology at the University of North Carolina at Chapel Hill, where he also serves as director of the Center for Competitiveness and Employment Growth. He is the coauthor of six books and more than fifty scholarly articles on demography, formal organizations, and urban economic development. His current research focuses on job creation and the spatial redistribution of people and industry.

NOTE: This article benefited immeasurably from the input and assistance of John J. Beggs and Robert L. Boyd. Maria T. Cullinane assisted in table preparation.

RESEARCH broadening our understanding of urban opportunity structures can be traced back to the early Chicago school.[1] Scholars documented how the dynamic economies of our emerging industrial cities generated excesses of low-skilled jobs that attracted waves of foreign-born and rural migrants in search of employment and a better life. Their field studies vividly described how each migrant group initially concentrated in highly segregated enclaves within deteriorating inner-city zones, where they faced suspicion, distrust, discrimination, and outright hostility from earlier ethnic arrivals. Yet these studies also showed how, with the passage of time, each group was able to carve out a niche in the economy, adjust to city life, assimilate into mainstream institutions, climb the socioeconomic ladder, and eventually move to desegregated housing beyond the core ghettos and slums—only to be residentially replaced by another wave of immigrants who replicated this spatial and temporal process of assimilation and mobility. It was these successive movements from first-generation settlement in the core followed by residential progression outward toward the periphery that accompanied the assimilation processes that were responsible for the reported correspondence between (1) length of residence of the ethnic group in the city, (2) the group's socioeconomic status, (3) its degree of segregation, and (4) the average distance that group members resided from the urban core.

1. Robert Park, Ernest Burgess, and R. D. McKenzie, eds., *The City* (Chicago: University of Chicago Press, 1925); Louis Worth, *The Ghetto* (Chicago: University of Chicago Press, 1928); Harvey W. Zorbaugh, *The Gold Coast and the Slum* (Chicago: University of Chicago Press, 1929); Roderick D. McKenzie, *The Metropolitan Community* (New York: McGraw-Hill, 1933).

Congruent processes of social and spatial mobility that characterized earlier disadvantaged residents of cities apparently do not apply to large numbers of underprivileged blacks currently residing in our largest cities. Indeed, the economic and social plight of a substantial segment of the urban black population is actually worse now than it was a generation ago as we have witnessed the formation of an immobilized subgroup of spatially isolated, persistently poor ghetto dwellers characterized by substandard education and high rates of joblessness, mother-only households, welfare dependency, out-of-wedlock births, and crime. The economic and social conditions of this subgroup, labeled the urban underclass, have deteriorated despite targeted infusions of public assistance, affirmative action, and civil rights legislation—programs traditionally supported by liberals—and have persisted in the face of national and urban economic recovery, solutions espoused by many conservatives.

One reason why neither liberal nor conservative prescriptions worked, I propose, is that both were overwhelmed by fundamental changes in the structure of city economies affecting the employment prospects of disadvantaged urban blacks. These structural changes led to a substantial reduction of lower-skilled jobs in traditional employing institutions that attracted and economically upgraded previous generations of urban blacks. Loss of these employment opportunities, in turn, had devastating effects on black families, which further exacerbated the problems of the economically displaced.

In this article I demonstrate the close relationship between urban industrial transition and black joblessness, especially among the poorly educated. I begin with a brief overview of urban employment change during the past two decades.

Next, data from the Census Bureau's 1950, 1970, and 1980 Public Use Microdata Sample (PUMS) Files are drawn together to explicate changes in the structure of employment in major Northern cities and associated increases in unemployment among blacks ill-equipped to work in new urban growth sectors. I then consider why recent ethnic immigrants to cities, including those with limited education, have been less affected by the urban industrial change and have been climbing the socioeconomic ladder while so many blacks have slipped off. The article concludes with a discussion of policies apropos the black underclass.

URBAN EMPLOYMENT IN TRANSITION

America's major cities are different places today from what they were in the 1960s, when our assumptions about urban poverty were formed. Advances in transportation, communication, and industrial technologies interacting with the changing structure of the national and international economy have transformed these cities from centers of the production and distribution of goods to centers of administration, finance, and information exchange. In the process, many blue-collar jobs that once constituted the economic backbone of cities and provided employment opportunities for their poorly educated residents have either vanished or moved. These jobs have been replaced, at least in part, by knowledge-intensive white-collar jobs with educational requirements that exclude many with substandard education. For example, by 1980, New York City and Boston each had more employees in information-processing industries—where executives, managers, professionals, and clerical workers dominate—than in their manufacturing, construction, retail, and wholesale industries combined. This is a dramatic metamorphosis compared to the situation in the mid-1950s, when employment in these more traditional urban industries outnumbered information-processing employment in Boston and New York by a 3-to-1 margin.[2]

Blue-collar employment decline was accelerated by the urban exodus of white middle-income residents and the neighborhood business establishments that once served them. This exodus further weakened secondary labor markets for lower-skilled consumer and personal services that, along with goods-processing industries, had employed the largest numbers of urban blacks.

The implications of urban industrial transition for the changing nature of jobs available in major Northern cities and their suburban rings are illustrated in Tables 1, 2, and 3. These figures, assembled from place-of-work data from the 1970 and 1980 PUMS Files, show changing characteristics of jobs—including jobs held by commuters—and their occupants by the actual location of employment.

Table 1 reveals that while the suburban rings of the six largest Northern cities added employment across every occupational classification, the central cities lost substantial numbers of jobs in clerical, sales, and blue-collar occupations. These losses were responsible for overall central-city employment declines between 1970 and 1980. At the same time, all cities exhibited considerable growth in employment of managers, professionals, and employees engaged in higher-level technical and administrative support functions. New York City, for instance, added over 260,000 workers in these two information-

2. John D. Kasarda, "Urban Change and Minority Opportunities," in *The New Urban Reality,* ed. P. Peterson (Washington, DC: Brookings Institution, 1985), pp. 33-67.

TABLE 1
CHANGE IN NUMBER OF JOBS IN SELECTED CENTRAL CITIES
AND SUBURBAN RINGS, BY OCCUPATIONAL SECTOR, 1970-80

Metropolitan Area	Managerial and Professional	Technical and Administrative Support	Clerical and Sales	Blue-Collar	Total
Boston					
Central city	26,120	30,300	−40,400	−62,500	−46,480
Suburbs	104,660	75,820	69,460	116,440	366,380
Chicago					
Central city	51,560	68,400	−89,760	−118,860	−88,660
Suburbs	156,120	120,660	115,360	237,900	630,040
Cleveland					
Central city	2,900	14,240	−25,280	−34,580	−42,720
Suburbs	30,140	26,160	16,960	23,800	97,060
Detroit					
Central city	4,700	15,840	−35,540	−89,860	−104,860
Suburbs	51,860	62,500	43,240	29,320	186,920
New York					
Central city	90,460	173,780	−187,820	−171,500	−95,080
Suburbs	200,140	210,800	51,060	27,080	489,080
Philadelphia					
Central city	23,040	35,360	−54,060	−75,200	−70,860
Suburbs	50,280	55,880	36,240	29,500	171,900

SOURCES: U.S. Department of Commerce, Bureau of the Census, Machine Readable Public Use Microdata Sample File, 5% A Sample, 1980; ibid., 15% County Group Sample, 1970.

intensive occupational categories while losing more than 170,000 jobs in blue-collar occupations.

Cross-classification of blue-collar employment change by industry, presented in Table 2, reveals that central-city blue-collar job losses were heavily concentrated in traditional urban employment sectors.[3]

3. The goods-producing sector comprises all those working in agriculture, forestry, fisheries, mining, construction, and manufacturing. The trade sector includes those in wholesale and retail trade. The producer-services sector is made up of those in finance, insurance, real estate, business services, and professional services. Those in transportation, communications, other public utilities, repair services, personal services, and entertainment and recreation services are in the consumer service sector. Public sector workers include those employed by all levels of government.

Goods-producing industries—primarily manufacturing—accounted for the majority of city blue-collar employment declines in each of the six central cities. Corresponding to the industrial shifts initially noted, all central cities also lost substantial numbers of blue-collar jobs in retail and wholesale trade and the consumer-service sector. The smallest losses were in producer-service industries—primarily financial and business services—and the public sector. In fact, both New York City and Chicago added blue-collar jobs in their public sectors and producer-service industries, the latter reflecting growth in custodial and maintenance jobs that accompanied the downtown boom in these office building industries during the 1970s.

TABLE 2

CHANGE IN NUMBER OF BLUE-COLLAR JOBS IN SELECTED CENTRAL CITIES
AND SUBURBAN RINGS, BY INDUSTRIAL SECTOR, 1970-80

Metropolitan Area	Goods Producing	Trade	Producer Services	Consumer Services	Public Sector	Total
Boston						
Central city	−36,760	−7,780	−2,200	−9,220	−6,540	−62,500
Suburbs	56,220	24,840	13,360	6,720	15,300	116,440
Chicago						
Central city	−84,360	−20,860	4,320	−23,340	5,380	−118,860
Suburbs	112,220	53,960	18,700	30,380	22,640	237,900
Cleveland						
Central city	−20,020	−5,200	−940	−6,500	−1,920	−34,580
Suburbs	6,640	13,460	980	880	1,840	23,800
Detroit						
Central city	−53,560	−15,880	−6,280	−14,680	540	−89,860
Suburbs	−13,140	19,420	8,340	8,320	6,380	29,320
New York						
Central city	−108,060	−24,340	6,060	−49,560	4,400	−171,500
Suburbs	−33,200	37,980	13,340	−10,300	19,260	27,080
Philadelphia						
Central city	−48,780	−9,980	−1,280	−13,820	−1,340	−75,200
Suburbs	1,700	16,700	7,600	−2,400	5,900	29,500

SOURCES: Bureau of the Census, Machine Readable Public Use Microdata Sample File, 5% A Sample, 1980; ibid., 15% County Group Sample, 1970.

Whereas the Northeast and Midwest were characterized by marked deindustrialization between 1970 and 1980, the suburbs of Boston, Chicago, Cleveland, and Philadelphia all added blue-collar jobs in their goods-producing industries. Boston and Chicago represent particularly striking city-suburban contrasts in blue-collar employment change in goods-producing industries, with suburban increases substantially exceeding central-city job losses. Retail and wholesale trade industries also significantly expanded the number of their blue-collar employees in the suburban rings of all metropolitan areas, in sharp contrast to blue-collar employment decline in these same industries in the central cities.

Central-city employment increases in managerial, professional, and high-level technical and administrative support occupations that occurred concurrently with precipitous drops in blue-collar and other jobs requiring lower levels of education contributed to major changes in the educational composition of occupants of central-city jobs. Table 3 displays the net change and the percentage change in the number of central-city jobs by education of the occupants.[4] For instance, the number of jobs in Boston held by those who did not complete high school declined by 80,260 between 1970 and 1980, which

4. The 1980 PUMS File is a 5 percent sample of the U.S. population. For reasons of economy, the Census Bureau coded only the information on

TABLE 3
CHANGE IN NUMBER OF CENTRAL-CITY JOBS,
BY EDUCATION LEVEL OF JOBHOLDERS, 1970-80

Central City	Less than High School	High School Only	Some College	College Graduate	Total
Boston	−80,260	−48,980	25,700	58,280	−45,260
(%)	(−58.7)	(−28.9)	(32.9)	(71.4)	(−9.7)
Chicago	−211,400	−81,020	91,320	112,500	−88,600
(%)	(−41.8)	(−18.6)	(43.9)	(56.7)	(−6.5)
Cleveland	−64,660	−20,220	26,300	15,980	−42,600
(%)	(−48.2)	(−14.0)	(53.5)	(31.0)	(−11.2)
Detroit	−107,300	−55,460	35,320	22,320	−105,120
(%)	(−55.0)	(−28.7)	(48.4)	(35.3)	(−20.0)
New York	−443,800	−161,180	237,580	266,360	−101,040
(%)	(−40.4)	(−15.8)	(61.0)	(47.3)	(−3.2)
Philadelphia	−144,060	−31,640	48,280	55,540	−71,880
(%)	(−47.2)	(−11.1)	(60.5)	(57.4)	(−9.3)

SOURCES: Bureau of the Census, Machine Readable Public Use Microdata Sample Files, 5% A Sample, 1980; ibid., 15% County Group Sample, 1970.
NOTE: Percentages in parentheses denote percentage change.

represents a 58.7 percent drop. Conversely, the number of Boston's jobs held by college graduates grew by 58,280, a 71.4 percent gain. There was also a major contraction in the number of jobs in all cities held by those with only a high school degree. Thus, in our industrially transforming cities, there are declining employment prospects not only for workers without a high school degree but also for those with just a high school degree. At the same time, slots being filled by those with formal education beyond high school have mushroomed.

Portions of the decrease in city jobs occupied by those without a high school

degree and growth in jobs held by those with higher education reflect improvements in the overall educational attainment of the city labor force during the 1970s. These improvements, however, were not nearly as great as the concurrent upward shifts in the education levels of city jobholders. As a result, much of the job increase in the college-graduate category for each city was absorbed by suburban commuters while many job losses in the less-than-high-school-completed category were absorbed by city residents.

The figures in Table 3 strikingly highlight the direction that urban labor markets are taking vis-à-vis the hiring of persons with different levels of educational attainment. Given that structure is formed by the relative growth rates of component parts, the educational structure of city employment experienced a major shift between 1970 and 1980. This shift is described in Table 4, which dis-

travel to work and workplace for half of the sample questionnaires. Thus the information on jobholders is only a 2.5 percent sample of the population. We used this 2.5 percent sample for all analyses. There is also a small group for whom occupation is not reported. This causes the totals and differences based on occupation to be slightly different from those based on education only.

TABLE 4
PERCENTAGE DISTRIBUTION OF CENTRAL-CITY JOBS,
BY EDUCATION LEVEL OF JOBHOLDERS, 1970-80

Central City	Less than High School	High School Graduate	Some College	College Graduate
Baltimore				
1970	48.3	29.2	10.2	12.2
1980	29.6	32.3	19.4	18.6
Boston				
1970	29.4	36.4	16.8	17.5
1980	13.4	28.6	24.7	33.2
Chicago				
1970	37.5	32.3	15.4	14.7
1980	23.4	28.2	23.8	24.7
Cleveland				
1970	35.4	38.0	13.0	13.6
1980	20.7	36.8	22.5	20.1
Detroit				
1970	37.3	36.8	13.9	12.0
1980	21.1	32.8	25.8	20.3
New York				
1970	35.8	33.1	12.7	18.4
1980	22.0	28.8	21.2	28.0
Philadelphia				
1970	39.9	37.0	10.4	12.6
1980	23.2	36.3	18.4	22.0
St. Louis				
1970	43.4	33.0	11.0	12.5
1980	25.4	33.5	22.1	19.0
Washington, D.C.				
1970	22.7	31.9	17.7	27.8
1980	11.3	24.1	24.0	40.6

SOURCES: Bureau of the Census, Machine Readable Public Use Microdata Sample File, 5% A Sample, 1980; ibid., 15% County Group Sample, 1970.

plays the percentage distribution of city jobs by education of their occupants in the six cities listed in Tables 1, 2, and 3 plus three additional cities—Baltimore, St. Louis, and Washington, D.C.—for which central-city resident data for 1970 and 1980 could be assembled from the PUMS Files.

In just 10 years, the percentage of Baltimore's jobs occupied by those who had less than a high school degree dropped from 48.3 percent to 29.6. Roughly analogous declines occurred in other cities in the proportions of jobs occupied by persons with less than a high school degree. All but Baltimore and St. Louis also experienced declines in the percentage of jobs held by persons with only a high school degree. Both Baltimore and St. Louis actually had net declines in jobs

occupied by those with only a high school degree but the percentage rose as an artifact of the precipitous drop in the number of jobs held by those with less than a high school degree. At the higher-education end of the continuum, job-holder percentages rose considerably in all cities. Combining the "some college" and "college graduate" percentages, we find that by 1980, 65 percent of all those employed in Washington, D.C. had at least some higher education, 58 percent in Boston, and 49 percent in both Chicago and New York. Except for Baltimore, more than 40 percent of all jobs in the cities shown in Table 4 were, by 1980, occupied by persons with educations beyond high school.

In sum, Tables 1 through 4 illustrate the dramatic changes that have occurred since 1970 in urban economies both in terms of the types of jobs performed—occupational changes—and the educational qualifications of those occupying city jobs. As major cities have transformed industrially from centers of goods processing to centers of information processing, knowledge-intensive, white-collar jobs have mushroomed while jobs typically filled by those without education beyond high school have shrunk considerably. The next section assesses the implications of these structural changes for employment opportunities for urban blacks.

<h2 style="text-align:center">CONSEQUENCES FOR
URBAN BLACK EMPLOYMENT</h2>

While overall educational attainment of black city residents improved during the 1970s, it was not sufficient to keep pace with even faster rises in the educational attainment of those persons being employed by city industries. Moreover, general improvements in city residents' education levels meant that lesser-educated jobless blacks fell further behind in the hiring queue. Particularly affected were those large numbers of urban blacks who had not completed high school, especially younger ones. For city black youth, school drop-out rates ranged from 30 to 50 percent during the 1970s and early 1980s, with case studies of underclass neighborhoods and schools suggesting even higher drop-out rates among the most impoverished.[5]

Table 5 illustrates the structural dilemma facing sizable portions of the black urban labor force. This table compares the 1980 educational distributions of those employed by city industries, including the self-employed, with the educational distributions of all out-of-school black males aged 16-64 and out-of-school black males aged 16-64 who are not working. The contrasts are dramatic. Despite their educational gains, black urban labor still remains highly concentrated in the education category where city employment has rapidly declined—the category in which people have not completed high school—and greatly underrepresented in the educational-attainment categories where city employment is quickly expanding, especially the category of college graduate. As late as 1980, the modal education-completed category for out-of-school black male residents in all cities except Boston was less than 12 years.

Those out-of-school black males who are jobless display an even more disadvantaging educational distribution. In Baltimore, for example, while 54.4 percent of all black males who were out of school had less than 12 years of education

<hr>

5. G. Alfred Hess, Jr., "Educational Triage in an Urban School Setting," *Metropolitan Education,* Fall 1986, no. 2, pp. 39-52; William S. Kornblum, "Institution Building in the Urban High School," in *The Challenge of Social Control,* ed. G. Suttles and M. Zald (Norwood, NJ: Ablex, 1985), pp. 218-29.

TABLE 5

**EDUCATIONAL DISTRIBUTION OF JOBHOLDERS IN SELECTED CENTRAL CITIES
AND EDUCATIONAL DISTRIBUTION OF OUT-OF-SCHOOL BLACK MALES
AGED 16–64 RESIDING IN THESE CITIES, 1980**

Central City	Less than High School	High School Only	Some College	College Graduate
Baltimore				
City jobholders	29.6	32.3	19.4	18.6
Black male residents	54.4	26.9	14.2	4.4
Black male residents not working	67.5	20.0	10.4	2.1
Boston				
City jobholders	13.4	28.6	24.7	33.2
Black male residents	35.4	38.6	17.4	8.6
Black male residents not working	47.6	34.7	12.0	5.8
Chicago				
City jobholders	23.4	28.2	23.8	24.7
Black male residents	44.7	29.2	19.6	6.6
Black male residents not working	58.1	26.6	12.8	2.5
Cleveland				
City jobholders	20.7	36.8	22.5	20.1
Black male residents	46.4	34.1	15.1	4.4
Black male residents not working	56.7	30.8	11.0	1.5
Detroit				
City jobholders	21.1	32.8	25.8	20.3
Black male residents	43.3	30.5	20.3	5.9
Black male residents not working	56.1	28.9	13.6	1.3
New York				
City jobholders	22.0	28.8	21.2	28.0
Black male residents	39.3	33.2	18.8	8.7
Black male residents not working	52.5	28.3	14.9	4.4
Philadelphia				
City jobholders	23.2	36.3	18.4	22.0
Black male residents	46.0	35.1	13.3	5.6
Black male residents not working	60.1	28.8	9.2	1.9
St. Louis				
City jobholders	25.4	33.5	22.1	19.0
Black male residents	50.9	28.1	15.5	5.5
Black male residents not working	63.8	24.7	9.3	2.2
Washington, D.C.				
City jobholders	11.3	24.1	24.0	40.6
Black male residents	40.7	29.5	17.8	12.0
Black male residents not working	55.5	24.8	13.5	6.1

SOURCE: Bureau of the Census, Machine Readable Public Use Microdata Sample File, 5% A Sample, 1980.

in 1980, 67.5 percent of black males out of school and jobless had not completed high school. With the exception of Bos-

ton, where 47.6 percent of jobless black males did not complete high school, more than 50 percent of jobless black males in

all cities had completed less than 12 years of schooling, including a remarkable 60-plus percent in Philadelphia and St. Louis, along with Baltimore. Comparing these figures with the percentage of city jobs filled in 1980 by those with less than a high school degree (top left figure of each city panel) and with changes in city jobs occupied by the poorly educated between 1970 and 1980 (Tables 3 and 4) exemplifies the substantial educational disparity faced by urban blacks in general and those not at work, in particular.

This educational disparity between city jobs and black residents poses a serious structural impediment to major improvements in urban black employment prospects. It may be the case that any individual black male who has not completed high school can secure employment in the city—some vacancies almost always exist, even in declining employment sectors. But, given the distributions shown in Table 5, if large portions of out-of-work urban blacks all sought the jobs available, they would simply overwhelm vacancies at the lower end of the education continuum.

The disparities between city jobs and black labor that are displayed at the higher-education end of the continuum help explain why policies based primarily on urban economic development have had limited success in reducing urban black joblessness. Most blacks simply lack the education to participate in the new growth sectors of the urban economy. While city jobs taken by college graduates have mushroomed, the percentage of urban black males who have completed college remains extremely small. For those who are out of work, the disparity at the higher-education end is even greater.

Confinement of poorly educated blacks in cities rapidly losing jobs that do not require knowledge associated with a high school education poses another serious impediment to lowering their unemployment rates. As blue-collar and other less knowledge-intensive jobs expanded in the suburbs, whites were able to relocate much more easily than blacks. Between 1972 and 1982, the U.S. censuses of manufacturers show that New York City lost 30 percent of its manufacturing jobs, Detroit 41 percent, and Chicago 47 percent. During approximately the same period, 1970-80, the non-Hispanic white population declined by 1.4 million in New York, by 700,000 in Chicago, and by 420,000 in Detroit, while the black populations of these three cities increased by 180,000, by 111,000, and by 102,000, respectively.[6]

Decline in manufacturing jobs, we have seen, is by no means the only pertinent indicator of losses in traditional blue-collar employment, but it corresponds to other indicators of the capacity of a city to sustain large numbers of residents with limited educational attainment. This reduced capacity had direct bearing on the employment status of undereducated blacks during the three decades ending in 1980, as is illustrated in Table 6.[7] Between 1950 and 1970 there was considerable growth in all cities in the number of blacks employed who had not completed 12 years of education. Aside from St. Louis, this growth occurred across all major industrial sectors. After 1970, the bottom fell out in urban industrial demand for poorly educated blacks. This was particularly the case in goods-producing industries. While goods-producing industries in Philadelphia, for instance, added over 14,000 blacks who

6. Kasarda, "Urban Change."
7. Cities selected are those for which residence as well as place of work could be determined for all years from the PUMS Files.

had not completed high school to their payrolls between 1950 and 1970, from 1970 to 1980, the number of blacks without a high school degree in Philadelphia's goods-producing industries dropped by over 20,000. Overall, Philadelphia's employment declines during the 1970s among blacks who had not completed high school (–57,760) nearly equaled the total numbers of poorly educated blacks it added to its job rolls between 1950 and 1970 (63,050).

Corresponding to these employment declines between 1970 and 1980 were dramatic drops across all cities in the percentage of poorly educated black males who worked full-time and a leap in the percentage not working. By 1980, fewer than half in each city had full-time jobs. Conversely, the percentage not working at all rose in Baltimore from 24.7 to 45.0; in New York from 28.2 to 43.9; in Philadelphia from 26.7 to 50.6; in St. Louis from 31.8 to 48.4; and in Washington, D.C., from 23.4 to 42.1. Clearly, the loss of low-education-requisite jobs in traditional city industries had at least an accelerating effect on the growth of joblessness among their least-educated black residents.

THE ROLE OF SPACE

Since John Kain's seminal article in 1968 on the effects of metropolitan job decentralization and housing segregation on black employment, spirited debate has surrounded the question of whether spatial factors play a role in the rise of joblessness among urban blacks.[8] At issue

is whether the suburbanization of blue-collar and other lower-skilled jobs has worked to the economic disadvantage of blacks who remain residentially constrained to inner-city housing. David Ellwood's impressive study[9] has been accepted by many as conclusive evidence that spatial factors—more specifically, differential residential proximity to jobs—account for little to nothing in understanding black unemployment. Ellwood systematically analyzed employment rates of out-of-school youth aged 16-21 in Chicago in 1970 using three methods: (1) multiple regression analysis of census tract and local community employment rates, (2) comparison of unemployment rates of blacks in two different sections of Chicago that purportedly had vastly different degrees of job accessibility, and (3) comparison of black and white employment rates in the same section of the city. Based on these analyses Ellwood concluded that it is "race, not space," that accounts for black-white differences in employment.

While there is no question that race, including outright discrimination, plays a potent—and probably the most power-

8. John Kain, "Housing Segregation, Negro Unemployment, and Metropolitan Decentralization," *Quarterly Journal of Economics*, 82:175-97 (May 1968); Paul Offner and Daniel Saks, "A Note on John Kain's Housing Segregation, Negro Employment and Metropolitan Decentralization," *Quarterly Journal of Economics*, 85(1):147-60 (Feb.

1971); Bennett Harrison, *Urban Economic Development* (Washington, DC: Urban Institute Press, 1974); Mahlon Strazheim, "Discrimination and the Spatial Characteristics of the Urban Labor Market for Black Workers," *Journal of Urban Economics*, 7(1):119-40 (Jan. 1980); Richard Price and Edwin S. Mills, "Race and Residence in Earnings Determination," *Journal of Urban Economics*, 17:1-18 (1985); David T. Ellwood, "The Spatial Mismatch Hypothesis: Are There Teenage Jobs Missing in the Ghetto?" in *The Black Youth Employment Crisis*, ed. R. B. Freeman and H. J. Holzer (Chicago: University of Chicago Press, 1986), pp. 147-85; Mark Alan Hughes, "Moving Up and Moving Out: Confusing Ends and Means about Ghetto Dispersal," *Urban Studies*, 24:503-17 (1987); Jonathan S. Leonard, "The Interaction of Residential Segregation and Employment Discrimination," *Journal of Urban Economics*, 21:323-46 (1987).

9. Ellwood, "Spatial Mismatch Hypothesis."

TABLE 6

CHANGE IN CENTRAL-CITY EMPLOYMENT OF BLACKS WITHOUT A HIGH SCHOOL DEGREE, BY INDUSTRIAL SECTOR, 1950-80, AND EMPLOYMENT STATUS OF BLACK MALE CITY RESIDENTS AGED 16-64 WHO ARE OUT OF SCHOOL AND DO NOT HAVE A HIGH SCHOOL DEGREE, 1970 AND 1980

	Baltimore	New York	Philadelphia	St. Louis	Washington, D.C.
Industrial sector					
Goods producing					
1950-70	6,860	34,350	14,200	−1,580	6,080
1970-80	−12,540	−29,460	−20,040	−7,440	−8,560
Trade					
1950-70	4,160	19,790	6,150	4,660	8,820
1970-80	−3,520	−18,840	−8,560	−2,980	−7,280
Producer services					
1950-70	8,690	30,790	11,440	5,840	10,390
1970-80	−1,280	−6,200	−3,960	−1,780	−2,660
Consumer services					
1950-70	8,020	32,270	14,500	1,530	12,180
1970-80	−8,660	−26,780	−16,340	−5,660	−9,720
Government					
1950-70	15,890	30,180	16,760	4,150	23,160
1970-80	−2,800	−1,020	−8,860	−120	−15,260
All					
1950-70	43,620	147,380	63,050	14,600	60,630
1970-80	−28,800	−82,300	−57,760	−17,98C	−43,480
Employment status of out-of-school black males with no high school degree					
Employed full-time (percentage)					
1970	69.1	65.2	66.7	59.2	72.1
1980	47.6	49.2	43.3	43.3	49.6
Not working (percentage)					
1970	24.7	28.2	26.7	31.8	23.4
1980	45.0	43.9	50.6	48.4	42.1

SOURCES: Bureau of the Census, Machine Readable Public Use Microdata Sample File, 5% A Sample, 1980; ibid., 15% County Group File, 1970; idem, Machine Readable Public Use Microdata Sample File, 1950.

ful—role in the relatively poor employment performance of blacks, one should be cautious in using the Ellwood study to dismiss space as a contributing factor. Let me briefly elaborate.

It should be recognized that in Ellwood's regression analysis of census tract data, the dependent variable was not black-white differences in employment rates but rather census tract employment rates with all races aggregated together. Inferences drawn must correspond to the measure. Nevertheless, while percentage black was consistently the most powerful

predictor of the aggregate employment rates, a number of the job-accessibility indicators had significant effects in the expected direction despite their likely low measurement reliability.[10] These significant effects remained after controls were introduced not only for percentage black but also for percentage Spanish speaking, percentage of high school graduates, percentage of persons in the tract over age 25, average family income, percentage of persons in poor families, and percentage of children in single-parent families (see footnote to Ellwood's Table 4.6). Related to this, Ellwood's findings that the inclusion of job-proximity variables did not alter the regression coefficient of census tract employment rate on percentage black is not evidence that job proximity has no effect on employment. It may simply mean that proximity has some effects on census tract employment rates distinct from racial composition.

While statistical critique inevitably seems to follow even carefully crafted aggregate-level analyses such as Ellwood's,[11] what appears far more devastating to job-proximity arguments are the results of his comparison of black youth unemployment rates in the South Side ghettos of Chicago with those on the West Side. According to Ellwood, Chicago's West Side ghettos were flush with spatially accessible jobs in 1970 while few jobs existed on the South Side. Yet, his results show that black youths on the West Side had nearly the same high unemployment rates as black youths on the South Side, leading him to conclude that in "what appeared to be the purest of natural experiments, reasonably identical populations with reasonably different labor markets, the labor market results were not measurably different."[12]

In point of fact, data for Chicago's West Side ghettos in 1970 suggest that their labor markets were not different from those of the South Side, at least with respect to job access for black youth. Between 1960 and 1970, Chicago lost 211,000 jobs, the bulk of them in manufacturing, trade, and blue-collar services.[13] Particularly hard hit were the West Side ghetto areas that prior to the 1960s had large concentrations of manufacturing and distribution facilities as well as commercial establishments. The spatial and economic core of this area was North Lawndale, which lost 75 percent of its industries and businesses between 1960 and 1970.[14]

Temporal patterns are important here. The loss of low-skilled jobs accelerated following the West Side ghetto uprising in 1966, which markedly raised insurance rates of commercial establishments.[15] On 4 April 1968, following the assassination of Martin Luther King, Jr., the West Side ghettos exploded with rioting, burning, and looting, cutting a nearly two-mile swath of devastation from Madison Avenue to the Horner Homes housing project. That night alone, 559 fires were reported on the West Side.[16] Madison Avenue, its main commercial strip, was totally destroyed.

10. See Jonathan S. Leonard, "Comment on David Ellwood's 'The Spatial Mismatch Hypothesis,'" in Black Youth Employment Crisis, ed. Freeman and Holzer, pp. 185-93.

11. Ibid.

12. Ellwood, "Spatial Mismatch Hypothesis," p. 180.

13. Pierre DeVise, "The Suburbanization of Jobs and Minority Employment," Economic Geography, 52(4):348-62 (Oct. 1976).

14. Loïc J.D. Wacquant and William Julius Wilson, "Poverty, Joblessness and the Social Transformation of the Inner City," in Reforming Welfare, ed. D. Ellwood and P. Cottingham (Cambridge, MA: Harvard University Press, forthcoming).

15. David Farber, Chicago 1968 (Chicago: University of Chicago Press, 1988).

16. Ibid.

Although some large job sites remained functioning on the West Side in 1970, the dynamics of the area were those of rapid blue-collar employment decline. This loss at the employment margin would be expected to affect new labor force entrants—for example, teenagers—most severely as, in fact, is revealed in Ellwood's finding that "fully half of the school dropouts in both areas (south and west sides) reported that they were interested in work but unable to find it."[17] The point is that the labor markets for new entrants were not measurably different on the West Side and South Side ghettos in 1970. It is not surprising, then, that black youth unemployment rates in the two areas were similar.

Nevertheless, we are still left with Ellwood's third major finding, leading him to conclude that the problem is not space, but race.[18] In the same West Side area, 79.4 percent of white out-of-school youths were employed compared to 54.3 percent of black out-of-school youths. Whereas the small sample size (N = 100) could have played a role here, the reason for the discrepancy may well be that residential constraints on whites were less than those on blacks, enabling jobless white youths to flee an area of declining employment prospects, thus depressing their rates of unemployment compared to blacks who remained behind. Evidence supporting this interpretation is provided by Kain and Zax, who found that when integrated firms relocated from the central city to the suburbs, white employees were much more likely to follow in order to keep their jobs.[19] Such an interpretation

is also consistent with reports that black unemployment is higher relative to whites where jobs are most suburbanized and black populations least so.[20]

What this implies is that future research on underclass joblessness might prove more profitable if it were cast in terms of race and space, including their interactions, rather than race versus space. That both play a role in affecting the economic opportunity of urban blacks is suggested by a number of other studies. On the wage front, Price and Mills find that while blacks earn 19 percent less than whites due to poorer labor qualifications and 15 percent less due to employment discrimination, they also lose an additional 6 percent due to their concentration in the central city.[21] An analogous study by Vrooman and Greenfield concludes that 40 percent of the black-white earnings gap could be closed by suburbanization of central-city black labor.[22] Consistent with both studies, Strazheim reports a positive wage gradient from city to suburban employment among lesser-educated blacks, in contrast to whites.[23]

Regarding space and employment, Leonard's study of census tracts in Los Angeles shows that the ratio of jobs to population is lowest in areas surrounding black census tracts and that blacks have the highest commuting times,[24] the latter also reported by Ellwood. Leonard finds that job accessibility significantly affects

17. Ellwood, "Spatial Mismatch Hypothesis," p. 178.

18. Ibid., p. 181.

19. John Kain and J. Zax, "Quits, Moves and Employer Relocation in Segregated Housing Markets" (Paper, 1983) cited in Leonard, "Interaction."

20. John E. Farley, "Disproportionate Black and Hispanic Unemployment in U.S. Metropolitan Areas," *American Journal of Economics and Sociology*, 46(2):129-50 (Apr. 1987).

21. Price and Mills, "Race and Residence."

22. John Vrooman and Stuart Greenfield, "Are Blacks Making It in the Suburbs?" *Journal of Urban Economics*, 7:155-67 (1980).

23. Strazheim, "Discrimination."

24. Jonathan S. Leonard, "Space, Time and Unemployment: Los Angeles 1980" (Paper, University of California, Berkeley, 1985).

teenage employment rates after controlling for percentage black and a full range of census tract socioeconomic variables, though, as in Ellwood's study, percentage black is the most potent predictor. In a detailed study of individual establishments, Leonard reports that establishment distance from the ghetto is the most significant determinant of blacks' employment share.[25] The farther the establishment is from the ghetto, the fewer blacks it employs and the more slowly it adds black employees over time. Because most new job growth in metropolitan areas is toward their peripheries, those concentrated in the urban core are spatially disadvantaged. This disadvantage is reflected in the longer commuting times of blacks to suburban jobs.

Table 7 extends Ellwood's and Leonard's results by looking at black-white differences in commuting times among lesser-educated central-city residents working in the suburbs of nine major metropolitan areas. In every city, blacks have longer commuting times than whites whether one compares those without a high school degree or those with only a high school education. Additional analysis revealed that racial differences are not accounted for by transit mode, because nearly the same percentages of blacks who work in the suburbs commute by private automobile as do whites.

The final column of Table 7 reveals the great dependence lesser-educated black city residents have on private vehicles to reach suburban work. The percentage relying on private vehicles ranges from 68 percent in Boston to 91 percent in Detroit. On average, across the nine cities, four out of five of the least-educated blacks depend on a private vehicle to travel to their suburban jobs. What about those who are jobless?

25. Leonard, "Interaction."

When complementary analysis was conducted using the PUMS Files of the percentages of unemployed black males aged 16-64 who resided in households with no private vehicle, and out-of-the-labor-force, out-of-school black males aged 16-64 who resided in households with no private vehicles, the figures were remarkable—in New York, for example, 72 percent of the males who were unemployed resided in a household with no private vehicle, while 78 percent of those who were neither in school nor in the labor force had no vehicle in their household. The figures for Chicago are 45 percent and 55 percent, respectively, and for Philadelphia 54 percent and 60 percent, respectively. I then analyzed the 1980 Census Tract Machine Readable Files to look at automobile availability in Chicago's low-income black census tracts. In the near West Side, the area studied by Ellwood, more than three out of four households did not have an automobile in 1980. In Chicago's South Side ghetto of Oakland the figure was the same. In those black census tracts with the greatest joblessness, more than 80 percent of the households did not possess a private vehicle in 1980. Residential confinement of disadvantaged blacks in areas of blue-collar job decline together with their limited automobile ownership—the latter increasingly necessary to obtain employment in a dispersing metropolitan economy—would surely seem to contribute to their high rates of unemployment.

Finally, that space—including distance from appropriate jobs—plays a role is suggested by Table 8, which presents, by region, changing jobless rates of black males who have not completed high school and who resided in the central cities and suburban rings from 1969 to 1987. Over this entire period, jobless rates generally climbed in both the central

TABLE 7

MEAN ONE-WAY TRAVEL TIME TO SUBURBAN JOBS BY CENTRAL-CITY MALES
AGED 16–64 AND EMPLOYED FULL-TIME, BY EDUCATION AND RACE, AND
PERCENTAGE OF CENTRAL-CITY BLACKS WITHOUT A HIGH SCHOOL DEGREE
WHO USE A PRIVATE VEHICLE TO COMMUTE TO SUBURBAN JOBS, 1980

	Mean Travel Time (minutes)				Blacks without a High School Degree Who Commute by Private Vehicle (percentage)
	Less than high school		High school degree only		
	Blacks	Whites	Blacks	Whites	
Baltimore	41.0	29.4	37.2	34.1	73.3
Boston	36.2	32.3	39.0	29.3	67.9
Chicago	46.2	35.9	46.3	33.3	85.5
Cleveland	31.6	24.0	32.7	22.9	83.6
Detroit	29.2	23.9	28.2	23.5	90.9
New York	54.4	44.1	53.2	44.4	81.8
Philadelphia	40.3	36.4	44.8	34.8	86.1
St. Louis	33.4	29.2	35.9	27.7	79.0
Washington, D.C.	38.8	32.0	35.6	31.3	75.0

SOURCE: Bureau of the Census, Machine Readable Public Use Microdata Sample File, 5% A Sample, 1980.

cities and the suburban rings, reflecting, in part, the growing employment handicap of a limited education. Yet joblessness among poorly educated black males tended to rise more in the central cities, reaching 50 percent in 1987 for the combined regions, compared to 33 percent in the suburban rings. More important, the post-1982 economic recovery left poorly educated black males in the city essentially untouched, while poorly educated blacks residing in the suburbs of each region experienced declines in joblessness. Why?

Despite the economic recovery of major cities with significant underclass populations, employment growth was selective, with white-collar service industries demanding greater education levels leading the way, while many traditionally lower-education-requisite industries continued to decline. For example, spurred by a 245,000 employment gain in its service sector, New York City added 329,100 jobs between 1980 and 1988, a 10 percent

overall increase, while losing 125,100 manufacturing jobs, a greater than 25 percent employment decline in this sector. Furthermore, employment growth in the recovering cities was far overshadowed by job increases at all skill levels in the suburbs. For instance, while employment in Washington, D.C., increased by 49,000 between 1980 and 1988, employment increased in its suburbs by 497,000.[26]

What is especially troubling given these rends is that black migration to the suburbs apparently slowed during the 1980s, compared to the 1970s.[27] Between 1970 and 1980, black suburban population growth averaged 177,000 annually. Between 1980 and 1986, black suburban

26. U.S. Department of Labor, Bureau of Labor Statistics, *Employment and Earnings*, vol. 22, 1975; ibid., vol. 33, 1986.

27. Eunice S. Grier and George Grier, "Minorities in Suburbia: A Mid-1980's Update" (Report to the Urban Institute Project on Housing Mobility, Mar. 1988).

TABLE 8
PERCENTAGE NOT AT WORK OF OUT-OF-SCHOOL CENTRAL-CITY
AND SUBURBAN BLACK MALE RESIDENTS AGED 16-64
WHO HAVE NOT COMPLETED 12 YEARS OF EDUCATION, 1969-87

Region of the United States and Metropolitan Residence	1969	1977	1982	1987
All regions				
Central city	18.8	38.3	49.5	49.5
Suburban ring	16.3	31.4	38.2	33.4
Northeast				
Central city	21.1	42.8	44.8	44.0
Suburban ring	15.1	27.0	34.4	30.8
Midwest				
Central city	19.5	42.6	54.3	55.5
Suburban ring	8.0	44.3	43.6	41.3
South				
Central city	15.4	32.0	47.3	45.8
Suburban ring	15.9	24.9	37.9	32.1
West				
Central city	27.4	42.3	60.4	60.8
Suburban ring	38.9	44.2	37.7	34.2

SOURCES: Bureau of the Census, Current Population Survey, Annual March Demographic File: Machine Readable, 1969; ibid., 1977; ibid., 1982; ibid., 1987.

growth averaged 156,000 annually, with over 75 percent of it occurring in the South. The slowing suburban black migration also continued to be selective, leaving behind those blacks with the lowest education and the least resources.[28]

HOW HAVE THE NEW ETHNIC IMMIGRANTS ADAPTED?

If spatial confinement and poor education are such handicaps to gainful employment in industrially transforming cities, why is it that America's new urban immigrant groups, especially Asians, have had such high success in carving out employment niches and climbing the socioeconomic ladder? Like blacks, many Asian immigrants arrived with limited

28. Ibid.

education and financial resources and are spatially concentrated in inner-city enclaves. Recent research on ethnic entrepreneurism casts light on the reasons and is suggestive for reducing underclass problems.[29] These studies show the critical importance of ethnic solidarity and kinship networks in fostering social mobility

29. Ivan Light, *Ethnic Enterprise in America* (Berkeley: University of California Press, 1972); Edna Bonacich and John Modell, *The Economic Basis of Ethnic Solidarity* (Berkeley: University of California Press, 1980); Kenneth L. Wilson and Alejandro Portes, "Immigrant Enclaves: An Analysis of Labor Market Experiences of Cubans in Miami," *American Journal of Sociology,* 86:295-319 (1980); Roger Waldinger, *Through the Eye of the Needle: Immigrants and Enterprise in New York's Garment Trades* (New York: New York University Press, 1986); Thomas R. Bailey, *Immigrant and Native Workers: Contrasts and Competition* (Boulder, CO: Westview Press, 1987).

in segregated enclaves through self-employment.

Unlike most urban blacks, many Asian immigrants and certain Hispanic groups have been able to utilize ethnic-based methods to (1) assemble capital, (2) establish internal markets, (3) circumvent discrimination, and (4) generate employment in their enclaves that is relatively insulated from both swings in the national economy and urban structural transformation. Ethnic businesses are typically family owned and operated, often drawing upon unpaid family labor to staff functions during start-up periods of scarce resources and upon ethnic contacts to obtain credit, advice, and patronage. The businesses are characterized by thriftiness and long hours of intense, hard work, with continuous reinvestment of profits. As they expand, ethnic-enclave establishments display strong hiring preferences for their own members, many of whom would likely face employment discrimination by firms outside their enclave. They also do business with their own. A San Francisco study found that a dollar turns over five to six times in the Chinese business community while in most black communities dollars leave before they turn over even once.[30]

Kinship and household structures of ethnic immigrants have significantly facilitated their entrepreneurial successes. Among recently arrived Asian immigrants, for instance, "other relatives," those beyond the immediate family, constitute a substantial portion of households: 55 percent among Filipinos and Vietnamese, 49 percent among Koreans, 46 percent among the Chinese, and 41 percent

among Asian Indians.[31] In addition to serving as a valuable source of family business labor, these extended-kin members enable immigrant households to function more efficiently as economic units by sharing fixed household costs such as rents or mortgages, furnishing child-care services, and providing economic security against loss of employment by other household members.[32] In short, by capitalizing on ethnic and family solidarity, many new immigrant businesses, ranging from laundries to restaurants to green groceries, have started and flourished in once downtrodden urban neighborhoods, providing employment and mobility options to group members in what in other respects is an unfavorable economic environment.[33]

Native urban blacks, in contrast, have been burdened by conditions that have impeded their entry and success in enclave employment, including lack of self-help business associations, limited economic solidarity, and family fragmentation. A survey by *Black Enterprise* magazine, for example, reported that 70 percent of self-employed blacks consider lack of community support as one of their most formidable problems.[34] This, together with the documented flight of black-earned income to nonblack establishments, led well-known black journalist Tony Brown to comment, "The Chinese are helping the Chinese, the Koreans help the Koreans, Cubans help Cubans, but blacks are

30. Joel Kotkin, "The Reluctant Entrepreneurs," *Inc.*, 8(9):81-86 (Sept. 1986); Rick Wartzman, "St. Louis Blues: A Blighted Inner City Bespeaks the Sad State of Black Commerce," *Wall St. Journal*, 10 May 1988.

31. Peter S. Xenos et al., "Asian Americans: Growth and Change in the 1970s," in *Pacific Bridges: The New Immigration from Asia and the Pacific Islands*, ed. J. Fawcett and B. Carino (Staten Island, NY: Center for Migration Studies, 1987), p. 266.

32. Ibid.

33. Robert L. Boyd, "Ethnic Entrepreneurs in the New Economy" (Paper, University of North Carolina, Chapel Hill, 1988).

34. Kotkin, "Reluctant Entrepreneurs," p. 84.

helping everyone else. We have been conducting the most successful business boycott in American history—against ourselves."[35] Apparently, racial political unity that has led to significant black electoral successes in major Northern cities during the past two decades has not carried over to the economic sphere.

Given the demonstrated importance of family cohesiveness and kinship networks in pooling resources to start businesses, provide day-care assistance, and contribute labor to family business ventures, the black underclass is at a distinct disadvantage. As Wilson found, approximately two-thirds of black families living in Chicago's ghettos are mother-only households.[36] These households are the poorest segment of our society, with female householders earning only a third as much as married male householders.[37] In short, it takes discretionary resources to start a small business and it requires patrons with money to sustain that business, both of which are in limited supply in underclass neighborhoods.

All the factors previously mentioned have converged to depress black self-employment rates during the past two decades, especially in the inner city.[38] Table 9, computed from the 1980 PUMS Files, shows for major cities the consistency with which lesser-educated blacks are underrepresented in self-employment,

particularly when compared to Asians. Among more recent Asian immigrants, self-employment rates are even higher. Data from the same source show that Korean immigrant self-employment rates range from a low of 19 percent in Chicago to a high of 35 percent in New York.[39]

Just as striking are Asian-black contrasts from the most recent census survey of minority-owned businesses. Between 1977 and 1982 the number of Asian-American-owned firms with paid employment expanded by 160 percent. During the same period, the number of black-owned firms with employees actually declined by 3 percent.[40] With small business formation becoming the backbone of job creation in America's new economy, blacks are falling further behind in this critical arena.

Financial weakness and family fragmentation among the black underclass not only preclude capital mobilization for self-employment but also create barriers to their children's social mobility. Living in a mother-only household was found to increase the risk of young blacks' dropping out of school by 70 percent.[41] The link between female headship and welfare dependency in the urban underclass is also well established, leading to legitimate concerns about the intergenerational transfer of poverty. At the root of this concern is the paucity of employment among welfare mothers and how this affects attitudes of their children toward work. Of those receiving welfare benefits, 85 percent have no source of income other

35. Ibid.

36. William Julius Wilson, *The Truly Disadvantaged* (Chicago: University of Chicago Press, 1987).

37. Sara McLanahan, Irwin Garfinkel, and Dorothy Watson, "Family Structure, Poverty, and the Underclass," in *Urban Change and Poverty*, ed. M. McGeary and L. Lynn (Washington, DC: National Academy Press), pp. 102-47.

38. Eugene H. Becker, "Self-Employed Workers: An Update to 1983," *Monthly Labor Review*, 107(7):14-18; Kotkin, "Reluctant"; Wartzman, "St. Louis Blues."

39. Roger Waldinger et al., "Spatial Approaches to Ethnic Business," in *Ethnic Entrepreneurs: Immigrant Business in Industrial Societies*, by R. Waldinger et al. (Newbury Park, CA: Sage, forthcoming).

40. Boyd, "Ethnic Entrepreneurs."

41. Sara McLanahan, "Family Structure and the Reproduction of Poverty," *American Journal of Sociology*, 90:873-901 (1985).

TABLE 9
PERCENTAGE SELF-EMPLOYED OF ALL EMPLOYED MALES,
AGED 16-64, WITH LESS THAN HIGH SCHOOL EDUCATION AND
RESIDING IN SELECTED CENTRAL CITIES, BY RACE OR ETHNICITY, 1980

Central City	Non-Hispanic blacks	Hispanics	Asians and others	Non-Hispanic whites
Baltimore	3.5	14.3	9.1	5.5
Boston	3.1	4.4	6.7	8.1
Chicago	3.4	2.5	15.2	6.2
Cleveland*	2.3	NA	15.4	3.9
Detroit	3.3	5.9	NA	6.0
New York	3.1	3.6	8.5	11.1
Philadelphia	3.4	4.2	17.3	7.4
St. Louis	2.4	10.0	25.0	16.7
Washington, D.C.	3.2	NA	18.2	16.4

SOURCE: Bureau of the Census, Machine Readable Public Use Microdata Sample File, 5% A Sample, 1980.
*Includes those with high school degree only.

than public assistance.[42] Furthermore, 65 percent of the recipients of Aid to Families with Dependent Children at any one point in time are in an interval of dependency that has lasted for at least eight years.[43] One does not require a deep sociological imagination to sense the attitudinal and behavioral consequences of growing up in an impoverished household where there is no activity associated with the world of work and a household that, in turn, is spatially embedded in a commercially abandoned locality where pimps, drug pushers, and unemployed street people have replaced working fathers as predominant socializing agents.

REKINDLING UNDERCLASS MOBILITY

It is clear from a substantial amount of research that strengthening the black family and reducing the exceptionally high percentage of impoverished mother-only households must be key focuses of policies to rekindle social mobility among today's urban underclass. These policies should be complemented with programs that improve opportunities for ghetto youths to be reared in household and neighborhood environments where adult work is the norm and to attend public schools that will provide them with necessary skills and social networks for employment in a rapidly transforming economy. In this regard, it has been shown that low-income black youths who moved from inner-city Chicago to predominantly white suburbs as part of a subsidized housing experiment performed remarkably well, both academically and socially.[44]

It was also shown herein that, as cities have functionally changed from centers of goods processing to centers of information processing, there has been a signifi-

42. Irwin Garfinkel and Sara S. McLanahan, *Single Mothers and Their Children* (Washington, DC: Urban Institute Press, 1986).

43. David T. Ellwood, "Targeting the Would-Be Long-Term Recipients of AFDC: Who Should Be Served?" (Report, Harvard University, 1985).

44. James Rosenbaum et al., "Low Income Black Children in White Suburban Schools: A Study of School and Student Responses," *Journal of Negro Education,* 56(1):35-43 (1987).

cant rise in the education required for urban employment. If greater portions of disadvantaged black youths do not acquire the formal education to be hired by the white-collar service industries beginning to dominate urban employment bases, their jobless rates will remain high. For this reason and because demographic forces portend potential shortages of educationally qualified resident labor for the white-collar industries expanding in the cities, there have been appropriate calls from both the public and private sectors to upgrade city schools, reduce black youth drop-out rates, and increase the proportion who continue on for higher education.

Such policies, however, are unlikely to alleviate the unemployment problems currently facing large numbers of economically displaced older blacks and yet-to-be-placed younger ones with serious educational deficiencies—those caught in the web of urban change. Their unemployment will persist because the educational qualifications demanded by most of today's urban growth industries are difficult to impart through short-term, nontraditional programs.[45]

The implausibility of rebuilding urban blue-collar job bases or of providing sufficient education to large numbers of displaced black laborers so that they may be reemployed in expanding white-collar industries necessitates a renewed look at the traditional means by which Americans have adapted to economic displacement—that is, spatial mobility. Despite the mass loss of lower-skilled jobs in many cities during the past decade, there have been substantial increases in these

jobs nationwide. For example, between 1975 and 1985, more than 2.1 million nonadministrative jobs were added in eating and drinking establishments, which is more than the total number of production jobs that existed in 1985 in America's automobile, primary metals, and textile industries combined.[46] Unfortunately, essentially all of the net national growth in jobs with low educational requisites has occurred in the suburbs, exurbs, and nonmetropolitan areas, which are far removed from large concentrations of poorly educated minorities. It seems both an irony and a tragedy that we have such surpluses of unemployed lower-skilled labor in the inner cities at the same time that suburban businesses are facing serious shortages in lower-skilled labor.

The inability of disadvantaged urban blacks to follow decentralizing lower-skilled jobs has increasingly isolated them from shifting loci of employment opportunity and has contributed to their high rates of joblessness. To reduce this isolation, a number of strategies should be considered, including (1) a computerized job-opportunity network providing up-to-date information on available jobs throughout the particular metropolitan area, the region, and the nation; (2) partial underwriting of more distant job searches by the unemployed; (3) need-based temporary relocation assistance, once a job has been secured; (4) housing vouchers for those whose income levels require such assistance, as opposed to additional spatially fixed public housing complexes; (5) stricter enforcement of existing fair-housing and fair-hiring laws; (6) public-private cooperative efforts to van-pool unemployed inner-city residents to suburban businesses facing labor short-

45. John D. Kasarda, "Jobs, Migration and Emerging Urban Mismatches," in *Urban Change and Poverty,* ed. M.G.H. McGeary and L. E. Lynn, Jr. (Washington, DC: National Academy Press, 1988), pp. 148-98.

46. U.S. Department of Labor, Bureau of Labor Statistics, Establishment Data 1939-1986 Machine Readable Files, Washington, DC.

ages; and (7) a thorough review of all spatially targeted low-income public assistance programs to ensure that they are not inadvertently anchoring those with limited resources to distressed areas in which there are few prospects for permanent or meaningful employment.

The aim of these people-to-jobs strategies is not only to bring a better balance between local supplies and demands for labor, but also to facilitate the means by which disadvantaged Americans have historically obtained economic opportunity and a better life. In this regard, it is not fortuitous that the three great symbols of social and economic opportunity for America's disadvantaged all relate to spatial mobility—the Statue of Liberty, the Underground Railway, and the covered wagon.

4

Absent Fathers in the Inner City

By MERCER L. SULLIVAN

ABSTRACT: The influences of structural economic factors, social ecology, and culture on producing young absent fathers in the inner city and on defining their relationships to their children are examined. Ethnographic data on three low-income urban neighborhoods are reported and compared with respect to the careers of young males, patterns of sexual activity and contraception, and responses to early pregnancy.

Mercer L. Sullivan received his Ph.D. in anthropology from Columbia University. He has conducted studies of school desegregation, youth crime and employment, and the male role in teenage pregnancy and parenting. He is a senior research associate at the Vera Institute of Justice in New York City.

NOTE: The research reported here could not have been carried out without the sensitive and dedicated work of three field research assistants: Carl Cesvette, for Projectville; Richard Curtis, for Hamilton Park; and Adalberto Mauras, for La Barriada. Our research on the role of young males in teenage pregnancy and parenting has been supported by the Ford Foundation and the W. T. Grant Foundation.

THE long-standing and increasing relationship between officially female-headed households and poverty has prompted much recent speculation that absent fathers are a major cause of concentrated and persistent poverty in the inner cities. Child support enforcement is now widely touted as a major solution to the emerging formation of a so-called underclass. As part of this strategy for reducing poverty, many proponents of reform do recognize the need for addressing the employment, education, and training difficulties of young men. Yet current welfare-reform proposals are more emphatic about the need to collect child support payments from young men than they are about the need to improve their economic opportunities. Meanwhile, knowledge of the economic circumstances of young, unmarried, officially absent fathers and of their relationships to the households in which their children live is sadly lacking. Official statistics do not convey an accurate picture of the extent to which officially absent fathers are really absent from the households and lives of their children or of the extent to which these men are actually able to support families.

Explanations of the relationship between family form and poverty have long been controversial in social science and in discussions of public policy. Although the association between poverty and female headship of households has been apparent for some time, the direction of causal relationships between the two has been hotly debated. Because poverty and female-headed households both occur at high rates among members of cultural minority groups in the United States, there has also been much controversy about the role that culture plays in the processes that produce both female-headed households and poverty. The culture-of-poverty theories of the late 1960s drew harsh criticism because they seemed to imply that cultural values concerning the control of sexual activity and the value of marriage were the causes rather than the results of poverty.

These theories provoked such heated reactions that research on family patterns among the poor was virtually suspended during the 1970s. During that decade, however, the proportions of female-headed households increased across society and soared among minority residents of inner-city areas. The associations between female headship of households, welfare dependency, and concentrated and persistent poverty became stronger than ever, eventually prompting social scientists and leaders of minority groups to pay renewed attention to family patterns among the poor. Fortunately, much of the recent research on these questions has maintained a steady focus on structural causes of both poverty and family disruption. Recent work by William Julius Wilson has sharpened this focus on structural factors by linking economic changes to powerful demographic shifts that have concentrated poor blacks in certain central-city areas while upwardly mobile blacks have left these areas.[1]

Unfortunately, the role of culture in these social changes remains as neglected as it has been since the days when overly vague notions of the culture of poverty brought disrepute to the culture concept as a tool for understanding the effects of the concentration of poverty among cultural minorities. This neglect of culture is unfortunate because it leaves us in the dark as to how people deal collectively with economic disadvantage, prejudice,

1. William Julius Wilson, *The Truly Disadvantaged: The Inner City, the Underclass, and Public Policy* (Chicago: University of Chicago Press, 1987).

and the dilemmas of procreating and raising families under such conditions. Lacking such an understanding, we are left with two sorts of explanatory framework, structural and individual, both of which beg crucial questions of how people in real communities devise collective responses to their problems. Too extreme an emphasis on individual causation ignores growing evidence of the proliferation of low-wage jobs and increasing joblessness in inner-city labor markets. Too much emphasis on structural causation ignores evidence that postponing childbearing leads to greater occupational success even within inner-city populations.

The neglect of culture stems both from a lack of ethnographic research, which alone can portray culture, and from theoretical confusion concerning the ways in which individual action, culture, and social structure are interrelated. The comparative ethnographic research on young fathers in three inner-city neighborhoods reported here attempts to resolve some of these issues, first by providing data on cultural processes and, second, by relating these cultural processes both upward to the structural constraints of the political economy and downward to the choices and strategies of particular individuals, which vary even within these neighborhoods.

A key to the theoretical approach employed here is the concept of social ecology, the idea that each neighborhood we studied is distinctive not just because of primordial cultural values that may have been retained from a distant past but, perhaps more important, because each neighborhood occupies a distinctive ecological niche in relation to the regional economy, the educational system, and other institutions of the larger society. Though even the early culture-of-poverty theorists maintained that culture is adap-

tive to structure,[2] their tendency to portray pathology and not adaptation led to the unfortunate current tendency either to dismiss culture or to reify it as a set of mysterious and immutable values. By focusing on social ecology, the present comparison of the adaptive strategies of young people in three different inner-city communities attempts to portray cultural process in a more complex way, as the collective adaptations of different groups of people with different group histories to similar yet distinctive difficulties in obtaining a living income, procreating, and supporting and raising children.

THREE NEIGHBORHOODS AND A RESEARCH PROJECT

The three neighborhoods we have studied are in Brooklyn, New York. In order to maintain the confidentiality of the very detailed and personal data we have gathered, we refer to these places using the pseudonyms Hamilton Park, Projectville, and La Barriada. The three neighborhoods are all relatively low income, yet they differ in class and in culture. Hamilton Park is a predominantly white, Catholic area many of whose adult residents are third- and fourth-generation descendants of immigrants from Italy and Poland. Though census figures show this neighborhood to have some of the lowest income levels among predominantly white, non-Hispanic neighborhoods in New York City, median income levels are still significantly higher than those in the two minority neighborhoods. Less than 12 percent of families are below the poverty level and less than 10 percent of households receive Aid to Families with Dependent Children (AFDC). Projectville

2. Oscar Lewis, *La Vida: A Puerto Rican Family in the Culture of Poverty—San Juan and New York* (New York: Vintage Books, 1965), p. xliv.

is a predominantly black neighborhood whose adult residents are first- or second-generation immigrants from the southern United States. La Barriada is a predominantly Hispanic area in which all of the families we have contacted are headed by first- or second-generation immigrants from Puerto Rico. Family poverty levels and household AFDC enrollment levels are around 50 percent in both these areas.

We began research in these areas in 1979 in a study of the relationships between schooling, employment, and crime in the careers of young males. In that study, we described distinctive career patterns in each neighborhood and related these patterns to the distinctive social ecology of each neighborhood.[3] In 1984, we began to look at young men who had become fathers at an early age and how their responses with respect to marriage, child support, and household and family formation related to the career patterns we had already been studying.[4] At that time, we recontacted some of the young males who had become fathers during our study a few years earlier; we also were introduced by them to younger males in their neighborhoods whose sexual partners had become pregnant. Some of the similarities and differences within and between these neighborhood-based groups of young men in how they became fathers and what they did about these critical life-cycle transitions are reported and compared here.

In order to assess the influences of both culture and economic opportunity on the ways in which young men become fathers and how they react, the three

3. Mercer L. Sullivan, *Getting Paid: Economy, Culture, and Youth Crime in the Inner City* (Ithaca, NY: Cornell University Press, forthcoming).
4. Mercer L. Sullivan, "Teen Fathers in the Inner City: An Exploratory Ethnographic Study," mimeographed (New York: Vera Institute of Justice, 1985).

neighborhoods are compared in terms of (1) the careers of young males; (2) patterns of teenage sexual activity; and (3) responses to pregnancy, including whether abortions are sought, whether marriage and coresidence are entered into, and how the children of young mothers are supported. The data are reported for 16 young males from Projectville, 17 from La Barriada, and 15 from Hamilton Park. These are not random samples but were recruited by ethnographic snowballing techniques. In addition, there is considerable variation within each sample. Each includes about a third who are nonfathers and each includes fathers who have been more and less effective in providing support for their children. Nonetheless, variation within each neighborhood sample falls within a distinctive range that reflects both community values and the resources available within that community.

All of those referred to as fathers fathered children by teenage mothers. Many of the fathers, however, were one to two years older and not themselves teenagers at the time they became fathers.

THE CAREERS OF YOUNG MALES

The higher employment rates and median family incomes of Hamilton Park residents are associated with more employment for young males and better wages when they are employed. Although work can also be scarce for them, they enjoy much better access to jobs, both while they are still of school age and subsequently, than their minority counterparts. The jobs that they do find are located almost entirely through neighborhood-based and family-based personal networks. While they are still of school age, this work is almost entirely off the books, yet it usually pays better than minimum

wage. As they get older, some find their way into relatively well-paying and secure unionized blue-collar jobs. Education plays very little role in their access to work. Most have attended a public vocational high school, but only about a third of them have obtained any sort of diploma.

Young males from the two minority neighborhoods fare much worse. They suffer more from lack of employment, and they earn very low wages when they do work, both as teenagers and as young adults. Yet the career patterns differ between these two minority neighborhoods in distinctive ways that are related to the neighborhoods' social ecology. La Barriada's young males leave school earlier than their peers in the other two neighborhoods. They tend to work in unskilled manual jobs in nearby factories and warehouses when they do work. Projectville's young males stay in school longer than their counterparts in La Barriada or in Hamilton Park. Nearly half of our sample from Projectville had either completed a diploma or were still working toward one. As a result of their prolonged participation in schooling, they tend to enter the labor market somewhat later than the others. They then tend to move into clerical and service-sector jobs in downtown business districts. Many of these jobs require a high school diploma. As a result, though they enter the labor market somewhat later than young males in La Barriada, they have better prospects for upward mobility. Yet they still tend to earn less than their less educated counterparts in Hamilton Park.

In our earlier study of crime and employment, we found that, although many young males in each of these neighborhoods are involved in exploratory economic crimes, the blocked access to employment among the minority youths leads to more sustained and prevalent involvement in intensive criminal activities and to periods of probation and incarceration. Census and police statistics generally support our findings concerning the relative involvements of those in the three neighborhoods in schooling, work, and crime.

These career patterns are described as background for understanding the different ranges of responses to early pregnancy within each of the neighborhoods.

SEXUAL ACTIVITY

Before looking at how young males in the three neighborhoods respond to early pregnancy and whether or not they become absent fathers, it is necessary to compare their patterns of early sexual activity and contraceptive use. If we had found substantial differences, we might conclude that differences in becoming fathers at an early age were due to later or less frequent sexual activity or, alternatively, to greater use of contraceptives. In fact, our data show relatively few such differences between the neighborhood groups, although we do find such differences within each group. Almost all those in each group had experienced intercourse by the age of 15, and few had used contraceptives in their first acts of intercourse.

These findings differ somewhat from survey findings that indicate a greater likelihood of early intercourse among blacks than among whites,[5] although Hamilton Park's whites are much poorer than the middle-class whites often sampled in these surveys. In fact, we found in each neighborhood that, from their early teens

5. Freya L. Sonenstein, "Risking Paternity: Sex and Contraception among Adolescent Males," in *Adolescent Fatherhood*, ed. Arthur B. Elster and Michael E. Lamb (Hillsdale, NJ: Lawrence Erlbaum, 1986), pp. 31-54.

on, males are almost entirely outside of adult supervision, except when they are in school, as they frequently are not. They also are encouraged to prove their manhood by sexual adventures and receive little consistent encouragement or instruction in the use of contraceptives.

What our data do suggest, however, is variations within each neighborhood in the use of contraceptives. We first sought out young fathers in each place and subsequently interviewed four or five friends of the fathers who were not themselves fathers. The nonfathers generally began sexual activity as early and heedlessly as the fathers. Some seemed to have avoided becoming fathers through chance, but others reported developing contraceptive practices that prevented their becoming fathers. These practices included some use of condoms but more often involved careful use of withdrawal or a long-term relationship with a partner who used birth-control pills.

RESPONSES TO PREGNANCY

In contrast to this relative lack of difference between the neighborhoods in patterns of early sexual activity and contraception, the ranges of response to early pregnancy differed between the neighborhoods in quite distinctive ways that can be related to differences in culture, class, and social ecology. After the discovery that the partners of these young males had become pregnant, those involved in each community faced a number of choices. The first choice was whether or not the young female should seek an abortion. If not, then it had to be decided whether the young couple should get married and / or establish coresidence and what extent and manner of support and care the young father should be expected to provide for his child. These choices

usually involved not just the conceiving young couple but also their parents and even extended families. In this way, individual choices became embedded in the context of the wider neighborhood community and its values and resources.

In all these choices, we found distinctive neighborhood patterns, although a range of choices was apparent within each neighborhood group. These patterns are described separately for each neighborhood. We begin with Projectville, which fits many of the stereotypes of underclass neighborhoods with high rates of out-of-wedlock childbearing by teenage mothers and related high rates of absent fatherhood. We then compare these patterns with Hamilton Park in order to assess the effects of different levels of economic opportunity. Finally, we examine La Barriada, an area that is similar to Projectville in class but different in culture and social ecology.

In Projectville, we found very ambivalent attitudes and behavior concerning the decision to seek abortions or not. Most of the young males reported extreme disapproval of abortion, often calling it murder and saying that they had urged their partners not to abort. Yet the same individuals would often say that their mothers might support abortions for their sisters. Three of them reported that they had been involved in pregnancies that terminated in abortions. In two of these cases, the decision was made by the female and her family, and the males were not involved. In the other case, the abortion was of a second pregnancy. Health statistics, which cover a fairly homogeneous area in this neighborhood, indicate that more than half of all teen pregnancies in Projectville end in abortion.

Attitudes toward marriage as a response to early pregnancy, however, were more uniform. Projectville residents gener-

ally did not encourage immediate marriage or coresidence for young parents. Two couples eventually did marry, though not until over a year after the birth, during which time the father's employment status had improved, in one case because the father had joined the military and had completed basic training. Another marriage occurred when a young mother married another male, not the father of her first child. The other fathers would be classified officially as absent. They neither married, nor, in most cases, did they establish coresidence.

Yet the absence of marriage and coresidence did not mean that they had no further relationships with the mothers and children. Although romantic commitments to the mothers tended to be volatile, most of the fathers reported strong commitments to their children. Their paternity was recognized within the neighborhood. Most eventually also established legal paternity. Further, most provided some measure of care and support, to the extent that they were able. They contributed money, some from employment, usually part-time and/or low-wage, others from criminal activities. Some continued with education and training for a time after the birth, unlike their counterparts in the other neighborhoods. In these cases, the mothers' families saw the young fathers' continued education as being in the best long-term interests of the children. These unmarried young fathers also visited regularly and frequently took the children to their own homes, for weekends or even longer periods of time. Many reported providing direct child care when they were with their children, to a greater extent than fathers in either of the other two neighborhoods.

The only ones who provided no care or support at all for some period of time were those who became heavily involved in crime or drug use and underwent incarceration, including 6 of the 16 at some point. Even these were involved with their children before or after incarceration.

These data were, of course, collected from a self-selected sample of young fathers who were willing to talk with researchers. All also reported that they knew of fathers who had "stepped off," as they put it, from their children. They attributed stepping off in some of these cases to the young fathers' inability to make contributions. Despite the self-selected nature of our sample, however, participation by young, unmarried fathers in informal systems of care and support for their children does seem to be quite common in this neighborhood. Other studies have shown that poor, black, officially absent fathers actually have more contact with and provide more informal support for their children than middle-class, white absent fathers.[6]

In Hamilton Park, we found quite different patterns of abortion, marriage, coresidence, and support. None of the young males we interviewed expressed strong condemnations of abortion, and several openly supported abortions in cases where the couple was not ready to get married. One of those who had not become a father as a teenager had avoided doing so by encouraging an abortion. Another nonfather said he would "slip her the two hundred dollars" if his partner

6. Ron Haskins et al., "Estimates of National Child Support Collections Potential and Income Security of Female-Headed Families: Final Report to the Office of Child Support Administration, Social Security Administration" (Bush Institute for Child and Family Policy, Frank Porter Graham Child Development Center, University of North Carolina, 1985).

became pregnant. Even one of the young fathers and his partner had aborted a first pregnancy and then married after a second pregnancy and before the birth.

Marriage was also more common in this group. Over half the fathers in this group married after conception and before the birth. One married before conception, he being the only one whose child was planned. Marriage also entailed setting up coresidence in apartments of their own. This pattern of family formation has deep roots in working-class tradition. Early sexual activity is a recognized form of risk taking that is often understood to lead to marriage if a pregnancy occurs.

This pattern of family formation is also strongly linked to the traditional working-class career patterns that are still maintained in this neighborhood, despite the recent pressures of economic change that threaten this way of life. Decent jobs are available, through neighborhood and family contacts, that do not depend on educational credentials and that allow young males to establish independent households and support their families. Those who got married found both work and housing through these local channels. These early unions were often troubled, and household arrangements did shift over time. Significantly, the only case of court-ordered child support we encountered in any of the three neighborhoods was among this group of relatively economically advantaged youths.

The relatively well-paying, blue-collar jobs that have sustained this neighborhood are disappearing from the regional economy, however, and the effects of this economic erosion are evident throughout the neighborhood. Many young people leave the area for the suburbs or western states. Others become heavily involved in drugs and hang out on the streets, working

irregularly. The differences in career and family-formation patterns between the neighborhoods are not absolute but matters of degree. Two of the nonmarrying fathers in Hamilton Park, for example, resembled some of their peers in Projectville, working irregularly and making regular contributions and visits but not marrying. The other nonmarrying fathers were all heavy drug users who made poor marriage prospects. One of them did not learn that he had become a father until two years later. Their children and the mothers of their children were among the AFDC recipients who, though less heavily concentrated than in the minority neighborhoods, still accounted for about 10 percent of the households in Hamilton Park.

In La Barriada, young males whose partners became pregnant also faced disappointing economic opportunities. Like their peers in Projectville and unlike some of their peers in Hamilton Park, they had relatively poor chances of being able to find jobs that would allow them to marry and provide full support for their children. Yet culture and social ecology led them to a different set of responses to their predicament.

Their attitudes toward abortion were even more negative than those we discovered in Projectville, yet some of them also had been involved in abortions. One of the nonfathers reported an abortion. In addition, three of the fathers reported abortions of second pregnancies. They said that they still disapproved of abortions but simply could not afford a second child right away. Health statistics for La Barriada and Hamilton Park were not readily comparable to those for Projectville, but statistics for the city as a whole did show the same patterns that we found: among pregnant teens, whites had

the highest rate of abortions, followed by blacks and then by Hispanics.[7]

Though even less likely than those in Projectville to see abortions as a solution, the young males in La Barriada were far more likely to pursue marriage and co-residence, despite formidable obstacles in the way of their being able to support families. Only 5 of 11 fathers did not marry legally, but 3 of these described themselves as being in common-law marriages and had established coresidence. Common-law partners openly referred to themselves as "husband" and "wife," unlike the unmarried but still involved couples in Projectville.

One father, a highly religious Pentecostal, married as a virgin at 18, indicating the relatively young age at which even so-called normal marriage and parenting can occur in this group. The others married after conception, either before or after the birth. Marriage entailed coresidence, though usually in the household of one of the young couple's parents. Most coresident couples lived with the father's parents, a distinctive pattern not found in the other neighborhoods and tied to cultural expectations that the father and his family are responsible for the child and mother.

Despite their willingness to marry and establish coresidence, however, these fathers' prospects for finding jobs that paid enough and were steady enough to allow them to support families remained poor. As a result, they entered the labor market somewhat earlier than those in Projectville, yet with fewer prospects for advancement. All the young fathers ceased

attending school after they became fathers, though some later returned to school or training programs. None of them remained in school continuously, as did some of the Projectville fathers.

Structural circumstances also discouraged marriage for some in La Barriada. The mothers and children in the common-law marriages, for example, all received AFDC. Refraining from marriage concealed their unions from scrutiny by the AFDC program.

Even though the young fathers from La Barriada were more likely to marry, their own family backgrounds suggested that the future of these marriages was highly doubtful. Most of them came from families in which the parents had been married, by ceremony or common-law arrangement, yet almost all their own fathers had left the households when they were young children. The departure of their own fathers was usually related to employment difficulties and led to household AFDC enrollment.

Crime and drugs also were involved in the inability of some of these young fathers to support their families. Two were incarcerated at some point and five others had some history of heavy drug use.

None of the officially absent fathers from La Barriada or Projectville had ever been involved in legal child support proceedings. Local child support agencies assigned a low priority to young fathers and especially to young, unemployed fathers. Young fathers who themselves lived with families on AFDC were automatically excluded from child support actions.

CONCLUSION

These comparisons of young males in three neighborhoods demonstrate the in-

7. Adolescent Pregnancy Interagency Council, *A Coordinated Strategy on the Issues of Adolescent Pregnancy and Parenting* (New York: Mayor's Office of Adolescent Pregnancy and Parenting Services, 1986), p. 10.

terrelated influences of structural economic factors, culture, and social ecology in shaping processes of family and household formation. The high rates of female-headed and AFDC-receiving households in the two minority neighborhoods are clearly related not only to an overall lack in this region of jobs paying wages that could allow men to assume traditional breadwinning roles but also to social-ecological factors that link the different neighborhoods to the regional labor market in quite different ways. The distinctive range of responses to early pregnancy in each community depends heavily on the resources that are available within that community.

Culture also plays a role in shaping local responses to teenage pregnancy. When cultural values are seen in relation to social ecology, however, they appear not as unchanging, primordial entities but rather as collective responses of people with distinctive group histories to different and changing structural positions in society. Hamilton Park's residents most closely adhere to a long-standing working-class tradition, in which teenage sexual activity is understood to be a risk-taking enterprise that should lead to marriage when pregnancy results. The erosion of well-paying entry-level jobs that have made this way of life possible, however, threatens these understandings as more young men, unable to find such jobs, turn to drugs and away from marriage.

Projectville's residents have known the link between lack of jobs and lack of marriage longer and live with much greater concentrations of joblessness and dependency, yet they have well-defined attitudes toward how to cope with these problems. They put great faith in education, despite its frequently disappointing payoffs in the job market, and they have developed complex ways of supporting children in kin-based networks.[8] Young males play important roles in these networks, which are highly flexible and adaptive to shifting circumstances.

La Barriada's residents are the most recent immigrants and cling tenaciously to a traditional culture even as its assumptions about a male's role in the family clash harshly with the realities of the low-wage labor market and the welfare system.

The influences of structural economic factors, culture, and social ecology on the actions of young men demonstrated in this analysis are not intended as disavowals of individual potential; nor are they intended as claims for an absolute cultural relativism, which would imply that processes of family formation in these neighborhoods, though different from those in the mainstream, are entirely satisfactory for local residents. To the contrary, the relationships between early pregnancy, absent fatherhood, and persistent poverty are quite evident to the residents of these communities. Some individuals in these communities do manage to escape these and other hazards of life in the inner cities. These struggles are particularly evident among Projectville residents, for example, as seen in their perseverance with education and their ambivalence toward abortion.

In none of these communities is any honor given to fathers who do not at least try to support their children. All the accounts we have heard indicate that failure to support one's children is experienced as a loss of manhood. The standards for judging individual fathers are clear within each neighborhood but differ somewhat between the neighborhoods in terms of relative emphasis on immediate cash

8. Carol B. Stack, *All Our Kin: Strategies for Survival in a Black Community* (New York: Harper & Row, 1974).

contributions, continued education, marriage, and the provision of child care. The higher rate at which young men in the two minority neighborhoods fail to meet such standards is a function neither of the random occurrence of high rates of pathological individuals in these areas nor of the content of ethnic culture but rather of blocked access to decent jobs.

Social policy that hopes to deal effectively with persistent poverty must move beyond assumptions that uncontrolled sexuality and an undeveloped work ethic are at the root of the problem. Policies and programs must recognize not only the powerful structural economic factors that concentrate poverty and dependency in the inner cities but also the unique ways in which individual communities attempt to reconcile their lack of access to jobs and their universal, human desire to reproduce.

At present, young males in these areas are particularly ill served by the job market, the schools, and the social welfare system. Males must be redefined as important parts of the solution and not merely as the sources of the problem. Some recent innovative efforts have been undertaken. Programs for the prevention of unwanted early pregnancy have begun to include males in their services. Some discussion has also begun concerning ways to alter the child support enforcement system to provide incentives for young fathers to acknowledge paternity. Such incentives could include connecting them to job-training and employment programs, encouraging continued education, recognizing in-kind contributions and not just cash payments, and expanding the amount they could contribute to AFDC households without having their contributions deducted from that household's AFDC budget. In order to be effective, these efforts will need to be part of an overall program of intensive and comprehensive services for inner-city children and adolescents.

5

Sex Codes and Family Life among Poor Inner-City Youths

By ELIJAH ANDERSON

ABSTRACT: Sexual conduct among poor black inner-city adolescents is resulting in growing numbers of unwed parents. At the same time, many young fathers are strongly committed to their peer groups. They congregate, often boasting of their sexual exploits and deriding conventional family life. These two interconnected realities are born of the extremely difficult socioeconomic situation prevailing in ghetto communities. The lack of family-sustaining jobs or job prospects denies young men the possibility of forming economically self-reliant families, the traditional American mark of manhood. Partially in response, the young men's peer group emphasizes sexual prowess as a mark of manhood, at times including babies as its evidence. A sexual game emerges and becomes elaborated, with girls becoming lured by the boys' often vague but convincing promises of love and marriage. As the girls submit, they often end up pregnant and abandoned, but eligible for a limited but sometimes steady income in the form of welfare, which may allow them to establish their own households and, at times, attract other men, in need of money.

Elijah Anderson is professor of sociology and associate director of the Center for Urban Ethnography at the University of Pennsylvania. He is the author of A Place on the Corner *and other urban ethnographic studies.*

NOTE: The author acknowledges the support of the U.S. Department of Health and Human Services' Office of Minority Health.

S EXUAL relations and out-of-wedlock pregnancy among poor black inner-city adolescents is a major social problem, yet we know little and understand less about these phenomena. To be sure, many studies deal in whole or in part with the subject, and they offer valuable insights into the dynamic of sexual interaction between youths in the ghetto and other socioeconomically circumscribed settings.[1] The wealth of information, however, tends to be fragmented and has led to differing, even contradictory, assessments of the state of such relations. My purpose in this article is to present a holistic account of the situation in the form of an informal ethnographic essay that focuses on actual behavior and the motivation behind it.

To this end, I interviewed some forty people who are personally involved with this issue, including teenage mothers, pregnant teenagers, teenage fathers, and prospective teenage fathers, and grandmothers, grandfathers, sisters, brothers, fathers, and mothers of youthful parents. I conducted those interviews in what could be described as natural settings: on stoops, on trolleys, in respondents' homes, in restaurants, and in other neighborhood places. Through these conversations, my goal was to generate a conceptual essay on the general subject of sex and pregnancy among poor inner-city black young people ranging in age from 15 to 23.

Sexual conduct among poor inner-city black youths is to a large extent the result of the meshing of two opposing drives, that of the boys and that of the girls. For a variety of reasons tied to the socio-economic ituation in which they find themselves, their goals are often diametrically opposed, and sex becomes a contest between them. To many boys, sex is an important symbol of local social status; sexual conquests become so many notches on one's belt. Many of the girls offer sex as a gift in their bargaining for the attentions of a young man. As boys and girls try to use each other to achieve their respective ends, the reality that emerges in the eyes of the participants sometimes approximates their goals, but it often results in frustration and disillusionment and the perpetuation or even worsening of their original situation.

In each sexual encounter, there is generally a winner and a loser. The girls

1. This literature includes Lee Rainwater, *And the Poor Get Children* (Chicago: Quadrangle Books, 1960); idem, "Crucible of Identity: The Lower-Class Negro Family,"*Daedalus,* 45:172-216 (1966); idem, "Sex in the Culture of Poverty," in *The Individual, Sex, and Society,* ed. Carlfred B. Broderick and Jessie Bernard (Baltimore, MD: Johns Hopkins University Press, 1969), pp. 129-40; idem, *Behind Ghetto Walls* (Chicago: Aldine de Gruyter, 1970); Elliot Liebow, *Tally's Corner: A Study of Negro Street Corner Men* (Boston: Little, Brown, 1967); Ulf Hannerz, *Soulside* (New York: Columbia University Press, 1969); Frank Furstenberg, *Unplanned Parenthood* (New York: Free Press, 1976); Boone E. Hammond and Joyce A. Ladner, "Socialization into Sexual Behavior in a Negro Slum Ghetto," in *Individual, Sex, and Society,* ed. Broderick and Bernard, pp. 41-51; Arnold W. Green, "The Cult of Personality and Sexual Relations," *Psychiatry,* 4:343-48 (1941); Conrad M. Arensberg, *The Irish Countryman* (New York: Macmillan, 1937); William Foote Whyte, "A Slum Sex Code," *American Journal of Sociology,* 49:24-31 (1943); Terry M. Williams and William Kornblum, *Growing up Poor* (Lexington, MA: D. C. Heath, 1985); David A. Schulz, *Coming up Black: Patterns of Ghetto Socialization* (Englewood Cliffs, NJ: Prentice-Hall, 1969); Ruth Horowitz, *Honor and the American Dream* (New Brunswick, NJ: Rutgers University Press, 1983); Carol B. Stack, *All Our Kin* (New York: Harper & Row, 1974); Robert Staples, ed., *The Black Family* (Belmont, CA: Wadsworth, 1971); idem, *The Black Woman in America* (Chicago: Nelson Hall, 1973); Marian Wright Edelman, *Families in Peril: An Agenda for Social Change* (Cambridge, MA: Harvard University Press, 1987); Allen R. Walter, "The Search for Applicable Theories of Black Family Life," *Journal of Marriage and the Family,* 40:117-29 (1978); Joyce Ladner, *Tomorrow's Tomorrow* (New York: Doubleday, 1973).

have a dream, the boys a desire. The girls dream of being taken off by a Prince Charming who will love them, provide for them, and give them a family. The boys often desire sex without commitment or, if they do impregnate a girl, babies without responsibility for them. It becomes extremely difficult for the boys to see themselves enacting the roles and taking on the responsibilities of conventional fathers and husbands on the basis of the limited employment opportunities available to them. Yet the boy knows what the girl wants and plays the role in order to get her to give him sex. Receptive to his advances, she may think that she is maneuvering him toward a commitment or, even better, that getting pregnant is the nudge the boy needs to marry her and give her the life she wants. What she does not see is that the boy, despite his claims, is often incapable of giving her that life. For, in reality, he has little money, few prospects for gainful employment, and, furthermore, no wish to be tied to a woman who will have any say in what he does, for his loyalty is to his peer group and its norms. Consistent with this, when the girl becomes pregnant, the boy tends to retreat from her, although she, with the help of local social pressure from family and peers, may ultimately succeed in getting him to take some responsibility for the child.

SEX: THE GAME AND
THE DREAM

To an inner-city black male youth, the most important people in his life are members of his peer group. They set the standards for his conduct, and it is important for him to live up to those standards, to look good in their eyes. The peer group places a high value on sex, especially what many middle-class people call casual sex. Although the sex may be casual in terms of commitment to the partner, it is usually taken quite seriously as a measure of the boy's worth. Thus a primary goal of the young man is to find as many willing females as possible. The more "pussy" he gets, the more esteem accrues to him. But the young man must not only get "some"; he must also prove he is getting it. Consequently, he usually talks about girls and sex with every other young man who will listen. Because of the implications sex has for local social status and esteem for the young men, there are many of them willing and ready to be regaled by tales of one another's sexual exploits. The conversations include graphic descriptions of the sex act.

The lore of the streets says there is something of a contest going on between the boy and the girl even before they meet. To the young man, the woman becomes, in the most profound sense, a sexual object. Her body and mind become the object of a sexual game, to be won over for the personal aggrandizement of the young man. Status goes to the winner, and sex becomes prized not so much as a testament of love but as testimony of control of another human being. Sex is the prize and sexual conquests are a game, the object of which is to make a fool of the other person, particularly the young woman.

The young men variously describe their successful campaigns as "getting over [the young woman's sexual defenses]." In order to get over, the young man must devise and develop a "game," whose success is gauged by its acceptance by his peers and especially by women. Relying heavily on gaining the confidence of the girl, the game consists of the boy's full presentation of self, including his dress, grooming, looks, dancing ability, and conversation, or "rap."

The rap is the verbal element of the game, whose object is to inspire sexual

interest in the boy. It embodies the whole person and is thus extremely important to the success of the game. Among peer-group members, raps are assessed, evaluated, and divided into weak and strong. The assessment of the young man's rap is, in effect, the evaluation of his whole game. Convincing proof of the effectiveness of one's game is in the "booty": the amount of pussy the young man appears to be getting. Young men who are known to fail with women often face ridicule at the hands of the group, thus having their raps labeled "tissue paper," their games seen as inferior, and their identities discredited.

After developing a game over time, through trial and error, a young man is ever on the lookout for players, young women with whom to try it out and perhaps to perfect it. To find willing players is to gain a certain affirmation of self, though the boy's status in the peer group may go up if he is able to seduce a girl considered to be "choice," "down," or streetwise. When encountering a girl, the boy usually sees a challenge: he attempts to "run his game." Here the girl usually is fully aware that a game is being attempted; however, if the young man's game is sophisticated, or "smooth," or if the girl is very young and inexperienced, she may be easily duped.

In many instances, the game plays on the dream that many inner-city girls evolve from early teenage years. The popular love songs they have listened to, usually from the age of seven or eight, are filled with a wistful air, promising love and ecstasy to someone "just like you." This dream involves having a boyfriend, a fiancé, a husband, and the fairy-tale prospect of living happily ever after in a nice house in a neighborhood with one's children—essentially the dream of the middle-class American life-style, complete with the nuclear family. It is nurtured by a daily involvement with afternoon television soap operas, or "stories," as the women call them. The heroes or heroines of these stories may be white and upper middle class, but for many, these characteristics only make them more attractive as role models. Many girls dream of the role of the comfortable middle-class housewife portrayed on television, even though they see that their peers can only approximate that role.

When approached by a boy, the girl's faith in the dream helps to cloud or obscure her view of the situation. A romantically successful boy has the knack for knowing just what is on a girl's mind, what she wants from life, and how she wants to go about obtaining it. In this regard, he is inclined and may be able to play the character the script calls for. Through his actions, he is able to shape the interaction, calling up those resources needed to play the game successfully. He fits himself to be the man she wants him to be, but this identity may be exaggerated and only temporary, until he gets what he wants. He shows her the side of himself that he knows she wants to see, that represents what she wants in a man. For instance, the young man will sometimes "walk through the woods" with the girl: he might visit at her home and go to church with her family, showing that he is an "upstanding young man." But all of this may only be part of his game, and after he gets what he wants, he may cast down this part of his presentation and reveal something of his true self, as he reverts to those actions and behavior more characteristic of his everyday life, those centered around his peer group.

In these circumstances, the girl may see but refuse to accept evidence of the boy's duplicity. She may find herself at times defending the young man to her

friends and family who question her choice of a boyfriend. In those cases in which the male is successful, the young woman may know she is being played, but, given the effectiveness of his game, his rap, his presentation of self, his looks, his wit, his dancing ability, and his general popularity in the peer group, infatuation often rules. Many a girl fervently hopes that her boy is the one that is different, while some boys are very good actors and can be extremely persuasive.

In addition, the girl's peer group supports her pursuit of the dream, implicitly upholding her belief in the young man's good faith. But it is clear that the goals and interests of the girl and the boy often diverge. While many girls want to pursue the dream, the boy, for the immediate future, is generally not interested in "playing house," as his peer-group members derisively refer to domestic life.

While pursuing his game, the boy often feigns love and caring, pretending to be a dream man and acting toward the girl as though he has the best intentions. Ironically, in many cases, the young man does indeed have the best intentions. He may experience profound ambivalence on this score, mainly because of the way such intentions appear to relate to or conflict with the values of the peer group. At times, these values are placed in sharp focus by his own deviance from them, as he incurs sanctions for allowing a girl to "rule" him or gains positive reinforcement for keeping her in line. The peer group sanctions its members with demeaning labels such as "pussy," "pussy-whipped," or "househusband," causing them to posture in manners that clearly distance themselves from such characterizations.

At times, however, some boys earnestly attempt to enact the role of the "dream man," one with honorable intentions of "doing right" by the young woman, of

marrying her and living happily ever after, according to their versions of middle-class norms of propriety. But the reality of the poor employment situation for young black males of the inner city makes it extremely difficult for many to follow through on such intentions.[2]

Unable to realize himself as the young woman's provider in the American middle-class tradition, which the peer group often labels "square," the young man may become ever more committed to his game. With ambivalence, many young men will go so far as to "make plans" with the women, including house shopping and window shopping for items for the prospective household. A 23-year-old female informant who at 17 became a single parent of a baby girl said the following:

Yeah, they'll [boys will] take you out. Walk you down to Center City, movies, window shop (laughs). They point in the window, "Yeah, I'm gonna get this. Wouldn't you like this? Look at that nice livin' room set." Then they want to take you to his house, go to his room: "Let's go over to my house, watch some TV." Next thing you know your clothes is off and you in bed havin' sex, you know.

Such shopping trips carry with them important psychological implications for the relationship, at times serving as a kind of salve that heals wounds and erases doubt about the young man's intentions. The young woman may report to her

2. See Elijah Anderson, *A Place on the Corner* (Chicago: University of Chicago Press, 1978); William Julius Wilson, *The Declining Significance of Race* (Chicago: University of Chicago Press, 1978); Bernard E. Anderson and Isabel V. Sawhill, eds., *Youth Employment and Public Policy* (Englewood Cliffs, NJ: Prentice-Hall, 1980); Elijah Anderson, "Some Observations of Black Youth Employment," in ibid.; William Julius Wilson, *The Truly Disadvantaged: The Inner City, the Underclass, and Public Policy* (Chicago: University of Chicago Press, 1987).

parents or to her friends on her latest date or shopping trip, indicating the type of furniture looked at and priced and the supposed terms of payment. She continues to have hope, which he supports by "going" with her, letting her and others know that she is his "steady," though in order for him to maintain a certain status within his peer group, she should not be his only known girl.

Such actions indicate a certain level of involvement on the part of the couple, particularly the young man. For him, the making of plans and the successive shopping trips may simply be elements of his game and often nothing more than a stalling device he uses to keep the girl hanging on so that he may continue to have the benefit of her sexual favors.

In many cases, the more he seems to exploit the young woman, the higher his status within the peer group. But to consolidate this status, he feels moved at times to show others that he is in control. There may be a contest of wills between the two, with arguments and fights developing in public places over what may appear to be the most trivial of issues. In order to prove his dominance in the relationship unequivocally, he may "break her down" in front of her friends and his, "showing the world who is boss." If the young woman wants him badly enough, she will meekly go along with the performance for the implicit promise of his continued attentions, if not love. Again, a more permanent relationship approximating the woman's dream of matrimony and domestic tranquility is often what is at stake in her mind.

As the contest continues, and the girl hangs on, she may be believed to have been taken in by the boy's game but particularly by his convincing rap, his claims of commitment to her and her well-being. In this contest, anything is

fair. The girl may become manipulative and aggressive, or the boy may lie, cheat, or otherwise misrepresent himself to obtain or retain the sexual favors of the girl. In many of the sexual encounters related by informants, one person is seen as a winner, the other as a loser. As one informant said:

They trickin' them good. Either the woman is trickin' the man, or the man is trickin' the woman. Good! They got a trick. She's thinkin' it's [the relationship is] one thing, he playing another game, you know. He thinkin' she alright, and she doing something else.

In the social atmosphere of the peer group, the quality of the boy's game tends to emerge as a central issue. In addition, whatever lingering ambivalence he has about his commitment to the role of husband and provider may be resolved in favor of peer-group status, which becomes more clearly at stake in his mind.

In pursuing his game, the young man often uses a supporting cast of other women, at times playing one off against the other. For example, he may orchestrate a situation in which he is seen with another woman. Alternatively, secure in the knowledge that he has other women to fall back on, he might start a fight with his steady in order to upset her sense of complacency, thus creating a certain amount of dynamic tension within the relationship, which he tries to use for his own advantage. The result is that the young woman can begin to doubt her hold on the man, which can in turn bring about a precipitous drop in her self-esteem.

In these circumstances, the boy may take pride in the fool he thinks he is making of the girl, and, when he is confident of his dominance, he may work to "play" the young woman, "running his game," making her "love" him. Some young men, in such instances, will brag

that they are "playing her like a fiddle," meaning that they are in full control of the situation. The object here, for the young man, is to prove he "has the girl's nose open," that she is sick with love for him. His goal is to maneuver her into a state of blissful emotionality with regard to himself, showing that she, and not he, is clearly the "weak" member in the relationship.

Strikingly, it is in these circumstances that the young girl may well become careless about birth control, which is seen by the community, especially the males, as being her responsibility. Depending upon the effectiveness of the boy's game, she may believe his rap, becoming convinced that he means what he has said about taking care of her, that her welfare is his primary concern. Moreover, she wants desperately to believe that if she becomes pregnant, he will marry her or at least be obligated to her in a way he is not to others he has been "messing with." Perhaps all he needs is a little nudge.

In these circumstances, however, the girl thinks little of the job market and job prospects for the boy. She underestimates peer-group influences and the effect of other "ladies" she knows or at least strongly suspects are in his life. She is in love, and she is sure that a child and the profound obligation a child implies will make such a strong bond that all the other issues will go away. Her thinking is clouded by the prospect of winning at the game of love. Becoming pregnant can be a way to fulfill an old but persistent dream of happiness and bliss. Moreover, for numerous women, when the man is determined to be unobtainable, just having his baby is enough. Often a popular and "fine," or physically attractive, young man is sought out by a woman in hopes that his physical attractiveness will grace her child, resulting in a "prize," or a beautiful baby. Moreover, for the young woman, becoming pregnant can become an important part of the competition for the attentions or even delayed affection of a young man, a profound if socially shortsighted way of making claim on him.

THE ISSUE OF PREGNANCY

Up to the point of pregnancy, given the norms of his peer group with regard to male and female relations, the young man could be characterized as simply messing around. The fact of pregnancy brings a sudden sense of realism to the relationship between the young man and the young woman. Life-altering events have occurred. The situation is usually perceived as utterly serious. She is pregnant, and he could be held legally responsible for the long-term financial support of the child. In addition, if the young couple were unclear about their intentions before, things now may crystallize. She may now consider him seriously as a mate. Priorities may now begin to emerge in the boy's mind. He has to make a decision whether to claim the child as his or to shun the woman who for so long has been the object of his affections, often for reasons of peer-group concerns.

To own up to such a pregnancy is to go against the peer-group ethic of "hit and run." Other values at risk of being flouted by such an action include the subordination of women and freedom from formal conjugal ties, and in this environment, where hard economic times are a fact of daily life for many, some young men are not interested in "taking care of somebody else," when to do so means having less. In this social context of persistent poverty, young men have come to devalue the conventional marital relationship, easily viewing women as a burden and children

as even more so. Moreover, with regard to such relationships, a young man wants "to come as I want and go as I please," thus meeting important peer-group values of freedom and independence. Accordingly, from the perspective of the peer group, any such male-female relationship should be on the man's terms. Thus in coming to an understanding of the boy's relationship with the girl, his attitudes toward his limited financial ability and his need for personal independence and freedom should not be underestimated.

Another important attitude of the male peer group is that most girls are whores: "If she was fucking you, then she was fucking everybody else." Whether there is truth to this with respect to a particular case, a common working conception says it is true about young women in general. It is a view with which so many young men approach females, relegating them to a situation of social and moral deficit. The proverbial double standard is at work, and for any amount of sexual activity, the women are more easily discredited than the men.

To be sure, among the young men and women there is a fair amount of sexual activity. In this social atmosphere, ambiguity of paternity complicates many pregnancies. Moreover, in self-defense, the young man often chooses to deny fatherhood; few are willing to "own up" to a pregnancy they can reasonably question. Among their peers, the young men gain ready support. Peer-group norms say that a man who is "tagged" with fatherhood has been caught up in the "trick bag." The boy's first desire, though he may know better, is often to attribute the pregnancy to someone else.

In these general circumstances, the boy may be genuinely confused and uncertain about his role in the pregnancy, feeling a great deal of ambivalence and

apprehension over his impending fatherhood. If he admits paternity and "does right" by the girl, his peer group likely will negatively label him a chump, a square, or a fool. If he does not, however, there are few social sanctions applied, and he may even be given points for his stand, with his peers viewing him as fooling the mother and "getting over," or avoiding the trick bag. But here there may also be some ambivalence, for there is a certain regard to be obtained by those of the group who father children out of wedlock, as long as they are not "caught" and made financially responsible to support a family on something other than their own terms. Hence, the boy, in these circumstances, may give, and benefit socially from, mixed messages: one to the girl and perhaps the authorities, and another to his peer group. Generally, to resolve his ambivalence and apprehension, the boy might at this point attempt to discontinue his relationship with the expectant mother, particularly as she begins to show clear physical signs of pregnancy.

Upon giving birth, the young woman wants badly to identify the father of her child, if primarily at the insistence of her family and for her own peace of mind. When the baby is born, she may, out of desperation, arbitrarily designate a likely young man as the father. As mentioned, there may be genuine ambiguity surrounding the identity of the father. In this atmosphere, there are often charges and countercharges, with the appointed young man usually easing himself from the picture over time. There is at times an incentive for the young woman not to identify the father even though she and the local community know whose baby it is. Given that job prospects for young black men are so limited as to be effectively nil, the woman may be better off denying that she knows the father, for a check

from the welfare office is much more dependable than the irregular support payments of a sporadically employed youth.

To be sure, there are many young men who are determined to do right by the young woman, to try out the role of husband and father, often acceding to the woman's view of the matter and working to establish a family. Such young men tend to be those who are only marginally related to their peer groups. They tend to emerge from nurturing families, and religious observance plays an important role in their lives. Strikingly, these men are usually gainfully employed and tend to enjoy a deep and abiding relationship with the young woman that is able to withstand the trauma of youthful pregnancy.

Barring such a resolution, a young man may rationalize his marital situation as something of a "trap" into which the woman tricked him. This viewpoint may be seen as his attempt to make simultaneous claims on values of the peer group as well as those of the more conventional society. As another young man said in an interview:

My wife done that to me. Before we got married, when we had our first baby, she thought, well, hey, if she had the baby, then she got me, you know. And that's the way she done me. [She] thought that's gon' trap me. That I'm all hers after she done have this baby. So, a lot of women, they think like that. Now, I was the type of guy, if I know it was my baby, I'm taking care of my baby. My o'lady [wife], she knowed that. She knowed that anything that was mine, I'm taking care of mine. This is why she probably wouldn't mess around or nothing, 'cause she wanted to lock me up.

In general, however, persuading the youth to become "an honest man" is not at all simple. It is often a very complicated social affair involving cajoling, social pressure, and, at times, physical threats.

An important factor in determining whether the boy does right by the girl is the presence of the girl's father in the home.[3] When a couple first begins to date, some fathers will "sit the boy down" and have a ritual talk; some single mothers will play this role as well, at times more aggressively than fathers. Certain males with domineering dispositions will, "as a man," make unmistakable territorial claims on the dwelling, informing or reminding the boy that "this is my house, I pay the bills here," and that all activities occurring under its roof are his singular business. In such a household, the home has a certain defense. At issue here essentially are male turf rights, a principle intuitively understood by the young suitor and the father of the girl. The boy may feel a certain frustration due to a felt need to balance his desire to run his game against his fear of the girl's father. Yet, the boy is often able to identify respectfully with the father, thinking of how he himself might behave if the shoe were on the other foot.

Upon encountering each other, both "know something," that is, they know that each has a position to defend. The young boy knows in advance of a pregnancy that he will have to answer to the girl's father and the family unit more generally. If the girl becomes pregnant, the boy will be less likely to treat the situation summarily and leave her. Further, if the girl has brothers at home who are her approximate age or older, they, too, may serve to influence the behavior of the boy effectively. Such men, as well as uncles and male cousins, possess not only a certain degree of moral authority in these circumstances but often the believable threat of violence and mayhem in

3. See Williams and Kornblum, *Growing up Poor*.

many cases. As one boy said in an interview:

The boys kinda watch theyself more [when a father is present]. Yeah, there's a lot of that going on. The daddy, they'll clown [act out violence] about them young girls. They'll hurt somebody about they daughters. Other relatives, too. They'll all get into it. The boy know they don't want him messing over they sister. That guy will probably take care of that girl better than the average one out there in the street.

In such circumstances, not only does the boy think twice about running his game, but the girl often thinks twice about allowing him to do so.

A related important defense against youthful pregnancy is the conventional inner-city family unit. Two parents, together with the extended network of cousins, aunts, uncles, grandparents, nieces, and nephews, can form a durable team, a viable supportive unit engaged to fight in a most committed manner the various problems confronting so many inner-city teenagers, including drugs, crime, pregnancy, and social mobility.[4] This unit, when it does survive, tends to be equipped with a survivor's mentality. It has weathered a good many storms, which have given it wisdom and a certain strength. The parents are known in the community as "strict" with their children; they impose curfews and tight supervision, demanding to know their children's whereabouts at all times. Determined that their children not become casualties of the inner-city environment, these par-

ents scrutinize their children's friends and associates carefully, rejecting those who seem to be "no good" and encouraging others who seem to be on their way to "amount to something."

In contrast, in those domestic situations in which there is but one adult—say, a woman with two or three teenage daughters and with no male presence— the dwelling may be viewed by young boys, superficially at least, as essentially an unprotected nest. The local boys will sometimes become attracted to the home as a challenge, just to test it out, to see if they can "get over," or be successful in charming or seducing the women who reside there. In such settings, a man, the figure the boys are prepared to respect, is not there to keep them in line. The girls residing in these unprotected situations may become pregnant more quickly than those living in situations more closely resembling nuclear families. A young male informant had the following comment:

I done seen where four girls grow up under their mama. The mama turn around and she got a job between 3 p.m. and 11 p.m. These little kids, now they grow up like this. Mama working 3 to 11 o'clock at night. They kinda raise theyself. What they know? By the time they get 13 or 14, they trying everything under the sun. And they ain't got nobody to stop 'em. Mama gone. Can't nobody else tell 'em what to do. Hey, all of 'em pregnant by age 16. And they do it 'cause they wanta get out on they own. They then can get their own baby, they get their own [welfare] check, they get their own apartment. They want to get away from mama. They really want to be grown.

As indicated in the foregoing statement, a woman may have an overwhelming desire to grow up, a passage best expressed by her ability to "get out on her own." In terms of traditional inner-city poverty experience, this means setting up

4. See Schulz, *Coming up Black;* Charles V. Willie and Janet Weinandy, "The Structure and Composition of 'Problem' and 'Stable' Families in a Low-Income Population," in *The Family Life of Black People,* ed. Charles V. Willie (Columbus, OH: Charles E. Merrill, 1970); Eugene Perkins, *Home Is a Pretty Dirty Street* (Chicago: Third World Press, 1975).

one's own household, preferably with a "good man" through marriage and family. As indicated previously, some single young women may attempt to accomplish this by purposely becoming pregnant, perhaps hoping the baby's father will marry her and help to realize her dream of domestic respectability. At the same time, there are an undetermined number of young women, unimpressed with the lot of young single men, who wish to establish their households on their own, without the help or the burden of a man.[5] It has become increasingly socially acceptable for a young woman to have children out of wedlock—significantly, with the help of a regular welfare check.

Because the woman emerges from such poor financial circumstances, the prospect of a regular welfare check can seem like an improvement. In this way, the social situation of persistent poverty affects norms of the ghetto culture such as the high value placed on children, thus having a significant impact on decisions to bear children.[6] Hence, among many young poor ghetto women, babies have become a sought-after symbol of status, of passage to adulthood, of being a "grown" woman. In such circumstances, babies can become valued emblems of womanhood. Moreover, it is not always a question of whether the young girl is going to have children, but when. Thus, given the young woman's limited social and financial outlook, she may see herself as having little to lose by becoming pregnant and, coinciding with the culturally reinforced perception, as having something to gain.

5. See the discussion of the male marriageable pool in Wilson, *Truly Disadvantaged.*

6. See Diane K. Lewis, "The Black Family: Socialization and Sex Roles," *Phylon,* 36:221-37 (1975); Warren Tenhouten, "The Black Family: Myth and Reality," *Psychiatry,* 2:145-73 (1970).

The reality of pregnancy, however, is often a bitter pill. As previously indicated, as the girl begins to show signs of pregnancy, becoming physically bigger, she often loses the connection with her mate, although she may gain the affirmation and support of other women who have followed the same path as she.

In their small, intimate social groups, women discuss their afternoon stories, or soap operas, men, children, and social life, and they welcome prospective members to their generally supportive gatherings. Interestingly, although the women tend to deride the men for their behavior, especially their lack of commitment to their girlfriends, at the same time they may accommodate such behavior, viewing it as characteristic of men in their environment. Yet, in their conversations, the women may draw distinctions between "the nothin'" and the "good man." The nothin' is "a man who is out to use every woman he can for himself. He's somethin' like a pimp. Don't care 'bout nobody but himself." As one older single mother, who now considers herself wiser, said in an interview:

I know the difference now between a nothin' and a good man. I can see. I can smell him. I can tell nothings from the real thing. I can just look at a guy sometimes, you know, the way he dresses, you know. The way he carries himself. The way he acts, the way he talks. I can tell the bullshitter. Like, you know, "What's up, baby?" You know. "What's you want to do?" A nice guy wouldn't say, "What's up, baby? What's goin' on?" Actin' all familiar, tryin' to give me that line. Saying, "You wanna joint? You wan' some blow? You wan' some 'caine?" Hollerin' in the street, you know. I can tell 'em. I can just smell 'em.

The good man is one who is considerate of his mate and provides for her and her children, but at the same time he may run the risk of being seen as a pussy in the eyes

of the women as well as his peer group. This inversion in the idea of the good man underscores the ambivalent position of the girls squeezed between their middle-class dreams and the ghetto reality. As one woman said with a laugh, "There are so many sides to the bad man. We see that, especially in this community. We see more bad men than we do good. I see them [inner-city black girls] running over that man if he's a wimp, ha-ha."

Family support is often available for the young pregnant woman, though members of her family are likely to remind her from time to time that she is "messed up." She looks forward to the day when she is "straight" again, meaning the time when she has given birth to the baby and has regained her figure. Her comments to others who are not pregnant tend to center wistfully on better days when she was not messed up. As her boyfriend stops seeing her so regularly, she may readily attribute this to the family's negative comments about the boy, but also to her pregnant state, saying time and again that when "I get straight, he'll be sorry; he'll be jealous then." She knows in a sense that her pregnant status is devalued by her family as well as her single peers, who have the freedom to date and otherwise consort with men. She may long for the day when she will be able to do that again.

When the baby arrives, however, the girl finds that her social activities continue to be significantly curtailed. She is often surprised by how much time being a mother actually takes. In realizing her new identity, she may very consciously assume the demeanor and manner of a grown woman, emphasizing her freedom in social relations, her independence. At times, during what is really a period of adjustment to a new status, she has to set her mother straight about "telling me

what to do." This is usually a time when other family members go through a learning process as they become used to the young woman's new status, which she tries on with a variety of stops and starts. In fact, she really is involved in the process of growing up.

Frustrated by the continued curtailment of her social activities, especially as she becomes physically straight again, the girl may develop an intense desire to get back into the dating game. Accordingly, she may foist her child-care responsibilities onto her mother and female siblings, people who initially are eager to take on such roles. In time, however, they tire, and otherwise extremely supportive relations can become strained. In an effort to see her daughter get straight again, the young woman's mother, often in her mid-thirties or early forties, may simply informally adopt the baby as another one of her own, in some cases completely usurping the role of mother from her daughter. In this way, the young parent's mother may attempt to minimize the deviance the girl displayed by getting pregnant while simultaneously taking genuine pride in her new grandchild.

OF MEN AND WOMEN, MOTHERS AND SONS

The relationship between the young man and woman undergoes a basic change during pregnancy; once the baby is born, he or she draws in other social forces, most notably the families of the couple. The role of the girl's family has been discussed. The role of the boy's family is also important, but in a different way. There is often a special bond between a mother and her grown son in the community that effectively competes with the claims of his girlfriend. The way in which this situation is resolved has important

consequences for the family and its relationship to the social structure of the community.

In numerous cases of teenage pregnancy among the poor, the mother of the boy plays a significant role, while the role of the father, if he is present at all, is often understated. Depending on the personality of the woman, her practical experience in such matters, and the girl's family situation, the mother's role may be understated or explicit. At times she becomes quite involved with the young woman, forming a female bond that becomes truly motherly, involving guidance, protection, and control of the young woman.

From the moment the mother finds out that the young woman is pregnant, an important issue is whether she knows the girl or not. If the young woman "means something" to her son, she is likely to know her or at least know about her; her son has spoken of the girl. On hearing the news of the pregnancy, the mother's reaction might be anything from disbelief that her son could be responsible to certainty, even before seeing the child, that her son is the father. If she knows something about the girl's character, she is in a position to make a judgment for herself. Here her relationship with the girl before "all this" happened comes into play, for if she liked her, there is a great chance the boy's mother will side with her. The mother may even go so far as to engage in playful collusion against her son, a man, to get him to do right by the girl. Here, it must be remembered that in this economically circumscribed social context, particularly from a woman's point of view, many men are known not to do right by their women and children. To visit such inner-city settings is to observe what appears to be a proliferation of small children and women, with fathers and husbands largely absent or playing their roles part-time. These considerations help to place in some context the significance of the mother's role in determining how successful the girl will be in having the boy claim and take some responsibility for her child.

For in this role, the mother is usually constrained, at least initially, because she is often unsure whether her son has actually fathered the child. She may, however, be careful about showing her doubt, thinking that when the baby arrives, she will be able to tell "in a minute" whether her son is the father. Thus during the pregnancy, the mother of the young man nervously waits, wondering whether her son will be blamed for a pregnancy not of his doing or whether she will really be a grandmother. In fact, the whole family, both the boy's and the girl's, is often an extended family-in-waiting, socially organized around the idea that the "truth" will be told when the baby arrives. Unless the parties are very sure, marriage, if agreed to at all, may be held off until after the birth of the baby.

When the baby arrives, real plans may be carried out, but often on the condition that the child passes familial inspection. The young man himself, the presumed father, generally lays low in the weeks after the baby's birth. He usually does not visit the baby's mother in the hospital on a regular basis; he may come only once, if at all. In an effort to make a paternal connection between the child and father, some mothers name the baby after the father, but, by itself, this strategy is seldom effective.

In a number of cases of doubtful paternity, the boy's mother, sister, aunt, or other female relatives or close family friends may form informal visiting committees, charged with going to see the baby, although sometimes the baby is brought to them. This kind of familial

inspection is often surreptitious and usually takes place without the acknowledgment of the girl or her own family. The visiting committee may even go by the girl's house in shifts, with a sister going now, the mother another time, and a friend still another. Social pleasantries notwithstanding, the object is always the same: to see if the baby "belongs" to the boy it is said to. Typically, after such visits, these women will compare notes, commenting on the baby's features, saying whom the baby favors. Some will blurt right out, "Ain't no way that's John's baby." People may disagree, and a dispute may ensue. In the community, the identity of the baby's father becomes a hot topic of conversation. The viewpoints have much to do with who the girl is, whether she is a "good girl" or "bad girl" or whether she has been accepted and taken in by the boy's family. If the girl is well integrated into the family, doubts about paternity may even be slowly put to rest with nothing more being said about it.

As previously indicated, the word carrying the most weight in this situation, however, is often that of the boy's mother. The following account of a young man is relevant:

I had a lady telling me that she had to check out a baby that was supposed to be her grandbaby. She said she had a young girl that was trying to put a baby on her son, so she said she fixing to take the baby and see what blood type the baby is to match it with her son to see if he the daddy. 'Cause she said she *know* he wasn't the daddy. And she told the girl that, but the girl was steady trying to stick the baby on her son. She had checked out the baby's features and everything. She knowed that the blood type wasn't gon' match or nothing. So, the young girl just left 'em alone.

If the child very clearly physically favors the alleged father, there may be strong pressure for the boy to claim the child and approach the attendant responsibilities. This may take a year or more, as the resemblance may not be initially so apparent. But when others begin to make comments such as, "Lil' Tommy look like Maurice just spit him out [is his spitting image]," the boy's mother may informally adopt the child into her extended family and signal for all other family members to do the same. She may see the child on a regular basis and develop a special relationship with the child's mother. Because of the social acknowledgment by the boy's mother of her son's paternity, the boy himself is bound to accept the child as his own. Even if he does not claim the child legally, in the face of the evidence he will often claim the child in the sense of "having something to do with him." As one informant said:

If the baby look just like him, he should admit to hisself that that's his. Some guys have to wait 'til the baby grow up a little to see if the baby gon' look like him 'fore they finally realize that was his's. Because yours should look like you, you know, should have your features and image.

Here the young man informally acknowledging paternity may feel that pressure to "take care of his own."

But due to his limited employment and general lack of money, he "can only do what he can" for his child. In such circumstances, many young men will enact the role of the part-time father. In self-consciously attempting to fulfill this role, the young man may be spied on streets of the inner-city community with a box of "Pampers," the name used as a generic term to refer to all disposable diapers, or cans of Similac, liquid baby formula, in his arms, on his way to see his child and its mother. As the child ages, a bond may develop, as the young man

may take the child, if it is a boy, for a haircut or shopping for shoes or clothes. He may give the woman token amounts of money. Such support symbolizes a father providing for his child. In fact, however, the support often comes only sporadically and, importantly, in exchange for the woman's favors, be they social or sexual. The woman's support may thus depend upon the largess of the young man and may function as a means of her control.

When and if the woman "gets papers" on the man, or legalizes his relationship to the child, she may sue for regular support, what people of the community call "going downtown on him." If her case is successful, the young man's personal involvement in the making of support payments to the child may be eliminated: his child support payments may be simply deducted from his salary, if he has one. Sometimes the incentive for getting papers may emerge in the young woman's mind when and if the young man obtains a "good job," particularly one with a major institution that includes family benefits. While sporadically employed, the youth may have had no problem with papers, but when he obtains a good job, he may be served with a summons. In some cases, particularly if the young man has two or three children out of wedlock by two or three different women, young men lose the incentive to work at such good jobs when to do so only ensures that much of their pay will go to someone else. In the case of one of my informants, after the mothers of his four children got papers on him and he began to see less and less of his money, he quit his job and returned to the street corner.

There are conditions under which the male peer group will exert pressure on one of its members to admit paternity. Most important is that there be no ambiguity in the group members' own minds as to the baby's father. This is established on the basis of the baby's features. When it is clear that the baby resembles a peer-group member, the others may strongly urge him to claim it and go on to help the mother financially. If the young man fails to claim the baby, group members may do it themselves by publicly associating him with the child, at times teasing him about his connection with the mother and his failure "to take care of what is his." As one informant said:

My partner's [friend's] girlfriend came up pregnant. And she say it's his, but he not sure. He waitin' on the baby, waitin' to see if the baby look like him. I tell him, "Man, if that baby look just like you, then it was yours! Ha-ha." He just kinda like just waitin'. He ain't claimin' naw, saying the baby ain't his. I keep tellin' him, "If that baby come out looking just like you, then it gon be yours, partner." And there [on the corner] all of 'em will tell him, "Man, that's yo' baby." They'll tell him.

While the peer group may urge its members to take care of their babies, they stop short of urging them to marry the mothers. In general, young men are assumed not to care about raising a family or being a part of one. Some of this lack of support for marriage is due to the poor employment prospects, but it also may have to do with the general distrust they have of women. As my informant continued:

They don't even trust her that they were the only one she was dealing with. That's a lot of it. But the boys just be gettin' away from it [the value of a family] a whole lot. They don't want to get tied down by talkin' about playing house, ha-ha, what they call it nowadays, ha-ha. Yeah, ha-ha, they saying they ain't playing house.

In a great number of cases, peer group or no, the boy will send the girl on her way even if she is carrying a baby he knows is his own. The young man very often lacks a deep feeling for a female and children as a family unit. He often does not want to put up with married life, which he sees as life with a woman who will have something to say about how he spends his time. This emphasis on "freedom" is generated and supported in large part by the peer group itself. Even if a man agrees to marriage, it is usually considered to be only a trial. After a few months, many young husbands have had enough.

This desire for freedom, which the peer group so successfully nurtures, is deeply rooted in the boys. It is, in fact, often nothing less than the desire to perpetuate the situation they had in their mothers' homes. A son is generally well bonded to his mother, something the mother tends to encourage from birth. It may be that sons, particularly the eldest, are groomed in this way to function as surrogate husbands because of the commonly high rate of family dissolution among poor blacks.[7]

With respect to family life, so many young boys really want what they consider an optimal social situation. In the words of peer-group members, they want it all: they want a "main squeeze," or a steady and reliable female partner who mimics the role played by their mothers in their original families, a woman who will cook, clean, and generally serve them with few questions about the "ladies" they may be seeing and even less to say about their male friends. The young man has grown accustomed to the good home-cooked meals, the secure company of his family in which his father was largely absent and thus unable to tell him what to do. He was his own boss, essentially raising himself, with the help of his peer group and perhaps any adult who would listen but not interfere. Many of the young men have very fond memories of the situation in which they grew up. For an undetermined number, such a life is too much to give up in exchange for the "problems of being tied down to one lady, kids, bills, and all that." In this sense, the young man's home situation with his mother competes quite effectively with the household he envisions with a woman whom he does not fully trust and whom his peer group is fully prepared to discredit.

Now that he is grown, the young man wants what he had growing up plus a number of ladies on the side. At the same time, he wants his male friends, whom he is required to impress in ways that may be inconsistent with being a good family man. As the young men from the start have little faith in marriage, little things can inspire them to retreat to their mothers or other families they may have left behind. Some men spend their time going back and forth between two families; if their marriage seems not to be working, they may easily ditch it and their wife, although perhaps keeping up with the children. At all times, they must show others that they run the family, that they "wear the pants." This is the cause of many of the domestic fights in the ghetto. When there is a question of authority, the domestic situation may run into serious trouble, often resulting in the young man's abandoning the idea of marriage or of "dealing" with only one woman. To "hook up" with a woman, to marry her, is

7. See Schulz, *Coming up Black;* Jerold Heiss, *The Case of the Black Family* (New York: Columbia University Press, 1975); Perkins, *Home Is a Pretty Dirty Street;* Garth L. Mangum and Stephen F. Seninger, "Ghetto Life Styles and Youth Employment," in *Coming of Age in the Ghetto* (Baltimore, MD: Johns Hopkins University Press, 1978).

to give her license to have something to say about what "you're doing, or where you're going, or where you been." For many young men, such involvement on the woman's part is simply unacceptable.

In endeavoring to have it all, many men become, in effect, part-time fathers and part-time husbands, seeing women and children on their own terms, when they have the time, and making symbolic purchases for the children. In theory, the part-time father is able to retain his freedom while having limited commitment to the woman and the little ones "calling me daddy." In many instances, the man does not mind putting up with the children, given his generally limited role in child rearing, but he does mind putting up with the woman, who is seen as a significant threat to his freedom, as someone with a say in how he runs his life. As one informant commented about marriage:

Naw, they [young men] getting away from that. They ain't going in for that 'cause they want to be free. Now, see, I ended up getting married. I got a whole lot of boys ducking that. Unless this is managed, it ain't no good. My wife cleans, takes care o' the house. You got a lot of guys, they don't want to be cleanin' no house, and do the things you got to do in the house. You need a girl there to do it. If you get one, she'll slow you down. The guys don't want it.

Unless a man would be able to handle his wife so that she would put few constraints on him, he may reason that he had better stay away from marriage. But as indicated earlier, with a generalized sense of increasing independence from men, financial and other, there may be fewer women who allow themselves to be so handled.

As jobs become increasingly scarce for young black men, their roles as breadwinners and traditional husbands decline. The notion is that with money comes a

certain control and say in the domestic situation. Without money or jobs, many men are increasingly unable to "play house" to their own satisfaction. It is much easier and more fun, some say, to stay home and "take care of mama," when taking care consists of "giving her some change for room and board," eating good food when possible, and being able "to come as I want to and to go as I please." Given the present state of the economy and the way in which the economy affects the employment situation of young black men, such an assessment of their domestic outlook appears in many respects adaptive. The peer group, largely with poor employment prospects, has nurtured and supported the idea of freedom and independence from family life, in which one would have to face bills and a woman having a say in one's affairs. From an economic and social standpoint, it seems very attractive for the young man to stay home with mama, to maintain his freedom, and to have a string of ladies, some of whom contribute to his financial support.

CONCLUSION: SEX, POVERTY, AND FAMILY LIFE

In conclusion, the basic factors at work here are youth, ignorance, the receptivity of the culture to babies, and the young male's resort to proving his manhood through sexual conquests that often result in pregnancies. These factors are exacerbated by the impact of present economic conditions and persistent poverty on the inner-city community.

In the present hard economic times, a primary concern of many inner-city residents is to get along financially as best they can. In the poorest communities, the primary sources of money include low-paying jobs, crime, including drugs, and

public assistance. Some of the most desperate people devise a variety of confidence games, the object of which is to separate others from their money. A number of men, married and single, incorporate their sexual lives into their more generalized efforts at economic survival. Many will seek to "pull" a woman with children on welfare mainly because she usually has a special need for male company, time on her hands, and a steady income. As they work to establish their relationships, they play roles not unlike the roles played in the young male's game to get over sexually with a female. There is simply a more clear economic nexus in many of these cases, for when the woman receives her check from the welfare department or money from other sources, she may find herself giving up a part of it just to obtain or retain male company and interest.

The economic noose constricting so much of ghetto life encourages both men and women to attempt to extract maximum personal benefit from sexual relationships. The dreams of the middle-class lifestyle nurtured by young inner-city women become thwarted in the face of the harsh socioeconomic realities of the ghetto. Young men without job prospects cling to the support offered by their peer groups and their mothers and shy from lasting relationships with girlfriends. In this situation, girls and boys alike scramble to take what they can from each other, trusting not in each other but often in their own ability to trick the other into giving them something that will establish or perpetuate their version of the good life, the best life they feel they can put together for themselves in the inner-city social environment.

It is important to remember the age of the people we are talking about; these are kids—mainly 15, 16, and 17 years old.

Their bodies are mature, but they are emotionally immature. These girls and boys often do not have a very clear notion of the long-term consequences of their behavior, and they have few trustworthy role models who might instruct them.

The basic sexual codes of inner-city youths may not differ fundamentally from those expressed by young people of other social settings. But the social, economic, and personal consequences of adolescent sexual conduct vary profoundly for different social classes. Like adolescents of all classes, inner-city youths are subject to intense, hard-to-control urges and impulsiveness. Sexual relations, exploitative and otherwise, are common among middle-class teenagers as well, but middle-class youths take a strong interest in their future and know what a pregnancy can do to derail that future. In contrast, the ghetto adolescent sees no future to derail, no hope for a tomorrow very different from today, hence, little to lose by having an out-of-wedlock child.

Another difference between middle-class and poor youths is their level of practical education. The ignorance of inner-city girls about their bodies is startling to the middle-class observer. Many have only an abstract notion of where babies come from and generally know nothing about birth control until after the birth of their first child, and sometimes not even then. Parents in this culture are extremely reticent about discussing sex and birth control with their children. Many mothers are ashamed to "talk about it" or feel they are in no position to do so, as they behaved like their daughters when they were young. Education thus becomes a community health problem, but most girls come in contact with community health services only when they become pregnant, sometimes many months into their pregnancies.

Many women in the underclass black culture emerge from a fundamentalist religious orientation and practice a pro-life philosophy. Abortion is therefore usually not an option.[8] New life is sometimes characterized as a "heavenly gift," an infant is very sacred to the young women, and the extended inner-city family appears always able to make do somehow with another baby. In the community, a birth is usually met with great praise, regardless of its circumstances, and the child is genuinely valued. Such ready social approval works against many efforts to avoid an out-of-wedlock birth.

In fact, in cold economic terms, a baby can be an asset. The severe economic situation in the inner city is without a doubt the single most important factor behind exploitative sex and out-of-wedlock babies. With the dearth of well-paying jobs, public assistance is one of the few reliable sources of money in the community, and, for many, drugs is another. The most desperate people thus feed on one another. In these circumstances, babies and sex are used by some for income; women receive money from welfare for having babies, and men sometimes act as prostitutes to pry the money from the women. The community seems to feed on itself.

The lack of gainful employment opportunities not only keeps the entire community in a pit of poverty, but it also deprives young men of the traditional American way of proving their manhood, namely, supporting a family. They must thus prove their manhood in other ways. Casual sex with as many women as possible, impregnating one or more, and getting them to "have your baby" brings a boy the ultimate in esteem from his peers and makes him a "man." Casual sex is therefore not so casual but is fraught with social significance for the boy who has little or no hope of achieving financial stability and so can have no sense of himself as caring for a family.

The meshing of these forces can be clearly seen. Adolescents, trapped in poverty, ignorant of the long-term consequences of their behavior but aware of the immediate benefits, engage in a mating game. The girl has her dream of a family and a home, of a good man who will provide for her and her future children. The boy, knowing he cannot be that family man because he has no job and no prospects yet needing to have sex with the girl in order to achieve manhood in the eyes of his peer group, pretends to be the good man and convinces her to give him sex and perhaps a baby. He may then abandon her, and she realizes that he was not the good man after all, but a nothing out to exploit her. The boy has received what he wanted, but the girl learns that she has received something, too. The baby may enable her to receive a certain amount of praise, a steady welfare check, and a measure of independence. Her family often helps out as best they can. As she becomes older and wiser, she can use her income to turn the tables, attracting the interest of her original man or other men.

In this inner-city culture, people generally get married for "love" and "to have something." This mind-set presupposes a job, the work ethic, and, perhaps most of all, a persistent sense of hope for, if not a modicum of belief in, an economic future. When these social factors are present, the

8. See William Gibson, "The Question of Legitimacy," in *Family Life and Morality* (Lanham, MD: University Press of America, 1980), pp. 41-54; idem, "The Alleged Weakness in the Black Family Structure," in ibid., pp. 55-73; Hallowell Pope, "Negro-White Differences in Decisions Regarding Illegitimate Children," *Journal of Marriage and the Family,* 31:756-64 (1969).

more wretched elements of the portrait presented here begin to lose their force, slowly becoming neutralized. But for so many of those who are caught up in the web of persistent urban poverty and become unwed mothers and fathers, there is little hope for a good job and even less for a future of conventional family life.

6

Employment and Marriage among Inner-City Fathers

By MARK TESTA, NAN MARIE ASTONE,
MARILYN KROGH, and KATHRYN M. NECKERMAN

ABSTRACT: This article uses data from the Urban Poverty and Family Structure Survey of inner-city residents in Chicago to examine the effect of employment on the likelihood that single fathers marry. Our results show that employed fathers are twice as likely as nonemployed fathers to marry the mother of their first child. These results run contrary to Charles Murray's argument that welfare discourages employed, low-income men from marrying. They are consistent with William Julius Wilson's hypothesis that the rise in male joblessness is linked to the rise in never-married parenthood in the inner city. Our analysis also shows that couples are more likely to marry when the woman is a high school graduate. In this population, the enhanced earnings potential of a woman increases, not decreases, the likelihood of marriage. This result is inconsistent with the hypothesis that the closer a woman's earnings potential is to a man's, the less likely the couple is to marry. Neither employment nor education fully accounts for the racial and ethnic differences we observe in the marriage rates of fathers in inner-city Chicago.

Mark Testa, Ph.D. in sociology, is an assistant professor in the School of Social Service Administration at the University of Chicago.

Nan Marie Astone, Ph.D. in sociology, is a postdoctoral fellow at the Institute on Aging and the Center for Demography and Ecology at the University of Wisconsin at Madison.

Marilyn Krogh is a Ph.D. student in the Sociology Department at the University of Chicago.

Kathryn M. Neckerman is a Ph.D. student in the Sociology Department at the University of Chicago.

NOTE: Financial support is gratefully acknowledged from the Ford Foundation, the Carnegie Corporation, the U.S. Department of Health and Human Services, the Institute for Research on Poverty, the Joyce Foundation, the Lloyd A. Fry Foundation, the Rockefeller Foundation, the Spencer Foundation, the William T. Grant Foundation, and the Woods Charitable Fund. Support was provided to Nan Astone by the National Institute for Aging under grant no. AG00129-02.

SINGLE-MOTHER families are among the most economically vulnerable groups in the United States. They are more likely than other families to be poor, to be dependent on welfare, and to live in inner-city neighborhoods. Their numbers have grown dramatically during the past two decades. Concern over the association between poverty and family structure has led policymakers and researchers to examine the economic and social changes related to the growth in the number of single-mother families.

Of course, for every child of a single mother there is also a father. Yet we know little about the factors leading to single fatherhood in the inner city. A lack of appropriate data has hampered our understanding in several ways. First, there is little detailed fertility and marital data about men. Consequently, fathers are often left out of analyses of one-parent families. Second, researchers often lack sufficient numbers of respondents for whom parenthood precedes marriage. This leads to their focusing on marital separation and divorce—the more typical middle-class experience—rather than on the decisions leading to an out-of-wedlock birth. Third, proportionately fewer whites than blacks have low incomes and live in poor neighborhoods. As a result, it is difficult to distinguish the effects of race from those of class or neighborhood. Fourth, although Hispanics are a significant and growing presence in the inner city, surveys rarely sample Hispanics by national origin. Mexicans, Puerto Ricans, and other Hispanic groups are lumped together even though their experiences and characteristics are distinctive.

Our purpose in this article is to redress these gaps in research on single fathers by examining the fertility and marital experiences of a sample of inner-city Chicago residents. We examine the influence of economic variables and race or ethnicity on whether men legitimate premaritally conceived births or marry the mother of their first child after the child's birth. Following a review of the literature, we describe our data, dependent variables, and sample-selection effects. Next, we describe the statistical models and methods used in our analysis, and then report the findings. Our discussion draws out the implications of these findings for several recent theories of poverty and family formation and suggests directions for future analyses.

LITERATURE REVIEW

Ethnic variation in levels of single parenthood has become a central issue in most discussions of the underclass. Even though the percentage of mother-only families has risen as sharply for whites as for blacks, there are significant racial differences both in the absolute levels and in the processes of becoming single parents. Most whites become single parents through marital breakup, while most blacks become single parents by having children before they marry.[1] In 1985, for example, 60 percent of black births were to unmarried mothers compared to 15 percent of white births.[2] Most of these out-of-wedlock births were to never-married mothers.

Blacks are more likely than whites to become never-married parents for several reasons. Among them are a younger age

1. Irwin Garfinkel and Sara S. McLanahan, *Single Mothers and Their Children: A New American Dilemma* (Washington, DC: Urban Institute Press, 1986).

2. U.S. Department of Commerce, Bureau of the Census, *Statistical Abstract of the United States: 1988* (Washington, DC: Government Printing Office, 1987).

at sexual initiation,[3] lower levels of contraceptive use,[4] and lower rates of legitimation.[5] Blacks are also less likely than whites to marry after the child's birth.[6]

Although some attention has been paid to cultural differences,[7] explanations for racial disparities in marriage tend to emphasize economic variables.[8] Researchers have focused on three key factors: welfare, the joblessness of males, and the economic independence of women.

Charles Murray's book, *Losing Ground,* contends that the proportion of out-of-wedlock births has risen because welfare rewards low-income parents for avoiding marriage.[9] Arguing within a "rational choice" framework, he asserts that low-income parents have abandoned the traditional norms of family formation in order to maximize their joint income under existing welfare eligibility rules. He argues

that since the mid-1960s, when the Great Society welfare policies were instituted, low-income parents have intentionally avoided marriage so that the mother could continue to collect Aid to Families with Dependent Children even if the father were employed. As long as the couple lives together without marriage, the wage earnings of the father are not included in the calculation of the family's eligibility for Aid to Families with Dependent Children. Thus in the absence of vigorous paternity determination and child support enforcement, the rational choice for a low-income couple is to live together unmarried.

In *The Truly Disadvantaged,* William Julius Wilson dismisses Murray's argument as inconsistent with welfare and illegitimacy trends after 1972.[10] Instead, he argues that recent trends and racial differences in levels of never-married parenthood reflect more traditional concerns over whether a potential husband can provide a steady income. If the father is stably employed, Wilson argues, then a couple with a child or expecting a child view marriage as financially viable; otherwise, they are likely to remain unmarried.

According to figures compiled by Wilson and Neckerman, black women face a shrinking pool of stably employed, or "marriageable," men.[11] Trends in joblessness, incarceration, and mortality show that the number of employed black men per 100 black women of the same age has decreased over the past twenty years. Trends in employment and family struc-

3. Sandra L. Hofferth, Joan R. Kahn, and Wendy Baldwin, "Premarital Sexual Activity among U.S. Teenage Women over the Past Three Decades," *Family Planning Perspectives,* 19(2):46-53 (1987).

4. Christine A. Bachrach, "Contraceptive Practice among American Women, 1973-1982," *Family Planning Perspectives,* 16(6):253-59 (1978).

5. Martin O'Connell and Maurice J. Moore, "The Legitimacy Status of First Births to U.S. Women Aged 15-24, 1939-1978," *Family Planning Perspectives,* 12(1):16-25 (1980).

6. Martin O'Connell and Carolyn C. Rogers, "Out-of-Wedlock Births, Premarital Pregnancies and Their Effect on Family Formation and Dissolution," *Family Planning Perspectives,* 16(4):157-62 (1984).

7. Nicholas Lemann, "The Origins of the Underclass," *Atlantic Monthly,* 257:31-61 (1986).

8. Charles Murray, *Losing Ground: American Social Policy, 1950-1980* (New York: Basic Books, 1984); William Julius Wilson, *The Truly Disadvantaged: The Inner City, the Underclass, and Public Policy* (Chicago: University of Chicago Press, 1987); Reynolds Farley, "After the Starting Line: Blacks and Women in an Uphill Race," *Demography,* 25(4): 477-495 (1988).

9. Murray, *Losing Ground.*

10. Wilson, *Truly Disadvantaged.*

11. William Julius Wilson and Kathryn M. Neckerman, "Poverty and Family Structure: The Widening Gap between Evidence and Public Policy Issues," in *Fighting Poverty: What Works and What Doesn't,* ed. Sheldon H. Danziger and Daniel H. Weinberg (Cambridge, MA: Harvard University Press, 1986).

ture, they argue, support the hypothesis that the rise of never-married parenthood among blacks is directly related to increasing black male joblessness. Further, indirect empirical support for an economic argument can be found in both historical and demographic research. Historically, out-of-wedlock births become more common during periods of economic dislocation.[12] Demographers also report that unfavorable economic conditions lead to marital delay[13] and that high unemployment and low wages are associated at the aggregate level with the incidence of single-parent families.[14]

In some respects, Wilson and Neckerman's male-marriageable-pool hypothesis resembles the demographic hypothesis of the marriage squeeze. This hypothesis links variation in women's marital behavior to sex-ratio imbalances caused by changes in birthrates. Because women tend to marry slightly older men, increases in the birthrate create larger cohorts of younger women who are attempting to find spouses among smaller cohorts of older men.[15] The marriage squeeze resulting from the post-World War II baby

boom, however, ended in the 1970s. Consequently, black women who have reached marriageable age in the 1980s have faced a larger pool of prospective husbands than did their predecessors of a decade ago.

Because this marriage squeeze ended in the 1970s, Reynolds Farley disputes that the rise in black single-mother families is linked to a shortage of black men for black women to marry.[16] He also cites the rising rates of never-married parenthood among more educated blacks to question the importance of male joblessness as the key determinant of family structure among blacks.

Instead, Farley suggests, the narrowing earnings differential between men and women opens up alternative family lifestyles to all women by lessening their dependence on marriage for economic support. Because black women are approaching economic parity with black men far more rapidly than white women are approaching parity with white men, Farley reasons that trends toward never-married parenthood should be more pronounced among blacks than whites. If white women continue to approach economic parity with white men, he suggests, the trends in family structure that we observe among blacks may be leading indicators of what may happen among whites in the near future.

Whether trends in never-married parenthood are being driven by greater economic parity between the genders, male joblessness, welfare incentives, or a mixture of economic and cultural factors has important implications for the development of policies to deal with the problems of persistent family poverty. Yet for the reasons mentioned earlier, very few studies have used individual-level data to examine the impact of economic status

12. Cissie Fairchilds, "Female Sexual Attitudes and the Rise of Illegitimacy," *Journal of Social History,* 8(4):627-67 (1978); Louise A. Tilly and Joan W. Scott, *Women, Work, and Family* (New York: Holt, Rinehart & Winston, 1978).

13. Richard Easterlin, *Births and Fortune* (New York: Basic Books, 1980).

14. See Sara McLanahan, Irwin Garfinkel, and Dorothy Watson, "Family Structure, Poverty, and the Underclass" (Paper prepared for the Committee on National Urban Policy of the National Research Council, Washington, DC, 1986), for an overview of these studies. Frank F. Furstenberg, Jr., *Unplanned Parenthood, the Social Consequences of Teenage Childbearing* (New York: Free Press, 1976), is one of the few individual-level studies of the effect of economic status on entry into marriage.

15. Noreen Goldman, Charles F. Westoff, and Charles Hammerslough, "Demography of the Marriage Market in the United States," *Population Index,* 50(1):5-25 (1984).

16. Farley, "After the Starting Line."

on whether a father marries the mother of his child.

DATA

Data for our analysis come from the Urban Poverty and Family Structure (UPFS) Survey of 2490 inner-city residents in Chicago. The UPFS Survey was developed under the direction of William Julius Wilson and fielded by NORC, a social science research center. It contains extensive retrospective data on fertility, marriage, and employment for parents 18 to 44 years old who lived in Chicago poverty tracts in 1986. A poverty tract is defined as a census tract in which 20 percent or more of the residents enumerated in the 1980 census had family incomes below the federal poverty line. At last census count, 1,283,000 persons, or 40 percent of the Chicago population, resided in poverty tracts.

The sample was stratified by parental status and race or ethnicity. There were 784 completed interviews with fathers, 1506 interviews with mothers, and 190 interviews with a subsample of blacks without children. The overall survey completion rate was 79 percent, which compares favorably to completion rates for other surveys of similar populations. The highest completion rate was for black parents, 83 percent; followed by black nonparents, 78 percent; Mexican parents, 78 percent; Puerto Rican parents, 75 percent; and non-Hispanic white parents, 74 percent.

Dependent variables: Legitimation and postpartum marriages

Table 1 shows the percentage of fathers in our sample whose first child was conceived after marriage, conceived before marriage and legitimated, or born out of wedlock. The time of conception

was dated as seven months before the birth of the child. The data show substantial racial or ethnic differences in the percentage of men who fathered their first child after marriage. While 22 percent of black fathers and 42 percent of Puerto Rican fathers conceived their first child after marriage, 64 percent of the Mexicans and 62 percent of the non-Hispanic whites did. There are also group differences in the legitimation of first births. Both Puerto Ricans and blacks were less likely than Mexicans to marry the mother of their first child between the time of conception and the child's birth. The figures in the second to last column of Table 1 show that about 8 percent of black and Puerto Rican premaritally conceived births were legitimated, compared to about a third of Mexican and non-Hispanic white premaritally conceived births.

Most studies of never-married parenthood end at this point—an out-of-wedlock birth. With our data, however, we can consider whether unwed parents eventually marry each other after the child's birth. The estimates in Table 2 show the cumulative proportion of fathers who married the mother of their first child by that child's first, second, and third birthday. The percentage "censored" refers to the proportion of fathers who were still single at the date of the survey or had married other women.

The group differences in postpartum marriage parallel those observed for legitimation. Both Puerto Rican and black single fathers were much less likely than Mexican and non-Hispanic white single fathers to marry the mother of their first child. By the child's third birthday, about 20 percent of the Puerto Ricans and blacks had married the mother, compared to 43 percent of Mexicans and 60 percent of non-Hispanic whites. The cumulative effect of ethnic differences in the probabilities of marriage before parenthood,

TABLE 1

FIRST BIRTHS BY ETHNICITY AND MARITAL STATUS
OF FATHER AT CONCEPTION AND BIRTH

| | | | | Conceived before Marriage | | | |
| | Total Births | | Conceived after Marriage (percentage) | Married at birth (percentage) | Single at birth (percentage) | Legitimation | |
Ethnicity	Number	Percentage				Percentage	Odds*
Black	290	100.0	21.5	6.6	71.9	8.4	0.092
Mexican	216	100.0	64.0	12.1	23.9	33.6	0.506
Puerto Rican	137	100.0	42.1	4.4	53.5	7.6	0.082
Non-Hispanic white	123	100.0	61.6	14.5	23.9	37.8	0.607

SOURCE: Urban Poverty and Family Structure Survey, 1986.
NOTE: Fathers were aged 18-44 and lived in Chicago poverty tracts, 1986. Percentages calculated from weighted sample.
*Legitimation odds = married at birth ÷ single at birth.

TABLE 2

CUMULATIVE PERCENTAGE OF FATHERS MARRYING MOTHER
OF FIRST CHILD AT SELECTED AGES OF THE CHILD

| | Premarital Births (number) | Cumulative Percentage of Fathers Marrying Mothers When Child Is Aged: | | | | Censored* (percentage) |
Ethnicity		6 months	12 months	24 months	36 months	
Black	206	5.8	8.8	17.8	23.1	68.0
Mexican	51	9.8	17.7	26.9	43.4	43.1
Puerto Rican	66	5.3	8.4	14.9	20.4	68.2
Non-Hispanic white	29	21.3	41.9	54.2	60.2	34.5

SOURCE: Urban Poverty and Family Structure Survey, 1986.
NOTE: Fathers were aged 18-44 and lived in Chicago poverty tracts, 1986.
*Fathers still not married at date of survey and fathers who married other than the mother of the first child.

during pregnancy, and after the child's birth is such that by age 3, an estimated one-half, or 54 percent, of the first children born to black fathers in Chicago poverty tracts had parents who had never been married to one another, compared to an estimated 42 percent of Puerto Ricans, 13 percent of Mexicans, and under 10 percent of non-Hispanic whites.

Sample-selection effects

The race and ethnic differences in marriage that we observe in a poverty-tract population are smaller than those in the general population. These differences are smaller because a poverty-tract sample is more economically homogeneous than a sample of the entire population; most poverty-area residents are low-income if not poor. Therefore, any race or ethnic differences in family structure that are related to class are attenuated in our data.

In order to see how restricted the race or ethnic differences might be, we compared UPFS Survey statistics on the legitimacy status of first children born between 1960 and 1981 to similar statistics computed from the June 1980 and June 1982 Current Population Surveys.[17] In the Current Population Surveys, 10 per-

17. O'Connell and Rogers, "Out-of-Wedlock Births."

cent of white infants and 50 percent of black infants were born out of wedlock. In the UPFS Survey sample, by contrast, 33 percent of white infants and 68 percent of black infants were born out of wedlock. Thus the racial difference in the legitimacy status of first births is smaller in our poverty-tract sample.

Although the higher levels of out-of-wedlock births in our data are not surprising, we also expect that the statistics we generate from the UPFS Survey will tend to understate the actual rates of legitimation and postpartum marriages in poverty-tract neighborhoods. Because our sample is a cross section of poverty areas, it includes recent immigrants and a residual population of persons who over the years have stayed in these neighborhoods. To the extent that marriage is related to geographical mobility, the marriage rates that we calculate from the retrospective data will tend to be lower than if we had data on all persons who ever lived in poverty tracts. In this sense, our estimates will be biased because they are weighted toward the experiences of never-married residents of poverty tracts. While the effects of this sample selectivity on our analysis need to be evaluated in greater detail, our guess is that the nature of the statistical bias works against our finding significant employment effects on marriage.

MODELS AND METHODS OF ANALYSIS

While Murray, Wilson, and Farley stress economic variables, they arrive at different conclusions about the intensity and, in some cases, the direction of particular economic effects. One of the more intriguing implications of Murray's argument is that father's employment ought to lower or at best have a neutral effect on the probability of legitimating a premarital pregnancy. In Murray's thought experiment, the couple with the largest incentive to avoid marriage is the one in which the man is employed. This couple should be less likely to legitimate a premarital pregnancy compared to the couple in which the man is unemployed. According to Wilson, on the other hand, couples are more likely to marry if the man has a steady income. Finally, Farley's argument suggests that couples tend to marry when the woman is most dependent on the man's earnings. Because earnings tend to rise with years of school completed,[18] the gap in potential earnings is greater when the man's education exceeds the woman's. Therefore, one would infer from Farley's argument that for similarly educated men, couples in which the man's education is greater than the woman's are more likely to marry than couples in which the man's education is equal to or less than the woman's.

We will test these predictions by fitting a set of logistic and hazards regression models to our data. The logistic regression model relates individual characteristics to the odds of legitimation, that is, marriage after conception but before birth. The hazards regression model relates individual characteristics to rates of marriage after childbirth.

Our approach will be to fit four separate models to the data. Model 1 includes only the effects of race or ethnicity. A significant race or ethnicity effect means that the odds of legitimation or the rate of postpartum marriage differs between ra-

18. U.S. Department of Commerce, Bureau of the Census, *Current Population Reports,* series P-60, no. 146, *Money Income of Households, Families, and Persons in the United States: 1983* (Washington, DC: Government Printing Office, 1985), tab. 12, "Years of School Completed—Households with Householder 25 Years and Older, by Total Money Income in 1983."

cial and ethnic groups. Model 2 includes race or ethnicity and paternal employment status. This analysis will test Murray's and Wilson's predictions about the effect of father's employment on the likelihood of marriage; Murray's work suggests a negative effect, while Wilson's predicts a positive effect.

Model 3 adds the effects of the man's and the woman's educational status. Like Farley, we are using educational attainment as a proxy for lifetime earnings. If Farley's hypothesis is correct, the couples in which the man's education exceeds the woman's should be the most likely to marry, and the couples in which the woman's education exceeds the man's should be the least likely to marry.

Finally, in addition to the independent variables whose effects are the main concern of this article, we control for a number of other variables reported in the literature as affecting the likelihood of marriage in the general population.[19] Although these studies usually do not distinguish between potential spouses who are childless and those who have children, we included these variables in our final model to see if they would predict fathers' first marriages. These variables include socioeconomic characteristics of the family of origin, religion, cohort, and age effects.

Table 3 shows the means of the independent variables to be used in the analy-

19. See Robert T. Michael and Nancy Brandon Tuma, "Entry into Marriage and Parenthood by Young Men and Women: The Influence of Family Background," *Demography,* 22(5):515-44 (1985), for a theoretical explication of these effects. See Ronald R. Rindfuss, S. Phillip Morgan, and C. Gary Swicegood, "The Transition to Motherhood: The Intersection of Structural and Temporal Dimensions," *American Sociological Review,* 49(3):359-72 (1984), for a good critical summary of the research on the effects of age, cohort, and period on family formation.

sis. These statistics are calculated separately for each of three groups of fathers: those who legitimated the birth of their first child, those who married after the birth, and those who had not married the mother of their child at the time of the survey.

FINDINGS

In this section, we present the findings from our multivariate analysis of ethnic variation in both the odds of legitimating a premarital pregnancy, and in rates of marriage after the first birth, among fathers in Chicago poverty tracts.

Racial and ethnic differences

Model 1, in Tables 4 and 5, includes only race or ethnicity. The estimated effects for all models are expressed as changes in the expected odds of legitimation or rate of postpartum marriage relative to a baseline group, non-Hispanic whites. For instance, Table 4 shows that the relative odds of legitimation for Mexicans are 0.775; in other words, Mexicans are three-quarters as likely as non-Hispanic whites to legitimate a premaritally conceived birth. By contrast, the relative odds for Puerto Ricans, 0.146, and blacks, 0.156, are only one-sixth the odds for non-Hispanic whites.[20] In both tables, estimates marked with an asterisk are not statistically significant.

The results of Model 1 in Table 5 show that the relative rate of marriage to the mother after the first child's birth among Mexicans, 0.554, is slightly above one-half the marriage rate among non-Hispanic whites. Puerto Ricans, with 0.272,

20. These relative odds are approximately the results one obtains from Table 1 by dividing each group's legitimation odds by the odds for non-Hispanic whites, the reference group.

TABLE 3
MEANS OF INDEPENDENT VARIABLES FOR FATHERS WHOSE
FIRST CHILD WAS CONCEIVED BEFORE MARRIAGE

Variable	Fathers Who Married before Birth	Fathers Who Married after Birth	Fathers Who Never Married Mother of Child
Black	.290	.489	.645
Mexican	.362	.219	.101
Puerto Rican	.087	.153	.207
Non-Hispanic white	.261	.139	.046
Employed*	.725	.518	.424
Is a high school graduate[†]	.397	.295	.308
Partner is a high school graduate[†]	.538	.554	.468
Mother graduated from eighth grade	.541	.488	.545
Sibship greater than four	.478	.625	.604
Catholic	.536	.409	.304
Family of origin ever received welfare	.102	.241	.295
Mother-only family of origin at age 14	.377	.314	.438
Mother and stepfather at age 14	.043	.087	.064
Year of birth	52.8 (5.8)	52.6 (6.0)	56.0 (6.6)
Age at conception of first child	22.3 (3.5)	21.4 (4.3)	21.1 (4.0)
Partner's age at conception of first child	20.5 (4.5)	18.8 (3.2)	19.6 (4.3)
Year of child's birth	75.8 (6.7)	74.6 (6.1)	77.7 (6.3)
Number of observations	69	137	217

SOURCE: Urban Poverty and Family Structure Survey, 1986.
NOTE: Standard deviations in parentheses.
*Any employment reported for the period from seven months before the birth of the first child to that child's birth.
†Status at conception of first child.

and blacks, with 0.251, have postpartum marriage rates that are one-quarter the non-Hispanic white rate.[21]

Father's employment

Model 2 extends our analysis by estimating the effects of father's employ-

21. Again, these relative rates are approximately each group's log complement of the cumulative proportion of fathers marrying divided by the log complement of the cumulative proportion of non-Hispanic white fathers marrying. The hazards regression model simplifies the comparison by assuming that the proportional differences between groups are constant at each duration after the child's birth.

ment status. Our results show that paternal employment is positively related both to the odds of a father's legitimating a premarital pregnancy and to his likelihood of marrying the mother after the first child's birth.

More specifically, Model 2 in Table 4 shows that fathers who were employed at the time of pregnancy are over two and a half times more likely to legitimate the birth than men who were not employed: the relative odds of legitimation among employed fathers was 2.557. In Table 5, the relative rate of marriage for employed fathers at each period after the first child's

TABLE 4
RELATIVE ODDS OF LEGITIMATION OF A PREMARITAL CONCEPTION BY MALES 18-44 YEARS OLD IN CHICAGO POVERTY TRACTS, 1986

Characteristic	Relative Odds		
	Model 1	Model 2	Model 3
Race or Ethnicity			
Black	0.156	0.177	0.169
Mexican	0.775	0.744	0.914*
Puerto Rican	0.146	0.146	0.154
Non-Hispanic white	1.000	1.000	1.000
Employment			
Male employed		2.557	2.945
Male not employed		1.000	1.000
Education of partners[†]			
Male < HS, female < HS			1.000
Male < HS, female HS+			1.448*
Male HS+, female < HS			1.740*
Male HS+, female HS+			2.414
Number of observations	423	423	366
Goodness-of-fit p value		.927	.236

SOURCE: Urban Poverty and Family Structure Survey, 1986.
NOTE: Baseline levels are indicated by relative odds of 1.
*Estimates not statistically significant at the .05 level.
[†]"< HS" stands for less than high school education; "HS+" stands for high school education or more.

birth, 1.87, is nearly twice as large as the rate for unemployed fathers.[22] Both sets of findings are inconsistent with Murray's hypothesis that employed fathers have a disincentive to marry, and they are consistent with Wilson and Neckerman's male-marriageable-pool hypothesis. Still, father's employment does not explain the large racial and ethnic differences we observe between inner-city fathers in Chicago in levels of never-married parenthood: the race or ethnicity estimates change only slightly from Model 1 to Model 2.

22. In this analysis, we allowed paternal employment status to change in value over time using the retrospective data on stable employment recorded on the life-history calendar. Stable employment was defined as any full- or part-time job that lasted six months or longer.

Education of the man and woman

Model 3 provides a partial test of Farley's hypothesis that the shift away from marriage, particularly among blacks, is caused by the narrowing of the earnings differential between men and women. Although we have no direct measure of the man's and woman's potential earnings, we use the joint educational attainment of the man and woman, which indexes lifetime earnings, as a proxy for potential earnings differential. We find in Table 4 that the likelihood of legitimation increases as the man and woman's joint education level increases. The increased likelihood is statistically significant only for high-school-educated couples. Model 3 in Table 5 shows a similar pattern for postpartum marriage, with one anomaly.

TABLE 5
RELATIVE RISKS OF MARRIAGE TO MOTHER OF FIRST BORN AFTER CHILDBIRTH FOR MALES 18-44 YEARS OLD IN CHICAGO POVERTY TRACTS, 1986

Characteristic	Relative Risks		
	Model 1	Model 2	Model 3
Race or Ethnicity			
Black	0.251	0.265	0.268
Mexican	0.554	0.506	0.679*
Puerto Rican	0.272	0.267	0.315
Non-Hispanic white	1.000	1.000	1.000
Employment			
Male employed		1.870	1.790
Male not employed		1.000	1.000
Education of partners[†]			
Male < HS, female < HS			1.000
Male < HS, female HS+			1.907
Male HS+, female < HS			1.323*
Male HS+, female HS+			1.639
Number of observations	301	301	301

SOURCE: Urban Poverty and Family Structure Survey, 1986.
NOTE: Baseline levels are indicated by a relative risk of 1.
*Estimates not statistically significant at the .05 level.
†"< HS" stands for less than high school education; "HS+" stands for high school education or more.

Couples in which the mother is a high school graduate but the father is not are more likely to marry after the child's birth than other couples. Two of these effects are statistically significant at the .05 level. These effects are net of the effect of male employment status on marriage, which changes little with the introduction of the education variable (compare Models 2 and 3 in both tables).

These education findings run counter to Farley's expectation that marriage occurs less among couples when the woman's earning potential equals or exceeds the man's. In our data, higher male and female education generally improves the probability of legitimation and postpartum marriage, and significantly so in the latter case. Although controlling for education reduces the difference between Mexicans and non-Hispanic whites to statistical insignificance, Puerto Ricans and blacks still show lower rates of marriage compared to whites.

Interaction effects

In separate analyses not shown, we examined whether the effects of male employment and education of the partners on marriage differed significantly by race or ethnicity. There are plausible reasons for believing this might be true. For instance, employment could increase marriage more for whites than for blacks if whites have less tolerance for unemployed husbands than blacks do. In addition, the female independence effect might be especially strong among blacks, given that, of all women, black women are closest to parity earnings with men of the same education.

We tested the first hypothesis by adding a term for the interaction of race or ethnicity and employment to Model 2 in Tables 4 and 5. We found that the interaction term was statistically insignificant and that the coefficients for the other terms changed very little. This means that the effect of male employment on marriage is equally strong among white, black, Mexican, and Puerto Rican fathers.

Similarly, we tested the second hypothesis by adding a term for the interaction of race or ethnicity and joint education to Model 3 in Tables 4 and 5. In this case, the interaction term did not significantly improve the model's fit to the data. Thus we found no evidence that allowing for different female independence effects by ethnic group improves our explanation of marriage rates among inner-city parents. Finally, we found no strong interaction between male employment status and the joint education of the partners.

Other explanatory variables

In our final model, also not shown, we added the other explanatory variables stepwise and as a group into the logistic regression predicting the likelihood of legitimation. Only one variable, the father's year of birth, had a statistically significant effect: the younger the father, the less likely he was to marry. This effect, however, was modest and did not change the coefficients of the ethnic, employment, or joint-education variables.

We also entered these variables as a group into the hazards regression predicting the likelihood of marriage after the birth of the child. We found significant effects of the father's year of birth, his age at conception of his first child, and his partner's age at that time. These effects, however, did not substantially change the coefficients of the ethnic, employment, or joint-education variables.

DISCUSSION

Our analysis provides direct evidence that employed men are more likely than jobless men to marry after the conception of their first child. These results are consistent with Wilson's male-marriageable-pool interpretation of changes in family structure; indirectly, they contradict Murray's argument about the impact of welfare incentives on the marriage of low-income couples. The effect of male employment on marriage is equally strong among white, black, Mexican, and Puerto Rican inner-city men. High school graduates are also more likely to marry than high school dropouts, suggesting that both short-term economic realities and long-term prospects shape the marriage decisions of inner-city couples.

Regardless of their own education level, men whose partners are high school graduates are also more likely to marry than those whose partners are high school dropouts. With the exception of one group, the higher a man and a woman's joint earnings potential, the more likely they are to marry. For this population, at least, the economic viability of the couple is more important than any independence effect a woman may derive from having her own source of income. These findings are inconsistent with Farley's interpretation of changing family structure. But, under the joint pressures of poverty and family responsibilities, it is not surprising that inner-city parents would marry if the match were economically viable. Farley's explanation remains a highly plausible account of marriage patterns in the rest of the population.

These results leave some questions

unanswered. Substantial differences remain in the marriage rates of racial or ethnic groups. We used very simple measures of economic status—current employment and high school graduation. It is possible that a more refined measure of economic status of men and women might decrease the size of racial or ethnic differences. In addition, it is possible that neighborhood characteristics influence marriage behavior over and above their correlation with individual characteristics. Although our poverty-area sample greatly reduces the variation between racial or ethnic groups in neighborhood status, blacks and, to a lesser extent, Puerto Ricans tend to live in much poorer areas than Mexicans or whites, and these differences are not controlled in our analysis. Finally, it is possible that racial or ethnic differences in the networks of family support available to unmarried parents influence the propensity to marry.

Nevertheless, these initial findings show that employed men are more likely than jobless men to marry the mothers of their children. We also can tentatively conclude that men are more likely to marry women with good economic prospects. Although one needs to be cautious about drawing policy prescriptions from observational findings, one message for policymakers is clear: improvements in the economic status of both low-income men and women promise to enable more parents to marry and thus provide a financially and, it is hoped, socially better environment for themselves and their children.

7

Single Mothers, the Underclass, and Social Policy

By SARA McLANAHAN and IRWIN GARFINKEL

ABSTRACT: This article focuses on the question of whether mother-only families are part of an emerging urban underclass. An underclass is defined as a population exhibiting the following characteristics: weak labor force attachment, persistence of weak attachment, and residential isolation in neighborhoods with high concentrations of poverty and unemployment. We find that only a small minority of single mothers fit the description of an underclass: less than 5 percent. But a small and growing minority of black, never-married mothers meet all three criteria. We argue that welfare programs are necessary but that too heavy a reliance on welfare can facilitate the growth of an underclass. In contrast, universal programs such as child support assurance, child care, health care, children's allowances, and full employment would discourage such a trend and promote economic independence among single mothers.

Sara McLanahan is an associate professor in the Department of Sociology and the Institute for Research on Poverty at the University of Wisconsin, Madison. Her research focuses on the intergenerational consequences of family disruption. Irwin Garfinkel is the Edwin Witte Professor in the School of Social Work and the Institute for Research on Poverty at the University of Wisconsin, Madison. His major interest is in income transfer policy, most recently child support. Professors Garfinkel and McLanahan are coauthors of the book Single Mothers and Their Children: A New American Dilemma.

NOTE: Support for this research was provided by the National Institute for Child Health and Development under grant HD19375-03 and by the Ford Foundation.

FAMILIES headed by nonmarried women have increased dramatically during the past three decades. Whereas in 1960 about 7 percent of all children were living with a single mother, in 1987 the proportion was more than 21 percent.[1] Over half of all children born today will spend some time in a mother-only family before reaching age 18, about 45 percent of all white children will do so, and about 85 percent of black children will.[2] Clearly, the mother-only family will have a profound effect on the next generation of Americans.

Increases in marital disruption and single parenthood have stimulated considerable debate during the past few years and there is much disagreement over whether recent trends are a sign of progress or decline. On the one hand, the growth of mother-only families is viewed as evidence of women's increasing economic independence and greater freedom of choice with respect to marriage.[3] On the other, it is often treated as a proxy for social disorganization. With respect to the latter, three aspects of divorce and single motherhood are seen as especially problematic: (1) the high rate of poverty among families headed by women, variously referred to as the "feminization of poverty" and the "pauperization of women"; (2) the lower rates of socioeconomic attainment among children from mother-only families as compared with children from intact families; and (3) the potential role of mother-only families in the growth and perpetuation of an urban underclass in American cities.

In our book, *Single Mothers and Their Children,* we describe in detail the first two problems: poverty and intergenerational dependence.[4] In this article, we focus on the last question, whether mother-only families represent the crystallization of an urban underclass. We begin by discussing various definitions of the underclass and by presenting our own views on the subject. Next we ask whether there are mother-only families who fit the description of an underclass, and, if so, what proportion might belong in this group. Finally, we review domestic social policy from the perspective of whether the current system and recent proposals for reform serve to perpetuate or break down the boundaries that isolate mother-only families from the rest of society.

DEFINITIONAL ISSUES

The underclass has been the focus of considerable discussion during recent years, beginning with the publication of a series of articles in the *New Yorker* magazine in the early 1980s.[5] While there is no general consensus on whether the underclass is a place or a group of people, most analysts agree that it is more than just another name for those at the bottom of the income distribution. Auletta defines the underclass as a group of people who suffer from "behavioral as well as income deficiencies" and who "operate outside the mainstream of commonly accepted values."[6] He includes street criminals, hustlers and drug addicts, welfare mothers, and the chronically mentally ill in his characterization of the underclass.

1. U.S. Department of Commerce, Bureau of the Census, *Current Population Reports,* series P-20, nos. 105, 106, and 423 (Washington, DC: Government Printing Office, 1960, 1961, and 1988).

2. Larry L. Bumpass, "Children and Marital Disruption: A Replication and Update," *Demography,* 21(1):71-82 (Feb. 1984).

3. Barbara Bergmann, *The Economic Emergence of Women* (New York: Basic Books, 1986).

4. Irwin Garfinkel and Sara S. McLanahan, *Single Mothers and Their Children: A New American Dilemma* (Washington, DC: Urban Institute, 1986).

5. Ken Auletta, "The Underclass: Part I," *New Yorker,* 16 Nov. 1981; idem, "The Underclass: Part II," ibid., 23 Nov. 1981; idem, "The Underclass: Part III," ibid., 30 Nov. 1981.

6. Auletta, "The Underclass: Part III," p. 105.

Whereas Auletta bases his definition of the underclass on individual behavior, others have used the word to describe particular geographical or residential areas. Sawhill and her colleagues at the Urban Institute speak of "people who live in neighborhoods where welfare dependency, female-headed families, male joblessness, and dropping out of high school are all common occurrences."[7]

Finally, Wilson speaks of the underclass as poor people, mostly black, who live in urban ghettos in the north-central and northeastern regions of the country and who are "outside the mainstream of the American occupational system."[8] He contends that changes in these communities during the 1970s, including deindustrialization and the exodus of middle-class blacks, greatly altered the conditions of families left behind. Ghetto residents are worse off today than they were in the 1960s, not only because their environment is more dangerous but also because they have fewer opportunities for social mobility and fewer positive role models.

Weak attachment to the labor force

A common thread running through all of these definitions is an emphasis on weak labor force attachment. Underclass people are generally described either as living in neighborhoods with high rates of unemployment or nonemployment, or as marginally attached to the labor force themselves. Weak attachment is viewed as problematic for several reasons. First, nonemployment clearly has costs for the individual, given that in a market society such as ours wages are the primary source of income for all nonelderly adults. Those who are not attached to the labor force, either directly or indirectly, are very likely to be poor or to be involved in some form of criminal activity. Moreover, their chances of gaining access to valued resources and/or power in the future are significantly lower than are the chances of those who are part of the labor force.

Weak attachment to the labor force also has costs for the rest of society, whose members ultimately must pay for high levels of nonemployment either through direct income transfers such as Aid to Families with Dependent Children (AFDC) or indirectly through the crime and social disorganization that accompany unemployment and a large underground economy. In addition, conservatives and liberals express concern that weak attachment undermines the work ethic and thereby reduces productivity, whereas Marxists worry that it undermines the solidarity of the work force and thereby reduces the likelihood of successful collective action.

Disabled workers, widows, and married homemakers may be indirectly attached to the labor force either through their personal work history or through the current or past employment history of their spouse. In the case of disabled workers and widows, the primary source of household income comes from social insurance, which is linked to the past work history of the individual and the individual's spouse, respectively. In the case of married homemakers, the primary source of income is the partner's current earnings.

7. Isabel V. Sawhill, *Challenge to Leadership: Economic and Social Issues for the Next Decade* (Washington, DC: Urban Institute, 1988); Robert D. Reischauer, "The Size and Characteristics of the Underclass" (Paper delivered at the conference of the Association for Public Policy Analysis and Management Research, Washington, DC, 1987).

8. William Julius Wilson, *The Truly Disadvantaged: The Inner City, the Underclass, and Public Policy* (Chicago: University of Chicago Press, 1987), p. 8.

Persistence of weak attachment

Weak attachment to the labor force is a necessary but not sufficient condition for defining an underclass. Individuals who are temporarily out of work or ill or dependent on welfare are usually not viewed as part of the underclass, even though they may be living below the poverty line. Rather, it is the persistence of weak attachment that distinguishes underclass behavior and underclass neighborhoods from poverty areas and the poor in general. Persistence may occur either over time, as when a person is unemployed and/or dependent on welfare for a long period, or it may occur across generations, as when a child of a welfare recipient also becomes dependent on welfare. We argue that persistence across generations is a necessary condition for establishing the existence of an underclass.

The emphasis on persistence for individuals and across generations highlights the fact that the underclass does not simply signify a particular structural position or group at the bottom of the income distribution. Rather, it means that certain individuals and their offspring occupy this position over a period of time. Thus the problem is not merely inequality—the fact that some locations or statuses in society carry with them fewer rewards than others—but an absence of social mobility—the fact that some persons do not have the chance to improve their situation. When Wilson and his colleagues talk about those left behind in the ghettos of the central cities, they are expressing concern for what they view as declining opportunity and increasing immobility.[9]

Concern about the persistence of weak attachment to the labor force has resurfaced recently. The predominant view among poverty researchers during the 1970s was that nonemployment and dependence on public assistance were relatively short-term phenomena. According to researchers at the University of Michigan, nearly 25 percent of the population was poor at least 1 year during the 1970s whereas less than 3 percent were poor for at least 8 of 10 years.[10] This perspective, which emphasized the fluidity of the poverty population, was seriously challenged in the early 1980s by Bane and Ellwood, who noted that a nontrivial proportion of those who became dependent on welfare were dependent for 10 or more years.[11] Bane and Ellwood's findings coincided with a new interest in the underclass and fueled concern that certain forms of poverty, especially those associated with weak labor force attachment, might be self-perpetuating. Mother-only families have been a particular concern, because they appear to experience longer periods of economic dependence than other poor groups and because the intergenerational implications of their prolonged dependence may be of greater consequence.

Social isolation

A final characteristic essential to our definition and common to most discus-

9. Ibid.; William Julius Wilson et al., "The Ghetto Underclass and the Changing Structure of Urban Poverty," in *Quiet Riots: Race and Poverty in the United States,* ed. Fred R. Harris and Roger W. Wilkins (New York: Pantheon, 1988); Loïc Wacquant and William Julius Wilson, "Poverty, Joblessness and the Social Transformation of the Inner City," in *Reforming Welfare,* ed. David Ellwood and Phoebe Cottingham (Cambridge, MA: Harvard University Press, forthcoming).

10. Greg J. Duncan and Richard D. Coe, *Years of Poverty, Years of Plenty: The Changing Economic Fortunes of American Workers and Families* (Ann Arbor: University of Michigan, Institute for Social Research, Survey Research Center, 1984).

11. Mary Jo Bane and David T. Ellwood, "Slipping into and out of Poverty: The Dynamics of Spells," *Journal of Human Resources,* 21(1):1-23 (Winter 1986).

sions of the underclass is the notion that its members are isolated from the rest of society in terms of both their connection to mainstream social institutions and their values. Isolation, be it in urban ghettos or rural areas of the South, is of concern because it reduces knowledge of opportunities. Isolation combined with spatial concentration, as occurs in urban ghettos, is especially worrisome in that it may lead to the development of a deviant subculture. Isolation is a mechanism by which weak labor force attachment persists over time and across generations.

Not all analysts agree that the underclass has a unique culture, that is, its own set of norms and values. In fact, since the late 1960s, liberal scholars have tended to avoid discussions that attribute a different set of attitudes to those at the bottom of the income distribution. Most recall that in the 1960s scholars who expressed concern over the so-called culture of poverty, even those who cited unemployment as the fundamental cause of deviant attitudes and behavior, were accused of blaming the victim.[12] Thus recent discussions of social isolation have tended to emphasize macroeconomic conditions and the institutional aspects of isolation as opposed to its norms and culture. For example, Wilson and his colleagues describe urban ghettos as communities with few employment opportunities and lacking in the leadership and interorganizational networks that facilitate job search and sustain community morale during times of high unemployment. Weak institu-

12. Daniel Patrick Moynihan, *The Negro Family: The Case for National Action* (Washington, DC: Department of Labor, Office of Policy Planning and Research, 1965); Lee Rainwater and William L. Yancey, eds., *The Moynihan Report and the Politics of Controversy: A Transaction Social Science and Public Policy Report* (Cambridge: MIT Press, 1967).

tions are viewed as the driving force behind cultural differences.

THE SPECIAL CASE OF SINGLE MOTHERS

Some would argue that single mothers are engaged in household production and therefore cannot be part of an underclass, even if they are not working in the paid labor force. Certainly, raising children is a valued activity that contributes to the public good by producing the next generation of young workers. A large proportion of married women devote full time to child care, at least while their children are very young, and many experts believe that this is the best use of their time. Furthermore, most industrialized countries provide children's allowances and various forms of parental leave, which make explicit the social value of children as well as the value of parental time spent on infant care. Yet in the United States, only those single mothers who are widows are provided sufficient public benefits to allow them to invest in full-time child care without paying the penalty of stigma and poverty. The fact that widowed mothers are treated differently from other single mothers suggests that something other than the mother's lack of paid employment and the cost of public transfers underlies the recent concern over welfare mothers.

One explanation for the negative attitudes toward welfare mothers is that they serve as proxies for nonemployed men, who are the primary concern of many analysts. According to this view, for every welfare mother, there is potentially a nonworking father who is part of the underclass. For critics of the welfare system, such as Murray, the AFDC mother is not only a proxy for the nonemployed father; she and the system that

supports her are a cause of his unemploy-ment.[13] According to Murray, single moth-erhood encourages male irresponsibility, which in turn undermines the work ethic and social productivity. In stark contrast, Wilson argues that the welfare mother is an indicator of a failing economic system in which low-skilled men can no longer support their families. According to this view, unemployment and low-paying jobs lead to family dissolution and nonmarriage, which give rise to single motherhood.

Although the causal relationship be-tween single motherhood and male employ-ment is opposite in these two views, both Murray and Wilson focus on male employ-ment as the primary problem. Concern for male employment also explains why widowed mothers are treated differently from other single mothers, even though they work fewer hours and receive higher public benefits. First, widowhood is caused by the death of a spouse and therefore is not a voluntary event. Provid-ing for widows does not encourage male irresponsibility or reduce the motivation to work. Second, Survivors Insurance (SI), like all aspects of social insurance, is closely tied to the previous work attach-ment of the spouse—in the case of widows, the deceased spouse—and thus it enhances rather than undermines the work ethic. In sum, widowed mothers who are eligible for SI are indirectly attached to the labor force even though they are not currently employed.

Quite apart from what it suggests about male employment, nonemployment among single mothers appears to be a growing concern in and of itself. The issue is not simply whether weak attach-ment to the labor force increases welfare costs, although for some this is the major problem, but whether full-time mothering has personal costs for women and children and social costs for the rest of society beyond the immediate transfer payments. Recent trends in the labor force participa-tion of married mothers suggest that social norms about women's employment are changing, and this in turn affects how policymakers and the general public view nonemployment among single mothers. When Mothers' Pensions programs were instituted in the beginning of the century and when SI and AFDC were instituted in the 1930s, the prevailing view was that mothers should stay home and care for their children.[14] Today, this view is chang-ing to reflect the fact that a majority of married mothers spend at least part of their time working in the paid labor force. The fact that over half of married mothers with young children work outside the home suggests that policies that encourage long-term economic dependency are not likely to be tolerated by the public. The welfare mother is increasingly isolated from mainstream society by virtue of the fact that she is not in the labor force.

EXTENT OF PERSISTENT
WEAK ATTACHMENT

Are single mothers weakly attached to the labor force, and if so does weak attachment persist over time and across generations? Both the absence of earnings and the presence of welfare are indicators of weak attachment. Although the former is the better measure in that it measures attachment directly, research on the dura-tion of welfare dependence is more readily available. In 1987, 69 percent of single mothers reported earnings whereas 33

13. Charles Murray, *Losing Ground: American Social Policy, 1950-1980* (New York: Basic Books, 1984).

14. Garfinkel and McLanahan, *Single Mothers and Their Children.*

percent reported receipt of some welfare.[15] Both the earnings and welfare figures suggest that about one-third of single mothers could be classified as weakly attached to the labor force. Of this group, 56 percent will be dependent on welfare for 10 years or more.[16] Multiplying the 33 percent of single mothers who report weak attachment by the 56 percent who are destined for long-term dependence yields an estimate of 18 percent of current single mothers who are potentially at risk for being in the underclass.

As discussed previously, nonemployment and economic dependency alone do not constitute sufficient evidence for classifying single mothers as part of the underclass, because these women are engaged in socially productive activity—taking care of children. Hence the more important question is, what happens to the children in these families? If the offspring of nonemployed single mothers become productive, independent citizens, the underclass characterization is inappropriate. Thus although some people may complain that the cost of supporting these families is too high or unfairly imposed

on the rest of society, their concern is different from that of whether welfare mothers are socially productive.

To address the question of intergenerational welfare dependence, detailed family histories over at least two generations are required. Such data are only now becoming available from longitudinal studies such as the Panel Study of Income Dynamics and the National Longitudinal Survey of Youth, both of which follow families and their offspring over a long period of time. Based on research by Gottschalk, we estimate that about 60 percent of the daughters from families who experience long-term welfare dependence will receive welfare themselves for at least 1 year.[17] Based on Ellwood's research, we estimate that about 40 percent of these daughters will receive welfare for 10 or more years.[18]

To combine and summarize these crude estimates: about 18 percent of single mothers in 1987 were dependent on welfare for a long period of time, and about 24 percent of their daughters will be

15. U.S. Department of Commerce, Bureau of the Census, *1987 Current Population Survey* (Washington, DC: Government Printing Office, 1987). Although there is underreporting of welfare receipt in the Current Population Survey data, for our purposes this is not likely to be a problem. There is also underreporting in the data that Ellwood uses to determine what proportion of those who receive AFDC receive it for a long period of time. See David T. Ellwood, *Targeting "Would-Be" Long-Term Recipients of AFDC* (Princeton, NJ: Mathematica Policy Research, 1986). So long as those who fail to report receipt of AFDC are not long-term recipients—a reasonable assumption—multiplying the proportion of single mothers reporting receipt of some welfare by the estimated proportion of long-termers gives an accurate estimate of the proportion of single mothers who are dependent on welfare for an extended period.

16. Ellwood, *"Would-Be" Long-Term Recipients of AFDC.*

17. Peter Gottschalk, "A Proposal to Study Intergenerational Correlation of Welfare Dependence," mimeographed (Madison: University of Wisconsin, Institute for Research on Poverty, May 1988). Using the National Longitudinal Survey, Gottschalk finds that 50 percent of white and 70 percent of black daughters of mothers who experience any welfare dependence will themselves experience at least one year of welfare dependence within seven years of leaving home. Greg J. Duncan, Martha S. Hill, and Saul D. Hoffman report much smaller intergenerational dependence. Only 36 percent of daughters whose mothers received welfare received welfare themselves between ages 21 and 23. By limiting their examination to these three years of age, however, they severely underestimate welfare receipt of daughters. Duncan, Hill, and Hoffman, "Welfare Dependence within and across Generations," *Science,* 239:469 (Jan. 1988).

18. Ellwood, *"Would-Be" Long-Term Recipients of AFDC.* We use the figure for unmarried mothers, which is 38 percent. We also assume that the estimates for daughters would apply as well to sons.

dependent on welfare for 10 more years. We conclude, therefore, that about 4 percent (0.24 × 0.18) of single mothers can be classified as members of an emerging underclass.

On the one hand, the figure of 4 percent is an overestimate of the association between single motherhood and underclass status, given that only a portion of those women who ever experience single motherhood are single mothers in any particular year. Half of all women who divorce remarry within five years, and presumably most of these are not at risk for being part of an underclass.[19]

On the other hand, 4 percent is an underestimate for some groups.[20] Persistence of welfare dependence among single mothers varies substantially. Ellwood finds, for example, that whereas 20 percent of whites who ever receive welfare will be dependent for 10 or more years, the figure for blacks is 32 percent.[21]

19. Andrew Cherlin, *Marriage, Divorce, Remarriage* (Cambridge, MA: Harvard University Press, 1981).
20. More generally, the figure in the text should be considered a lower bound. To see this, suppose each mother has only one daughter who either does or does not become dependent on welfare for a long period of time. If the daughters do not become long-term dependents, we classify the mothers as outside the underclass because they have raised a productive child, which is in itself productive. But in reality, many mothers have more than one daughter. In some cases, one or more of the daughters will become long-term dependents while one or more will not. By multiplying the 36 percent of daughters of long-term welfare-dependent mothers who themselves become long-term dependents by the 18 percent who are long-term dependents, we are implicitly assigning a portion of each mother with multiple children to underclass or nonunderclass status. An argument can be made, however, that even if only one of several daughters of a mother with long-term nonattachment to the labor force exhibited the same behavior, that family would be appropriately included as part of an underclass.
21. Ellwood, *"Would-Be" Long-Term Recipients of AFDC.*

Similarly, Gottschalk finds that whereas half of white daughters of welfare-dependent mothers become recipients themselves, the figure for blacks is 70 percent. Even more striking, whereas only 14 percent of divorced mothers who ever receive welfare will be dependent for 10 or more years, the figure for unmarried mothers is nearly 40 percent. Thus among some subgroups of single mothers—in particular, young unwed black mothers— the risk of being in the underclass is high.

EXTENT OF SOCIAL ISOLATION

Are mother-only families more socially isolated than other families, and does their isolation lower their mobility? As noted earlier, social isolation may occur because the community no longer functions as a resource base for its members, as when a neighborhood has no jobs, no networks for helping to locate jobs, poor schools, and a youth culture that is subject to minimal social control. Cultural isolation, on the other hand, refers to deviations from normative standards, such as the absence of a work ethic or a devaluation of family commitments.

One way to measure social isolation is to ask what proportion of mother-only families live in urban neighborhoods with high proportions of poor people. Table 1 presents information on the proportion of different types of families in the United States who live in neighborhoods in which 20 percent or more of the population is poor or in which 40 percent or more is poor. Poverty areas are restricted to neighborhoods in the 100 largest cities.

Several findings in Table 1 merit attention. First, families headed by single mothers are more likely to live in poor urban neighborhoods than other families. Second, only a small proportion—about 5.6 percent—of mother-only families live in extremely poor neighborhoods. Final-

TABLE 1
PROPORTION OF U.S. FAMILIES LIVING IN URBAN POVERTY AREAS IN 1980

	20 Percent Poverty Areas	40 Percent Poverty Areas
Mother-only families	16.5	5.6
Other families	4.7	1.0
White mother-only families	4.5	1.0*
Black mother-only families	34.2	10.0*
Black persons	26.0	8.0

SOURCE: U.S. Department of Commerce, Bureau of the Census, 1985.

*Information is not available on the proportion of white and black mother-only families living in areas that are 40 percent poor. We estimate these percentages by extrapolating from the proportions observed in 40 percent areas for other families and black persons. The estimate for white mother-only families was obtained by assuming that the ratio of white mother-only families to other families that pertains to the 20 percent areas also pertains to the 40 percent areas. The estimate for black mother-only families was obtained by assuming that the ratio of mother-only families to black persons that pertains to the 20 percent areas also pertains to 40 percent areas.

ly, there are huge racial differences in the degree of isolation of mother-only families. Whereas less than 5 percent of white mother-only families live in areas in which 20 percent of the residents are poor, over 34 percent of black mother-only families live in such areas. About 10 percent of black mother-only families and less than 1 percent of white mother-only families live in areas of extreme poverty.

To what extent did black mother-only families become more socially isolated during the 1970s? Our research suggests that the proportion of black mother-only families who reside in neighborhoods in which at least 20 percent of the residents are poor declined. Yet the proportion of those who reside in neighborhoods that are at least 40 percent poor increased dramatically—by about 30 percent. In other words, in the face of general economic progress for black families in the last 25 years, the proportion of poor mother-only families who are isolated increased. Finally, these extremely poor

neighborhoods became more desolate with respect to the proportion of males employed and the proportion of families on welfare.[22]

In addition to residential characteristics, offspring from mother-only families also differ with respect to certain community resources and parental values. Research based on data from High School and Beyond, a survey of 50,000 high school sophomores and seniors, shows that black adolescents in mother-only families attend lower-quality high schools and are more accepting of nonmarital births than their counterparts in two-parent families, even after controlling for socioeconomic status. In contrast, the educational aspirations of their mothers are no different from those in two-parent families.[23]

22. Sara S. McLanahan, Irwin Garfinkel, and Dorothy Watson, "Family Structure, Poverty, and the Underclass" (Discussion paper no. 823, Institute for Research on Poverty, University of Wisconsin, 1987).

23. Sara S. McLanahan, Nan Astone, and Nadine Marks, "The Role of Mother-Only Families

In sum, whereas only a small proportion of mother-only families live in extremely poor—or what might be called underclass—neighborhoods, there is evidence that this group is growing. Moreover, there is some evidence that children from mother-only families are more accepting of the single-parent status than children from two-parent families. The issue of intergenerational female headship and its consequences is especially important for blacks, given their higher concentration in urban poverty areas and their high prevalence of mother-only families. An important question, which we have not attempted to answer here, is whether an increasing proportion of new birth cohorts are being born to single mothers in extremely poor neighborhoods, and, if so, how this will affect the gains in socioeconomic status made by blacks during the past three decades.

SOCIAL POLICY TOWARD SINGLE MOTHERS AND THE UNDERCLASS

All communities develop institutions to aid dependent persons. As capitalism replaced feudalism, providing for the poor became a public responsibility. In the United States, we have always had public welfare programs, and they have been the most important source of government income for poor single mothers.[24] Though welfare programs are necessary, too heavy a reliance on them is conducive to the emergence of an underclass.

AFDC and other means-tested welfare programs undermine the indirect labor force attachment of poor single mothers by promoting female headship and reducing the likelihood of marriage.[25] While the effect of welfare on the aggregate growth in mother-only families is quite small, its effect on the poorest half of the population is more substantial. Our own crude estimate suggests that the threefold increase in AFDC and welfare-related benefits between 1955 and 1975 may account for as much as 20 or 30 percent of the growth in mother-only families among the bottom half of the income distribution.

Welfare also undermines direct attachment to the labor force by imposing a high tax rate on earnings. Welfare recipients lose nearly a dollar in benefits for each dollar earned, and they may also lose health care and other income-tested benefits. Because of the high tax rate and loss of benefits, and because their earnings capacity is very low, many single mothers would be worse off working full-time than depending on welfare.[26]

Finally, AFDC promotes social isolation by creating a separate institution for the poor and by encouraging nonemployment at a time when married mothers are entering the labor force in increasing numbers. Ironically, whereas AFDC was originally designed to allow single mothers to replicate the behavior of married women—that is, to stay home with their children—it currently functions to separate the two groups further.

So why not reduce dependence by simply cutting or even eliminating welfare benefits as some have suggested? Unfortunately, such a strategy would do great harm to families who rely on welfare

---

in Reproducing Poverty" (Paper delivered at Poverty and Children, a conference at the University of Kansas, Lawrence, 20-22 June 1988).

24. For a brief historical account of public aid to single mothers, see Garfinkel and McLanahan, *Single Mothers and Their Children,* chap. 4.

25. For a critical summary of the literature, see ibid., chap. 3.

26. Sheldon Danziger, Robert Haveman, and Robert Plotnick, "How Income Transfers Affect Work, Savings, and the Income Distribution: A Critical Review," *Journal of Economic Literature* 19:975-1028 (Sept. 1981).

at some point but who are in no danger of becoming part of the underclass. Such families constitute the overwhelming majority of those who ever become dependent on welfare.[27] Furthermore, such a strategy would leave the mothers with the fewest skills and least experience worse off and even more desperate than they are today. Reducing welfare could lead to increased dependence on illegal sources of income and even further isolation for those families at the bottom of the income distribution.

In this connection, it is important to recognize that the existence of intergenerational welfare dependence is not prima facie evidence of the ill effects of welfare. In the absence of welfare, intergenerational transmission of poverty is to be expected. Indeed, one justification for welfare programs is to break this intergenerational link. Whether welfare ameliorates or exacerbates the intergenerational transmission of poverty is a complicated question that merits further research.[28]

Whereas welfare programs discourage work and isolate the poor, universal programs have the opposite effect. Because benefits in universal programs are not eliminated as earnings increase, they provide an incentive to work for those who would otherwise be dependent on welfare. That is, benefits from universal

programs make low-wage work more competitive with welfare. Aiding the poor through institutions that serve all income classes is itself integrative.

Universal programs are also more successful in preventing poverty and reducing economic insecurity. By providing a common floor to everyone, they lift the standard of living of the poorest, least productive citizens without stigmatizing them as economic failures. The common floor facilitates the efforts of such citizens to escape life on the dole, by making life off the dole more attractive. Universal programs therefore prevent both poverty and welfare dependence. The common floor, of course, also cushions the fall of middle- and upper-income families who come upon hard times.[29] Finally, because universal programs provide a valuable good or service to all citizens, they develop a more powerful political constituency and are therefore funded far more generously than programs for the poor.[30] A

29. In addition to the cushion provided by a common floor, social insurance programs—which, along with free public education, are the two most important universal systems in the United States— provide additional protection to middle- and upper-income families by providing higher benefits to workers with histories of higher earnings.

30. For a discussion of the politics of universal and income-tested programs, see Gordon Tullock, "Income Testing and Politics: A Theoretical Model," in *Income-Tested Transfer Programs: The Case For and Against,* ed. Irwin Garfinkel (New York: Academic Press, 1982); David Berry, Irwin Garfinkel, and Raymond Munts, "Income Testing in Income Support Programs for the Aged," in ibid.; ibid., pp. 499-513; Hugh Heclo, "The Political Foundations of Antipoverty Policy," in *Fighting Poverty: What Works and What Doesn't,* ed. Sheldon H. Danziger and Daniel H. Weinberg (Cambridge, MA: Harvard University Press, 1986); Margaret Weir, Ann Orloff, and Theda Skocpol, eds., *The Politics of Social Policy in the United States* (Princeton, NJ: Princeton University Press, 1988); Sheila Kamerman and Alfred Kahn, *Mothers Alone: Strategies for a Time of Change* (Dover, MA: Auburn House, 1988).

27. Ellwood, *"Would-Be" Long-Term Recipients of AFDC.* Although this statement about the proportion of families ever receiving welfare who become long-term recipients may appear to be inconsistent with the earlier estimates of the proportion of welfare families at a point in time who are long-term recipients, there is no inconsistency. The point-in-time estimate will always be higher than the lifetime exposure estimate because the short-term recipients are less likely to be on welfare at any point in time.

28. Gottschalk has proposed to address this issue. See Gottschalk, "A Proposal to Study Intergenerational Correlation of Welfare Dependence."

recent comparison of six industrialized countries shows that the poverty rates of single mothers are substantially lower in countries that rely most heavily on universal and employment-related income transfer programs as compared to countries that rely heavily on means-tested programs.[31]

Although universal programs have clear benefits for the underclass, some analysts have argued that they are inefficient. The small amount of research that directly addresses this issue, however, suggests that whether universal or welfare programs are more efficient is difficult to ascertain and that, in any case, the differences are not likely to be large.[32] What is clear is that universal programs will be more costly than welfare programs to upper-middle- and upper-income families.

The new child support assurance system (CSAS), which is being implemented in Wisconsin and other parts of the country, encourages labor force attachment and reduces isolation.[33] Under CSAS, the financial obligation of the nonresidential parent is expressed as a percentage of his or her income and is withheld from

31. Barbara B. Torrey and Timothy Smeeding, "Poor Children in Rich Countries" (Paper prepared for the meeting of the Population Association of America, New Orleans, LA, 21-23 Apr. 1988).

32. See David Betson, David Greenberg, and Richard Kasten, "A Simulation Analysis of the Economic Efficiency and Distributional Effects of Alternative Program Structures: The Negative Income Tax versus the Credit Income Tax," in *Income-Tested Transfer Programs*, ed. Garfinkel; Jonathan R. Kesselman, "Taxpayer Behavior and the Design of a Credit Income Tax," in ibid.; Efraim Sadka, Irwin Garfinkel, and Kemper Moreland, "Income Testing and Social Welfare: An Optimal Tax-Transfer Model," in ibid.; ibid., pp. 503-9.

33. Irwin Garfinkel and Patrick Wong, "Child Support and Public Policy" (Discussion paper no. 854, Institute for Research on Poverty, University of Wisconsin, 1987).

earnings as income and payroll taxes are. The child receives the full amount paid by the nonresident parent, but no less than a socially assured minimum benefit. When the nonresident parent is unemployed or has very low earnings, the government makes up the difference just as it does with the social security pension. CSAS is at least a cousin of our social insurance programs, which require a contribution from all member families but guarantee a minimum pension irrespective of the contribution. CSAS increases indirect attachment to the labor force by providing a link between the mother-only family and the nonresidential parent who is employed, and it increases direct attachment by providing a source of income that supplements rather than replaces earnings.

Universal child care, health care, and child allowance programs also help to integrate the poor into mainstream society. At present, the government has two different mechanisms for subsidizing the cost of raising children. Middle- and upper-middle-income families receive their subsidies through three provisions in the tax code: the dependent-care tax credit, the personal exemption for children, and the exclusion of employer-financed health-insurance benefits from taxable income. Lower-income families receive subsidies primarily through two welfare programs, AFDC and Medicaid. To beat welfare, unskilled single mothers need health care, child care, and cash outside of welfare.

Replacing the personal exemptions for children in the federal income tax with an equally costly refundable credit or child allowance would shift resources toward the bottom half of the population and provide a small cash supplement to earnings. Making the child-care tax credit refundable and more generous at the bottom would help the poor pay for child

care.[34] Adopting a universal health insurance program would reduce the incentive to remain on welfare as a way of ensuring health-care coverage.

The most universalistic policy of all, and the one most important to poor single mothers, is full employment. High unemployment promotes both loose attachment to the labor force and female headship. Despite some gaps and anomalies, there is now a strong body of empirical research that documents that one of the costs of increased unemployment is increased female headship.[35] With the exception of the Vietnam war, unemployment rates for blacks have gone up steadily since the 1950s. William Julius Wilson has argued, and our own examination of the evidence has led us to concur, that this increase in unemployment has probably been the single most important cause of the increase in female headship among poor blacks.[36]

For single mothers themselves, a high demand for labor increases both the availability of jobs and their rate of pay. It also increases the ability of nonresidential fathers to pay child support. In sum, nothing will do more to forestall the development of an underclass than a full-employment policy.

SUMMARY

Although the vast majority of single mothers do not fit the description of an underclass, there is a small group of predominantly black single mothers concentrated in Northern urban ghettos that is persistently weakly attached to the labor force, socially isolated, and reproducing itself. Although welfare programs are necessary for those who are failed by or who fail in—depending upon one's political perspective—the labor market and other mainstream institutions, too heavy a reliance upon welfare can facilitate the growth of an underclass. In contrast, aiding single mothers through more universal programs such as a child support assurance system, child care, health care, children's allowances, and a full-employment macroeconomic policy will retard the growth of an underclass.

34. Another alternative is for the government to provide child care for all and to charge a sliding-scale fee based upon income.

35. For a summary of the literature, see Garfinkel and McLanahan, *Single Mothers and Their Children*. See also Scott South, "Economic Conditions and the Divorce Rate: A Time Series Analysis of the Postwar United States," *Journal of Marriage and the Family,* 47:31-42 (1985); Andrew Cherlin, *Social and Economic Determinants of Marital Separation* (Berkeley: University of California Press, 1976); Wilson, *Truly Disadvantaged;* Moynihan, *Negro Family*.

36. Wilson, *Truly Disadvantaged.*

8

Puerto Ricans and the Underclass Debate

By MARTA TIENDA

ABSTRACT: This article uses data from the Current Population Surveys of 1975, 1980, and 1985 and the 1980 census of population to investigate why the economic status of Puerto Ricans has declined more than that of Mexicans and Cubans. The working hypothesis—that structural factors, namely, rapidly falling employment opportunities in jobs where Puerto Ricans traditionally have worked and the concentration of Puerto Ricans in areas experiencing severe economic dislocation, are largely responsible for their disproportionate impoverishment—finds considerable support. Results based on the Current Population Surveys show that Puerto Ricans are distinct from Mexicans and Cubans in that their labor market instability and complete withdrawal began earlier—in the mid- compared to the late 1970s—and was more extreme. Furthermore, the analysis of census data shows that the constraints on Puerto Ricans resulting from ethnic labor market divisions and high unemployment rates are stronger than those on Mexicans or Cubans, lending support to structural interpretations of the Puerto Ricans' economic distress.

Marta Tienda is professor of sociology at the University of Chicago and associate director of the Population Research Center. She is coauthor of The Hispanic Population of the United States *(1987) and coeditor of* Divided Opportunities: Poverty, Minorities and Social Policy *(1988) and* Hispanics in the U.S. Economy *(1985). Her current research interests include the work and welfare consequences of amnesty and the migration and employment patterns of Puerto Ricans.*

NOTE: This research was supported by grants from the Ford Foundation, the Office of the Assistant Secretary for Planning and Evaluation of the U.S. Department of Health and Human Services under a grant to the Institute for Research on Poverty at the University of Wisconsin, Madison, and the College of Agricultural and Life Sciences at the University of Wisconsin, Madison. Institutional support was provided by the Population Research Center of the National Opinion Research Center and the University of Chicago. The opinions expressed are those of the author and not of the sponsoring institutions.

DESPITE the appreciable drop in poverty since 1960, recent empirical work on the economic status of minorities has documented persisting and in some instances widening differentials in poverty and economic well-being according to race and national origin. Among Hispanics, between 1970 and 1985 Puerto Ricans experienced a sharp deterioration in economic well-being while Mexicans experienced modest, and Cubans substantial, improvement in economic status.[1]

A few indicators illustrate the extent to which economic disparities between the three major Hispanic populations have widened. Puerto Rican family income declined by 7.4 percent in real terms during the 1970s and by an additional 18.0 percent between 1979 and 1984. Mexican and Cuban real family incomes increased during the 1970s, then fell after 1980; but the decline for neither group approached the magnitude experienced by Puerto Ricans. Unlike that of Puerto Ricans, black real family income rose gradually during the 1970s, then fell 14.0 percent following the recession of the early 1980s.[2] While real family incomes of all population groups—minority and non-minority alike—fell between 1979 and 1984, the decline was steepest among minorities, Puerto Ricans in particular.

Equally disturbing are findings that family income concentration has increased for Puerto Ricans since 1970. The share of Puerto Rican families with income below one-quarter of the median income of whites rose from 11 percent in 1960 to 15 percent in 1970, 26 percent in 1980, and 33 percent in 1985.[3] A similar pattern was not discerned among Mexicans or Cubans, indicating that Puerto Ricans are diverging from other Hispanics. William Julius Wilson and others claim that black family incomes have become bifurcated, with increasing shares of families concentrated at the upper and lower tails of the income distribution.[4] So severe has the decline in Puerto Rican economic status been that this minority group has fared worse than blacks in the 1980s, a reversal of the situation prevailing during the 1960s. This generalization obtains whether based on national data or those for New York City, which houses the single largest concentration of Puerto Ricans.[5]

Although the reasons for the measured increases in racial and economic inequality are not well understood, there is a growing consensus that three interrelated sets of circumstances are involved: (1) uneven changes in family composition and labor market position according to race and national origin; (2) a heavier toll of cyclical downturns on the job prospects of minority workers; and (3) the persisting significance of race in allocating social position. By themselves, these factors do not explain why some minority groups, such as blacks and Puerto Ricans, have lost more economic ground than others, such as Cubans, Mexicans, or Native Americans, nor do they enable us to

1. Marta Tienda and Lief Jensen, "Poverty and Minorities: A Quarter Century Profile of Color and Socioeconomic Disadvantage," in *Divided Opportunities: Minorities, Poverty and Social Policy,* ed. Gary D. Sandefur and Marta Tienda (New York: Plenum Press, 1988) pp. 25-33.

2. Ibid., tab. 1, p. 27.

3. Ibid., tab. 2, p. 31.

4. William Julius Wilson, "The Ghetto Underclass and the Social Transformation of the Inner City" (Paper delivered at the Annual Meeting of the American Association for the Advancement of Science, Chicago, IL, 1987). See also Walter R. Allen and Reynolds Farley, "The Shifting Social and Economic Tides of Black America, 1950-1980," *Annual Review of Sociology,* 12:227-306 (1987).

5. Terry J. Rosenberg, *Poverty in New York City: 1980-1985* (New York: Community Service Society of New York, 1987).

predict the future course or magnitude of inequality.

Signs of economic distress among Puerto Ricans have fostered considerable speculation that Puerto Ricans have become part of the urban underclass, but the available evidence is more suggestive than conclusive. Answering this question in the affirmative requires, at a minimum, longitudinal data showing that extreme economic deprivation is both chronic and concentrated among a segment of the Puerto Rican population; that chronic deprivation is accompanied by labor market detachment; and that both conditions are sustained by social and spatial isolation from mainstream institutions and activities. Although inadequate for demonstrating the coincidence of these three conditions for Puerto Ricans, repeated cross-sectional census surveys can shed some light on the emerging debate about whether and to what extent the deteriorating economic status of Puerto Rican families is accompanied by one form of social dislocation, namely, labor market detachment.

One objective is to examine the labor market position of Puerto Rican men in comparison with that of Mexicans and Cubans. A second objective is to document the influence of structural factors, namely, ethnic labor market concentration and ethnic job queues, on Puerto Ricans' earnings. The working hypothesis guiding the analysis is that structural factors—to wit, rapidly falling employment opportunities in jobs where Puerto Ricans traditionally have worked, and the concentration of Puerto Ricans in areas experiencing severe economic dislocation—are major factors accounting for the impoverishment of this minority group.

The following section sets forth theoretical issues bearing on the significance of national origin in producing and main-taining labor market inequality. The next sections compare the labor market standing of Mexican, Puerto Rican, and Cuban men from 1970 to 1985, emphasizing the uniqueness of the Puerto Rican labor force withdrawal process both in timing and magnitude, and then assess the economic consequences of ethnic job queues and ethnic labor market concentration on earnings. The concluding section discusses these empirical findings in light of growing speculation that Puerto Ricans are becoming part of the urban underclass.

THEORETICAL CONSIDERATIONS

Evidence from cross-sectional data suggests that the declining economic status of Puerto Ricans can be traced both to poor economic performance and to the low stocks of human capital possessed by Puerto Rican workers. Although a substantial literature documents the importance of education for labor market success, the low educational achievement of Mexicans challenges the completeness of the human-capital explanations. Mexicans have not experienced declines in labor market standing and economic well-being comparable to those of Puerto Ricans, even though their educational levels are similar.

That a steep increase in poverty was not experienced by all Hispanic groups raises questions about the salience of structural factors in restricting these effects to Puerto Ricans. My case is that the weakened labor market position of Puerto Ricans and their consequent impoverishment have roots in their placement at the bottom of an ethnic hiring queue coupled with residential concentration in a region that experienced severe economic decline and industrial restructuring after 1970. Each of these ideas is elaborated in the following pages.

ETHNIC HIRING QUEUES

The significance of ethnicity for the labor market stratification of minority workers depends not only on local employment conditions but also on how individual ethnic traits circumscribe choices, how ethnic traits are evaluated in the marketplace, and how ethnic traits are used to organize the labor market. If national origin is used as a criterion to define and maintain job queues, then the economic costs and benefits of residential concentration will derive not only from opportunities to interact with members of like ethnicity but also from the role of national origin in channeling minority workers to particular categories of jobs.

The viability of ethnic hiring queues, however, is related to patterns of ethnic geographical concentration. Stanley Lieberson, who succinctly summarized the ecological foundations of racial or ethnic occupational differentiation, claimed that a discriminatory hiring queue results when employers activate their prejudices and preferentially hire workers on the basis of ethnic traits rather than market skills.[6] Two aspects of Lieberson's queuing premises have direct implications for the ensuing analyses. One is that the job configuration of groups will vary in accordance with their share of the labor force in a given labor market. Second, because of

the existence of ethnic hiring queues, shifts in unemployment will be highest for the group or groups at the bottom of the queue in the event of a wave of unemployment.[7] This interpretation appears to be consistent with the Puerto Rican experience after the mid-1970s.

Lieberson's argument has considerable appeal for explaining the growing economic inequality among Hispanic workers. For example, Mexicans have been preferred workers in agricultural jobs at least since the mid-1800s. While the incomes of agricultural workers are low compared with those in other low-skilled jobs, when evaluated against the alternative of unemployment or nonparticipation in the labor force, agricultural work is preferable because it at least ensures some earnings. Puerto Ricans, unlike Mexicans, never have been preferred laborers for specific jobs, with the possible exception of women in garment and textile industries. Unionization initially protected textile and garment workers, but the massive industrial restructuring in the Northeast,[8] which has resulted in the elimination of many unskilled and unionized jobs, has dimmed the employment prospects of all Puerto Ricans, including youths and mature men.

Viewed in this way, the declining economic status of Puerto Ricans may have resulted partly from the rapid decline in the types of jobs in which they were disproportionately concentrated and part-

6. See Stanley Lieberson, *A Piece of the Pie* (Berkeley: University of California Press, 1980). His ideas about the existence and operation of an ethnic job queue are derived from the following propositions: (1) that the occupational composition of a community is independent of the ethnic or racial composition of its population; (2) that groups differ in their objective qualifications for various occupational activities; (3) that group membership directly affects occupational opportunity, owing to employer preferences and tastes; (4) that occupations—jobs—differ in their desirability; and (5) that groups differ initially in their dispositions toward certain jobs.

7. Alternatively, during periods of labor shortage, groups at the bottom will experience broadened employment opportunities because the preferred groups will not fill all of the traditional employment opportunities. Under these circumstances, employment shifts could be most favorable for groups at the bottom of the queue. This is consistent with the experience of Puerto Ricans during the 1960s.

8. See George Borjas and Marta Tienda, eds., *Hispanics in the U.S. Economy* (Orlando, FL: Academic Press, 1985), esp. chaps. 10 and 11.

ly from a loss in relative earning power owing to low stocks of human capital in a market whose demand for labor increased in some sectors while it decreased in others.[9] That Cuban men did not have a similar experience, despite their disproportionate representation in two of the same labor markets as Puerto Ricans—in New York and New Jersey—suggests either that Cubans are ranked higher in an employment queue or that Cuban workers displaced by the employment-restructuring processes were more successful finding alternative employment by moving from New York and New Jersey to Miami.

LABOR MARKET CONCENTRATION

The burgeoning literature on structural aspects of labor market outcomes has identified both positive and negative effects of ethnic residential concentration on employment outcomes.[10] For present purposes it suffices to note that positive effects of minority labor market concentration are consistent with an overflow or power thesis: the former would derive from the spillover of minorities into higher-status jobs and/or the reorganization of labor markets along ethnic lines, while the latter would stem from greater political leverage of minority groups as a function of increasing group size. Negative effects would be consistent with the discrimination and subordination theses, whereby minorities are systematically excluded from jobs or relegated to the least desirable jobs. This process would be

accentuated by the demarcation of hiring queues along ethnic lines.

These ideas concerning how ethnic density and ethnic typing of jobs influence employment outcomes suggest two working hypotheses. First, I hypothesize that the unequal labor market experiences of Mexican, Puerto Rican, and Cuban men during the 1970s reflect their unequal placement in a hiring queue, with Cubans at the top of the Hispanic queue and Puerto Ricans at the bottom. Second, the disadvantaged labor market status of Puerto Ricans results partly from the unequal benefits of minority labor market concentration reaped by each group. These ideas will be empirically evaluated here, after a brief review of the extent of labor market detachment experienced by Puerto Ricans since 1970.

LABOR MARKET DETACHMENT IN
COMPARATIVE PERSPECTIVE

Failure to participate in the labor market, along with social isolation and persisting deprivation, is a defining feature of the urban underclass. Although national data on chronicity of poverty and labor force nonparticipation do not exist for Puerto Ricans, annual Current Population Survey data permit an initial foray into questions of labor market detachment and withdrawal. For this purpose, Hispanic men were classified into three categories based on their employment status at the time of, and five years prior to, the 1975, 1980, and 1985 Current Population Surveys:[11] the stable active category consists of persons, including

9. Some indirect evidence on this point is afforded by comparisons of Puerto Rican unemployment rates in industries where they historically have been concentrated. These tabulations are available from the author.

10. Marta Tienda and Ding-Tzann Lii, "Minority Concentration and Earnings Inequality: Blacks, Hispanics and Asians Compared," *American Journal of Sociology,* 2 July 1987, pp. 141, 165.

11. The uniform series of March Current Population Survey files was created under the direction of Robert D. Mare, of the University of Wisconsin, and Christopher Winship, of Northwestern University, with financial support from the National Science Foundation through grant SOC-7912648, "Social and Demographic Sources of Change in the Youth Labor Force." Current Population Survey

the unemployed, who were in the labor force at both points in time;[12] persons who were in the labor force at the beginning of the five-year period but not at the end, or vice versa, are classified in the unstable active category; the stable inactive category includes persons who were out of the labor force, and not looking for work, at both the beginning and the end of the period.[13]

While less than ideal for evaluating the hypothesis of labor market detachment because these cross-sectional data do not represent the continuous employment history of the same individuals over the entire time span, results summarized in Table 1—first row for each panel—clearly show a steeper rise in labor market instability and incomplete withdrawal from the work force among Puerto Ricans. Whereas the category of stable inactive was virtually nonexistent prior to the onset of economic decline in the mid-1970s, the share of unstable employment rose between 1970 and 1985, a

---

data for 1970 were not analyzed, owing to space constraints.

12. Including the unemployed in the category of stable active overstates the share of workers with some income. For the present purposes, however, this classification procedure is reasonable because the goal is to characterize changes in labor market activity. For individuals to be classified as in the labor force, they had to be looking for work, itself an indicator of commitment to work or attachment. Inactivity, that is, classification as out of the labor force, indicates that individuals were neither actively employed nor searching for work.

13. The unstable active employment category largely reflects withdrawal from the market over the five-year period, because only a trivial share of workers moved from inactive to active status over the interval. My decision to pool the two unstable active categories was based on the rule of parsimony. Also, it bears emphasizing that the cross-sectional nature of the data makes it impossible to ascertain whether additional employment-status changes occurred during the interval for which we have observed beginning and ending states.

period characterized by slow growth and two major recessions.

The share of men experiencing unstable employment hovered around 8 to 9 percent among Mexicans and 4 to 7 percent among Cubans. For Puerto Ricans it was not only considerably higher than that for either Mexicans or Cubans throughout the period but also rose more steeply between the 1975-80 and the 1980-85 intervals, from 13 to 19 percentage points. An increase in unstable employment experiences is significant because it appears to be a precursor to complete withdrawal. By 1985, the share of chronic detachment among Puerto Ricans had reached nearly 6 percent, compared to 1 percent for Mexicans and 3 percent for Cubans.

The notable rise in Cuban labor market instability and withdrawal during the 1980-85 interval partly reflects the presence of a large segment of low-skilled immigrants whose labor market integration process was more difficult than that of earlier Cuban immigrants.[14] A similar period-immigration-effect cannot be claimed for Puerto Ricans, yet among them labor market withdrawal was even more pronounced. Moreover, the lower levels of market withdrawal and detachment among Mexicans, who also have become increasingly diversified by a high influx of immigrants since 1970, challenge any simplistic explanations that international migration or, in the case of Puerto Ricans, circular migration—between island and mainland—was largely responsible for the observed instability and withdrawal.

Table 1 also provides information about social and economic characteristics

14. Alejandro Portes, Alex Stepick, and Cynthia Truelove, "Three Years Later: The Adaptation Process of 1980 (Mariel) Cuban and Haitian Refugees in South Florida," *Population Research and Policy Review,* 5:83-94 (1986).

TABLE 1

SELECTED CHARACTERISTICS OF ADULT HISPANIC MEN AGED 25-64 BY LABOR FORCE EXPERIENCE (Means or percentages)

Period and Work Experience Category*

	1970-75			1975-80			1980-85		
	Stable active	Unstable active	Stable inactive	Stable active	Unstable active	Stable inactive	Stable active	Unstable active	Stable inactive
Mexicans									
Category total (percentage)	91.0%	9.1%	0.0%	91.5%	7.8%	0.8%	89.8%	9.0%	1.1%
Education (years)	8.5	7.4	NA	9.3	8.6	7.1	9.5	7.6	8.2
(s.d.)†	(4.5)	(4.1)	—	(4.5)	(4.7)	(4.9)	(4.3)	(4.6)	(3.4)
Family income (1974 dollars)	$8,015	$5,935	—	$8,890	$5,601	$4,849	$8,031	$5,579	$4,484
(s.d.)†	(4,947)	(4,411)	—	(5,602)	(5,188)	(3,266)	(5,650)	(4,522)	(3,438)
Poverty rate (percentage)	15.5%	27.5%	—	9.9%	38.3%	34.5%	17.7%	39.5%	44.1%
[N]‡	[652]	[67]	[0]	[1773]	[157]	[18]	[1814]	[176]	[24]
Puerto Ricans									
Category total (percentage)	86.8%	13.2%	0.0%	84.3%	13.4%	2.2%	74.8%	19.3%	5.9%
Education (years)	9.2	5.3	NA	10.1	7.5	5.1	10.8	6.9	8.0
(s.d.)†	(3.6)	(3.2)	—	(3.7)	(3.8)	(5.5)	(3.5)	(4.4)	(4.3)
Family income (1979 dollars)	$7,752	$4,750	—	$8,453	$4,343	$4,425	$7,908	$3,956	$4,293
(s.d.)†	(4,287)	(3,721)	—	(5,280)	(5,951)	(2,360)	(5,107)	(3,574)	(4,715)

128

Poverty rate (percentage)	11.6%	49.4%	—	11.1%	65.1%	34.1%	12.2%	49.2%	46.7%
[N]‡	[152]	[24]	[0]	[287]	[49]	[9]	[320]	[69]	[22]
Cubans									
Category total (percentage)	95.8%	4.2%	0.0%	95.7%	4.3%	0.0%	90.0%	6.8%	3.2%
Education (years)	11.1	8.2	NA	11.2	10.5	—	11.3	8.8	10.9
(s.d.)†	(4.0)	(3.7)	—	(3.6)	(4.6)	—	(3.9)	(4.0)	(3.9)
Family income (1984 dollars)	$9,565	$4,280	—	$10,199	$8,283	—	$10,499	$3,656	$8,152
(s.d.)†	(5,427)	(2,581)	—	(5,963)	(5,553)	—	(7,829)	(3,383)	(4,732)
Poverty rate (percentage)	5.5%	22.3%	—	6.4%	8.3%	—	5.3%	51.2%	0.0%
[N]‡	[114]	[5]	[0]	[199]	[9]	[0]	[227]	[14]	[7]

SOURCE: Current Population Survey, standardized files, 1975, 1980, and 1985. See note 11.

NOTE: Unless otherwise indicated, the figures in this table are weighted to approximate population parameters.

*Stable active: in labor force at beginning and end of interval; unstable active: changed labor force status during interval; stable inactive: out of labor force at beginning and end of interval.

†Standard deviation.

‡Unweighted sample size.

129

of the men according to employment-experience categories. Although the sample characteristics are weighted to approximate those of the total population, the small sample sizes warrant cautious comparisons between some categories, particularly for Cubans. Nevertheless, the contrasts between Mexicans and Puerto Ricans are striking and instructive.

That labor market position is directly associated with economic well-being is clearly apparent in the poverty and income data, which show substantially higher poverty risks for men whose labor market experience was characterized by instability or inactivity. Of course, stable employment does not always preclude poverty, because a share of the poor are full-time, year-round workers whose poverty status derives from low wages, but the incidence of poverty for the stable active experience category is considerably less than for workers in the other two categories.[15]

While real family incomes declined for most groups between 1980 and 1985, they did so differentially according to employment category and national origin. Cuban men illustrate one pattern: essentially, stably employed men did not experience a decrease in real family incomes throughout the period, although the rate of growth slowed during the early 1980s, from roughly 6.6 percent for the 1975-80 period to 2.9 percent for the 1980-85 interval.

In sharp contrast to the Cuban experience, family incomes of Mexicans and Puerto Ricans who were stably employed during the 1975-80 period rose roughly 11 and 9 percent in real terms, while the family incomes of men unstably employed—unstable active—fell by 5.6 percent and 8.6 percent, respectively. During

15. Poverty among those in the stable active category results in part from unemployment and low-wage experiences.

the 1980-85 interval, among Mexicans real incomes of those stably employed fell 9.7 percent, incomes of the unstably employed were virtually constant, and those of chronically inactive men dropped substantially, by 7.5 percent. Puerto Ricans fared somewhat worse in the 1980s: family incomes fell 6.4 percent among men stably employed, 9.0 percent among those unstably employed, and 3.0 percent among those who were out of the labor force continuously. Thus the declining economic status of Puerto Ricans appears to be rooted in two factors: the rising shares of prime-age men with unstable employment and chronic inactivity, and sharper declines in the incomes of those with unstable labor market experiences. The latter may contribute to the withdrawal process, as chronically low earnings and unstable work lead to total discouragement and alienation from the market.

Arguments about the importance of education for labor market success also find some support in the tabulations reported in Table 1. For all groups, labor force withdrawal and detachment were associated with lower stocks of education. The average educational attainment of Mexican and Puerto Rican men was roughly similar at the beginning of the period, 8.4 and 8.6 years, respectively, but over time, as the average schooling stocks for these groups rose, differentials within experience categories increased, favoring Puerto Ricans over Mexicans among those stably employed, and Mexicans over Puerto Ricans among those unstably employed or chronically out of the labor force. If human capital were the major determinant of labor market withdrawal and detachment, then the shares of Mexicans with unstable and inactive work trajectories would be greater than those of similarly classified Puerto Ri-

cans. In fact, just the opposite occurred. This justifies a search for structural explanations, which is the topic of the following section.

JOB QUEUES AND DECLINING LABOR MARKET OPPORTUNITIES

The theoretical and substantive issues raised earlier focus on how residence in ethnic labor markets—that is, whether individual workers reside in labor markets with high levels of ethnic concentration[16]—and ethnic job segmentation—whether jobs were ethnic typed, Anglo typed, or not ethnically differentiated[17]—operate to stratify the annual earnings of Hispanic-origin men. The data used for this part of the analysis are from the 5 percent sample of the Public Use Microdata Samples of the 1980 census.[18]

My arguments about the influence of ethnic concentration and ethnic segmentation of jobs in shaping the economic opportunities and outcomes for Hispanic workers integrate two structural attributes of labor markets—the ethnic segmentation of jobs and the ethnic composition of markets—and assess their influence on logged annual earnings. I evaluate these premises by regressing the log of annual earnings of Mexicans, Puerto Ricans, and Cubans on measures of ethnic labor market concentration and incumbency in an ethnic job queue.

Table 2 reports descriptive statistics for samples of Mexican, Puerto Rican, and Cuban men who worked during the year prior to the 1980 census. The rank ordering of the groups according to average annual earnings shows Cubans well above Mexicans—23 percent higher—and Puerto Ricans—30 percent higher—while a difference of less than 6 percent separates the latter two groups. Equally striking are the educational gaps according to national origin. Beyond the average schooling differentials reported in Table 1, these data show appreciable discrepancies in the credentials held by Hispanic men. At one extreme, roughly two-thirds of Mexican and Puerto Rican adult men had completed less than 12 years of formal schooling; at the other extreme, about 4 percent had attended college, in contrast with 18 percent of Cuban men. Mexicans and Puerto Ricans thus appear quite similar in terms of human-capital characteristics as well as hours and weeks of labor supply. Only in English proficiency do Cubans appear to

16. The distinction between high- and low-ethnic-density labor markets is derived from an analysis of both the ethnic composition of labor markets and the distribution of each ethnic group among them. Briefly, a labor market area was defined as one of high ethnic density for a given reference group if the group was overrepresented relative to its share of the total population, based on standardized, or z, scores.

17. The statistical procedures we used are detailed in Marta Tienda and Franklin D. Wilson, "Ethnicity, Migration and Labor Force Activity" (Paper delivered at the National Bureau of Economic Research Workshop on Migration, Trade and Labor, Cambridge, MA, 11-12 Sept. 1987). A log-linear analysis was used to determine whether each ethnic group was overrepresented (ethnic-typed), underrepresented (Anglo-typed), or approximately equally represented (nontyped), after adjustments for group differences in education and age composition.

18. The sample includes approximately half of the men aged 25-64 who self-reported their race or national origin as Mexican, Puerto Rican, or Cuban. Restricting the lower end of the age distribution to 25 rather than 16 ensured that most respondents had completed school at the time of the

census, hence school enrollment would not limit labor force participation. Additional restrictions on the sample excluded individuals who met the following conditions: (1) never worked, or were out of the labor force continuously during the five years prior to the census; (2) were enrolled in school or in the military in either 1975 or 1980; or (3) resided outside the United States in 1975.

TABLE 2
DEMOGRAPHIC AND LABOR MARKET CHARACTERISTICS
OF HISPANIC MEN AGED 25-64, 1980

	Mexicans	Puerto Ricans	Cubans
Dependent variable			
Annual earnings (logged)	9.23	9.18	9.43
(s.d.)	(.89)	(.87)	(.82)
Annual mean earnings	$13,342	$12,587	$16,368
	(9,414)	(8,647)	(13,069)
Individual characteristics			
Education (percentage)			
Did not complete high school	62.3%	59.9%	41.2%
High school graduate	33.3%	36.1%	40.9%
Some college	4.4%	4.0%	17.9%
Age (years)	39.3	39.5	46.1
(s.d.)	(10.6)	(10.1)	(10.0)
Good English (percentage)	78.0%	82.7%	63.6%
Foreign born (percentage)	36.3%	77.3%	93.3%
Work disabled (percentage)	5.0%	5.8%	3.5%
Weeks worked	46.2	46.7	48.1
(s.d.)	(11.0)	(10.8)	(9.2)
Average hours worked weekly	41.7	40.0	42.6
(s.d.)	(10.2)	(10.0)	(11.1)
Household head (percentage)	85.2%	79.6%	89.6%
Married (percentage)	81.3%	71.7%	81.8%
Market characteristics			
Ethnic job queue (percentage)			
Ethnic typed	13.0%	18.0%	13.0%
Anglo typed	4.3%	6.6%	14.4%
Nontyped	82.7%	75.4%	72.6%
Concentrated area (percentage)	85.9%	83.2%	84.4%
Area wage rate	$7.21	$7.88	$7.37
	(0.97)	(0.72)	(0.61)
Area unemployment rate	6.19	6.69	5.66
	(1.98)	(1.23)	(1.30)
[N]	[5,726]	[5,908]	[3,895]

SOURCE: Public Use Microdata Samples, A-File, 1980.
NOTE: The sample includes approximately half of the men aged 25–64 who self-reported their race or national origin as Mexican, Puerto Rican, or Cuban. Restricting the lower end of the age distribution to 25 rather than 16 ensured that most respondents had completed school at the time of the census, hence school enrollment would not limit labor force participation. Additional restrictions on the sample excluded individuals who met the following conditions: (1) never worked, or were out of the labor force continuously during the five years prior to the census; (2) were enrolled in school or in the military in either 1975 or 1980; or (3) resided outside the United States in 1975. In this table, standard deviations appear in parentheses; they are descriptive statistics based on a sample with nonzero earnings in 1979.

bc disadvantaged relative to Mexicans and Puerto Ricans, reflecting the shorter immigration history of the Cuban population. The national-origin groups also differ in terms of their family status: among men aged 25-65, Puerto Ricans were less likely to be married and to be household heads than either Mexicans or Cubans.

My argument about the influence of structural factors in explaining the weakened labor market position of Puerto Ricans finds some support in the summary market characteristics. Puerto Ricans' residential configuration afforded them the highest unemployment rates and the highest average wage rates. Cubans, on the other hand, resided in labor markets with relatively lower unemployment—a difference of nearly one percentage point, on average, compared to Puerto Ricans—while the unemployment rates where Mexicans resided were between the Puerto Rican and Cuban extremes.

Space restrictions preclude a full discussion of the implications of market conditions for the labor supply decisions of Hispanic men. Suffice it to note that, in a separate analysis, area unemployment rates exerted a significant negative effect, and average area wage rates a significant positive effect, on the labor force decisions of Puerto Ricans, while for Cubans and Mexicans these effects were essentially zero.[19] This appears to indicate that the labor market behavior of Puerto Ricans is more sensitive to labor market conditions than that of either Cubans or Mexicans, but why this is so is less obvious. Moreover, among those individuals who do secure employment, uneven placement in the job queue further

weakens their labor market position, leaving them vulnerable to economic cycles and ethnic prejudices.

Support for this proposition is found in Table 2, which shows that Puerto Ricans were more likely to work in ethnic-typed jobs than either Mexicans or Cubans, and in Table 3, which shows that Puerto Rican incumbents of ethnic-typed jobs were penalized 17 percent relative to their statistically equivalent counterparts engaged in nontyped jobs. For Mexicans, the earnings penalty for incumbency in ethnic-typed jobs was somewhat lower, roughly 12 percent, while incumbency in Anglo-typed jobs sustained economic rewards 19 percent above those received by incumbents of nontyped jobs. These effects are net of individual productivity characteristics—for example, education, English proficiency, disability status, age, and the conditional probability of being in the wage sample. Puerto Ricans, however, did not reap additional earnings bonuses from incumbency in Anglo-typed jobs.

Equally interesting are the earnings consequences of labor market conditions. Whereas both Mexicans and Cubans gained significant financial rewards from residence in high-wage areas—13 percent and 3 percent, respectively—no such benefit accrued to Puerto Ricans. Moreover, residence in labor markets with high concentrations of the respective nationality groups translated into an economic liability for each group, but less for Puerto Ricans than for either Mexicans or Cubans. This suggests that residential concentration does not increase the ability of these groups to protect ethnic workers via political leverage derived from group size, nor does group concentration result in massive spillover into high-status and well-paying jobs. That Mexicans and

19. These results were based on a probit regression of 1980 labor force participation and are available from the author.

TABLE 3
EFFECTS OF ETHNIC JOB QUEUES ON EARNINGS OF
HISPANIC MEN AGED 25-64, 1980 (Metric coefficients)

	Mexicans	Puerto Ricans	Cubans
Ethnic job queue			
Ethnic typed	−.116*	−.170*	−.257*
	(.029)	(.025)	(.033)
Anglo typed	.193*	.067	.112*
	(.048)	(.039)	(.031)
Labor market			
Area wage	.126*	.016	.035*
	(.010)	(.014)	(.018)
Concentrated area	−.172*	−.079*	−.180*
	(.029)	(.027)	(.031)
Education			
High school graduate	−.253*	−.068	−.238*
	(.050)	(.064)	(.037)
Did not complete high school	−.412*	−.183*	−.283*
	(.052)	(.070)	(.045)
Age	.042*	.032*	.025*
	(.008)	(.008)	(.010)
Age^2	−.0004*	−.0003*	−.0002
	(.0001)	(.0001)	(.0001)
Good English	.185*	.126*	.206*
	(.027)	(.026)	(.026)
Foreign born	−.029	−.080*	−.070*
	(.024)	(.024)	(.044)
Work disabled	−.135*	−.192*	−.200*
	(.045)	(.042)	(.060)
Lambda[a]	.120*	.096*	.083*
	(.015)	(.014)	(.016)
Constant	5.552	6.330	6.708
R^2	.334	.300	.336
[N]	[5,726]	[5,908]	[3,895]

SOURCE: Public Use Microdata Samples, A-File, 1980.
NOTE: Effects of ethnic job queues are adjusted for the effects of weeks worked and usual hours worked. Standard errors are in parentheses. The sample includes approximately half of the men aged 25-64 who self-reported their race or national origin as Mexican, Puerto Rican, or Cuban. Restricting the lower end of the age distribution to 25 rather than 16 ensured that most respondents had completed school at the time of the census, hence school enrollment would not limit labor force participation. Additional restrictions on the sample excluded individuals who met the following conditions: (1) never worked, or were out of the labor force continuously during the five years prior to the census; (2) were enrolled in school or in the military in either 1975 or 1980; or (3) resided outside the United States in 1975.
[a]Inverse of Mills ratio to correct for self-selection into the wage sample.
*Significant at the 95 percent level.

Cubans were more residentially concentrated than Puerto Ricans in 1980 partly explains why the effects of concentration were more pronounced for them, but it is also conceivable that discrimination has intensified because of the loss of low-skilled jobs in New York City coupled with the growing presence of Dominican and Colombian immigrants willing to work in jobs that offer low wages and poor working conditions.[20]

Substantively, the findings in Table 3 suggest that the process of channeling Puerto Ricans into so-called Puerto Rican jobs, coupled with the absence of earnings bonuses for securing nontyped jobs, reinforces the low earnings of Puerto Ricans who do manage to secure employment. But, as the analyses in Table 1 show, since 1975 increasing shares of adult Puerto Rican men have not secured jobs, and residence in high-concentration areas has not improved the chances of employment for Hispanics, irrespective of national origin.

DISCUSSION

During the 1960s and 1970s it was commonplace to attribute the existence of racial and economic inequality to discrimination and to direct policy initiatives aiming toward equal employment opportunity and affirmative action. The experience of the 1980s, however, has reaffirmed that a healthy economy is a necessary, albeit insufficient, condition for reducing inequality. The economic experiences of Puerto Ricans provide stark testimony concerning the deleterious consequence of economic decline.

Although discrimination may still be a major factor accounting for the disadvantaged economic status of Puerto

20. See Borjas and Tienda, eds., *Hispanics in the U.S. Economy*, chaps. 10 and 11.

Ricans, it does not address the issue of why the economic status of Cubans and especially Mexicans has not followed suit. While not denying the importance of prejudice in maintaining socioeconomic inequality along racial and ethnic lines, a structural interpretation is consistent with the uneven regional effects of economic growth and decline that occurred during the late 1970s and early 1980s. But a simple Rustbelt-Sunbelt dichotomy set against the backdrop of major recessions also is inadequate to explain the impoverishment of Puerto Ricans; their increasing labor market instability and withdrawal (Table 1) can only partly be understood in these terms.

Additional and equally important insights into the declining economic status of Puerto Ricans obtain from the results showing that the existence of ethnic labor market divisions also places constraints on the earnings frontiers of Hispanic workers, and Puerto Ricans in particular. This is evident in results (Table 3) showing strong negative penalties for incumbency in Puerto Rican jobs, and no additional compensation or bonus for the small share of Puerto Ricans who manage to secure Anglo-typed jobs. Yet these results also raise many questions about the economic significance of ethnic job queues, which appear to operate differently for Mexicans and Cubans. While both groups benefit financially from incumbency in Anglo-typed jobs, the share of each group able to secure these better-paying jobs differs (Table 2). Moreover, both groups are penalized for incumbency in ethnic-typed jobs, Cubans more so than Mexicans.

On balance, the empirical results presented are more suggestive than conclusive as to the importance of structural factors in explaining the declining economic status of Puerto Ricans. While the evidence

of labor force withdrawal has aroused speculation about the emergence of an underclass among Hispanics, largely concentrated among Puerto Ricans, the absence of longitudinal data prevents examination of the duration of labor market detachment.

My results place the Puerto Rican experience in a comparative perspective and emphasize the promise of a structural interpretation of labor force withdrawal. While evidence of growing labor market instability and withdrawal is consistent with one of the premises of the persisting poverty syndrome, further scrutiny of the concentration of labor market withdrawal and social isolation is needed before concluding that Puerto Ricans have become part of the urban underclass. Priority issues worth investigating include establishing whether increased labor market competition from immigrants—Dominicans and Colombians in particular—has exacerbated the economic problems of Puerto Ricans and the extent to which industrial restructuring has been responsible for the labor market withdrawal of Puerto Rican men. Beyond these structurally focused lines of inquiry, additional study of labor market trajectories is essential to determine whether the patterns of nonparticipation based on repeated cross sections represent the accumulation of chronic spells and permanent withdrawal among a segment of the total population, or whether the observed increase in nonparticipation among Puerto Ricans reflects the increasing prevalence of short spells of nonparticipation among the total population. Until these questions are satisfactorily answered, discussions about the development of a Puerto Rican urban underclass will be largely speculative.

9

Immigration and the Underclass

By ROBERT D. REISCHAUER

ABSTRACT: The size and nature of recent immigration to the United States have raised the possibility that immigrants have diminished the labor market opportunities of low-skilled, native minority workers and, thereby, might have contributed to the emergence of the urban underclass. To the extent that immigrants and native workers are substitute factors of production, immigrants may reduce the wage rates of native labor, increase their unemployment, lower their labor force participation, undermine working conditions, and reduce rates of internal mobility. While casual empiricism would seem to support the notion that immigrants have depressed the opportunities of low-skilled native workers, careful and sophisticated analyses by a number of social scientists provide little evidence that immigrants have had any significant negative impacts on the employment situation of black Americans. Thus competition from unskilled immigrants should not be included on the list of factors that have facilitated the growth of the underclass.

Robert D. Reischauer is a senior fellow in the Economic Studies Program of the Brookings Institution, where he is completing a book on America's underclass. He served as senior vice-president of the Urban Institute from 1981 to 1986 and before that was the deputy director of the Congressional Budget Office. Reischauer has written extensively on domestic policy issues, fiscal federalism, and the federal budget. He received a Ph.D. in economics and an M.I.A. in international affairs from Columbia University.

NOTE: The views expressed in this article are those of the author and should not be attributed to the Brookings Institution, its trustees, or its funders.

IN recent years, a large number of immigrants, both documented and undocumented, have entered the United States. Some observers have feared that this wave of immigration might have contributed to the emergence of the urban underclass by eroding the labor market prospects of low-skilled native minorities. The size and nature of the recent immigration make such concerns plausible. Over the decade 1975-84, some 5.1 million aliens entered the country legally and an estimated 1 to 3 million persons entered in an undocumented status.[1] In raw numbers, this inflow came close to equaling the nation's largest immigration wave, which occurred during the first decade of the twentieth century. Relative to the size of the nation's population, however, the recent inflow is substantially below that of the first three decades of this century.

The recent flow of immigrants has been notable not only for its magnitude but also for its characteristics. After the enactment of the National Immigration Act of 1965, an increasing fraction of the new arrivals were drawn from Asia, Latin America, and other less developed areas. Compared to previous immigrant waves, fewer of these newcomers came from Europe and Canada, more were nonwhite, and more had relatively low skill and educational levels.[2] For example, while 68 percent of legal immigrants

came from Europe, Canada, Australia, and New Zealand during the 1951-60 period, less than 15 percent of the immigrants arriving during the 1980s came from these areas.

The impetus behind immigration has also changed somewhat over time. As travel costs have fallen, desperate economic conditions, population pressures, and civil strife have continued to push many from their countries of birth. But the American economy has not been very vibrant. Rising unemployment and slow wage growth have characterized the economy during this period of increasing immigration.

The size and characteristics of these recent immigrant flows, and their occurrence during a period of high unemployment, have rekindled fears that immigration may be hurting the labor market prospects of native labor, in particular low-skilled, minority workers. This possibility has generated particular concern because certain minority groups, most notably black males with few skills, have experienced significant labor market problems during the past decade and a half. Black unemployment rates have risen dramatically, the incomes of less educated blacks have not kept pace with those of whites, and black male labor force participation rates have fallen. Specifically, the unemployment rate for black males aged 25 to 34 rose from 8.5 percent in 1974 to 13.8 percent in 1985 while the rates for white males of the same age rose from 3.6 percent to only 5.7 percent. The incomes of less educated black males rose at a rate that was under two-thirds of that of whites with similar levels of educational attainment. Finally, the fraction of the black males aged 25 to 34 participating in

1. For estimates of the number of legal immigrants, see U.S. Department of Justice, Immigration and Naturalization Service, *Statistical Yearbook;* idem, press releases. For estimates of the number of illegal entrants, see *Economic Report of the President,* Feb. 1986, pp. 216-19; Jeffery S. Passel, "Estimating the Number of Undocumented Aliens," *Monthly Labor Review,* 109(9):33 (Sept. 1986).

2. The occupational-preference visas provided by the 1965 act tended to increase the skill and educational levels of immigrants relative to those of the native population while the kinship preferences and the growth of undocumented immigration had the opposite effect. See Barry R. Chiswick, "Is the

New Immigration Less Skilled than the Old?" *Journal of Labor Economics,* 4(2):169-92(1986).

the labor force fell from 92.8 percent to 88.8 percent over the period from 1974 to 1985.[3]

This article explores the possibility that the size and character of recent immigration have hurt the labor market prospects for low-skilled minorities and thereby might have contributed to the emergence of the urban underclass. The next section of the article summarizes the theoretical framework used by labor economists to analyze the impact of immigration on the native labor force. This is followed by a description of the specific avenues through which the arrival of immigrants might worsen the labor market prospects of the native workers with whom they compete. The next section reviews the circumstantial evidence of these effects, evidence that has clearly influenced public impressions. This is supplemented with a summary of the findings of some recent social science research that examines these issues. The concluding section discusses several reasons why there appears to be so little evidence that immigration has played any appreciable role in the deterioration of minority job prospects and the growth of the urban underclass.

THE IMPACT OF IMMIGRATION: THE THEORY

Immigration both increases the supply of labor and raises the overall level of

3. The unemployment and labor force participation rates are taken from U.S. Department of Labor, Bureau of Labor Statistics, *Handbook of Labor Statistics,* Bulletin 2217 (Washington, DC: Government Printing Office, June 1985), tab. 5, pp. 20-21, and tab. 27, pp. 71-72. The income figures are derived from data contained in U.S. Department of Commerce, Bureau of the Census, *Money Income in 1974 of Families and Persons in the United States,* series P-60, no. 101, Jan. 1976, tab. 58; idem, *Current Population Reports,* series P-60, no. 156, *Money Income of Households, Families and Persons in the U.S.: 1985* (Washington, DC: Government Printing Office, 1987), tab. 35, p. 34.

economic activity as the immigrants who work and those who do not increase the demand for the goods and services needed for daily existence. The popular discussion has focused solely on the increase in the supply of labor and has assumed that this increase must lower the wages of native workers. In other words, it has been assumed that immigrant labor and native workers are what economists refer to as substitute factors of production.

While an increase in the labor supply caused by immigration should act to reduce the labor market prospects for some groups of native workers, this may not be the case for all or even most types of native labor. In other words, some groups of native labor may be complements to immigrant labor and may find their labor market prospects improved and their wages bid up as a result of increased immigration. Whether immigrant workers are a complement or a substitute for a certain category of native workers will depend very much on the characteristics of the immigrants, the relative numbers and characteristics of the native workers living in the labor markets in which the immigrants settle, and the strength of those local labor markets.

Under certain circumstances, immigrants could even prove to be a complementary factor of production for all categories of native workers. This would be the case if the immigrants filled an empty niche in the labor force; in other words, if they were willing to do the jobs that no native worker would accept at the prevailing wage. Such a situation could lead to an increase in the demand for all types of native labor. For example, a certain type of manufacturing might be unprofitable in the United States because no native workers are willing to do the most unpleasant tasks required by the production process even for the highest

wage that the manufacturer could pay and still compete effectively with imports. When immigrants who are willing to do this work at a low wage arrive, an industry is created. This then increases the demand for native workers who fill the other jobs in the new industry and in the industries that supply goods and services to the new industry. The apparel and furniture industries in Los Angeles conform to this pattern as does much of the fruit and vegetable farming in the West and Southwest.

A similar situation could occur if the positions of native workers, whom one might expect to be competitive with the immigrants, were somehow protected. For example, it has been suggested that Mexican immigration into southern California might have raised incomes for black workers because a significant portion of California's blacks are employed by the public sector and immigration has driven up the demand for public services. Because citizenship or legal entry is a prerequisite for public-sector employment, many of the immigrants were precluded from competing with the blacks for these government jobs.

The more normal situation would be one in which the immigrants compete with some segments of the native labor force and complement other segments. Those for whom they act as substitutes would find their labor market prospects damaged, while those for whom they are complements would be helped. The characteristics of the immigrants, both actual and those perceived by employers, would be important in determining which specific groups of native workers were helped and which were hurt.[4]

The price reductions and increases in economic activity caused by immigration should act to offset some of the detrimental labor market effects of an increased supply of a particular type of labor. Under some extreme circumstances, the increase in economic activity could completely offset any detrimental labor market impacts and all groups of native workers could find themselves as well or better off after the immigration. For example, an influx of wealthy political refugees—Iranians, for instance—few of whom intended to work, or an increase in the number of immigrants who were the retired relatives of natives could produce this result.

AVENUES OF IMPACT

Most of the public discussion of the impact of immigration on labor markets has focused on wage rates, but wages are only one of five possible avenues through which the impact of immigration might be felt. Unemployment represents a second avenue. Institutional rigidities could make wages relatively inflexible. The minimum wage and collective-bargaining agreements are two such rigidities, but there are others. For example, many large national companies have uniform wage policies across geographic areas, some of which are affected by immigrants and others of which are not. Such rigidities would preclude the full expression of the impact of immigration on wages and instead may lead to increased unemployment among those groups who must compete with recent immigrants. To the extent that immigrants are viewed as better, less troublesome, or harder workers, they would be preferred at any fixed wage over native labor. If this is the case,

---

4. There is no reason why the negative impact of immigration need be confined to the unskilled portion of the labor force. For example, at the top end of the skill spectrum, a case can be made that the influx of foreign medical professionals has reduced the earnings of native doctors.

native labor may suffer more unemployment because of immigration but little noticeable reduction in the wage rates of those who remained employed.

A third avenue through which the impact of increased immigration might be felt is the labor force participation of competing workers. In recent years, the labor force participation rate for black youths has fallen significantly. Most analyses indicate that many of the young persons who are out of the labor force do want to work. At first glance, their reservation wages do not seem to be unreasonably high; in fact, they are slightly below those for white youths.[5] These reservation wages may, however, be considerably above those of competing immigrant workers. The net result may be that competition from recent immigrants has increased the fraction of native youths who have dropped out of the labor market. Those remaining in the labor force may be disproportionately in protected jobs, such as the government sector, or in positions that require a strong communications ability. In other words, they may be protected or complementary factors of production.

A fourth avenue through which immigration could affect the prospects of competing groups of native labor is internal migration. U.S. history is replete with examples of vast internal flows of workers seeking better opportunities. The movements west during the Gold Rush, the flight of the Okies from the Dust Bowl in the 1930s, the migration from rural areas to the industrializing cities that took place during the world wars, and the post-World War II exodus of

blacks from the South to the cities of the North and Midwest are just some examples. One possible effect of the recent influx of immigrants may have been to slow down the pace of internal migration. Thus the major impact of the flow of immigrants into such expanding metropolitan areas as San Diego, Phoenix, Los Angeles, and Miami may not be found among the unskilled native work forces of those cities but rather in St. Louis, Gary, Newark, and Detroit, where potential migrants to these more vibrant labor markets might now be trapped because they cannot compete successfully for the available jobs in the boom areas.

Finally, the impact of immigration may manifest itself not in wages, employment, migration, or labor force participation but rather in the working conditions and fringe benefits of the jobs taken by immigrants. If significant numbers of blacks also hold these jobs, the effects of immigration on black workers may be felt through a relative reduction in the generosity of the health insurance, vacations, pensions, and workplace safety offered by these jobs.

To summarize, there are a number of different channels through which immigration might affect the labor market prospects for native workers, and it is unlikely that the impact of immigration would be expressed through just one or two of these. The most probable situation would be for all to be active to some degree.

THE CASUAL AND CIRCUMSTANTIAL EVIDENCE

The public has long been fearful that immigration has a harmful effect on native workers. Periodically, this fear has erupted into political movements to restrain immigration. The nation's first restrictions on immigration—the Chinese

5. Harry J. Holzer, "Black Youth Nonemployment: Duration and Job Search," in *The Black Youth Employment Crisis,* ed. Richard B. Freeman and Harry J. Holzer (Chicago: University of Chicago Press, 1986), pp. 23-70.

Exclusion Act of 1882 and the 1907 agreement to stop the entry of Japanese—were manifestations both of this fear and of racism.

Public opinion polls suggest that these concerns are strong today and represent some of the impetus behind the immigration reform legislation that Congress passed in 1986 after four years of debate. For example, a poll conducted in mid-1986 found that one-third—34 percent— of the total population and 44 percent of blacks felt that immigrants were taking jobs away from Americans.[6] A June 1983 poll of the Los Angeles area, which ranks second only to Miami among metropolitan areas most affected by recent immigration, found that almost half— 48.2 percent—of the respondents felt that undocumented aliens were taking jobs away from native workers and over two-thirds—68.6 percent—felt that immigrants lowered the wage levels in at least some occupations.[7] When compared to whites and Asians, black respondents expressed significantly stronger convictions that undocumented aliens were undermining the labor market and that this was affecting black workers the most.

Casual observation of labor market trends in large American cities would seem to support these popular views. Many of the low-skilled jobs that one might expect to find filled by minority workers with little education appear to be held by immigrants. Taxicab drivers are one noticeable example. The skills required for this job are an ability to communicate in English, an ability to

drive a car, and some knowledge of the geography of the local area. A dropout from an inner-city high school should certainly have an advantage on all of these dimensions over a recent immigrant from a Third World nation. Yet, in some cities, disproportionate numbers of cab drivers are recent immigrants. For example, a recent survey found that 77 percent of those applying for new hack licenses in New York were born outside of the continental United States.[8]

Cab driving is not the only low-skilled occupation in which immigrants appear to have a strong foothold. In many cities, the crews that clean large office buildings are increasingly dominated by recent immigrants, as are the kitchen staffs of many restaurants, the personnel hired by upper- and middle-income working women to care for their children, and operators, fabricators, and laborers in low-wage manufacturing industries. A well-publicized example of the latter was the composition of "the New York 21," the group of 21 workers at the Hantscho, Inc., plant in Mount Vernon, New York, who, on 22 August 1985, won one-third of what, at the time, was the nation's largest lottery prize. Only two of the workers were native-born, the remainder having come from such countries as Paraguay, the Philippines, Poland, Trinidad, China, the Dominican Republic, Thailand, Yugoslavia, and Hungary.

Some crude indication of the potential for competition between immigrants and black workers can be obtained by examining the changes in employment, unemployment, and labor force participation that

6. New York Times/CBS News poll conducted by Gallup in mid-1986, New York Times, 1 July 1986.

7. Thomas Muller and Thomas J. Espenshade, The Fourth Wave: California's Newest Immigrants (Washington, DC: Urban Institute Press, 1985), app. C, pp. 199-202.

8. Anne G. Morris, "The Impact of a Mandated Training Program on New Taxicab Drivers in New York City" (Report no. NY-11-0034, Center for Logistics and Transportation, Graduate School and University Center of the City University of New York, Dec. 1985), pp. 15-17.

occurred between 1970 and 1980. During this period the size of the immigrant working-age population—aged 20 to 64—increased by roughly the same amount as the working-age black population: 3.29 million blacks versus 3.39 million immigrants. Recent immigrants, however, filled a disproportionate number of the new jobs created during the decade. Of every 8 new jobs, 1 was filled by a recent immigrant, while blacks filled only 1 out of every 11 new jobs.

Over the same decade, the unemployment rates and labor force participation rates of blacks and immigrants diverged. Black male unemployment grew from 6.3 to 12.3 percent between 1970 and 1980, while the unemployment rate for male immigrants rose from 3.7 to 6.5 percent. The labor force participation rate for all black males fell from 69.8 to 66.7 percent over this period, and for those in their prime working years—ages 25 to 44—it fell from 87.8 to 84.6 percent. In contrast, the labor force participation of all male immigrants rose from 64.0 to 68.9 percent and that for prime-working-age immigrants fell slightly from 91.8 to 89.4 percent.[9]

While these divergent trends are disturbing, there may be little causative connection between the labor market behavior of blacks and immigration. A more detailed look at the employment changes by occupation over the decade does not provide any strong evidence of competition or displacement. Black job growth took place disproportionately in the more rapidly growing occupational categories such as managerial, professional, and technical workers, sales and clerical workers, and nonhousehold service workers.

Immigrant job growth was more heavily concentrated in the slower-growing occupations. Of course, it is possible that blacks were forced out of these more slowly growing occupations. This, however, does not seem to be a likely source of the problem because not much of black male employment had been in these occupations.[10]

A simple comparison of black unemployment, labor force participation, net migration rate, and earnings in the metropolitan areas that have experienced the largest recent inflow of immigrants with comparable data from those metropolitan areas that have experienced little new immigration also does not reveal any striking evidence that immigration has had a substantial impact. The average unemployment rate for black males in the metropolitan areas with the greatest immigration rose less than did the average rate for the areas that experienced little immigration (see Table 1). Similarly, in the metropolitan areas experiencing the most immigration, the average black male labor force participation rate fell less and the average earnings of black workers increased more than was the case in the metropolitan areas with little immigration. The change in net black out-migration, however, was slightly greater in the high-immigration metropolitan areas.

Of course, these measures of labor market performance are affected by many factors that are not controlled for in the crude comparisons presented in Table 1. Therefore, these data do little more than rule out the possibility that immigration has had an overwhelming effect on black labor market performance. If the effects are subtle, more complex and sophis-

9. U.S. Department of Commerce, Bureau of the Census, *1970 Census of Population,* subject reports, *National Origin and Language,* PC(2)-1A, June 1973; unpublished data from the U.S. Bureau of the Census.

10. Joseph Altonji and David Card, "The Effects of Immigration on the Labor Market Outcomes of Natives" (Paper delivered at the NBER Conference on Immigration, Trade and Labor Markets, Cambridge, MA, 1987).

TABLE 1

CHANGE IN BLACK LABOR-FORCE PARTICIPATION RATES, UNEMPLOYMENT RATES, MEDIAN EARNINGS, AND NET MIGRATION RATES FOR METROPOLITAN AREAS THAT EXPERIENCE SUBSTANTIAL AND INCONSEQUENTIAL IMMIGRATION, 1970-80

Metropolitan Area	Recent Immigration* (a)	Labor Force Participation† (b)	Unemployment Rate‡ (c)	Median Earnings§ (d)	Net Migration‖ (e)
High immigration					
Miami	16.64	−5.4	218.5	106.2	−2.16
Los Angeles	12.93	−6.3	15.5	102.1	−4.21
New York	8.40	−9.5	53.1	88.0	−6.72
San Francisco–Oakland	6.88	−6.9	70.2	107.6	−2.84
Houston	4.97	−0.3	96.6	159.5	2.03
Washington, D.C.	4.48	−3.1	252.0	104.8	−2.69
Average	9.05	−5.3	117.7	111.4	−2.77
Low immigration					
Indianapolis	0.58	−3.7	−11.9	113.9	−1.29
Cincinnati–Hamilton	0.58	−12.3	236.7	89.5	0.0
St. Louis	0.63	−5.0	104.7	115.2	−3.59
Pittsburgh	0.66	−2.2	187.4	122.7	0.48
Kansas City	0.87	−11.0	71.4	80.1	−2.87
Buffalo	0.93	−21.6	134.4	113.8	−6.53
Average	0.78	−9.3	120.5	105.7	−2.30

SOURCES: For columns a and e, U.S. Department of Commerce, Bureau of the Census, *1980 Census of Population*, vol. 1, chap. C, subject reports, PC 80-2-2C, *Geographic Mobility for Metropolitan Areas* (Washington, DC: Government Printing Office, 1985). For columns b, c, and d: idem, *1970 Census of Population*, subject reports, PC (2)-2B, *Negro Population* (Washington, DC: Government Printing Office, 1973); idem, *1980 Census of Population*, vol. 1, chap. C, subject reports, PC 80-1-C1, *General Social and Economic Characteristics*, pt. 1, *United States Summary* (Washington, DC: Government Printing Office, 1984).

*Percentage of 1980 population composed of immigrants arriving between 1970 and 1980.
†Percentage change from 1970 to 1980 in labor force participation for black males aged 25 to 29.
‡Percentage change from 1970 to 1980 in unemployment rate for black males aged 25 to 29.
§Percentage change from 1969 to 1979 in earnings of black males working full-time, full-year.
‖Percentage-point change from 1970 to 1980 in five-year net black migration rate.

ticated statistical procedures would be required to ferret them out.

THE ANALYTICAL EVIDENCE

A number of recent analyses, using sophisticated statistical techniques, have attempted to measure the degree to which immigrants have hurt the labor market prospects of native workers. These studies have used three approaches. The first of these employs a generalized Leontief production function framework to estimate the factor price elasticities of various categories of native labor with respect to increases in immigrant labor. These models are estimated across samples of individuals. The second approach examines in detail the experience of a particular labor market, one that contains a large number of recent immigrants. The third approach involves analyzing labor market outcomes across standard metropolitan statistical areas (SMSAs) or industries to determine whether native labor in areas or industries with high immigrant shares have been affected by this immigration.

The major contributions based on the production function approach are contained in a series of articles written by

George J. Borjas and several others contributed by Frank D. Bean, B. Lindsay Lowell, and Lowell Taylor. These articles utilize several different data sources to estimate the effects of various types of immigrants on the wage rates, earnings, and participation rates of different groups of native workers. Using data from the Survey of Income and Education, Borjas found no evidence to support the view that Hispanic male labor—either immigrant or native—depressed the wages of black male workers.[11] Instead, this study uncovered some weak evidence to support the view that Hispanics and blacks are complements.

In another paper, using 1970 and 1980 census data, Borjas examined the impact of immigration on the annual earnings of various classes of native workers.[12] Annual earnings, of course, are a product of wage rates and hours worked and thus encompass unemployment, the second avenue through which immigration may affect the native labor force. Borjas's estimates suggest that male immigration increased the earnings of both young and older black males in 1970; that is, that male immigrants were a complementary factor of production to black male workers. Black male earnings were unaffected by female or Hispanic immigration. Similar estimates using data from the 1980 census provided no statistically significant evidence that black male earnings were reduced either by recent—occurring between 1970 and 1980—or earlier—pre-1970—immigration.

In a third study, using data from the 1970 census, Borjas separated the impact

of Hispanic and non-Hispanic immigrants and found that neither group appeared to reduce the wages or annual earnings of black males.[13] Under certain circumstances, however, native Hispanic males appeared to be a substitute for black males. Borjas also found that women were substitutes for men and that the increase in the labor force participation of women has had a particularly large impact on black male labor market prospects. Borjas also looked at effects of immigration on labor force participation rates and found some evidence that white male immigration and the increase in female participation had reduced the participation rate of black males.

In yet another paper, Borjas examined the impact of four separate categories of male immigrants—black, white, Hispanic, and Asian—on five categories of native workers—black, white, Hispanic, and Asian males, and all females—utilizing data from the 1980 census.[14] All immigrant groups were found to depress the earnings of white native males, but only black and Hispanic immigrants had an even marginally negative effect on the earnings of native black males. The depressive effect of Hispanic immigrants was confined to Mexican—as distinct from Cuban, Puerto Rican, and other Hispanic—immigrants, but the magnitudes of these effects were minuscule. For example, one set of Borjas's estimated parameters indicated that a doubling of Mexican immigration would reduce the earnings of black native males by less than 1 percent.[15]

11. George Borjas, "Substitutability of Black, Hispanic, and White Labor," *Economic Inquiry*, 21:101 (Jan. 1983).

12. George Borjas, "The Impact of Immigrants on the Earnings of the Native-Born," in *Immigration: Issues and Policies*, ed. V. M. Briggs, Jr., and M. Tienda (Salt Lake City, UT: Olympus, 1984).

13. George J. Borjas, "The Demographic Determinants of the Demand for Black Labor," in *Black Youth Employment Crisis*, ed. Freeman and Holzer, p. 225.

14. George Borjas, "Immigrants, Minorities and Labor Market Competition," *Industrial and Labor Relations Review*, 40:382-92 (Apr. 1987).

15. Ibid., p. xxx.

Frank Bean and his colleagues have used a similar methodology and 1980 census data to examine the impact of undocumented Mexicans on the annual earnings of native workers in 47 SMSAs in the Southwest.[16] Their results suggest that the size of the undocumented Mexican population has no depressive effect on the annual earnings of black males or females and that legal Mexican immigrants and native Mexicans are complementary to blacks. The major detrimental impact of immigration, both legal and undocumented, was found to be on the earnings of other immigrants. A second study confirmed these findings and extended them to cover black females and blacks working in blue-collar occupations.[17] While the findings of these studies are significant, their relevance may be limited by the fact that they focused only on the SMSAs of the Southwest, many of which have very small black populations.

A number of studies have employed the second approach, which involves careful examination of the interactions between immigrants and native workers in a particular labor market. One of the most detailed of these is the Urban Institute's analysis of the impact of immigration on the economies of southern California and the Los Angeles metropolitan area.[18] This analysis found that the large inflow of unskilled immigrants

into Los Angeles did not seem to have any negative labor market consequences for the native black population. Over the 1970-82 period, labor force participation of black adults in Los Angeles was consistently higher than the national average. The labor force participation rate for black females rose more than the national average over this period, while the participation rate for men fell less than elsewhere. Similarly, the unemployment rates for blacks in the Los Angeles area increased far less dramatically than they did in the nation as a whole over this period despite the substantial inflow of immigrants into the area.

The Urban Institute analysis concluded that there was little direct job competition between blacks and Mexican immigrants in the Los Angeles area. Over 90 percent of the net increase in black employment occurred in white-collar jobs, and, as a result, black wage gains in the area seemed to outpace those in the nation as a whole. The institute's researchers did find considerable evidence, however, that the influx of immigrants had depressed wages in certain low-skilled occupations where immigrant labor was concentrated.

Researchers at Rand have also examined the impact of Mexican immigration on the economy and social structure of California.[19] They found that wage growth in California and Los Angeles over the 1970-80 decade was slower than in the nation as a whole probably because of immigration. While immigration affected the earnings of native whites and

16. Frank D. Bean, B. Lindsay Lowell, and Lowell Taylor, "Undocumented Mexican Immigrants and the Earnings of Other Workers in the United States," *Demography*, 25(1):35-52 (1986).

17. Frank D. Bean et al., "Mexican Immigration and the Earnings of Other Workers: The Case of Undocumented Females" (Paper no. 9.014, Texas Population Research Center Papers, series 9:1987, University of Texas at Austin, 1987).

18. Muller and Espenshade, *Fourth Wave*, pp. 91-123; Donald M. Manson, Thomas J. Espenshade, and Thomas Muller, "Mexican Immigration to Southern California: Issues of Job Competition and Worker Mobility" (Policy Discussion Paper,

Urban Institute, Aug. 1985); Thomas J. Espenshade and Tracy Ann Goodis, "Recent Immigrants to Los Angeles: Characteristics and Labor Market Impacts" (Policy Discussion Paper, Urban Institute, May 1985).

19. Kevin F. McCarthy and R. Burciaga Valdez, *Current and Future Effects of Mexican Immigration in California,* Executive Summary, R-3365/1-CR (Santa Monica, CA: Rand, 1985).

blacks, their earnings still remained considerably above the national averages at the end of the period.

The Urban Institute researchers are among those who have employed the third approach, which involves examining the effects of immigration across metropolitan areas or industries using the areas or industries as the unit of observation.[20] They used regression analysis to examine the effect of Mexican immigration on black unemployment rates and family incomes in a sample of 51 metropolitan areas in the Southwest and to estimate the effects of variation in the size of the Hispanic population on black unemployment and family incomes across 247 of the nation's metropolitan areas. These models uncovered no evidence of any significant effects on unemployment rates and only a very small effect on family incomes in the sample of 247 metropolitan areas.

CONCLUSION

The empirical work that was reviewed in the previous section provides no strong evidence that immigration has significantly diminished the labor market prospects for black workers. This conclusion appears to be fairly robust; it is based on studies that use a variety of analytical approaches and a number of different data sources. Therefore it is unlikely that recent immigration has played an appreciable role in the emergence of the underclass.

Nevertheless, there are several reasons why this conclusion should be regarded as tentative. Prime among them are the limitations of the available data. Most of the studies reviewed in the previous section are based on fairly old data, data that

20. Muller and Espenshade, *Fourth Wave.*

were collected in 1970, 1976, or 1980. Labor market dynamics could have changed some during the 1980s. About 5 million additional immigrants have entered the United States since the 1980 census, many local labor markets have become extremely weak, and the minimum wage has not been increased since 1981.

Not only are the available data old, but they also may not be sufficiently detailed to isolate the types of effects that are of interest. These effects may be quite localized, may affect only small groups of native workers—for example, young minority workers with limited educational attainments—and may be caused by only certain types of immigrants—for example, recent immigrants with few skills. Analyses that examine national data may not be able to uncover effects that are felt in only a few geographic areas. The concentration of recent immigration suggests that this shortfall could be a problem. The metropolitan areas of Miami, Los Angeles, New York, Houston, San Francisco, and Chicago absorbed more than 40 percent of the net increase in immigrants over the 1970-80 period; the post-1980 immigration may have been even more concentrated.

Similarly, it may be necessary to disaggregate immigration even more than has been done to uncover the effects it has had on certain small segments of the native labor force. The labor market characteristics of the various groups of immigrants differ greatly. One would not expect many of these immigrant groups to diminish the labor market prospects of poorly educated, native minorities. For example, immigrants from Western Europe and Canada have characteristics that are very similar to those of the native white work force, while those from India have very high educational levels and are

disproportionately competing for professional jobs. Some 66 percent of the Indian immigrants enumerated in the 1980 census had completed four years of college and 43 percent of those employed were in professional specialty occupations.

It is also possible that the effects of immigration are being manifest less on the wages, earnings, and unemployment that the existing studies have examined and more on the dimensions—such as labor force participation, fringe benefits, working conditions, and internal migration—that have received less attention.

While there are these reasons to reexamine the question when data from the 1990 census become available, the existing evidence suggests that immigration has not been a major factor contributing to the emergence of the urban underclass.

10

The Urban Homeless:
A Portrait of Urban Dislocation

By PETER H. ROSSI and JAMES D. WRIGHT

ABSTRACT: In this decade, homelessness has been recognized as a serious and growing urban social problem. Using a new research approach to the study of undomiciled urban populations, we describe the social, economic, and demographic characteristics of the literally homeless population in Chicago. The homeless in the Chicago sample are unaffiliated persons living in extreme poverty, with high levels of physical and mental disability. Homelessness is interpreted as a manifestation of extreme poverty among persons without families in housing markets with declining stocks of inexpensive dwelling units suitable for single persons.

Peter H. Rossi, S. A. Rice Professor of Sociology, is acting director of the Social and Demographic Research Institute at the University of Massachusetts, Amherst, and the recipient of the Common Wealth Award for contributions to sociology. His latest work, Down and Out in America, *a monograph on homelessness and extreme poverty, will be published in 1989.*

James D. Wright is the Charles and Leo Favrot Professor of Human Relations in the Department of Sociology at Tulane University. He has authored or coauthored more than 80 scholarly papers; among his 11 books the most recent is Homelessness and Health, *coauthored with Eleanor Weber.*

F EW of our contemporary social problems rival homelessness in the public attention received in this decade.[1] There are ample and obvious reasons for this attention, for the plights of the homeless easily evoke sympathy and concern. In a society that places so high a value on the concept of home and devotes so much attention to housing and its accoutrements, the vision of being without a home is clearly a frightening one, bound to evoke sympathy for persons so afflicted.

The high level of concern about homelessness has not produced much in the way of empirically adequate knowledge about the extent of homelessness and the conditions that produce it. Estimates of the size of the national homeless population vary from about a quarter million to upward of 3 million;[2] equally wide variations exist in the estimates for specific cities and states. The sources of homelessness are also not understood in any detail. Is homelessness primarily a housing problem, an employment problem, a condition created by deinstitutionalization of the chronically mentally ill, a manifestation of the breakdown of family life, a symptom of the inadequacies of our public welfare system, or a combination of these and other factors? To be sure, there have been many dramatic and moving descriptive accounts of the plight of homeless persons, but these do not cumulate to precise knowledge about the extent and character of the problem of homelessness.

Reasonably valid data on homelessness is unquestionably difficult to obtain. National statistical series contain little or no information on the homeless population. The U.S. census essentially counts the homed population; conventional surveys are ordinarily derived from samples of households and therefore miss those without conventional dwellings.[3] This article describes the findings from research using an adaptation of modern sample-survey methods, a study that is the first to provide reasonable valid data on the homeless of a major city, Chicago.[4]

A major significant obstacle to the study of the homeless is the lack of an agreed-upon definition of homelessness.[5]

1. The rather sudden welling up of concern can be indexed by the number of listings under "homelessness" in the *Reader's Guide to Periodical Literature* (New York: H. A. Wilson, 1976, 1983-85). In 1975, there were no listings; in 1981, 3; in 1982, 15; in 1983, 21; and in 1984, 32.

2. U.S. Department of Housing and Urban Development, *A Report to the Secretary on the Homeless and Emergency Shelters* (Washington, DC: Office of Policy Development and Research, 1984); U.S. Department of Health and Human Services, *Helping the Homeless: A Resource Guide* (Washington, DC: Government Printing Office, 1984); U.S. General Accounting Office, *Homelessness: A Complicated Problem and the Federal Response*, 1985.

3. The 1980 population census included some partial attempts to enumerate persons living in shelters and in public places, such as train and bus stations, but this effort did not cover all places where homeless persons might be found nor did the census cover all cities. U.S. Department of Commerce, Bureau of the Census, *Persons in Institutions and Other Group Quarters, 1980 Census of Population*, pub. PC80-2-4D (Washington, DC: Government Printing Office, 1984). Virtually all survey- or census-based estimates omit homeless persons, and most pass over institutionalized persons as components of such estimates, leading to corresponding underestimates of poverty-impacted populations.

4. A full account of the methodology and the findings can be found in Peter H. Rossi, Gene A. Fisher, and Georgianna Willis, *The Condition of the Homeless of Chicago* (Amherst: University of Massachusetts, Social and Demographic Research Institute; Chicago: University of Chicago, National Opinion Research Center, 1986).

5. On the definitional problem, see Edward Baxter and Kim Hopper, *Private Lives, Public Spaces: Homeless Adults on the Streets of New York City* (New York: Community Service Society of New York, Institute for Social Welfare Research, 1984); Steven Crystal, *Chronic and Situational Dependence: Longterm Residents in a Shelter for Men* (New York: Human Resources Administration of the City of New York, 1982).

On the most general level, the homeless can be defined as those who do not have customary and regular access to a conventional dwelling or residence. But what is a conventional dwelling or residence, and what is customary and regular access? There is a continuum running from the obviously domiciled to the obviously homeless, with many ambiguous cases to be encountered along that continuum. Any effort to draw a line across that continuum, demarcating the homed from the homeless, is of necessity somewhat arbitrary and therefore potentially contentious.

These definitional ambiguities are not simply scholastic issues. A definition of homelessness is, *ipso facto,* a statement as to what should constitute the floor of housing adequacy below which no member of society should be permitted to fall. It is equally obvious that the number and existential conditions of the homeless depend in no small part on how the phenomenon is defined.

In dealing with these definitional problems, we have found it useful to distinguish between (1) the literally homeless, persons who clearly do not have access to a conventional dwelling and who would be homeless by any conceivable definition of the term; and (2) precariously, or marginally, housed persons, with tenuous or very temporary claims to a conventional dwelling of more or less marginal adequacy. This distinction, of course, does not solve the definitional problem, although it does more clearly specify subpopulations of likely policy interest.

METHODOLOGY USED IN THE CHICAGO STUDY

Most conventional quantitative social research methods depend on the assumption that persons can be enumerated and sampled within their customary dwelling units, an assumption that fails by definition in any study of the literally homeless. The strategy devised for the Chicago study therefore departed from the traditional sample survey in that persons were sampled from nondwelling units and interviews were conducted at times when the distinction between the homed and homeless was at a maximum. Two complementary samples were taken: (1) a probability sample of persons spending the night in shelters provided for homeless persons—the shelter survey; and (2) a complete enumeration of persons encountered between the hours of midnight and 6 a.m. in a thorough search of non-dwelling-unit places in a probability sample of Chicago census blocks—the street survey. Taken together, the shelter and street surveys constitute an unbiased sample of the literally homeless of Chicago, as we define the term.

Our research classified persons as literally homeless if they were residents of shelters for homeless persons or were encountered in our block searches and found not to rent or own a conventional housing unit.

In the street surveys, teams of interviewers, accompanied by off-duty Chicago police officers, searched all places on each sampled block to which they could obtain access, including all-night businesses, alleys, hallways, roofs and basements, abandoned buildings, and parked cars and trucks.[6] All persons encountered

6. Instructions to interviewers were to enter all places until they encountered locked doors or were forbidden—for example, by managers or proprietors—to go further. Police escorts were hired to protect interviewers. Cooperation rates were 81 percent in the shelter surveys and 94 percent in the street surveys. The majority of the shelter respondents not interviewed were not present at the time of interview, being temporarily out of the shelter for one reason or another.

were queried to determine whether they were homeless, and they were interviewed if found to be homeless.

We believe the Chicago Homeless Study to be the first attempt to apply modern sampling methods to the study of the homeless, and, as such, it provides the first scientifically defensible estimates of the size and composition of the homeless population in any city.

ECONOMIC, SOCIAL, AND DEMOGRAPHIC CHARACTERISTICS OF THE LITERALLY HOMELESS

Being homeless is predominantly a male condition; three out of four—76 percent—of the homeless were men, in sharp contrast to the proportion of the Chicago adult population that is male, 46 percent.[7] Blacks and Native Americans constituted considerably more than their proportionate share of the homeless, with whites and Hispanics proportionately underrepresented. Although the average age of the homeless—40 years—was not far from that of the general adult population, there were proportionately fewer of the very young—under 25—and the old, or those over 65. Nor were the homeless very different from the general population in educational attainment, the typical homeless person being a high school graduate.

The modal homeless person was a black male high school graduate in his middle thirties. Average characteristics, however, obscure an important fact, namely, that the homeless population is somewhat heterogeneous. Especially significant was a minority of young black women—about 14 percent of the homeless—who were, typically, homeless with their young children and apparently in transition from unsatisfactory housing arrangements to establishing new households with those children. In addition, older males—over 40—tended to be white and were usually homeless for relatively long periods of time.

In the wealth of social and economic detail contained in our interview data, three salient characteristics of the homeless stand out: extreme poverty; high levels of disability resulting from poor physical and mental health; and high levels of social isolation, with weak or nonexistent ties to others.

Extreme poverty

The literally homeless are clustered at the extreme lower boundary of the American population that is in poverty. Within the rather narrow income range found, there was some heterogeneity, as the differences between the various measures of central tendency show. The mode comprised the almost one in five—18 percent—who reported no income at all in the month prior to the survey; median income for the month was $99.85, and average, or mean, income for the same period was $167.39. Given that the 1985 poverty level for single persons under 65 was $5250, the official poverty level was 2.6 times the average annual income and 4.4 times the median annual income of Chicago's literally homeless.[8] On average, the literally homeless survive on substantially less than half the poverty-level income.

---

7. The percentage of women—24 percent—among the homeless is in stark contrast to the homeless, or skid row, population of Chicago as studied in the late 1950s, virtually all of whom were men. See Donald Bogue, *Skid Row in American Cities* (Chicago: University of Chicago, 1963).

8. Poverty levels for households of various sizes and for various years are given in *The Statistical Abstract of the United States* (Washington, DC: Government Printing Office, 1986).

In Chicago there is almost no afford-able housing at these levels of income. In 1985, the average monthly rental for SRO rooms, among the cheapest accom-modations available for single persons, was $195,[9] $27 above the average monthly income of the homeless. At this level of extreme poverty, spending one's entire available income would still not be quite enough to afford the cheapest available housing, much less also cover the costs of food and other necessities. That the liter-ally homeless manage to survive at all is a tribute to the laudable efforts of the shel-ters, soup kitchens, and charitable orga-nizations that provide most necessities.

The homeless make some contribution to their own support. Although a very small percentage—4 percent—held full-time jobs, almost two in five had worked for some period over the previous month, mostly at casual, poorly paid part-time jobs. Remarkably, work and other eco-nomic activity was, on average, the source of 29 percent of total monthly income. Even more of a surprise, income transfer payments accounted for very little of their income, with only about a quarter—28 percent—receiving Aid to Family with Dependent Children (AFDC) or General Assistance (GA)—mostly the latter. In-come transfer payments amounted to 30 percent of the total income; another 21 percent was accounted for by pension and disability payments, received by about one in five, or 18 percent.

Job histories of the literally homeless suggest that they have been among the extremely poor for years. On the average it was more than 4.6 years, or 55 months, since their last steady job, defined as full-time employment lasting three or more months; the median amount of time was 3.3 years, or 40 months. Interestingly, elapsed time since last steady job was very much greater than time currently home-less, the latter averaging about 22 months, with a median of 8 months.[10] This suggests that many among the literally homeless were helped by their families and friends through relatively long periods of unem-ployment,[11] but that the patience, forbear-ance, or resources of these benefactors eventually ran out, with literal homeless-ness then added to chronic unemployment as a problem experienced daily.

Disability

Many disabling conditions plague the homeless, ones that would ordinarily make it difficult or impossible for a person to lead a full life—to obtain employment, participate in social life, or maintain relationships with others. Of course, disability is a matter of degree, so that it is difficult to calculate precise proportions; nevertheless, it is abundantly clear that the proportions among the literally homeless are much higher than in the general adult population.

More than one in four reported that they had some health problem that pre-vented their employment. Prominent among the conditions reported were men-

9. Jewish Council on Urban Affairs, *SRO's, An Endangered Species: Single Room Occupancy Hotels in Chicago* (Chicago: Jewish Council on Urban Affairs and Community Emergency Shelter Organization, 1985).

10. "Time currently homeless" is counted as months elapsed since last domiciled. Many homeless people have been homeless more than once; among those who had become homeless sometime in the year prior to the interview, 11 percent had had one or more homeless episodes in previous years.

11. Research on recipients of General Assistance in Chicago documents that many of the extremely poor survive mainly through the goodwill of family and friends. See Matthew Stagner and Harold Richman, *General Assistance Profiles: Findings from a Longitudinal Study of Newly Approved Recipients* (Chicago: University of Chicago, Na-tional Opinion Research Center, 1985).

tal illness, cardiovascular ailments, and gastrointestinal disorders. Likewise, more than one in three—37 percent—reported themselves as being in only "fair" or "poor" health, a level of self-reported ill health about twice that found in the general adult population, 18 percent. Behavioral indicators support these self-reports, with more than one in four reporting a hospital stay of more than 24 hours during the previous year.[12] High levels of alcoholism and drug abuse are also indicated by the one in three who reported stays in detoxification centers.

Relatively high levels of mental illness are evident in the data. Almost one in four—23 percent—reported having been in a mental hospital for stays of over 48 hours, more than eight times the level found in the general population. Among those who had been in mental hospitals, three out of five, or 58 percent, had had multiple hospitalizations. Nearly one in five—16 percent—reported at least one suicide attempt.

In addition to the self-report data, two short scales were administered to measure psychiatric symptomatology.[13] On a scale

12. For the self-reported health status of the U.S. adult population for 1982, see the first Special Report of the R. W. Johnson Foundation (1983). Additional data on the health status of the homeless are reported by P. W. Brickner et al., *Health Care of Homeless People* (New York: Springer-Verlag, 1985); James Wright et al., in *Research in Social Problems and Public Policy,* ed. M. Lewis and J. Miller (Greenwich, CT: JAI Press, 1987), 4:41-72.

13. The first scale was a shortened version of the CES-D scale measuring symptoms of depression, developed by the Center for Epidemiological Studies of the National Institute of Mental Health for the national Health and Nutritional Examination Survey; the second was a shortened version of the Psychiatric Epidemiological Research Interview developed by Dohrenwend and associates. Barbara S. Dohrenwend et al., "Social Functioning of Psychiatric Patients in Contrast with Community Cases in the General Population," *Archives of General Psychiatry,* 40:1174-82 (1983); Bruce P.

measuring symptoms of depression, nearly half—47 percent—of the Chicago homeless registered levels suggesting a need for clinical attention, compared to about 20 percent in the national Health and Nutritional Examination Survey. On a second scale, measuring psychotic thinking, one in four showed two or more signs of disturbed cognitive processes; almost every item showed significantly higher levels of psychotic thinking than a comparison group tested in a New York City working-class neighborhood.

Contacts with the criminal justice system represent yet another, albeit qualitatively different, disability that is rather widespread. Such contacts at least indicate prior adjustment difficulties, some of a rather serious nature. Two of five—41 percent—had experienced jail terms of two or more days, 28 percent had been convicted by the courts and placed on probation, and 17 percent had served sentences of more than one year in state or federal prisons, presumably for felony offenses.

The cumulative incidence of these various disabilities is staggering. More than four out of five—82 percent—of the homeless either reported fair or poor health, or had been in a mental hospital or a detoxification unit, or received clinically high scores on the demoralization scale or on the psychotic-thinking scale, or had been sentenced by a court. A majority had had two or more such experiences or conditions. Although these data clearly do not sustain precise estimates of the degree of disability among the literally homeless, it is clear that the prevalence is several magnitudes above that encountered in the general adult population.

Dohrenwend et al., "Nonspecific Psychological Distress and Other Dimensions of Psychopathology," ibid., 37:1229-36 (1980).

Social isolation

A high degree of social isolation is also endemic among the homeless. Most—57 percent—have never married; of those ever married, most are separated or divorced, on either count in sharp contrast to the patterns of the general adult population.[14] The very few—9 percent—who are still with families are almost exclusively homeless women with dependent children.

The literally homeless are relatively isolated from extended family and from friends. Nearly nine in ten—88 percent—have surviving relatives and family members, but only three in five—60 percent—maintain even minimal contact with them—visiting, writing, talking with, or telephoning them at least once every two or three months. Similar low levels of contact with families of procreation—spouses, ex-spouses, or children—were also reported; 55 percent had such persons, but only one in three maintained contact with them. Overall, one in three reported no contact with any relatives and almost one in four reported no contacts with either relatives or friends.

Further evidence on strained relations with family and relatives was shown in replies to a sequence of questions on preferred living arrangements. We asked whether respondents would like to return to their families and whether their families would take them. Among the young homeless women, very few wanted to return; many of the young men would have liked to but believed they would not be welcome.

The social isolation of many of the homeless implies that they lack access to extended social networks and are there-

fore especially vulnerable to the vagaries of fortune occasioned by changes in employment, income, or physical or mental health.

AN INTERPRETATION OF HOMELESSNESS

The characteristics of the homeless as derived from the Chicago Homeless Study pertain only to the literally homeless and are not necessarily descriptive of the precariously homed. Indeed, there is some evidence that the latter may also be in extreme poverty but differ in other important respects. The Illinois GA rolls for the city of Chicago in 1985 contained about 100,000 individual recipients, most of whom were single-person households, largely male, and with annual incomes below $1848, the eligibility cutoff point. Given that GA monthly payments of up to $154 are by themselves insufficient to bring recipients above $1848 per year, we can consider GA clients as among the extremely poor. Because only few are literally homeless, we may regard the clients as reasonably representative of the precariously homed of Chicago or at least of some large portion thereof.

Stagner and Richman's study of those receiving GA in 1984 provides a description of this group showing them to be similar to the literally homeless in demographic composition.[15] Most—68 percent—are male, 71 percent are black, and 91 percent are unmarried; they tend to be slightly younger—the average age was 34—than the literally homeless. GA recipients contrasted strongly with the literally homeless in three important respects. First, GA recipients are considerably more integrated socially, with half living with relatives and friends and an addi-

---

14. It is interesting that, despite their marital histories, more than half—54 percent—had children, but current contact with these children tended to be minimal.

15. Stagner and Richman, *General Assistance Profiles.*

tional 30 percent receiving financial assistance from such sources. Second, disability levels among GA clients are much lower. Far fewer—9 percent—have physical-health conditions that prevented employment or had been in mental hospitals, the latter amounting to 1 percent. Third, GA clients had work histories with shorter median periods—19 months—since their last full-time jobs.

There are undoubtedly other persons in Chicago, as poor or poorer, who are not on the GA rolls. Some of the precariously homed extremely poor participate in other income-maintenance programs such as AFDC or Supplemental Security Income (SSI), receive payments under Old-Age and Survivors Insurance (OASI) or other retirement plans, or are receiving unemployment benefits. It is difficult to estimate the total number of the extremely poor of Chicago, although the magnitude is at least 100,000 and possibly as many as 200,000 persons whose annual incomes from all sources are under $2000, 38 percent of the official poverty level. Most, if not all, of these extremely poor persons are at high risk of becoming literally homeless.

Considering jointly the special and distinctive features of the literally homeless in relation to the contrasting characteristics of other extremely poor persons, we offer the following interpretation of homelessness and some speculation about the forces that influence changes in the size of the homeless population.

At the base of our interpretation is the viewpoint that literal homelessness is primarily a manifestation of extreme poverty. Literal homelessness, or the proportion of persons being literally without conventional housing, is a function of extreme poverty, in a housing market that has an inadequate supply of very low cost housing to offer to single-person

households. The incidence of literal homelessness falls very heavily on persons who are unaffiliated with households and upon those who have been extremely poor for long periods of time. The homeless therefore are the long-term very poor who have been unable to maintain supportive connections with—or have been rejected by—their parental families and friends and who have not been able for a variety of reasons to establish their own households.

Why the literally homeless have been extremely poor for so long, why they have been rejected, and why they have difficulty establishing such households are issues very likely connected with their disabilities. Persons with serious disabilities are likely to experience difficulty connecting with full-time lasting employment and also difficulty maintaining their shares in the webs of reciprocity that constitutes the support structures of kin and friends. It should be noted that because their parental families and friends likely also are among the poor and have few resources to share with others, the burden of taking on the support of an additional adult is high. If the adult in question presents behavioral difficulties and a prospect of being dependent indefinitely, it is quite understandable why relatives and friends may be reluctant to take on a burden that would strain both resources and patience.

The literally homeless constitute only a very small fraction of the very poor, most of whom manage somehow to avoid literal homelessness. Using the size of the Chicago GA rolls, 100,000, as a conservative estimate of the magnitude of the very poor, the literally homeless constitute about 2.7 percent of the very poor. To understand literal homelessness properly and to predict its course, we need to know more about how most of the very

poor manage to avoid that condition. We can speculate, on the basis of some knowledge, that they do so mainly by either overspending on housing or being subsidized by their families and friends.

Overspending on housing

Some of the extremely poor may avoid literal homelessness by spending all or mostly all of their cash income on housing. These are persons who live in single-room-occupancy hotels or furnished rooms or share inexpensive apartments and who obtain food through food stamps or handouts from food kitchens; clothing from charitable sources; and medical care from free clinics and through Medicaid. To pursue this pattern of life consistently, one must also have a consistent source of income as provided by minimum OASI payments, small pensions from other sources, GA, disability payments, and perhaps small remittances from relatives or ex-spouses. They must also live close to facilities that can provide free or low-cost meals, casual employment, and the other amenities.

We suspect that the reason why there were so few very old persons among the literally homeless is because even minimum OASI payments provide sufficient consistent income to enable retired persons or their surviving spouses to live alone or share dwellings with others. The same line of reasoning can explain why so few of the literally homeless were receiving disability payments: SSI recipients received enough consistent income from SSI payments to connect with the lowest end of the housing market. The homelessness literature is full of references to persons in extreme poverty who spend as much as they can on housing from their small pensions or other remittances but find that they do not have enough money

to be in rented quarters all the time. Their small pensions or welfare checks can be stretched to cover, say, all but the last few days before the next check arrives. These are persons who are homeless on a part-time basis, supplementing their rented quarters by spending some nights in shelters or on the streets.

Private subsidies

Most of the extremely poor avoid literal homelessness by being given housing and subsistence at little or no charge by their relatives—mainly parents and siblings—and friends. The households that provide these subsidies incur the marginal costs of adding another person to be housed and fed. Note that these costs may not be a severe financial drain on the household in question, especially if the person in extreme poverty provides some payments to the subsidizing household or shares in household chores. For example, adding another adult person to a household may not mean any additional rent outlay, nor may it be necessary to purchase any additional food, if the rations given to every household member are diminished in order to share with the additional member. But there are other, nonfinancial costs, including increased space pressures, reduced privacy, lower food quality and quantity, and increased wear and tear on facilities. In addition, there is also the potential for interpersonal conflict.

Private subsidies may be virtually the only way that extremely poor single persons can live on the income-maintenance payments to which they may be entitled. Illinois's GA payments of $154 per month are simply not enough to allow a recipient to enter the private housing market. AFDC payments to single-parent households, although more

generous than GA, also fall short of providing enough to live on without additional income in kind or cash.

The foregoing suggests that the size of the literally homeless population is driven by those macro processes that affect the availability of low-skilled employment, the ability of poor families to help their less fortunate members, the market conditions affecting the supply of very low cost housing for single persons, and the coverage of income-maintenance programs for disabled and single persons, as follows:

1. Changes in demand for low-skilled workers. The employment prospects for low-skilled workers can affect the number of literally homeless in two ways: directly, by influencing the job prospects for low-skilled single persons and hence their abilities to earn sufficient income to keep them from being extremely poor; and indirectly, by influencing the abilities of families to provide subsidies to their long-term unemployed peripheral adult members. A major difference between the description of Chicago's skid row in the late 1950s[16] and the portrait emerging from the our 1985-86 study is that in the earlier period a strong market demand apparently existed for casual labor from which the homeless men living in the flophouses and cheap hotels could earn enough to pay their rents and buy food. Side by side with the flophouses on Madison Street in Chicago were employment exchanges for casual laborers. With the decline in demand for low-skilled casual labor such employment exchanges are no longer available.

2. Changes in the level of income-maintenance support for poor families and for poor single persons. The more generous the levels of welfare support, the more likely families are to put up with their long-term unemployed and disabled adult relatives. Many commentators on the homeless problem suspect that cutbacks in social welfare programs have led to an increase in homelessness. In this connection as well, the processes involved may work indirectly, by providing lower incomes to poor families and thereby lowering their abilities to subsidize their adult unemployed members, and directly, by lowering the coverage and real value of income-maintenance programs available to single persons. Income transfer payments over the past two decades have not kept pace with inflation. The recent rise in the size of the literally homeless population may be at least a partial reflection of the lowered real value of welfare payments and the consequent decreased ability of poor families on AFDC or other income-maintenance programs to subsidize their peripheral unemployed adult members. Similarly, the decline in the real value of GA payments implies a correspondingly decreased ability of single-person households in that program to afford rentals available at the bottom of the housing market.

3. Changes in the coverage of income-maintenance support programs for disabled persons, including admission into total-care institutions such as mental hospitals. The greater the coverage of disability payment programs, the more likely are disabled single persons to be able to afford low-cost housing for single persons. Hence the less likely are such persons to become homeless. Similarly, changes in the coverage of indoor support programs, such as mental hospitals, can also influence the numbers of persons who are literally homeless. In this view, being institutionalized may be regarded

16. Bogue, *Skid Row in American Cities.*

as a form of public subsidy for the maintenance of extremely poor persons. Deinstitutionalization forces such extremely poor persons either into the literally homeless group or into the privately subsidized poor.

4. Quantitative and qualitative changes in the supply of very low cost housing. As low-cost housing units for low-income families become short in supply or smaller in size, the greater becomes the burden imposed on such families by support for their long-term unemployed and disabled peripheral adult relatives. Similarly, the shorter the supply and the higher the cost of inexpensive housing for single-person households, the more likely single-person households are to be homeless. In city after city, the supply of low-cost housing for single-person households has experienced precipitous declines in the past decade. In Chicago, single-room occupancy capacity has been estimated to have declined by almost 25 percent in the period 1980-83. This trend almost surely has contributed heavily to the growth of the literally homeless experienced in the past decade.

5. Changes in the numbers of persons who are disabled in middle adulthood. Although disability levels in a population ordinarily may be only indirectly and weakly influenced by social policy, the special character of the disabilities of the literally homeless may be more amenable to such purposeful policy moves. Many of the homeless men are disabled mainly because of alcohol and, to a lesser extent, other substance abuse. Measures taken to reduce the amount of alcohol abuse during early adulthood, particularly among males, would do much to reduce the prevalence of disability in their middle years.

These macro processes suggest both short-term and long-term remedies for the extremely poor and the literally homeless in America. Short-term measures that would considerably ameliorate the condition of the homeless include measures that would increase the amount of income available to the extremely poor. In particular, more generous income-maintenance programs and wider coverage for disability programs would both help poor families to provide help to their long-term unemployed adult members and help such members directly. Indeed, one may even consider some of the possible programs as Aid to Families with Dependent Adults! The long-term measures would include increasing the supply of low-cost housing, particularly for single persons; providing more low-skilled employment opportunities in ways that would be accessible to the extremely poor; and measures designed to lower the prevalence of disabling conditions among young adult males. In the meantime, support for shelters, food kitchens, and other charitable organizations serving the literally homeless is necessary at least to lessen the extreme hardships imposed by that condition.

11

Equal Opportunity and the Estranged Poor

By JENNIFER L. HOCHSCHILD

ABSTRACT: This article is concerned with people who so lack marketable skills and material resources that they are excluded from mainstream society, and who lack faith that they can succeed through conventional means. They are usually poor, but they are a small subset of the poor and are not necessarily poor throughout their lives. Most are excluded because the American rhetoric of equal opportunity for all is belied by political choices that deny to some any chance of success. Programs to enable the estranged poor to enter mainstream society must provide skills, a starting place, and faith in the possibility of achievement. Such programs are long-lasting, intensive, and comprehensive—thus costly. To ensure that estrangement is not reproduced in the next generation, programs to aid the poor must, furthermore, eliminate gender biases in their prescriptions and must change the structural conditions that create the gap between the promise and practice of equal opportunity. These programs should not necessarily be targeted on minorities or the poor, but should build on Americans' support for social policies that give everyone a chance for at least some success.

Jennifer L. Hochschild, professor of politics and public affairs at Princeton University, received her Ph.D. in political science from Yale University in 1979 and has taught at Duke University and Columbia University. She is the author of What's Fair?: American Beliefs about Distributive Justice *and* The New American Dilemma: Liberal Democracy and School Desegregation *and a coauthor of* Equalities. *She is a panelist on the National Academy of Sciences Committee on the Status of Black Americans and was a fellow at the Center for Advanced Study in the Behavioral Sciences.*

NOTE: My thanks to Princeton University, the Center for Advanced Study in the Behavioral Sciences, and the Spencer Foundation for sponsoring this research.

A N early contributor to the recent upsurge of interest in poor Americans claims that "the underclass is distinguished from the lower class principally by its lack of mobility."[1] This definition is imprecise and incomplete, but it points toward the core problem of American poverty: in a land dedicated to opportunity for all, some people lack the skills and resources they need to get ahead and lack faith that they can obtain them through conventionally accepted means. Enabling those people to escape their condition and reducing the gap between the promise and practice of equal opportunity in the future are not impossible but will require levels of political understanding and commitment beyond what American citizens and especially policymakers have recently offered. This article seeks to further that understanding and suggest appropriate avenues for that commitment. My starting—and ending—point is the assertion that the problem of severe poverty and its attendant behaviors and emotions can be solved only when Americans choose actually, not merely rhetorically, to open the opportunity structure to all regardless of their race, class, or gender.

THE PROBLEM OF BEING LEFT OUT

A defining characteristic of American society is its faith in equality of opportunity and the likelihood of success. At least since the early nineteenth century, most Americans have agreed that in principle all men are created equal, all have the inalienable right to pursue happiness, the government should help in that pursuit, and most people should be able to succeed to some extent if they deserve to. That

mixture of faith, hope, and political demand is full of ambiguity: until recently "all men" did not include blacks or women; the government is sometimes directed to stay out of the economy and sometimes to intervene; definitions of success and desert vary widely. Those ambiguities are philosophically and politically significant, but they should not be allowed to obscure the underlying ideological unity behind the phrase "equal opportunity." Americans who lack the skills or resources to enable their participation in the opportunity system, or who are given no chance to participate, and who have no hope or faith that they might get ahead through conventionally acceptable channels, are seriously out of step with the dominant American culture.[2]

My concern in this article is that small but important group of profoundly estranged Americans. Readers of this volume are by now familiar with poor blacks' increasing concentration in urban ghettos, unmarried teenage mothers' dismal prospects, young blacks' high unemployment rate, children's increasing involvement in drug use and sales, and all of the other social, economic, and demographic problems of the urban poor. But the ideological and political context of the apparently growing underclass[3] has

1. Douglas G. Glasgow, *The Black Underclass* (San Francisco: Jossey-Bass, 1980), p. 8.

2. Over 95 percent of Americans agree that "every citizen should have an equal chance to influence government policy" and "everyone in America should have equal opportunities to get ahead." Herbert McClosky and John Zaller, *The American Ethos* (Cambridge, MA: Harvard University Press, 1984), tabs. 3-5, 3-9. For an analysis of the equal-opportunity theme in popular literature of the nineteenth century—perhaps the closest analogue to modern opinion polls—see Irvin Wyllie, *The Self-Made Man* (New York: Free Press, 1954).

3. At least one scholar, however, sees the apparent rise in underclass behavior as mainly a rise in "deviant" behavior at all levels of society. See Mark Hughes, "Moving Up and Moving Out: Confusing Ends and Means About Ghetto Dispersal," *Urban Studies*, 24:503-17 (1987).

not received as much attention as it warrants.

Not all of the poor have lost faith in achieving success through conventional means. Indeed, as the vast literature on why there is no socialism in the United States shows, most poor Americans historically have kept their faith in the promise of opportunity long after it was clear to observers that they had no realistic chance to improve their circumstances. Other poor Americans have found alternative ideologies and social networks that give them dignity, self-respect, and hope for the future outside the equal-opportunity framework. They include members of the Nation of Islam, fundamentalist Christians, and egalitarian socialists, to give but a few examples. Thus only a small proportion of the poor are included among the estranged Americans who are my subject here.

Conversely, some people start life with resources and skills and therefore a reasonable chance to maintain or improve their situations, but they lack the talents, gumption, emotional strength, or simple luck to sustain themselves. They fall into poverty and despair and thereby join the group with whom I am concerned. Others start out poor but attain wealth for at least part of their lives; an obvious example is drug dealers who amass large fortunes in their usually brief and violent careers. In short, the estranged Americans who are my subject here may spend part of their lives out of poverty.

People manifest in varied ways their lack of faith in getting ahead through conventional means. Some simply drop out of society, living lives of quiet—or noisy—misery. Others sell drugs, leave high school and the labor force, or have children with no means of supporting them except welfare because they are responding rationally to the incentives

they face. Still others can hardly be said to make a choice, in that no one has taught them that to keep a job, for example, one must report to work on time every day, respond appropriately to a supervisor, maintain decent relations with coworkers, and so on. Finally, a few simply reject conventional values as well as conventional means of achieving their goals; they will take what they want however they can.

Obviously I am not providing a rigorous definition of the underclass, nor would this combination of objective and subjective characteristics necessarily be a fruitful start toward a rigorous definition. My goal here is not to define and measure but rather to add an ideological context, a political explanation, and policy suggestions to the standard sociological and economic definitions. Let us turn, then, to that context and explanation.

THE GAP BETWEEN RHETORIC AND REALITY

Some people lack skills, resources, and faith because they have not taken advantage of the chances they were given. Everyone knows, indirectly at least, of people who were so witless, emotionally damaged by some experience or relationship, or slothful that they sank far below their original status and were abandoned in despair by their families and friends. Enabling these people to improve their circumstances is part of my concern here, but their reasons for falling in the first place are not, because those reasons are more personal and idiosyncratic than political and general. Once a pattern is found—such as middle-class wives' being beaten or abandoned by their husbands—a political analysis becomes appropriate, but up to that point, individual disasters are more the province of psychologists than of political scientists.

Let us, then, consider the pattern of choices made by American policymakers—with the support or at least the acquiescence of most citizens—that have created or increased estrangement among a minority of the poor. Those choices are best understood in terms of a gap between the rhetoric and reality of opportunity for all.

Much of American history can be read as a set of political choices that created and consolidated racial, ethnic, and gender disparities in wealth and power. I have no room to consider them here, but they form the backdrop for the thirty-year period I do want to examine. Americans' response to poverty and discrimination since the 1960s has been curiously double sided. On the one hand, citizens from President Kennedy to the average television watcher were genuinely shocked by the evidence of malnourishment and vicious racial prejudice that confronted them in the early 1960s. Their response was sincere and vehement; these things had to be stopped. Congress passed three civil rights acts with bite in quick succession after stalling for decades over much weaker proposals; presidents and mayors made eloquent speeches about breaking the shackles of the past; money and energy flowed into ghettos, barrios, rural hinterlands, and even suburban households.

This new commitment to opening channels of opportunity had effects. Poor blacks who were in a position to take advantage of their new legal and economic resources did so; by the late 1970s, young, married, well-educated, professional blacks living in the Northeast had average incomes greater than their white counterparts. The number of black voters rose considerably and the number of black elected officials rose dramatically. Women moved in unprecedented num-

bers out of unpaid housework and low-paid office work into professional and white-collar jobs, and by the 1980s their salaries and political power had begun to rise accordingly. Legally immigrating Hispanics began to resemble older white ethnic groups in their range of incomes, occupations, and residential and marital choices.

This is a familiar and justly celebrated story. Opportunities really did become more equal than they had ever been in American history, and many women and minorities took advantage of them. Then came the 1970s, with oil cartels, combined inflation and unemployment, the glut of new female and young workers, the movement of many factories to newly industrializing nations. Political and psychological changes accompanied these demographic and economic shocks. Citizens grew weary of the so-called excesses of the 1960s. Politicians and academics cautioned against too much democracy and overly high expectations. Books about people taking advantage of the welfare system and the decline of academic and personal standards hit the best-seller lists. The number of whites who preferred "something in between" to either "desegregation" or "strict segregation" rose from 48 to 61 percent between 1964 and 1978.[4] Even incumbent politicians ran for office against government.

Americans' apparent rightward move is an equally familiar story with perhaps less familiar results. "The real value of the median state's maximum AFDC [Aid to Families with Dependent Children] payment declined by 27 percent between 1970 and 1983."[5] By 1983 a family of four

4. Philip Converse et al., *American Social Attitudes Data Sourcebook, 1947-1978* (Cambridge, MA: Harvard University Press, 1980), p. 61.
5. Rebecca Blank and Alan Blinder, "Macroeconomics, Income Distribution, and Poverty," in

at the poverty line was paying more than 16 percent of its income in direct taxes, almost double the percentage paid in 1965. Between 1979 and 1985, the annual median family income for the poorest 40 percent of the population declined $918 (in constant 1986 dollars) whereas the wealthiest 40 percent of families gained $2775, and the wealthiest 10 percent gained $6369.[6] Courts stopped ordering mandatory school desegregation and in a few cases reversed long-standing busing plans; racial segregation in schools increased over 13 percent in the Northeast between 1968 and 1980.[7] Policymakers decided that the concept of full employment permitted an official unemployment rate of around 6 percent, a figure that many had considered unacceptably high in the late 1950s.[8] The minimum wage

declined sharply in real value during the late 1970s and early 1980s. The Equal Rights Amendment was defeated. It is important to note that these and other changes were policy choices, not simply unintended or inevitable outcomes of uncontrollable economic, social, or demographic forces.

In short, the 1960s' fervor to improve opportunities for those left out ran out of steam before its promises were fulfilled for all of the poor. Legally and normatively, all minorities and women benefited; socially, economically, and politically, only some did. By the 1980s the rhetoric and memories of the 1960s, but little of the political commitment, remained.

Into this context came the children of the 1960s' generation. Their grandparents often expected little from the larger society, so they were not surprised when they received little. Their parents were led to expect and demand more, especially for their children, and for some the dreams came true. But today's poor youths have inherited convictions of their rights and hopes for their future with few of the structural conditions for fulfilling them.

Albert Hirschman describes this gap between promise and fulfillment as the "tunnel effect," as when drivers of cars in a traffic jam in a tunnel are initially pleased that cars in the adjacent lane are beginning to move. The tunnel effect

Fighting Poverty: What Works and What Doesn't, ed. Sheldon Danziger and Daniel Weinberg (Cambridge, MA: Harvard University Press, 1986), p. 196. Note, however, that this decline in AFDC payments may have been a deliberate response by state legislatures to the rise in noncash federal benefits during the same period, in order to keep the welfare package worth about the same as the lowest-paid employment. See Robert Moffitt, "Has State Redistribution Policy Grown More Conservative?" (Discussion paper no. 851-88, Institute for Research on Poverty, University of Wisconsin, 1988).

6. Sheldon Danziger and Daniel Weinberg, "Introduction," in *Fighting Poverty,* ed. Danziger and Weinberg, p. 17; Center on Budget and Policy Priorities, "Gap between Rich and Poor Widest Ever Reported" (Press release, Center on Budget and Policy Priorities, 17 Aug. 1987). Data are from U.S. Department of Commerce, Bureau of the Census, *Current Population Reports* (Washington, DC: Government Printing Office, 1985).

7. The percentage of black students in schools with more than half minority students went from 66.8 percent in 1968 to 79.9 percent in 1980 in the Northeast. Gary Orfield, *Public School Desegregation in the United States, 1968-1980* (Washington DC: Joint Center for Political Studies, 1983), p. 4.

8. Christopher Jencks, "Deadly Neighborhoods," *New Republic,* 13 June 1988, pp. 23-32.

operates because advances of others supply information about a more benign external environment; receipt of this information produces gratification; and this gratification overcomes, or at least suspends, *envy*. . . . As long as the tunnel effect lasts, everybody feels better off, both those who have become richer and those who have not.

At some point, however, those left behind in the tunnel come to believe that their

heightened expectations will not be met; not only are their hopes now dashed, but they are also left in a relatively worse position than when the upward mobility began.[9] "Nonrealization of the expectation [that my turn to move will soon come] will at some point result in my 'becoming furious,' that is, in my turning into an enemy of the established order."[10] Some of the infuriated will be galvanized into extraordinary efforts to pull themselves up by their bootstraps; others will unite in political rebellion or withdraw into an alternative social order. A few will sink into apathy or erupt into violence; they are the estranged poor.

Particular forms of relative deprivation will probably vary by race and gender.

Blacks of both genders will focus on persisting racial discrimination in the face of white insistence that discrimination has almost disappeared.[11] Women of both races may be attuned to intractable gender discrimination in jobs and households.[12] Poor Hispanics may especially react against inflated promises that the United States is the land of milk and honey. But all could plausibly respond to both past promises and present discrepancies between themselves and others like them with the question, "Why not me, too?"

Another gap between the rhetoric of the 1960s and the reality of the 1980s is more cultural than material. Many white Americans stopped demanding that blacks and ethnic minorities assimilate into mainstream—that is, white—styles and mores and started proclaiming the virtues of cultural pluralism. Similarly, some people stopped expecting employed women to act just like employed men, and began praising nurturant men and professional women who no longer hid their children. Blacks, ethnic minorities, and women took new pride in their distinctiveness and began to expect new accommoda-

9. Both poor nonwhites and poor whites have lost ground compared to wealthy members of their own group in the past three decades. Consider the average family income of families at the ninety-fifth and twentieth percentiles of the income distribution during the recession years of 1961, 1971, 1975, and 1983. (I used recession years in order to control roughly for unemployment rates.) The income ratio of the lower to the higher percentile for whites rose from .206 in 1961 to .219 in 1971, then declined to .212 in 1975 and .186 in 1983. The income ratio remained lower but followed the same pattern for nonwhites, rising from .138 in 1961 to .158 in 1971, then declining to .154 in 1975 and .118 in 1983. U.S. Department of Commerce, Bureau of the Census, *Current Population Reports,* series P-60, no. 146, *Money Income of Households, Families, and Persons in the United States: 1983* (Washington DC: Government Printing Office, 1985), pp. 49-50.

10. Albert Hirschman with Michael Rothschild, "The Changing Tolerance for Income Inequality in the Course of Economic Development," *Quarterly Journal of Economics,* 87:546, 552 (Nov. 1973). John Johnstone, "Social Class, Social Areas, and Delinquency," *Sociology and Social Research,* 63:49-72 (Oct. 1978), shows that poor youths commit more crime when they live in affluent neighborhoods than when they live in poor neighborhoods; he explains this finding as a manifestation of relative deprivation. Relative deprivation is not, of course, uniquely a property of the poor, but well-off sufferers are unlikely to become part of the estranged poor as a result.

11. In 1978, fewer than one-fourth of white Americans perceived discrimination against blacks in acquiring jobs, pay, and promotions or in treatment by police, teachers, labor unions, or home owners. Up to 75 percent of blacks felt discriminated against in at least one of these arenas. Of white respondents, 39 percent in 1964 and 63 percent in 1976 felt that there has been "a lot" of "real change in the position of [blacks] in the past few years." Blacks' views were the mirror image; the proportion who saw a lot of real change declined from 60 percent in 1964 to 32 percent in 1978. Louis Harris and Associates, *A Study of Attitudes toward Racial and Religious Minorities and toward Women* (New York: Louis Harris, 1978), pp. 4-34; Converse et al., *American Social Attitudes,* p. 79. Surveys in the 1980s show similar results.

12. Barbara Reskin, "Bringing the Men Back In," *Gender and Society,* 2:58-81 (Mar. 1988).

tions. But however sincere the proclamations and praise, practice was something else again. Employers found that blacks with nonstandard English and unconventional styles made white customers and coworkers nervous. They found that female employees who became pregnant, sought maternity leave, and needed good day care added new and unwanted complexities to personnel management. Californians declared English to be the only official state language. Too many middle-class white male Americans seemed unable or unwilling to distinguish what they liked and were used to from what was really crucial for running a business or society. Cultural pluralism went the way of the war on poverty, leaving behind high expectations and unsatisfying results.

Poor urban blacks already angry at withdrawn promises of opportunity and pluralism may be tipped into fury or despair by a weakening sense of community. A middle-class white author can easily romanticize in hindsight blacks' sense of mutual commitment in the days of racial segregation. But blacks themselves, like ethnic whites whose enclaves are also broken up by physical and social mobility, mourn the decline of the solidarity forced upon them by a common enemy. That curiously bittersweet loss is worsened by a simpler but more devastating problem. Poor blacks, like poor whites in Appalachia and ethnic slums, survive as well as they do by sharing resources and responsibilities.[13] But if their resources decline past a certain point, they must choose which responsibilities to fulfill and which to abandon. The weakening of community among urban blacks may be due not only to the

13. Carol B. Stack, *All Our Kin* (New York: Harper & Row, 1974). I also owe the next point in this paragraph to Carol Stack.

movement of middle-class blacks to the suburbs but also to the rise in unemployment and decline in incomes during the 1970s and 1980s. At some point, people must choose to feed themselves and their young children and let their cousins and older children fend for themselves. If those older children are already inclined to hostility or despair, they may slide from the merely poor into the estranged poor. Thus the deterioration of well-off Americans' general commitment to their poorer fellows can lead to a deterioration of poor Americans' particular commitment to their even poorer neighbors and relatives. Even if only a small minority of the poor are forced into such triage, the people at the very end of the line could well experience a devastating loss of place and faith.

Even the decline in old-fashioned racism and sexism during the last three decades may do little to help poor minorities enter the mainstream. White employers have invented new ways to discriminate without admitting prejudice. One method is statistical discrimination: denying positions of responsibility to members of some group because of a belief—perhaps correct—that that group causes more problems than other kinds of people. Young black men, for example, may be more likely to come to work late, borrow petty cash, or talk back to obnoxious customers than young white men or older black women, so employers behave rationally by choosing older, white, or female employees. The difficulty, of course, is that a likelihood of 5 percent more thefts leads to a nearly 100 percent denial of employment to young black men, thereby punishing many more innocent than guilty. Surveys of employers show that statistical discrimination is especially likely in jobs that require at most a high school education—just the

jobs, of course, that most poor youths are able to pursue.[14] To the degree that statistical discrimination is a cover, conscious or not, for lingering racial or gender prejudice, would-be workers face an additional barrier to their efforts to prove themselves exceptions to the rule. No wonder so many eventually give up.

Combining employers' suspicions of no-longer-deferential adolescents with poor youths' suspicions of proclamations of equal opportunity is lethal.

Self-consciously aspiring toward . . . self-respect, many young blacks see themselves and are seen by others as not taking "the stuff" that has traditionally been dished out to black Americans. . . . Add to this new image of militancy a . . . stereotype of black [male] youth as being primarily responsible for urban street crime . . . and general incivility, and one is faced with the specter of a nearly "unemployable" person.[15]

Then add poor education and lack of work experience among many ghetto youths, and the recent excess of potential workers, and the "nearly" may well drop out of that verdict.

There are many other ways in which the gap between the promise and reality of equal opportunity works to create the physical, social, economic, political, and psychological conditions that add up to estrangement from mainstream America. My main point should, however, be clear:

14. Jomills Braddock III and James McPartland, "How Minorities Continue to Be Excluded from Equal Employment Opportunities," *Journal of Social Issues,* 43:15-17 (Spring 1987).
15. Elijah Anderson, "Some Observations of Black Youth Unemployment," in *Youth Employment and Public Policy,* ed. Bernard E. Anderson and Isabel V. Sawhill (Englewood Cliffs, NJ: Prentice-Hall, 1980), p. 85; Toby Herr et al., "Early Job Turnover among the Urban Poor" (Report, Center for Urban Affairs and Policy Research, Northwestern University, 1987).

Political choices ranging from slavery to a preference for unemployment over inflation in the context of a particular ideological framework helped to create a group of people with no resources, no skills, and no faith. But political choices can undo what they have done; I turn now to that possibility.

NARROWING THE GAP BETWEEN RHETORIC AND REALITY

Two strategies are necessary to help the estranged poor, but neither suffices alone. The first addresses particular individuals—and their children—as they are now; the second seeks to halt the reproduction of a similar group of people in the future.

The most urgent task is to enable the estranged poor to enter mainstream society or to find a satisfying alternative. Teaching skills and even providing a starting place without restoring faith will not work, and trying to instill faith without giving a material grounding also will not work. Thus either workfare alone or social services alone—never mind simple income maintenance—are insufficient.

The literature on programs to help the poor supports this claim powerfully if unsystematically. Despite controversy over what the underclass is and whether and why it is growing, analysts surprisingly concur on what to do about it. Consider the following programs and recommendations. The directors of an extensive research program on black male unemployment conclude that "public or private policies . . . should include not only government jobs programs for youth and aggressive anti-discrimination activity, but also the efforts of a broad range of public and private social institutions, ranging from the welfare system to employers to schools, to the criminal

justice system, and to families."[16] The *New York Times* praises a program that has prevented pregnancies among 32 teenage girls through "care that is as multidimensional as the care that's supposed to come from one's own family.... Institutional programs can work, but require a lot of money."[17] In 1981, Eugene Lang promised to pay college costs for a class of Harlem sixth-graders and to make himself and a full-time counselor available for tutoring, advising, companionship, and intervention on their behalf; as of June 1987, 27 of the 48 students remaining in Harlem had graduated, the rest were expected to, and so far 25 had been admitted to college.[18] The most extensive analysis of job-training and placement programs concludes that "income maintenance should be deemphasized.... More intensive investments are needed."[19]

The common thread in these disparate programs and analyses is that successful efforts to aid the estranged poor cost a lot, last a long time, and involve a wide array of activities aimed at changing skills, views, and life circumstances.[20]

The political implications of this conclusion are clear. On the one hand, politics as usual will not suffice. On the other

16. Richard Freeman and Harry Holzer, "Young Blacks and Jobs—What We Now Know," *Public Interest,* 78:31 (Winter 1985).

17. "The Editorial Notebook: Pregnancy Prevention," *New York Times,* 16 June 1986.

18. Jane Perlez, "In Harlem, Millionaire's Promise Still Inspires," *New York Times,* 21 June 1987.

19. Robert Taggart, *A Fisherman's Guide: An Assessment of Training and Remediation Strategies* (Kalamazoo, MI: W. E. Upjohn Institute for Employment Research, 1981), p. ix.

20. More systematic compilations of "programs that work at the local level" concur. See National League of Cities, *Children, Families, and Cities: Programs That Work at the Local Level* (Washington, DC: National League of Cities, 1987); idem,

hand, the situation is not hopeless; if the United States chose to devote enough private resources and public actions to the effort, many of the worst-off could be moved into the ideological, behavioral, and economic mainstream.

The costs of such an effort would be substantial, but the benefits greater. Some analysts argue that programs such as the Women, Infants and Children Feeding Program, Head Start, Chapter I—addressing compensatory education—of the Education Consolidation and Improvement Act, the Jobs Corps, the California Conservation Corps, and others "not only improve the lives of participating children, but 'save public moneys as well'" by raising wages and reducing health problems, crime, welfare dependency, and unemployment.[21] None of these programs serves more than a fraction of the eligible population, and the staff members of all

Reducing Urban Unemployment: What Works at the Local Level (Washington DC: National League of Cities, 1987); William T. Grant Foundation Commission on Work, Family, and Citizenship, *The Forgotten Half: Non-College Youth in America* (Washington, DC: W.T. Grant Foundation Commission, 1988); Robert Woodson, ed., *Youth Crime and Urban Policy* (Washington DC: American Enterprise Institute, 1981); Andrew Hahn and Robert Lerman, *What Works in Youth Employment Policy?* (Washington, DC: National Planning Association, Committee on New American Realities, 1985); Manpower Demonstration Research Corporation, *Summary and Findings of the National Supported Work Demonstration* (Cambridge, MA: Ballinger, 1980). Poverty programs in the 1980s, unlike those in the 1960s, ignore empowerment of individuals or local communities. That seems a serious mistake; political efforts ranging from neighborhood anticrime watches to campaigns for political offices could be important in reducing the underclass and inhibiting its reproduction. Obviously, this additional ingredient makes the political component of social policy reform that much more central, and difficult.

21. Grant Foundation Commission, *Forgotten Half,* p. 31, quoting from U.S. Congress, House,

of them have had enough experience to know how to start and maintain high-quality programs. Their expansion seems an obvious first step.

Other analysts are less sanguine about both the ratio of financial benefits to costs and the long-term social benefits of these programs.[22] But the question is not whether these programs are as successful as we would like—they are not—or as successful as many programs that serve a less disadvantaged population—they are not. The issue is whether Americans are willing to let some fellow citizens destroy their own and others' lives without using the available knowledge to stop some of the destruction. I am not simply calling for throwing money at the problem, for two reasons: money is not enough, and we know with some precision where to throw it most effectively. What we now need is a political decision to spend what it will take to give faith, skills, and a starting place to people who lack them all.

A second cost of successful programs is personal rather than financial. They take a lot of people, time, and emotional energy. We could, however, turn a potential flaw into a virtue by relying on local talent that is now mostly wasted. Peer tutoring teaches the tutor even more than the pupil; peer counseling reduces juvenile crime and teenage pregnancy and improves race relations; parents' involvement in the schools improves children's learning. Again we must beware roman-

ticization. Programs for citizen participation often increase disparities between middle-class and poor families, camouflage bureaucratic ineptitude and patronization, or simply die from inertia.[23] At best, using even highly trained community members as counselors and teachers raises unexpected and complex problems.[24] But here, too, the main issue is political will. There are enough successful models of how to train and employ community members to help the poor that the appropriate question remains, Why don't we do more of it? rather than, What should we do?

Successful programs will also be costly to organizational stability. Public officials traditionally tackle problems one at a time. Legal-aid lawyers jostle with social workers about clients' rights and responsibilities, and both perceive the police as competitors for public resources. Local officials, perhaps especially new black urban administrators, mistrust suburban- and rural-dominated state legislatures. Both fear federal control as much as they want federal dollars. But helping the estranged poor requires attacking racial and gender discrimination and poverty and crime and lousy schools and anger, frustration, ignorance. No feature in our policymaking system prohibits such coordination, but conventional American political practice inhibits it.[25]

Select Committee on Children, Youth and Families, *Opportunities for Success: Cost-Effective Programs for Children,* Aug. 1985.

22. Laurie Bassi and Orley Ashenfelter, "The Effect of Direct Job Creation and Training Programs on Low-Skilled Workers," in *Fighting Poverty,* ed. Danziger and Weinberg, pp. 138-51; Christopher Jencks, "Comment" [on Nathan Glazer, "Education and Training Programs and Poverty"], in ibid., pp. 175-79.

23. Jennifer Hochschild, *The New American Dilemma: Liberal Democracy and School Desegregation* (New Haven, CT: Yale University Press, 1984), pp. 108-12.

24. Judith Musick, "A Chain of Enablement," *Zero to Three,* 8(2):1-6 (Dec. 1987).

25. A simple example of interorganizational suspicion is the case of Judge Leonard Edwards, who is spearheading an acclaimed effort to reform the juvenile justice system in California. Administrators from almost all agencies are cooperating; the holdout agency is the Department of Social Services, which supervises cases under court jurisdiction. The public defender says, "I've heard social

Institutional constraints on successful programs go even beyond these three costs. They include "a strong need for overselling whatever is to be done," which generates backlash and a proclamation of failure; "the tendency of our political processes to accord special treatment only to groups that are well organized, politically active, and sophisticated in pursuing a uniform set of interests"; politicians' inability to refuse any claimant, so that new resources are spread too thin; and a history of weak administrative capacity in federal labor market programs. Perhaps the most severe institutional constraint is the politician's "strong need for overselling whatever is to be done." That means that the inevitable failure of a large proportion of programs to help the estranged poor—and the inevitable failure of a large proportion of the participants in even the most successful programs—will make the whole effort seem futile, not merely risky. Add the fact that public opinion polls show over and over that "Americans favor government action to help the poor, but they generally dislike the subset of government programs that are intended to be targeted on the poor," and the prospects become dismal for expensive programs for the worst-off of the poor.[26]

It is just as well that I am focusing here on only the extreme end point of poverty and despair. I cannot say just how many people need such a comprehensive commitment, but it is surely a minority of the poor and of any ethnic or racial group. Perhaps the best political strategy for overcoming the daunting constraints just described would emphasize how small the group of estranged poor is. That would permit two arguments: (1) the disproportion between the number of targeted people and the amount of damage and misery they represent suggests that the benefits of aiding even some will have large social payoffs; and (2) these almost unmanageable problems are of a manageable scope. We do not, after all, need very many foster homes, or public jobs, or Eugene Langs to make a big impact.

Arguments about the small number of estranged poor will have bite only if it is clear that current members who escape will not simply be replaced by a new generation. That point brings us to the other essential set of policies—those needed to reorganize the economy and polity to minimize the number of people who grow up with no skills, place, or faith in the opportunity system.

My first observation about the next generation focuses on the children of the existing poor, or more specifically, on a curious set of common recommendations for the parents of those children. Bearing and raising a child, even at too young an age and without a husband, does not automatically make a mother a member of the underclass. The amount of damage to mother and child depends on the emotional well-being of the mother and the social circumstances of the family. If unwed teenage motherhood is problematic mainly because of the mother's poverty, it is not obvious why providing jobs for fathers—mostly unmarried—is the best way to solve the problem. At best, it

---

workers say hundreds of times over the years that they don't care what a judge says, they have the power and they are going to do what they think is best." A spokesperson for the social workers disagrees; "The system works well, even though we all have distinct roles and are not always in agreement." John Hubner, "Childhood's Friend," *West* [magazine of *San Jose Mercury News*], 1 May 1988, pp. 34-35.

26. All quotations in this paragraph are from Hugh Heclo, "The Political Foundations of Antipoverty Policy," in *Fighting Poverty*, ed. Danziger and Weinberg, pp. 330, 332-35.

is one step removed from the mother's and child's poverty, and because any program to aid the poor has a high failure rate and is very costly, indirectness adds a needless inefficiency. After all, not all of those newly employed fathers will marry—and stay married to—the mothers, or support their children. Why not, then, concentrate just as much on jobs for mothers?[27] At worst, increasing the number of marriageable men by improving their skills and providing them jobs without providing the same service for women reifies a patriarchal social structure in which women are dependent upon individual men—rather than on men collectively, as in the welfare system—for their and their children's livelihood.[28]

Caution is clearly called for here; I am not arguing that public policies should encourage unmarried women to have children or that public policies should not make strenuous efforts to help men finish school, secure a job, and support their children. I am simply arguing that the common recommendation of a "macroeconomic dating service," in Adolph Reed's brilliant phrase,[29] has worrisome norma-

tive implications and the potential for more spillage than necessary from the proverbial leaky bucket of social policy.

As my argument for providing jobs for women as well as for men implies, policies to prevent the reproduction of the estranged poor should begin with skills and, especially, a starting point, rather than with faith, if for no other reason than that it is probably easier to provide skills and a starting point and then let faith grow than to create and sustain faith in an empty promise.

That reasoning implies programs to reduce gender and racial discrimination, improve schools and ease the transition to work, reduce teenage pregnancies and births, provide jobs to inner-city youth, break down the barriers between jobs in the primary and secondary labor markets, assert more political control over plant closings and industrial relocation, give previously disenfranchised people more control over local political decisions, and so on. It may imply even broader policies if race- and poverty-specific programs cannot sustain popular support, especially during economic downturns, when they are most needed.[30] In that case, the United States needs programs in which the downwardly redistributive component is submerged economically and politically in the horizontally redistributive component. Social Security is one such program; family allowances, full-employment policy, and national youth service programs are others.

The broader the policy, the more controversy there will be over how to

27. Women in job-training and placement programs increase their income more than comparable men do, even though women have been generally underrepresented in the programs and disproportionately placed in their least successful tracks. Lynn Burbridge, "Black Women in Employment and Training Programs," in *Slipping through the Cracks,* ed. Margaret Simms and Julianne Malveaux (New Brunswick, NJ: Transaction Books, 1986), pp. 97-114. The rise occurs more because women increase the number of hours they work than because their wages rise; thus programs of comparable worth or steering women into traditionally male-dominated jobs could produce even greater benefits for previously unemployed poor women. Bassi and Ashenfelter, "Direct Job Creation," pp. 140-47.

28. Carol Stack, "Viewpoint," *Signs,* in press.

29. Adolph Reed, "The Liberal Technocrat," *Nation,* 6 Feb. 1988, p. 168.

30. William Julius Wilson, *The Truly Disadvantaged* (Chicago: University of Chicago Press, 1987); Charles Hamilton and Dona Hamilton, "Social Policies, Civil Rights, and Poverty," in *Fighting Poverty,* ed. Danziger and Weinberg, pp. 287-311; Robert Kuttner, *The Life of the Party* (New York: Viking, 1987).

achieve it and the less we know about the links between efforts and results. Those facts imply that even the best-designed programs will be inefficient, full of flaws, and less successful than we hope. In addition, these programs must be downwardly redistributive to some degree really to affect poverty. The political strategy for embarking on such ambitious programs should therefore focus on the conservative, stabilizing outcomes of these apparently radical reforms. Public opinion surveys have shown repeatedly that Americans want to be generous toward people in need; they want to be free from gender and racial discrimination; they want peo-

ple to have jobs that support them and their children. Above all, Americans want to believe that equal opportunity is neither a sham nor the privilege of a few. The estranged poor challenge these beliefs and deny these desires. American citizens may be willing to do more—both as individuals and through their chosen policymakers—than is normally assumed in order really to open the system to all. So far, the American policymaking system has made a lot of wrong choices, but there is no reason why we cannot change our course, and lots of reasons why we should.

12

The Logic of Workfare:
The Underclass and Work Policy

By LAWRENCE M. MEAD

ABSTRACT: Much of today's entrenched poverty reflects the fact that poor adults seldom work consistently. The problem cannot be blamed predominantly on lack of jobs or other barriers to employment, as the chance to work seems widely available. More likely, the poor do not see work in menial jobs as fair, possible, or obligatory, though they want to work in principle. Government has evolved policies explicitly to raise work levels among the poor. Workfare programs, linked to welfare, show the most promise but still reach only a minority of employable recipients. Welfare reform should, above all, raise participation in these programs, as the share of clients involved largely governs their impact. Welfare should also cover more nonworking men to bring them under workfare. While work enforcement may seem punitive, the poor must become workers before they can stake larger claims to equality.

Lawrence M. Mead is an associate professor of politics at New York University, where he teaches public policy and American government. He is the author of Beyond Entitlement: The Social Obligations of Citizenship *and other works on social policy, especially welfare and employment programs. He has been involved in deliberations on welfare reform in Washington, D.C. He received his Ph.D. in political science from Harvard University in 1973.*

AN important reason for entrenched poverty and dependency in American cities is that poor individuals and families no longer work with the regularity they once did. In 1959, 32 percent of the heads of poor families worked full-time, and only 31 percent did not work at all, even though 22 percent of those heads were elderly, or beyond the normal working age. In 1984, in contrast, only 17 percent worked full-time, and 51 percent did not work at all, even though the proportion of elderly had fallen to 10 percent, due to growing Social Security payments.[1]

The change primarily reflects rising welfare dependency by single mothers and less regular work by single men, many of them the fathers of welfare children. In ghetto neighborhoods today, welfare is the economic mainstay while many more men and youths are jobless than would have been true a generation ago. Aid to Families with Dependent Children (AFDC), the main welfare program, supports 4 million families, mostly female headed, yet only 5 percent of the mothers work at a given time compared to 53 percent for all single mothers with children under 18.[2] In 1960, 83 percent of both black and white men were either working or looking for work, but by 1982 the rate had fallen to 70 percent for blacks, as against 77 percent for whites;[3]

the drop was apparently even greater for the low-skilled black men with the highest unemployment. Many, though not all, of these poor but nonworking adults have problems severe enough for them to be included in the underclass.

We are far from the world of the turn of the century when whole families of immigrants on New York's Lower East Side labored long hours six or seven days a week, yet still were destitute.[4] In the intervening century, rising real wages have lifted the vast majority of working-aged Americans above need—if they work. At the century's turn, the poor were needy despite employment. Today, on the whole, they are poor for lack of it. Their overwhelming economic problem is nonwork, in which I include both inability to obtain a job and failure even to look for one. Rising nonwork by working-aged adults is the main reason the overall poverty rate, now 14 percent, has fallen little in the last twenty years despite economic growth and decreasing need among the elderly.

The reasons for nonwork remain controversial, but both liberals and conservatives have given up hope that the problem will yield to general measures such as an expansionary economic policy or civil rights enforcement. Government has had to embark on policies and programs aimed specifically at raising work levels among the poor. Of these, much the most important is workfare, or recent requirements that employable welfare recipients work or prepare for work in return for support. In this article, I summarize the reasons behind this development, describe what current workfare programs achieve, propose some further developments in

1. U.S. Department of Commerce, Bureau of the Census, *Characteristics of the Population below the Poverty Level: 1984*, series P-60, no. 152 (Washington, DC: Government Printing Office, June 1986), tab. 4, p. 15.

2. Robert Moffitt, "Work and the U.S. Welfare System: A Review" (Study prepared for the U.S. Department of Health and Human Services, rev. version, Oct. 1987), tabs. 1, 4.

3. U.S. Department of Commerce, Bureau of the Census, *Statistical Abstract of the United States: 1984* (Washington, DC: Government Printing Office, 1983), p. 407.

4. Jacob A. Riis, *How the Other Half Lives: Studies among the Tenements of New York* (New York: Dover, 1971).

work policy, and consider the implications of workfare for equality.

THE ECONOMIC CONTEXT

The tradition among American policymakers has been to blame poverty on barriers to opportunity. It has been assumed that poor adults will work if they have access to jobs, so poverty can only be due to a lack of jobs or to other practical impediments to employment. The great fact shaping the work debate today is that these barriers no longer seem as compelling as they once did.

Those seeking barriers ask, above all, whether jobs are accessible to nonworking adults, most of whom are low skilled and live in urban areas. Groups that are heavily poor—minorities, women, and youths—typically have much higher unemployment rates than normal for the economy, reaching, in the case of inner-city black youths, catastrophic levels of 40 percent or more. Such figures seem to compel the conclusion that jobs must be lacking. They arouse deep-seated memories of the Great Depression, when an economic collapse threw a quarter of the labor force out of work.

But in the postwar era, the economy has suffered no contraction comparable to that of the 1930s, not even the severe recession of the early 1980s. Decade after decade, it has generated new jobs on a scale never seen before. Total employment rose 35 percent between 1970 and 1985. Millions of immigrants, legal and illegal, have flooded into the country to do jobs for which, apparently, citizens are unavailable. At this writing, overall unemployment has fallen close to 5 percent, a level many economists consider close to full employment.

As the special editor of this volume has noted, confidence in prosperity caused the architects of the war on poverty in the 1960s almost to dismiss structural economic causes of poverty. They assumed jobs existed for the poor. The emphasis was all on compensatory education and training programs to make poor adults more able workers.[5] In the current tight labor market, that conviction remains compelling.

The nation has, however, experienced economic troubles since 1970 that have given new life to the belief that the economy might deny employment to many low-skilled workers. In the 1970s, shocks including higher oil prices led to recessions that pushed the overall jobless rate into double digits. Employment growth was for several years outpaced by a massive growth in the labor force due to the maturing of the baby-boom generation. Most seriously, the economy encountered competitiveness problems that seemed to constrict opportunity for low-skilled job seekers. Industry and manufacturing, formerly staples of well-paid manual employment in the Northern cities, declined due to foreign competition, and the remaining jobs tended to shift to the suburbs, the Sunbelt, or overseas.

While new employment has mushroomed, it is predominantly in service trades, which pay less than unionized factory jobs, and there are more jobs in the suburbs than in the urban centers where most jobless poor people live. Better-paying urban jobs are mostly in the new high-technology economy based on information processing, which typically requires more education than earlier employment. But in the inner city, education levels have fallen due to high drop-

5. William Julius Wilson, *The Truly Disadvantaged: The Inner City, the Underclass, and Public Policy* (Chicago: University of Chicago Press, 1987), pp. 129-33.

out rates and the failure of many students to absorb even minimal skills.

In short, there appears to be a mismatch between available jobs and unskilled job seekers. The inability of poor adults to commute to or qualify for today's employment might explain the catastrophic rates of joblessness found in the inner city, even if the surrounding economy is prosperous.[6] Unemployment, in turn, explains high illegitimacy and dependency in the ghetto, since poor mothers prefer welfare to marrying poor men who cannot support them. From the decline of family stability, many of the other social problems of the underclass follow.[7]

To date, however, proponents of the mismatch theory have appealed mostly to the high-level trends in the labor market just mentioned. They have not demonstrated a concrete connection between the workers victimized by deindustrialization and jobless poor people in the inner city. Research that does look at individual workers suggests, rather, that many jobs are still available in the inner city, even if they are usually not very good jobs.

If the ghetto were depressed in the 1930s sense, we would expect to find that most job seekers were unemployed long-term. But, while a minority are, most are out of work for only a few weeks. Among the groups with the highest measured unemployment—minorities, women, and youths—employment and unemployment tend to be highly transient. There is rapid turnover, with workers moving quickly into or out of employment or the labor force, not a pattern that suggests

that jobs are absolutely lacking in the ghetto.[8] We do not know that there would be enough jobs if all unskilled workers sought them at once, but jobs clearly seem available at the margin. It is inconsistent work, not a total lack of employment, that largely explains today's adult poverty and dependency.

The poor themselves say that jobs of a kind usually are available. Only 40 percent of poor adults working less than full-time give inability to find work as the main reason for their short hours, and only 11 percent of those not working at all do so. Much more often, the constraint is that they are ill, retired, in school, or keeping house. These figures rise to 45 and 16 percent among poor blacks and to 59 and 23 percent among poor black men, the main focus of the mismatch theory.[9] Even among jobless inner-city black youths, the group with the highest unemployment, 71 percent say it is fairly easy to get a job at the minimum wage. They complain, rather, about the quality of these jobs, which are mostly menial and low paid.[10]

Research has also failed to show that employment is really inaccessible to inner-city job seekers due to distance or qualifications. Black workers do have to commute further than others to find work, but this fact is only a minor reason for their much

6. John D. Kasarda, "The Regional and Urban Redistribution of People and Jobs in the U.S." (Paper prepared for the Committee on National Urban Policy, National Research Council, Oct. 1986).

7. Wilson, *Truly Disadvantaged*, passim.

8. Robert E. Hall, "Why Is the Unemployment Rate So High at Full Employment?" *Brookings Papers on Economic Activity*, no, 3, pp. 369-402 (1970); Kim B. Clark and Lawrence H. Summers, "Labor Market Dynamics and Unemployment: A Reconsideration," ibid., no. 1, pp. 13-46 (1979).

9. Calculated from Bureau of the Census, *Characteristics of the Population below the Poverty Level: 1984*, tab. 10, pp. 37, 45, 47.

10. Harry J. Holzer, "Black Youth Nonemployment: Duration and Job Search," in *The Black Youth Employment Crisis*, ed. Richard B. Freeman and Harry J. Holzer (Chicago: University of Chicago Press, 1986), chap. 1.

higher unemployment compared to other groups; differences of race and education are much more important.[11] The increase in education requirements for available jobs has been overstated, in that the share of positions requiring more than a high school education has actually changed little despite high technology.[12] Also, some part of rising credentialism reflects, not a real demand for higher skills, but an attempt by employers to compensate for falling standards in the schools.

THE SOCIAL CONTEXT

Such findings leave it a mystery why nonworking adults do not take and hold available jobs more consistently. Inquiry has sought out barriers of a more social nature, but these, too, turn out to be less substantial than often claimed.

Nonwork has frequently been blamed on racial discrimination, since most of today's long-term poor are nonwhite. However, minority employment rates were much higher before civil rights than they are now, and working blacks today earn wages closer to those of comparable whites than ever before. Such trends make it implausible that nonworking blacks are being denied all employment. There is some evidence that employers prefer to hire women, both black and white, rather than unskilled black men and youths, whom they view as uncoopera-

tive,[13] but this preference reflects experience and is not entirely invidious.

Many have supposed that welfare deters employment because recipients typically have their grants reduced dollar for dollar for any earnings they make. But extensive research has failed to show that these disincentives are strong enough to explain the very low work levels found in the ghetto. Most welfare mothers would be better off, at least economically, if they worked, yet few do, and work levels vary little with welfare benefit levels. It has been estimated that even the total abolition of AFDC would raise working hours by the recipients by only 30 percent.[14]

Nor is it clear, as is commonly asserted, that poor women fail to work because of the burdens of children or their inability to find child care. While numbers of children do deter work, most welfare mothers now have only one or two dependents, and those with preschool children are as likely to work their way off welfare as those with older children.[15] Surveys have shown that most working mothers, rich and poor, manage to arrange child care fairly easily, mostly informally with friends and relatives. Only 9 percent make use of organized facilities, yet only 6 percent lose working time in a given month due to a breakdown in child care.[16] Government must clearly

11. David T. Ellwood, "The Spatial Mismatch Hypothesis: Are There Teenage Jobs Missing in the Ghetto?" in *Black Youth Employment Crisis*, ed. Freeman and Holzer, chap. 4; Jonathan S. Leonard, "Space, Time and Unemployment: Los Angeles 1980" (Paper, School of Business Administration, University of California, Berkeley, Sep. 1986). These studies use census data from, respectively, 1970 and 1980.

12. Thomas Bailey and Roger Waldinger, "A Skills Mismatch in New York's Labor Market?" *New York Affairs*, 8(3):3-18 (Fall 1984).

13. George J. Borjas, "The Demographic Determinants of the Demand for Black Labor," in *Black Youth Employment Crisis*, ed. Freeman and Holzer, chap. 5.

14. Moffitt, "Work and the U.S. Welfare System," pp. 20-35.

15. Mary Jo Bane and David T. Ellwood, "The Dynamics of Dependence: The Routes to Self-Sufficiency" (Study prepared for the U.S. Department of Health and Human Services at Urban Systems Research and Engineering, Cambridge, MA, June 1983), pp. 34, 44-45.

16. U.S. Department of Commerce, Bureau of the Census, *Who's Minding the Kids? Child Care*

pay for care if it wants welfare women to work, and it already does pay, but there appears little need for more center-based child care.

Nor is lack of skills usually an impediment to work in some job. Welfare mothers with education and work experience are more likely to work than those without, but the influence of these and other demographic variables is less than one would expect. For example, younger, black mothers are just as likely to work their way off the rolls as older, white women.[17]

Work for the poor involves real burdens, but they are mostly the demands inseparable from finding jobs and organizing one's life to hold them, not impediments peculiar to the needy. On the whole, economic and social barriers explain inequality rather than nonwork. That is, they explain why the poor do poorly if they work, not why so many fail to work at all. Unquestionably, most poor adults lack the education and background to succeed in the sense of obtaining good jobs, and recent trends in the economy may have made prospects more difficult for them. But these factors cannot explain why so many do not work even enough to escape poverty and welfare. By implication, barriers cannot explain the existence of an underclass.

CULTURAL FACTORS

If barriers to work are not prohibitive, we must finally reconsider the orthodox presumption that poor job seekers seek out employment as assiduously as the better-off. Studies suggest that the poor

want to work as strongly as other people,[18] but since they do not work as consistently in practice, this finding has to be interpreted.

One reading is that they want to work, but only if they can also succeed, that is, attain jobs paying mainstream wages. They reject jobs that pay little, especially if they are "dead-end." That is, nonwork has a political element. It is in part a protest against the menial jobs the economy offers the unskilled. This view has some plausibility for nonworking inner-city men and youths, who, studies show, can be fractious employees. Many black youths insist on earning the same wages white youths earn, but since they are less able to attain them, they more often remain jobless for long periods. When they do work, they more often come into conflict with employers, causing them to leave jobs or be fired.[19]

Another interpretation is that nonworkers, despite their professions, do not really seek work. They are oriented to private life and have abandoned advancing themselves through employment. Economic fatalism is a feature of poverty culture, particularly on the part of minorities who, until recent decades, saw little chance to get ahead. The ghetto culture of today's Northern cities may, in part, reflect the defeatism poor blacks learned under Jim Crow in the South.[20] In the

18. Leonard Goodwin, *Do the Poor Want to Work? A Social-Psychological Study of Work Orientations* (Washington, DC: Brookings Institution, 1972).

19. Freeman and Holzer, eds., *Black Youth Employment Crisis*, chaps. 1-3, 7, 10; Elijah Anderson, "Some Observations of Black Youth Employment," in *Youth Employment and Public Policy*, ed. Bernard E. Anderson and Isabel V. Sawhill (Englewood Cliffs, NJ: Prentice-Hall, 1980), chap. 3.

20. Nicholas Lemann, "The Origins of the Underclass," *Atlantic*, June 1986, pp. 31-55.

Arrangements: Winter 1984-5, series P-70, no. 9 (Washington, DC: Government Printing Office, May 1987), tabs. B, E.

17. Bane and Ellwood, "Dynamics of Dependence," pp. v, 29-45.

background is the fact that the most heavily dependent American ethnic groups—blacks, Hispanics, and American Indians—have origins outside the West. Where Western culture has sought to overcome material hardships through rationalizing economic activity, non-Western culture, on the whole, has counseled acceptance. That heritage helps to explain why today's poor seem more passive in the face of apparent opportunity than other ethnic immigrant groups, even if most blacks and Hispanics have absorbed the acquisitive individualism of the mainstream culture.

However, the most persuasive interpretation of nonworking psychology, especially for welfare mothers, is what in the 1960s was referred to as culture of poverty. In this view, the poor *want* to work and observe other mainstream mores, but they do not feel they actually *can* work given the impediments they face.[21] While the barriers to work do not seem unusual to an impartial eye, nonworkers often feel them to be. They feel that someone else, typically government, must find them a job and arrange child care and other logistics before they actually can work. Thus they have absorbed orthodox values but not with the force needed to bind actual behavior. For them, work is something they would like to do, but not something they feel they must do at any cost. It is an aspiration but not an obligation.

This psychology is no doubt longstanding, but it has become more visible due to changes in the inner city. Under Jim Crow, when blacks of all classes were confined to separate residential areas,

better-off blacks provided the role models and supported the social institutions—such as churches—needed to uphold work and other mainstream mores for the group as a whole. But after the advent of civil rights, these leading elements departed for the suburbs. Many poorer blacks then rejected legal but low-paying jobs in favor of welfare, crime, and the underground economy. The ghetto lost its connection with the legitimate economy, and far fewer residents now have regular contact with working people. They thus find it more difficult to locate "straight" jobs even if they want to.[22]

In this analysis, the major task of work policy is not to dismantle barriers to work, because they seldom literally bar employment. Rather, it is to restore conventional work norms to the authority they had in the inner city before civil rights. Public programs and policies must somehow take over the leadership role previously exercised by the black middle class. They must reconnect the ghetto with the legitimate economy, for only through the workplace can poor blacks enter mainstream society.

POLICY DEVELOPMENT

Federal policymakers have gradually accepted that work by the poor must be enforced, not simply facilitated by expanded opportunities. Work policy has been closely tied to welfare, as it is nonwork by welfare adults that is most controversial, and it is only the recipients of benefits whom government has the authority to require to work.

The approach given the longest trial was work incentives, or the attempt to give recipients stronger financial inducements to work. As mentioned earlier,

21. Daniel P. Moynihan, ed., *On Understanding Poverty: Perspectives from the Social Sciences* (New York: Basic Books, 1969), chaps. 2-3, 7-9; Hyman Rodman, "The Lower-Class Value Stretch," *Social Forces*, 42(2):205-15 (Dec. 1963).

22. Wilson, *Truly Disadvantaged*, pp. 46-62, 137-38, 143-44.

welfare seems to remove the material payoff to work by deducting any earnings from assistance. To reduce this "tax" on work, reforms in 1967 allowed working recipients to keep somewhat over a third of their earnings. But work levels did not rise, and the Reagan administration largely eliminated the incentives in 1981. Research, too, has shown that changes in the payoff to work, like varying benefit levels, have surprisingly little effect on work effort by recipients. The reality is that welfare recipients, especially the long-term cases, are not very responsive to economic incentives. Indeed, if they were, they would seldom be poor in the first place.

A later strategy was public employment. Provide disadvantaged adults with attractive, temporary jobs within government, the argument went, and they will become more involved in work and will move on to regular employment. As many as 750,000 such jobs a year were funded under the Comprehensive Employment and Training Act (CETA) during the 1970s. While the recipients usually contributed useful labor, they seldom made the transition to private employment. Most went back on welfare or unemployment benefits or, at best, took other jobs within government. The problem was that the level of pay and amenity necessary to raise clients' commitment to work was more than they could usually command in the private sector. Thus the jobs were in part disguised welfare and did not really solve the work problem. For this and other reasons, Congress killed the program in 1981.

Increasingly, work policy has relied on administrative work requirements, or stipulations that welfare recipients look for work or enter training as a condition of receiving assistance. Such a test was added to AFDC in 1967 and was stiffened

in 1971 and 1981. The requirement differs from an incentive in that employable recipients are faced with a cut in welfare if they do not seek to work, rather than promised higher income if they do. The offender's share of assistance is eliminated from the family's welfare grant, which, however, continues for the rest of the family.

The work requirement bears on recipients who are employable, which is currently defined to include unemployed fathers, teenagers not in school, and mothers whose children are aged 6 or over. That constitutes only about 38 percent of all recipients over 16, chiefly because of the exemption of mothers with preschool children. Furthermore, while all the employable must register with a work program, only a third to a half ever participate actively in work-related activities, due to funding limitations and the reluctance of staff to work with the more disadvantaged clients.[23]

The participants mostly look for jobs under staff direction, but some enter training or government jobs. The term "workfare" originally applied only to assignments where clients "worked off," or earned, their grants in unpaid public positions, but it has acquired a broader meaning, preferred here, that includes all the mandatory, work-related activities in which clients may engage, including job search, training, or education, as well as work.

Work programs hitched to welfare show potential. Many new programs have appeared since 1981, when Congress allowed states and localities to develop alternatives to the Work Incentive (WIN)

23. U.S. General Accounting Office, *An Overview of the WIN Program: Its Objectives, Accomplishments, and Problems* (Washington, DC: Government Printing Office, 21 June 1982), chap. 2.

program, which previously had been the nationwide AFDC work structure. Evaluations of several of the recent initiatives by the Manpower Demonstration Research Corporation (MDRC) make them look promising. In most instances, welfare clients who were involved in the programs worked more hours, earned more money, and drew less welfare afterward than comparable clients not so exposed. While running the programs cost money, it was usually more than recouped due to savings in welfare grants as more recipients went to work.[24]

In most cases, the economic gains are still marginal. Workfare's main effect is not to reduce dependency, at least not right away. In the typical work program, 52 percent of the clients entering jobs earn enough to leave welfare,[25] but many will return later. Rather, the effect is to make the welfare experience less passive. The major potential of workfare is simply to increase work effort, to raise the share of the employable recipients who are doing something to help themselves, whether or not they leave welfare, whether it be training, looking for work, or actually working. Short of abolishing welfare, this is government's best hope to enforce the work norm in the inner city.

Despite its long history, however, workfare has only begun to be implemented seriously in the United States. Few states have programs that levy a real work demand on more than a token slice of the employable caseload. Workfare is still too controversial in most places to be instituted more forcefully. Even where the will to enforce work is strong, difficult statecraft lies ahead. A serious program requires that welfare departments and other local agencies coordinate many services and change many routines. In most states, that process has only begun. There is still doubt as to whether government can carry out workfare in practice, whatever its potential.[26]

WHAT WORKFARE DOES

Workfare reflects the analysis of the work problem presented earlier. It assumes that jobs exist but that jobless recipients must be motivated to take them. For motivation to exist, work must be enforced, much as other public obligations—such as tax payment—are by other public agencies. The aim is not to resocialize the poor, a task probably beyond the capacity of government. It is only to close the considerable gap that now exists between the desires of the poor to work and their actual behavior.

Workfare involves more than an inducement to work. Recipients are not left to respond to work opportunities on their own, as with work incentives. Rather, there is a definite program to follow up on them. Special personnel help them look for work and provide necessary support services, particularly child care. And because participation is mandatory, the staff have an authority over clients lacking in voluntary employment programs. They can demand effort and cooperation from the client *in return* for the benefits they are receiving.

The combination of services and requirements places clients in a structure where they find they can work and also

24. Judith M. Gueron, "Reforming Welfare with Work" (Paper, Manpower Demonstration Research Corporation, New York, Dec. 1986), pp. 18-25.

25. U.S. General Accounting Office, *Work and Welfare: Current AFDC Work Programs and Implications for Federal Policy* (Washington, DC: Government Printing Office, Jan. 1987), pp. 105-6.

26. Lawrence M. Mead, *Beyond Entitlement: The Social Obligations of Citizenship* (New York: Free Press, 1986), chaps. 6-7.

that they must. Previously, welfare was essentially an entitlement, a right to support regardless of effort made to overcome dependency. Now that right is balanced with an onus to work or seek work. Previously, work was only a hope for most clients. Now it becomes an obligation, something they actually have to do here and now, in many instances for the first time.

The power of such requirements to raise work effort is potent. The rhetoric of barriers has convinced many welfare experts that to insist on work could have little impact. In reality, the degree of obligation in work programs is the main determinant of their performance. One measure of that expectation is the participation rate, or the share of all the employable clients who participate actively in a work program. That rate is generally low, for reasons given earlier, but it varies widely across state and local programs. In WIN, that variation was the strongest determinant of the share of clients in those programs who entered jobs. This was so even controlling for the alleged barriers, that is, the disadvantages of the clients and economic conditions.[27] It has probably been by raising participation, more than for any other reason, that the recent work programs have improved on WIN.

Opponents typically view workfare as coercive, but it should rather be seen as an exercise in authority. Enforcement assumes that the poor want to work, not that they do not, for otherwise work would be unenforceable, just as Prohibition was. If workfare clients truly participated against their will, we would find many being penalized for noncooperation. In fact, sanction levels are low, with only about 5 percent of participants losing their benefits,[28] even though the penalty for noncooperation is now very limited.

The MDRC studies of recent programs reveal that most participants approve of them. They think the work requirement is fair, and they feel positively about their work experience under the program. The main reservation is that those working off their grants would prefer regular jobs.[29] This reaction is not what one would expect from middle-class people, and it reveals much about the psychology of workfare. Those who have not fully internalized the work norm resist requirements less, not more, than those who have. It is better-off people who resist being told what to do by government, quite rightly, because they are more able to tell themselves. My impression is that the clients who are sanctioned in WIN tend to be the most self-reliant, not the least. Most activists who oppose requirements are not themselves dependent. Conversely, those on welfare usually appreciate the guidance workfare provides. They know they need that structure to work in practice.

The notion that workfare is repressive projects a middle-class psychology on the poor. Actually, effective programs work against repression. Typically, welfare clients coming to workfare are profoundly withdrawn. They have often been failures in school and earlier jobs and see little opportunity around them. They have the same belief in insuperable barriers evinced

27. Lawrence M. Mead, "The Potential for Work Enforcement: A Study of WIN," *Journal of Policy Analysis and Management*, 7(2):264-88 (Winter 1988); idem, "Expectations and Welfare Work: WIN in New York State," *Polity*, 18(2):224-52 (Winter 1985).

28. General Accounting Office, *Work and Welfare*, p. 62.
29. Gueron, "Reforming Welfare with Work," pp. 17-18.

by liberal analysts of the work problem, but it leaves them powerless. Hence their reluctance to do more to help themselves. We think of social deviance as something assertive, akin to breaking the law, but for this group it rather arises from defeatism. Some are aggressive, but many more are passively aggressive.

Much that workfare does, besides help recipients with the logistics of work, is prompt them to be more assertive. Only then can they seize opportunities and control their lives. Two activities dominate in most programs, both of them dedicated to this end. One is job search, in which staff send individual recipients to interviews with employers. The other is job clubs, a form of job seeking in which groups of recipients support each other in the endeavor to find work. Group members encourage each other, but they also levy expectations to keep each other from "shirking." The dynamic works against passivity, as defeated individuals are drawn out of themselves.

Besides aiming for high participation, successful workfare programs encourage intensive interaction between clients and staff and among the clients themselves.[30] The work obligation is levied more through these interchanges than impersonal bureaucratic requirements. Recipients are not coerced; they are expected to participate and then to work by other human beings whose demands they experience as just and unavoidable.[31] Relationships are the main lever that forces them to become more active. Programs that rely heavily on legal coercion are much more passive, more impersonal, less able to motivate, and thus less successful.[32]

Workfare should be seen in the broadest sense as a form of public education. Just as we require children to attend school, so we should require adults to do something to improve themselves if they are employable yet on welfare. Just as in public education, mandatoriness is essential to achieve participation, to draw recipients out of their homes and into constructive activities. The message is that defeatism is not acceptable, that able-bodied adults must do something to help themselves. But, given participation, the developmental objectives of workfare can be uppermost. Learning is directed inward as well as outward. Participants have much to learn about themselves as well as the outer world. The emphasis is on opportunity and hope.

According to MDRC, the new work programs are upbeat and not punitive in tone.[33] Most of them do not seek primarily to cut welfare but rather to reduce passivity on the rolls. Most of them offer training and education options alongside immediate work. Some, indeed, include "learnfare," or requirements that teenage welfare mothers remain in school rather than drop out, a policy that makes explicit the parallel to education. All embody a presumption, deep-seated in the culture, that both education and work are public activities to be expected of all competent citizens, for their own good and society's.[34]

WELFARE REFORM

The success of recent work programs has prompted many work-oriented proposals for welfare reform in Washington.

30. Mark Lincoln Chadwin et al., "Reforming Welfare: Lessons from the WIN Experience," *Public Administration Review*, 41(3):375-76 (May-June 1981).

31. For a vivid portrayal of such interaction within a comparable program, see Ken Auletta, *The Underclass* (New York: Random House, 1982), chaps. 1, 3-4, 6, 8-11, 15-16.

32. Mead, "Expectations and Welfare Work," pp. 237, 244-45.

33. Gueron, "Reforming Welfare with Work," p. 17.

34. Mead, *Beyond Entitlement*, chaps. 5, 10-11.

At this writing, however, little change is foreseeable. The reform bills most likely to become law, drafted by Democrats Daniel Moynihan in the Senate and Thomas Downey in the House, would increase welfare benefits in marginal ways, but states would control most parameters of work programs, as they have since the 1981 reforms. They could define as employable welfare mothers with children as young as 3—rather than 6, as now—and the participation rate, or the share of the employable clients actively involved, could remain low.

Changes on this scale would not alter the token character of most existing work programs, which typically "cream," or work with only the most employable recipients. The tendency among liberal legislators is to play down the mandatory aspect of workfare in favor of the new services it provides for willing job seekers. This approach suits their political needs, which are to satisfy public concerns about work on welfare without disturbing large, entrenched urban caseloads. But programs that cream tend to serve recipients who might well go to work without special assistance. Thus they have little impact on the more seriously dependent cases, those most central to the underclass.

Rather, reform should expand participation in workfare so that many more of the employable recipients share actively in work activities. This is the only way to ensure that work effort becomes an integral part of the welfare experience. Federal rules now set a minimum participation rate in state work programs of only 15 percent. As a counter to the Democratic proposals, House Republicans, with the support of the Reagan administration, drafted a plan that would have raised the floor to 70 percent over several years. The effect on work effort and job entries would have been sharp. At present, some 2 million recipients are registered in work programs in a given year, but only about 700,000 have to participate actively. According to the Congressional Budget Office, the Downey bill would have added only 210,000 participants and would have caused only 15,000 families to leave welfare over five years; the comparable figures for the Moynihan bill were only 86,000 and 10,000. The Republican plan, however, would have raised participation by 935,000 and caused 50,000 families to leave the rolls. It also cost less—$1.1 billion versus $5.7 billion for Downey and $2.3 billion for Moynihan—because more of the new services would have been defrayed by welfare savings.

The defeat of the Republican proposal means that no version of reform will expand workfare very much. However, it is likely that some minimal participation standard will be added to the final legislation. At the urging of the White House, the Moynihan bill was amended, when it passed the Senate in June 1988, to specify that 22 percent of the employable recipients had to participate actively in workfare by 1994. That, at least, is somewhat above the 15 percent in current law. The possibility of higher participation levels will also be studied. A level of 50 percent is probably achievable over several years, as this is the level reached in the more demanding of the recent workfare programs.[35]

Besides the small scale of the work programs, the other main limitation of current work policies is that they affect women much more than men. Workfare can obligate only the adult recipients of assistance, most of whom are welfare mothers. It cannot directly reach nonworking men, few of whom are on welfare but

35. Gueron, "Reforming Welfare with Work," p. 16.

whose employment problems are even more central to the underclass. At best, there is the hope that to require welfare mothers to work will make them less tolerant of nonworking men as sexual partners.

Work effort by men outside welfare must be enforced by suppressing the alternatives to legal employment, meaning crime, particularly drug trafficking, and the underground economy, or work that is legal but done off the books to escape taxes. The defenses sometimes made of illegal work are unpersuasive. It is not true that crime is a rational choice for unskilled black youths, since over a year most will make more money in legal jobs.[36] Nor is illegal work morally or socially equivalent to legal employment. Few underground workers are successful husbands or fathers, nor can they earn full acceptance by other citizens. The way forward for today's poor, like yesterday's, lies through the legitimate economy.

As a secondary measure, I would also expand welfare to cover more low-skilled fathers, so that more of them could be reached by workfare programs. At present, states may cover two-parent families under AFDC, but only if the father has a work history and is unemployed. If he works more than 99 hours a month, the family loses all benefits, even if it is still needy; his earnings may not be supplemented up to the welfare level, as those of working mothers may be. Only about half the states cover unemployed parents, and the small size of the programs indicates that few welfare fathers find the rules attractive. The current Democratic reform proposals would mandate cover-

36. W. Kip Viscusi, "Market Incentives for Criminal Behavior," in *Black Youth Employment Crisis*, ed. Freeman and Holzer, pp. 308, 314-15.

age in all states but would still forbid the father to work and remain on welfare.

It would be better to cover the father but require him to work. That is, a father could receive welfare provided he was working and his family was still needy. He would have the same right to supplementation as a working mother, except that he would face a much tougher work test. He would have to be working full-time in a legitimate job or a workfare job even to apply for aid, and he would have to keep working to maintain eligibility. That requirement is also what differentiates this proposal from the many plans offered in the 1960s and 1970s to extend welfare from single-parent to two-parent families. One move in this direction was another amendment added to the Moynihan bill on its passage by the Senate, a requirement that unemployed fathers work at least 16 hours a week in workfare jobs. But there is no need to confine them to government employment. Private-sector jobs would satisfy the work norm as well or better.

Obviously, this proposal would help only workers with the lowest wages and sizable families, particularly in states paying high welfare benefits. For others, to work steadily in virtually any job places one above the welfare level. But more welfare fathers might accept these rules than the current ones, and for that portion, government would have more leverage to enforce work than it does now.

WORKFARE AND EQUALITY

The leading objection to any steps to strengthen work policy is that they would condemn the poor to a life of drudgery in "dirty jobs." The dead-end quality of such jobs is exaggerated, as poor and black people show mobility comparable

to that of the better-off over time—if they work.[37] But there is no question that, for many low-skilled adults, to work initially means menial labor. Should they have to work under such conditions?

It is hard to argue otherwise as long as the public so clearly wants the poor to work more than they do.[38] It is easier to argue for raising job quality. Workfare can enforce work only in jobs that pay the minimum wage and meet other rules for conditions and benefits set by government. Those standards could be raised— for instance, by increasing the minimum wage or requiring that all jobs include health benefits. But they would have to be raised for all workers, an expensive proposition. To offer "better" jobs just to the poor, as experience with public employment shows, does not achieve integration, as the beneficiaries do not meet the norms faced by other workers.

Work policy presumes that even dirty work is preferable to the distress now faced by the working-aged poor both on and off welfare and that it would help to integrate the underclass. About two-thirds of recipients who work their way off welfare escape poverty.[39] Even if the effect of enforcement were only to increase the number of working poor, the latter would have much greater resources, both economic and political, to demand redress than the nonworking poor have now. New economic claims can be made only by citizens in full standing, who in this culture must have a work history.

Workfare is not opposed to greater equality, but it addresses rather the problem of economic participation that must be solved before issues of equity can even get on the agenda. The last generation has given poverty unprecedented attention, but finally at the expense of equality. Poverty raised issues of social order, including nonwork, that ultimately took priority. For a generation, those who would have government do more to promote equality have been stymied by the charge that the poor are undeserving. Likewise, those who want government to do less, including the Reagan administration, have faced the charge that the poor would be hurt. The underclass is the albatross around the necks of social reformers, on both the Left and the Right.

A rise in work effort among the poor, more than any other change, would give both sides freer rein. Both the collectivist and the free-market ideology would become more defensible, for both are visions on behalf of *working* citizens. The country would much rather argue about these New Deal options than about poverty, for both presume exactly the competence among the poor that has recently been in question.

37. Greg Duncan et al., *Years of Poverty, Years of Plenty: The Changing Fortunes of American Workers and Families* (Ann Arbor: University of Michigan, Institute for Social Research, 1984), chaps. 2, 4.

38. Mead, *Beyond Entitlement*, pp. 233-40.

39. Bane and Ellwood, "Dynamics of Dependence," pp. 56-57.

13

Institutional Change and the Challenge of the Underclass

By RICHARD P. NATHAN

ABSTRACT: This article calls for greater emphasis on the institutional challenge of the urban underclass, particularly on implementation studies of new social programs. The need for such a shift in emphasis is examined in historical context, stressing the pluralistic and competitive nature of the American policy process, the structure of American federalism, and the critical role of state governments in chartering and overseeing the major institutions that provide social services. Two types of action are proposed to give greater attention to institutional dimensions of the challenge of the urban underclass: (1) evaluation research that incorporates institutional, attitudinal, and community variables; and (2) new consultative arrangements involving panels of academics and experts to assist government agencies in the implementation of social policies focused on the urban underclass.

Richard P. Nathan is professor of public and international affairs at the Woodrow Wilson School, Princeton University. He received his Ph.D. degree in political economy and government from Harvard University in 1967. Nathan has written extensively on welfare, urban affairs, and federalism. He is a former U.S. government official and senior fellow of the Brookings Institution. His most recent book is Social Science in Government, Uses and Misuses.

FIVE years ago, Ken Auletta's book *The Underclass* was published. In the intervening period, William Julius Wilson, Isabel Sawhill, Robert Reischauer, Ronald Mincy, Erol Rickets, Mark Hughes, Greg Duncan, and others have wrestled with the issues involved in defining and measuring the elusive condition of what is widely believed to be a growing urban underclass in America. This special issue of *The Annals* of the American Academy of Political and Social Science presents a cross section of the views of these and other leading experts on the subject of the urban underclass. I was asked to write the penultimate article, focusing on the institutional challenge of the urban underclass. Rather than use valuable space in this compendium to present my ideas on the reasons for and character of the urban underclass, I begin with a series of assumptions and then turn my attention to two questions that fascinate me. First, given the existence of an urban underclass, what can we do about it? And more specifically, what can be done to assure that the institutions in the society whose actions are critical to the nation's response to the problem of an urban underclass rise to this challenge? I particularly focus on the second question in this article.

ASSUMPTIONS

I assume that the dramatic increase over the past two decades in the geographic concentration of multi-problem poor persons—predominantly members of racial-minority groups—in large cities in the United States is more than a difference of degree from past periods. It is a new condition that is, and should be, deeply troubling to the nation. In part, this condition is a function of the success—not complete, but substantial nonetheless—of the civil rights revolution in America. As William Julius Wilson has pointed out, one of the reasons for the concentration of the multi-problem minority poor in large cities is the out-migration of role models—teachers, merchants, civil servants, professionals—from the distressed areas of cities as opportunities have opened up for them to live and work in other and better-off areas.[1]

By "multi-problem," I refer to three interconnected conditions: (1) economic needs as measured by such indicators as poverty, unemployment, and educational deficiencies; (2) behavioral problems such as long-term welfare dependency, family instability, drugs, crime, and prostitution; and (3) attitudinal problems of deep isolation and alienation. All three of these conditions are extremely difficult to measure, especially when they coexist. Moreover, even in those situations where national or local data are available, they usually are cross-sectional rather than longitudinal, so our knowledge of the character, depth of severity, size, and duration of the urban-underclass condition is limited.[2]

Despite these and other measurement problems, we have become increasingly aware in recent years of the existence of a growing and ever more isolated urban underclass.[3] One indicator is the greater

1. William Julius Wilson, *The Truly Disadvantaged: The Inner City, the Underclass, and Public Policy* (Chicago: University of Chicago Press, 1987).
2. A new study of the urban underclass under the auspices of the Social Science Research Council and sponsored by the Rockefeller Foundation includes neighborhood ethnographic studies. Similar research at the neighborhood level, which will add an important dimension to our knowledge in this field, is being conducted by William Julius Wilson in Chicago.
3. My views on this subject are summarized in "Will the Underclass Always Be with Us?" *Society*, Mar.-Apr. 1987, pp. 57-62.

concentration in urban census tracts of multi-problem conditions. Decennial census data for 1970 and 1980 show that the number of tracts with high concentrations of poverty and other social problems increased in the 1970s, although the population of these tracts in many cases declined.[4] This latter phenomenon—the thinning out of urban distress—has been widely noted in the literature. It is obvious in windshield surveys of what formerly were concentrated ghetto neighborhoods that now have large numbers of abandoned and burned-out buildings and vacant lots.

In my view, the striking characteristic of this underclass situation, a characteristic that has tended to be left out of our analysis, is that it is spatial. A recent study by the Urban Institute shows that in the 1970s, "a significant proportion of the black population shifted away from established ghetto areas."[5] The increased geographical concentration of the urban underclass has the effect of reinforcing the behavior and attitudes that draw people into the patterns of deviance— deviance, that is, from prevailing social norms—that characterize the urban underclass. My assumption is that this greater concentration of problem conditions differentiates this issue of the urban underclass from that of high levels of poverty and related concerns in rural areas. In the summer of 1987, just a few months before he died, Bayard Rustin referred to this situation as the rise of a "lumpen black underclass" in our cities, which he said required a new and expensive governmental response unlike that of the civil rights policies begun in the 1960s.[6]

Instead of devoting more attention here to a diagnosis, I turn now to the response. This subject falls naturally under two headings, one involving the character of the response, the other its execution. As stated earlier, my main interest is in implementation—the institutional challenge of the underclass. First, however, we need to consider the policies and programs that can be part of the kind of new response as advocated by Bayard Rustin.

THE RESPONSE

The first and critical point to make about the response to the underclass is that it is bound to be extraordinarily difficult to reach into this hardened social-problem milieu and save even a relatively small proportion of the people trapped in the urban underclass. The cultural isolation, danger, and depth of severity of the social environment we are considering is hard to exaggerate. The people who need help are often resentful, alienated, and prone to hostile acts. This makes the politics of response much more difficult than in an earlier period, when a war on poverty included helping the old and the sick, that is, a much larger number of persons whom the society defines as the deserving poor. In short, the political challenge of putting together a coalition of supporters for what Bayard Rustin said have to be "new and expensive" government programs to affect the problem of the urban underclass adds a dimension of great difficulty.[7]

4. Research by Mark Alan Hughes being conducted at the Woodrow Wilson School, Princeton University, uses detailed mapping analyses of 15 major cities for all census tracts to study conditions and trends relevant to the urban underclass.

5. "Trends in Residential Segregation," *The Urban Institute Policy and Research Report*, Winter 1987, p. 20, based on a study by Scott McKinney and Ann Schnare, "Trends in Residential Segregation by Race, 1960-1980."

6. Television interview, "Commentary," 5 July 1987.

7. This challenge is discussed in other articles in this issue of *The Annals* of the American

Despite the fact that both the social and the political conditions involved are so difficult, there are arguments for action and types of action that I believe are feasible in terms of both their chances for success and the prospects for winning support for their adoption.

A number of the authors of the articles in this special issue of *The Annals* were part of the working seminar on family and American welfare policy sponsored jointly by the American Enterprise Institute and Marquette University and chaired by Michael Novak.[8] The seminar included a group of experts on domestic and social issues who reflected a wide range of ideological positions. In its report, issued in May 1987, the working seminar emphasized the emergence of what it called "the new consensus" between liberals and conservatives on social policy. This new consensus is grounded in the concepts of "mutual obligation" and behavioral change. It involves a political bargain in which, on the one hand, conservatives are willing to support programs that instill the dominant social values of the society, such as the obligation to obtain an education, to work, and to fulfill family and community responsibilities and, on the other hand, liberals are willing to highlight these values as a trade-off for obtaining more money for social programs.

Recent developments in the field of welfare policy give concreteness to this treaty on the part of political actors in the field of social policy. Such developments include, for example, the state programs adopted during the past five years to institute a combination of work and welfare, or so-called new-style workfare reforms. Under these state programs, able-bodied heads of welfare families— mostly females in single-parent families—are obligated to enter into what is often called a social contract. This social contract requires them to participate in services like training, remedial education, and job search and to accept employment. In exchange, the state provides the needed services to make this bargain work. Similar concepts are embodied in the inner-city education reforms emanating from the program developed by Eugene Lang, a businessperson and philanthropist in New York City. His approach involves a deal whereby students—typically in junior high school—agree to stay in school in exchange for a commitment on the part of an individual, such as Mr. Lang, or an organization, such as the Boston Compact, to provide help to those who stay in school and to guarantee a fully paid opportunity for higher education when they graduate from high school.

Likewise, in the field of corrections, where there has been rapid growth in the prison population and in the proportion of blacks and Hispanics in prison, state governments are experimenting with new approaches that at their roots involve institutional change. Examples are programs for closely supervised probation, including daily check-ins and frequent contact with parole officers, and intensive, supervised corrections facilities for youths with rehabilitation programs that emphasize behavior change, job training, and education.[9]

The political bargains reflected in these approaches for reaching in and saving

Academy of Political and Social Science, including Jennifer L. Hochschild, "Equal Opportunity and the Estranged Poor."

8. *The New Consensus on Family Welfare* (Washington, DC: American Enterprise Institute for Public Policy Research, 1987).

9. See Joan Petersilia, *Expanding Options for Criminal Sentencing*, R-3544-EMC (Santa Monica, CA: Rand, 1987); John J. DiIulio, Jr., "True Penal Reform Can Save Money," *Wall Street Journal*, 28 Sept. 1987.

some of the people in the urban underclass have now been sufficiently noted, and in some cases tested, so that there is substance to the idea of a new consensus as embodied in the report from the seminar sponsored by the American Enterprise Institute and Marquette. I should add that this agreement does not entail the commitment of large amounts of resources to new social programs, but it does translate into support for more spending and more intensive programs focused on the urban underclass on the part of many state and local governments and private groups. Moreover, even though it is not widely known, the national government under the Reagan administration has provided some support, though not huge, for program innovations in this area, particularly in the welfare field, where various federal waivers have enabled state governments to use federal matching funds for new-style workfare initiatives.

My own view is that these quiet incremental steps are promising. One reason for optimism is that the steps have been taken without the expansive rhetoric and overpromises typical of new federal social programs. Some states—Massachusetts, Michigan, Pennsylvania, California, and New Jersey, to mention examples—have been embarked on efforts to institute new-style workfare systems for as long as five years. They are developing concepts and systems to do this without the spotlight of attention that accompanies new federal social programs and often produces inflated expectations and impatience for rapid results. Another positive factor is the support of business groups like the Committee for Economic Development, which stress the need to upgrade the nation's human capital because of the projected decline in the labor force.

While these developments bode well, there are also negative factors that bear mention. One is that liberal groups that in the past have been important to efforts to adopt new social programs have tended to drag their heels on or even oppose these relatively small steps, which in some cases—notably workfare—involve obligations that they oppose.

In sum, there is wider agreement now on some potentially effective responses to the problem of the urban underclass, but it is not wholehearted and general agreement and it does not at this time entail a willingness to devote large amounts of new money to such programs on a broad basis. Nevertheless, an agenda is forming that is grounded in the diagnosis, given previously, of the urban underclass that for many of its proponents is refreshingly realistic about the depth of the problem and the immensity of the challenge involved. Implicit in this formulation is the recognition that it will take a long time to achieve change, that even then only some people will be affected, and that the politics involved are very difficult.

For me, this situation is hopeful—with one big caveat. The caveat concerns institutions and implementation. The key to the new consensus is institutional change of welfare systems, school systems, child-care systems, and other institutions that deliver social services to needy people in troubled inner-city neighborhoods. The remainder of this article deals with the institutional challenge of the new consensus. Both in social science and in social policy, I see this institutional dimension as the neglected frontier that is an important key to success in dealing with the problem of a growing urban underclass.

THE NEGLECTED FRONTIER

Generally speaking, the bulk of the attention of political actors and experts on social issues is devoted to the diagnosis

of problems and to the formulation and adoption of policy. The rewards—publicity for policymakers, and publication for experts and scholars—tend to favor these activities. The task of implementing new policies is left to people who are less central to the intellectual process, and the implication often is that they are less important players in the policy game.

Yet implementation is a special challenge in the American setting. The American political system is distinctively open, pluralistic, and competitive; Tocqueville called it full of "striving and animation." As a result, public policy decisions often are complex political bargains made under the pressure of a deadline without much, if any, attention to how they will be carried out. The more controversial the policy areas that are addressed, the more complex, turbulent, and unstable the political bargains that emerge. In the social policy field in the United States, we are almost immune now to the fact of constant change in program requirements and resources.

What is more, the special character of our political system involves a high level of uncertainty and instability in the staffing for implementation processes. The chief officials of many public agencies are relatively short-term political appointees, often with little experience, who are constantly looking to the next rung on the career ladder. This characteristic of the American political system is compounded by the division of authority and responsibility, often along lines that are unclear, between federal, state, and local governments. It comes to roost, for the purposes of this article, in troubled inner-city neighborhoods, where both public agencies and community organizations deal with the complex web of problems and pathology of the urban underclass in the provision of public services.

One can think of the American polit-ical system of checks and balances as having both a horizontal dimension and a vertical dimension. The horizontal dimension is reflected in the sharing of powers between the executive, the legislature, and the courts, with the latter coming to have an ever more assertive role in many areas of social policy. The vertical dimension is that of federalism, which involves the replication of this threefold sharing arrangement—executive, legislative, judicial—at many levels of government. Structurally, culturally, and intellectually, this dynamic, competitive political system places heavy pressure on those charged with the task of implementation in an issue area as basic and complex as dealing with the problems of the urban underclass.

In political science, the academic literature on implementation is relatively new and not extensive; the principal theme of the best work in the field highlights the immensity of the gap between an idea and its execution in the American governmental setting.[10] This academic literature has its roots in an earlier period in the work of specialists in public administration as a subfield of political science. Now out of fashion, the leaders in public administration at one time had much higher standing. They taught courses in personnel management, coordination, budgeting, auditing, and accounting as elements of a paradigm that viewed policymaking as the work of politicians and its execution as the work of professionals with neutral competence in administrative processes. But wiser heads took charge in the discipline, with their central point being a critique of the idea that policy and

10. See, for example, Eugene Bardach, *The Implementation Game: What Happens after a Bill Becomes a Law* (Cambridge: MIT Press, 1977); Jeffrey L. Pressman and Aaron Wildavsky, *Implementation*, 3d ed., expanded (Berkeley: University of California Press, 1984).

administration can be separated and assigned to different political actors. Their point, surely a legitimate one, is that the policy process is continuous and that values are brought into play in both the legislative and the administrative processes. As public administration has fallen away in political science, a focus on economics, statistics, and organizational behavior has replaced it in graduate education in public affairs.

Political science's sister discipline of economics has contributed to this shift. In an earlier day, economics gave more attention to institutions. John R. Commons, at the University of Wisconsin, and his followers stressed the idea that institutions behave differently from the sum of the rational men and women who make them up. This insight caused Commons and others, including a generation of labor economists at Princeton University, to view the workings of social programs on a basis that highlighted the role and importance of the way institutions behave in the public sector. All of this is gone now in economics.

To put together several of the ideas in this section, I believe that both the character of the American policy process—not unique, but distinctive in these pluralistic, Madisonian terms—and the intellectual heritage of the social sciences are such that we must now find ways to give more attention more systematically to institutional aspects of governance and specifically to the implementation process in the conduct of social policy. How do we do this?

"A NEW INSTITUTIONALISM"

In political science, James G. March and Johan P. Olsen have called for "a new institutionalism" that holds promise for change and redirection toward imple-

mentation studies in the social sciences.[11] They stress the importance of symbolic action and the "interdependence between relatively autonomous social and political institutions." In turn, March and Olsen "deemphasize the simple primacy of micro processes in favor of relatively complex processes and historical inefficiency."[12] Their call for "a new institutionalism" and that of others are beginning to influence a number of scholars. This is all to the good. In particular, I see the need to have this movement be interdisciplinary, encompassing both political science and economics. It is also important for other disciplines, especially sociology and social psychology.

To extend the argument here about the need for institutional and particularly implementation studies in the social sciences, and specifically to connect it to the challenge of the urban underclass, the next two sections of this article deal with areas in which this linkage can be made. Specifically, I believe that evaluation research in the social sciences can make an important contribution on the institutional side of the urban-underclass issue. I also believe that we can be creative in devising new consultative arrangements to involve scholars, experts, and universities, particularly schools of public affairs, in explicit and helpful ways to assist in the implementation process for new social policies.

EVALUATION RESEARCH

Evaluation research in the field of social policy came into prominence in the late 1960s. Actually, it includes two types

11. James G. March and Johan P. Olsen, "The New Institutionalism: Organizational Factors in Political Life," *American Political Science Review*, 78:734–49 (1984).

12. Ibid., p. 738.

of studies: demonstration studies, to test new policies; and evaluation studies, to assess the effects of existing, ongoing programs. The large-scale and systematic practice of both types of policy research in the field of social policy in the United States dates from the Great Society period, especially the inception of the New Jersey demonstration studies to test the idea of a negative income tax. A number of evaluation studies were also conducted of President Johnson's Great Society programs. Later, under Presidents Nixon and Ford, demonstration studies were undertaken to test other new social policies. These studies included the health insurance experiments, the housing experiments, and education vouchers.

My experience in this field involves both demonstration and evaluation research. The demonstration studies I know best are closely related to the topic of the underclass, namely, the studies undertaken by the Manpower Demonstration Research Corporation (MDRC) to test new employment and training and work/welfare programs to assist disadvantaged population groups, which, for the purposes of this article, in most cases would be included in the underclass.[13] I have also had experience conducting field network evaluation studies of the implementation of new federal grant-in-aid programs, including employment and training and community development programs targeted on disadvantaged people and distressed places.

In an important sense, the rise of these two types of large-scale applied social science studies—demonstration and evaluation studies—can be seen as a fallback position to the earlier, ambitious effort

13. See Judith Gueron, *Work Initiatives for Welfare Recipients: Lessons from a Multi-State Experiment* (New York: Manpower Demonstration Research Corporation, 1986).

by Lyndon Johnson to adopt a planning-programming-budgeting system on a governmentwide basis. It was not possible, as Johnson had envisioned, to identify the goals and measure the results of all domestic programs and policy alternatives as a way to make the budget process more scientific and rational. Demonstration and evaluation research is selective, involving large-scale studies of those programs, either potential new programs or existing programs, that are believed to warrant special attention.

In the 1960s, when demonstration and evaluation research rose in prominence—it has fallen from grace in the Reagan years—economists were far and away the dominant group among social scientists in the design and conduct of these studies. This is to their credit; however, the down side of the strong influence of economists in this area is that subjects that economists have not been interested in have received short shrift. The most important subject in this category, for the purposes of this article, is the institutional dimension of the policy process. Political scientists and sociologists were not featured guests at demonstration and evaluation research banquets, although sometimes they were invited to fill in at the back tables. This has meant that certain variables in the research equation—both independent and dependent variables—have been given no or relatively little attention. They include institutional variables and also attitudinal and community variables.

In my opinion, these omissions are not as serious in the case of demonstration research as they are in the case of evaluation research. When the issue is what works, as it is in demonstration research, we tend to be most interested in specific economic values like the effect of a new program on income, earnings, employment, and the like. The work/welfare

demonstrations conducted by MDRC are a case in point. Tests by MDRC in eight states involved the random assignment of 35,000 people to treatment and control groups, with the principal dependent variables being earnings and welfare benefits. But what if new-style workfare worked?

When a government decides to generalize a work/welfare program tested in a demonstration study, the research challenge is transformed. Politicians in this situation are likely to be interested in whether we can change the pertinent institutions so that the program will be put in place effectively and as intended. They have ideas, even data, about what they want to do. The question now becomes, Can government do it? In the case of work/welfare initiatives, for example, can the governmental entities involved change the behavior of schools, the welfare systems, the employment service, and child-care services in ways that focus on the rehabilitative needs of welfare recipients on an interconnected basis? In the assessment of such programs, we are likely to be interested in individual economic impacts like earnings, employment, and welfare recipiency. But the funders of such research—government agencies and foundations—are likely to be much more interested in political and institutional variables and processes. This is the kind of knowledge that can help us cross the frontier of institutional change critical to dealing with the stubborn, hard problems of the urban underclass.

The bottom line for this discussion is that we need broader, multidisciplinary evaluation studies that incorporate the idea of "a new institutionalism." This entails moving back—or, if you like, forward—in terms of pushing policy-oriented social science into the administrative arena. While I favor doing this for good intellectual reasons that go beyond the topic of the urban underclass, such a development would be highly beneficial in enhancing our knowledge base and our capacity for acting in this area. The intellectual mode of evaluation research as envisioned here would be more inductive and descriptive than evaluation research driven by economics. Likewise, it would rely more heavily on qualitative, as opposed to quantitative, research methods and data. It would focus on questions involving the degrees to which, and the ways in which, the major organizational actors involved in implementing a new policy responded to changed policy purposes and signals. It would make heavier use of interviews, survey data—especially on attitudes toward policy change—and program information.[14]

NEW CONSULTATIVE
ARRANGEMENTS

Not only should the members of the fraternity I belong to, policy-oriented institutional social scientists, augment our research capacity to deal with the underclass challenge, but we also ought to bring this capacity to bear in a more direct and immediate way in the execution of new programs. Here, I think we need to do some institution building of our own. The aforementioned MDRC work/welfare demonstrations indicate the kinds of possibilities involved. These demonstrations were conducted in eight states. On the basis of the findings of the research and also for other reasons, a number of state governments decided in effect to replicate the demonstrated programs and program ideas on a larger scale. California is a case in point.

14. The ideas presented in this section are discussed further and in greater detail in Richard P. Nathan, *Social Science in Government, Uses and Misuses* (New York: Basic Books, 1988).

MDRC did its first and probably best-known work/welfare demonstration to test new approaches to job search linked with community work experience for welfare applicants and recipients in San Diego County, California. Some 5000 persons participated in this demonstration, and the results were encouraging. Significant, though not huge, increases in earnings and lower welfare benefits were found for the participants compared to the controls. Based on these findings and also taking into account other ideas and purposes, the state of California in 1985 enacted a statewide program called Greater Avenues to Independence (GAIN). The program involves an intricate set of interconnected steps to provide continuous service—education, job counseling, training, work experience, child care—to heads of welfare families. These services are to be provided by a multitude of social agencies under the supervision of county governments, of which there are 58 in California. The law gives counties two years to plan their program, which must be approved by the state.

At its roots, the idea of GAIN is to convert the welfare system from a payment system into a service system focused on work preparation and facilitation. Now, nearly two years into the GAIN program, it is abundantly clear that the ambitious system-reform objectives of this new law stretch the state's capacity to design and oversee changes in social programs and administrative procedures across a broad array of communities and agencies. The logistics involved for the service agencies that are called on to participate—schools, the employment service, junior colleges, training programs, child care—and the task of keeping integrated records and making timely payments for welfare assistance to the individual participants and to service providers

are appreciable hurdles to the achievement of the goal despite the fact that the goal is widely shared.

The state of California has committed itself to a major evaluation of the GAIN program. In the normal course of affairs, however, the main outputs of such a study follow, rather than coincide with, the implementation process. As state officials turned their attention to implementing the GAIN program, it became increasingly apparent that the task was a formidable one.

It is in this kind of territory that I believe we would benefit from some inventive institution building that would bring the intellectual community—experts and academics—closer to the implementation process. I have in mind the creation of on-the-scene advisory panels that would work with government officials and prepare material for their internal use and periodic reports for public dissemination. I realize that such arrangements are often made and furthermore that they involve many and diverse kinds of special political conditions and interests. Nevertheless, I believe there would be value in having some central organization develop, organize, and oversee the creation of consultative arrangements for panels of academic experts and consultants to have formal ties to implementation processes for important new social policy initiatives. A group like the National Academy of Public Administration, for example, could play this role on a national basis whereby it would develop the expertise to identify participants, provide staff, and perhaps also help obtain funding for such arrangements.

The advantage of having a central organizing unit is that there would be a body of experience—not unlike the case of MDRC as a research intermediary in this field—that could be drawn upon in

arranging for the auspices, time commitment, publications, funding arrangements, and staff for the panels to aid in the implementation process for social policy initiatives, especially those focused on the intractable problems of the urban underclass. If nothing else, the central unit would provide a sounding board and discussion arena for defining key issues and considering problems as they arise in the execution of important and complex new social policies. At some points along the way in the implementation process, it could also help to clear the air or obtain support on key issues just by the fact of having independent and well-developed analyses of the major choice points and issues in the implementation process.

My image of these central groups is that they would involve multidisciplinary panels of academics and experts, including former officials in the field, perhaps using faculty members and graduate students at schools of public affairs or other similar programs as principals and support personnel. The groups would have a single chair or director and a specified relationship with program officials. There would be financial resources and space for staff and an agreed upon schedule of their tasks and main products. The work of these special panels would be time limited. They would go out of existence once the program being considered had been developed and put in place. They could operate at different levels of the political system—in state government or in large local jurisdictions, including counties, cities, and school districts.

Under the general heading of inventing mechanisms for institutional change, I would go one step further. With respect to the earlier discussion of the pluralism and diversity of American domestic government, we need to return to the federalism dimension of the American policy process. It is state governments that have the dominant policy and oversight role for many of the services that are critical to addressing effectively the hardened social problems of the urban underclass. Historically, the main role of the U.S. national government in domestic affairs has been in the area of income transfers, such as social security, unemployment compensation, and welfare. In the service area, its role has been more limited, focusing on stimulating and supporting state and local social services. The emphasis of federal policy has been on grants-in-aid for social service programs, and not so much—as I argue is needed now—on promoting institutional change. We need to shift our attention from specific and narrow programs to a broader concern for systems—schools, welfare, corrections, hospitals—in providing for the poor. This requires rethinking the federal role. The National Institutes of Health could be considered as a model, with the aim being to give both financial and intellectual support on a systematic basis to state governments and through them to their major local entities—big cities, urban counties, and school districts—to transform the institutions critical to dealing with the problems of the urban underclass.

RECAPITULATION

The articles in this special issue of *The Annals* reflect a convergence in their diagnosis of the problem of a hardened, troubled, and predominantly minority urban underclass. The underlying challenge of racial differences is the main story line of the history of social conditions and social policy in the United States. Our capacity to deal with this challenge is the critical test of the American democratic idea.

There is now an emerging consensus in the social policy community about strategies that are likely to make a dent in these intractable problems. The missing ingredient in dealing with these problems that is highlighted in this article is greater and concentrated attention on the institutional dimension of the policy changes needed to reach the problems of the urban underclass, particularly the implementation process for new strategies and programs. This article examines the reasons why this ingredient is so often missing and the consequences of its absence. It highlights ways in which intellectual resources, both evaluation research and new consultative arrangements, could be brought to bear in more systematic ways to help turn goals into accomplishments in the field of social policy related to the urban underclass. It is in the interest of lighting a dark area of government that this article offers suggestions for dealing with the institutional challenge of the urban underclass.

Index

Please remember that this is a library book,
and that it belongs only temporarily to each
person who uses it. Be considerate. Do
not write in this, or any, library book.

DATE DUE

Acknowledgments

For Nina, John, and Amy

And with special thanks to Jette and Randi!

Picture credits

211 Corbis: Edmund D. Fountain/Zuma Press (far center right)

Special Photography

Tim Trøjborg Matthäi (Billund shoot), Brian Axel (cover).

Additional Photography

Joseph Pellegrino (pp.242–3), Ben Ellermann, Johannes Koehler, Yaron Dori, (pp.66–7, pp.68–9, pp.90–1, pp.92–3), Daniel Rubin (pp. 78–9), Sarah Ashun (p.35), PHOTO: OOPSFOTOS.NL. (Mount Rushmore, p.22), Steve Scott (Bilofix image, p.20), Nick Ricks of TT Games (pp. 228–9).

Brick Film Stills

Chris Salt, Curt Werline, Steffen Troeger (with Sandra Abele).

LEGO® Brick Artists

Nathan Sawaya, Jørn Rønnau, Ego Leonard, Andrew Lipson & Daniel Shiu, Sean Kenney, Nicholas Foo.

Adult Fans of LEGO (AFOLs)

Lino Martins, Paweł Michalak, Nannan Zsang, Jürgen Bramigk, Marcin Danielek, Maciej Karwowski, Jaime Spencer, Rainer Kaufmann, Bill Ward, Sachiko Akinaga, Bryce McGlone, Chris Giddens, Marcin Danielek, Aaron Andrews, Peter Reid, Dan Rubin.

Dorling Kindersley would like to thank the following for their help with the visual content of this book

Andy Crawford, Erik Andresen, Alexander Pitz, Monica Pedersen, Anders Gaasedal Christensen, Mona B. Petersen, Dale Chasse, Erik Varszeg, Steve Gerling, Dan Steininger, Paul Chrzan, Mark Roe.

The Author and Dorling Kindersley would like to thank the following for their help in producing this book

Randi Kirsten Sørensen, Jette Orduna, Stephanie Lawrence, Keith Malone, Christina Bro Lund, Mona B. Petersen, Anja Sølvhviid, Annemarie Kvist, Dawn Stailey, Gregory Farshtey, Haakon Smith-Meyer, Lluis Gilbert, Tobias Roegner, Valerie Barnes, Holger Matthes, Anders N. Ravnskjær, Flemming Lund Kristensen, Jan Beyer, Richard Stollery, Anders Gaasedal Christensen, Monica Pedersen, Peter Hobolt Jensen, Kristin Robinson, Hanne Bornstein, Jesper Just Jensen, Matthew James Ashton, Ronald Turcotte, Benjamin Jackson, Annmarie Lomonaco, Nicholas Ricks, James Hall, Bill Vollbrecht, Valerie Barnes, Mike Pastor, Nicholas Groves, Heidi Bailey, the entire international LEGO® Club team, Steve Witt, Jordan Schwarz, Jeramy Spurgeon, Daniel Rubin, Mark Sandlin, Ben Ellermann, John McCormack, Brian Regini, Sanne Østergaard Jacobsen, Kelly McKiernan, Danielle Ezold, Lisa Chiarella, Yole Anna Russo, Tine Froberg Mortensen, Kristian Hauge, Shawn Curtis, Jason Cosler, Melinda Oakes, Phillip Ring from TT Games, Erni Marlina, Dawn Stailey, Ali Sayers, Ali Slayton.

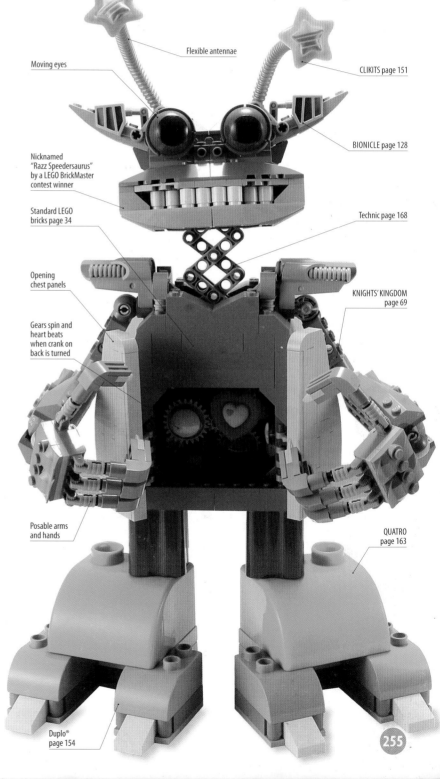

Constructed by a LEGO® Master Builder in 2005 to celebrate the 50th anniversary of the LEGO System of Play (see p. 18), this big green monster combined pieces from many different LEGO themes to show how they can all be built together.

Flexible antennae

Moving eyes

CLIKITS page 151

BIONICLE page 128

Nicknamed "Razz Speedersaurus" by a LEGO BrickMaster contest winner

Standard LEGO bricks page 34

Technic page 168

Opening chest panels

KNIGHTS' KINGDOM page 69

Gears spin and heart beats when crank on back is turned

Posable arms and hands

QUATRO page 163

Duplo® page 154

255